WEYERHAEUSER ENVIRONMENTAL BOOKS

William Cronon, Editor

WEYERHAEUSER ENVIRONMENTAL BOOKS

Weyerhaeuser Environmental Books explore human relationships
with natural environments in all their variety and complexity. They seek
to cast new light on the ways that natural systems affect human
communities, the ways that people affect the environments of which
they are a part, and the ways that different cultural conceptions of
nature profoundly shape our sense of the world around us.

The Natural History of Puget Sound Country by Arthur R. Kruckeberg

*Forest Dreams, Forest Nightmares: The Paradox of Old Growth
in the Inland West* by Nancy Langston

Landscapes of Promise: The Oregon Story, 1800–1940,
by William G. Robbins

*The Dawn of Conservation Diplomacy: U.S.-Canadian Wildlife
Protection Treaties in the Progressive Era* by Kurkpatrick Dorsey

*Irrigated Eden: The Making of an Agricultural Landscape
in the American West* by Mark Fiege

*Making Salmon: An Environmental History of the Northwest
Fisheries Crisis* by Joseph E. Taylor III

WEYERHAEUSER ENVIRONMENTAL CLASSICS

*The Great Columbia Plain: A Historical Geography,
1805–1910,* by D. W. Meinig

*Mountain Gloom and Mountain Glory: The Development
of the Aesthetics of the Infinite* by Marjorie Hope Nicolson

CYCLE OF FIRE BY STEPHEN J. PYNE

World Fire: The Culture of Fire on Earth

*Vestal Fire: An Environmental History, Told through Fire,
of Europe and Europe's Encounter with the World*

Fire in America: A Cultural History of Wildland and Rural Fire

Burning Bush: A Fire History of Australia

The Ice: A Journey to Antarctica

MAKING

Salmon,

An Environmental History
of the Northwest Fisheries Crisis

JOSEPH E. TAYLOR (III)

University of Washington Press

SEATTLE AND LONDON

To
Mom and Dad,
Bill and Joyce,
&

Harvey and Lavonne

Copyright © 1999 by the University of Washington Press
Printed in the United States of America

Library of Congress Cataloging-in-Publication Data

Taylor, Joseph E.
Making salmon : an environmental history of the
Northwest fisheries crisis / Joseph E. Taylor III.
p.   cm. — (Weyerhaeuser environmental books)
Includes bibliographical references.
ISBN 0-295-97840-6 (alk. paper)
1. Pacific salmon fisheries—Northwest, Pacific—
Management—History.   I. Title.
II. Series: Weyerhaeuser environmental books.
SH348.T39   1999   99-35414
333.95'656'09795—dc21   CIP

The paper used in this publication is acid-free and recycled from 10 percent post-
consumer and at least 50 percent pre-consumer waste. It meets the minimum
requirements of American National Standard for Information Sciences—Permanence
of Paper for Printed Library Materials, ANSI Z 39.48–1984. ∞ ♲

Contents

List of Maps   *vii*

Foreword: Speaking for Salmon,
by William Cronon   *ix*

Acknowledgments   *xiii*

Introduction: A Durable Crisis   *3*

1 / Dependence, Respect, and Moderation   *13*

2 / Historicizing Overfishing   *39*

3 / Inventing a Panacea   *68*

4 / Making Salmon   *99*

5 / Taking Salmon   *133*

6 / Urban Salmon   *166*

7 / Remaking Salmon   *203*

8 / Taking Responsibility   *237*

Citation Abbreviations   *259*

Notes   *263*

Bibliographic Essay   *379*

Index   *411*

Maps

1. Salmon Habitat—1800, West of Mountains *8*

2. Salmon Habitat—1800, East of Mountains *9*

3. Oregon Country Indians and Salmon Fisheries *16*

4. Mining Activity before 1900 *48*

5. Salmon Habitat by 1900 *58*

6. Salmon Hatcheries, 1877–1899 *93*

7. Transfer of Salmon Stocks, 1877–1905 *97*

8. Clackamas River Hatcheries and Egg Harvests, 1877–1955 *110*

9. Siuslaw River Hatcheries and Egg Harvests, 1892–1904 *127*

10. Lower Columbia River Fisheries, c. 1890–1910 *142*

11. Upper Columbia River Fisheries, c. 1879–1936 *143*

12. Rogue River Hatcheries and Egg Harvests, 1877–1939 *152*

13. Salmon Habitat by 1930 *178*

14. County Voting Majorities for Fishwheel Restriction Bill
in Oregon's 1908 June Election *186*

15. County Voting Majorities for Gillnet Restriction Bill
in Oregon's 1908 June Election *187*

16. County Voting Majorities for Nestucca Closure Bill
in Oregon's 1927 Special Election *197*

17. Salmon Hatcheries, 1900–1940   *223*

18. Transfer of Salmon Stocks, 1906–1960   *231*

19. Salmon Habitat by 1960   *234*

20. Salmon Habitat by 1990   *240*

Speaking for Salmon

Conservation biologists speak these days of "keystone species," organisms so central to the functioning of an ecosystem, so tied to a multitude of other creatures, that their removal can have far-reaching, even devastating consequences. In the face of growing extinction rates worldwide, the possibility that the disappearance of one particular organism might carry away many others in its wake is especially frightening to contemplate. What is less often remarked upon is that the ecological characteristics we associate with such keystone species are often accompanied by corresponding and no less essential *cultural* characteristics as well. The radical depopulation of bison herds on the Great Plains during the nineteenth century had profound implications not just for the grassland environment but for the cultures and ways of life of virtually every Indian community on the Plains, to say nothing of American culture more generally. Dislodge the keystone, and the architecture of which it is a part is altered and put at risk in ways that are almost impossible to predict.

In the Pacific Northwest, this role of keystone has long been played by the several species of salmon whose migrations between river and sea have been as crucial to human cultures as they have to natural ecosystems. For millennia, native peoples have gathered beside the Columbia and its tributary streams to harvest an incredible treasure of shining flesh as these extraordinary fish have sought to complete their thousand-mile journey back to the sites of their birth. In the two centuries since Euro-Americans first arrived in the Oregon country, salmon have been subjected to a host of new pressures from human activities: intense harvesting by commercial fisheries, radical disruption of watersheds by dams and land use changes, competing demand from sportfishing, changes in water quality, and a variety of conservation efforts focused in strikingly different ways on preserving salmon runs. The story of salmon has been entangled with that of human beings for so long in this region that it is almost impossible to imagine the two in isolation from each other. The salmon is not just a keystone species but a cultural icon of the first order, a powerful symbol of all that the Pacific Northwest is and has been.

In *Making Salmon*, Joseph Taylor weaves together these different stories as skillfully and compellingly as any scholar has ever done. Tracing the history of the Oregon salmon runs over the past century and a half, he has produced what will surely be regarded as the standard scholarly account of this subject for the next generation. And because the subject is so important, because Taylor's analysis is so germane to arguments now raging about the steps most needed to protect these endangered species, his work will be of interest far beyond the academy. What is so impressive about this book is its refusal to caricature any group of people that have ever declared an interest in Pacific Northwest salmon. They are all here: the natives, the commercial fishers, the dam builders, the sportfishers, the conservationists. Taylor is absolutely scrupulous about presenting the perspectives of each as fairly as he can—just as he is absolutely scrupulous about criticizing the self-interested lenses through which each has viewed the fish they sought to use and protect. The range of his intellectual sympathies is enhanced not only by his training as a first-rate environmental historian but by his experiences working in the commercial fishing fleet of the Pacific Coast and his obvious concern for the fate of the fish and people about whom he writes. One of his most striking arguments is that although many people have sought in the past to "speak for salmon"—to declare what these remarkable fish "need" in order to remain sustainably present in the ecosystems and human cultures of the Pacific Northwest—in fact they have all too often done a far better job of articulating their own needs and perspectives than those of the fish. Speaking for salmon turns out to be far more difficult than many of the fish's most passionate advocates have been willing to recognize, no matter which side of which debate they have been on.

A central strand of Taylor's argument has to do with the role of hatcheries in creating many of the most troubling problems now facing salmon in the Pacific Northwest. The ironies here could hardly be more striking. Hailed in the nineteenth century as a triumphant example of science and technology wedded together to sustain a crucial natural resource for the long run, the hatcheries fostered what environmental historian Paul Hirt, writing in a different context, has called "a conspiracy of optimism." By seeming to prove that human beings could intensively harvest vast quantities of fish as long as the animals were managed almost as a form of agriculture, the hatcheries made it possible to pretend for far too long that subtle ecological and genetic changes which in the long run threatened the very survival of the salmon runs were not occurring. Although Taylor identifies endlessly recurring examples of critics who declared Pacific Northwest salmon to be in a state of crisis, he also shows that responses to this "crisis" have remained ineffective right down to the present.

Taylor's is a chastening story, and its core argument does not leave one hopeful that "solving" the "salmon problem" will be even remotely easy. Quite the contrary. Taylor's purpose is to help us understand just how hard it is to grapple with ecological problems that are also intensely cultural and political and economic. His message in this is not that we should despair, that salmon are inevitably doomed, but that we err grievously when we imagine that simple solutions to complex problems are ever likely to be successful: we must never permit ourselves to believe that "speaking for salmon" is easy. By showing us how complicated the human history of salmon has been in the past, Taylor assembles the essential tools we need for thinking more clearly about its future as well.

WILLIAM CRONON

Acknowledgments

My name stands alone on the cover of this book, but I accrued many fiscal, intellectual, and personal debts during its writing. The following institutions and individuals deserve my deepest thanks. The Department of History at the University of Oregon helped me with a one-year teaching fellowship; the University of Washington and its Department of History offered generous assistance via a John Calhoun Smith Memorial Scholarship, a two-year teaching assistantship, and a W. W. Stout Fellowship for research; the Smithsonian Institution awarded me two separate Predoctoral Fellowships during the summers of 1994 and 1995; the National Science Foundation gave me a Dissertation Improvement Grant in 1996; and Iowa State University funded some eleventh-hour research trips to resolve troublesome questions.

This study would not have been possible without access to documents and staff assistance at various research institutions around the country. I wish to thank Jack Marincovich of the Columbia River Fishermen's Protective Union; Anne Witty, Barbara Minard, and David Pearson at the Columbia River Maritime Museum; Dwight Miller at the Herbert Hoover Presidential Library; Marty West at the Lane County Historical Society; Joe Schwartz and Jim Rush at the National Archives; Ron Overman at the National Science Foundation; the Northwest Fisheries Science Center Library at the National Marine Fisheries Service in Seattle; Gloria Bourne, Steve Johnson, Steve King, and Wayne Rawlins of the Oregon Department of Fish and Wildlife; M. C. Cuthill at the Oregon Historical Society; James Clark and Timothy Backer at the Oregon State Archives; William Deiss, Mary Dyer, Libby Glenn, Pam Henson, and Bruce Morrison at the Smithsonian Institution; M. Wayne Jensen Jr. at the Tillamook County Pioneer Museum; Vicky Jones and Duffy Nelson of Special Collections at the

Knight Library, University of Oregon; and Richard Engeman of Special Collections at the Allen Library, University of Washington.

Many people have contributed important insights and timely advice. I want to thank Dauril Alden, Dean Allard, James Anderson, Keith Benson, Richard Maxwell Brown, Bob Bunting, Ham Cravens, Bill Cronon, Matt Dennis, Bob Eaton, John Findlay, Susan Flader, Bob Francis, Chris Friday, John Halver, Ron Hardy, Bob Haskett, Ray Hilborn, Richard Johnson, Matt Klingle, Bill Lang, Nancy Langston, Nate Mantua, George McJimsey, Gregg Mitman, Kathy Morse, Linda Nash, Jeff Ostler, Paul Pitzer, William Ricker, Bill Robbins, Randall Schalk, Robert Self, Bruce Stadfeld, Ellen Stroud, J. Michael Wallace, John Winton, Warren Wooster, and Chris Young. Each contributed substantially through their insights on fields and issues they understood much better than myself.

This book has gone through several permutations. It began as an honors and then masters thesis at the University of Oregon, where Edwin Bingham and Richard Maxwell Brown helped me discover this story's complexity. Their sage advice and loose rein enabled me to follow odd hunches that profoundly altered research. When I transferred to the University of Washington, my committee of Richard White, John Findlay, Keith Benson, and Ray Hilborn offered advice and encouraged me to pursue even my weirdest ideas. Richard White, who served as chair, holds the dubious distinction of having read every draft of every chapter. His wisdom permeates every sentence, and I am a better scholar and person for knowing him, my other committee members, and the members of the Departments of History at the University of Oregon, University of Washington, and Iowa State University. The people at University of Washington Press have been especially helpful. Keith Benson, Bill Robbins, Bill Cronon, Julidta Tarver, and Pamela J. Bruton helped make this monster a more readable work, and I owe all a debt of gratitude. Any residual errors are, of course, mine.

Higher education can be incredibly rewarding, but it can also be a circus of excruciating contradictions. Although professors train their students to think as individuals, the system remains essentially paternalistic and feudal. Advisors simultaneously encourage catholicity and specialization; intellectual criticism can crush egos; and intense competition for funding and employment encourages social and emotional asceticism. The only thing worse may be getting a job. Seventy-hour work weeks are standard, and the pressures that accompany the process of promotion and tenure are nothing short of hideous. My colleagues at Iowa State University have been wonderfully supportive of my teaching and research, yet I no longer wonder why personal relationships suffer, anxiety is commonplace, and neuroses abound in this profession. Higher education is damn hard work.

For all its intellectual rewards (this is not a profession for those seeking wealth), the experience would be intolerable without the emotional support of good friends. Thus I need to pay special thanks to a number of important people. Dauril Alden, John Beatty, Keith Benson, Rick and Sue Braithwaite, Dick Brown, Ham Cravens, John Findlay, the late Sid Fisher, Jack Gilman, April Hatfield and John Maxwell, Doug Hurt, the late Victor Learned, George McJimsey, Ruth McPherson, Wendy Pfeuffer, and Richard White offered me hospitality and support during school, research trips, and conferences. Others helped in less tangible ways. Tracy Curtis, John Eby, Mike Frome, Chris Galbraith, Jen Hakel, Julian Madison, Ray Monroe, Byron Nakamura, Margaret Paton Walsh, Wendy Pfeuffer, Mark Spence, Rachel Standish, Michele Thompson, and Sam Truett let me rant and made me laugh. Jen Boyd, Sue Curtis, Claire Strom, Moran Tompkins, and my brother Craig Taylor kept me sane. Matt Klingle has been a true friend.

Over the course of this project I have come to think of books as children. Authors conceive and nurture their works with the same mixture of hope and dread common to parents, and for both groups the object of their affection soon takes on a life of its own. Such is the case here. This book is a vessel of dreams fulfilled and dashed, and seeing it to publication has taught me much about faith, fealty, and sacrifice. It has also enhanced my respect for the art of parenting, so it is fitting that I should use this opportunity to honor six people who nurtured me: my parents, Barbara and Joseph Taylor, gave me a love of education and of the North American West; Bill and the late Joyce Curtis taught me the meaning of love; and Harvey and Lavonne Hellwege opened doors and introduced me to worlds I never knew existed. This book would not have occurred without their sacrifices as well.

[U]nless some scheme for replenishing the stock of fish is carried to successful completion . . . the hope for future generations of salmon in the waters of the Columbia will indeed be very thin.

—*Astoria Daily Astorian*, 1877

[Unless Oregon] does something for the fishing interests that interest will be a thing of the past.

—Oregon State Senator L. T. BARIN, 1887

The utter disappearance of the salmon fishery of the Columbia is only a question of a few years.

—Ichthyologist DAVID STARR JORDAN, 1894

[T]he decrease in the catch becomes more pronounced each year and the industry is assuredly facing a crisis unless some steps are taken.

—*Portland Morning Oregonian*, 1907

[Because of] the increased appropriation of water . . . spawning grounds on these rivers are being rapidly destroyed or depleted.

—Oregon Fish Commission, 1917

The Columbia is headed for the same type of destruction as the Sacramento, namely, the extermination of the salmon.

—U.S. Fish Commissioner HENRY O'MALLEY, 1929

The construction of numerous great dams . . . may well result in the extermination of a large part of the remaining runs of both Chinooks and bluebacks.   —Zoologist WILLIS H. RICH, 1939

It would indeed be a calamity if provision should be made for artificial propagation only and then it should fail.

—Biologist PAUL R. NEEDHAM, 1945

Must power turbines mean the end of migratory fish runs?

—U.S. Senator RICHARD L. NEUBERGER, 1958

The destruction of [Pacific salmon] is so notorious that we cannot believe that Congress through the present Act authorized their ultimate demise.

—Supreme Court Justice WILLIAM O. DOUGLAS, 1967

The salmon and steelhead runs of the upper Columbia basin are at a critical crossroads.   —Biologist ED CHANEY, 1978

Salmon management in the Pacific Northwest is at a major turning point.

—Biologist CARL J. WALTERS, 1988

In the 1990s, native anadromous Pacific salmonids . . . are at a crossroads.

—Biologists WILLA NEHLSEN, JACK E. WILLIAMS, and

JAMES A. LICHATOWICH, 1991

Making Salmon

INTRODUCTION

A Durable Crisis

Pacific Salmon have mattered for millennia, but the bond between humans and fish has changed radically over time. Huge runs once sustained aboriginal societies and later enriched industrial and sports fisheries, but now their scarcity threatens lives and economies. Salmon are still revered and coveted by some, but others fear and dismiss them. For many people salmon hold little cultural or economic relevance except as their interests conflict with water and land use policies. Pacific northwesterners have seen sport and commercial fishing seasons dwindle from nine months to zero days; Indians have to purchase Alaska salmon because local runs are protected by the Endangered Species Act; industrialists pay higher electricity bills; irrigators water fewer acres; loggers cut fewer trees; ranchers graze farther from streams; and urbanites ration water. Since 1981, when Congress made the Bonneville Power Administration give salmon equal consideration when managing Columbia River dams, the region has invested three billion dollars to save these fish, and the only thing everyone can agree upon is that the effort has largely failed.[1]

This is the modern "salmon crisis," but its roots extend to the earliest days of settlement. Pacific northwesterners have been prophesying the imminent demise of salmon for 125 years. As early as 1875, the *Portland Morning Oregonian* worried about the "almost total extinction of salmon in our waters." U.S. Fish Commissioner Marshall McDonald warned Oregon's governor in 1893 about "the disastrous outlook for the future of the salmon fisheries of the Columbia." Throughout these years pundits spoke of killing the goose that laid golden eggs and compared declining runs to the vanishing buffalo. In 1939 fishery biologist Willis Rich anticipated the rapid "extermination of a large part of the remaining runs of both Chinooks and bluebacks," and more recently biologists have declared repeatedly that

3

salmon are at a "crossroads." One can read these alarms like Alfred E. Neuman and see their authors as so many Chicken Littles. But the toll of declining and extinct runs contradicts such dismissals. These protests in fact contain subtle and surprising lessons.[2]

The litany of jeremiads reveals not only the magnitude of the problem but also the fickle character of social memory. Nothing suggests the size of former salmon runs more than the length of time it took them to collapse. The sheer loss is stunning to contemplate, yet the urgency that has gripped the many Cassandras suggests a second insight we must consider. Alarmists have usually portrayed salmon decline in immediate terms because the problem appeared as novel to speaker and audience in, for example, 1991 as it did in 1939, 1907, or 1877. Collapsing runs seemed like an event, but this excruciatingly long disaster was actually a process. The inability to see decline as a process, let alone a complicated process, has everything to do with natural resource politics.[3]

The essence of the salmon crisis is the struggle to define and solve a complicated environmental and social problem, but resolution has been elusive because participants have little in common. How people respond to declining runs depends on who they are, where they live, what they do for a living, and how they think it happened. How people remember the past, and the stories they tell about that past, are inextricably linked to identity and interest. Fishers and fish culturists who want more salmon criticize dams and changes in hatchery policies; anglers and environmentalists who covet wild fish and scenery charge resource users with destroying habitat; smelters, irrigators, bargers, and dam agencies who depend on the industrialized river blame trollers, netters, and Indians for overfishing; Indians who value salmon for subsistence and spirituality accuse governments of conspiring to deprive them; and almost everyone blames seals, sea lions, birds, and ocean conditions for consuming too many young salmon. What these explanations have in common is that all are simple stories which deflect blame onto other groups or activities.

The persistence of simple stories about the past has been an obstacle to restoring salmon runs. For a century and a quarter northwesterners have tried in vain to save salmon. Their failure, however, has stemmed less from ignorance or insincerity than from asking the wrong questions of the wrong histories. Many have wanted and do want to save salmon, but few have been willing to accept responsibility and bear the costs of recovery. Instead, they have tried to reframe history to indict rival users of fish, water, and land, and to shift the burden onto less powerful groups. Advocates simplified the past to create scapegoats and relied on technology to solve social problems. They justified these convenient solutions by invoking simple stories. And though they failed to halt decline, their stories, strategies, and solutions have retained considerable legitimacy to this day.[4]

The purpose of this book is to subvert the way people have thought about salmon management for the last 125 years. The history of the salmon crisis is far more complicated than most stories admit, and the preferred political and technological strategies have perpetuated, rather than resolved, problems. A detailed history of those efforts should remind readers of the complexity of the forces driving decline. It should also caution readers against uncritical faith in technology and temper the tendency to moralize and scapegoat.

To understand the history of the salmon crisis, we must first understand the life history of Pacific salmon (*Oncorhynchus*). Pacific salmon belong not only to different species than Atlantic salmon (*Salmo salar*) but to a different genus as well. These scientific classifications matter because they help us approximate evolutionary relationships between organisms and, as will become apparent later, occasionally determine who can exploit certain species.[5]

Pacific salmon possess some of the most complicated life cycles in nature. Their life stages and physiological changes are as complex and amazing as a caterpillar's metamorphosis into a butterfly. Most salmon are anadromous, which means that they begin and end their lives in freshwater but grow to maturity in the ocean. After two or more months of incubation, salmon emerge from eggs as alevins. For the next forty-five to sixty days they hide in river gravel and feed off the nutrients in their yolk sacs. Once they absorb the sacs, alevins become fry, swim out of the gravel, and begin to feed on small aquatic organisms. Some salmon immediately descend toward the ocean. Others remain in their natal streams or lakes for up to three years before departing, and some steelhead (*O. mykiss*) and sockeye (*O. nerka*) spend their entire lives in freshwater as rainbow trout and kokanee, respectively. During this freshwater stage fry grow into parr, develop vertical stripes, and in many respects resemble other western trout, which are also members of the *Oncorhynchus* genus.

As salmon fry and parr descend toward the sea, however, they undergo a series of physiological changes that quickly distinguish them from other river fish. These changes, called smoltification, are essential for surviving in salt water. Smolts develop a different blood chemistry, grow scales, and assume the silvery appearance we associate with salmon. They then migrate to sea. Those that survive the first critical months can migrate as far north as the Gulf of Alaska, where they spend one to five or more years feeding and growing to prodigious sizes. Pink (*O. gorbuscha*) and sockeye reach five to eight pounds before returning to spawn in one to three years; chum (*O. keta*), steelhead, and coho (*O. kisutch*) occasionally grow to eighteen to twenty-two pounds during the same period; and chinook (*O. tshawytscha*) can reach between eighteen and sixty pounds in three to six years.

When Pacific salmon are ready to spawn, they return to their place of birth and undergo another series of radical physiological changes. The fish stop feeding, their digestive tracts shrink, and their sexual organs grow rapidly. Salmon live off their body fat for the remainder of their lives as they travel upstream and spawn. These spawning runs provided the dietary staple of aboriginal society and formed the economic backbone of the later industrial fishery. By the time the fish arrive at the reach of stream or lake (in the case of sockeye) from which they emerged as alevins, hormonal changes have caused secondary physical changes. Most fish change color to a deep brown or brilliant red and green, and males develop distended backs and hooked jaws, especially pink (called "humpies" colloquially) and sockeye.

What sets *Oncorhynchus* apart from *Salmo* is that most Pacific salmon spawn only once and then die. Life and death merge in a grotesque spectacle during spawning season. As Pacific salmon mature sexually, they also fall apart. The grueling migrations and bodily changes that accompany spawning exhaust the fish. Salmon grow thin and attenuated from consuming their own fat, and they have lost most of their energy reserves by the time they reach their spawning grounds. Salmon literally starve to death to bring life, and many succumb to fungal infections or diseases during these migrations. Those that do reach the spawning grounds pair off with mates, claim a pile of gravel, dig a hole, release their milt and eggs, and cover the eggs with gravel. They do this repeatedly until exhausted and then guard the gravel mound, called a redd, until death and current carry them away in a few days. Steelhead and an occasional coho or sockeye may survive to spawn again, but even these fish will die after a second or possibly a third spawning run.[6]

The salmon's complicated life cycle exposes the fish to many social and natural influences. Aside from Arthur McEvoy's groundbreaking history of the California fisheries, however, nobody has examined the interplay of nature, economy, culture, and science in the fisheries. Most historians concentrate only on human impacts upon salmon, ignoring nature's impact on history. Yet from fish biology to droughts, floods, and fires, nature has constantly shaped the plight of salmon and human efforts to save these fish. The unseen effects of fluctuating ocean environments, most dramatically in the case of the climatic phenomenon known as El Niño, have been especially important.[7]

Of course, human activities have also affected salmon in many ways. The most obvious of these was harvest. Using many forms of fishing gear, Indians and non-Indians alike took salmon in incredible numbers, but methods and impact have ranged widely. Spears and leisters had relatively little impact on salmon runs; dipnets, gillnets, and seines could capture salmon in much larger numbers; and weirs, traps, poundnets, and fishwheels could devastate entire runs. Both Indians and non-Indians used every form of gear. Both also exchanged fish for goods and services. Thus calling their fisheries "Indian" and "non-Indian," or "Indian" and "commercial," fails to articulate their complexity. The terms "aboriginal" and "industrial" do a much better job of differentiating the economic and cultural uses of salmon over time. This pertains not only to fishing but to all the activities that shaped salmon runs (see maps 1 and 2). Oregon country[8] Indians were nonagrarian, but their constant use of fire could alter water chemistry and increase soil erosion. As Euro-Americans multiplied the uses of nature, they also increased the threats to salmon. By tilling soil, damming streams, and diverting water, they increased siltation, blocked migration, reduced flows, and warmed water; they also logged, mined, milled, and congregated at unprecedented rates.[9]

In some respects the decline of salmon has been a function of numbers. The more people who lived in the region, the greater the material pressure on indigenous plants and animals. Yet there is more to this story than simple demographics. The way people used nature also reflected their technological sophistication and intellectual concerns. How they made collective sense of these and other issues is what we call *culture.* Seemingly ethereal matters of the mind, it turns out, matter greatly when trying to understand the material consequences of everyday life. This is as true of the aboriginal first-salmon ceremony as of the capitalistic commodification of nature, the development of scientific salmon management, or the preservation of ecosystems. Both then and now, salmon's fate has been inextricably linked to culture and economy.

But *culture* has a dual meaning in this study. Although at times it will refer to the anthropological focus on social meaning, it will also retain its original link to husbandry when used to describe modern attempts to increase fish populations. This second usage, which we call *fish culture* or *artificial propagation,* is central to this book. Ranging from constructing fishways and eliminating predators to capturing fish, removing eggs, manual fertilization, and

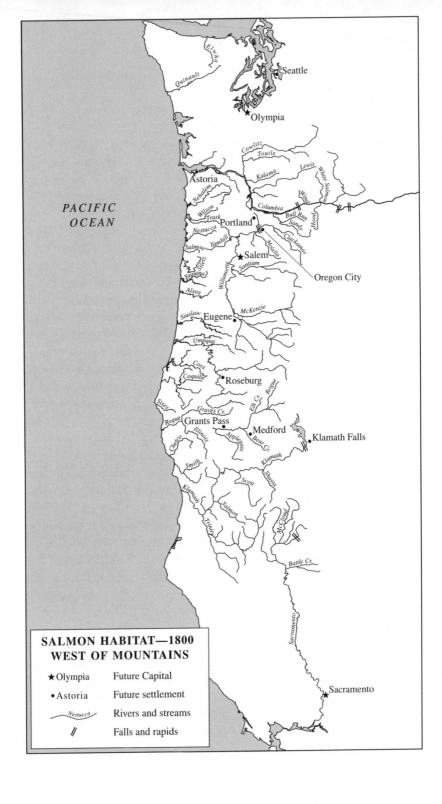

PACIFIC
OCEAN

Elwha

Quinault

Seattle

Olympia

Cowlitz
Toutle
Lewis
Kalama
White Salmon

Astoria

Nehalem
Wilson
Trask
Nestucca
Salmon
Siletz
Yaquina
Alsea

Wind
Columbia
Bull Run
Hood
Sandy
Clackamas
Molalla

Portland

Yamhill

Salem

Santiam
Willamette

Oregon City

Siuslaw

McKenzie

Eugene

Umpqua

Coos
Coquille

Roseburg

Sixes

Elk Cr.
Graves Cr.
Rogue

Grants Pass

Chetco
Illinois
Applegate

Bear Cr.

Medford

Klamath Falls

Smith

Klamath
Scott
Shasta

Klamath
Salmon
Trinity

McCloud

Battle Cr.

Sacramento

Sacramento

SALMON HABITAT—1800
WEST OF MOUNTAINS

★ Olympia   Future Capital

● Astoria   Future settlement

〜 Nestucca   Rivers and streams

⁄⁄   Falls and rapids

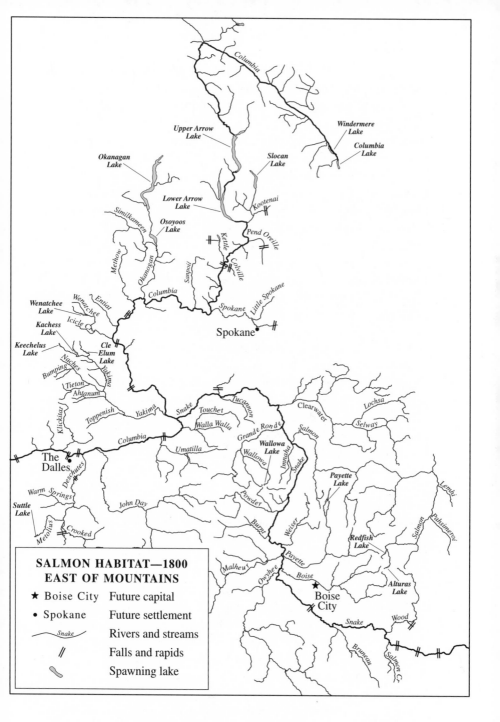

MAPS 1 and 2. Extent of salmon habitat in selected western (*facing page*) and eastern (*above*) Oregon country streams prior to Euro-American settlement.

rearing ponds, all practices emanated from a belief that humans could make salmon more efficiently than nature. Confidence in these measures rested on a pair of assumptions: science's progress toward truth, and technology's ability to mitigate social problems. Since the 1870s, these twin faiths have encouraged Pacific northwesterners to fund a burgeoning hatchery system rather than limit their destructive activities. The policy would have worked if salmon had responded as fish culturists predicted, but salmon were not so malleable. Adults died before spawning, eggs failed to hatch, juveniles succumbed to diseases, and releases became prey. Over time hatchery salmon grew smaller, weaker, and fewer because of cultivation practices, while wild populations dwindled because fish culture reduced the perceived need to protect natural habitat. In short, policies developed out of genuine concern for salmon unintentionally channeled fishery management and salmon evolution onto paths that contributed significantly to the mounting disaster.[10]

Science played a key role in legitimating the use of fish culture. As science gained stature in nineteenth-century America as an objective measure of the world, fish culture became a leading branch of fishery science. And although they eventually lost their scientific prestige, fish culturists' initial ability to portray themselves as production-oriented scientists helped them make grandiose claims about artificial propagation, argue that it was a scientifically proven art, and persuade politicians and taxpayers to fund a burgeoning program of government-sponsored hatcheries. Most observers assumed that progressive science would refine whatever technological problems emerged. They were sure that hatcheries would cure society's ills. The cultural power of science was a critical force of persuasion, so it is imperative to examine it in context. Science, which some nineteenth-century Americans regarded as absolute truth, was really just another cultured way of knowing nature. And although scientific knowledge could be precise and flexible, its understanding of salmon and fish culture was often wanting. Where science faltered, bureaucratic concerns and cultural acceptance helped shield hatcheries for half a century. By the time systematic criticisms of fish culture emerged in the 1920s, other management options had largely disappeared.[11]

The political culture that buttressed hatcheries has also shaped our understanding of fishers, producing over time a dissonance between the way we discuss the environmental history of salmon fisheries and the reality of those fisheries. In the past, historians have tended to fixate on whether the "tragedy of the commons" is an apt metaphor to explain decline. This debate has circled around the question of whether unrestricted access to salmon runs led fishers to harvest as many fish as they could. In its bluntest form, the commons model proposes that because competitors would consume anything left in the water, it was economically irrational for fishers to moderate their activities. This argument seems salient. License records indicate that salmon fishers multiplied inexorably until 1910, and the fisheries seem like an open-access industry. But calling the Columbia or any other stream a "commons" ignores a central reality of the fishery's spatial and racial politics. Rivers were not open fields for anyone to enter. Many social barriers existed based on one's race, ethnicity, class, and gender. Fishing gear also formed physical barriers to access on many rivers and streams. Because the salmon fisheries were neither perfectly open nor closed, we need a better way to discuss their environmental history than the perpetuation of inapt metaphors and impotent debates.[12]

The geographer's concept of space may be a more fruitful way to analyze the historical development of salmon management. Geographers have criticized historians for too often portraying the past as if people "were packed solidly on to the head of a pin." In discussing temporal change, we do tend to slight the other three dimensions of human activity, yet spatial arrangements have been as critical to the realization of social power as any other category of analysis. Every day in every way people delimited their and their neighbors' opportunities through location and action. As geographer Allan Pred notes, "Power relations, while abstract and intangible, are always somehow associated with the concrete conduct of social life in place. . . . Thus, struggles, of whatever focus and scale, are always at some level struggles over the use and meaning of space and time." In chronicling change, we should also examine "the social production of space and the restless formation and reformation of geographical landscapes."[13]

Integrating a spatial perspective helps us to envision complex cultural and material relationships people have developed toward salmon and salmon environments. Pacific northwesterners regarded salmon in sometimes radically different ways depending on identity, location, and interest. The relative economic and political capital that each group possessed was crucial when interests collided in environmental management. Mapping those features spatially as well as temporally helps illustrate the distribution of social power in society, the social and environmental consequences of policies, and the internal contradictions of salmon management. The forces driving decline were far more complicated than previous tellings have conveyed. We need such a rendition of the past to demonstrate why simple stories have failed us and why a multidimensional perspective is essential for resolving the salmon crisis. Both the problem and potential solutions are, and have always been, our collective responsibility.

1 / Dependence, Respect, and Moderation

To understand what went wrong with the industrial fishery and why modern management has failed, we should first step back and ask whether there was ever a successful fishery and what success might mean. Indians, as they do so often in environmental issues, have come to represent a native Eden. In popular literature and commercial advertisements alike, they stand as a symbol of natural simplicity. In the Pacific Northwest, popular culture imagines that an aboriginal balance and harmony existed between Indian fishers and salmon from which later fisheries devolved. Historians also portray the aboriginal fishery as benign in their critiques of the open-access policies of modern management. But their portrayal and critique falter because they also argue that Indians lacked both the numbers and the technology to harm the nineteenth century's massive runs. If Indians could not influence salmon populations, then their fishery does not matter in any historical sense. But look closer. Indians had a greater impact on salmon than we assume, and the success of their fishery has far more significance than Edenic myths suggest.[1]

The aboriginal salmon fishery provides a useful lens for analyzing the intersection of economy, culture, and nature in the fisheries because Indians did influence salmon populations. Salmon were the largest single source of protein in the aboriginal diet, Indians' fishing techniques were potentially as effective as modern methods, and food storage practices and trade patterns extended consumption in both time and space. Cultural reliance on salmon and technological developments in the fishery allowed Oregon country Indians to consume a huge proportion of the region's runs. Indians' material and cultural relationships with salmon were both more influential and more complicated than popular mythology suggests.

The scale of the aboriginal fishery and the Indians' dependence on salmon posed a potentially significant threat to runs, yet Oregon's rivers still teemed with salmon when whites arrived. How did this happen? The answer lies in the way Indians managed their landscapes. According to anthropologists Eugene Hunn and Nancy Williams, social and environmental management is always a cultural act. "Hunter-Gatherers *actively manage* their resources" as actively as modern society does. In the Oregon country, historical, ethnological, and archeological evidence suggests that aboriginal spiritual beliefs, ritual expressions, social sanctions, and territorial claims effectively moderated salmon harvests. Myths, ceremonies, and taboos restrained individual and social consumption, while settlement patterns and usufruct rights restricted access to salmon. Oregon country Indians' dependence on salmon yielded forms of respect for the fish that sustained life, and respect shaped human actions that retarded consumption. Indian culture and economy produced a sustainable tension between society and nature.[2]

In early December 1805, Lewis and Clark's Corps of Discovery hunkered down at the south end of Youngs Bay near the mouth of the Columbia River. After a journey of almost two years, the sojourners now had to endure Fort Clatsop's soggy monotony. During an uncharacteristically buoyant moment, however, William Clark remarked, "We live sumptuously on our Wappatoe [*sic*] and sturgeon." Years later trappers and traders would echo Clark by noting the abundant herds of elk and deer that wandered into their gun sights. Their reports helped foster a popular impression of the Oregon country as a cornucopia that was both accurate and misleading. The region did contain an amazing array of resources, but Indians did not exploit everything available. Rather, they were specialists.[3]

Indians relied primarily on salmon and a few other items for subsistence. They preferred salmon to other animals because of their abundance and reliability. Salmon runs fluctuate wildly at the extreme northern, southern, and eastern edges of their range, but Oregon country rivers were once among the most accommodating environments for salmon. Moreover, because salmon are anadromous and spawn in freshwater, they appeared at predictable places at predictable times. Fishing was thus a far more efficient way of procuring protein than hunting. It offered Indians a massive and timely supply of protein and carbohydrates. It is no wonder that salmon was a staple of aboriginal diets.[4]

Although virtually all Oregon country Indians (see map 3) specialized in salmon, individual groups employed markedly different subsistence strategies. Geography, environment, and culture thus produced a variety of subsistence patterns within this homogeneous salmon culture.

An individual group's subsistence strategy depended largely on whether it lived on the coast, the Columbia River, the Plateau, or an interior valley. Indians living in coastal and estuarine environments had local access to shellfish, berries, and roots throughout the year, and four species of salmon (chinook, coho, chum, and steelhead) spawned in these streams. Overlapping runs and food storage provided coastal groups a nearly constant supply of protein, so they migrated little and developed dense populations. People living away from the coast had to make greater efforts to procure food. Although six species of salmon (the same as above plus pink and sockeye) spawned in the Columbia River basin, river sites contained fewer additional resources. Groups residing along the lower Columbia still lived in dense, semisedentary populations, but they migrated more often during food quests. They also compensated for local and seasonal scarcities by trading with others along the river. Lush environments ended abruptly at the eastern edge of the Cascade Range. The arid climate widened the spaces between plants, animals, and humans alike. Plateau Indians lived in smaller kin units and searched for roots, plants, berries, and game over vast areas for much of the year. They congregated in larger populations only at fishing sites, root-gathering rendezvous, and winter villages. The people of the Willamette and other interior valleys lived a life similar to Plateau groups except that they often spent more time harvesting roots and less time fishing.[5]

When salmon began their spawning runs, coastal Indians established temporary camps at opportune fishing sites such as waterfalls and riffles. Nature helped determine where people fished, but culture organized human labor by gender. Men migrated directly to the fishery to repair and install fishing gear. Women and children took a slower course, gathering herbs and firewood for meat drying. During the harvest men fished and women prepared the catch. Spring and summer fishing could be leisurely, but fall was all business; people concentrated on stocking supplies for winter meals, trade, and ceremonies. Once they secured their stores, Indians dismantled their fisheries and returned to permanent villages. Coastal groups usually ended their food quests in September and retired to plank houses until the following March.[6]

Lower Columbia groups also relied on salmon, but in general the farther inland one went, the more time Indians spent harvesting other resources. Indians living along the lower Columbia and lower Willamette Rivers spoke a common dialect, Chinook, and oriented life around waterways and salmon. In spring before the salmon arrived women harvested wapatos, a bulbous root growing in shallow mud banks, which they consumed or

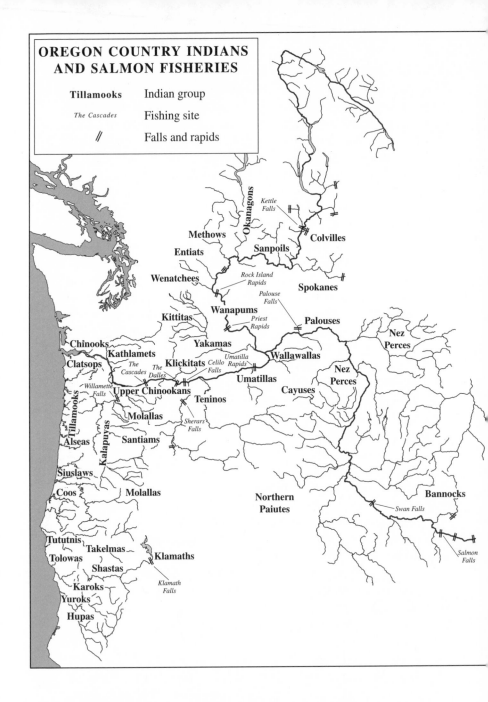

OREGON COUNTRY INDIANS AND SALMON FISHERIES

Tillamooks Indian group

The Cascades Fishing site

// Falls and rapids

Okanagons

Kettle Falls

Methows

Colvilles

Entiats

Sanpoils

Wenatchees

Rock Island Rapids

Spokanes

Kittitas

Wanapums

Palouse Falls

Priest Rapids

Palouses

Nez Perces

Chinooks

Kathlamets

Yakamas

Clatsops

The Cascades

Klickitats

Umatilla Rapids

Wallawallas

The Dalles

Celilo Falls

Umatillas

Nez Perces

Willamette Falls

Upper Chinookans

Cayuses

Teninos

Tillamooks

Molallas

Sherars Falls

Alseas

Kalapuyas

Santiams

Siuslaws

Coos

Molallas

Northern Paiutes

Bannocks

Swan Falls

Tututnis

Takelmas

Tolowas

Shastas

Klamaths

Salmon Falls

Karoks

Klamath Falls

Yuroks

Hupas

MAP 3. Selected groups of aboriginal salmon fishers in the Oregon country. These are modern groupings. Indians normally organized themselves into far smaller conglomerations of villages or kin associations.

traded. In between runs Indians made sorties for roots, berries, and game. Chinookan speakers fished at locations on both the main river and its tributaries, but the sites at Willamette Falls, Cascade Rapids, The Dalles, and Celilo Falls, where the river tumbled through narrow channels or over falls, provided some of the most prolific fisheries on earth. By October lower-river groups had cached enough food to last until March.[7]

Indians living east of the Cascade Range migrated more frequently and for longer periods, but Plateau life still centered on rivers. Indians defined their territories by drainage basins. They spent much of the summer at fishing sites along tributaries of the Columbia and Snake Rivers, moving away to protected sites only with the onset of winter. Even one hundred miles up the John Day River, on the upper Owyhee River, on the Drewsey River, and at Salmon Falls on the Snake River, small bands of Paiutes and Shoshones gathered annually to fish the salmon runs. Food quests on the western Plateau began in March and ended in October. Farther east in the Snake River basin groups had to wait until May and did not winter until November.[8]

The environment placed limits on dependence, however. The flows of the Columbia and Snake were always heavy enough to accommodate large runs, but where stream size decreased or elevation increased, water levels fluctuated more severely. In areas like the upper Burnt and Grande Ronde Rivers, stream flows were less stable and salmon runs less predictable. Thus the Cayuses, Nez Perces, and other groups relied less on salmon than westward groups. The Blue Mountains of eastern Oregon marked a rough boundary for the region's salmon culture.[9]

The Willamette, Camas, and upper Rogue River valleys presented a different set of subsistence challenges. Salmon were scarce above Willamette Falls and in the upper Coquille drainage. To compensate, resident Indians instead developed subsistence patterns similar to those of the Plateau. Migrating frequently to exploit abundant supplies of camases, wapatos, and berries, they then traded these items to coastal or Columbia River groups for salmon. Perhaps predictably, inland groups had fewer ceremonies and myths related to salmon than their neighbors. Indians along the middle and upper Rogue River also migrated seasonally to harvest acorns, berries, and game, but salmon remained the staple food because of the Rogue's abundant runs. Despite varied subsistence patterns, however, salmon bound the disparate peoples and environments of the Oregon country into a coherent culture. Throughout the region, access to salmon influenced the location of villages, group wealth and power, and emphases of culture.[10]

Salmon's importance as a staple was unmistakable, and it has become a key factor in population estimates. Ecologists use the term "carrying capacity" to describe the upper population limit an environment can sustain. In the Oregon country salmon seem to be the crucial factor determining human carrying capacity. Demographers repeatedly link aboriginal population to local historic abundances of salmon. The correlations are highly suggestive, but they do not by themselves either prove a causal link between salmon and human population or demonstrate that the aboriginal fishery stressed salmon runs. It is possible, for example, that inefficient fishing techniques could have limited human consumption and thus population. It is also possible that Indians were inclined to take no more than they needed to sustain themselves for short periods. The ability of groups to suspend foraging and spend winters in permanent villages suggests a different answer, however. Aboriginal fishing methods *could* fully exploit the region's salmon runs.[11]

Indians used a wide array of fishing techniques, but local circumstances dictated which devices prevailed. The middle Columbia River is an example. As the river tumbled through the narrow basaltic cliffs of The Dalles, the swift currents simultaneously aided and frustrated fishers by forcing salmon close to shore and limiting the types of fishing tools used. Only a few implements worked well in those dangerous conditions. Wasco and Wishram fishers living at the great narrows of the Columbia had access to salmon migrating up the largest spawning river in the world, but standing on rock ledges and wood platforms at the edge of the torrent, they could catch salmon only with long-handled spears and dipnets. These methods may seem crude, but they required immense skill. Fishers had to thrust their tools with precision, and a momentary loss of balance could mean death. Farther upstream, Colville Indians suspended reed baskets to trap salmon as they jumped over Kettle Falls. Although spears, dipnets, and traps were not the most efficient devices available, the Wascos, Wishrams, and Colvilles enjoyed the most productive fisheries in North America.[12]

Where the waters calmed and salmon dispersed, Indians switched to other fishing methods. A few groups used poisons to stun fish before spearing or netting them, but this was rare—poisoning required dense concentrations of fish and very slow currents. Instead, most Indians favored seines and gillnets. Coastal and Columbia River groups constructed these devices using local plant material such as iris, cedar bark, and silk grass, or Indian hemp and bear grass obtained from the Plateau. To keep their nets vertical in the water, Indians attached wood floats and rock sinkers to the top and bottom. Both methods were considerably more efficient and sophisticated than spears, dipnets, and poisons.[13]

Gillnets and seines possessed different advantages depending on water conditions. Seines worked best in calmer waters like estuaries and eddies, but Indians also used them to create impenetrable barriers on smaller streams. Seines were especially good at efficiently sweeping broad, shallow areas, as James Swan observed of a Clatsop seining party in the early 1850s.

> Two persons get into the canoe, on the stern of which is coiled the net on a frame made for the purpose, resting on the canoe's gunwale. [The canoe] is then paddled up the stream, close in to the beach, where the current is not so strong. A tow-line, with a wooden float attached to it, is then thrown to the third person, who remains on the beach, and immediately the two in the canoe paddle her into the rapid stream as quickly as they can throwing out the net all the time. When this is all out, they paddle ashore, having the end of the other tow-line made fast to the canoe. Before all this is accomplished, the net is carried down the stream, by the force of the ebb, about the eighth of a mile, the man on the shore walking along slowly, holding on to the line until the others are ready, when all haul in together. As it gradually closes on the fish, great caution must be used to prevent them from jumping over: and as every salmon has to be knocked on the head with a club for the purpose, which every canoe carries, it requires some skill and practice to perform this feat so as not to bruise or disfigure the fish.

The nets Swan saw were one hundred to six hundred feet in length and seven to sixteen feet deep. Indians used similar nets in the eddies below Celilo Falls.[14]

Gillnets were even more sophisticated. While seines corralled fish into a confined area, gillnets entangled them in the net's webbing. Indians sized the mesh so fish could swim only partially through the net. When they attempted to back out, gill plates and fins tangled with the mesh. Weaving a useful net required great skill because sizing the mesh was critical. An opening slightly too large or too small rendered the net useless. Fishing a gillnet was also demanding, and keeping it taut and properly aligned in the current required years of practice, especially when one remembers that gillnets were only used at night or in muddy water because salmon avoided the thick-twined nets during daylight.[15]

Weirs were the ultimate fishing device, and most groups away from the Columbia used them. These "salmon dams" were basically permeable walls built across small rivers, streams, and estuaries. They let water pass downstream but kept salmon from swimming upstream. Indians generally chose shallow locations above tidewater but below spawning grounds; they then drove posts deep into the river bed to support the fencing. This was important because the barrier would back up the stream and put considerable pressure on the structure. Fences were lattices of sticks and branches assembled on portable frames, and each year fishers repaired damaged posts and reinstalled the frames. Some structures were fully portable, posts and all, and many used double weirs and basket traps to corral salmon into small enclosures.[16]

Fishing demanded prolonged and intense labor. Once they installed the weir, Indians could easily capture trapped salmon with dipnets and spears, but they battled not only the fish but time and the elements as well. Weirs and nets could hinder runs for a time, but eventually the rains would begin. Nature imposed its own time schedule, which Indians could not afford to ignore. They had to catch enough salmon to meet their winter needs and disassemble their stations before the fall freshets or risk losing weirs, platforms, and nets to the rising waters.[17]

Taken as a whole, the aboriginal fishery represented a serious effort to exploit salmon runs to their fullest extent. Aboriginal techniques could be frighteningly efficient, and in many respects they compare favorably to modern practices. Weirs blocked all passage to spawning grounds; seines corralled large schools of salmon; and basket traps collected without discrimination. Indians in fact possessed the ability to catch many more salmon than they actually did. The Nez Perce claimed at least fifty different fishing sites in the Snake River basin, each of which could produce between 300 and 700 salmon a day. On the southern Oregon coast a Takelma woman claimed her father caught 300 salmon in a single night. Such figures were not representative of all places at all times, but they do suggest the potential intensity of the fishery.[18]

Estimates of the annual harvest provide a basis for comparing the aboriginal fishery with the industrial fishery, but arriving at figures presents a complicated historical problem. The most direct method involves multiplying per capita consumption by total population. The task is mired in controversy, however, because population figures vary considerably depending on the assumptions of demographers. A basic problem with calculating populations hinges on how many epidemics Indians experienced, which is not always known with precision. The impact of various epidemics also varies

(*Facing page*) "Indian seining at Chenook." With seines up to 600 feet in length and 16 feet deep, Indian fishers such as those depicted in this 1857 etching from the lower Columbia River could be incredibly effective. (James G. Swan, *The Northwest Coast* [1857; repr., Seattle: University of Washington Press, 1972], 105.)

according to where and how groups lived, because diseases thrive in some environments but not others. Differences in the ways Indian groups consumed salmon and in the amount of salmon consumed add to the variables confounding the calculations of harvest.[19]

Researchers have tried to resolve these problems for the Columbia River basin for more than fifty years. The studies have grown increasingly sophisticated as scholars have altered their assumptions about aboriginal America. Even the earliest estimate posited a substantial fishery, but each successive attempt, incorporating more ethnographic and demographic information, has yielded ever higher figures for total harvest. The most recent estimate suggests an aboriginal fishery fully comparable to the industrial fishery during its heyday.

Early estimates of the aboriginal fishery relied on figures that later turned out to be either overly conservative or based on simplistic assumptions. During the 1930s scholars assumed a precontact population in the Pacific Northwest of 50,000. The estimate for annual per capita consumption was the suspiciously convenient figure of 1 pound per day, or 365 pounds a year. In 1940 Joseph Craig and Robert Hacker used these figures to calculate the annual aboriginal harvest in the Columbia basin at 18 million pounds. Noting that the industrial fishery harvested 26 million pounds in 1933, Craig and Hacker argued that the aboriginal fishery represented "a very significant proportion of the commercial catch of today." Another researcher later speculated that eighteen million pounds "may have been near the maximum sustainable yield for Columbia River salmon."[20]

The first estimate was challenged almost immediately. Edward Swindell suggested coastal groups probably consumed more than the 365 pounds per person annual estimate, while Gordon Hewes recalculated the aboriginal harvest to include loss for wastage, a factor Craig and Hacker had ignored. Hewes also used an updated population estimate of 61,500. He increased the Columbia River catch to 22,274,500 pounds, and the coastal catch to 5,600,000 pounds. His work placed the Indian fishery on a par with catches in the 1940s, although by then the Columbia was clearly a declining fishery.[21]

As impressive as these early estimates were, they nevertheless reinforced the stereotype of an Edenic fishery. For all that they consumed, Indians would not have significantly threatened salmon runs. The Hewes's estimate of 22 million pounds represents about 2.3–3.4 million salmon. This was a *lot* of fish, but it would have barely dented the Columbia's historic runs of 11–16 million salmon. Yet we know that Indians possessed the ability to harvest as many salmon as they wished, and anthropologists such as Alex

Krieger argue that Indians fully exploited local runs. The numbers conflict with observations.[22]

More recent research has reconciled this conflict by casting doubt on earlier estimates from two independent directions. In the 1980s demographer Robert Boyd revisited the question of aboriginal populations. Boyd reviewed disease histories throughout the region and noted far more epidemics than previously considered. He then recalculated attrition to account for these additional episodes and arrived at a significantly higher aboriginal population. Anthropologists also reexamined estimates of per capita consumption and discovered significant discrepancies. Although some groups clearly ate less than the 365-pound standard, many others ate considerably more.[23]

In 1986 anthropologist Randall Schalk returned to the question of aboriginal harvest. Using updated data on salmon usage, carbohydrate demands, and salmon biology, Schalk revised the aboriginal harvest to 41,754,800 pounds, or about 4.5–6.3 million salmon out of a run of 11–16 million. Aboriginal harvests were probably fairly consistent due to constant dietary needs, but salmon runs fluctuated considerably in response to changing river and ocean conditions. Thus the impact of the fishery varied considerably. In abundant years the fishery took only about 28 percent of the run, but in poor years it could exceed 57 percent. Schalk's estimate represents a harvest fully comparable to the industrial fishery during its heyday between 1883 and 1919, which surpassed 41 million pounds only nine times.[24]

Schalk's and Boyd's estimates seem the most plausible. Their figures harmonize best with current understandings of aboriginal demography, and consumption meshes with regional correlations between run size and local populations. If accurate, their research suggests that Indians put considerable pressure on salmon runs yet avoided permanent harm.

Two factors help explain what appears to be Indians' long-term success at exploiting the fisheries without seriously diminishing runs. The first is spatial. Unlike the industrial fishery, which concentrated itself on the lower Columbia, aboriginal fishers dispersed over the entire basin. Their behavior helped match harvests to local run sizes, creating a better fit between consumption and abundance than the almost limitless demand that developed around canned salmon. The second reason involved salmon behavior. Large runs can lead to fierce competition on spawning beds. Salmon will mortally wound their rivals during courting, and spawners often destroy previously fertilized eggs while excavating gravel during mating. When space on spawning beds is limited, there can indeed be such a thing as too many salmon. Superabundance retards reproduction, but thinning a run, if done evenly throughout the system, may actually increase productivity. Thus intensive fishing did not necessarily destroy runs.[25]

But food storage and trade practices did threaten salmon by extending consumption in both time and space. For at least 2,500 years, Oregon country Indians have preserved salmon for winter consumption. As Indians learned to preserve food, they began to establish more sedentary patterns. This represented an extraordinary development for a nonagricultural society, but food storage also increased pressure on runs by extending the period Indians could consume the seasonal food. Indians began to eat salmon not just during fishing season but all year. As Indians perfected their techniques over the next several millennia, harvests intensified and populations increased. Some groups dried salmon in the open air, while others jerked the meat outdoors or in smokehouses. Breaking it into tiny pieces before drying slowed deterioration even further. The curing process altered the flavor, but coastal groups developed a dip using whale oil or seal blubber that enhanced the taste and became a popular trade item. By the time William Clark descended to the Pacific in 1805, he noted drying stations all along the Snake and Columbia Rivers. The center of production, however, was at The Dalles.[26]

Biology, culture, and geography intersected to make The Dalles fishery a unique natural and social space, and the rendezvous that developed around salmon produced complex webs of material, social, and cultural exchanges. Wasco and Wishram Indians combined salmon biology with Plateau geography to develop a unique food called salmon pemmican, which exceeded all other salmon preparations in durability and value. Salmon ceased to feed when they left the ocean, living off stored fats for the remainder of their fading lives. By the time they reached The Dalles, their fat content was considerably lower than at the mouth of the river. After men captured the salmon, women would pulverize the meat, spread it on open-air racks, and let nature take its course. The lean meat cured extremely efficiently in the warm, desiccated air of the Plateau. Within days it was completely dried and ready to be packed in ninety-pound baskets. The resulting product reportedly stayed edible for years. A fifteen-mile stretch of the Columbia supported a permanent population of well over 1,000 people. Each household prepared about 3,000 pounds of pemmican for subsistence and another 1,000 pounds for trade.[27]

The pemmican trade brought Wascos and Wishrams a privileged position that they jealously guarded. For over 1,300 years Indians came from as far away as the Great Plains, Northern California, and Puget Sound to visit and exchange with the resident "merchant fishermen" and other visiting groups. Both William Clark and Alexander Ross likened the atmosphere to a "great mart." But the "mart" was actually a complicated system of material, intellectual, social, and cultural exchanges. Indians from the Plateau and Plains traded furs, skins, slaves, buffalo meat, berries, wool, camases, and obsidian for salmon, shellfish, fish and seal oil, seal meat, hemp, wood carvings, wapatos, and native copper from the lower Columbia and coast. Fishing groups sought bear grass and Indian hemp from the Plateau for net making. Inland groups coveted dentalia, haliotis, and olivella shells as forms of currency and prestige. Pemmican traveled in all directions because of its durability. Indians also gathered information on food abundance and military affairs. Although participants consumed massive amounts of salmon during these rendezvous, trade was never strictly economic. At The Dalles material exchanges melded with social intercourse, gambling, and marriage arrangements.[28]

Marriage negotiations were especially important because kinship established trading relationships and access to resources, and food issues were a primary concern when creating alliances in the Oregon country. Marriages involved a series of material and social exchanges that influenced individuals and communities alike. Intermarried families took turns visiting their relations and bestowing gifts of shells and food. Hosts used these occasions to display wealth and increase prestige by impressing guests. Meals could turn into orgiastic feasts of salmon, salmon eggs, and other delicacies. Although the host reaped the rewards of the event, the entire community contributed because all shared the benefits of advantageous alliances. An abundant supply of salmon was an invaluable asset in the pursuit of prestige. A Nestucca myth allegorized the point. One day a man found a salmon filled with dentalia shells, a form of currency throughout western North America. As long as he treated the salmon properly, it continued to generate shells for the increasingly wealthy Indian. The connection between access to salmon, proper treatment, and wealth was unmistakable.[29]

Displays of wealth and power were critical moments in aboriginal life. A performance that increased one's prestige produced a spiraling sequence of benefits that translated into greater power for individuals and greater security for communities. An impressive distribution of gifts enhanced prestige; greater prestige enhanced bargaining power in marriage arrangements; and opportune alliances gave access to additional resources. Maintaining access to fishing, hunting, and gathering sites over a wide area was also an important hedge against the failure of local resources. In times of scarcity, groups relied heavily on their relations.[30]

As a conduit for resources, kinship had both spatial and temporal implications. The desire for widespread access encouraged exogamous marriage with distant groups. Individual villages were thus socially heterogeneous and polyglot. To maintain these alliances through time, most Oregon country groups practiced not only exogamy but also forms of the sororate and levirate, which extended kinship beyond death through ritual remarriage of the surviving spouse to an appropriate brother or sister of the deceased. Kinship was thus a complicated system of exchanges involving people, food, wealth, and prestige; as will be discussed later, access to salmon also influenced forms of property transfer.[31]

This broad, salmon-based trading network enabled Indians to extend the spatial boundaries of consumption by exchanging local surpluses for distant surpluses. The Kalapuya of the upper Willamette Valley were salmon-poor because Willamette Falls usually blocked migration. What the upper Willamette lacked in salmon, however, it more than made up for in camases, wapatos, and berries. These plants were valuable trade items, so Kalapuyas harvested and exchanged them for salmon at Willamette Falls or the coast. In 1826 trapper Alexander McLeod encountered two separate parties of Kalapuyas on their way to the coast to trade camases and berries for salmon. Such exchanges increased pressure on salmon runs by expanding the spaces of consumption, and the trade was so important that not even war could interrupt it.[32]

Food storage and trade were mundane matters during times of abundance, but they became critical activities when scarcity threatened. Fluctuating ocean conditions, droughts, and floods depleted salmon runs independent of human agency. Salmon runs could appear too soon or too late or pass too quickly to be harvested. In such instances a group could easily find itself with insufficient stores for winter. Seasonal changes in salmon biology further complicated matters. Salmon that ran in spring had more body fat than fall fish because they had longer migrations in time and distance. More fat provided more carbohydrates, but it also made the meat harder to preserve—this is why pemmican came from The Dalles and not closer to the ocean. Fall salmon presented a trade-off. Fall fish had less fat because they made shorter journeys and spawned sooner. This made the meat easier to cure but also less nutritious. Poor preparation further eroded nutritional quality, and no matter how well prepared, all dried salmon except pemmican went bad within six months—regardless of fat content. Even abundant supplies of salmon did not necessarily ensure a sufficient supply of protein.[33]

Episodes of scarcity reveal the genius of social organization in the Oregon country. When starvation threatened, Indians called in their markers and visited kin with more resources. White explorers recorded several of these incidents. During their journey east in 1806, Lewis and Clark encountered a group from The Dalles descending the Columbia in search of food. Clark wrote that the Indians "had consumed their winter store of dryed fish. . . . & that they did not expect the Salmon to arrive untill the full of the next moon which happens on the 2d of May." Peter Skene Ogden witnessed similar episodes in eastern and southern Oregon, but there is a danger of overstating the problem. Starvation was a real threat, yet the sight of desperate hunger was traumatic for both victim and observer. Although emotions might have exaggerated impressions, discussions were not confined to outsiders. The ubiquity of aboriginal myths about famine suggests that privation was an omnipresent concern. The issue of prevalence aside, such episodes clearly demonstrated that Indians could exhaust their supplies of salmon.[34]

Aboriginal fishing and the extension of consumption through food storage and trade posed significant threats to salmon. That Indians did not overfish despite heavy consumption suggests that they practiced some form of restraint. The question is how, and the answer runs to the core of aboriginal culture. Restraint flowed from the concepts and practices of Oregon country Indians, who filled their world with spirits that demanded respect. The way they understood this relationship resulted in a series of activities dedicated to propitiating salmon, and although conservation was not the stated purpose, moderation of harvests was the effective result.[35]

Dependence on salmon created complicated forms of respect. Indians feared the disappearance of salmon, and episodes of scarcity underscored the need to treat the fish carefully. These themes pervaded cultural forms of celebration and deference. Myths revealed the rationale for moderating behavior; ceremonies and taboos became the means.

American Indians developed a sense of empathy for their environments. Empathy manifested itself in a series of customs that circumscribed social behavior toward nature, but respect varied with importance and not all in nature was equal. Animals, plants, and forces that were central to aboriginal life tended to possess spiritual power and demand deference, and some animal spirits were clearly stronger than others. Generally speaking, the more important the material relationship, the stronger the spiritual connection. In the Oregon country, salmon stood above all.[36]

As a result, subsistence, worldviews, and cultural activities had a circular relationship in the Oregon country. Abundant salmon runs encouraged subsistence specialization. Specialization and food storage enabled more sedentary social patterns, denser populations, and winter hiatuses. Winter villages became the loci for such complex rituals as myth festivals and spirit dances. These annual gatherings hinged on and paid homage to salmon. Oral traditions related the importance of salmon to the continuation of life; ceremonies paid ritual respect; taboos circumscribed behavior to prevent offense; and all these practices moderated harvests. Culture helped sustain the fish that sustained the society that sustained the culture. The circle was complete.[37]

And the circle began and ended with salmon. As food, salmon profoundly influenced subsistence patterns; in trade, they were currency in the pursuit of prestige, power, and alliances. Salmon's material importance matched its cultural position. Indians imbued salmon with spiritual value and elevated it to cultural icon. Salmon became potent symbols of renewal and sometimes even culture heroes. They were at once food, currency, and icon.[38]

The oral traditions of Oregon country Indians explained the Indians' place in nature. Indians told how transformers (mystical beings) prepared the world for them. These mythic characters were demigods with personalities that resembled the animals they were named after: Wolf was predatory and socialized in groups; Fox, intelligent and crafty; Bear, ponderous but dangerous; Salmon, ever decaying and reborn in silvery beauty. At the end of the mythic age, transformers changed into the animals, plants, and geologic features of the aboriginal world. The narrative of transmogrification symbolically linked humans with nature.[39]

Interpreting these myths is complicated and problematic. Original meanings are not easily determined. Depopulation, relocation, and acculturation have drastically altered both the content and context of myths, and the catalog of stories has dwindled drastically since the late eighteenth century. Some stories died with their narrators during epidemics; others lost meaning or gained new ones. Ethnographers and linguists did not record these stories until the late nineteenth century, and too often they used only a few or even one informant for information. Franz Boas relied heavily on Charles Cultee for his information about the Lower Chinook, while Edward Sapir based his entire interpretation of Takelma society on interviews with Frances Johnson and Molly Orton. Such strategies severely limited what could be known because Indians often segregated women and men during subsistence and ceremonial activities. Thus gender delimited knowledge of such activities as fishing, birthing, and ceremonies. The result has been a radically reduced selection of myths for modern research.[40]

Understanding a myth is further complicated by the medium of presentation. Much of a story's content was embedded in the gestures and intonation of oral performance, so important visual and tonal information was lost in written translation. Myths also served functions beyond instruction. Stories were sources of entertainment, a way of relieving boredom and anxiety during the long, cold nights of winter. The ribald, scatological humor of some stories may have ameliorated concerns about dwindling resources or tensions arising from living in close quarters for prolonged periods, or such stories may have been enjoyed simply because they were funny. After all, sometimes a cigar *is* just a cigar.[41]

Nevertheless, the ubiquity of certain plots and themes suggests a common relationship between Indians and salmon throughout the Oregon country. Many stories emphasized equality between humans and other species through allegorical or physical interchangeability. Some myths anthropomorphized plants and animals so they could converse like humans. Other stories transmogrified animals into human form. A Shasta myth described how the culture hero Coyote transformed a girl into a steelhead and then himself into the form of the girl. Tillamooks told stories about salmon that turned into men and danced on water, while the Nez Perce ended a tale with a woman leaping into a stream and changing into a salmon. Others relied on important similes. A Shasta myth described Beaver eating wood but calling it salmon. Another prevalent feature was the notion that salmon were a gift from the mythic era. The Tillamooks explained how Tk'a created the world and placed salmon in the rivers for humans. In the end Tk'a transformed himself into a famous rock on Siletz Bay, but his soul returned to the country of salmon and became their master.[42]

Stories of Coyote were particularly widespread, and several related directly to humans' inheritance of salmon. In some stories Coyote created and gave order to the world in preparation for humans. In others he played the trickster, representing the wicked and bawdy side of humanity. One plot common to groups from the Plateau to the lower Klamath River told how Coyote gave salmon to humans. A group of women had built a dam so they could hoard salmon. Humans living upstream began to starve, so Coyote tried to release the fish. The women knew about Coyote's plans, so he deceived them by assuming the guise of an orphaned baby. The women gave refuge to the disguised Coyote, but whenever they left him alone he would work feverishly to free the fish. By the time the women discovered the subterfuge it was too late. Coyote destroyed the dam and then, in punishment, turned the women into frogs or swallows that reappear each spring with the first salmon runs. Some groups replaced Coyote with local culture heroes, but the narrative structure remained essentially similar throughout the Oregon country.[43]

Indians living along the lower Columbia regarded Salmon as their culture hero. One myth chronicled an allegorical journey by Salmon (the mythic character) up the Columbia during a time of late-winter privation. The upriver procession reenacted the majestic salmon runs that coursed the Columbia each spring, and many of the characters accompanying Salmon also reappeared with the spring salmon runs. Salmon greeted various plants as "brother" or "nephew" and paid tribute to their importance as food sources during the weeks before the spring salmon runs. Linguist Dell Hymes has described Salmon's role in these stories as the "one who determines future destinies."[44]

Another myth highlighted the notion of regeneration. In the story Salmon was murdered, but one of "his" eggs survived to spawn a son. In one version the son was another Salmon; in another he became Steelhead. That Steelhead's mother could also be his father, Salmon, underscores the very different rules governing causality in aboriginal culture. The story illustrated the belief that salmon were literally reincarnated from the bones or organs of the previous year's ceremonial fish.[45]

The story also recounted how salmon's return abruptly reversed the subsistence fortunes of Indians. Abundance replaced privation in a dramatic moment as the salmon reappeared in runs so large they churned the rivers like boiling water. Less than a month after meeting starving villagers, William Clark witnessed the emotional force of that moment: "There was great joy with the nativs last night in consequence of the arrival of the Salmon; one of those fish was cought, this was the harbenger of good news to them. They informed us that those fish would arive in great quantities in the course of about 5 days. this fish was dressed and being divided into small pieces was given to each child in the village."[46] The festival revealed the emotional impact of salmon runs. The radical shift in fortunes fused a powerful spiritual element to salmon, while the regularity of runs reinforced notions of immortality. It appeared as though salmon knew exactly when to return. Indians consequently believed that salmon willfully surrendered themselves and that as long as they treated salmon with respect the cycle would continue. Indians were bound to salmon by a spiritual and material symbiosis. Humans depended on salmon for subsistence, while salmon required deference to remain immortal.[47]

Myths extolled the necessity of respect. Some stories featured culture heroes advising humans to leave nothing to waste or to take no more than needed. In a Tillamook myth Thunderer admonished an Indian, "Don't catch more than you are able to eat." Others warned both characters and audience to respect salmon or else. In the Coos myth "Salmon Did Ill to

Boys," mischievous boys used a salmon to play a trick on a younger boy. The following spring salmon avenged the insult by bringing a tidal wave that swept away all disrespectful villagers.[48]

Other tales were more allegorical. In a Kathlamet tale Crab belittled a school of young salmon for being too small, but when Crab attempted to grab the fish, they were so heavy they broke his claws. When other characters behaved similarly, salmon disappeared. One common tale featured a magical trap that caught salmon and called the owner when full. The trap did not know when to stop, however, so the owner was forever tending the filled basket. Unable even to start a cooking fire, the exasperated owner (often in the guise of Coyote) eventually cursed the basket. The basket immediately lost its magic and the salmon disappeared. Such stories made clear both the burdens of honoring salmon and the consequences of failure.[49]

The Nez Perce myth "The Maiden and Salmon" encapsulates many of the themes of Oregon country myths. The story begins with Salmon (as a human) instructing his wife (also a human) to return some part of his body to the water if he is killed. Otherwise he will not regenerate. The Five Wolves then hire Rattlesnake to bite Salmon while they kidnap Salmon's wife. Rattlesnake complies, but a drop of Salmon's blood reaches the river. Thus reborn, Salmon begins a quest to avenge his murder and rescue his wife. Along the way he meets a kindly elder and rewards him with a stream full of salmon. He also encounters foolish Coyote making a net to "ravage" the fish. Salmon punishes Coyote by instructing the fish to avoid Coyote's river. Salmon also captures Rattlesnake but spares his life because the snake regrets his disrespect. Salmon finally reaches the Five Wolves' den at the headwaters of a river "where Salmon can never arrive." He releases his wife and together they kill four of the Wolves, but the fifth proves too wary to be trapped. Salmon and Maiden make their escape by diving into the stream and transforming themselves into fish. Immortality, restoring salmon to the waters, upstream migration, respect repaid, offense punished, naturalistic similes, and transmogrification: "The Maiden and Salmon" epitomizes Oregon country Indians' cultural construction of salmon.[50]

Scholars have focused on the cultural and spiritual aspects of ceremonies, but few have noted that fear played as strong a role as reverence in shaping worship. As stories explained time and again, to offend salmon was to court disaster. The Coos described how a fisher discarded a salmon heart and the fish disappeared, leaving him to starve. A Tillamook myth warned, "Don't burn the salmon when you roast them, for they do not like it. They may take revenge." Catastrophe plagued Indians enough in real life to be accorded a conspicuous place in their mythic world. The dark side of dependence was a fear of failure, which engendered respect for the fish that sustained life.[51]

Myths also explicated rituals and taboos. Characters behaved properly and improperly to delineate correct behavior. A Tillamook myth relates a hunter's visit with Thunderer and the lessons he learns of how not to offend spirits. When the hunter returns to his village and conveys his knowledge, he is proclaimed a great shaman. An Alsea myth describes a culture hero catching and preparing salmon. The hero proclaims, "My children will habitually do this to [salmon] after they shall become people."[52]

Clatsop stories conveyed the very particular knowledge necessary to ensure the return of salmon. Coyote attempted to catch salmon near a Clatsop village but repeatedly failed because he did not know the local taboos. Following each failure, Coyote asked his excrement why he could not catch salmon, and his excrement mocked "foolish Coyote" for not knowing a particular fishing or cooking taboo. The story was necessarily long because Coyote had to break every taboo for the audience's sake. The ordeal of trial and error exhausted Coyote, but in the end he declared, "The [people] shall always do in the same manner." The nearby Kathlamet told a similar story but altered the taboos to fit local customs. Although such myths instructed through magical discourse, the setting and activities depicted everyday events. Story mythologized life; life mimicked art. Ideology and action affirmed one another.[53]

What myths expressed in words, ceremonies expressed in deed; they were interrelated halves of a coherent ideology. The first-salmon ceremony was the foremost example of this integration. Indians throughout the Oregon country performed the ceremony with the arrival of the first run of the year, and although timing and customs varied widely, it was consistently the most elaborate festival of the year, choreographing the entire community in a series of rigidly prescribed activities. The ceremony wove respect and gratitude into ritual just as myth integrated belief into plot.[54]

Groups went to great lengths not to offend the precious fish. Tillamook festivals lasted about a week, and strict local customs governed capture, conveyance, and preparation. The meat had to be cut lengthwise to avoid severing the backbone. If Indians destroyed the integrity of the fish, its spirit would not fully regenerate. This would offend the salmon, and they would not return. The Tillamook roasted the fish and presented it to the headman, who ate the entire fish, tail and all. At the end of the ceremony they carefully burned the bones and blood to ensure the fish's immortality. The Tillamook feared that if salmon were handled carelessly, "The master of the salmon would become angry and take back the salmon, and the people would become sick."[55]

These disposal rites varied considerably. The Alsea boiled their first fish; other groups differed on who handled and ate the fish, what remained, and how they disposed of it. Ceremonies along the southern coast used priests called formulists. Formulists recited a set pattern of words (the formula) over the fish, and the person who conducted the ceremony might change from year to year. Ceremonies along the lower Columbia diverged significantly from those nearer The Dalles or across the Plateau. The Tillamook explained these differences in functional terms: each stream had its own salmon master, such as Ecahnie, Tk'a, As'ai'yahal, or Seu'ku, so Indians had to devise a range of fishing, cutting, and bone rituals to help masters recognize the correct stream to which each fish must be sent.[56]

The first-salmon ceremony was not a universal practice, however. Neither the Nez Perce, the Cayuse, the Kalapuya of the upper Willamette Valley, nor the Indians living around Klamath Lakes observed it. Salmon were seasonally important for the Nez Perce and Cayuse, but the undependability of runs in the far interior discouraged the sort of specialization usually associated with the ceremony. Klamaths did observe a "first-fish" ceremony, but they honored the locally important sucker fish, not salmon. Similarly, Northern Paiutes observed a "first-fruits" ceremony that included salmon but was hardly dedicated to it.[57]

Bone and organ rites epitomized the concept of regeneration. The Coos believed that the essence of salmon resided in its bones, and ubiquitous taboos against severing backbones revealed this belief's wide currency. Coquilles told of how Salmon warned Coyote not to cut the bones of Salmon's children (actual fish) lest they not be reborn, and Kathlamets spoke of a time of hunger that ended only when they replaced salmon bones in the river. Returning salmon bones and organs to the water (or burning them) manifested the Indian notion of the immortality of a salmon's soul. All coastal groups and most inland fishers performed some form of ritual disposal of the ceremonial salmon.[58]

Taboos shared by many Oregon country Indians further illustrate the elevated stature of salmon. Groups typically banned impure members from participating in ceremonies, touching fishing gear, or eating fish. The list of untouchables included pubescent girls, menstruating women, new parents, murderers, mourners, and anyone who handled corpses. Blood seems to be the binding theme. Such taboos reveal a concern for maintaining good relations with salmon. As anthropologist Erna Gunther notes, "In every ritual it is clear that the welfare of the animal is most important, and the taboos regulate conduct that [the] spirit may not be offended." The first-salmon ceremony was a powerful social event that confirmed social inequalities even as it bound communities together in reverence for a fish.[59]

Myth and ritual were inseparable in everyday activity, and the relationship is crucial for explaining how Indians tempered their exploitation of salmon runs. Myths projected a complex understanding of salmon: revered and cursed, immortal and rotting, avenging and merciful, killer and victim—salmon were at once icon, currency, and food. Oregon country Indians thrived by consuming what was sacred; they compensated by holding elaborate rituals of respect that produced incidental results that helped moderate consumption.

Born out of respect and fear, ceremonies and taboos significantly moderated aboriginal consumption of salmon. Some groups restricted access to scarcer species such as chum and steelhead, thus relieving pressure on runs at risk. Many restricted consumption during ceremonial periods by limiting fishers to what they could eat before sunset. Groups living along the lower Columbia dictated the number of times a net could be fished, while others ceased fishing entirely during ceremonies or mourning. Because Indians conducted ceremonies throughout the Oregon country, a uniform pattern of behavior unfolded across temporal and physical space. When salmon arrived, Indians restrained their activities. They caught only what they could eat for the duration of the first-fish ceremony, a period sometimes lasting two weeks or longer. Isolated instances of such behavior might not have been significant, but when every group acted similarly, conservation gained spatial coherence. The ceremony retarded harvests and helped ensure adequate escapement.[60]

By the early nineteenth century, whites were well acquainted with Indian customs. The strength of aboriginal taboos repeatedly frustrated trappers and traders wishing to trade for salmon during ceremonial periods. Indians implored whites to observe rules for cutting, cooking, and eating salmon, and when they balked, Indians would intervene to preserve good standing with the fish. Non-Indians still received salmon, but Indians took care to cut and cook the fish before the exchange. They also refused to trade more than a day's supply of salmon and made certain that whites understood they had to consume it before sunset. Such encounters frustrated non-Indians. Trappers needed to replenish their stores through trade, but as long as Indians controlled the fisheries, the trappers were at a distinct disadvantage. By the 1830s some groups decided not to trade salmon to non-Indians during ceremonial periods. Their actions demonstrated an obsession with maintaining good relations with salmon, even at the risk of antagonizing whites.[61]

For all its spiritual content, ceremony was also relevant to group survival. In the midst of the festivities at The Dalles, William Clark noted that the "custom is founded on a supersticious opinion that it will hasten the arrival of the salmon." Indians used spiritual means to ensure material consequences. Propitiation revealed both spiritual and utilitarian motives. Out of a "desire to treat the fish so runs [would] be plentiful," Indians propitiated salmon spirits lest the fish withhold its favors.[62]

The very dependence on salmon may have restrained the adoption of salmon as a personal spirit. Indians engaged in spirit quests throughout the Oregon country. The quest was a rite of passage for adolescents. Young men and women journeyed to sites of great spiritual importance to fast, bathe, exercise, and meditate for days in preparation for visions. The object was to acquire through revelation or dream a personal animal spirit that would accompany them through life. The form of the animal spirit determined what powers an individual could acquire. Deer spirit helped hunters stalk deer; sturgeon spirit made warriors brave and indestructible; rattlesnake spirit protected people from bites.[63]

But spirit powers also entailed responsibilities. Some groups observed taboos against eating the animal form of one's spirit—thus someone with deer spirit could not eat deer. This presented a clear conflict, however, between salmon specialists and salmon spirit, and interestingly, only the Klamath Lakes Indians mentioned the possibility of acquiring salmon spirit. They were also one of the few groups that did not depend upon salmon. This suggests complex relationships between material dependence and spiritual value. Some Indians even courted spirits that preyed on salmon. Guardian spirits such as Iqamia'itx and Itcli'xyan were valued for their ability to help fishers locate and capture salmon. Indians who would supplicate spirits to help them capture salmon, even as they propitiated spirits to prevent the destruction of salmon, are a challenge to understand. Although we tend to separate the pragmatic from the spiritual and accord primacy to one or the other, Oregon country Indians did not necessarily make such rigid distinctions. Their relationship with salmon reveals a more complicated view of the world.[64]

There is some evidence to suggest that Oregon country Indians possessed what we would define as an ecological understanding of nature. They developed an encyclopedic knowledge of resources, and their ability to identify salmon eggs and spawning grounds suggests that they clearly understood the function of reproduction. They also may have recognized the need for escapement. During the twentieth century, Indians at The Dalles appointed "salmon chiefs," who would open and close fishing daily to ensure escapement. It seems reasonable therefore to acknowledge at least the possibility that Indians may have devised their ceremonies and rituals with an eye to their impact on a specialized subsistence economy.[65]

At the same time, it would be anachronistic to portray Indians as conservationists, in the sense of anticipating the rationale and logic of modern conservation. Myths did counsel listeners to take no more than needed and taboos restricted consumption, but the explicit motive was propitiation, not conservation. The concern was to prevent offense. Moreover, it is hard to demonstrate causal links between many rituals and conservation. Bone rites and taboos against cutting the backbone have no direct causal link to abundant runs. Similarly, the Clatsops once buried a man alive because they thought the individual might die during the salmon run. They did not want to offend salmon with the presence of a dead person. Such actions do not easily fit into a modern definition of conservation. Aboriginal ceremonies and taboos nevertheless moderated harvest *effectively, if not intentionally.* They retarded consumption across time and space so significant portions of runs could escape upstream to spawn. Belief and action produced an emotional and material symbiosis between humans and salmon. Massive salmon runs sustained a thriving society, and humans acknowledged their debt in ways that helped sustain those runs.[66]

Ceremony did moderate harvests, but Indians also took steps to limit access to salmon by claiming usufruct rights to fishing sites and restricting access to kin. In doing so, they imposed territorial practices that further limited salmon harvests. For all its spiritual significance, salmon remained above all a food. Indians explicitly noted its economic importance. In story after story salmon are reserved for humans as food. A Coos tale states, "Someone must have given us this food"; one Wishram story announces, "People will soon come who will want these salmon"; another declares, "Those fish will be the people's food"; a Takelma story prophesies, "People shall spear salmon, they will go to get food"; a Kalapuya myth proclaims, "You will be Chinook Salmon. You will be eaten"; and a Clackamas tradition instructs, "These things are food."[67]

Salmon's importance as food is crucial to a discussion of conservation, because exploitation intensified rapidly once ceremonies ended. Moderation, in other words, cannot be explained functionally based solely in terms of respect. Additional measures were also necessary, and controlling access to fish and fishing sites was critical. Many groups made claims to strategic resources, but in the scramble for salmon all Oregon country Indians asserted usufruct claims to coveted fishing sites. Since good sites were limited, restricted access throughout the region effectively throttled the number of harvesters.[68]

Both individuals and communities claimed fishing sites. Some coastal and Plateau groups acknowledged individual rights, but villages usually controlled major sites like falls or weirs. The distinctions often blurred in practice. Individuals could hold priority claims to a station, but all community members enjoyed access. Outsiders had to request permission, however, and villagers tightly monitored harvest. This was true even among Northern Paiutes, which was extraordinary for a culture generally noted for sharing resources. The universal practice of restricting access, even by groups who normally shared, underscores the importance of Oregon country salmon.[69]

Maintaining a claim required the social means to secure it, and here kinship took on special significance. The village was the dominant political unit in the Oregon country, but these were patrilineal societies in which men were related and women were outsiders. The village was essentially an extended kin group. Patrilineality had important consequences, however. Blood gave political identity genetic coherence, but consanguinity necessitated exogamy as a biological necessity. Exogamous marriages opened access to outsiders, so to retain title to fishing sites within the community fathers passed their claims to sons. Patrilineal inheritance was necessary because women left the village at marriage, and control would have dissipated rapidly under bilateral or matrilineal inheritance.[70]

Kinship also influenced sharing. Consanguinity tempered selfish behavior within the group. In villages where individual ownership prevailed, owners redistributed "their" salmon to the rest of the community to increase prestige and obligations. Under communal ownership the headman parceled out salmon to families. The material and social effects were identical. Sharing reinforced both cohesion and hierarchy. Oral traditions suggest that sharing was a moral imperative. In one story a brother dies from gluttony and greed because he would not share his salmon; in another myth villagers punish a girl for hoarding camases. Indians inculcated sharing early. Every group imposed taboos against eating a first kill or a first basket of gathered vegetables or fruits. Groups expected youths to give their initial harvests to other members or incur endless bad luck. Such taboos reinforced the ideal of interdependence.[71]

Anthropologist Deward Walker likens communal ownership to "stewardship" because Indians managed resources to support both present and future generations. Kinship exchange networks weakened exclusive claims because they expanded the community of consumers, but usufruct claims—even when not invoked—implied a right to restrict access if circumstances required. Territoriality was thus an important means of limiting access, further suggesting that Indians recognized a vested interest in conserving salmon.[72]

Oregon country Indians related to nature as cohabitants and consumers. Their complex thoughts and actions defy romanticism. They were hardly preternatural beings exuding environmental wisdom, those proverbial "children of nature." Nor were they timeless and unchanging. Indians' understanding of salmon was contextual and historical. Groups adapted their fisheries as cultural and environmental circumstances warranted. Culture and environment shaped each other reciprocally, and both were in constant flux. As oral traditions instructed time and again, knowledge was not immaculately conceived but wrought from much trial and error. Salmon conservation was the sum of centuries or millennia of social and cultural development.[73]

Thus Oregon country Indians' ability to sustain their intensive fisheries suggests that a new image is required: Indians were seasoned, rational fishers. They developed a culture and economy that meshed well with nature. Respect, propitiation, utility, and territoriality reinforced a coherent, moderate strategy of exploitation. The synergistic result was a culturally specific form of conservation. No single mechanism entirely mitigated the potential for destruction, but in combination they worked wonders. Fishing techniques could wreak havoc on salmon runs, and cultural routes to prestige encouraged heavy consumption; but cultural forms of respect moderated harvest, and the technical limitations of food preservation capped storage capacity. Nature also influenced consumption by presenting an inviting resource of astonishing proportion and regularity, yet runs fluctuated wildly and their ephemeral presence imposed limitations on exploitation that were independent of culture or technology. Thus culture, technology, and nature both encouraged and moderated exploitation. Dependence yielded respect for the fish that sustained life. Together they produced social and cultural customs that effectively moderated harvests.[74]

2 / Historicizing Overfishing

Popular imagination misconstrued the aboriginal fishery, simplifying it as a benign activity. By positing that Edenic past, we have been able to explain the subsequent decline of salmon as a fall from grace. This quasi-lapsarian story is tidy and linear. It begins with the expulsion of Indians from Eden. The wages of sin then descend in the shape of the industrial fishery, followed by the rise of modern civilization as Babylon. It ends with a flood of dams. The plot holds both cultural resonance and political utility, and writers, scholars, and managers alike have used it to shape public opinion and policy. As history, however, the tale is neither particularly accurate nor very enlightening.[1]

In real time, these events unfolded simultaneously, not sequentially. Indian populations did fall precipitously, but they never left the stage. Overfishing did occur, but it happened because of concurrent social, economic, cultural, and environmental changes. Dams did provide the coup de grâce, but they have been reducing salmon habitat since the 1840s. Thus the fisheries took too many fish not simply because there were too many nets in the water—that is a tautology—but because many more activities began to stress runs with the arrival of Euro-Americans. A complicated history of the salmon crisis offers messier, but far more interesting, lessons about declining salmon than a simple lapsarian tale.

The most significant environmental change during the nineteenth century was the demographic shift from Indians to Euro-Americans. The scale of change was astonishing. By 1900 the number of Oregon country Indians had declined 95 percent, while non-Indians had increased from fewer than 800 in 1840 to more than 1.1 million.

Anthropologist Robert Boyd has called disease "the single most important factor in the aboriginal depopulation" of the Pacific Northwest. Nonindigenous pathogens such as smallpox, measles, influenza, and malaria ravaged American Indians. These exotic sicknesses produced "virgin-soil epidemics" that swept over entire groups, and initial exposures killed between 33 and 90 percent of affected populations. High attrition rates stemmed from several interacting factors. Diseases often struck in combinations that produced a lethal synergism. In addition, because pathogens did not affect all bodies identically, they rarely decimated a genetically heterogeneous population. The entire Indian population of North America descended from a relatively small group of founders, however, and because they were so closely related, diseases that could kill one member were far more likely to kill many members.[2]

Virgin-soil epidemics unleashed a cascading series of consequences on society. Mild infections often developed into serious bouts because few members remained healthy enough to attend the sick or provide nourishment. If epidemics interrupted harvests, periods of famine often followed outbreaks. Aboriginal medicinal practices often exacerbated the course of an illness. Indian healers had no experience with European ailments. They did not know how to treat effectively the symptoms they encountered, and contagions easily spread from the unquarantined sick to uninfected members and from village to village. Smoke-filled and flea-infested plank houses and pit houses presented pathogens with the aboriginal equivalent of a petri dish, and frequent trade along the Columbia and other waterways ensured that diseases cut a wide swath across most of the Oregon country.[3]

Establishing a reliable chronology of epidemics is difficult. Some oral traditions suggest that first contact occurred before the 1770s; the earliest Europeans to visit the region may have arrived during the sixteenth and seventeenth centuries, but most demographers dismiss the impact of such explorers as Juan de Fuca (1592), Admiral de Ponte (1640), and Admiral Shapely (1640). Archeologist Sarah Campbell suggests that an epidemic may have occurred during the first half of the sixteenth century, but the evidence is sketchy and populations had rebounded to predisease levels by the 1770s in any case.[4]

Most demographers believe that population decline began with a smallpox epidemic sometime after 1775. It continued when a second wave of smallpox struck in 1801. The most likely source for the initial outbreak was the Spanish expedition of the *Santiago* and *Sonora*, which visited the Northwest coast in 1775. The second epidemic traveled across the Rockies from the northern Great Plains. Each episode likely killed about one-third of all Indians exposed to the disease. Indians quickly associated these catastrophic events with European contact. The Clallam of Puget Sound, for example, linked the arrival of a trading vessel in 1790 with Dokwebutl, a spirit that brought great sicknesses.[5]

Learning to recognize the link between Europeans and disease came quickly, but learning how to survive disease took much longer. During the next century epidemics ravaged the Oregon country. In 1824 and 1825 measles struck the coastal and Plateau regions, killing between 10 and 20 percent of the population. In 1837 and 1838 smallpox took a smaller toll along the coast. The deadliest epidemic was the "intermittent fever" of the 1830s. The fever, now recognized as malaria, nearly extirpated Indians in the Willamette Valley and along the lower Columbia River. Between 1830 and 1841 the death rate exceeded 85 percent. In some areas of the Multnomah basin losses reached 98 percent. The Hudson's Bay Company's (HBC) chief factor John McLoughlin estimated losses in 1830 alone at upward of 75 percent. Malaria reappeared three times between 1831 and 1833, taking a heavy toll with each recurrence.[6]

The way Indians and whites treated malaria reveals the limits of each culture's ability to understand the forces reshaping the region. Possessing some knowledge of malaria, McLoughlin and others administered quinine and cinchona to combat fever. They struggled mightily to save lives, but many Indians refused white medicines. They instead relied on indigenous treatments. Unfortunately, sweat baths and cold swims did not cure; they induced shock and pneumonia. Ignorance killed, but no race or culture had a corner on that condition. Some white settlers also rejected quinine in favor of prayer meetings. New diseases failed to respond to old remedies.[7]

Nonindigenous pathogens continued to kill Indians throughout the nineteenth century. During the 1840s, a series of "immigrant diseases," including measles, whooping cough, dysentery, and cholera, killed one-third of the Plateau Indians and about 10 percent along the lower Columbia. In 1851 smallpox, measles, and tuberculosis wracked southern Oregon Indians. Smallpox returned a fourth time in 1853, taking somewhat less than 40 percent of coastal Indians, and a fifth time in 1862 and 1863. Each episode further pared population. Malaria alone reduced the aboriginal population along the lower Columbia and Willamette from about 13,940 in 1830 to roughly 1,175 in 1841—a loss of 92 percent. Diseases were relatively less destructive on the Plateau because settlement and harvest patterns were more dispersed. The demographic decline was nevertheless catastrophic. Epidemics reduced Plateau populations from approximately 23,000 in 1775 to just over 6,000 by the 1860s—a decline of 74 percent. In the interior valleys of the Cowlitz, Willamette, Umpqua, and Rogue, populations fell from about 41,000 to "no more than 2,000." Even in the relatively isolated Great Basin, which included southeastern Oregon, population declined from about 40,000 to about 12,000.[8]

Indians remained highly susceptible to European diseases for 100–150 years after contact. Thus Oregon country Indians continued to lose numbers until after 1900. Acquisition of immunities and acceptance of new treatments helped a relative few persist into the twentieth century, but the survivors were a changed people. Ceremonies and oral traditions metamorphosed as populations decreased. Exchange ceremonies began to emphasize the destruction of property as a way of limiting the amount of wealth within the community so elites could protect their privileged status. The encyclopedia of aboriginal knowledge also narrowed as informants died before they could pass on their wisdom.[9]

The ramifications of disease extended to nature as well. Fewer Indians meant less use of fire to harvest food and to clear undergrowth. Forest fires became both less frequent and more destructive because fuel accumulated for longer periods before burning. Cottonwoods, firs, and oaks grew unhindered for the first time in millennia, and forests began to encroach on the previously open spaces of the Willamette, Camas, and other inland valleys. Declining consumption of salmon during the middle decades of the nineteenth century most likely increased the number of spawners, but this may have produced counterintuitive effects. In general, the larger the spawning run, the more pressure for space on spawning beds. Competition in such cases can be violent and destructive, and salmon reproduction may become more erratic. There is no inherent balance in fish populations, so reduced harvests did not necessarily result in greater reproduction. Contact and depopulation caused convulsive changes in the social, cultural, and physical landscape of the Oregon country.[10]

European pathogens and white settlement undid the aboriginal world. The Kalapuyas virtually disappeared during the malaria years, and neighboring groups lost many members. Fewer numbers meant less capacity to shape the new world. Indians were less able to resist immigrant pressures or to control the direction of social and environmental change. To survive they coalesced in polyglot villages both voluntarily and under duress. By 1850 the few Indians left in the Multnomah basin had gathered into two villages, one near Willamette Falls and the other on Wapato Island (now Sauvies Island), at the confluence of the Willamette and Columbia. Group distinctions were already diminishing, but cultural homogenization accelerated when settlers and the government forced Indians onto reservations in 1855. Most Indians in western Oregon moved to the Coast Reservation or the

Grand Ronde Agency. The resulting communities were a jumble of social fragments. To communicate, they initially spoke Chinook Jargon, a lingua franca used for centuries in trade. After 1900, however, English gained preference within these hybrid societies, and many native languages died soon after. In the process, a distinct Chinook culture also ceased to exist.[11]

Disease reshaped the Oregon country, but how people assessed these changes varied greatly. Indians had little reason to see epidemics as anything but a disaster. Confined to reservations, the Coos descended into nostalgia, fondly remembering a past when they were "numerous as the head hair" and their villages lined the rivers. Many whites, on the other hand, saw disease as a providential force. Traveling through southern Oregon in 1840, Reverend Gustavus Hines remarked, "Under the impression that the doom of extinction is suspended over this wretched race, and that the hand of providence is removing them to give place to a people more worthy of this beautiful and fertile country, we arrived at the place of our encampment." For Hines depopulation redeemed the landscape and bequeathed its bounty to a more virtuous body of Christian farmers. Other whites were more ambivalent. Although John McLoughlin was thankful that his white employees had not met a fate similar to the Indians, he realized that depopulation had severely strained the HBC's trading network.[12]

Depopulation and removal tell only half the demographic story of the nineteenth century, however, because the decline of Indians coincided with, partially resulted from, and encouraged an invasion of Euro-Americans. In 1841 fewer than 800 trappers, traders, and settlers lived in the Willamette Valley. In the next two years a few hundred entered the region, but in 1843 the trickle became a flood. One hundred and twenty wagons, more than 800 people, and over 5,000 livestock journeyed from Elm Grove, Kansas, to Oregon. By 1845 there were 2,100 non-Indians in western Oregon, and 3,000 more arrived that fall. Having already taken possession in fact, the United States claimed Oregon by treaty in 1846. The HBC acknowledged the fait accompli by withdrawing to Fort Victoria, and Great Britain agreed to a formal boundary, not at the Columbia, as it had hoped, but along the forty-ninth parallel. By 1850, 12,093 non-Indians lived in Oregon. Settlers built towns along the lower Willamette and Columbia, the most important of which became Oregon City, Portland, Salem, and Astoria.[13]

In the rush to settle Oregon, Americans laid the groundwork for further social and material conflicts between Indians and whites. The United States had an official policy of negotiating title to Indian lands *before* settlement by Americans. According to Commissioner of Indian Affairs A. S. Loughery,

"No effort should be untried to procure the removal of the whole [Indian population], thereby leaving the country free for settlement by the whites." But Congress vitiated its own policies by passing in 1850 the Donation Land Claim Act before negotiating treaties. The act awarded 320 acres of land to male settlers over eighteen years of age and an additional 320 acres for spouses. It recognized existing claims and set in motion a frenzied rush for additional farmland. Settlers poured into the Willamette and other interior valleys and usurped Indian lands with impunity. The federal government eventually issued 7,317 certificates for more than 2.5 million acres under the law. Settlers claimed just about everything in sight while federal agents negotiated Indian treaties that Congress promptly rejected because they had not removed Indians from agricultural areas. The result was a legal and social morass.[14]

Tensions escalated into war as invasions continued and Congress failed to respond. Farmers were only one of several groups of immigrants. During the early 1850s California miners also moved north. In 1851 they rushed into the Rogue River basin, and in 1855 they crossed to the Plateau. Farmers and grazers were close on their heels. Conflicts erupted wherever Indians resisted these incursions. In 1853 a series of retaliatory strikes escalated into full-scale war in southwestern Oregon. Miners vowed "extermination" and slaughtered Indians indiscriminately; Indians avenged themselves on isolated settlers. By 1855 the U.S. Army had entered the fray, broken Indian resistance, and forced the original inhabitants to sign a treaty and permanently vacate the region.[15]

In 1855 and 1856 Washington Territorial Governor Isaac Stevens and Oregon's Joel Palmer created similar problems east of the Cascades. In their rush to negotiate treaties, Stevens and Palmer coerced Plateau Indians and made empty promises. The treaty councils left Indians embittered and distrustful. Miners, farmers, and grazers exacerbated tensions by invading the Plateau before Congress could ratify the treaties. Outraged Indians resisted, and war erupted in 1855 and again in 1858. Each war and treaty expanded white opportunities to reorganize the landscape by pushing Indians farther toward the periphery.[16]

White immigration only accelerated in the ensuing years. By 1859 there were enough residents to justify statehood, and the smaller boundaries of the state of Oregon replaced the broader, more diffuse Oregon country on national maps. By 1860 there were 52,465 residents in the state. By 1870 the population almost doubled to 90,923, and it quadrupled in the next thirty years, gaining 84,000 by 1880, 143,000 by 1890, and 96,000 by 1900. By the turn of the century 413,536 people lived in Oregon, but only 4,951 were listed as Indian. The 1.1 million people living in the region once called the Oregon country but now known as the states of Oregon, Washington, and Idaho included only 19,216 Indians. The demographic transition from an aboriginal society to a Euro-American society was astonishingly swift and decisive. The Indian population had declined by 95 percent, while non-Indians increased more than a thousandfold.[17]

Demographic shifts provided the foundation for a rapid cultural, economic, and environmental reorganization of the Oregon country. American settlers set in motion far-reaching changes across the Oregon landscape.

Although many factors influenced how humans consumed the resources of the Oregon country—including the material necessities of subsistence, cultural preferences, and local environmental constraints—capitalism was the single most important force behind those activities that most affected salmon. Indians had harvested huge quantities of salmon and other animals and plants, but they consumed these resources primarily for local subsistence. Euro-Americans also relied on nature for subsistence, but increasingly they harvested for external markets. Trappers, miners, farmers, grazers, loggers, and fishers expanded the array of resources used, while transportation and market systems extended consumption over far broader expanses of the world. Traders sold otter furs in China and beaver pelts in Europe; farmers sold wheat in San Francisco and Minneapolis; grazers sold cattle in Chicago; loggers sold fir, spruce, and cedar in southern California, South America, northern China, and Australia; and industrial fishers sold canned salmon just about everywhere.[18]

The new economic rules altered the relationship between consumer and nature. Aboriginal spirits no longer mediated harvests. Instead, settlers increasingly redefined nature as a set of commodities. They ascribed worth according to market values, and reorganized the landscape to produce marketable items. Ecologically complex prairies gave way to fields devoted to a single species. Animals, plants, and rocks gained or lost prestige according to the market: some rocks became minerals; some grasses became grain and feed; some trees became lumber. Mammals gained or lost value according to their furs or skins, fish according to their meat or oil. Nature that did not sell lost value. Animals and plants that interfered with or competed for economically valued items became "enemies," "varmints," and "pests."[19]

The fur trade was the leading edge of the transition to capitalism. The trade began with Captain James Cook's expedition to Nootka in 1778, but it did not deplete inland fur-bearing populations until after 1810. Trading vessels had visited the lower Columbia since the 1790s. Boston and English traders traded beads, cloth, and metallic goods for otter and beaver pelts, but only gradually did trapping extend inland along existing aboriginal trade networks. Furs, exotic goods, and pathogens began to travel the same routes that salmon and shells had for millennia. Initially Indians continued to control the terms of trade. For decades the Clatsop headman Comcomly held a dominant position in this trade by keeping European traders and inland groups apart with rumors of cannibalism that engendered mutual fear and distrust. In the early nineteenth century, however, imperial rivalries turned the mouth of the Columbia into a coveted prize for the Americans and the British; Lewis and Clark's Corps of Discovery, the Astorians, the North West Company, and the HBC each made proprietary claims to the Oregon country in the subsequent rush.[20]

By the 1820s the HBC had gained ascendancy over its competitors. It successfully tapped into and redirected existing systems of exchange by controlling the flow of such coveted trade items as iron tools, guns, and cloth. In 1826 it moved from Fort George at the mouth of the Columbia to Fort Vancouver near the mouth of the Willamette River. The inland location allowed the HBC to intercept furs formerly channeled through Comcomly, and the Clatsop headman lost all influence when cannibalism failed to materialize. Inland groups instead traded directly with the fort or its emissaries, and some began to devote greater energy to harvesting fur-bearing animals than to salmon fishing. The changed emphasis had serious consequences. By 1825 Governor George Simpson noted numerous incidents of winter famine because Indians had neglected to fish. By 1841 the HBC was supplying Indians with upward of thirty barrels of salted salmon each winter. The new economy partially reversed the flow of salmon, which formerly had been from Indians to whites.[21]

From Fort Vancouver the HBC held a commanding position in the region's fur trade, a gateway between the Oregon country and a global trading network. The river location ensured direct access by ships traveling to Valparaiso, Boston, London, Canton, or Bombay. Indians flocked to Fort Vancouver to trade goods, while the chief factor sent traders and trappers in all directions to harvest furs: east to Spokane House on the upper Columbia, Fort Nez Percés on the lower Snake River, and Fort Hall on the upper Snake; north up the Cowlitz to Fort Nisqually and Puget Sound; south down Willamette Valley to Fort Umpqua; and west down the Columbia to Fort George and the coast. Vancouver became a nexus in a vast network of ocean and terrestrial systems.[22]

Beaver trapping also reorganized salmon habitats. During the twentieth century fishery biologists considered beavers an "enemy" of salmon because they built dams, but biologists misconstrued nature. Beaver dams sometimes did block salmon migration, but the structures were hardly permanent. Dams usually washed out during freshets, but because salmon wait for freshets before making their spawning runs, the dams were rarely an obstacle. Rather, the ponds beavers created supplied young salmon with important rearing habitat; they contained insects and water organisms on which juveniles fed, and the backwaters and side channels protected salmon from strong currents. Thus beavers maintained environments favorable to salmon, but after 1824 beavers grew scarce because the HBC tried to create a "fur desert" south and east of the Columbia. The HBC wanted to forestall American competition, but the policy undermined salmon habitat east of the Cascades. Without beavers, streams grew more linear, and salmon fry had fewer refuges in early life. Trapping had less impact west of the Cascades, but this was only a small fraction of the habitat in the Columbia River basin.[23]

The fur trade began the process of reshaping the social and environmental landscape, but its impact was minor compared to changes that followed resettlement. Oregon settlers tried to follow midwestern patterns and grow corn, but the climate west of the mountains was too cool and wet. They turned instead to wheat, barley, potatoes, fruits, vegetables, and nuts. They also raised cattle, mules, sheep, and pigs. In every case settlers grew exotic, rather than indigenous, plants and animals, rapidly transforming the biotic assemblage of the Oregon country to a more domesticated state. Nevertheless, agriculture was at best a modest activity until 1848. The discovery of gold in California boosted agriculture by creating an instant market for all the flour, livestock, and timber Oregonians could supply. The wheat crop jumped from 160,000 bushels in 1846 to 208,000 bushels in 1850.[24]

The mining boom soon spread to southwestern Oregon. In 1850 prospectors found gold on the Illinois River. Word leaked out, and in December 1851 miners rushed into the Rogue River basin. Jacksonville grew from a trail campsite into an instant supply center and Oregon's largest city. Additional strikes on Galice Creek in 1852, at Gold Hill in 1857, and at Phoenix in 1860 sustained the boom, and smaller discoveries along the numerous benches, bars, and tributaries of the Rogue, Illinois, and Applegate Rivers sustained activity for decades. Prospectors also explored east of the Cascades. In 1861 miners made another major strike in the Powder River basin. By 1862 the town of Auburn claimed 5,000 to 6,000 miners, while a similarly sized camp formed on the upper John Day River near Canyon City. Lewiston, Walla Walla, Wallula, Umatilla, and The Dalles grew as regional entrepôts, or "jump-off points." By 1864 mining had spread

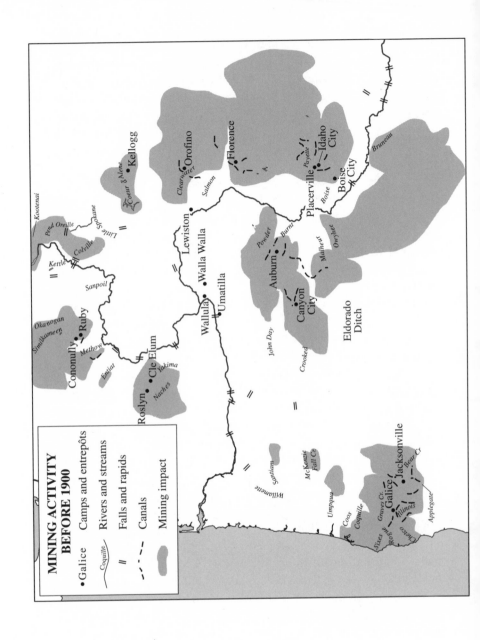

MINING ACTIVITY BEFORE 1900

- Galice   Camps and entrepôts
- Coquille   Rivers and streams
- =   Falls and rapids
- –·–   Canals
- ▨   Mining impact

Kootenai

Pend Oreille

Little Spokane

Coeur d'Alene

Kellogg

Colville

Kettle

Sanpoil

Okanogan

Similkameen

Cononully • Ruby

Methow

Entiat

Roslyn • Cle Elum

Naches

Yakima

Clearwater

Orofino

Lewiston

Salmon

Florence

Walla Walla

Wallula

Umatilla

Powder

Burnt

Auburn

Canyon City

John Day

Crooked

Malheur

Owyhee

Payette

Placerville

Idaho City

Boise

Boise City

Bruneau

Eldorado Ditch

Willamette

Santiam

McKenzie

Fall Cr.

Umpqua

Coos

Coquille

Sixes

Rogue

Groves Cr.

Galice

Illinois

Jacksonville

Bear Cr.

Applegate

Victor

MAP 4. Nineteenth-century mining activity in the Oregon country was both intensive and extensive.

48

throughout the region, and new strikes continually reinvigorated a highly profitable industry (see map 4). In the late 1870s miners were still making $5 per day on Beaver Creek, while the *Canyon City Times* estimated that the John Day placer mines yielded between $75,000 and $100,000 annually.[25]

Mining enveloped other areas as well. During the second half of the century, miners discovered gold along the Umpqua, Molalla, Santiam, Blue, and Coquille Rivers and several coastal beaches. They also moved into Washington Territory. In 1859, 1,200–3,000 miners worked the Similkameen basin, and by the 1870s they worked the Yakima as well. During the 1880s and 1890s miners also entered the Okanogan, Methow, Wenatchee, Chelan, and Entiat River valleys. Though these ventures were significant, they paled in comparison to Idaho's mining rushes. In 1860 and 1861 miners rushed up the Clearwater River to the Orofino District, harassing Nez Perce Indians as they went. They moved on to the Boise River basin the following year, and by 1863 there were 25,000 people in southern Idaho working the Boise, Payette, and Snake Rivers. Cities grew overnight, placing greater pressure on water resources and salmon habitat. Town construction at Ruby and Conconully "essentially destroyed" Salmon Creek in the Okanogan basin.[26]

Mining involved far more than just gold. Settlers also excavated gravel, sand, and limestone from streambeds as early as the 1850s. By the 1870s miners were digging silver, copper, and iron in southwestern Oregon. Coal mining began in the 1870s at Coos Bay, and in the 1890s at Cle Elum and Rosalyn in the Yakima basin. In the 1860s miners discovered quicksilver deposits along Calapuya Creek in the Umpqua River basin, and in 1868 on the upper Rogue. Fluctuating prices halted operations repeatedly, and production figures suggest a minimal industry before 1900. The peak year for mercury production was 1887, with 65 flasks. Production dropped by half the next year, and by another third the year after. There was no recorded production during the 1890s, but the records are most likely incomplete since there are no figures for before 1887 either.[27]

When an Oregon journalist reviewed the first quarter-century of mining, he remarked, "Here, as in California and Nevada, the light placers were soon worked out. The men who worked them were only the pioneers of a branch of mining more enduring." The writer identified several major characteristics of mining in the West. Although booms passed, mining remained a steady activity throughout the nineteenth century. When new strikes drew people from older districts, other miners replaced them, but the identity of those miners and the methods they used differed significantly.[28]

The era of the classic gold panner was indeed short-lived. "Pioneer" panners quickly exhausted surface deposits in southwestern and eastern Oregon and then moved to new fields. The capital necessary for more intensive mining exceeded their resources, but their claims rarely remained idle. In their wake came two distinctly different groups. White laws prohibited Asians from staking claims, but when whites moved to new grounds, Chinese laborers often stayed behind to rework the abandoned claims. In southern Oregon, Chinese miners first appeared in 1852. By 1857 they constituted a significant part of the workforce, and by 1864 they dominated some districts. They entered eastern Oregon and Idaho in the 1860s and were numerically dominant by 1870. Thus gauging the impact of mining by tracing booms and busts misses the continuity of activity.[29]

The other group of miners consisted of entrepreneurs who possessed large amounts of capital. In the mid-1850s wealthy individuals and corporations began to invest in Oregon claims, squeezing out individuals with fewer economic resources. In southern Oregon local investors like Alexander Ankeny, Gin Lin, and Lum Sing were colorful participants, but the major players were corporations like the Red River Gold Mining Company, which invested $80,000 in a single flume. To recover investments rapidly they adopted hydraulic mining, which processed far more gravel far more quickly by shooting large volumes of water through high-pressure nozzles. According to the *Portland Morning Oregonian,* "The amount of dirt [a nozzle] will wash out in a day is enormous," but the equipment was expensive. One company on the Applegate spent $2,500 for 1,500 feet of fifteen-inch pipe. The price of the 400-pound nozzle was unlisted but presumably even more expensive. Hydraulic mining nevertheless spread rapidly. The first nozzles typically appeared a few years after the rush—1856 on the Rogue, 1863 in eastern Oregon, and 1864 and 1865 in Idaho—and over time their design and efficiency improved. The investments often paid large dividends. In one six-week period, a Rogue River mine cleaned up $10,000 in gold, no small sum in 1878.[30]

Bringing water to the nozzle required not only flumes and pipes but ditches and dams. Corporations employed gangs to dig extensive ditch systems. In 1860 Chinese laborers dug the first major ditch in southern Oregon on Galice Creek. Others soon followed, including ditches of nineteen and twenty-seven miles on the Applegate, and twelve miles on Graves Creek, as well as many smaller networks. Miners dug even longer ditches in eastern Oregon and Idaho. Early efforts included the Auburn Ditch (1863), the Rye Valley Ditch (1864), and the Sparta Ditch (1873). The crowning achievement was the Eldorado Ditch, which, when completed in 1873, extended 136 miles from the headwaters of the Burnt River to claims on the upper Malheur River. Labor gangs worked on it for ten years, and it cost over $500,000. As with other aspects of mining, Idaho miners operated on an even larger scale. The *Boise News* remarked, "Throughout the entire length of all the various paying creeks and gulches between [Idaho City] and Placerville, we observe an almost continuous network of sluices, ditches and hydraulics."[31]

Although mining had little impact on the Chelan, Okanogan, Entiat, Willamette, and Deschutes Rivers, it buried spawning habitat in heavily mined areas of the Rogue, John Day, Yakima, Grande Ronde, Powder, and Owyhee, as well as numerous streams in Idaho. By 1865 mining had eliminated salmon runs from the Boise River. There were several reasons for the decline. As biologist Henry Ward noted, mining amounted to a "violent overturning of natural soil." Operations often occurred a few feet from water. Detritus washed into streams, smothered spawning beds, and made it impossible for eggs to hatch. Early mining dumped enough material into the Rogue that the water turned a reddish yellow that carried far out to sea. The entire John Day and Grande Ronde Rivers were similarly muddied by placer mining near their headwaters, while acidic chemicals leached from gold and coal mines and altered the chemical balance of streams.[32]

Mechanical changes caused additional harm to streams. Diversion dams rarely included fishways, and both juvenile and adult salmon were sucked into ditches and blown through nozzles. For those salmon that remained in the river, water levels often fell precipitously in summer. This happened not just on smaller tributaries. In 1871 miners turned about half the Rogue River into the works at Big Bar. Temperatures rose considerably as water levels fell during summer. Miners also used wing dams to divert streams temporarily while they uprooted the beds in search of color, and some streams were blocked entirely. By 1892 mining dams cut off salmon from large sections of the Bruneau and Boise Rivers in Idaho and from the Grande Ronde River above La Grande in Oregon. At the end of the century, miners also began using dredges to root through streambeds at an even faster, and more destructive, pace. Mining rearranged salmon habitat on a massive scale, rerouting streams into nozzles and hillsides into streams.[33]

Mining was an economic boon for Oregon farmers, but the increased farming to fill the stomachs of miners also harmed salmon habitat. Mining attracted single men who depended on others for materiel and foodstuffs, and in their rush for wealth they were willing to pay inflated prices. The succession of western mineral strikes between 1848 and the 1870s provided farmers with a strong regional market, while steamboats and railroads improved access to overseas markets. Wheat production accelerated rapidly from 211,000 acres in 1850 to 2,389,000 acres in 1870. During the same period dairy cows increased from 9,000 to 48,000 and sheep from 15,000 to 318,000. The more farmers tilled soil, the greater the sediment loads became in streams. Heavy silt loads grew noticeable in the Columbia by the mid-1880s. Siltation and increased precipitation brought more flooding, so farmers began to dike their fields and dredge streams to move goods to market, but this only further reduced the rearing habitat for juvenile salmon.[34]

The growth of irrigation during the nineteenth century increased pressures even further. Irrigation began in 1844 on the Walla Walla River at the Whitman Mission, and Catholic missions established irrigation in the Yakima Valley during the 1850s. These were small projects designed to feed Indian neophytes. Significant growth came with the initiation of commercial irrigation in the 1860s and 1870s. Farmers moved east of the Cascades to exploit mining markets and the Plateau's warmer and drier climate, but arid conditions required irrigation during summer. Farmers opened ditches on the John Day in 1860, on the Boise in 1864, on the Powder and Yakima in 1866, on the Burnt in 1870, and on the Wenatchee in 1872. Wheat production boomed. In 1866 the Grande Ronde Valley alone produced over a half million bushels of wheat. By the 1880s wheat fields spanned the Hood River, Umatilla, middle Columbia, Methow, Okanogan, Wallowa, Malheur, Owyhee, and Bruneau Valleys. Farmers dug a few ditches in western Oregon as well, but these were small by comparison.[35]

Irrigation escalated again following the arrival of the railroads in the 1880s. Farmers and civic boosters had long desired railroads to improve their market opportunities. In one instance a group of Umatilla Valley farmers petitioned the Northern Pacific for a feeder line. They complained that the great distance to the Oregon Railway and Navigation Company's railhead made "wheat raising on an extensive scale [un]profitable: therefore the advancement of our country will necessarily be slower" until a feeder line reached them. The rhetoric may have been formulaic, but it was grounded in a clear understanding of the relationship between agriculture, transportation, and markets: without markets, there was no reason to develop agriculture; without development there would be no "advancement" of the country. Thus the arrival of the Northern Pacific in 1883 unleashed another population and agricultural boom. Areas like Chelan County in Washington doubled their population annually, and irrigation projects multiplied. By 1905 the Northern Pacific and other private investors had developed five separate projects on the Yakima River alone, where irrigated land jumped to 388,111 acres.[36]

Increased irrigation meant a decrease in salmon. Most farmers used simple gravity systems with headgates, but some employed low dams to divert water. While a few of these dams extended only partly into the current, most spanned entire streams and none had fishways. During high water fish could pass these barriers, but low water during summer often precluded all passage. This was the problem on the Bruneau River by the early 1890s. During summer farmers sometimes diverted the entire stream into their ditches. In 1897 the problem on the Yakima grew so alarming that residents of Easton begged the U.S. Fish Commission to take action after local officials refused to tear down a dam. Like hydraulic miners, irrigators never installed screens across their ditches. Thus even ditches with simple headgates diverted juvenile and adult fish into fields, where they died in appalling numbers. Farmers did return excess water to the streams, but this was laden with silt and significantly warmer. In 1893, for example, the Yakima reached sixty degrees.[37]

The impact on salmon hardly went unnoticed. As early as 1877, U.S. Fish Commission employee Livingston Stone noted that the Umatilla River was already deficient in salmon, and in the 1880s settlers complained that runs were also declining on the Deschutes River. In 1888 the Oregon fish commissioners complained that farmers had taken "nearly all the water from" the Bruneau River. By 1892 irrigation dams blocked much of the Umatilla, and in 1901 settlers leveled similar complaints against irrigators on the Wallowa River. The literal low point came in the summer of 1906, when the Yakima dropped from an average flow of 3,900 to 105 second-feet. Irrigators had taken "practically all of the water in the Yakima River," and what little remained was actually recycled from fields. In 1903 Portland resident A. W. Anthony complained to the U.S. Fish Commission that irrigation ditches killed 90 percent of the migrating juvenile salmon. The commission considered the figure "undoubtedly exaggerated," but they were concerned, and with good reason. By 1900 irrigation dams had destroyed perhaps 90 percent of the sockeye runs on the Yakima River, while other dams began to alter the timing of runs. An official later admitted, "The low water flow of the Yakima was over-appropriated long before the [federal] Government began its work in the Yakima valley [in the early 1900s,] and serious water shortages had occurred prior to that time."[38]

Milling operations further harmed salmon. After 1850 increases in wheat production spurred mill construction throughout Oregon. The largest operations were located on the Willamette at Milwaukie, Oregon City, Jefferson City, Salem, and Albany, while smaller mills appeared on the Yaquina, Umpqua, Clackamas, and elsewhere. By 1900 there were 150 flour mills in

Oregon alone. Sheep raising encouraged construction of several woolen mills on the lower Willamette as well. Most mills required dams to build a sufficient head to turn machinery, but none had workable fish ladders. Thus when the Northern Pacific arrived at Spokane in 1882, mill construction jumped and salmon runs plummeted on the Spokane River. In 1885 settlers near Hilgard complained about dams that obstructed fish passage on the Grande Ronde, and the following year Thomas Day voiced similar concerns about three dams "that stop the fish from coming up" Hubbard Creek on the Umpqua. By the 1890s settlers were reporting on dams blocking fish passage everywhere from the Rogue and Klamath in southwestern Oregon to the Little Spokane in northeastern Washington.[39]

Livestock grazing also expanded in the wake of the mining booms. Herders had exploited the miners' huge demand for beef, wool, and mutton since 1849, and grazers followed when miners moved north and east during the 1850s and 1860s. By the early 1860s one rancher was running more than 100,000 cattle and 20,000 horses in the Yakima Valley, while others moved herds into the Grande Ronde and John Day basins. Livestock increased rapidly. Dairy herds grew from 9,000 in 1850 to 48,000 in 1870 and 122,000 in 1900; beef cattle expanded from 24,000 in 1850 to 69,000 in 1870 and 715,000 in 1900; sheep increased from 15,000 in 1850 to 318,000 in 1870 and a whopping 1,961,000 in 1900. By the turn of the century, a nondescript rail stop in eastern Oregon named Shaniko was a world leader in wool production.[40]

This expansion did not unfold evenly—dairy herds predominated in the wetter climates of western Oregon, while cattle and sheep dominated the Plateau—but grazing damage did follow a general pattern. Animals concentrated in the lower reaches of river basins during winters and moved to higher pastures during summer. By the 1870s the Yakima basin was already overcrowded, and corporate grazers like Phelps and Wadleigh moved their herds to the Okanogan. Plateau cattle populations peaked in the early 1880s and then plummeted after a series of severe winters bankrupted most cattle barons, but the ranges gained no rest from misfortune. In the 1890s sheep grazers spread their herds across the Blue Mountains and other ranges. While there were fewer than 2,000 sheep in Okanogan county in 1890, by 1904 there were 31,757, and Yakima County herds had reached 147,000.[41]

The tremendous increase in livestock created further pressure on salmon habitat. The ranges of the Plateau were not virgin fields when livestock arrived in the 1850s. Indians had grazed horses for more than a century, and the vast herds of the Nez Perces, Cayuses, and Shoshones left an impact on the landscape. Consequently, "When whites brought cattle in and grazing pressure tripled after the 1870s, the grasslands were less resistant to cattle than they might have been otherwise." Grazing practices exacerbated the pressure on grasslands. In order to claim valuable watering holes, herders kept livestock in small areas for extended periods, but this damaged both plant cover and riparian areas. Animals had to eat, so they clipped grasses to the nub and prevented seeding; they also had to drink frequently, and repeated visits to watering holes eroded stream banks, increased siltation, and disturbed spawning beds. Cattle demonstrated a particular talent for turning streams into bovine toilets. Herders further concentrated the impact of grazing whenever they moved animals along trails.[42]

These activities altered the landscape significantly. Cattle had overgrazed parts of the upper Grande Ronde by the 1880s and the Applegate by the 1900s. Sheep extended the damage in the following decades. Not only were the river bottoms in trouble, but high meadows suffered as well. Plant communities altered under intense grazing. Native bunchgrasses gave way to less nutritious species like cheatgrass, while the suppression of fire encouraged the growth of sages and shrubs. Degraded habitat exacerbated grazing pressure because herbivores had to eat more plants to sustain themselves. Over time cattle and sheep also began to compact the soil, and the ground lost its ability to retain water. Runoff increased in winter and spring, causing downcutting of riverbeds and banks, but dropped precipitously in summer, leaving some spawning beds high and dry. Salmon got few breaks from these changes.[43]

Logging also reduced salmon habitat. Most early logging in Oregon involved clearing land for farming, but the discovery of gold increased the demand for lumber in rapidly growing San Francisco. Logging only expanded as mining moved north and populations increased in Oregon. The Puget Sound area was the leading exporter of lumber in the Pacific Northwest, but with time production drifted south and east. In Oregon, lumbering activity centered mostly in the Willamette Valley and the lower Columbia, Tillamook, Yaquina, Coos, and Umpqua estuaries, but the amount exported was substantial. In 1872 sixteen vessels arrived in Coos Bay for lumber each week. Logging also followed mining east of the Cascades, and by the 1880s there were substantial logging operations along the Powder and Grande Ronde Rivers, where, according to historian Nancy Langston, "[l]ogging was almost as heavy one hundred years ago as it was in the late 1980s." By the end of the century, Oregon loggers were cutting nearly a billion board feet annually.[44]

As with the effects of other activities, the impact of logging was not evenly distributed across the landscape. Loggers cut primarily along riparian areas and nearby hillsides, and they focused on preferred species like cedars, Sitka spruce, and Douglas fir west of the Cascades, and ponderosa pine on the Plateau. They went through forests repeatedly, harvesting one species after another. Each time, they left more debris, so when fires erupted they burned much hotter, consuming not only more trees but soil minerals as well. Fires grew far more catastrophic with settlement. In the late 1840s fires destroyed about 500,000 acres between the Siuslaw and the Nestucca Rivers; in 1850 a fire burned two-thirds of the main valley of the Naches River; in 1853 another 500,000 acres burned in the Yaquina basin; between 1857 and 1868 more fires burned near Yaquina Bay and Coos Bay; and in 1878 fires swept large areas of the Blue Mountains. Smaller fires broke out almost every summer. Each time, forests became less able to hold runoff, and soil erosion and siltation increased.[45]

Logging hewed close to streams in order to float logs to mills. Concentrated harvesting reduced streamside cover, eroded banks, and increased sediment loads. Wayward logs often jammed in streams and prevented salmon passage. During the mid-1800s eleven western Oregon streams had logjams of between 100 and 1,500 feet in length. Loggers used explosives to clear these obstructions, but this probably did as much harm as good. To rationalize transportation and use smaller streams, loggers also built splash dams to regulate streamflows. Splash dams allowed loggers to retain water and then flush logs downstream on precise daily or weekly schedules. The dams also helped extend operations well into the dry season. Loggers began using splash dams in coastal streams in the early 1870s. By 1910 there were 56 dams on lower Columbia tributaries in western Washington, 55 on portions of the Willamette and Deschutes Rivers, and 160 dams on coastal and lower Columbia tributaries in Oregon. Loggers also built dams in eastern Oregon on the Grande Ronde River.[46]

Splash dams have largely escaped historical memory, but they caused significant problems for salmon. Some dams were temporary structures meant to last only a season, but others lasted more than fifty years—or fifteen generations of salmon. The average was twenty years. Many dams totally blocked passage and very few had fishways that worked. Thus splash dams further concentrated salmon spawning in the lower reaches of streams, reducing available habitat and causing crowding on the remaining redds. But the effect of splash dams was not simply spatial. Because loggers regulated the stream to facilitate transportation, flows fluctuated wildly. When they closed the dam gates, streams dried to a trickle and then were inundated by scheduled flash floods. The sudden rush of water and logs scoured spawning beds and rechanneled streams, harming any salmon, eggs, and juveniles caught in the torrent. Such floods also eroded river-banks, widened streambeds, and buried the deep pools salmon needed for migration and rearing.[47]

Logging continued to plague salmon even after logs reached the mills. Like other industries, early sawmills used stored water to turn machinery. The earliest mills appeared along the lower Columbia and Willamette Valleys. In 1862 loggers built the first sawmill in eastern Oregon on the John Day River, and by the 1880s logging was a thriving industry in the Blue Mountains. By 1870 there were 173 sawmills in Oregon, 138 of which used water-power. By 1900 the number of mills had grown to nearly 500. Most had switched to steam power, but there were still 115 waterwheels in use. Damage was not limited to dams, however. Mills often stored logs in backwaters, and some logs sunk and smothered bottom dwellers, while others emitted naturally toxic chemicals. The waters most affected by these practices were those bays and estuaries along the coast and lower Columbia and Willamette that were critical environments for juvenile salmon during smoltification.[48]

Mills also dumped untold tons of sawdust into streams and bays. The sawdust covered streambeds, smothered plants, and consumed oxygen in the water. Incubating eggs and alevins literally suffocated. Many settlers recognized the damage done by sawdust and complained to officials. In 1887 the *Portland Morning Oregonian* criticized Governor Sylvester Pennoyer for dumping sawdust into the Willamette from his Portland mill, and in 1890, C. A. Wright wrote to the U.S. Fish Commission about a mill on the Grande Ronde River that had "for some time past been running the saw-dust from their saw-mill directly into the Grand Ronde River, and the river is now in such a condition that not a fish can live in it any where near the place." George Milhan voiced similar concerns about sawdust "driving all of the fish out of the creeks."[49]

Finally, there is the role of cities in the transformation of the Oregon country. Oregon's population grew exponentially during the nineteenth century, but people did not live evenly across the land. Although Oregon was predominantly rural before 1900, the region's population had increasingly shifted toward urban areas. Civic boosters energetically encouraged this migration. In 1874 the *Portland Morning Oregonian* editor warned, "The real situation of Oregon becomes more and more apparent every day. Greater and more pressing than any other want to the State of Oregon, is the want of people—population." The editor need not have worried. Portland had 8,293 residents in 1870; by 1900 it had grown to 90,426. Spokane grew similarly after the railroad arrived, mushrooming from 350 in 1880 to 36,848 in 1900.[50]

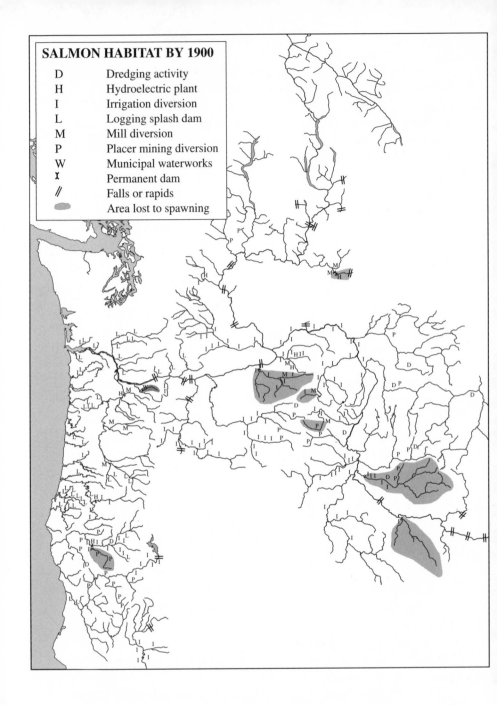

MAP 5. By 1900, the concentration of reproduction in downstream areas was well under way. Development had already extensively altered salmon habitat. Note especially the loss of several watersheds east of the Cascades.

As towns grew, they altered a swath of land that extended far beyond their boundaries. Urbanites imported much of what they consumed, so urban growth required additional farming, logging, and fishing. Portland, Spokane, and Salem made increasing demands on distant resources, and civic leaders lobbied for river improvements and rail links to facilitate trade. The federal government responded beneficently. In the 1860s the Army Corps of Engineers began to channel rivers and build jetties, dikes, and locks throughout the region, while Congress gave generous land grants to foster stage roads and transcontinental railroads. Such "improvements" created both growth and harm. River projects redirected currents and dredged spawning channels, while railroads filled in rivers with debris and slides. As cities grew, officials diverted more and more water from salmon streams for domestic use. Salmon mistook storage ponds in East Portland for spawning creeks, and in 1895 Portland dammed Bull Run River and diverted it twenty-four miles to the city waterworks. In 1888 Portland General Electric built a hydroelectric dam at Willamette Falls; in 1896 the Washington Water Power Company erected a similar dam farther up the Columbia basin on the Spokane River.[51]

Oregon country Indians had harvested massive quantities of salmon for many centuries before whites arrived, but their impact on the rest of the landscape was relatively benign. Salmon encountered a far different world in the second half of the nineteenth century (see map 5). Trappers, farmers, miners, irrigators, loggers, and boosters transformed nature in ways that made it less hospitable to aquatic life. The clear, cool, unimpeded streams of precontact times had become dirtier, warmer, and more often obstructed. By 1900, Euro-American settlement had already reduced significantly the spawning ranges of salmon in the Columbia and other basins. This was the ecological context of the industrial fishery during the late nineteenth century.[52]

Changes in the fisheries mirrored changes on the land. Aboriginal exchange systems slowly gave way to a market economy as British and American traders vied for fish as they had for furs. Indians supplied this trade initially, but disease eroded their numbers, and by the 1860s markets and demography had transformed the social, economic, and spatial organization of the fisheries.

The arrival of whites introduced new meanings and relationships with salmon. Lower Columbia Indians had traded salmon with visiting ships since 1792, but these were small-scale seasonal exchanges. The establishment of Fort Astoria in 1810 created conditions for a permanent and far more substantial trade in salmon. Clatsops and Chinooks delivered canoe loads of fish, which they exchanged with trappers for cotton cloth, brass buttons, knives, files, and beads, but aboriginal rules still shaped the exchange. During ceremonial periods Indians continued to restrict consumption and insist that salmon be consumed before sunset. Non-Indians grudgingly obeyed as long as Indians could force compliance, but repeated epidemics undermined aboriginal control.[53]

This shift in social power coincided with an expansion of the range of consumption. Seeking ways to increase their profits, in 1823 officers of the HBC began developing additional markets for salmon. That year they shipped a barrel of salted salmon to London, but the fish spoiled during the long trip around Cape Horn. When a second batch went rancid in 1824, the HBC tried markets closer to Fort Vancouver. In 1826 Chief Factor John McLoughlin proposed a vigorous escalation of the salmon trade in the Pacific basin. McLoughlin saw possibilities for profit, and he feared that Americans would seize control if the HBC did not. He warned, "We must avail ourselves of all the resources of this Country if we have to Compete for the trade of it with the Americans as we may depend they will turn every thing they possibly can to account." Thus in 1827 he made a trial shipment to Monterey in Alta California, where one 250-pound barrel of salmon sold for thirty dollars. Success encouraged further forays and the trade extended to Acapulco and Lima. The number of salmon harvested and shipped was less important, however, than controlling the resources of the region.[54]

Despite McLoughlin's efforts, the Americans came. Captain John Dominis and the brig *Owyhee* had visited the Columbia regularly since 1820. At first salmon was only a secondary concern between Dominis and the HBC. Furs were the real prize, but during the struggle all resources became fair game. Once the HBC began to show a profit, the struggle for salmon took on a life of its own. In the fall of 1829 the *Owyhee* returned with its sister ship the *Convoy*. During the next six months the crews of the two vessels purchased and salted salmon at Fraser River and Willamette Falls. When Dominis returned to Boston eight months later, he could only sell a few barrels as curiosities. Like McLoughlin's shipments to London, Dominis's cargo spoiled during the voyage around Cape Horn. Meanwhile, McLoughlin sold sixty barrels at Monterey.[55]

Historians have written much about contests between British and American traders in the Pacific Northwest but little about the effect those struggles had on Indians or Indians' impact on imperial rivalries. Indians were the sole suppliers of salmon before 1850. The logistics of trade placed Indians as producers and whites as consumers. Indians guarded their fishing sites jealously, and traders could not afford to import labor. As a result, Indian men continued to fish while wives, sisters, and daughters exchanged salmon with traders anchored nearby. Initially Indians dictated the terms of trade, but as malaria ravaged the lower Columbia in the early 1830s, the rules of exchange began to shift. Traders stopped negotiating each transaction and instead issued tickets that could be redeemed at the end of the season. The ticket system regularized exchange rates and thus accelerated the delivery of perishable flesh, while malaria undermined the Indians' ability to resist these changes. Under different conditions, the cutthroat competition and limited financial backing of traders might have worked to the Indians' advantage. They might have been able to use their control of salmon fishing to dictate the terms of trade, but disease undermined their ability to resist coercion.[56]

Meanwhile the *Owyhee* venture inspired other Americans. While Dominis peddled rotten salmon, Boston merchants fitted the brig *Sultana* with supplies to put up a thousand barrels of salmon in case the crew failed to fill the hold with seal skins. In 1832 Nathaniel Wyeth also journeyed west in search of salmon and furs, but his misadventures instead seemed to doom the American salmon trade. Disaster plagued Wyeth in 1832 and 1834. When he failed to procure enough salmon to cover expenses in 1835, Wyeth admitted defeat, sold his enterprise to McLoughlin, and fled east.[57]

Although McLoughlin reveled in outlasting Americans, he struggled constantly to control the fishery. He tried to extend the salmon trade by pursuing contacts in Mexico, South America, Alaska, the Sandwich Islands, Tahiti, China, and London. Hawaii proved the most lucrative and stable market, but McLoughlin never relaxed his efforts. American traders remained a ubiquitous threat in his letters and on the river. In 1840 the *Maryland* made a beeline for Willamette Falls, and in 1841 the *Thomas Perkins* followed suit. Like their predecessors, both enterprises fell short. The captain of the *Thomas Perkins* grew so desperate that he purchased salmon from McLoughlin at Hawaii prices, allowing McLoughlin to crow endlessly of his ability to squeeze the profit out of American ventures. In 1842, however, two American vessels finally unlocked the secret of the Willamette Falls fishery. By arriving early in spring, they were able to procure a huge amount of salmon while the flesh was still fresh. Though the H B C salted more barrels, American traders finally learned the logistics of catching salmon on the Columbia. Procuring the fresh, high-fat, spring run chinooks was the key to success.[58]

American traders inherited the Oregon salmon trade by default when the HBC moved north in 1846, but they took remarkably little notice. Technical obstacles still hampered the shipment of salted salmon around Cape Horn, while agriculture and mining captured the attention of American settlers. The acquisition of California drew commercial fishers south to the Sacramento River, and a small group from Maine began to experiment with canning technology. In Oregon, Indians continued to do the majority of fishing for subsistence and markets, but after 1850 a few whites also fished commercially. Immigration made the fish trade more lucrative, and in 1861 Washington Territory granted two men the exclusive right to fish their gillnets on a mile-long stretch of the lower Columbia near Oak Point.[59]

The grant was a narrowly focused act, but it highlighted several significant shifts occurring in the social organization of fishing. The grant reflected the transfer of power from Indians to the state, while its purpose symbolized the transition from a regional subsistence fishery to a capitalist market fishery. Markets were redefining the meaning and organization of labor and space. Fishing centers such as Willamette Falls, The Dalles, and Kettle Falls were giving way to new sites more accessible to urban markets. The exclusive grant represented the opening wedge for a new racialization of fishing space as well. Many of these changes were already under way in 1861; others would not be fulfilled until the 1870s. The grant nevertheless foreshadowed, if not predicted, the coming of the industrial fishery.

People were already eating Oregon-country salmon in far-flung places when canneries arrived on the Columbia, but changes in the harvest, preservation, and transportation of fish further expanded the scale and scope of consumption, escalating the pressure on salmon dramatically.

Industrial fishing was still in its infancy when it came to the Columbia in 1866, but the fishery had already established its central characteristics in California. By 1864, expatriates fleeing the failed Atlantic salmon fisheries had combined efficient capture methods, (dis)assembly line processing, canning technology, and global marketing into a formidable enterprise on the Sacramento River. The fishery enriched a few canners, but by the mid-1860s the Sacramento runs were in full retreat. Hydraulic placer mining had devastated spawning beds, and fishing competition undermined profitability. Running out of money and fish, Andrew Hapgood and William, George, and R. D. Hume began to scout new prospects. They visited the Columbia in 1865 and decided to erect a small cannery at Eagle Point. During the next decade the Humes became the first family of the salmon fisheries. Their talents as fishers and technological innovators produced remarkable success, and other East Coast fishers took notice. Interest grew and the "swidden fishery" migrated once more from an exhausted river to a new Eden. What began as a couple of broke fishermen looking for a new stream soon became the second largest economic activity of the region.[60]

Let a few numbers begin to tell the story. In 1866 there was one cannery: Hapgood, Hume and Company. It packed 272,000 pounds of salmon in cans. By 1870 there were five canneries processing 10 million pounds. By 1875 fourteen canneries packed 25 million pounds. Fishers and capitalists continued to pour into the region, and aside from a brief but alarming downturn in 1877, production grew steadily. By 1884 thirty-seven canneries packed 42 million pounds of salmon, or about the same amount as the annual aboriginal harvest.[61]

The problem with numbers, though, is that they can hide as much as they reveal. Aboriginal and industrial harvests appear statistically similar, but the fishery had changed radically. Indians had harvested various runs and species from March to November, but Euro-American consumers preferred the deep orange meat of chinook and sockeye. Canners quickly learned to concentrate on the runs of favored species between April and July, and fishing time shortened from nine months to four. Fishing space collapsed as well. The aboriginal fishery was scattered throughout the river systems, but the industrial fishery evolved differently. Salmon meat degrades quickly, so canners located their operations near fishing sites. The high capital costs of canning also required large supplies of fresh fish and access to transportation to remain profitable. The industrial fishery thus gravitated toward deepwater harbors. As the *Portland Morning Oregonian* noted in 1874, "The canning establishments are tending towards Astoria. . . . Here the salmon are just in from the seas, fat and in the highest condition for curing to perfection." By 1880, a once-dispersed fishery had congealed into a forty-mile stretch of the lower Columbia. Culture and economy transformed the temporal and spatial shape of the fishery, increasing pressure on some runs while alleviating it on others. A simple recital of numbers cannot tell the whole story.[62]

The industrial fishery introduced other changes as well. To increase their competitiveness, gillnetters attached additional layers of webbing and weights on their nets. The improved versions entangled salmon more ways and fished more layers of the river. In the late 1870s fishers also introduced traps, poundnets, and fishwheels. These stationary structures created deadly gauntlets in areas where the current ran too slow or too fast for gillnets, and after 1880 fishing space expanded once again. When the Northern Pacific Railroad arrived in 1883, packers rushed to The Dalles, colonized aboriginal

fishing sites, and erected fishwheels seemingly everywhere. Along tidewater, canners improved haul seines by adding teams of horses to pull larger
nets. In some senses the gear that industrial fishers used was no more
destructive than that used by aboriginal fishers—after all, weirs could block
an entire run—but technology is meaningless without a cultural context.[63]

What distinguished the two fisheries was their raison d'être. Aboriginal
fishers harvested for local use, and technology, demography, and culture
combined to moderate catches. By contrast, only the technical limitations
of harvest, preservation, transportation, and markets constrained the industrial fishery. Capitalism freed fishers from the governing influence of ceremonies and taboos, and fishmongers harnessed ships and, after 1883, railroads to create a global market for salmon. Quite suddenly the East Coast,
Great Britain, and Europe consumed more Pacific salmon than northwesterners. The implications of these intersecting developments are nowhere
more evident than in the canneries, where packers remained competitive
through constant innovation. They streamlined delivery systems and processing techniques. They accelerated production and improved product reliability. They reduced waste and developed markets for such by-products as
fish oil and fish meal.[64]

But waste could never be completely eliminated in an open-access fishery, and profligacy plagued the industry's reputation. During large runs
fishers sometimes caught more salmon than the canneries could handle,
and huge piles of fish rotted in the open. A huge run of salmon entered the
Columbia between 24 July and 10 August 1896. According to one canner,
the chinook were so big and numerous "that the canneries, run to there [sic]
greatest capacity, could not put up near all the fish, probably about one-
half." When canneries imposed quotas to limit deliveries to processable
amounts, fishers highgraded their catches (a practice of continuing to fish
after a quota was reached in order to replace smaller fish with larger ones to
maximize profit). In the process fishers killed many salmon but kept only
the largest of preferred species. Many observers attributed these episodes to
sheer greed, but as sociologist Patricia Marchak points out, "Competition
by fishers [was] a consequence of the structure of that market." Government
refused to restrict economic activity. Thus canners had to increase production and reduce costs to remain competitive in a laissez-faire market, and
fishers had to catch more, or larger, fish to offset falling wages and quotas.
Without restrictions on participation or harvest, cutthroat practices were
almost inevitable.[65]

The subtlety of this argument was lost on observers though, because
numbers tended to confirm the thesis of greed. Participation continued to

grow after 1884. By 1888, 3,538 fishers worked the Columbia, another 80 the Willamette, and more than 100 were Indian dipnet fishers at The Dalles. The following year 1,226 gillnets, 40 seines, 164 traps, and 40 fishwheels worked the Columbia, and in the next decade all types of gear continued to proliferate. Meanwhile harvests faltered. Catches plummeted by 50 percent between 1884 and 1889, rebounded briefly in the mid-1890s, and then fell again. Observers prophesied doom, that salmon runs would soon "be a thing of the past," and the swidden fishery fled once more. Canners began to test the upper Columbia and coast in the late 1870s. After 1884 the trickle became a flood. Dispersal and consolidation reduced the number of Columbia River canneries from a high of thirty-nine in 1887 to only twenty-one two years later, and Alaska quickly eclipsed the Columbia in both harvests and control of the market.[66]

Again, the numbers obscure many of the details. Government census takers labored vigorously, but they depended on voluntary reporting, canners rarely submitted timely figures, and no one counted losses due to spoilage. Moreover, most packers conflated species for the sake of convenience. Lower Columbia canners tended to lump coho, sockeye, chum, and steelhead with their chinook totals, since the latter was the species that predominated; upper Columbia records favored sockeye for similar reasons. This practice masked the decline of spring and summer chinook during the 1880s because canners compensated by exploiting fall runs and other species. Thus the statistical rebound in the early 1890s resulted largely from greater reliance on sockeye and coho. On the other hand, observers of waste rarely noted that canners often salted or mild-cured excess catches or shipped them to other canneries. People were so fixated on canneries that they largely ignored other modes of consumption. Nobody systematically quantified subsistence fisheries, fresh-fish markets, or industrial uses of salmon even though there was a sizable market fishery on the Snake during the 1890s and subsistence and market fishers severely damaged runs on the Okanogan in the 1860s and at Wallowa Lake in the 1880s.[67]

Lastly, though largely unrecognized at the time, nature also had a hand in shaping salmon runs. Climatic events interrupted harvests repeatedly, and not always to the benefit of salmon. Heavy rains and snowmelts unleashed floods in 1861, 1878, 1879, 1881, and 1890 that probably scoured the spawning grounds. Conversely, in 1894 the Columbia rose to its highest level ever and wrecked almost every fishwheel on the river. Such floods did not affect all streams equally. Topography ensured that some watersheds received inordinate precipitation. The Wilson, Trask, and Siletz Rivers on the northern coast, the Bull Run and Santiam in the Willamette Valley, and the Umpqua and Rogue in southern Oregon tended to draw the brunt of storms. Droughts, on the other hand, spread their misery widely. In 1889, 1897, and 1900 smaller streams were too dry to use nets or fishwheels for much of the year. In 1909 fishers got drought and flood. Warm weather kept coastal streams dry for much of the summer and fall; then freshets inundated the fisheries the remainder of the year. Yet the impact of severe weather on spawning beds remains speculative, because no one bothered to measure their effects until much later.[68]

The physical and biological conditions of the Pacific, which fluctuate periodically, also affected salmon. Seasonal and annual shifts have long been recognized, but major changes also occur over decades in response to broad atmospheric forces. Fishery biologists have only recently begun to recognize these long-term climate shifts and their effects on salmon runs. They have divided the northeast Pacific into two zones, the Central Subarctic Domain (CSD) and the Coastal Upwelling Domain (CUD), which seem to oscillate over several decades. When the low-pressure zone that hovers over the Aleutian Islands intensifies, the CSD grows cooler and plankton density increases, thus creating better conditions for salmon; meanwhile, the CUD grows warmer and less fecund. Instrument records only go back to the turn of the century, but if the patterns they reveal prevailed in the late nineteenth century, then the CUD, which played host to Oregon country salmon, may have been in a down cycle during the industrial fishery's time of troubles in the late 1800s.

Ocean climates can also fluctuate interannually. The reasons vary, but the most famous phenomenon is El Niño, a sometimes intense event of marine warming that can affect continental weather patterns. When El Niño struck in the late 1870s, floods ravaged much of the Pacific coast and salmon runs plummeted. Although El Niño will be discussed in more depth in the next chapter, for now it should be noted that it too shaped salmon runs in ways no one recognized at the time.[69]

In 1854, fishery investigator John Cleghorn coined the term "over-fishing" to explain the reduction of the British herring fisheries. In its original application, the term described the impact of fishing effort on a pelagic species, but in the last century society has applied it uncritically to far more complicated situations. In popular usage, we tend to extract fishing from its social and ecological context. We reduce dynamic processes to a tale of too many nets and let the thesis of greedy fishers overpower our memories. "Overfishing" is no longer just an analytical device. It has been freighted with social and political connotations that, as anthropologist Courtland Smith notes, lump "together several processes that are difficult to separate." When we use this term, we invariably place the onus for declining runs squarely at the feet of fishers, yet as Patricia Marchak reminds us, they were "not the sole participants in the industry, and it is on this point that the typical arguments about fishers depleting the resource are most blind." The history of overfishing is more complicated than a simple tale of "too many fishers."[70]

Yet as abused as it sometimes is, "overfishing" does retain explanatory power—it just needs a more dynamic and historical application. When we broaden our focus, we see how critical the nineteenth century was to the fate of the region's salmon runs. Demographic shifts initiated broad transformations of the social, cultural, economic, and ecological landscapes of the Oregon country. Trapping, farming, mining, irrigating, logging, urbanization, and industrialization reshaped salmon habitat, while the industrial fisheries altered harvesting in ways that increased pressure on some runs but reduced it on others. The environment became less amenable to salmon reproduction, yet fishing remained as intensive as ever. No one acknowledged responsibility or accepted the need for limitations, and salmon runs dwindled like a candle burned at both ends.

3 / Inventing a Panacea

Although many Americans recognized the inroads which development was making on salmon habitat, they regarded change as an unfortunate but unavoidable cost of "civilization." Their solace was the burgeoning notion that science would enable civilization to compensate for the destruction it caused. Science, the modern panacea, would save salmon. To understand this faith, we need to trace the historical development of ideas about science and fishery management, their incorporation into the U.S. Fish Commission (USFC), and that agency's political and fiscal dependence on the artificial propagation of fish.

Critics have attributed this reliance on fish culture to larger cultural imperatives: to biblical commandments to subdue nature; to "our collective impulse to domesticate"; and to an "unwillingness to take responsibility." But such explanations are too broad, timeless, and unnuanced. The more muddled reality is that fishery management developed from a tangled alliance of politics, science, and technology during a specific period of history. Managers built fish hatcheries during the 1860s and 1870s because they offered a technological solution to a series of vexing social and political problems. Fish culture gained scientific legitimacy and popular support, which administrators used to build formidable institutions for fishery management. By 1900 federal management was so dependent on fish culture that it had become an end in itself.[1]

Federal administrators designed a management system around fish culture to balance strategies of production with hesitant regulation and federal authority with states' rights. Ideally, the federal government would assist the fisheries by providing scientific information and running hatcheries; states would pass laws to regulate fishing. Funded by Congress, the USFC tried to cultivate a national agenda that was less concerned with increasing runs per se than repairing depleted fisheries and establishing new ones. Its job was to make and distribute fish. States might also run hatcheries, but their primary responsibility was to set seasons, define gear restrictions, and enforce laws. Although federal managers never realized this idealized model, the underlying assumptions continued to shape fishery management well into the twentieth century despite their increasingly apparent shortcomings.

Fish culture dates to ancient China, but it did not appear in the United States until 1850. What began as an avocation among a few eastern professionals soon intrigued state politicians. In 1870 interest shifted to Congress, which created the U.S. Fish Commission to investigate interstate problems. The legacy of these early efforts and the commissioner's experiences during his first year solidified the future course of American fishery management.

American fish culture grew in response to declining fisheries in the eastern United States. Agriculture and industrialization had driven many Atlantic salmon and shad runs into sharp decline or extinction during the late eighteenth and early nineteenth centuries. By the 1850s there were few anadromous runs left, but then a few medical doctors and wealthy individuals in Ohio, New York, and New England began to tinker with artificial propagation as a way of replenishing streams. In 1853 the physicians Theodatus Garlick and H. A. Ackley read European reports and began to fertilize trout eggs near Cleveland. Two years later E. C. Kellogg and D. W. Chapman began their own experiments in New England. Anglers, fishmongers, and reformers soon embraced fish culture for its potential to increase preferred species and end hunger. Kellogg prophesied, "From what has been done in Europe, prophetic vision is unnecessary to see that at no distant period . . . our rivers and streams . . . will teem with salmon and trout, as well as with delicate fish from foreign waters, affording food and luxury to all."[2]

Such prophecies garnered considerable attention, but what fish culturists meant by success needs examination. In the 1850s and 1860s, Garlick, Ackley, Kellogg, and Seth Green mastered the basic problems of artificially fertilizing and incubating fish eggs. In doing so they significantly increased the rate of reproduction over natural methods, but their claims extended far beyond successful incubation in the hatchery. In their minds, more efficient reproduction led directly to increased harvests. Canadian fish culturist Samuel Wilmot compared artificial hatch rates of 80 or 90 percent to a dubious natural rate of 1 percent and claimed, "The superiority of the former over the latter system will be easily understood, even by the great masses of the people, who are as yet wholly uninformed as to the novel science of artificial fish culture." Thus "a judicious application of the natural and artificial methods of propagation, together with thorough protection during the close seasons, would soon reproduce ... a large supply of fish, both for domestic purposes and foreign trade. The outlay required to achieve this object will be found to be trifling ... in comparison to the ultimate benefits that would assuredly flow from its application." Science would triumph.[3]

These golden promises captured the attention of politicians and led to the coining of a peculiarly American version of fish conservation by George Perkins Marsh. In 1856 and 1857 state legislators commissioned a series of studies to investigate fishery problems and fish culture. Marsh conducted the most important of these studies for Vermont. His report amounted to a definitive statement of the art and science of fish culture. He began with a sophisticated analysis of ecological changes. He noted that mills and factories dammed streams, polluted waters, and killed fish, and he also implicated "the general physical changes produced by the clearing and cultivation of the soil." Farming and logging reduced the forest's ability to retain precipitation. Freshets were "more violent" and dry seasons more arid. Reduced cover increased siltation and temperatures and decreased the availability of insects that fish consumed. Marsh concluded, "It is enough to say that human *improvements* have produced an almost total change in all the external conditions of piscatorial life."[4]

Marsh gave a deft description of causation, but solutions were far less evident.

> The unfavorable influences which have been alluded to are, for the most part, of a kind which cannot be removed or controlled. We cannot destroy our dams, or provide artificial water-ways for the migration of fish ...; we cannot wholly prevent the discharge of deleterious substances from our industrial establishments into our running waters. ... It is therefore not probable that the absolute prevention of taking fish at improper season, or with destructive implements, or indeed that any mere protective legislation, however faithfully obeyed, would restore the ancient abundance of our public fisheries ... [even] if the legal and moral power of the legislature ... were somewhat greater.

Thus habitat restoration, while environmentally "desirable," was politically "impractical."[5]

Marsh's pessimism arose from a realistic assessment of the central tenets of American political economy. In the early part of the century fishers and industrialists had waged bitter contests over the damming of New England streams. Each side won battles, but victory always hinged on the economic benefits at stake—a situation that would repeat itself in the twentieth century when fishers and developers clashed over dams in the Pacific Northwest. Nineteenth-century courts and legislatures hesitated to limit profitable activities, and they insisted that the fisheries were open-access commons. Thus Marsh was justified in regarding environmental problems as the sad but inevitable price of progress. "The final extinction of the larger wild quadrupeds and birds, as well as the diminution of fish, and other aquatic animals, is everywhere a condition of advanced civilization and the increase and spread of a rural and industrial population." With nature and civilization as polar opposites, it became "for obvious reasons, impracticable to restore a condition of things incompatible with the necessities and the habits of cultivated social life."[6]

Marsh discounted legal proscriptions, but he did not despair for nature. He had reviewed the literature on fish culture and cited such authorities as Swiss naturalist Karl Vogt, American fish culturist J. C. Comstock, and French fish culturist Jules Haime. Vogt had cautioned against believing the outlandish claims of fanatics, yet he noted, "Nature loses more than ninety per cent. of the material capable of development which she provides, and all her economy is calculated for this proportion of loss. . . . [Thus] it should be our aim to preserve this superabundance of material, and to adopt such methods as will secure development and growth to the largest possible proportion of it." Comstock emphasized the need for hatcheries and fishways, and he estimated profits from fish culture that bordered on the marvelous. Haime made an even more forceful endorsement. "Every thing, then, gives reason to hope that at an early period pisciculture will be naturalized among the useful sciences, and that it is destined to solve one of the important terms of the great problem of cheap living."[7]

Marsh saw much promise in fish culture. He hoped that society might "still do something to recover at least a share of the abundance which, in a more primitive state, the water kingdom afforded," and he thought that artificial propagation was "not only practicable, but may be made profitable, and . . . our fresh water may thus be made to produce a vast amount of excellent food."[8]

But doubt tempered enthusiasm. The language and metaphors experts adopted suggested lingering confusion. J. C. Comstock preferred to call fish culture a "long neglected art." Marsh characterized fish culture as "simple and easy," yet it also needed redeeming by "competent scientific men." E. C. Kellogg favored terms from husbandry and suggested that fish be "stall fed . . . and fattened as well as animals." Jules Haime mixed industrial and agricultural metaphors when he suggested that a "piscifactory" prepare the waters "by regular sowing." The lack of rhetorical consistency—this wavering between art and science, husbandry and industry—reflected larger uncertainties. Haime, Marsh, and others admitted that there was much they did not know and that natural history still had much to offer fish culturists.[9]

The central practical issues facing Americans were the questions of jurisdiction over fish and responsibility for fish culture; the solutions people offered reveal a tangled relationship between nature, political economy, and technology. Salmon and shad frustrated attempts to protect them because their lives did not conform to the political boundaries that humans imposed on nature. Vogt and Haime suggested what Marsh considered a European approach to management: centralized authority and government-supported fish culture. J. C. Comstock too favored federal oversight of interstate waters, but he preferred that the states compel dam owners to install fishways. Marsh resolved the problems of environmental change, technological uncertainty, and political economy like a classic Jeffersonian republican. He dismissed state management as inapplicable in America, where government "policy is to protect and promote industry with the least possible amount of legislation." It was impossible to manage an anadromous fishery in interstate waters like the Connecticut River or Lake Champlain. "Our main reliance," he insisted, "must be upon the enterprise and ingenuity of private citizens." Vermont should instead protect investors by awarding property rights to fish produced in private hatcheries.[10]

Marsh's ideas reflected the essential optimism of American individualism and capitalism, and his prescription of minimal governmental interference and technological solutions would become the foundation of American fishery management in the following decades. The Vermont legislature refused to institute Marsh's recommendations because of "the present state of information," but part of Marsh's agenda went forward nonetheless. In the next decade most New England and middle Atlantic states formed fish commissions to investigate problems, and private fish culture prevailed as the favored solution. Richard Nettle hatched an anadromous species for the first time in 1857 with Atlantic salmon, and ten years later Seth Green hatched shad in the Hudson River. That same year the Canadian Samuel Wilmot built the first salmon hatchery near Lake Ontario, and in 1868 Livingston Stone transplanted salmon eggs from the Canadian province of New Brunswick to various New England states.[11]

Yet a critical element of Marsh's plan was missing. The inability or reluctance of states to maintain open streams and limit fishing deterred fish culturists from investing in anadromous fish as property. As salmon and shad runs continued to decline, states began to fill the breach. Maine built a hatchery in 1870 and neighboring states passed more stringent fishing regulations. In the late 1860s fishery troubles extended from rivers to the ocean. Tensions increased between trap and net fishers in southern New England over declining alewife and scup numbers. Massachusetts and Rhode Island tried to resolve the conflict, but investigators soon discovered that the debate was hopelessly mired in ignorance and partisanship. Neither state would fund the necessary research, and as with shad and salmon on the Connecticut River, the problems of managing a migratory fish eclipsed the powers of individual states.[12]

By 1870 observers were frustrated by the provincial attitudes and jurisdictional limitations that were thwarting fishery management. Private enterprise faded as a solution, and a few observers began to hope that the federal government would investigate and manage interstate fisheries. Fishers, state representatives, and Smithsonian staff began to lobby Congress for assistance, but Congress was reluctant because most Americans distrusted intrusions by the state. The evidence of problems was overwhelming, however, and in 1871 Congress responded with what political scientist Stephen Skowronek calls a "patchwork" solution. Rather than create a new department with broad powers, Congress devised the U.S. Commission on Fish and Fisheries as an unaffiliated temporary agency with no regulatory functions. Its sole initial purpose was to investigate fishery problems. Congress then hired Spencer Fullerton Baird as commissioner of the USFC.[13]

Spencer Baird's appointment was a critical event in the development of American fishery management. Baird had made a name for himself as a systematic zoologist classifying species in ornithology and herpetology, but he also had a knack for politics. He cultivated connections with many of the leading lights of American science, including John James Audubon, Louis Agassiz, James Dwight Dana, Joseph Henry, and George Perkins Marsh. His connection to Marsh was particularly fortuitous. As a congressman in the late 1840s, Marsh had lobbied the Smithsonian on Baird's behalf, and in 1850 Baird received a position as assistant secretary. Through Marsh, Baird also met Vermont senator George Franklin Edmunds, who encouraged Baird's interest in the fisheries, helped create the USFC, and ushered his appointment as commissioner. But Baird knew birds and reptiles, not fish, so he relied extensively on the advice of others, the most important of whom was Marsh.[14]

Baird investigated the scup fisheries in much the same way as Marsh had tackled Vermont's problems. In order to discover whether alewives and scup were actually declining and if so why, he and Addison E. Verrill, a natural history professor at Yale, made as comprehensive an examination of the fish and fisheries as possible on a limited budget. The duo learned the natural history of the fish by sampling local waters to determine predators, prey, and food availability. They also surveyed fishers to learn the economic landscape, identify problems with pollution, and assess the impact of rival fishing practices. By the fall of 1871, Baird had some tentative conclusions. Neither marine resources nor pollution were limiting fish populations, but the increasing use of large poundnets to entrap whole schools of fish, especially in Massachusetts, and an alarming number of scup in bluefish stomachs seemed to explain the decline. Baird could do nothing about the bluefish, but he was sure that poundnets could be controlled.[15]

Baird's conclusion drew him into the murky waters of regulation and toward a conflict he could not hope to win. Like Marsh, Baird believed in a minimalist federal state. He tried to persuade Massachusetts and Rhode Island to close their poundnets on weekends. He used his authority as a scientist and his summer's research to cajole legislators to take action, but his plan backfired horribly. Rhode Island legislators played to the large contingent of gillnetters in their state by curtailing poundnets severely, while Massachusetts legislators played oppositely to a majority of poundnet owners in their state. Baird tried to break the stalemate by predicting an imminent collapse of the scup fishery, but his science failed him. Massachusetts fish commissioner Theodore Lyman used his own detailed research to refute Baird's conclusions about bluefish and the decline of scup. Baird grew desperate and threatened a federal takeover of fishery management, but his bluff fooled no one.[16]

Baird's first year as fish commissioner ended disastrously. By rejecting federal authority, Baird had backed himself into a management conundrum. He had abdicated control to the states but then had to admit that the states were not "disinterested enough" to pursue conservation measures where "the benefits are likely to be shared . . . [with] other States." Turning Marsh's ideas into policy proved much harder than anticipated.[17]

Baird devised a new approach to management by reintroducing the other half of Marsh's managerial vision: technology. His solution came from another group advocating federal involvement: fish culturists. Hatchery boosters such as Seth Green and Robert Barnwell Roosevelt had lobbied Baird since early 1871, but only after the debacle with Rhode Island and Massachusetts did Baird seriously consider supporting a federal program of fish culture. He privately endorsed the idea but maintained a discreet distance by publicly advocating voluntary cooperation. He instructed Vermont fish commissioner M. C. Edmunds to build a coalition with neighboring states, and he asked private fish culturist William Clift to similarly organize his fellow fish culturists.[18]

Baird and his allies quietly welded disparate agendas into a successful movement for a federal program by portraying the USFC as a natural organ for fish culture. Commissioner Edmunds wanted to transplant Pacific salmon eggs in eastern streams, but the expense was too great for any one state and, as Baird had already admitted, interstate cooperation was unlikely. Only the federal government had the breadth and resources to conduct such a transplant program. For similar reasons, Clift argued that the USFC should distribute shad eggs in the Mississippi basin. Edmunds and Clift combined their proposals at the annual meeting of the American Fish Culturists' Association (AFCA), a new organization of fish culturists, managers, and anglers. New York fish commissioner George Shepherd Page drafted the proposal and lobbied Congress; New York congressman and AFCA member Robert Roosevelt regaled the House of Representatives with the wonders of fish culture and the problems of interstate management; and honorary AFCA members Baird and Senator Edmunds worked the cloakrooms of the Capitol.[19]

The campaign was politically astute; it promised to benefit state and private interests at little cost while solidifying the role of the USFC. Federal hatcheries provided states a means of restocking rivers at federal expense. The USFC afforded private fish culturists a means of expanding the market for shad while procuring free salmon eggs from California. Fish culture offered Baird a way to rejuvenate fisheries without treading the political minefield of regulation. And most important of all, a national distribution system allowed Baird to claim that fish culture would benefit all sections of the country. Baird could cultivate broad congressional support by promising fish for everyone. Oregon senator Henry Corbett sealed the deal when he added an amendment requiring the USFC to plant shad on the Pacific slope (streams entering the Pacific Ocean) while harvesting Pacific salmon eggs for the East. Congress appropriated $15,000, and the new federal agency had found its mission: making fish.[20]

During the last decades of the nineteenth century, Baird tried to implement Marsh's vision of minimal regulation and restoration of fisheries through technology. In doing so, however, he unwittingly altered his mission from scientific investigation to promotion of fish culture.[21]

Baird had originally envisioned the USFC as a convenient tool for pursuing scientific research that the Smithsonian could not afford, but his inter-

ests failed to fire the imagination of Congress. To generate support, he had
to straddle the worlds of politics and science. Fish culture was his bridge;
it promised practical results painlessly, and science would improve its methods over time. Hatcheries allowed him to build and maintain political
backing and funding for less obviously utilitarian science projects such as
investigations of tiny aquatic life or an encyclopedic classification of North
American fish species. Baird had become what historian Charles Rosenberg
calls a "scientist-entrepreneur." As an administrator of a government-
sponsored program, he mediated "between the world of science . . . [and]
the social and economic realities of a particular state constituency."[22]

Baird used this pragmatic combination of economy and science to build
a national conservation program founded on fish culture. He concentrated
on charismatic species like shad and salmon, and he distributed fish to every
congressional district as a way of demonstrating the utility of fish culture.
He also insisted that applications for eggs be submitted through congressional representatives to remind them of the USFC's popularity.[23]

The political undercurrents of his project emerged early. In 1872 Baird
hired Seth Green to distribute shad in the Mississippi basin, but when the
project stumbled Baird admitted: "Anxious as I am to make a demonstration the present season, & thus prove to Congress that we are in earnest, I
do not object to paying the apparently disproportionate expense. I am very
glad that you placed the Shad in the Allegheny, but am sorry you could not
have made the number larger; as 30,000 does not make a great show for a
big experiment." On another occasion Baird told an employee that the fate
of the eggs was less important than the planting. "The object is to introduce
[fish eggs] into as many states as possible and have credit with Congress
accordingly. If they are there, they are there, and we can so swear, and that
is the end of it." Political considerations drove fish culture practices from
the beginning.[24]

Restoring Atlantic salmon runs required a more elaborate solution than
shad because of the sheer scale of the losses. Baird developed a two-part
strategy. He used the state hatchery at Bucksport, Maine, to restore the
relatively healthy runs of northern New England; for streams farther south
he wanted to import Pacific salmon. But this required building an infrastructure from scratch. Baird knew next to nothing about salmon, so he hired
Livingston Stone as assistant commissioner and charged him with Pacific
Coast operations. Stone was a perfect choice. He had trained to be a
Unitarian minister, but poor health forced him from the pulpit. Stone
transferred his religious zeal to fish culture, and by 1872 he had become a
founding member of the AFCA, its first secretary, and a leading authority on

salmon propagation. Stone desperately wanted the job, and he gladly sacrificed business and professional interests to pursue what he called *"the one great work, above all others, in the restoration of salmon to the American rivers and lakes."*[25]

Stone became an apostle for Baird's ideas about management. Like Marsh and Baird, Stone believed that fish culture would "relieve in a great measure the excessive restrictions, which must otherwise be placed on the fishing of the restocked rivers, and which will hardly be less obnoxious to the people than not stocking them at all." He gave numerous speeches and interviews extolling the virtues of artificial propagation and advocating state-imposed limits on fishing and pollution. Baird gave Stone great leeway in these activities. Together they melded science and technology into a coherent program as much concerned with alleviating economic restrictions as conserving natural resources.[26]

Stone traveled to the Pacific Coast in 1872, and there he faced the practical constraints on fish culture. Baird had left most of the details to Stone, including the location of the hatchery and the species to be bred, but to appease angling interests he insisted that the salmon take a hook and taste good. Baird and Stone considered the Columbia as an egg source, but in the early 1870s the necessity of locating near a railhead precluded areas outside the Sacramento Valley. Stone settled on the chinook runs of the McCloud River, a tributary of the upper Sacramento. During the next few years he developed a reliable method for transporting fertilized eggs across the continent. He learned how to pack eggs in wood crates, insulate them with moss, and cool them with ice. The combination weathered the long, hot, bumpy trip across the continent, and Stone's associates on the East Coast soon had a reliable and inexpensive supply of Pacific salmon eggs.[27]

Baird turned the commission into a biological clearinghouse. He arranged for free transportation on railroads and distributed liberal assignments of Pacific salmon eggs not only to state and private hatcheries throughout the East but to such exotic locales as Australia, New Zealand, South America, Europe, Iowa, and the Great Salt Lake. Egg transfers became quite popular, especially after the triumphal boasts of hatchery boosters. In 1875, for example, Stone called a shipment of salmon eggs to Australia "a success" simply because the eggs hatched. Such claims were not completely unwarranted—fish culturists *had* increased the rate of hatching over natural reproduction—but the assumption that depositing young fish in streams equaled victory illustrates the tremendously different standards of nineteenth-century science.[28]

Throughout this period neither Stone nor Baird nor anyone else knew much about the biology of Pacific salmon. When Stone arrived in California, he viewed western nature through eyes trained in the East. He saw *Salmo*, not *Oncorhynchus*. Phenomena such as multiple runs, suspension of feeding, distorted and rotting bodies, and death after spawning perplexed and appalled him. By the end of his first season in California he admitted that conditions were "entirely different here from any previous experience at the East." "I do not understand it." He considered many traits "paradoxical," "unreasonable," and "incredibly contradictory to nature's laws of life."[29]

Critics recoiled at such waste, but Stone defended his observations. The irrationality of nature in fact confirmed his sense of a higher mission: "Nature, perhaps more aptly speaking, Providence, in the case of fish . . . produces great quantities of seed that nature does not utilize or need. It looks like a vast store that has been provided for nature, to hold in reserve against the time when the increased population of the earth should need it and the sagacity of man should utilize it. At all events nature has never utilized this reserve, and man finds it already here to meet his wants." Stone combined theology and technology into a righteous cause. In the Jeffersonian tradition, Man would complete the pastoral project of finishing nature.[30]

Pastoral ideals were not the sole inspiration of fish culture, however. In an 1871 speech before the AFCA, M. C. Edmunds blended technology and civic progress for a different sort of crusade. Edmunds noted, "The great desideratum with Yankee enterprise is, 'Does it pay?' and to which all other considerations must bend." Edmunds assured listeners that hatcheries would produce profits, yet they need not involve a descent to base materialism. They could combine gain with finishing nature and alleviating misery. "The stocking of our rivers with the salmon is above price, the great and good work for us all— the final consummation of which will bring blessings to millions of people; establishing the fact that man is not living wholly for self."[31]

Fish culturists incorporated profit into the pastoral. Edmunds implored his audience, "Let us labor onward and upward, looking for the success ultimately to be realized." "I conceive of no higher ambition for any man or set of men than the ultimate restocking of our streams with the migratory sea fish, more especially the salmon. It at once gives all classes the advantages of cheap and desirable food. And, gentlemen, are we not commanded 'to feed the hungry,' and how better can this great duty be performed than by laboring to restock our lakes and rivers with fish of all kinds? To this end let us labor and eventually perpetuate a blessing."[32]

The pastoral was the realm of small producers—common people—but fish culture demanded experts. In 1886 another Baird disciple, George

Brown Goode, insisted that "to be efficient, [fish culture] must be conducted by men trained in scientific methods of thought and work." This,
thought Edmunds, was "making progress in the right direction." Fish culture had become a sign for science, technology, efficiency, and progress.[33]

This rhetoric of finishing, of combining the pastoral and the technical to
create a more efficient nature, indicates that the shift to so-called Progressive conservation may not have been as abrupt as some historians suggest.
Historians trace the origin of government-sponsored conservation to the
Progressive Era and Gifford Pinchot's Forest Service. They emphasize the
importance of progress and efficiency as guiding principles of the period,
yet these themes were already in play thirty years earlier. Progressive conservation was not cut from whole cloth but emerged over a longer period of
economic and social change. The speeches of Stone, Edmunds, and Goode
reveal an intellectual flux. The Jeffersonian ideal of a pastoral middle
ground held elements of perfecting nature that proved amenable to newer
priorities of industrial efficiency in the service of social progress. The USFC
was the epicenter of nascent efforts to get the federal government to manage the nation's natural resources.[34]

The political economy of government conservation thus has a prehistory
of sorts. It begins not in the forests but on the water, and it reveals not one
but a spectrum of strategies for conserving resources. Baird agreed to manage fish rather than fishers, whereas Pinchot preferred to control both trees
and loggers. The Taylor Grazing Act offered a third approach by regulating
ranchers instead of grass, while the Agricultural Adjustment Act restrained
production to rationalize markets.[35]

Fishery managers may have played politics to solve some problems, but
they still had to contend with the strange nature of salmon. In reconciling
Atlantic and Pacific salmon, Stone developed a theory that emphasized the
plasticity of salmon. He saw "nothing yet to indicate that there is more than
one species of salmon in the Sacramento River." Multiple runs and death
were accidents of climate and location. Salmon that spawned in the cold
waters of the McCloud River did die, but nothing seemed to prevent
spawners farther downstream from returning to the ocean. Out of this
observation emerged a convoluted latitudinal and climatic theory for transplanting salmon. "It seems . . . that the Delaware and more southern rivers,
should be stocked with the Sacramento salmon, they being warm rivers like
the Sacramento, and their headwaters being cold streams like the McCloud.
I cannot help but think that the *mortality* of the Sacramento salmon is an
objection to its introduction into the Eastern rivers, [but] it does not, by any
means, follow that the fish will continue to die when transferred to the

Atlantic rivers. The cause of the mortality may lie, not in the nature of the fish, but in the climate of the water." Stone favored Sacramento salmon over Columbia salmon for transplants simply because the Sacramento River was farther south.[36]

Stone's confusions about salmon bared a larger quandary. During the 1880s and 1890s scientists were only one of many groups engaged in the debate over the nature of salmon. Fishers, canners, anglers, editors, politicians, and engineers also claimed knowledge about salmon. Sacramento canners argued that chinooks moved freely between the Sacramento and Columbia. Rogue River canner R. D. Hume claimed he had proof that salmon returned to sea after spawning. Many believed that fall runs spawned on the sands of the lower Columbia. At least one Astorian believed that every cannery doubled as a hatchery because discarded spawn underwent spontaneous fertilization under the docks, while another Oregonian refuted him on the grounds that the wake from passing ships would destroy the spawn. No single theory of salmon or group of people controlled the debate. Rather, nearly everyone had some things right even when they totally bollixed other aspects.[37]

One scientist eventually gained the upper hand in these debates, but his victory was hardly a triumph of truth. When Stone visited the Columbia in 1875, he identified at least six different species and heard reports of at least six more. Observers eventually split *Oncorhynchus* into thirty-five species and four genuses before David Starr Jordan resolved the debate in favor of the present classification system devised by Johann Walbaum in 1792. Jordan's academic training as a naturalist helped him solve these problems of systematic ichthyology and incidentally gain standing as the premier expert on Pacific salmon, yet in many respects he was as confused as others. Jordan relied on untrained assistants to collect information about salmon, which he then processed into science, but he had little direct experience in observing salmon. These shortcomings revealed themselves in 1881, when he wrote a natural history titled "Story of Salmon." The tale was a fanciful invention that bordered on the goofy: juvenile salmon migrated to sea because "they began to grow restless and to sigh for a change"; adults returned to rivers when they "remembered how the cold water used to feel . . . and in a blundering, fishy fashion . . . wondered whether the little eddy looked as it used to"; and salmon hatched in southwestern Washington were as likely to spawn in the Bitterroot Mountains of Idaho as their natal stream.[38]

Jordan had no empirical evidence to support these claims, yet even when challenged he never altered his opinions. In 1894 he wrote another article systematically reiterating his earlier ideas about the natural history of salmon, again getting many details completely wrong. Borrowing from the "modern theory" on pelagic fish populations, Jordan insisted that salmon "probably remain not very far from the mouth of the river in which they were spawned." He also thought that "[c]ontact with cold fresh water, when in the ocean, in some way causes [salmon] to run toward it." Thus separate runs were an artifact of meteorological patterns. He also doubted whether all salmon died after spawning, and he saw "no reason to believe that the salmon enter the Rogue River simply because they were spawned there, or that a salmon hatched in the Clackamas River is more likely, on that account, to return to the Clackamas than to go up the Cowlitz or the Deschutes."[39]

Jordan's theories mattered because they carried weight and influenced policies. Jordan reasoned that "the non-molestation of this fall run therefore does something to atone for the almost total destruction of the spring run." When Columbia River canners, who correctly believed that there were discrete runs, objected to relying solely on fall salmon for eggs, USFC Commissioner Marshall McDonald replied, "There seems to be no natural reason why this difference in location of spawning should differentiate the salmon into distinct races having distinct habits. . . . I would not hesitate to establish a hatchery and base its operations upon the collection of eggs from the fall run of fish. . . . I have no doubt the results . . . would be the same as if the operations of the hatchery had been conducted entirely with the eggs from the spring run."[40]

McDonald was wrong. There *were* natural reasons for differentiation. Humans cannot take fall fish and make spring runs, but until scientists understood how genetics could explain the creation of discrete populations, which would not occur until after the rediscovery of Gregor Mendel's paper in 1900, neither fishers nor scientists would know how to refute the arguments of Jordan and McDonald. Not until the late 1930s did fishery biologists finally agree that discrete runs existed and that salmon returned to natal streams. In the meantime the fishing industry hammered spring and summer runs with the blessing of fish culturists because everyone assumed that science would make more salmon.[41]

Other scientists added their voices in favor of fish culture. Naturalist Stephen A. Forbes reasoned, "If man increases these natural losses [from predation], he must compensate the species, either by protecting it from some of its enemies which would otherwise appropriate what he takes himself, or else by increasing the rate of multiplication so that the species may be able to support the added drain." Baird added mathematical justification. He contrasted natural hatch rates of one-half percent with artificial propagation rates above 90 percent and posited ratios of two hundred to one. Success had become an arithmetical given.[42]

Baird used these arguments to build support for the USFC. In 1874 he boasted, "Wherever the California salmon . . . has come under the hands of the fish-culturist, it is acknowledged . . . to exceed all other species, which are propagated, in hardiness, in tenacity of life, and in freedom from tendency to disease." He promoted fish culture in the USFC's annual reports and bulletins and published a wide array of studies by American, Canadian, and European fish culturists. He also engaged lay readers through *Forest and Stream*, which became the official organ of the AFCA. The common message of these publications was that fish culture worked.[43]

Baird's stature as a scientist gave him great authority, and the media responded enthusiastically. He gained a reputation as America's leading authority on fish culture. Canada's director for fish breeding called him an "eminent scientist" and "the highest authority on matters relating to fish, fisheries, and fish culture in . . . America." Professional and amateur fish culturists asked Baird for advice on "the matter which has in a large degree contributed to make you [Baird] famous throughout the land, Pisciculture." Baird cultivated this impression by publicizing the USFC in grand terms. The *San Francisco Overland Monthly* called the McCloud River Station "a striking illustration of the valuable assistance rendered by science." The *New York Times* regaled the "wonders" achieved by fish commissioners and "scientific ichthyologists."[44]

But Baird's propaganda campaign redirected the USFC in unintended ways. In 1872 Congress allocated $8,500 for scientific investigations, which represented 100 percent of the USFC's annual budget. In the next seventy years, however, expenditures for science never again exceeded 21 percent (1875) and usually stayed below 7 percent. Meanwhile the budget for fish culture skyrocketed. From 1873 to 1875 Congress allocated an average of $25,000 for shad and salmon work. By 1887 that figure had risen to $185,000. Fish culture had become the fiscal engine driving the USFC, employing 105 people and consuming over 73 percent of the budget. The tail began to wag the dog. In 1882 George Goode noted that artificial propagation was "by far the most extensive branch of the work of the Commission."[45]

Fish culture was also important as propaganda. In 1885, for example, Baird decided to close the McCloud Station because it ceased to have promotional value. Hatcheries were creating potent impressions, and in 1889, J. W. Collins judged the West utterly dependent upon hatcheries: "No section of the country is probably more dependent on fish-culture for the successful continuance of its fisheries than the Pacific slope. . . . Artificial propagation of fish has now passed beyond the experimental stage, and there is no longer doubt in unprejudiced and well-informed minds as to its possibilities when conducted intelligently and on a scale equal to the objects aimed at." In terms of the efficacy of fish culture, Collins's statement was ill-founded. Western hatcheries had run intermittently at best. Moreover, few transplanted salmon eggs ever reached maturity, and Baird discontinued egg shipments to the East Coast in 1883. As an assessment of the political importance of fish culture, however, Collins was right. Americans everywhere demanded hatcheries to save their fisheries. By 1890 fish culture had indeed passed beyond the "experimental stage" to become a formidable institution in its own right.[46]

Spencer Baird had performed wonders during his long tenure. He had helped realize a management philosophy coined by George Perkins Marsh and rooted in a Jeffersonian faith of limited government and the power of private enterprise. But turning those assumptions into policy forced him to rely on technology to solve social problems: human destruction of habitat and overfishing. Fish culture helped turn a temporary agency into a fledgling bureaucracy, but it also deflected the mission of the agency. Baird never secured the institutional commitment to scientific research he so desired.

Instead, budgets and staff always tilted toward fish culture, which administrators endorsed in the strongest terms. In 1882 George Goode wrote, "The rude appliances of ten years ago have given way to scientifically devised apparatus, by which millions of eggs are hatched where thousands were [before], and the demonstration of the possibility of stocking rivers and lakes to any desired extent has been greatly strengthened." The only other way "to bring back the number of salmon to what it was when nature was supreme . . . would be . . . to undo our civilization, to let our meadows run again to unpruned forests." Hatcheries thus offered the best of all worlds: "All civilized Governments in the world [should] foster the science of fish culture."[47]

Baird died in 1887. The following year President Grover Cleveland appointed Marshall McDonald as the new commissioner. McDonald initiated convulsive changes in the USFC, but he only solidified the emphasis on fish culture. He imposed bureaucratic structure, reconfigured personnel, and explicitly emphasized production over science.

Change began almost immediately after Baird's death. George Brown Goode was already serving as temporary commissioner when Baird died. He continued in the post only five months, but during his brief term Goode gave the USFC a new structure. He reconfigured the growing commission for better management by organizing activities within formal divisions. The Division of Fisheries handled industry statistics; the Division of Scientific Inquiry managed fishery research and resource surveys; and the Division of Fish Culture managed hatchery programs. Change extended to the style of management with the appointment of McDonald.[48]

Baird and McDonald were a study in contrasts. Baird had been trained as a scientist and achieved a high degree of respect among fellow scientists and politicians. He cultivated a paternalistic relationship with his staff, which was largely composed of like-minded, genteel Republicans. He played father to appropriately awed children, lecturing errant employees and correcting mistakes. McDonald was trained as a military engineer at Virginia Military Institute, fought with the Confederacy, and was a lifelong Democrat. His tenure as commissioner was awkward and contentious. He imposed military order on employees, enjoyed neither the professional respect nor the social deference that had been granted Baird, and endured several attacks by Republican office seekers and disgruntled staff.[49]

These differences and their consequences emerged most starkly in the way McDonald handled personnel. By the time McDonald assumed office, Livingston Stone had worked for the commission for eighteen years, yet he was hardly an ideal bureaucrat. Stone never mastered the voucher system for submitting expenses to Washington and expected a high degree of autonomy out West. Baird tolerated these shortcomings and privileges because of Stone's value as a culturist and advocate, but McDonald was less patient. Trouble began in 1887 during negotiations with Oregon for the transfer of a state hatchery. To forestall speculators, Stone purchased the site with his own funds and then sold it to the USFC at cost. The land deal piqued McDonald, who wrongly suspected corruption. Tensions quickly worsened after Stone granted Oregon final say over the distribution of eggs and fry at the federal hatchery. Bargaining away the USFC's authority over its own operations and then failing to ship a consignment of salmon eggs to Oregon from the McCloud Station in January 1890 were the final straws.[50]

McDonald first attempted to remove Stone by making his professional life so onerous that he would quit. McDonald recruited Stone for a survey expedition to Alaska, then replaced him with individual supervisors at each hatchery, and finally reduced his rank from field superintendent to hatchery superintendent. An indignant and humiliated Stone wrote McDonald: "I have lost money, health, standing and everything else by coming here [to California]. Still, I have not lost my interest in the work of the Commission on this coast, and I am as willing to devote myself to it as ever, if I am fairly treated and with this end in view I ask you frankly to reinstate me in my former position of Deputy Commissioner, and I also ask you frankly to give me an increase in salary." McDonald ordered Stone to complete his report and return east. In the meantime McDonald also abrogated Stone's egg-transfer agreement with Oregon by shipping 600,000 salmon eggs to California and planning more consignments to the Société d'acclimation in Paris.[51]

Stone obeyed under the naive assumption that another opportunity would follow. McDonald terminated Stone's salary in March and severed communications. The moves stunned Stone. Having sold his business interests when he moved to California in 1872, Stone had to rely on his family and beg for jobs. In September he wrote to McDonald: "I have had no pay since last March and am entirely out of money and have no means of supporting my family this winter except by selling part of my real estate, which I cannot do except at a great sacrifice. I am therefore compelled to tell you of my great and pressing need of getting to work again." McDonald ignored this and many other requests, probably hoping that Stone would go away. Twenty-seven months and at least eleven pleading letters later, McDonald finally consented to give Stone the vacated position at McCloud River, but only after lecturing him on the necessity of toeing the line.[52]

McDonald's treatment of Stone exemplified the ruthless way he controlled the commission. In the name of bureaucratic efficiency, McDonald embraced civil service to resist patronage, imposed gag orders to throttle the dissemination of information, and centralized administration to increase the commissioner's power. By 1890 the entire commission reported directly to an increasingly powerful main office. As Staff Secretary Herbert Gill noted in his instructions to Stone, these changes increased both the power and political security of the commissioner: "It is absolutely necessary that the office should be in possession of all the facts in relations [sic] to the expenditures at the stations. . . . By careful attention to details . . . we were able, during the recent investigation of the Commission, to fully and satisfactorily reply to many statements made in regard to the conduct of the work, as well as to answer many inquiries which had been suggested by the charges. . . . It should be borne in mind, however, that it is not necessary that explanations be given subordinates for action taken or information called for; their duty is to obey instructions." Such militaristic practices represented a sharp break from Baird's genial and patrician-like tenure.[53]

McDonald was similarly ruthless with his staff in Washington, D.C. In the summer of 1892, Assistant in Charge of Statistical Inquiry Joseph W. Collins tried to depose McDonald. When the plot surfaced in September,

McDonald responded with a counteroffensive that quickly enveloped the larger scientific community. Collins, commission scientist Hugh M. Smith, Chief Clerk E. G. Bryan, and employee E. E. Race aligned with a group of Baird disciples that included George Brown Goode of the Smithsonian, Addison Emery Verrill of Yale, and William P. Seal of the World's Fair. McDonald countered with several notable scientists, including Alexander Agassiz of Harvard and Daniel Coit Gilman of Johns Hopkins, and New York politicos E. G. Blackford and Judge Long.[54]

The ensuing war revealed the political context of federal management. Collins had complained that McDonald was a Democrat and had interfered with his plans for the commission's exhibit at the Chicago World's Fair. McDonald professed to be "personally . . . indifferent to [politics], but I propose to fight this fight to a finish." He countercharged that opponents were malicious, insubordinate, venal, and corrupt. He accused Collins of "shameful prostitution of public service to private advantage," Postmaster John Wannamaker of being a "hypocrite both by inheritance and practice," and Verrill of stealing the commission's invertebrate collection.[55]

The dispute broke at a particularly fortuitous moment for McDonald. In September 1892 President Benjamin Harrison was running for reelection on the Republican ticket. Harrison had a reputation for supporting civil service and moving slowly on patronage appointments, and he seemed even less willing to make changes during an election campaign and with a Democratic Congress. McDonald used the opportunity to dispatch his opponents. By the end of September he had discharged Collins, Bryan, and another employee; assigned W. C. Titcomb to audit Collins's books; and replaced Collins with Hugh Smith and Bryan with William de Chastignier Ravenal. McDonald drummed up support during the remainder of Harrison's lame duck term and then attacked Collins mercilessly once Grover Cleveland entered office the following March. Cleveland quickly cleared his fellow Democrat of all charges.[56]

These triumphs allowed McDonald to remake the USFC in his own image. Promotions and bureaucratic reconfigurations elevated two fellow southerners to positions of significant authority. Hugh Smith, who was from Washington, D.C., ably directed the Division of Fisheries and the Division of Scientific Inquiry for many years before becoming commissioner in 1913. W. de C. Ravenal was a South Carolinian. He had little experience or training as a fish culturist and possessed a profound ignorance of salmon and western geography. McDonald nevertheless promoted Ravenal to assistant in charge of the Division of Fish Culture. The promotion effectively institutionalized ignorance about salmon. Ravenal privately ad-

mitted that "I am personally unfamiliar with the Columbia and its possibilities," yet frequent changes in personnel meant that he knew as much (or as
little) about salmon as his staff. Federal policy on salmon devolved into an
act of the blind leading the blind just as western fishery managers began to
emphasize egg production more than ever.[57]

McDonald radically altered the style and procedure of management, but
he did not so much change as accentuate the policies of Marsh and Baird.
Like his predecessors, McDonald advocated state regulation of fishing,
pollution, and stream obstructions. In 1888 he instructed Stone, "It is extremely important to the success of our work, and its proper appreciation,
that we should not take part in any controversy between antagonized interests on the west coast." He refrained from interfering with activities that
damaged habitat. The USFC instead redirected complaints about dams and
sawdust back to the states even when petitioners complained that state and
local authorities refused to act. According to McDonald, "The work of the
U.S. Fish Commission is limited to the measures of artificial propagation
for restocking the streams and maintaining supply by aid of fish culture,"
and he assured his audience that this was sufficient. "The percentage of
survival under artificial methods is so largely increased, that by hatching but
a small proportion of the total egg supply in any given field, we may equal
or surpass the results from natural reproduction in the same area, even when
nature's efforts are not contravened, restricted, or rendered abortive by the
adverse conditions under which the fisheries are prosecuted."[58]

Fish culture was the panacea. "By our methods we give to a small percentage of fish ova, the potentiality of the entire reproduction under unrestrained natural conditions." "Therefore, as we enlarge the means for artificial propagation may we ease or release our restraints upon the commercial
fisheries and permit a larger catch without . . . a deterioration of our fishery
resources."[59]

McDonald almost completely conflated management and fish culture.
Baird had continued to lobby, and sometimes coerce, states to impose
closed seasons, require fishways, and reduce pollution. McDonald also endorsed these measures, but his core interests lay elsewhere. He had used his
engineering skills to become a major innovator of hatchery technology. He
spent years improving techniques for egg incubation and fish passage, pat-
enting several hatching bottles and fish ladder designs during the 1880s.
Where Marsh and Baird offered sophisticated analyses of environmental
change in the decline of fish, however, McDonald favored technological
solutions like fishways and hatching jars and ignored the environment
almost completely.[60]

McDonald largely abandoned Baird's support of science. Baird had promoted science for its own sake, and he encouraged a wide range of studies of marine and freshwater life. The USFC published several major ichthyological studies, and Baird spearheaded the establishment of marine laboratories in America. McDonald preferred utilitarian research, and he insisted that the "Commission has always held that such investigations as it might properly undertake should have as their ultimate object the discovery of facts and the attainment of results which possess an economic value."[61]

McDonald transformed the Division of Scientific Inquiry into a tool of industry, whose main duty was to survey nature for marketable species and hatchery sites. In 1892 he sent USFC architect and engineer Charles Gorham to the upper Columbia River basin. Gorham's job was to determine whether salmon ascended the Clark's Fork in Montana and to locate a hatchery in Washington State, but the narrowly focused survey ended prematurely when Gorham died. The following year McDonald reassigned the project to a pair of ichthyologists, Charles Gilbert and Barton Warren Evermann, who inspected streams throughout the Columbia River basin. The pair found numerous examples of degraded or obstructed watersheds. On the Little Spokane River, for example, they noted: "The character of this stream is being materially changed by the advent of civilization, a fact which is, or has been, true of most streams of this country. The cutting away of the timber and brush on the immediate banks and the cultivation of the land within the drainage area of the stream have greatly increased the surface erosion and, in consequence, the impurities of the stream."[62]

When it came time to apportion blame, however, a much simpler explanation emerged. Demonstrating an increasing impatience with the fishing industry generally, McDonald believed that the "entire volume of this great river is strained through the meshes of the unnumerable [sic] nets which occupy and obstruct the passageway to the spawning grounds." He claimed that the "investigations . . . clearly indicate . . . that this deterioration is to be attributed in large part, if not entirely to the exclusion of the salmon from their spawning grounds by the operations of the net fisheries."[63]

Despite their own catalog of environmental damage, Gilbert and Evermann concurred in an odd argument.

While it is true that the salmon are shut out by falls and dams from a large area of the Columbia and especially the Snake River basins, and while it is also true that the limitations are increasing as streams become useful for irrigation purposes and for mining, it is nevertheless certain that the decrease in the numbers of salmon, due to ill-regulated fishing in the lower Columbia, has so far outstripped the decrease in area of spawning-beds that the latter are now more than ample for all the fish that appear. We do not, therefore, believe that increasing the spawning-grounds through the removal of obstructions would materially benefit the salmon industry. In our judgment, the streams can be repopulated only by regulating the fishing in the lower Columbia and at the same time increasing the output from the hatcheries.

These comments bare the core assumptions of fishery managers in the nineteenth century. Habitat destruction was an unfortunate cost of "civilization," but fish culture would ameliorate change. If salmon continued to decline despite fish culture, then fishers were solely to blame.[64]

These assumptions solidified the symbiotic relationship between fish culture and federal management. Congress was always more willing to fund utilitarian projects than basic research, and the budget for the Division of Fish Culture grew dramatically during McDonald's era. In 1890 funding jumped from $178,000 to $248,000, consuming over 70 percent of the USFC budget. The more salmon declined, the less curious Congress seemed about the cause of decline, and the more basic research dwindled and "practical" appropriations increased. Baird's emphasis on pure science fell by the wayside. The Division of Scientific Inquiry budget averaged $18,175, or less than 8 percent of all expenses. The little research that was conducted focused on surveys of economic species or improving fish culture practices. Fishery management had become synonymous with production, and fish culture was its sacred cow.[65]

McDonald died in 1895, but his narrow focus of management endured. Commissioners John J. Brice and George M. Bowers continued the USFC's reliance on hatcheries even as declining runs belied their faith. And when administrators did notice problems, they deflected public criticism and endorsed a vigorous expansion of existing policies.

Near the end of his tenure, McDonald began to recognize a need for scientifically trained workers, but his focus remained narrowly utilitarian. In 1894 he wrote to Charles Gilbert at Stanford: "Fish culturists and superintendents of Stations would be much better equipped for the practical work of the Commission if instructed in the branches of science. . . . I would then be able to accomplish what I have steadily looked forward to, namely, the making of each station a center and opportunity of high scientific value, which would enable us to solve many of the perplexing problems of practical fish culture, and so give better direction to our work." McDonald told the Stanford ichthyologists that if they would train scientific fish culturists, he would "furnish the means of acquiring practical experience to such of your students as may desire to enter this field of work, and . . . will always . . . place them upon the temporary roll with moderate pay, at such of our fish-cultural stations as it may be convenient or desirable for them to attend during the active period of fish-cultural operations." McDonald did not reject science so much as discriminate between what he regarded as more and less useful applications of science.[66]

John J. Brice, a naval officer who had commanded several USFC ocean surveys before succeeding McDonald in 1896, also turned to science to correct woefully erratic hatchery practices. Brice had the commission publish a manual on fish culture that standardized procedures. He also shipped microscopes to the stations and encouraged superintendents to make detailed studies of egg development. Embryology was a well-established discipline in the life sciences. Private and federal fish culturists had conducted extensive investigations of the development of fish eggs during the 1880s, but hatchery production-oriented superintendents were so unfamiliar with these practices that Brice had to include detailed instructions on how to use microscopes, prepare slides, and record observations.[67]

Brice also developed a research program on the life histories of fish. Baird and Stone had suggested such studies in the 1870s, but poor funding precluded investigations. McDonald had also contemplated a biological survey, but his main interest remained the instrumental goal of determining "the conditions of greatest productiveness of the fisheries," or "aquatic pasturage" as he phrased it. Brice's interest, by contrast, was more catholic. Wanting information covering the entire life cycle, Brice initiated two systematic studies of salmon in 1896. He sent Evermann and Seth Meek back to the Columbia to continue Evermann and Gilbert's work, and he sent Cloudsley Rutter to the Sacramento to construct a similar life history of chinook. Brice also instructed hatchery superintendents to make daily observations of the "habits, growth, food, etc." of released salmon, but the superintendents were as unskilled at this task as with microscopes.[68]

Brice's utilitarian goals remained the same: to increase the number of hatcheries and regularize and systematize their operation. As one of his employees stated, "It is a vain hope to expect nature to recover and hold lost ground by nature's methods alone." The USFC conducted surveys to identify hatchery sites, and Ravenal encouraged efforts to improve the transportation and incubation of salmon eggs.[69]

Brice's emphasis on science did not last, because political considerations led to a change in leadership that further eroded the expertise of the USFC. In 1898 President William McKinley replaced Brice with George Bowers as a reward to Senator Stephen B. Elkins for his support of McKinley at the Republican National Convention. Historians have cited Bowers as the commission's first "political" appointment, but this understates the influence of politics in previous decisions. The backroom machinations driving Baird's appointment in 1871 and Cleveland's choice of McDonald in 1888 were no less political, but their scientific backgrounds have obscured these links. Bowers was simply the most obvious case because he was clearly the least qualified for the job. His significance lies less in his "political" roots than in his impact on fishery management. By 1898 a rank amateur was running the commission. Without a strong advocate for scientific research at the helm, many of Brice's science initiatives quickly faded.[70]

Bowers's inexperience forced him to defer to assistants and policies that had originated with McDonald. Hugh Smith, William Wilcox, and William Ravenal continued to direct the Divisions of Scientific Inquiry, Fisheries, and Fish Culture; their opinions about fish culture continued to prevail. David Starr Jordan spoke for many when he claimed: "A well-ordered salmon hatchery is the only means by which the destruction of the salmon fisheries of the Columbia can be prevented." Livingston Stone reviewed a quarter-century of fish culture and declared victory: "People generally were so utterly ignorant . . . of the whole subject that almost any story told about fish eggs would pass unchallenged. How different from the present day, when the minute fish of the very bottom of the oceans is closely and thoroughly studied, and the [microscopic] fish food . . . of the fresh water lakes is measured and classified."[71]

But did fish culture work? Self-assured claims aside, there was little evidence to suggest that hatcheries had even stabilized fisheries, let alone improved them. Runs fluctuated wildly and harvests declined steadily in the 1880s and 1890s. Some noted these discrepancies and questioned authorities. One Canadian critic asked pointedly about failures in New Brunswick: "If thirteen years' operations at Newcastle and eight years at Restigouche and Miramichi have produced no visible results . . . how many years will be required to restore our salmon fisheries?" In Oregon a canner complained, "I cannot see any results which have been obtained by either the U.S. Commission or the State Fish Commissioners on the Pacific Coast. The rivers where propagation has been done have steadily decreased their output."[72]

Fishery managers handled criticism by assailing their critics and complaining about the lack of support. Canada's Samuel Wilmot defended the "maligned science of fish culture" and insisted that criticism stemmed from "the ignorance of some, the natural antagonism to every experiment in the direction of progress by others, and, I might add, the malice of an insignificant few." Wilmot instead blamed commercial and subsistence fishers. "Mankind, from his overweening selfishness, is not satisfied with killing these fish in the earlier seasons, when they are fat and wholesome . . . but would . . . relentlessly pursue and kill them up to the close of the year, whilst in the very act of spawning." Michigan's John Bissell defended the "practical art" of fish culture from charges of failure by claiming that the state had not built hatcheries on a sufficiently large scale or allowed sufficient time to prove themselves. Stone called opponents "ridiculous" and accused fishermen of being "like Jews. . . . the same all the world over."[73]

The USFC's response to disappointing hatchery returns was denial or the shifting of blame. In 1894 USFC workers privately admitted that their Siuslaw River hatchery had been a "total failure," but publicly they denied problems or deflected blame. In 1896 the fall salmon run on the Palouse River dwindled to two fish, prompting one reservation agent to suggest relocating the band of Indians who relied on the run to a reservation. The same year hatcheries failed on the Siuslaw, Clackamas, and Snake Rivers, yet John Brice insisted that these hatcheries had produced "the most satisfactory results" (see map 6).[74]

In 1899 runs plummeted all along the coast. Federal employees privately acknowledged the magnitude of the disaster. William Ravenal called Clackamas River Station "a complete failure," and Commissioner Bowers conceded that the "office has been aware . . . for a number of years that the Clackamas Station is badly equipped and as a collecting point for salmon eggs is almost a failure." But recognizing failure and admitting it and responsibility were hardly synonymous. The USFC was less than candid with outsiders. Bowers was "glad to furnish" salmon eggs when the Oregon fish protector requested help, but he did not mention that the USFC was also struggling to get eggs. A month later he informed the fish protector that the California runs had been "a total failure" but still said nothing about the Clackamas Station. Bowers also discussed hatchery complaints with an Oregon congressman, but he adamantly denied their validity. In the USFC annual report, Bowers noted blandly that "for reasons beyond the control of the Commission, the collections of quinnat-salmon eggs were not as large as in the past few years, and there was consequently a considerable falling off in the output of this species."[75]

By the turn of the century the USFC's institutional dependence on fish culture had compromised its assessment of efficacy. The fish culture budget had reached $331,000, or two-thirds of all USFC funds. Like agricultural colleges and experiment stations, the USFC was being "guided by institutional needs. Staff members needed support for research and salaries and

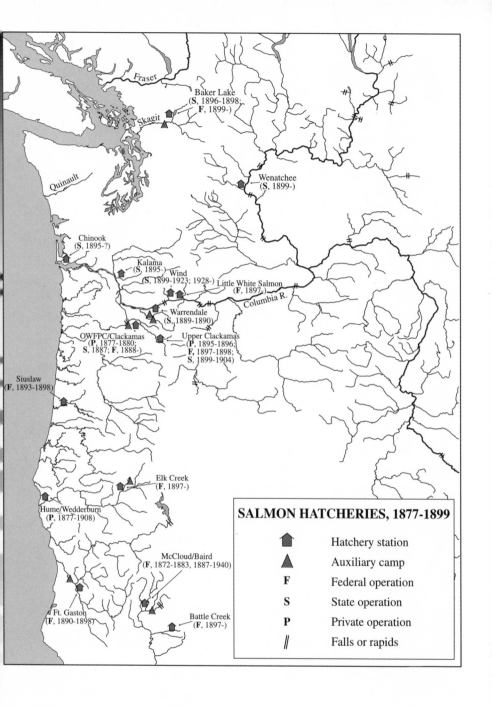

SALMON HATCHERIES, 1877-1899

🏠	Hatchery station
▲	Auxiliary camp
F	Federal operation
S	State operation
P	Private operation
∥	Falls or rapids

Baker Lake
(**S**, 1896-1898;
F, 1899-)

Fraser

Skagit

Quinault

Wenatchee
(**S**, 1899-)

Chinook
(**S**, 1895-?)

Kalama
(**S**, 1895-)
Wind
(**S**, 1899-1923; 1928-)
Little White Salmon
(**F**, 1897-)

Columbia R.

Warrendale
(**S**, 1889-1890)

OWFPC/Clackamas
(**P**, 1877-1880;
S, 1887; **F**, 1888-)

Upper Clackamas
(**P**, 1895-1896;
F, 1897-1898;
S, 1899-1904)

Siuslaw
(**F**, 1893-1898)

Elk Creek
(**F**, 1897-)

Hume/Wedderburn
(**P**, 1877-1908)

McCloud/Baird
(**F**, 1872-1883; 1887-1940)

Ft. Gaston
(**F**, 1890-1898)

Battle Creek
(**F**, 1897-)

MAP 6. By 1900, private, state, and federal hatcheries were trying to bolster declining salmon runs on many Pacific Northwest streams.

relief from physically exhausting . . . duties. Given the economic and political structure . . . the only way in which these goals could be achieved was through integrating the work of the institution with the economic needs of the community." The USFC had ingratiated itself to politicians and businessmen by providing a technology which alleviated the need to restrict economic activity.[76]

Once fish culture became an institutional crutch, criticism of the agency's raison d'être became intolerable. To protect his cash cow, Bowers extended his control over internal affairs, insisted that only the central office disseminate information, and reprimanded superintendents who spoke without permission. He also regularized hatchery procedures, terminology, equipment, and release schedules to minimize controversy. In reports he claimed, "The practical value of the Commission's work on artificial propagation has long since been removed from the realm of doubt, and is appreciated and conceded by all persons qualified to express an intelligent opinion thereon." Bowers's policies and arguments imposed a circular universe. Only qualified persons could speak, and the only intelligent opinion was already conceded.[77]

Not only was fish culture successful, Bowers contended, it was also the only possible strategy the federal government could embrace. He explained to the secretary of commerce:

The power of the general government with reference to the protection of fish in state waters is practically nil. This limitation imposed by the constitution has always been zealously defended by the states, and necessarily determined the course which the bureau laid out in the beginning of its career and has since followed for the maintenance and increase of the aquatic resources of the country—namely, that government aid to the fishing industry can be most effectively rendered by artificial propagation, leaving to the states the duty of maintaining . . . so much protection as might be necessary to conserve the fish supply.

"The general policy of the bureau," he insisted, "is to refrain from any aggressive work which is contrary to public sentiment." Bowers had thus internalized the limits on the USFC and, after 1902, on the Bureau of Fisheries (USBF).[78]

Having buried their doubts and limited the scope of their activities, federal administrators promoted hatcheries as necessary and sufficient. At the end of his 1857 report, George Marsh had suggested that hatcheries "should keep always on hand a sufficient stock of young fish of different ages to illustrate the processes of breeding and rearing in all their different stages." Baird and his successors took this advice to heart. They enthusiastically embraced any opportunity to promote fish culture as a synonym for federal management. Beginning with the 1876 Centennial Exposition in Philadelphia, the U S F C and U S B F installed exhibits in at least sixteen major fairs, exhibitions, and expositions during the next thirty years. Marshall McDonald turned the research vessel *Albatross* into a traveling demonstration of fish culture, and he instructed hatchery superintendents, "It is desirable, as a matter of policy, to conciliate public opinion by . . . allowing access to the [hatchery] grounds to those who desire to inform themselves in regard to the character of the work or are interested in the results [of fish culture]."[79]

Commission exhibits became didactic dioramas of the power of science and technology to improve society and nature. Organizers arrayed aquaria, fishing devices, scale models, and fish culture tools to create a sense of technical proficiency. The logistics of maintaining these displays were sometimes quite elaborate. A whole year before the 1893 Columbian Exposition in Chicago, McDonald instructed superintendents to construct a Noachian assemblage of fishes cultivated at stations. The collections included a male and female not simply of each species but of each life stage from one to five years. Each specimen was specially wrapped, labeled, and shipped, and thirty days later, duplicates were similarly prepared and shipped, to ensure preservation. When the fair started, McDonald placed field stations on alert and instructed them to reserve large supplies of fish and eggs for emergency shipment to Chicago.[80]

Exhibit organizers sought to create an ideal image of fish culture. At the 1905 Lewis and Clark Centennial in Portland, Oregon, the U S B F planned a typical exhibit of aquaria filled with exotic fish and other emblems of expertise. They also considered including a working hatchery with an official title: the Willamette Station. The exhibit became a theater of technical proficiency. According to J. W. Titcomb, "A battery of troughs, ranging from 10 to 100, would be kept full of salmon and trout eggs throughout the summer season, and distributions of fish could be made from this sub station just as if it were the Big White Salmon [hatchery] or any other station." Visitors would watch hatchery workers raise fish while a spieler explained operations. Fishery personnel devoted much effort to the aesthetics of the exhibit. They debated over which colored tub would best accentuate different fish, but all agreed that the unsightly "preparation of food is not a feature for public exhibition, although [one that] fish culturists may want to see."[81]

Exhibit planners insisted that this hatchery as theater be "properly provided for," even if it meant "curtailing expenses if necessary at other points in the field." Promoting hatcheries had become more important than running them. The exhibit was an elaborate sleight of hand. The USBF billed it as a self-contained hatchery serving the public, but it was in fact a heavily subsidized parlor trick. The bureau instructed regular hatcheries to reserve eggs and fish in case the exhibit needed replenishing, which it did on a chronic basis. Poor water quality at the exhibit killed many fish, and workers sometimes treated trout eggs like caviar and fed them to display fish. The USBF subordinated regular activities to the needs of the Willamette Station. Hatchery superintendents delayed distributions of salmon fry, while the exhibit director monopolized bureau railroad cars to refortify his theater. Salmon eggs and fry poured in from Clackamas in Oregon, Baker Lake in Washington, and Fort Gaston in California, while pike, perch, bass, crappie, and sunfish arrived from the rest of the country (see map 7).[82]

What had started as a tool for promoting the regular functions of the USFC and USBF had become an end in itself. The superintendent at Clackamas complained bitterly about the inconvenience of the exhibit, but he tolerated its existence because he had first claim on the equipment left over from the Centennial. The exhibit had something for everyone. It offered Bowers a powerful forum for advertising the USBF; it reassured the public that science and technology were indeed solving fishery problems; and it mollified the superintendent with promises of new goodies. Ultimately, the Willamette Station neither served the public interest nor distributed many fish. The exhibit was hardly a self-contained operation, but it was potent propaganda.[83]

American fishery management was never a pure science later fouled by politics. Political considerations have always mattered. When we look back to the mid-nineteenth century, we realize that politics, science, and technology were already hopelessly tangled by the time Congress created the USFC. Political culture had favored minimal regulation, and legislators preferred popular solutions. When fish culturists touted their abilities, politicians and administrators gravitated toward technological fixes. Marsh, Baird, and Stone fashioned these assumptions into the founding principles of American fishery management: courts and legislatures would encourage economic activity; states would regulate fishing; and federal agencies would conjure technological panaceas. These were neither self-evident strategies nor the inevitable outcomes of nineteenth-century science. They were political compromises.

This has remained a hidden history. By not looking more closely at

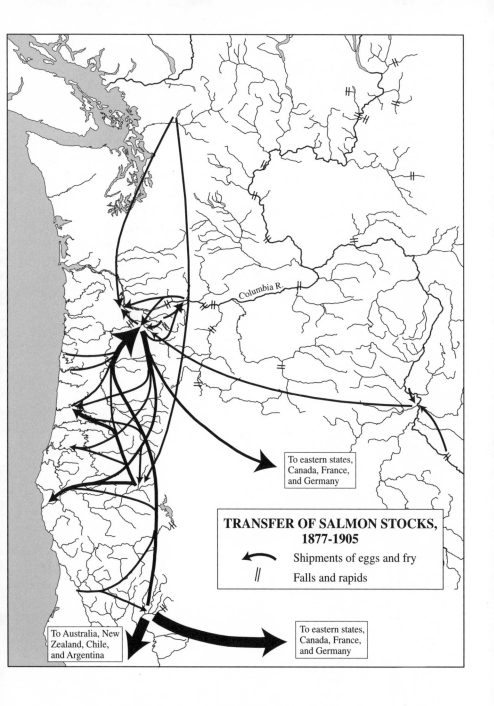

Columbia R.

To eastern states,
Canada, France,
and Germany

**TRANSFER OF SALMON STOCKS,
1877-1905**

Shipments of eggs and fry

‖   Falls and rapids

To Australia, New
Zealand, Chile,
and Argentina

To eastern states,
Canada, France,
and Germany

MAP 7. Most nineteenth-century fishery managers discounted the importance of evolutionary distinctions among runs and stocks of salmon and redistributed eggs and fry between streams in an effort to make salmon runs more profitable.

nineteenth-century developments, we have accepted an evolutionary narrative of honest mistakes made and environmental ignorance overcome. Policy turned on promises and the politically possible. Fish culture became the preferred tool of management because it offered to produce an endless supply of fish. Salmon hatcheries seemed to facilitate economic progress while alleviating resource conflicts. It was no wonder that Americans embraced fish culture, but neither were their choices timeless. Hatcheries were a logical product of a context. The logic was shaped by particular perspectives on government, science, and nature. While we may not share our ancestors' attitudes, it is purposeless to criticize their choices. Times change, and we can, and should, revisit those decisions. Hatcheries were a hopeful solution to vexing problems, but they had unexpected consequences. The pragmatic adoption of fish culture forced federal administrators to redefine the USFC's central mission from scientific inquiry to making fish. Over time, federal and state agencies became so fiscally dependent on fish culture that criticism became taboo. By the end of the nineteenth century, hatcheries had become an end in themselves.

4 / Making Salmon

George Perkins Marsh, Spencer Baird, Livingston Stone, and Marshall McDonald greatly influenced the course of American fishery management. The system that Baird envisioned placed the federal government in a supplementary role as technical advisor and supplier of fish. The U.S. Fish Commission (USFC) would introduce fish and restore runs, but it would not subsidize fisheries. Baird insisted that industry bear the costs of production as much as possible, and that states regulate fishing. But the history of the Oregon fisheries is more complicated than a simple tale of federal managers achieving wisdom and saving salmon. Federal administrators preferred a layered approach to fishery management, but some states preferred to rely solely on fish culture to solve their fishery woes.

This difference exposed a central problem of fishery management. Although it was easy to agree in principle on regulations or fish culture, such plans were virtually impossible to implement. Regulations required enforcement, which raised taxes and alienated constituencies; hatcheries cost money and still necessitated regulation. Oregonians tried to solve this conundrum by having the USFC make salmon. That way the federal government would bear the costs of production and make enough fish to avoid restrictions. But in practice even this simplified strategy induced a number of unavoidable spatial and fiscal struggles. The salmon fisheries contained a series of contested social and natural spaces in which fishers, fish culturists, and other groups exploited nature in competing and often inimical ways. Fishers, fish culturists, and Indians vied for the same fish; hatcheries and mills relied on the same streams. The question of who would fund salmon hatcheries was another source of friction and repeated conflict. Administrators resolved some tensions by suppressing politically marginal groups such as Indians, but other interests and problems proved more intractable.

Hatcheries supposedly solved these problems, yet we know that they did not. To understand why people continued to pour money into failure, we need to consider not only how politics shaped fishery management but how the rise of fish culture was inextricably linked to human conceptions of nature. From the habits of salmon to the influence of terrestrial and ocean climates, nature constantly shaped the fate of the fisheries. But nineteenth-century Americans understood these forces poorly. Observers regularly misconstrued events and attributed upturns to hatcheries and downturns to overfishing or an absence of propagation. Their interpretations lent fish culture considerable credibility despite declining runs. Persistent problems with hatcheries made some federal administrators skeptical, but their doubts failed to dampen public enthusiasm. The number of hatcheries grew rapidly, and by 1900 common wisdom deemed fish culture an unqualified success. This overweening faith in hatcheries led to a management debacle in 1904.

History hung heavy over the Oregon fisheries in the early 1870s. Federal managers, state officials, and private citizens saw the plight of Atlantic salmon as prophesying a dismal future for Pacific salmon. Their warnings and legislative efforts produced little immediate response, but they laid a foundation for the future by outlining the two competing models of fishery management.

Writers, editorialists, and politicians all warned Oregonians how the eastern past might become the western future. In 1870 a writer reminded readers, "Some of the older States of the Union . . . have suffered serious loss . . . from early neglect, which they are now endeavoring to repair at large cost." In 1874 the *Portland Morning Oregonian* counseled readers: "It will be the part of wisdom for our people to profit by the experience of those similarly situated on the Atlantic side of the continent, and avoid the misfortunes that befell them in consequence of improvident and reckless methods of conducting an industry which, with proper care might have remained always productive and of incalculable benefit to the country. We may copy their errors and succeed to the misfortune entailed, or we may be at once warned and taught, and preserve our fisheries as good as they are at present for an indefinite length of time." Governor Lafayette Grover echoed these concerns in his messages to the legislature. "We have been accustomed to think that this fish product was inexhaustible. But the river fisheries of all countries, where the laws have not intervened for their preservation, have one uniform history— first, decimation, then destruction."[1]

The intended point of these history lessons was to provide an abundant future for the West. Knowledge became a fulcrum for creating a utopian image of material prosperity. One writer argued, "We must somehow legislate so as not to kill the goose that lays this golden egg." The *Morning Oregonian* added, "This is a question of such moment to the prosperity of the State that it ought to command the serious attention of the Legislature of the State [of Oregon] and [Washington] Territory." Governor Grover concurred. "In Oregon we have in abundance, two of the best river fishes in the world, the salmon and the trout. To preserve these is worthy of careful legislative enactments."[2]

To avoid replicating the eastern experience meant understanding and preventing eastern mistakes. The *Morning Oregonian* gave front-page coverage of Spencer Baird's work in New England, and readers drew several lessons. Many began to fear the rapid expansion of canneries and "wasteful and destructive modes of carrying it on." A reporter worried, "These [new canneries], with the old fisheries, will make the capacity of all the establishments together sufficient to use up all the fish that can well be taken on the whole fishing ground from Rainier to the mouth of the river." A few Oregonians did worry about dams and pollution, but most wanted to blame fishing even though the commercial harvest at the time was probably only about half that of the peak aboriginal harvests.[3]

To forestall disaster, letter writers, the editor of the *Morning Oregonian,* and Governor Grover endorsed a series of technological and political solutions. The 1848 Territorial Constitution had prohibited obstruction of salmon streams, but the state had not enforced this provision. By the early 1870s observers were recommending new laws "to prevent the destruction of fish in our waters, either by taking them improperly or obstructing their passage up and down our streams." They also advocated copying the regulations of "older states" like Minnesota, state-funded fishways, a fish commission composed of "prominent and competent citizens," and joint regulation of the Columbia River with Washington Territory.[4]

Not trusting to older solutions, observers also expressed an interest in fish culture. The *Morning Oregonian* was the strongest advocate of this solution. It carried several articles on the subject in the early 1870s, including a lengthy story on Livingston Stone's McCloud River hatchery. In 1872 one article noted promisingly that "an acre of water is capable of producing more food for man, than an acre of land." Another insisted, "That our rivers may thus be made far more profitable than at present has been clearly proved by the results of the efforts made during the last few years." Governor Grover added, "A lively interest is now manifested throughout the States bordering on the Atlantic seaboard, seeking by fish culture, not only to recover lost fisheries, but to create new ones, and to introduce species of fish valuable for food, not before known in those waters."[5]

The legislature's response revealed what would become a persistent political problem with state management. Newspaper conversations reflected a largely lower Columbia and urban constituency, but the majority of legislators in Salem came from rural areas away from the river. This spatial division, and the parochial attitudes of many Oregonians, undermined the possibility of coordinated action. Farmers and ranchers from eastern Oregon blocked efforts to assist fishers west of the Cascades with tax dollars, and fishers in southern Oregon demanded local exemptions from restrictions written for the Columbia River fisheries. Moreover, Oregonians, who were famously resistant to taxation, recoiled at the idea of publicly aiding an industry that many considered overcapitalized.[6]

Faced with political divisions and fiscal conservatism, Oregonians instead turned to the deeply western tradition of seeking federal assistance. In 1874 legislators passed a resolution asking Congress to regulate fishing on the Columbia and suggested weekly and annual fishing seasons. Legislators recognized a need for coordinated regulation, but they argued that the Columbia was an interstate waterway and thus impossible for states to regulate.[7]

The issue was ostensibly about jurisdiction, but Oregon's excuse was contrived because it adopted contradictory positions. In 1876 Baird designed a set of regulations that would establish concurrent jurisdiction of the Columbia by Oregon and Washington Territory, but when Washington legislators approved them, Oregon immediately balked. Legislators insisted that Oregon's state charter granted it jurisdiction over the entire river. "If concurrent action in the passage of a law is necessary," they argued, "it will certainly be a long time before there is any law." This was true, because even under its altered position the legislature refused to pass laws that it had already admitted were needed. Oregon wanted to rule the Columbia while shifting expenses elsewhere.[8]

Concurrent jurisdiction was only one issue. Baird's full response to Congress concerning the Oregon resolution bears discussion because it reveals George Perkins Marsh's lasting influence on salmon management. Like Marsh, Baird began his reply with a general discussion of civilization as the cause of decline, surmising, "In all probability the experience of the salmon fisheries of the Columbia river will be similar to that of many other noted streams in the eastern United States and in Europe." He described the impact of "excessive fishing," dams, and "changes in the physical condition of streams" "consequent upon the progress of civilization." Baird warned that "the destruction of the forests and underbrush of the region, and the consequent alteration in the character of its drainage," increased problems with floods and dry seasons. He also noted the deleterious effect of industrial pollution. "Even now," Baird concluded, "the diminution is appreciable, and although it may be several years before this becomes very marked, yet such a result is sure to arrive in time."[9]

Baird then discussed possible solutions and their problems. He began by noting, "The methods by which the salmon fisheries of the Columbia river can best be kept up [by Congress], in at least the average degree of efficiency, are two-fold: first, by the enactment of suitable laws regulating the number, the periods, and the season of capture of the fish; and, secondly, by hatching them artificially at some suitable point." Unfortunately, history precluded the first option. "In the United States it has always been found very difficult [for the federal government] to enforce laws in regard to the fisheries." "A still better procedure," he continued, "would be to employ the now well understood methods of artificial multiplication of fish."[10]

Baird left regulation to the states, while fish culture became the federal panacea. Thus he "unhesitatingly recommend[ed] that, instead of the passage of protective laws which cannot be enforced except at very great expense and with much ill feeling, measures be taken, either by the conjoint efforts of the States and Territories interested, or by the United States, for the immediate erection of a hatching establishment on the Columbia river, and the initiation during the present year of the method of artificial hatching of these fish." Hatcheries would increase reproduction a thousandfold. A $10,000 investment would produce ten million eggs. "There can be no reasonable doubt," he assured Congress, "as to the success of such measures, and of their power not only to maintain the present supply of fish indefinitely, but to increase it if desirable." The plan made political sense, but by suggesting federal hatcheries Baird reinforced the inertia of state legislators.[11]

Baird made certain his strong policy statement had full public effect. In March 1875 the *Morning Oregonian* reprinted his recommendations on page 1 and advised readers to "carefully read [the letter] with a view to future action in the premises. . . . Unless steps are taken early to protect the salmon against destruction by reckless modes of taking them and changes in the physical condition of the streams they ascend, it will be but a few years till this industry will cease to be of any importance." Baird also directed Livingston Stone to inspect the Columbia for hatchery sites. He had considered collecting eggs on the river in 1872, but he thought it too far from a railroad to justify the effort. Although Baird still believed that the USFC's primary job was to introduce or rehabilitate runs, not subsidize local fisheries, his willingness to consider establishing a hatchery, even though no railroad yet existed, signaled a shift in his assessment of the role fish culture and the USFC should play in salmon management.[12]

Stone's 1875 survey was less important for the information it rendered than for the public attention it received. The *Morning Oregonian* covered Stone's journey and interviewed him before he returned to California. Its reports marked a shift in the discussion of salmon from a narrow focus on harvest to a broader vision of the problems plaguing the fishery. The paper introduced Stone as "thoroughly and practically versed" in the "sciences of piscatorial culture" and questioned him on issues surrounding the fisheries. The paper wanted to know whether the industrial fishery might "ultimately result in the almost total extinction of salmon in our waters," or whether dumping sawdust in the Willamette might also harm salmon spawn. Stone insisted that both concerns were groundless on large rivers, but he strongly recommended protecting "smaller streams" from pollution.[13]

The interview was an odd discussion; its participants operated at cross-purposes. The paper wanted to reassure readers that economic progress was compatible with the fisheries; Stone wanted to reassure readers that federal egg transfers would not harm local runs. These were opposed and oxymoronic agendas. Observers knew that development hurt salmon and interfered with hatcheries. Likewise, exporting eggs from a stream inevitably reduced the reproductivity and profitability of fisheries. Fish culture alone seemed to reconcile these contradictions.

The material and social conflicts inherent in salmon management, and fish culture's role in ameliorating them, emerged very early and very clearly in the battles surrounding an 1876 attempt to impose federal jurisdiction over the Columbia fisheries. The episode revealed the inevitability of conflict when government tried to regulate fishing. That year Oregon's John H. Mitchell submitted a bill to the U.S. Senate to shorten fishing seasons and prohibit all types of gear except gillnets, but the bill raised immediate opposition from rival-gear users. Over three hundred "leading citizens and merchants" signed a remonstrance that invoked classic American political symbolism. The petitioners portrayed themselves as "pioneer settlers," claimed the measure would destroy property values, and insisted that they knew how to protect salmon better than distant officials "who are not fishermen, and who never have seen one solitary salmon taken from the meshes of a net."[14]

The petitioners instead endorsed fish culture as the solution to their problems. They asked Congress to instruct Baird "to send a competent person to visit the State of Oregon, and the fisheries on the Columbia river, and make such arrangements as he may deem proper for the propagation of fish." They promised to support the endeavor financially but insisted, "This is the only protection we want for the future prosperity of this important business, and we are as solicitous about our fisheries as the farmer is about his land and crops." The protest was a masterful merger of political emblems with technological solutions that successfully killed the Mitchell bill.[15]

The defeat of the bill only increased the appeal of Baird's proposal for state regulation and federal hatcheries. Governor Grover again called for a state fish commission and coordinated regulation of the Columbia River; Baird and Stone planned an egg-taking station in Oregon; observers decried "the rapacity of catchers" and urged legislation; and history continued to haunt Oregonians. In 1876 the Portland Board of Trade warned, "While it is all very good to say that our rivers are practically inexhaustible we must *now*, before it is too late, learn the lesson which other salmon-producing countries have taught us—that unless this fish is placed under statutory regulations and its growth encouraged, that which certainly happened to those countries will come to us—extermination of the salmon industry." Their solution, and increasingly that of other groups, was fish culture. As the salmon canners confidently boasted, "We can now *preserve* and *increase* the production of our rivers."[16]

This, or a similarly optimistic position, was both expedient and necessary. Between 1870 and 1876 the number of Columbia River canneries had grown from five to seventeen, while the salmon harvest jumped from ten million to thirty million pounds. This rapid growth provoked historically informed concerns about overfishing and the future of the fisheries; fish culture seemed to alleviate these concerns without the pain of regulation. A consensus was forming around Spencer Baird's panacea. While Oregonians did little but talk before 1877, they did lay a philosophical groundwork for the future.[17]

It took a crisis to precipitate action. In 1877 what we now believe to be a major El Niño devastated salmon runs. Faced with a downturn in the catch, Oregonians blamed fishing and adopted Baird's advice. They built a hatchery.

Although latitude, longitude, barometric pressure, sea surface temperature, and ocean upwelling are abstract concepts that require sophisticated tools to measure, they nevertheless correspond to real places and events that can materially affect human and natural history. Such is the case with El Niño. Far out in the equatorial Pacific two atmospheric pressure zones shape ocean and terrestrial climates around the world. A zone of high pressure lies above Easter Island, and a zone of low pressure hovers above

Darwin, Australia. This atmospheric pairing drives a phenomenon known as the Southern Oscillation. Surface winds usually flow from east to west between these points. Over time the winds amass a pile of warm water in the western equatorial Pacific, but occasionally the pressure differential relaxes. When this happens, the gradient reverses, and Kelvin waves of warm water rush eastward toward South America. Peruvian fishermen long ago coined this secondary phenomenon "El Niño" (the child) because it often occurs around Christmas.[18]

El Niño events vary in intensity, scope, and duration. Most El Niños are relatively short, mild warming events confined to the Peruvian coast, but occasionally very intense episodes of warming alter ocean conditions as far away as the northeastern Pacific. These episodes seem to occur when Southern Oscillation reversals are extreme and Northern Hemispheric pressure zones align so they advect warm air and water laterally from the equator to the northeast Pacific on a more or less direct route. Oregon weather patterns change significantly in response. Winters are warmer and wetter than normal; summers are drier. Ocean environments also warm significantly, creating at least two important effects. First, warm water inhibits internal upwelling, the currents that draw nutrients from lower depths toward the surface to stimulate production of smaller organisms that salmon and other fish feed upon directly and indirectly. A suppression of upwelling can disrupt the fecundity of ocean environments. Second, hake, mackerel, and other warm-water dwellers migrate north during El Niños. When these species arrive in great numbers at the same time that ocean productivity is declining, they prey on juvenile salmon just entering the ocean phase of their life cycle.[19]

In severe instances these conditions can devastate salmon. Runs plummet, size decreases, and fecundity declines, but the effects are temporary. Subsequent runs can rebound quickly depending on the intensity and duration of the event. Moreover, these are unusual occurrences. During the last one hundred and twenty years only a few El Niños have affected salmon runs. Ocean records are sketchy before the mid-1920s, but the most likely candidates seem to be 1877, 1891, 1896–1900, 1926, 1943, 1957, and 1983. In 1983 an extremely intense El Niño wreaked havoc on salmon and garnered global attention, but its historical significance may rank below those of 1877, the late 1890s, and 1926 as a critical event in the development of salmon management. Earlier episodes were more important because human ignorance of natural events led to crucial misperceptions of causation. Observers did not know about El Niño and its effects, so they blamed fishing for downturns and credited hatcheries for rebounds when the ocean was probably more responsible in both cases.[20]

In September 1876 the Southern Oscillation tilted sharply toward the east. The pressure gradient inverted, and weather patterns went off kilter around the globe. The following January was warm enough for Oregonians to plant gardens on the coast and at The Dalles. By July the Willamette was so dry that riverboats needed shore lines to reach Corvallis. Salmon canners had prepared for a season "on a scale almost gigantic," but the runs disappointed. In May the *Morning Oregonian* noted darkly, "It is an acknowledged fact that the run of salmon this year is considerably lighter than common, while the number of nets in use is larger than ever before." While Umatilla Indians waited in vain for salmon to arrive, gillnetters tried to untangle warm-water porpoises from their nets on the lower Columbia. The fishing season was a disaster despite the largest fishing effort ever. Canneries ran at half time, and at least two went bankrupt. For the first time canners extended operations into August and onto other streams to recoup losses, but the harvest still fell five million pounds below the previous year. Fishers on Puget Sound and the Rogue River suffered similarly.[21]

The world beyond Peru would not know about El Niño for another half-century, so Oregonians instead interpreted the downturn as a manifestation of their worst fears. Livingston Stone concluded that the Columbia was "despoiled" in a "wholesale manner"; others called it "indisputable proof of the results of overfishing." The *Astorian* predicted that "this will be the last season for profitable salmon fishing interests on the Columbia for many years to come." The *Morning Oregonian* warned that "unless something is done to promote the propagation of salmon our fishing interests will be very materially injured and may eventually result in clearing the river of what is now and what may be made a constant source of income to the State at large."[22]

While most agreed on the need for a hatchery, consensus still broke down over who should build it. Baird quietly encouraged Columbia River canners to build a hatchery with private funds, but they would not budge as long as the Mitchell bill remained alive. Attitudes changed when the scope of the decline became clear in early April. After contacting "a gentleman in the East who is known for scientific skill in the breeding of fish," most likely Stone, the canners began to raise funds for a hatchery east of the Cascades. The *Morning Oregonian* drummed up support, arguing that fish culture "is no longer an experiment or theory; it has passed into the realm of practical certainty." To further influence readers, the paper printed portions of an 1872 speech by Robert Roosevelt that persuaded Congress to support federal fish culture.[23]

Senator Mitchell took a different tack. After the gillnetter bill died in committee, Mitchell asked the USFC to construct and run a hatchery, or "hotelling establishment" as he termed it, for salmon. Baird tried to meet Mitchell halfway. He pleaded poverty but encouraged Mitchell to submit an appropriation for a hatchery. He also offered to supply a superintendent if the canners built the hatchery. Mitchell held out for a government appropriation and threatened to sabotage the USFC budget if he did not get his way. This forced Baird onto the defensive until he learned that the canners had formed the Oregon and Washington Fish Propagating Company (OWFPC) to build a private hatchery on the Columbia. The OWFPC was run by a small cadre of Astoria canners and Portland merchants, but its subscribers included almost every canner on the river. Baird sent a telegram to Stone in New Hampshire and asked him to return to Oregon and superintend operations.[24]

Stone was enthusiastic, but his fervor dampened after arrival. The directors of the OWFPC had grandiose visions but little knowledge and less willingness to spend their own money. They wanted to build up the Columbia runs by incubating sixty million eggs a year for three years, but they budgeted a mere $10,000 a year. Furthermore, the canners challenged Stone when he concluded that the Clackamas River was the best location for a hatchery.[25]

The disagreement was rooted in the contested knowledge of salmon biology. Canners differentiated between runs and wanted Stone to propagate the more profitable spring chinook that spawned in the upper Columbia and Snake Rivers. Stone insisted that a salmon was a salmon—the plastic-body theory. Thus chinook that spawned in the Clackamas in fall were essentially the same as chinook that spawned in the headwaters in spring. Stone was technically correct as far as he went—all chinook were the same species—but the canners were right about the difference between spring and fall runs. The industry continually criticized the transplanting of salmon and fish culturists' reliance on fall runs, but they had no scientific basis for objecting to these practices until scientists discovered the role of genetics in differentiating runs and races during the 1930s.[26]

Stone was politic. He initially acquiesced and made a second survey of the Columbia, venturing as far east as the Umatilla River before retreating because of a lack of salmon and his fear of Indians. He next concocted a plan to take eggs near Cathlamet Bay and plant them upriver, but he eventually negotiated a second visit to the Clackamas and persuaded canners that it was "one of the great natural spawning grounds" of chinook. "I am amazed," he continued, "at the obstinacy of the Cannerymen in holding out against this river so long. Had they come here at the outset, as I then advised them to in the most emphatic terms, they might have had by this time a hatchery in good running order." The canners approved his choice and purchased twenty acres of land that "Professor" Stone, as the *Morning Oregonian* called him, claimed was "the best location" on "the best river in Oregon for hatching salmon" (see map 8).[27]

As hatchery proponents moved from principle—that hatcheries would produce salmon more efficiently than nature—to real-world operations, they spawned as many disagreements as salmon. Stone chose a site near the mouth of the Clackamas in order to intercept as many spawning salmon as possible, but industrial fishers thought similarly and set nets even farther downstream. Stone suddenly found himself competing for salmon with the very group he supposedly served. He complained to Baird: "There has been, and *is* so much fishing below our hatching station that the prospect of obtaining parent salmon is very discouraging. . . . There is nothing to prevent fishermen from coming close up to our dam with drift nets and taking our fish, *which they actually do.* . . . I am now entirely at the mercy of Bohemian fishermen." Some of those Bohemians turned out to be Clackamas Indians, whom Stone summarily evicted from the river, an act the Oregon fish and game protector would repeat twenty years later on the upper Clackamas. Stone also called for a "thorough reformation of the laws" to restrain fishing below his hatchery.[28]

As the eviction of the Indians and denunciation of "Bohemian" fishers revealed, the hatchery necessarily required control of social space; and as the relocation of the site of spawning showed, hatcheries also rearranged natural space. This need to control space quickly drew the federal government back into management struggles. The Portland Board of Trade, which hoped to monopolize the world market for salmon, wanted Congress to tax canners to support fish culture. The *Morning Oregonian* wanted to declare the Columbia "a national public highway" and asked Congress to "provide all needful laws for its protection. . . . [I]f the general government . . . provides for the propagation in the Columbia and its tributaries, these fisheries will not decline, but will grow to contribute millions annually to the trade and wealth of Oregon and Washington." Stone also asked Baird to help fund the OWFPC, but Baird did not want to create a precedent for private subsidies.[29]

Baird's unwillingness to subsidize or regulate fisheries revealed the fundamental conservatism of federal management. Baird did worry about unrestricted fishing, especially after hearing a rumor that a cannery at the

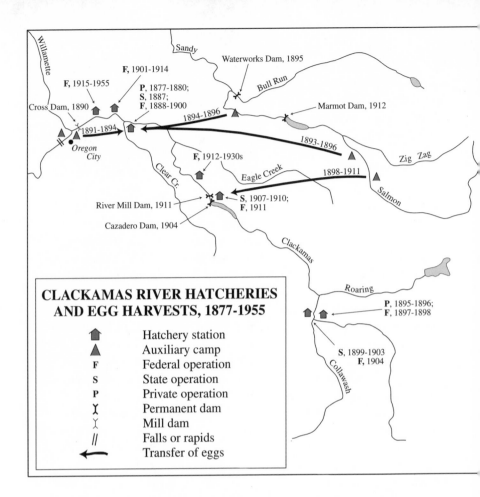

MAP 8. The Clackamas River hatchery began as a private venture, but fiscal and political problems shifted control to state and then federal agencies. Fish culturists began to exploit other streams following the installation of Cross Dam in 1890. Dams and biological transfers increasingly concentrated reproduction in the lower Clackamas and Sandy Rivers.

Cascade Rapids would barricade the entire Columbia with nets. The report was patently absurd, but Baird's ignorance about the size and force of the Columbia allowed him to imagine imminent disaster. He recommended that fishing be concentrated at the mouth of the Columbia and that hatchery streams be protected, but he left it to Oregon and Washington to impose these measures and advised the OWFPC to seek private or state funding. "If it be entirely a state enterprise," Baird reasoned, "it will be supported by public officers in the state, whereas, if it is a National establishment, Oregon will pay less heed to it." Baird's suspicions were well founded. The political impasse in Oregon meant that the only effort to protect salmon would be fish culture.[30]

In mid-August Stone and assistant Waldo Hubbard began their efforts to rearrange the spaces of reproduction. They stopped salmon runs by placing a fence across the river, but these "racks" harmed runs in several ways. Racks sometimes stopped fish so effectively that workers harvested every salmon in the river and endangered natural reproduction. Racks also harmed the fish they were meant to preserve. Salmon battered and scarred themselves trying to pass the structures, thus increasing the likelihood of fungal infections. Some fish tried to spawn below the racks, but concentrating reproduction in downstream areas led to overcrowded conditions, increased competition for spawning beds, and destruction of eggs from fights or repeated spawnings.[31]

Theoretically, such losses mattered little; the hatchery would compensate for destruction. Stone and Hubbard constructed buildings, hatching troughs, and a dam and flume to divert a nearby creek. Operations went smoothly until the middle of September when a sudden freshet washed away the rack and freed the fish. Stone's solution was to transfer 100,000 chinook eggs from the McCloud River Station in California. The transfers may have done little good because salmon adapted to one stream do not necessarily thrive elsewhere—this was why Baird eventually stopped transferring eggs to eastern streams—but Stone masked these setbacks with propaganda. He proclaimed the hatchery "the largest in the world." He sent regular updates to local papers, broadcasting the progress of work, hatchery oddities like Siamese twins, and alevin plantings. These massive releases seemed impressive, but they probably benefited local predators more than future runs.[32]

At the end of construction Stone returned to California and left Hubbard to struggle through the rest of the season. Unlike Stone, Hubbard had little experience managing a hatchery. Stone ranked Hubbard's talents as he might those of a draft animal: "faithful and industrious, very strong and capable of a great deal of endurance . . . though not of the brilliant sort." Hubbard and his equally overwhelmed helpers eventually released about one million alevins rather than the sixty million the canners envisioned, but the *Morning Oregonian* did not quibble. In the gloom of El Niño, the paper declared victory and remarked brightly, "The large amount of rain that has fallen during the past six weeks has greatly retarded operations, but by the energy of Prof. Stone, assisted by Mr. Hubbard, the foreman, and the determination on the part of the company to accomplish the work in spite of the difficulties in the way, the enterprize has been brought to a point where success is certain, and the only question now is to what extent shall it be carried." In 1877 the "science of fish culture" had only to release fish to prove itself. That they would return as adults was a foregone conclusion.[33]

The basic pattern established by 1877 continued for the next decade. State regulation faltered from internal conflicts, and Oregonians repeatedly tried to shift costs to the federal government. In 1881 the OWFPC ran out of money and closed the Clackamas hatchery, but a rebound in runs following El Niño led to more misinterpretations. Oregonians thought that the failed hatchery had, in fact, succeeded. They retained their faith in scientific pisciculture and pleaded for another hatchery. When runs plummeted after 1884, they grew desperate. Baird used their desperation as leverage, and he briefly succeeded in imposing coordinated regulation in exchange for assistance.

In the late 1870s Oregon legislators tried repeatedly to secure federal management on their own terms. In November 1877 Congressman Richard Williams reintroduced Senator Mitchell's bill calling for a three-month season from May through July, elimination of all gear except gillnets, and federal regulation of the Columbia River fisheries. When Williams's bill died in committee, Mitchell took a different tack. In January 1878 he submitted a bill that reflected an altered understanding of salmon biology and fishery politics. Believing that hatcheries could take fall eggs and make spring salmon, he reduced the closed season to August and September, assuming that this would still protect "the best portion of the spawning season." Mitchell also dropped opposition to traps and weirs to avoid another remonstrance, added penalties for pollution, and insisted on federal jurisdiction.[34]

Mitchell's second bill gained considerable support, but Baird subverted it in favor of a more conservative agenda. Newspapers reported favorably on the bill, and Stone recommended it despite what he thought were "excessive . . . penaltys [sic]." But Baird feared that any attempt to federalize the Columbia would create turmoil among representatives opposed to a strong central government. Baird did not want to endanger the main USFC appropriation, so he withheld support from Mitchell's second bill. When the Senate tabled it, Baird persuaded Mitchell to submit a third bill appropriating $5,000 for a hatchery. This fared no better than the others, but the USFC appropriation survived. Baird had preserved his agenda by channeling Senator Mitchell's energies into existing management policies and safe legislation.[35]

Congressional inaction moved regulation efforts back to the state. In

1878 the *Morning Oregonian* ran more articles promoting fish culture and encouraging state participation, and Governor William Thayer reminded Oregonians, "The history of salmon . . . ought to serve as a lesson to us; where they once abounded in profusion they have entirely disappeared, and negligence and rapacity will probably produce a like effect here, and the salmon return to our rivers no more." "As the matter now stands," he continued, "Congress believes it has no power to regulate our salmon fisheries, and therefore, the territory of Washington and state of Oregon can alone mutually pass laws on this point." Thayer asked legislators to create a fish commission that could "consider the subject of the introduction, propagation and culture of fish in the waters of this state. . . . by the known scientific methods."[36]

The 1878 legislature finally responded, but a weak state infrastructure and reluctant court system undermined the force of legislation. Late that year Oregon legislators passed all the pieces of Mitchell's second bill. They created a state fish commission, imposed weekly fishing closures, specified gear regulations, and prohibited industrial pollution. They also mandated fishing licenses as a way of funding the hatchery. But gillnetters called the fees burdensome, complained that canners and retailers did not have to pay, and defied the law. They and canners openly ignored the closed seasons and license requirements. The state responded weakly because the Oregon Fish Commission had few enforcement powers. The Oregon Supreme Court exacerbated matters by ruling the license unconstitutional, thus stripping the state of its means to fund fish culture and enforcement. The following year the *Morning Oregonian* observed sarcastically, "It may not be generally known that the law prohibiting the taking of salmon is now in operation." The paper openly worried that the runs would "soon be exterminated."[37]

The OWFPC also tried to shift costs, but not control, to the USFC. Canners initially succeeded at fund-raising, but donations dwindled by the end of 1877. During the next few years Stone and the OWFPC vacillated between lobbying Baird for support and trying to raise money locally. Both tactics failed. Baird had no spare funds, but when local sources dried up, he offered to cover expenses in exchange for control of the hatchery and the right to export eggs. Baird had come full circle: from viewing the Columbia as a source of eggs in 1872, to maintaining runs in 1875, back to seeing it as an egg source in 1878. But the OWFPC balked at the loss of control. As Stone explained, "I hardly think the Columbia River people will accept any money on the conditions which you suggest in your letter. They are a very touch-me-not sort of people." Baird claimed he only wished "to establish the principle of a willingness to sunder a quid pro quo in connection with private enterprises," but he refused to reduce the USFC to a cash cow for the canners.[38]

The problems at Clackamas were not solely fiscal. The 1878 season began amid great optimism. El Niño had relaxed by spring, and salmon runs rebounded strongly. Canners packed thirty-one million pounds of salmon, the largest harvest ever, and the OWFPC forecasted ten million eggs. Operations went smoothly at first. Workers captured many more males than females, yet still harvested two million eggs with a surfeit of males for milt. But in September a freshet destroyed the racks, and in November the diversion dam broke. Without a water supply, workers had to release 300,000 alevins prematurely and move the rest to a jury-rigged pen in the river. In December another freshet killed many of those fish. Workers moved the survivors back to the hatchery and released the last of the brood in January. Of the more than two million eggs gathered, Hubbard released 1.2 million juveniles. This still exceeded estimates of natural reproduction, but it was hardly the 95 percent efficiency that boosters touted.[39]

By 1881 the OWFPC had run out of money. The cost of repairing the 1878 flood damage exceeded assets, so the OWFPC reluctantly agreed to let Baird export eggs in exchange for USFC funds. Once they fixed the damage, however, they severed ties with the USFC. The divorce was shortsighted. The next two seasons went badly. Salmon runs on the Clackamas were light, and Hubbard scrambled for eggs. Workers used every means available, including spears, and a hard freeze in 1879 killed 2.5 million salmon. The hatchery did much better in 1880, releasing two million alevins, but the OWFPC was broke. Canners tried to sell its property to the USFC, and Baird briefly toyed with the idea after a flood damaged the McCloud River Station, but he ultimately declined. The OWFPC lost interest, the hatchery went into disuse, and subsequent flooding caused further damage.[40]

The OWFPC died with a whimper, but observers continued to believe in the science of fish culture, and nature serendipitously confirmed their faith. In 1881 ichthyologists David Starr Jordan and Charles Gilbert argued that a "well ordered salmon hatchery is the only means by which the destruction of the salmon in the Columbia river can be prevented." When a very large run of salmon appeared in 1883, the *Morning Oregonian* insisted: "Certainly it is not unreasonable to assume that the hopes of the propagators have been realized. The coincidence of an unprecedented run upon the year when the Clackamas hatched spawn was 'due' is too striking not to be a strong argument in favor of further experiment."[41]

The 1883 runs were large, but the evidence tying them to the hatchery was weak. Salmon runs had increased steadily after El Niño ended in 1878—not all at once when hatchery fish returned. The 1883 harvest was the largest to date at 42,799,200 pounds of fish packed in cans, but between 1878 and 1883 the fishing effort more than trebled while the pack only increased by a third. The great season was probably less a function of fish culture than a multiplication of harvesters and a more fecund nature, but observers conditioned to believe in fish culture saw only a confirmation of expectations. The same sequence of events and misperceptions would happen again at critical moments during a series of moderate and strong El Niños from 1896 to 1900.[42]

The rebound in runs nevertheless created potent impressions. In 1886 Army engineer W. A. Jones thought it "quite evident that satisfactory preservation and maintenance of this fishing industry can only be accomplished through the aid of a systematic study of the biology of the fish," yet enough was known "to show that hatcheries and a weekly close season should be established without delay." Jones presented arithmetical calculations of hatchery returns that by his own estimate bordered "on the marvelous." He concluded, "If artificial propagation can be insured there can be no objection to catching most of the fish. It has been demonstrated that the salmon can be bred artificially to any desirable extent." Oregonians completely accepted these claims over the next two decades.[43]

With private enterprise having failed and state management in disarray, Oregonians continued to seek help from a reluctant USFC throughout the 1880s. Legislators lobbied Baird vigorously; canners acknowledged the USFC's right to export eggs; boosters promoted the newly completed Northern Pacific as an ideal shipping route; and individuals, civic groups, and senators endorsed various sites for hatcheries. Baird resisted these appeals by returning to a narrow interpretation of the USFC's mission. "The province of the Commission under the law," he insisted, "is to *introduce* [fish] and not to *increase* [runs]." Baird's reply underscored both his belief that fish culture *would* increase runs and his aversion to subsidizing industry.[44]

Yet neither did Baird want to antagonize Oregonians. In 1883 he appeased petitioners by sending Livingston Stone to conduct yet another survey of the Columbia. His instructions to Stone reveal the political economy of hatcheries in the late nineteenth century. Baird wanted a site with access to large, consistent runs that could be completely blocked, but he also demanded a location convenient to shipping lines. Thus instead of searching the entire basin, Stone inspected only those sites close to railroads. The directives of the USFC narrowed his gaze to small sections of the Willamette, Sandy, Deschutes, John Day, Umatilla, Walla Walla, Snake, and Little Spokane. None gained his hearty endorsement and, by default, attention returned to the Clackamas.[45]

When the USFC failed to endorse a hatchery site, Oregonians tried again to get state help. During 1886 and 1887 fishers, canners, and politicians asked legislators to support fish culture. Most agreed with one gillnetter who warned, "Unless anything is done, and that quickly, our fisheries will be a thing of the past." Everyone believed in the necessity of fish culture, but thereafter consensus quickly evaporated. Fishers and canners divided on which taxation policy would best benefit themselves at the expense of rivals; on where to locate the hatchery to best serve particular interests; and on how to regulate different forms of gear. Others preferred to blame nature and kill seals, sea lions, and cormorants. Once again, people could agree in principle on hatcheries, but implementing policy created intractable conflicts.[46]

As runs continued to plummet, however, pressure mounted for someone, anyone, to make salmon. In 1887 the Oregon legislature leased the Clackamas hatchery from the OWFPC, but the effort was short-lived. The refurbished station released 1.5 million alevins in its first year, but in 1888 the biennial rivalry between eastern and western Oregon legislators doomed continued funding. Lobbying then turned to Congress. In 1886, Senators John Mitchell and Joseph Dolph had asked Baird to write an appropriation bill for a hatchery. Baird cooperated, but as with earlier encounters he stipulated conditions and demanded free transportation for USFC personnel and materiel via the Northern Pacific and Oregon Railway and Navigation Company. By 1888 the senators were desperate for assistance. They conceded to Baird's wishes and quickly negotiated agreements with presidents of both railroads.[47]

The impasse in Oregon gave Baird a unique opportunity to impose his preferred model of federal fishery management. He insisted that Oregon and Washington Territory pass regulations "sufficiently preventing salmon from improper capture or destruction." To minimize potential controversies, he also demanded that state fish commissioners "be [officers] charged with the artificial propagation and multiplication of fishes rather than with the enforcement of police regulations. It is essential for the economic conduct of the work of the Fish Commissions . . . that their Commissioners should be on the very best terms with the fishermen, and their duties should

(*Facing page*) "As It Should Be, If Hatcheries Were Well Maintained." This newspaper illustration evoked the promise of unlimited bounty many foresaw in fish culture during the late nineteenth and early twentieth centuries. (*Oregonian*, 24 July 1898.)

never be of such character as to make their presence objectionable or looked upon with suspicion by the fishermen with whom they should be in thorough accord." Baird wanted to institute a system of federal fish culture and state regulation which was liberated from politics, so he drafted a bill that made federal assistance contingent upon his conditions. Congress passed the bill in 1888, and in a singular victory, Baird obtained veto power over state regulations by withholding hatchery funds until Oregon complied with his standards.[48]

Baird died before the bill became law, but his efforts gained the USFC considerable leverage in later negotiations. When Oregon did not fund the Clackamas hatchery, interim commissioner George Brown Goode bargained for title to the property *and* complete control of operations by threatening to build a hatchery in Washington instead. The Oregon Fish Commission released its claim to the property but then reneged on the salmon egg agreement by invoking states' rights arguments and demanding that no salmon eggs leave Oregon. Happily accepting federal aid but flinching when it came time to pay, Oregon remained very much a "touch-me-not" state.[49]

Between 1888 and 1906 the lines between federal and state policies of management were clearly drawn. The USFC and U.S. Bureau of Fisheries (USBF) endorsed a combination of natural reproduction in rivers, artificial reproduction at federal hatcheries, and state regulation; Oregonians favored federal hatcheries and few restrictions. Federal administrators tried to persuade or coerce Oregon into compliance in two key battles, but their inability to impose their will ensured that Oregon's ideas prevailed by default. In 1904, however, Oregon's victory ended in disaster.

The official transfer of the Clackamas hatchery did not occur until March 1889, but McDonald assumed the lease early so he could send Stone and Hubbard for the 1888 season. Stone arrived a hero. He had worked diligently to bring the USFC back to Oregon, and the *Morning Oregonian* celebrated his return to his "old stamping [*sic*] grounds." Stone used the paper for free advertisement, giving tours to reporters and promoting fish culture and the USFC. He was so convincing that one enthusiastic reporter declared, "Artificial propagation has already begun to have its effect in the Columbia."[50]

Faith ran high that the USFC would refurbish the salmon fisheries. In January 1889 Commissioner McDonald wrote, "We congratulate ourselves and the Oregon Fish Commission upon the auspicious beginning of the work on the Columbia," and in October the *Morning Oregonian* declared,

"Artificial propagation is the only salvation of the salmon packing industry on the Columbia River." In 1889 a federal investigator argued, "It is within the power of man to increase the supply of fish, and thus restore what he has been so aggressively active in destroying." The *Morning Oregonian* noted, "Several things are combining to show forth a decided drift of public sentiment toward the artificial propagation of salmon. Of the benefits of its undertaking there has never been any doubt among scientific pisciculturists, though popular sneers have not been lacking concerning the work done by the government at its Clackamas hatchery." By 1898 the paper's editors had convinced themselves that "artificial propagation is the cure for salmon difficulties, and the scientific means for the industry's perpetuation. Fortunately, there is no longer need to argue the merits of hatcheries. That work has been done."[51]

Again, proof was in the runs. The reigning theory held that chinook broods returned invariably on a four-year cycle. Thus when harvests seemed to increase in the 1890s, the *Morning Oregonian* announced victory. "The quantity of fish ascending the Columbia in late years, notwithstanding the startling increase in gear and fishing activity, has come to be regarded as demonstrating the efficacy of turning young salmon loose into the Clackamas River." The following year the paper extended its argument. "In all probability but for the artificial propagation, the salmon fishery of the Columbia would have been a thing of the past some years ago." Such faith was in fact extraordinary. In 1894 a federal investigator noted that "in no other region in the United States are the people more generally impressed with the beneficial results of artificial propagation and more ready to aid and approve any fish-cultural measures."[52]

Almost anything became evidence of the efficacy of fish culture. Both good runs coinciding with hatchery production and bad runs coinciding with no production proved efficacy. These were obvious examples, but hatchery boosters could also turn to their advantage bad runs in hatchery years and good runs in nonhatchery years. When a huge run of fish entered the Columbia in 1880 rather than 1881, when the first Clackamas brood *should* have returned, David Starr Jordan explained that "the high water of that year undoubtedly caused many fish to become spring salmon which would otherwise have run in the fall." Boosters had several excuses for explaining away runs that failed to meet expectations. In 1890 they blamed the absence of freshets; in 1893 they blamed an insufficient effort at the hatchery; in 1894 they blamed overfishing; in 1898 they blamed floods for destroying alevins.[53]

The problem with these arguments was that they assumed a recovery that had not occurred. The results of fish culture were uneven at best. In 1888, for example, salmon eggs began to die at alarming rates due to warm water. Other disasters continually undermined production. Harvests did seem to rebound—the 1895 run of 43 million pounds was exceptionally good—but other years were uneven, and the content of the catch had changed substantially (see table 1). By the 1890s canners were no longer relying solely on chinook but were packing large amounts of sockeye and coho as well. Claims of recovery thus rested on a statistical sleight of hand, but these distinctions were lost at the time and fish culture gained credibility out of all proportion to its actual effect.[54]

This uncritically good press elevated the stature of the USFC, the Oregon Fish Commission, and anyone associated with them. F. C. Reed and Hollister D. McGuire headed the Oregon Fish Commission from 1887 to 1901. Neither had previous experience in fish culture; both supervised state hatcheries and formed state policy by relying on the USFC for advice. Yet the federal officials they deferred to were hardly omniscient. Waldo Hubbard advised Oregon and Washington on techniques and site locations, but other USFC employees regarded his ideas dubiously. Moreover, Hubbard's supervisor, William Ravenal, was himself rather clueless about salmon and Oregon geography. Expertise was, of course, relative, but the emerging hierarchy had less to do with individual knowledge than institutional prestige.[55]

The emerging hierarchy was the one the USFC had long sought. It made the USFC *the* leader in fishery management. To retain good relations, however, McDonald advised employees "to proceed with the utmost circumspection with the view of giving a patient hearing to all interests, and if possible to conciliate all antagonism; not being diverted, however, from our purpose" of running hatcheries. The USFC avoided controversy by avoiding political battles and law enforcement, which they insisted were the province of the states.[56]

Federal claims of expertise were important, but they were also limited and circumscribed. In 1890 McDonald wrote to Washington's fish commissioner, "I hardly felt that I have sufficiently definite knowledge of the habits of the salmon of the Columbia River to undertake to advise you as to the details of legislation for their protection." But states were no more knowledgeable and still unwilling to enforce laws. Illegal fishing was rampant, stream obstructions and pollution were unchecked, and license fees went uncollected. State managers quite literally put all their eggs in one basket and pursued only technological solutions. They requested more hatcheries and federal assistance, and the USFC happily dispensed advice on fish culture and fishways.[57]

Fish culture seemed to promise an end to restrictions, but in fact it increased the need to regulate space, even if on a limited scale. No sooner had Stone returned to the Clackamas than upriver settlers threatened to tear down the USFC's rack because it blocked the runs they harvested for winter stores. An unsympathetic Stone assigned someone to guard it from vandals. Oregon and the USFC also battled over control of the distribution of eggs. The conflict pitted Oregon's desire to stabilize runs locally against the USFC's mission to establish runs nationally. Both sides had compromised during negotiations over the Clackamas hatchery, but by December they were locked in a jurisdictional struggle that neither completely won. The USFC did export some eggs, but they imported many more eggs and, to reduce federal expenses, let Oregon operate the station each year from December to May. Oregon thus had control over the distribution of most eggs. To avoid future conflicts, Stone dreamed of creating a "National Salmon Park" in Alaska as a pristine nursery from which the USFC could harvest salmon eggs for the rest of the continent.[58]

The first major conflict erupted in 1890 when a local lumber mill built a dam across the Clackamas below the hatchery. State senator H. E. Cross, who owned the Gladstone Dam, began to log above the hatchery, float timber downstream, and disrupt operations at the hatchery rack. While the dam did have a fishway, netters commandeered it during runs, and repairs in 1891 made it completely useless. That fall Hubbard had to collect salmon below the dam to obtain eggs. The conflict quickly drew the commissioner into the fray. An outraged Marshall McDonald wrote to Oregon's governor and senators and threatened to abandon Oregon entirely unless someone built a proper fishway. Oregon fish commissioner F. C. Reed promised to look into it, but in 1892 the dam again blocked runs. To maintain appearances McDonald ordered Hubbard to "[g]et as many salmon eggs as you can even if you must go to other streams for them. Expenses of station may be reduced later if necessary, but the hatchery must be filled if possible." The USFC expanded the spaces of egg collecting but blurred genetic distinctions; it boasted the number of salmon eggs hatched but failed to mention their provenance.[59]

The Gladstone Dam created an intolerable situation for the USFC. McDonald faced two equally unappealing options: abandon his principle of noninterference or abandon the Clackamas. He chose both. In 1893 McDonald established "auxiliary stations" on other streams to collect and ship eggs to the Clackamas Station, which became a central site for incubating eggs from many streams. He also scheduled a trip to inspect the dam. McDonald and Oregon fish protector Hollister McGuire met with Senator

TABLE 1. Columbia River Salmon Catch, 1866–1936 (thousands of pounds)

Year	Chinook	Coho	Sockeye	Chum	Steelhead	Total
1866	272	—	—	—	—	272
1867	1,224	—	—	—	—	1,224
1868	1,904	—	—	—	—	1,904
1869	6,800	—	—	—	—	6,800
1870	10,200	—	—	—	—	10,200
1871	13,600	—	—	—	—	13,600
1872	17,000	—	—	—	—	17,000
1873	17,000	—	—	—	—	17,000
1874	23,800	—	—	—	—	23,800
1875	25,500	—	—	—	—	25,500
1876	30,600	—	—	—	—	30,600
1877	25,840	—	—	—	—	25,840
1878	31,280	—	—	—	—	31,280
1879	32,640	—	—	—	—	32,640
1880	36,040	—	—	—	—	36,040
1881	37,400	—	—	—	—	37,400
1882	36,808	—	—	—	—	36,804
1883	42,799	—	—	—	—	42,799
1884	42,160	—	—	—	—	42,160
1885	37,658	—	—	—	—	37,658
1886	30,498	—	—	—	—	30,498
1887	24,208	—	—	—	—	24,208
1888	25,328	—	—	—	—	25,328
1889	18,135	—	1,210	—	1,727	21,072
1890	22,821	—	3,899	—	2,912	29,633
1891	24,065	—	1,053	—	2,010	27,129
1892	23,410	283	4,525	—	4,920	33,139
1893	19,637	1,979	2,071	157	4,435	28,280
1894	23,875	2,908	2,979	—	3,565	33,327
1895	30,254	6,773	1,225	1,530	3,378	43,159
1896	25,224	2,999	1,155	—	3,377	32,755
1897	29,867	4,138	882	—	3,138	38,025
1898	23,180	4,449	4,534	—	1,787	33,950
1899	18,771	2,013	1,630	774	816	24,004
1900	19,245	3,055	895	1,203	1,401	25,799
1901	—	—	—	—	—	29,832
1902	23,034	716	1,159	707	584	26,200
1903	27,917	828	570	680	493	30,489
1904	31,783	2,125	878	1,407	671	36,864

Year	Chinook	Coho	Sockeye	Chum	Steelhead	Total
1905	33,029	1,824	528	1,751	668	37,800
1906	29,971	2,818	531	1,891	442	35,653
1907	24,250	2,159	374	1,534	403	28,720
1908	19,743	2,137	584	1,148	729	24,341
1909	17,119	2,868	1,704	1,669	1,175	24,535
1910	25,326	4,687	423	4,525	370	35,330
1911	36,602	5,400	407	3,636	584	49,480
1912	21,388	2,165	558	1,272	2,147	27,530
1913	19,384	2,786	758	904	2,168	26,556
1914	25,409	4,744	2,401	3,351	1,908	38,501
1915	32,127	2,267	371	5,884	2,690	43,839
1916	31,993	3,542	258	5,288	1,581	42,746
1917	29,522	4,372	542	3,649	2,233	40,448
1918	29,249	6,674	2,573	2,030	3,023	44,125
1919	30,326	6,170	494	5,134	1,900	44,934
1920	31,094	1,838	177	1,278	1,166	36,312
1921	21,552	2,338	411	328	1,021	26,713
1922	17,915	6,150	2,091	601	2,163	30,153
1923	21,578	6,965	2,605	1,735	2,684	35,668
1924	22,365	7,796	500	3,927	3,193	38,167
1925	26,660	7,937	384	3,795	2,907	42,333
1926	21,241	6,606	1,478	2,234	3,843	35,567
1927	24,011	5,209	468	4,655	3,147	37,688
1928	18,149	3,723	327	8,497	2,160	33,127
1929	18,151	6,701	685	3,714	2,870	32,321
1930	20,078	7,737	668	773	2,404	31,923
1931	21,378	2,714	281	239	2,126	27,032
1932	16,001	4,096	190	1,174	1,432	23,330
1933	19,528	2,702	471	1,659	1,958	26,847
1934	18,788	4,775	467	1,663	1,919	27,902
1935	15,266	7,108	89	1,054	1,472	25,756
1936	16,214	2,496	669	2,081	1,941	23,529

SOURCE: Figures from Joseph A. Craig and Robert L. Hacker, *The History and Development of the Fisheries of the Columbia River*, U.S. Bureau of Fisheries Bulletin 32 (Washington: Government Printing Office, 1940).

NOTE: Some totals do not match figures due to rounding. Totals for 1911 and 1913–16 are greater than the totals for the individual species due to idiosyncrasies in the tabulation of frozen-fish production figures for those years.

Cross at the dam site. McDonald declared the dam a menace, but he also criticized fishers at the mouth of the Clackamas for supposedly stretching their nets completely across the stream. In the short term McDonald recommended that the racks be moved below the dam so the hatchery would have at least a few eggs, but he threatened to remove the dam or the hatchery if things did not change.[60]

This was not an empty threat. Before his visit McDonald had ordered Barton Warren Evermann to prepare a report of Evermann's investigation of the Columbia "so that I may have the data with me upon which to base suggestions as to what [legislation] may be necessary." Thus McDonald came prepared to recommend major changes in the management of Oregon's fisheries and streams. He wrote to Governor Pennoyer and others demanding changes in the dam and "rigid protective regulations governing the catch on the river." McDonald had crossed his Rubicon. Forced into ultimatums, he gambled by threatening to quit the field unless Oregon changed the way it managed salmon and salmon environments. Senator Dolph encouraged cooperation and McGuire prosecuted Cross for illegally blocking the stream, but Oregon would not yield and a local jury deadlocked twice at eleven to one for conviction.[61]

McDonald followed through with his threat when Oregon failed to open the river. The USFC continued to operate the Clackamas Station in 1894, but it moved its egg collection operation to a tent camp on the Sandy River. McDonald hoped the strategy would circumvent the conflict on the Clackamas, but Waldo Hubbard soon found himself competing with a fishwheel for salmon on the Sandy as well. McDonald was livid. He informed Oregon's senators that he was "indisposed to advise any further appropriations for the construction of hatcheries in the Columbia River basin until the State has established such protective regulations as will enable us to make the hatcheries productive after they have once been established." McDonald demanded shorter fishing seasons and a complete closure of the Clackamas River. State legislators wired McDonald and promised to pass the needed legislation if he would approve a pending hatchery appropriation. McDonald encouraged and worked closely with them on the proposed bills, but he refused to budge until the states acted.[62]

Early in 1895 McDonald's gambit began to unravel. State legislators refused to pass new laws, and the courts refused to tear down the Gladstone Dam. H. E. Cross took the offensive in May. Cross jury-rigged a fish ladder by nailing a flume to the side of the dam. He then accused Hollister McGuire of selective enforcement, claiming that McGuire also owned a dam with no fish ladder. By July Oregon and Washington were at each other's throat over concurrent jurisdiction of the Columbia, and all hope for cooperation dissolved. Columbia River canners stepped into the breach and paid Cross $1,600 to have a five-foot opening cut in the dam. The USFC nevertheless had to import eggs from California to keep the Clackamas Station operating. The following year Cross made more trouble by logging directly above the station, sending logs down Clear Creek, destroying the station's bridge, suing Hubbard for interrupting his operations, and winning in court.[63]

McDonald's defeat was another decisive event in salmon management. Like Spencer Baird before him, McDonald had tried to influence state management. He warned McGuire that money was not the issue. "You may spend $100,000 in the construction of hatcheries, but under present conditions it will be money absolutely wasted." The pervasive reluctance to restrict economic activity undermined all efforts, however. Oregon was no more willing to save salmon by restricting fishing and milling on the Clackamas in the 1890s than the Interior Department would be willing to save salmon by prohibiting logging in eastern Oregon forests in 1903. This impasse moved salmon management irresistibly away from the federal model of production and regulation toward the Oregon model of production only.[64]

The preference for production over restrictions ensured that hatcheries were a point of agreement throughout the period. Both sides had something to gain from fish culture: the USFC's reputation rested on technical mastery; Oregon relied on hatcheries to avoid regulations. But who would pay was always a point of contention.

The transfer of the Clackamas initiated a pattern: build a hatchery with state or private funds, beg poverty, get the USFC to run the operation, and then try to keep federal managers on the ground. The strategy drew the USFC ever deeper into the role of hatching salmon while effectively shifting the cost of management from state to federal books. Oregonians lobbied for federal assistance on many streams, and they succeeded in transferring responsibility to the USFC on the Clackamas in 1888, 1897, and 1908, the Siuslaw in 1894, the Rogue in 1897, the Siletz in 1901, the Snake in 1903, and the Yaquina in 1904. Each transfer differed slightly, but the history of the Siuslaw illustrates the basic pattern.[65]

The USFC's introduction to the Siuslaw is a classic example of the way politics shaped salmon management (see map 9). In 1893 McGuire asked the USFC to oversee the construction of a state hatchery at Mapleton, on the Siuslaw River, but in early 1894 Columbia River canners sued the state to stop it from spending any more of their tax dollars to support competitors on other streams. McGuire wrote McDonald, "I have no funds available . . . and ask if you will not come to our aid in this matter and furnish operatives to run the hatchery this year." This afforded the best of both worlds. The *Morning Oregonian* noted that Oregon would "thus be assured of [the hatchery] being run on scientific principles, and at the same time shoulder the expense upon the general government." In May, McDonald promised that an "arrangement will be made for developing the work to its full capacity." McDonald's decision to help came not from sympathy but because the Siuslaw presented a way to move operations from the Clackamas, which the Gladstone Dam still blocked.[66]

The official explanation for the move was dry and bland. "Believing that this station could be successfully and profitably operated, the owner, through Mr. L. E. Bean, of Mapleton, kindly offered its free use to the United States Fish Commission for that purpose." The Siuslaw hatchery was neither free, profitable, nor successful. In 1894 Hubbard tried to propagate chinook but failed miserably. Rather than admit poor planning, however, the USFC blamed overfishing and admonished McGuire for lax enforcement. McGuire promised to punish offenders but he arrived late and prosecuted no one. The USFC did not hatch a single egg. In disgust, they declared the season "a total failure," blamed the state for inadequate protection, and vowed never to return.[67]

In reality the failure had less to do with fishing than with the nature of the stream. The state had located the hatchery at the head of tidewater, but this presented several problems. The river at Mapleton was too deep to install a rack, so workers tried without success to net fish. In addition, the USFC wanted chinook eggs, but coho predominated in the Siuslaw and most other coastal streams. Fishers repeatedly requested that the USFC hatch coho as well, but the USFC adamantly refused because it believed that coho were an economically inferior fish. Such conditions and attitudes doomed the season before it started.[68]

The USFC tried to write off the Siuslaw, but the hatchery became a Frankensteinian monster that would not die. In 1895 the son of the owner of the hatchery "undertook to investigate and experiment" with the hatchery. Louis Bean claimed he had hatched 60,000 eggs and released 40,000 alevins. The figures sounded impressive, but in reality he probably spawned twelve females and released about two-thirds of the offspring. Bean reported this success to his congressman, who then lobbied the USFC to give the hatchery another try. Bean followed up with a second letter, insisting that "I am quite sure that a more favorable place can not be found on the coast." Political pressure mounted, and the USFC relented in July 1896.[69]

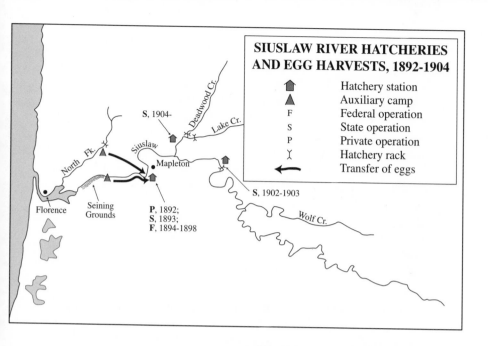

MAP 9. The Siuslaw River was another example of private ventures turned public and significant biological reorganizations. The location of fish racks tended to concentrate reproduction in both the main stem and tributaries.

The result was incompetence and a prelude to disaster. The USFC assigned Seth Meek as supervisor and hired Bean to assist. Meek was a University of Arkansas zoologist working for the USFC that summer. Neither Meek nor Bean had any experience running a mass production hatchery, nor did Bean's brothers or cousin, whom Meek hired as workers. Their methods were crude. Since the river was too deep to rack, Meek had fishermen collect salmon at the seining grounds, pack up to 200 in four "liveboxes," and float the huge wooden traps upstream to Mapleton. As a measure of his sophistication, Meek determined the fitness of salmon for transportation by tying several by the tail and rowing them a mile upstream to see if they survived.[70]

In their struggle to obtain fish, Meek and Bean introduced the same spatial problems plaguing other hatchery streams. In 1893 McDonald had noted, "Since 1878 . . . salmon have gradually been getting scarcer in the tributaries to the upper river[s] that once were favorite spawning grounds, and now it is difficult to get enough fish to supply the tables of [upstream] residents." Racks and development had progressively concentrated reproduction in the lower reaches of such hatchery streams as the Clackamas, Little White Salmon, and Chinook Rivers. Meek's live-boxes were a way of circumventing racks, but by the end of October some of the fish in the boxes were dying. The only fish ready to spawn came from gillnets at the hatchery, and most of these died as well. To obtain more fish, Bean rode to the North Fork of the Siuslaw and set up a rack. By the time he returned, many of the fish had already spawned on overcrowded redds. Before he could return again, a flood carried away the rack.[71]

The 1896 season devolved into a series of disasters for salmon. The same flood that destroyed the racks also wrecked one of the live-boxes, allowing about thirty chinooks to escape. More fish died in the next month, and Meek abandoned a live-box when strong currents made it impossible to tow the box upriver. High waters then washed the box onto a bank, where possibly half the fish escaped. At least five died, however, and three more tried to spawn in the box. On the Clackamas, the USFC tried to maintain appearances by transferring eggs from other streams, but huge numbers died in transit. In December a disgruntled neighbor poisoned the hatchery's water supply, killing all the fish. McDonald hid the incident by transferring three million fry from California.[72]

The USFC again tried to wash its hands of the Siuslaw. Meek and Bean gathered about 200,000 eggs and planted about 180,000. The numbers were unimpressive; but the accounting system had also excluded fish that died before spawning or after release, and most plantings were mass deposits of alevins, a technique far more beneficial to predators than to juvenile salmon. False accounting was an endemic problem. Commissioner John Brice actually fudged the number up to 240,000, but he still felt it would "be impracticable to do work there on a large scale under existing conditions."[73]

Locals hurried to the hatchery's defense. Bean insisted that "the work of the past season has fairly established what can be done and I am quite sure that far better results can be made in the future." Brice was doubtful. Four days after accepting an offer from R. D. Hume to work the Rogue River, Brice announced that the USFC would not operate the Siuslaw. Ravenal then transferred Bean to Clackamas, but Bean resisted. Local canners wanted the hatchery run. They flooded Congress and the USFC with correspondence. Brice defended his decision and outlined past efforts and costs, but mounting pressure eventually forced a reversal.[74]

William Ravenal announced that the USFC would return to the Siuslaw as part of an agreement whereby local merchants and canners would contribute $500 to the venture. Ignoring his earlier remarks that it was not worth the costs, Ravenal rationalized that another season "should permit of our testing very thoroughly the extent to which salmon propagation can be carried on in the Siuslaw River." This time Bean ran the hatchery by himself. He installed racks at the head of tidewater and on the North Fork, which freshets immediately destroyed. Bean replaced the racks, but he relied heavily on seiners to donate fish and half of these died.[75]

Problems mounted again. Local merchants reneged on financial promises; fish died in live-boxes by the score; netting operations killed more; the rack on North Fork forced fish to spawn on overcrowded redds; and Bean damaged many eggs during incubation. Bean eventually spawned 544,275 eggs, using 97 males and 117 females, but the uneven number of mates reduced the genetic diversity of the cohort and narrowed the pool in the next generation. Ravenal asked for a full accounting of the fish and eggs handled, not just those Bean succeeded in spawning, and hoped the evidence would damn the project. Bean submitted his report and added hopefully, "I trust this station will receive favorable consideration. . . . It is obvious that it can be operated with good results." But success was not obvious, and the USFC finally escaped the Siuslaw.[76]

Oregon wanted the federal government to fund and operate hatcheries, but when the USFC retreated, Oregonians believed they had to establish their own hatchery program to save salmon. In the late 1890s state fish commissioners escalated their budgets by trumpeting fish culture, asserting expertise, and prescribing massive production. In 1897, for example, Hollister McGuire privately criticized the late Marshall McDonald for being a "Do-Nothing" commissioner despite his heavy reliance on USFC expertise. Publicly, he predicted the size of runs and prophesied, "If hatcheries could be operated on the headwaters . . . uninterruptedly for 10 years, it would result in materially increasing the supply of our most valuable run of fish." Oregonians began to envision a system of hatcheries cranking out one hundred million eggs a season.[77]

In 1899 McGuire drowned while inspecting a hatchery site on the Umpqua River, but his successors shared his basic assumptions about the role of fish culture. McGuire, F. C. Reed, and H. G. Van Dusen hailed hatcheries as a scientific solution, yet they also used hatchery jobs as a patronage engine in ways that undermined their stated objectives. State fish commissioners would hire political cronies, present a copy of the federal fish culture manual, and unleash them on salmon. By 1910 Oregon boasted ten hatcheries, but the operators usually knew more about politics than fish. When production fell short, as it so often did, the Oregon Fish Commission inflated figures to maintain their prestige.[78]

Salmon management had evolved into a game of meeting production quotas by expanding operations over an ever widening field. The USFC conducted experiments to increase hatching efficiency, and it advised the public on fishing offshore grounds, raising fish, turning salmon into fertilizer, and shipping salmon abroad. These activities bolstered the USFC's popularity, but its authority still rested on the impression of technological mastery. To maintain that reputation, fish culturists had to demonstrate improvement. Thus the USFC subsidized the Siuslaw and other rivers through massive egg transfers from Clackamas and California. Ravenal encouraged his staff to push the work "to its utmost capacity" and capture every spawner possible. But erecting racks, concentrating reproduction, transferring eggs, and liberating alevins only exacerbated the decline of runs. Federal workers masked these problems by turning stations into incubation centers for eggs collected on many streams. By the end of the century, fish culture resembled a biological Chinese puzzle.[79]

Despite these problems, fish culture continued to gain prestige when runs rebounded after 1900. Although physical oceanographers would later attribute the recovery to improved ocean conditions, contemporary observers credited fish culture for saving the day. In 1902 H. G. Van Dusen proclaimed, "It is now a recognized fact, even by the most skeptical, that the salmon product in our rivers can be limited only by the number of young fry liberated from our hatcheries." Bureau of Fisheries Commissioner George Bowers added, "The history of salmon culture on the West coast shows that natural reproduction cannot be depended upon to furnish a supply of salmon equal to the demand, and that artificial propagation can do so." The *Morning Oregonian* concurred. "The experience of the past few years has proven that artificial propagation has practically guaranteed a supply of raw material which is certain to be available before the end of the season." Such claims required a selective reading of the past, however, one which ignored a decade's worth of failure and insisted that artificial propagation had not begun until 1896.[80]

Oregonians' faith in fish culture reached its logical conclusion during the 1904 fishing season. The previous year Oregon master fish warden H. G. Van Dusen fretted over the impact of irrigation on salmon. Van Dusen criticized unscreened ditches that destroyed salmon, but he also believed that neither farmers nor fishers should be "required to suffer to any great extent." His solution, of course, was fish culture. "Since it has been proven that the hatchery work is sure to take care of the product in a more substantial manner and at a trifling expense, it seems that these close-seasons, especially [on] the Columbia river . . . might just as well be done away with, and that in place of them fishing be stopped entirely on all salmon breeding tributaries to be set aside and designated as spawning streams." The *Morning Oregonian* seconded Van Dusen with a refrain of "Hatcheries, more hatcheries."[81]

In 1904 Van Dusen launched his plan with devastating results. Salmon arrived late that year, probably due to chronic overfishing of spring and summer runs and possibly a drought as well. Canners and fishers were suffering, so Van Dusen and Washington fish commissioner T. R. Kershaw effectively suspended the closed season. Fishing continued unmolested during August and September, but the lapse of enforcement created a domino effect. Van Dusen insisted that all was well, but by mid-October most hatcheries still had few or no eggs. In November, Portland and Oregon City gillnetters decided to defy the closed season as well since nobody else was obeying the law. Local juries sympathized and refused to convict violators.[82]

Criticism exploded when the final egg takes amounted to only a fifth of the previous year, but the resulting complaints had an old feel to them. The *Morning Oregonian* blamed Van Dusen and the fishery for the disaster; it grumbled about killing gooses that laid golden eggs, invoked comparisons to vanishing buffalo, and prophesied extermination and doom. The prescriptions observers offered were no more original. Rival fishing interests blamed each other; politicians called for concurrent jurisdiction of the Columbia; and federal administrators prospected for new streams and asked Oregon to prohibit fishing on hatchery streams. After thirty years, state and federal administrators had yet to reconcile their rival models of how to manage Oregon's salmon fisheries.[83]

Federal administrators tried to prescribe solutions to fishery problems, but Pacific northwesterners appropriated the medicine and made it their own. Boosters called fish culture a "science," but there was more political science than biology in their ideas. In practice, artificial propagation tried to alleviate economic and social conflict rather than restore runs. Hatcheries were technological band-aids that sustained production but did not rationalize management. Fish culturists nevertheless boasted success, and a combination of superficial logic and serendipitous natural events legitimated their claims. Hatcheries would offset the costs of development, so legislators gave fish culturists the power to reconfigure the natural and social spaces of production and reproduction on a massive scale.

But the rhetoric never matched material results. Good intentions could not compensate for the gaps in understanding, and procedures meant to increase production in fact undermined the industry's future. As one USBF scientist noted in 1919, early hatcheries "probably inflicted as much, or

more, damage to the salmon runs as they did service of value." Fish culturists compensated for insufficient production by descending into a vicious
spiral. When runs from one stream could not supply enough eggs to replenish that stream, hatchery workers expanded their search over an ever widening field to find more. This was robbing Peter to pay Paul on a grand scale,
and, not suprisingly, such efforts did little good. Runs continued to plummet, and those who depended on salmon began to wage a fratricidal war
over who would control and benefit from the dwindling resource.[84]

5 / Taking Salmon

Fish culturists prophesied an endless supply of salmon, but when hatcheries failed to deliver immediately on that promise, the dream of a fishery without restrictions seemed to falter. With that dream also went all hope for harmony among fishers. Starting in the early 1880s, fishers began to compensate for declining harvests by attacking their competitors. They divided into factions, and each group tried to influence state regulations and federal policies. Their underlying intent was to gain an advantage at the expense of rivals. Salmon management was devolving into a Spencerian struggle more concerned with identifying and excluding the politically weakest members of the fishery than with addressing the fundamental problems of overfishing.

But public rhetoric could leave a listener with a different impression. Fishers often claimed that these contests were a struggle by *The People* for conservation, but such arguments were usually self-serving rationalizations constructed to achieve economic gain. Battles between fishing interests were really about social legitimacy, and contestants did their best to portray opponents as liminal members of society. These early "fish fights" were ugly, violent affairs, and government officials did little to mediate disputes. Still unwilling to restrict economic competition, they kept their distance and clung to the forlorn hope that hatcheries would eventually solve all problems.

The Pacific Northwest's history of fish fights is well documented, but the environmental and social consequences of these battles have received less attention. Such episodes need to be understood *not only* as allocation struggles—for that they were—but also as contests to produce and control the social spaces of fishing. Contestants understood, at least implicitly, that before they could claim fish they first had to transform natural space into a social space that they could control. Fishers used many tactics to accomplish this end. They sorted themselves by race, ethnicity, class, gear, and place in order to exclude outsiders. They also made exclusive claims to sections of streams through physical alterations, social contracts, and legal fiat. The political contests to control fishing spaces did protect some salmon and salmon fishers, but by 1908 the struggles had also devastated communities and fractured the biological coherence of salmon management.[1]

Race was the first fault line. Contests for access to land and fish produced both official and unofficial policies that segregated Indians and Asians from the salmon fisheries. Both groups resisted efforts to exclude them, but few Indians and fewer Asians maintained access into the twentieth century.

During the 1850s and 1860s settlers bent the federal government to their desire to wipe Indians off the map. In the early 1850s treaty agents negotiated and renegotiated agreements until whites had effectively banned Indians from the Willamette Valley. Meanwhile in the Rogue Valley, miners and settlers precipitated a war of extermination. The bloody fighting forced the U.S. Army and Office of Indian Affairs to orchestrate the removal of Indians from southwestern Oregon. In 1855 President Franklin Pierce signed two emergency executive orders creating the Coast Reservation and the Grand Ronde Agency for these refugees. The treaties negotiated by Isaac Stevens and Joel Palmer in 1855 played a similar role in rearranging social space east of the Cascades. When Plateau Indians resisted invasions by settlers and miners in 1859, the army seized fishing sites and starved Indians into surrender. Impelled by the pressures of resettlement, the federal government became choreographer to a mass exodus of Indians away from the Willamette, Rogue, and Columbia Rivers.[2]

Relocation to reservations was only the beginning of a concerted effort to dismantle the aboriginal fisheries. Even after they were forced to move to the Grand Ronde Agency, Molallas, Clackamases, and Clowellas continued to visit Willamette Falls to catch salmon. Whites attacked these Indians so relentlessly that the reservation agent bribed Indians with an offer of free nets to persuade them to fish the Yamhill River instead. But the Yamhill turned out to have few salmon, so the agent asked the Indian Office to grant Grand Ronde residents access to the Salmon River on the Coast Reservation. Each change in policy diverted Indians farther from their former fisheries and from whites.[3]

Indians living on the Coast Reservation experienced an even more serious assault. President Pierce created the reservation by executive order rather than treaty. This accelerated the process of relocation, but it also left Indians vulnerable to later spatial adjustments. In 1865 Congress bisected the 200-mile reserve to satisfy demands that Yaquina Bay be opened to ships and settlers, and ten years later it amputated huge portions from the northern and southern ends for similar reasons. By 1875 presidential orders had whittled the Coast Reservation to a quarter of its original size. Oregonians celebrated such recisions. According to the *Morning Oregonian*, "The sooner these Indians are concentrated in [one] locality, and the country they occupy thrown open for settlement the better it will be for Oregon." Such arguments placed all Indians on the wrong side of a racial divide, and without treaties to protect them, coastal Indians remained highly vulnerable to the whims of federal policy.[4]

Yet even with treaties there was no guarantee that Indians could exercise their rights. Joel Palmer's 1855 treaty granted middle Columbia River Indians the right to fish at "usual and accustomed places," but settlers often refused to acknowledge these provisions. Whites claimed the shores of the Columbia River as private property after Indians moved to Warm Springs. They then beat and stabbed Indians who tried to fish ancestral sites. Settlers complained that the government had failed to protect private property, and in 1864 the commissioner of Indian affairs authorized Superintendent J. W. P. Huntington to renegotiate the treaty to eliminate off-reservation rights. It took Huntington a year to convene a council, but when he did he achieved spectacular results. For $3,500 Huntington claimed that he had persuaded Indians at Warm Springs Reservation to relinquish their right to fish, hunt, and gather beyond the reservation. To accomplish this feat, however, Huntington apparently misrepresented his intentions and the contents of the document, and Indians and agents alike have contested its legitimacy ever since. Congress nevertheless ratified the Huntington Treaty, which remained in effect de jure, if not always de facto, until 1969.[5]

By the turn of the century the Indian fishery had changed dramatically. Indians had lost control of most of their fishing sites, and they often needed state assistance to use those that remained. The content of fishing also changed. Coastal and Columbia River Indians continued to fish for subsistence and ceremonial purposes, but commercial fishing occupied an increasing amount of their time. In 1878 the Siletz agent tried to deemphasize the significance of salmon for subsistence, but ten years later he changed his mind. Watching the salmon industry expand along the coast, the agent suggested that fishing might, after all, be a legitimate economic activity for Indians. They were already fishing commercially on Yaquina Bay, so the government leased a section of land at the mouth of the Siletz in 1896 for the erection of a cannery. Salmon reemerged as an economic staple for Indians and reservation agents. Each fall Indians caught salmon and cured the meat or sold it to the cannery. They also used it as a form of currency at the reservation school. In 1899 the agent remarked that "the cannery has brought thousands of dollars to the Indians each year, as they do most of the fishing [for the cannery]."[6]

Commercial fishing also blossomed at The Dalles, but events there had darker consequences. In 1859 and 1871 the Warm Springs agent suggested that the government erect a salting station at The Dalles so Indians could fish commercially, but these efforts languished even though agents later admitted that salmon remained the Indians' "principle [sic] source of subsistence." In 1886 Army Engineer W. A. Jones noted: "The Indian has been driven from the field [at The Dalles]. White men have obtained from the Government the exclusive right to fish." In 1895 Commissioner D. M. Browning remarked in exasperation, "Inch by inch they have been forced back by the whites from the best fishing grounds and not allowed to fish with the whites in common as provided in the treaty. . . . They have borne this denial with patience, but urged that they be restored to their ancestral and treaty rights."[7]

Some Plateau Indians did fish for subsistence, but increasingly their energies fell under the control of the industrial fishery. They gained access only at the pleasure of the packers who now owned the ancient sites, and they traded fish on the canners' terms. Instead of an exchange for food or prestige, Indians sold salmon at a price set by the packers. While the old understandings of salmon did not die, Indians increasingly regarded the fish also as a commodity to be sold in a market economy controlled by others. During strong runs Indian fishers could profit handsomely, but during lean years Indian women and children were seen sitting on cannery floors, shivering as they waited for scraps of food.[8]

Indians did not accept their situation passively. As one agent noted, "Every new superintendent, every inspector and supervisor, and every missionary who meets these Indians in open council must listen to the story of the treaty robbery and land steal." Their protests eventually produced results. In 1886 the federal government dispatched investigators to record Indians' complaints, and the attorney general responded with lawsuits designed to resolve the issue of treaty rights. Between 1887 and 1919 the federal government waged numerous court battles on behalf of Indians, and they gained significant victories in the Supreme Court in 1905 and 1919. Congress also responded in 1917 by granting land for a permanent fishing village near Celilo Falls. Still, the number of Indians who benefited from these corrections was relatively small. Yakimas and some off-reservation Indians gained better access, but not the Indians from Warm Springs, whose 1855 treaty the government still refused to recognize.[9]

Whites also excluded Asians from the salmon fisheries. Packers began using Chinese labor in canneries in 1870. By the 1880s Chinese workers formed an elite corps in most plants, but they held few positions outside the factories. White fishers and packers would not allow Asians to compete for white men's jobs on the water. As George Brown Goode noted, "a Chinaman dare not fish in the Columbia, it being an understood thing he would die for his sport." David Starr Jordan and Charles Gilbert concurred: "There is no law regulating the matter, but public opinion is so strong . . . and there is such a prejudice against the Chinamen, that any attempt on their part to engage in salmon fishing would meet with a summary and probably fatal retaliation."[10]

Asians' status in the fishery rested on white acceptance. In the 1880s a few Chinese worked as tenders for boats, traps, and wheels, but this ended after gillnetters organized as the Columbia River Fishermen's Protective Union (CRFPU) in 1886 and opposed employment of Asians outside canneries. By the 1900s they were barred from freezing plants as well. Some Asians had better success farther north. Between the mid-1890s and World War II, Fraser River canners employed Japanese immigrants as both cannery laborers and fishers in order to suppress wages for white workers. On the whole, though, Asians fared little better than Indians, and their presence everywhere hinged on good harvests and tolerance among more powerful factions in the fishery. White exclusion of Indians and Asians became the leading edge of a kind of conservation by ostracism. Salmon management increasingly became a political process of determining who should benefit from salmon and who should be excluded.[11]

With the exclusion of Indians and Asians, the industrial salmon fishery became a white fishery, but this failed to alleviate tensions. Although production mushroomed during the 1870s and early 1880s, individual fishers lost ground. By the mid-1880s the industry began to fragment according to gear and social divisions, and management devolved into a series of turf wars over salmon.

Hatcheries had gained popularity because they seemed to alleviate the necessity of restrictive legislation, but without regulation fishing increased in a rapid, unrestrained manner (see table 2). In 1866 there was one cannery on the Columbia—Hapgood, Hume, and Company. It packed 272,000 pounds of salmon. By 1870 there were five canneries processing ten million pounds. In 1875 fourteen canneries packed twenty-five million pounds. By 1884 thirty-seven canneries packed forty-two million pounds. The number of fishers and the array of gear grew in similar fashion. In 1874 there were

TABLE 2. Columbia River Fishing Participation, 1866–1936

Year	Canneries	Gillnet Boats	Traps	Haul Seines	Fish-wheels	Dipnets	Trollers
1866	1	—	—	—	—	—	—
1867	1	—	—	—	—	—	—
1868	2	—	—	—	—	—	—
1869	4	—	—	—	—	—	—
1870	5	—	—	—	—	—	—
1871	6	—	—	—	—	—	—
1872	6	—	—	—	—	—	—
1873	8	—	—	—	—	—	—
1874	13	250	—	—	—	—	—
1875	14	300	—	—	—	—	—
1876	17	400	—	—	—	—	—
1877	29	450	4	5	—	—	—
1878	30	550	—	—	—	—	—
1879	30	750	—	—	1	—	—
1880	35	900	—	—	—	—	—
1881	35	1,200	20	—	—	—	—
1882	35	1,500	—	—	1	—	—
1883	39	1,700	—	—	4	—	—
1884	37	1,500	—	—	5	—	—
1885	37	—	105	—	—	—	—
1886	39	—	154	—	—	—	—
1887	39	1,600	156	—	7	—	—
1888	28	1,435	—	—	—	—	—
1889	21	1,226	164	40	40	—	—
1890	21	1,224	168	35	41	—	—
1891	22	1,410	238	49	44	—	—
1892	24	1,536	378	38	57	—	—
1893	24	—	—	—	—	—	—
1894	24	2,200	—	—	—	—	—
1895	24	2,207	378	84	57	—	—
1896	24	—	—	—	—	—	—
1897	22	—	—	—	—	—	—
1898	23	—	—	—	—	—	—
1899	17	—	—	—	76	—	—
1900	16	—	—	—	—	—	—
1901	13	—	—	—	—	—	—

Year	Canneries	Gillnet Boats	Traps	Haul Seines	Fish-wheels	Dipnets	Trollers
1902	14	—	—	—	—	—	—
1903	16	—	—	—	—	—	—
1904	20	2,596	393	92	49	—	—
1905	19	—	—	—	—	—	—
1906	19	—	—	—	—	—	—
1907	19	—	—	—	—	—	—
1908	14	—	—	—	—	—	—
1909	15	2,348	346	52	51	—	—
1910	15	—	—	—	—	—	—
1911	15	—	—	—	—	—	—
1912	15	—	—	—	—	—	—
1913	15	—	—	—	—	—	—
1914	17	—	—	—	—	—	—
1915	19	2,856	301	59	—	500	—
1916	20	—	—	—	—	—	—
1917	20	—	—	—	—	—	—
1918	20	—	—	—	—	—	—
1919	21	—	—	—	—	1,000	—
1920	22	—	—	—	—	—	—
1921	20	—	—	—	—	—	—
1922	23	—	—	—	—	—	—
1923	23	1,604	—	—	—	—	—
1924	22	—	—	—	—	—	—
1925	21	1,605	—	55	62	322	365
1926	21	1,790	506	94	48	291	342
1927	22	1,885	451	98	54	307	321
1928	24	1,589	374	104	30	331	349
1929	21	1,741	412	96	34	346	461
1930	21	4,608	442	98	39	306	442
1931	20	1,495	289	86	32	310	261
1932	15	1,307	207	49	29	261	183
1933	14	1,353	239	63	29	290	155
1934	13	1,359	238	57	27	311	179
1935	10	1,225	51	44	0	477	193
1936	11	1,239	38	42	0	471	206

SOURCE: Figures from Courtland L. Smith, *Salmon Fishers of the Columbia* (Corvallis: Oregon State University Press, 1979).

approximately 250 gillnet boats. By 1884 the number had risen to 1,500, and canneries used traps, seines, and fishwheels as well. By 1904 there were 2,600 gillnets, almost 400 traps, 92 seines, and 49 wheels (see maps 10 and 11). But growth produced a paradox. The total harvest increased with additional gear, but greater participation diluted earnings. In 1866 gillnetters averaged $900 annually; by 1883 income had dropped to $540. Greater production did not equal greater prosperity, and fishers realized they had reached a point of diminishing returns. Hatcheries still held promise for the future, but fishers needed more immediate solutions.[12]

Columbia River fishers adjusted to limited salmon by adopting a political strategy that continues today. They balkanized the fishery according to relations of production and social identity. Fishers divided themselves by gear, location, and ethnicity, and each group tried to claim exclusive use of fishery space. Gillnetters had tried to form unions since 1876, but only succeeded in 1886 with the establishment of the CRFPU. Trapmen soon followed with the rival Washington Fishermen's Association. Canners continued their cutthroat competition until the end of the century, when they too organized—first locally as the Columbia River Packers Association and later under the broader aegis of the Association of Pacific Fisheries. The process of economic consolidation did not in itself resolve perceived problems with overcrowding; rather, it created the social and economic context that has dominated contests to shape natural and social space for the last century.[13]

As competition increased and ocean and river habitat deteriorated, fishers began to shape and appropriate the river's spaces to exclude rival interests. The scale and scope of these activities varied considerably. At the local level bands of gillnetters formed small associations. They pooled resources, cleared the river bottom, and made fishing safer and more profitable. These "snag unions" then claimed prescriptive use of the resulting "drift," a stretch of fishable river resulting from their efforts. As snag unions multiplied during the 1890s and 1900s, fishermen began to divide the river into a series of exclusively allotted and increasingly formalized spaces. Groups wrote bylaws and rules and demanded annual dues. They delineated who could fish a net on a particular section of water, when, and in what order. Members held "rights" to the drift that could be sold or inherited. Their associations were typically ethnically homogeneous: Finns controlled the Smith Channel and Black Spar drifts; Swedes controlled the Tongue Point drift; and Greeks and Slavonians held Blind Channel.[14]

These social categories were not as firm as the rhetoric suggested, however. Fishers often worked several jobs, and their diversified activities blurred what seemed at first to be stark divisions between interests. Gillnetters and seiners were often at odds over territory, yet seine operators routinely refused to accept financial contributions from their laborers to defray the costs of clearing a drift because they feared that their employees would later claim a right to fish the drift with their own gillnets. Farmers and merchants criticized the scandalous behavior of rowdy fishers, yet some of those fishers were dairymen simply earning extra money after their cows dried up in fall. Similarly, while drift unions tended to be ethnically homogeneous, the fishery itself was far more socially heterogeneous. When rival associations fought over drifts or Old World issues, they revealed the fault lines of gear solidarity. Such tensions further fractured the river into a series of personally demarcated and exclusively allotted physical and social spaces. The river fishery was anything but a commons, yet neither was it ever completely atomized.[15]

Gear and ethnicity pulled fishers apart, but history and culture drew them together. Commercial fishers of whatever stripe often shared a common past. Well into the twentieth century, fishing was still an inherited life, and expertise was generally passed along gendered lines. Men caught the fish and women processed them. Families were repositories for generations of knowledge in the rhythms of nature and the pursuit of prey. Fishing was more than a job or a means to lucre; to paraphrase the CRFPU motto, their work was their joy. Camaraderie inevitably grew among people who worked the waters on long nights and in stormy weather. Netters would risk their lives to help strangers, and even bitter rivals would call a truce for the annual fishermen's ball. On the water or dock, along the street or across the fence, fishers could look at each other and see their reflection. Culture bound men and women into communities of fishers, while markets and politics bent them into rivals. The need to sustain access and opportunity constantly reminded fishers that their neighbors were also their competitors.[16]

So fishers made proprietary claims, and rivals contested them. Such challenges revealed the barely concealed role that violence played in ordering the fishery. In most cases gillnetters resolved disputes by "corking" a competitor. This involved setting fishing gear in front of rivals' nets so they could not catch fish. If coercion failed, fishers would sabotage a rival by cutting a net or sinking a boat. Gillnetters would occasionally drive a scow over a trap to remove what they considered a dangerous obstruction. Vandalism usually persuaded a challenger to move on, but sometimes violence escalated into fisticuffs or worse. During the 1880s there were several murders on the

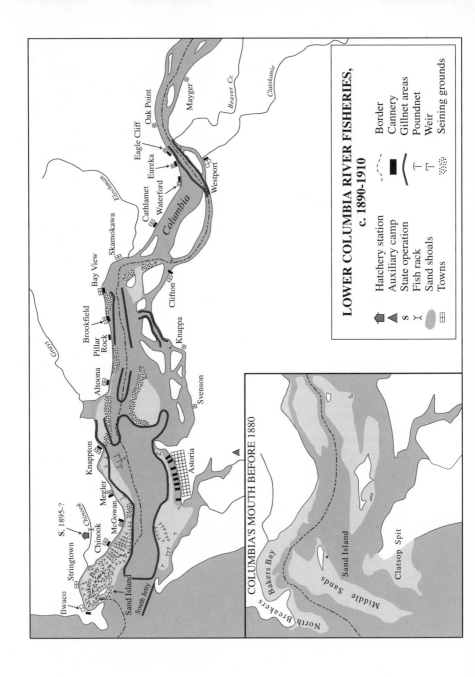

MAP 10. By the mid-1890s, fishers had already demarcated the lower Columbia River as a series of discrete fishing spaces. Note also the ethnic and economic imprint on town names and changes to the channel following the erection of poundnets and weirs in the late 1870s.

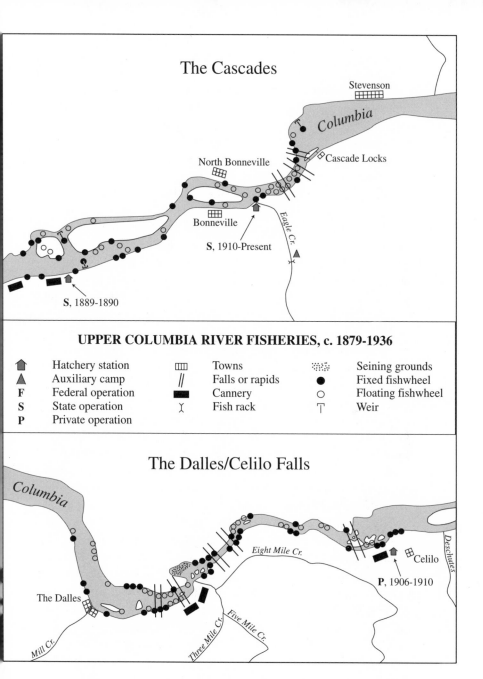

MAP 11. Fishwheels and weirs on the upper Columbia ensured that these fisheries were no more a commons than downstream areas. The very existence of wheels and weirs prevented rivals from using the same spaces. Floating wheels on scows were more mobile but generally less effective.

Columbia as gillnetters and trap owners struggled to control fishing space. Violence was an omnipresent threat in the fishery. It became a means for both challenging and legitimating fishermen's claims.[17]

Poundnet and fishwheel owners created similarly exclusive social spaces by driving posts, hanging nets, erecting wheels, and building weirs. Whites had used traps since the 1850s, but numbers mushroomed only in 1879 when fishers adopted the eastern-style poundnet. Property owners along the Washington shore employed long wings of netting to direct migrating salmon into the "heart," or inner trap, of the poundnet. The technology quickly overtook Bakers Bay. In 1881 there were 20 poundnets; by 1892 there were 378. An 1887 map shows the bay almost choked with traps. In 1879 fishers also adopted fishwheels. Fishwheels were an ingenious invention. Long weirs channeled salmon into a series of perpetually turning scoops driven by the river's current. These devices could be incredibly efficient. One investigator described wheels as "the apotheosis of the dipnet" and their success as "painful. . . . they [literally] pump the fish out of the river." Traps worked best in slow currents, while wheels excelled in strong currents. Thus poundnets and other types of trap technology proliferated in tidewater, and wheels reigned from the Cascade rapids to The Dalles and Celilo Falls. By 1900 there were seventy-six wheels along the middle Columbia River.[18]

Such "improvements" tended to monopolize river space by physically impeding the use of driftnets or other movable gear. Gillnetters hated both wheels and traps but for different reasons. Wheels deprived men of jobs; poundnets were downright dangerous. Tidal currents swept through these "permeable dams," and in the dark gillnetters became entangled in the netting and sometimes lost their lives. As one investigator noted, "The pounds are prejudicial to gill-net fishing by endangering lives of boat fishermen and rendering damage liable to fishing boats and nets . . . obliging gill-net fishermen to keep away from the locality of the pounds." Gillnetter George Johnson asked a representative of the trap men, "By what authority or right do you enclose spaces in water? What will become of the fish of our fish-hatchery when fish are murdered by the traps?" Poundnets also slowed the current and caused the river bottom to shoal. This complicated navigation north of Sand Island, and tensions erupted during 1883 and 1884 when several gillnetters drowned in poundnets.[19]

In 1886 the CRFPU complained about the poundnets to the federal government. The U.S. Fish Commission (USFC) politely declined involvement, so Congress asked the Army Corps of Engineers to investigate the entire fishery. Gillnetters wanted the government to eliminate poundnets from Bakers Bay because they obstructed navigation and posed a safety hazard to netters. They complained that traps had displaced them from the best fishing grounds onto the dangerous Columbia River bar and noted that the traps were responsible for several drownings. Gillnetters harped about safety to the Corps of Engineers and attacked traps in the newspapers. On one occasion they offered to help pay for a new hatchery if Oregon and Washington Territory would outlaw rival forms of gear; other times they claimed that traps, wheels, and seines destroyed juvenile fish migrating to sea; thus eliminating such gear would conserve salmon.[20]

The Washington Fishermen's Association, a group of Bakers Bay trap owners aligned with canners, countered with equally disingenuous claims. Trap men deflected criticism by claiming they were true conservationists. They portrayed themselves as "citizens and property owners and heads of families." They conserved salmon by selectively harvesting from their pens without undue mortality. Gillnetters, on the other hand, were rootless opportunists who wasted salmon by capturing more than canneries could handle and highgrading catches. Gillnetters also endangered navigation by crowding the shipping channels and entangling propellers with their nets. Trap owners answered the charge of endangering gillnetters with a casual shrug: "So pound nets are destructive of human life? . . . For every one you can count as a victim to pound nets I can count two as victims of murder by Columbia river gillnet 'fishermen.' As for there being scores of them, I could count them all on one-half the fingers of one hand."[21]

Violence ran close to the surface, and ignorance marked many debates. Gillnetters claimed that the small-mesh nets used by traps, seines, and wheels caught immature salmon. Poundnet owners countered that the only salmon in the Columbia were mature salmon. Both sides quoted authorities freely to prove their point. The head of the gillnetters' union claimed, "The threatened exhaustion of the Columbia river salmon, is in nowise due to the legitimate expansion of this industry, but is the result of permitting the small fish to be taken." A poundnet spokesman did not deny that the traps caught small salmon. Instead, he insisted that trapping small fish did not reduce spawning capacity, because those fish did not breed, but gillnets destroyed fertilized eggs buried in the sands near the mouth of the Columbia.[22]

All these claims revealed how little fishers understood their fishery. Gillnetters had tried to deflect criticism from themselves by attributing decline to the harvest of small fish. Their ploy fooled no one, but trap owners did no better. Their claim that small salmon did not spawn was spurious. Some salmon, called jacks, do mature sexually at a very young age. Similarly, their claim that gillnets harmed spawning grounds was absurd.

No salmon species spawned in the sands of the lower Columbia. No one had a corner on truth. Part of the reason both sides grasped at straws was because everyone still thought in terms of the Atlantic salmon most had grown up catching. Such arguments revealed the degree to which ignorance drove debates.[23]

Investigators eventually grew disgusted. Army engineer W. A. Jones concluded that "the real reason for the removal or retention of the Bakers Bay traps, as between the Columbia River Fishermen's Association and the cannery interests, is a local question of self-interest, based on competition in production by two methods of supply." An Oregon legislative committee agreed: "Many fishermen judge . . . the question solely with a view to what is most advantageous to them."[24]

The episode seemed to end in stalemate, but this was not so. Jones admitted that poundnets probably contributed to shoaling in Bakers Bay, but the Corps decided to encourage this. They wanted to rationalize shipping on the Columbia by eliminating one of the river's two main channels. Poundnets accommodated this by slowly filling in the channel north of Sand Island. Traps gained the sanction of the Corps and gillnetters lost access to Bakers Bay.[25]

The Corps punted on other issues. "If all, or nearly all, [salmon] die," Jones noted, "then there can be no objection to the catching of most of them, provided that artificial means are adopted for placing in the rivers each year a sufficient number of young fish to insure a good run four years thereafter, and this can be done with precision." "With two hatcheries and a weekly close season I do not see that any necessity would exist for placing restrictions upon the methods of catching fish." Federal agents leaned on fish culture to avoid having to restrict fishers, and they wrote off the issue of ensuring escapement as a state problem. Fish culture remained a political panacea that alleviated tensions by promising salmon for everyone.[26]

State governments took no more responsibility for conservation. Divisions within the industry were reproduced in both the Oregon and the Washington legislatures as competing factions tried to seize control of or limit access to resources. Most participants spoke in the name of conservation, yet that was rarely the primary impulse. In 1888, for example, social and economic concerns dominated when Oregon's Board of Fish Commissioners excused their failure to enforce conservation laws: "Had the literal law been enforced this year private property to the amount of $200,000 would have been rendered worthless, and while owing to the wealth of the packers they could have borne the loss without serious hardship. . . . [I]t is not so with the fishermen who have their all in their fishing gear." Conservation remained politically contingent on its social and economic costs.[27]

The struggle to oust competitors flared again in the 1890s. Gillnetters remained at center stage, but fishwheels replaced poundnets as their main foe. Class and ethnic tensions persisted, but spatial rivalries expanded. The contest over tidal areas gave way to struggles between upriver, downriver, and state interests.

Discussing the history of these conflicts is a slippery task. "Upriver," "downriver," "gillnetters," "wheel owners," and "canners" delineate significant factions of the fisheries, yet these social categories were themselves prone to factionalism. Gillnetters united during strikes for higher prices, but they would also break solidarity to sneak out and catch a big run or sabotage a comrade's gear. Packer alliances were just as fragile. In 1894 Oregon canners united when Sacramento River canners claimed they had caught a Columbia River salmon. The Sacramento canners attempted to undermine the marketing advantage of the Columbia packers by claiming that chinook moved freely between the two streams, but Oregon canners and the USFC demurred. Once the conflict passed, however, canners quickly fragmented. Some concocted schemes to monopolize riverfront space and drive out competitors; others mislabeled cans of fish to increase profits. Fishing atomized the industry, yet solidarity remained only a political crisis away.[28]

Between 1893 and 1896 a crisis did pull gillnetters and wheel owners back into their respective alliances. In 1893, Johnston McCormac wrote to Commissioner McDonald and appealed for federal intervention on the behalf of gillnetters. McCormac wrote, "I positively affirm that I do not believe there is a man in Astoria or on the Lower Columbia who does not know . . . that traps[,] wheel[s,] and seines are the true causes [of decline]. . . . [T]he great fishing industry of the Columbia river will come to an end unless these destructive appliances & their wholesale slaughter of young fish are removed."[29]

For McCormac and other gillnetters the basic issue was class privilege. McCormac cited examples of prolific waste and navigation hazards that endangered netters and asked, "what right have a few rich men thus to shut out poor gillnet fishermen from the very last portion of the common fishing ground & stake off lots for themselves?" Many downriver supporters concurred. Some asked the USFC for more information to help Oregon legislators resolve the problems in Salem; others requested federal regulation of the Columbia and the prohibition of fishing on hatchery streams.[30]

Upriver wheel owners likewise appealed to the federal government to eliminate their downriver rivals. I. H. Taffe was a former southerner who had a reputation for shooting Indians he caught fishing near his wheels or cannery at Celilo Falls. In 1892, Taffe wrote McDonald to complain about downstream fishers. "I will say to you in all confidence that the destruction of salmon is greater in other places on the columbia river than at the Cascades, although it is fearful there, at certain stages of water." Taffe tried to arrange a personal meeting with McDonald. When McDonald declined, Taffe spoke his piece anyway.[31]

While gillnetters focused on class, Taffe reduced the struggle to differences of ethnicity, patriotism, and manhood. "The principal portion of this fishermens union are composed of Rusian Finns and Italions, who care not half as much for the lives of their fishing brothers as they do for a fish that they can catch by being the first at the mouth of the river, with nets so close that it is almost impossible for a salmon to get in at all." Taffe's fishwheels, in contrast, were only "six feet wide in an obscure place on the river bank." His critics were simply a "worthless set of men . . . afraid to act like men."[32]

By 1895 the wheel owners were ready for war. They requested information to aid legislators while Taffe continued to lobby McDonald for support. He forwarded a note from the editor of a local newspaper as "a faint expression of the sentament of our people all over the States of Oregon and Washington, east of Astoria." The editor thanked "Providence" for protecting wheel men's property from the "Vandals of Astoria," but he advised wheel owners "to combine and put a stop to nets drifting over the natural spawning grounds with their miles of lead lines." He saw "no reason why I should . . . quietly submit to seeing Astoria destroy the only resource we have for a change of diet" and concluded, "In time of peace prepare for war." Taffe added, "The Russian fins and Italians who compose the fishermens Union, want and expect to controle the Columbia river and do away with all methods of fishing but theirs—no matter who sinks so they swim is the motto of Astoria and the fishermens Union who runs the place."[33]

The USFC regarded this conflict as trouble best avoided. When William Wilcox surveyed the Pacific fisheries in 1894, he inspected many gillnets, poundnets, and fishwheels without ever seeing the alleged slaughter of immature salmon. He concluded, "there is such jealousy existing among the American fishermen using pound nets and wheels and the foreigners who chiefly employ gill nets that no reliance can be placed on their statements as to the destruction or catch by the apparatus used by their rivals." Another USFC employee added, "I do not think the Commission can afford to make response to complaints of this kind from any one place in so large a river basin."[34]

McDonald was getting disgusted. He politely declined private meetings with fishing interests, but was politic enough to "receive [suggestions] in confidence and recommend such legislation as may be necessary to direct the attention of the Fish Commissioners of Oregon and Washington to the destruction of salmon in violation of law." He had lost patience with the industry's approach to conservation, however, and in a moment of exasperation noted that all fishers tried "to minimize the damage caused by their own operations, and to exaggerate the injurious influence of the methods employed by their competitors using different appliances. As a matter of fact all the methods in use for taking fish have concurred in bringing about the present and prospective decline in the salmon production of the River."[35]

But McDonald's politic solution was really no advance in policy. He wanted the states to regulate fishing, "impose no restraints that are not clearly necessary," and rely on artificial propagation to "make up the deficiencies of natural reproduction." Having lost the battle at Gladstone Dam, the USFC called for a comprehensive approach to conservation but in effect delegated these disputes to the states.[36]

Oregon's fish and game protector tried to fill the void in leadership, but the factional disputes in the fishery doomed his efforts. In 1894 Hollister McGuire wrote a bill that shortened fishing seasons, closed hatchery streams, and increased penalties for polluting and obstructing streams or possessing fish out of season. The bill also imposed fishing license fees and citizenship requirements that threatened ethnic gillnetters, so the Astoria representative added amendments outlawing traps, seines, and wheels. The bill collapsed of its own freight, and a frustrated McGuire wrote McDonald, "There is a constantly increasing strife here between those interested in gillnets and those operating wheels and traps."[37]

Political rivalries also shaped state management. A faction within the Republican party tried to upstage McGuire in 1894 by enlisting Congressman Binger Hermann to write a separate bill, and in 1901 the same faction purged the Oregon Fish Commission of rival Republicans. To facilitate patronage they installed the governor, secretary of state, and treasurer as the new Fish Commission. They also eliminated the position of fish and game protector held by F. C. Reed and replaced him with H. G. Van Dusen in the new office of master fish warden. The change made little difference in the level of expertise guiding state management—neither Reed nor Van Dusen knew much about fish culture—but it did influence the course of fishery politics. Van Dusen was a native Astorian and an open supporter of gillnetters.[38]

Washington State was equally hamstrung by legislative rivalries. In 1901 a representative from New Whatcom, at the north end of Puget Sound, tried to limit the use of traps, poundnets, fishwheels, and seines. As chair of the Fisheries Committee, H. A. Fairchild easily guided his bill to the floor, but then a representative from Brookfield, on the Columbia River, poisoned the bill by adding an amendment that forced Fairchild to vote against it. The bill did pass the House but died in the Senate Fisheries Committee, which was chaired by J. G. Megler, a salmon canner from Brookfield and state senator in his spare time.[39]

By the early 1900s these conflicts had paralyzed management. Many state laws were dead letters because the Oregon-Washington border ran along the Columbia River. The political division of the Columbia allowed fishers and canners to exploit the river's ambiguous jurisdiction. Gillnetters played the states against each other by buying licenses from whoever charged less or gave more privileges. In 1903 and 1904 they protested Oregon's attempt to license individual fishers by purchasing Washington licenses instead. The strategy crippled Oregon's hatchery system because of the loss of license revenues. Canners exploited Washington's lax enforcement to circumvent conservation efforts by Oregon. On several occasions Oregon wardens spied canners transporting and processing salmon out of season, but they were powerless to arrest the violators as long as they remained in Washington's unpatrolled waters.[40]

The political division of the Columbia continually undermined coherent regulation of the salmon fisheries. In 1905 Oregon gave in to the gillnetters and rescinded the personal license. Similarly, when Van Dusen refused to issue licenses to itinerant fishermen from California in 1905, they too exploited Washington's more lenient statutes until Oregon repealed its policy. Federal officials and local observers called repeatedly for concurrent jurisdiction of the Columbia, but Oregon and Washington legislators instead exacerbated tensions by changing fishery laws frequently and with little regard for their neighbors.[41]

The political and spatial tensions between Oregon and Washington were replicated in Oregon proper. In 1903, Master Fish Warden Van Dusen tried to reorganize state management by raising license fees on canneries and fishmongers to increase revenues for hatcheries, and by dividing the state into two management zones: District 1 covered the Columbia and its tributaries; District 2 included all coastal streams. Van Dusen's solutions reinforced his political allegiances. As a gillnet supporter, he shifted management costs from labor to capital; as an Astorian, he structured government space so Columbia revenues remained in the watershed; as a fish culture booster, he shaped fiscal policy to facilitate expanded hatchery production. But policy changes solved little. District 2 suffered chronic revenue shortages because the smaller coastal fisheries could not generate sufficient license revenues to cover hatchery expenses on these streams. Columbia River packers accepted the increased fees as a fait accompli after the fishing license fiasco, but the new license schedule solved none of the spatial tensions.[42]

In 1906 shifting sands and industry rivalries formed the backdrop for another series of contests over fishery space: first between states, then between individuals and the state, and last between fishers. These battles culminated in 1908 in a cataclysmic election that reshaped the political landscape of the fisheries.

Spatial battles bubbled over in 1906 during a dispute between Oregon and Washington over the Columbia River border. The location of the "main channel" was the central point of contention. When Oregon gained statehood in 1859, the Columbia emptied into the Pacific from two separate mouths in the unstable Clatsop Spit (see map 10). The state charter established the border along the "main channel," which at the time flowed on the north side of Sand Island. This situation changed in the 1880s. The Army Corps of Engineers allowed Bakers Bay to shoal, and it constructed a jetty to seal all but one entrance into the river. The north channel ceased to exist, and shipping traffic steered south of Sand Island.[43]

The ambiguous language of Oregon's charter provided Washington an opportunity to contest fishery space. Washington opposed a policy allowing canners to lease seining rights on Sand Island from the federal government after Oregon canners won most of the bids. Washington contested the government's right to lease the land. According to the *Pacific Fisherman*, an industry organ, "The island reserved [by the federal government in 1860 for military use] and the island of today are not one and the same." Washington used the shifting sands to argue that the border should be redrawn to reflect the change in traffic. That way Washington would control the lucrative seining operations at Sand and other islands and shoals along the lower river. Oregon insisted that the border ran along the north channel regardless of where the "main channel" existed. Monetary considerations were only part of the equation. With jurisdiction also went managerial control of the fishery. As Boundary Commissioner C. C. Dalton noted after the U.S. Supreme Court ruled in Oregon's favor, "The decision is a

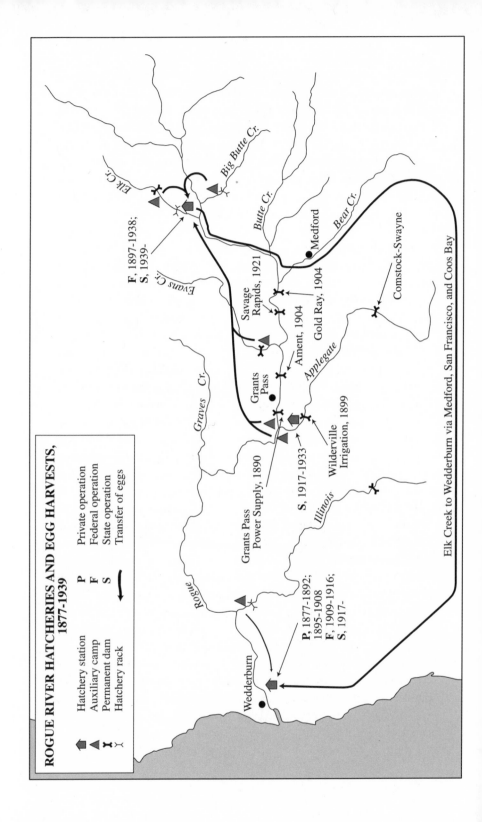

ROGUE RIVER HATCHERIES AND EGG HARVESTS, 1877-1939

Hatchery station   **P**   Private operation
Auxiliary camp   **F**   Federal operation
Permanent dam   **S**   State operation
Hatchery rack   Transfer of eggs

Elk Cr.

Big Butte Cr.

Butte Cr.

Bear Cr.

Medford

Comstock-Swayne

F, 1897-1938;
S, 1939-

Evans Cr.

Savage
Rapids, 1921

Ament, 1904

Gold Ray, 1904

Applegate

Graves Cr.

Grants
Pass

Wilderville
Irrigation, 1899

Grants Pass
Power Supply, 1890

S, 1917-1933

Illinois

Rogue

P, 1877-1892;
1895-1908
F, 1909-1916;
S, 1917-

Wedderburn

Elk Creek to Wedderburn via Medford, San Francisco, and Coos Bay great loss in territory and jurisdiction to the State of Washington. It gives to Oregon nearly exclusive control of the salmon fisheries and islands of the Columbia River."[44]

Similar spatial politics occurred elsewhere. By the early 1900s salmon canner R. D. Hume was locked in similar endgames with the state of Oregon and various rivals over control of the Rogue River fishery. At stake were Hume's monopolistic claims to the lower Rogue River and the state's power to tax his canning operations. Hume's battles highlighted both the environmental and social problems involved in managing Oregon's industrial salmon fishery and Hume's attempted solutions for restricting access and ensuring reproduction.

Robert Deniston Hume was an ornery and highly successful businessman. From southwestern Oregon during the late nineteenth century, Hume controlled operations scattered over two states and a territory. His interests included fish and vegetable canning, lumbering, land speculation, shipping, and retail sales. He also played an intermittent but significant role in Oregon's Republican party during the 1890s and early 1900s. Hume's activities earned him both ardent supporters and bitter opponents, the latter often antagonized by his tendency to imagine conspiracies and litigate at the drop of a hat.[45]

In many respects Hume epitomized the grasping capitalist of the period, yet he was more than a self-styled "pygmy monopolist." Hume possessed an incisive understanding of the nature of salmon and the dynamics of an open-access fishery. Raised on the Kennebec River, initiated on the Sacramento River, and seasoned on the Columbia River, he had witnessed the decline of once promising fisheries three times over. He had been a favored member of a failed swidden fishery on its way to depleting every salmon stream from Maine to Alaska. Yet unlike his competitors, Hume developed a holistic understanding of the fishery's problems (see map 12).[46]

While most canners saw rivers only as avenues for fish, Hume understood the fishery as a system. From experience he realized that the inability to limit fishing pressure and ensure reproduction were the industry's fatal flaws. Beyond that, he also understood that the competitive tensions within the industry and the scale of environmental changes taking place on major rivers limited the ability of the industry, let alone any one individual, to respond

MAP 12 (*facing page*). Similar to the experience of the Clackamas River, R. D. Hume's efforts to sustain Rogue River salmon produced a volatile mixture of private, state, and federal participation, and hatchery operations and economic development thoroughly altered the evolutionary pressures on runs.

effectively. Earlier than most, Hume recognized that a repetition of these conditions would eventually doom even the mighty Columbia, so in 1877 he decided to move his operations to the Rogue. The move was more than a simple relocation; it represented a brave and brazen experiment in sustainable exploitation. By 1877, Hume believed he might avoid past mistakes if he could control all aspects of the salmon's environment, but he needed the right river. Ideally, it would have runs large enough to ensure a handsome profit, yet not so large as to invite competition. Nor could development have yet undermined the natural river with dams, logging, or irrigation. In the Rogue, Hume thought he had found such a stream.[47]

Hume understood that success hinged on his ability to moderate not only his own but society's impact on salmon and their environments, yet he realized he could not control human activity over the entire length of even this smaller river system. Instead, he devised a plan for controlling only those sections strategic to his fishery. He, in effect, truncated the natural river into its constituent parts, identified the important fragments, and then monopolized or redesigned them to fit his needs. To control fishing on the lower river, Hume bought the tidal and shore rights to both banks for an extended distance upstream. He then lobbied state legislators to sanction this de facto monopoly by passing specious legislation granting him "ancient rights" to the river. He also harried state and federal fishery agencies to police dams, irrigation ditches, and mining operations that threatened his fishery. Meanwhile, he tried to restrain salmon runs by stretching a black seine across the river until fishing season opened.[48]

As aggressive as he was, Hume realized his control of the fishery remained incomplete, so he also invested tremendous sums of money and energy in artificial propagation. Hume built his first hatchery in 1877 to increase the river's disappointing runs. But to reduce transportation costs and rationalize reproduction, he located the hatchery not at the existing spawning grounds but next to his cannery at Wedderburn, near the mouth of the river. This raised new problems. Except for the economically unimportant chum, most salmon species are not ready to spawn the moment they enter freshwater but instead take up to six months to reach sexual maturity. To solve this problem, Hume dug and enclosed a holding pond to retain the fish until they were "ripe." Hume tried to collapse the spatial requirements of salmon by eliminating their need to travel upstream to spawn, thus reducing his own need to control nonfishing space.[49]

Fish culture thus became a central component for ensuring reproduction independent of upriver conditions. Hume's dedication to the scheme was complete. When the initial hatchery failed to sustain runs, Hume enlisted the help of the USFC to build a second hatchery farther upstream. Instead of pulling stakes and moving to Alaska like most of his competitors during the 1890s, he offered to underwrite the construction of the new hatchery. His only immediate demand was that he receive one-third of the eggs the government collected. When federal workers resisted his wishes, he tried unsuccessfully to get himself or one his allies appointed as hatchery superintendent for the Rogue.[50]

Embracing fish culture forced Hume to expand the domain of his fishery ever outward. The journey of the salmon eggs from the upper Rogue to his hatchery at the mouth required a long and circuitous route. Federal workers packed the eggs in wooden crates lined with moss and ice and then loaded them onto a wagon for the thirty-mile trip to Medford. Rugged mountains and rapids blocked the route between Medford and Wedderburn, so workers instead placed the eggs on a Southern Pacific railroad car bound for San Francisco. The eggs next went by steamer north to Coos Bay, by smaller steamer south to Wedderburn, and by wagon east to Hume's hatchery. In all, eggs taken 150 miles up the Rogue River journeyed over 1,000 miles to reach Hume's increasingly unnatural nursery. The spaces of Hume's fishery expanded even farther when federal agents transplanted eggs from the Columbia and Sacramento to restore the Rogue's dwindling runs. Salmon responded poorly to these manipulations. One shipment of eggs to Wedderburn arrived with severe freezer burn, and salmon transplanted from other streams probably fared poorly at best.[51]

Through purchase, legislation, and science, R. D. Hume had attempted to create and control a political space that was environmentally and economically conterminous with his fishery. Despite his holistic intentions, however, Hume fractured nature as decisively as did his contemporaries.

Hume's uneasily circumscribed space proved equally difficult to maintain. Rivals for salmon, water, or political supremacy fought him doggedly, and invariably these contests wound up in the newspapers and before judges. By 1908 Hume's battles had narrowed to two lingering court cases. One involved a long-standing dispute over his monopolistic claim to the Rogue River fishery; the other, the state's power to tax his canning operations. Hume justified his monopoly with a specious argument of "ancient rights" that had no legal precedent apart from a dubious state law passed at his behest in 1899. Rivals had challenged the monopoly in one way or another since the early 1890s, but as late as 1906 Hume appeared to be winning the fight. This was less the result of judicial confirmation, however, than of his opponents' habit of dying before hearings could be held. As Hume himself noted darkly, "It seems as if all the ones who oppose me here are bound to be drowned, and then fish improve." Like on the Columbia, salmon management on the Rogue devolved into a struggle to exclude rival interests.[52]

And like on the Columbia, the interests involved transcended the local and personal to include the state. Hume's intransigence in the monopoly case was mirrored by his resistance to the Oregon Fish Commission's efforts to license his cannery. Hume initially objected to a license fee that supported state hatcheries. As he rightly noted, the only hatcheries operating on the Rogue were run by himself and the federal government, not the state. Why, he asked, should he be required to support activities that gave him no benefit?[53]

Over time the license issue expanded into a general debate over whether the state or the federal government should manage Oregon salmon. By 1908 federalization had grown into a broad movement, and Hume's personal struggle drew increasing support. Portland attorney W. C. Hale agreed with Hume's "contention that the operation of hatcheries and control of fish industries and their protection should be placed in the hands of the United States Fish Commission, and would be pleased to render any assistance towards that result." Portland merchant J. O. Hawthorn concurred: "I hope that such will be the case. I, like yourself, think it is a matter that does not belong in politics, at all." But as Hume himself stated, politics was unavoidable. "Whichever way it goes, whoever attempts to fight us will come out the little end of the horn. Politics is at the bottom of the whole thing."[54]

In 1908 politics dominated the fisheries as various conflicts hurtled toward resolution. While the Supreme Court considered the Columbia River boundary case, and state courts heard appeals in the two Hume cases, another long-standing fish fight erupted into full-scale political war. Gillnetters had never conceded their fight against rival forms of gear. In 1896 the secretary of the CRFPU vowed, "Not until it is arranged to do away with small mesh gear, wheels, and traps can there be expected any protection to Columbia river fish." After 1900, however, gillnetters switched tactics. They ceased complaining about harvesting small fish and instead embraced another tried and true strategy: closing hatchery streams. Following the disastrous 1904 season, fishery managers forcefully insisted that the state ban net fishing on hatchery streams to ensure an adequate escapement of brood fish. In doing so, however, they unintentionally introduced a new factor that further destabilized the spatial politics of the industry.[55]

By legitimating the idea of closing streams for conservation purposes, managers unwittingly aided gillnetters in their fight against upriver competitors. Van Dusen was a longtime critic of poundnets and fishwheels. In 1904 he recommended, "Under no circumstances should a fish-trap or a fish-wheel be permitted at the mouth of a salmon-breeding stream or within miles of one." When runs continued to decline, he called for more drastic measures. Noting that "a sacrifice has to be made some place," Van Dusen recommended extending to the Columbia a law restricting commercial fishing to tidewater in Oregon's coastal streams. "The Columbia River should have been included in this measure at the time it was enacted," he noted, "but the influence brought to bear by the upper river interests was too strong."[56]

Van Dusen had distilled the problem and split it into a stark dichotomy: gillnets harvested fresh salmon near river mouths, but wheels preyed upon spawners near breeding grounds. Under such terms, and with the endorsement of federal fish culturists, fishing clearly needed to be restricted to tidewater. Van Dusen had deftly created a spatial argument in which wheel owners and the state legislature seemed to be obstructing a scientifically legitimated approach to conservation.

Gillnetters seized the opportunity in 1907. Ed Rosenberg, secretary of the CRFPU, reduced the contest to a fight between capital and labor. He claimed that "rich men's predatory practices" had stymied proper regulation of the fisheries "through legislative trickery." "The safest method [of conserving salmon]," argued Rosenberg, "is simply to aid Nature in spawning our salmon at or near our headwaters." To ensure escapement, the gillnetters made an end run on the state legislature, which had proved increasingly resistant to gillnetters, and issued an "Appeal to People." Gillnetters drafted a voter initiative to prohibit fishing above tidewater. The bill would have eliminated fishwheels by denying wheel men access to the fast water they needed to operate their devices. The gillnetters maintained, "Fishwheels, traps and dragseines all tend toward extermination of the salmon and hamper artificial propagation." Thus, "halting fishing at tidewater was the last best hope for saving the salmon." This was essentially a spatial contest, but Rosenberg's emphasis on class and gear helped mask the support gillnetters received from downriver canners.[57]

Upriver fishermen and trap owners responded with a two-pronged counteroffensive. They dismissed Rosenburg's claims as the un-American prattlings of an ignorant laborer. They then tried to dilute or confuse the gillnetter initiative by introducing a rival initiative measure restricting fishing to daylight hours in order to give "additional protection to the adult salmon." As wheel men and trap men well knew, the thick-twined gillnets were only effective at night and during muddy water conditions, so forcing gillnetters to fish during daylight would ensure their ruin. The wheel men also sought to replace Master Fish Warden Van Dusen, who was throwing fuel on the fire by recommending the elimination of fishing within ten miles of Celilo Falls. The wheel men accused Van Dusen of being a "catspaw" for the gillnetters and having abandoned all objectivity in the management of the salmon fisheries.[58]

Despite their sometimes radically different solutions, everyone claimed to be on the side of nature, including a third group, which tried to moderate the conflict between the gillnetters and wheel men. At the heart of this quiet effort were nonlegislative government officials from the courts and the Oregon Fish Commission, the publishers of the *Portland Morning Oregonian,* and a few discreet salmon canners. They attempted to defuse the spatial tug-of-war between upriver and downriver interests, and with it public dissatisfaction with fishery management, in order to avoid the threat of federalization. Their solution was to assert state hegemony over the fisheries.[59]

The movement had begun in the summer of 1907 with backroom efforts to find an "impartial" replacement for Van Dusen. Gillnetters tried to defend Van Dusen in early 1908, but by March the Fish Commission had found a replacement in Herman C. McAllister, a traveling salesman with no experience in the fisheries. McAllister's selection revealed how volatile salmon politics had become and how desperate Oregon politicians were to defuse tensions. As the *Morning Oregonian* noted, "Technical knowledge of the fishing industry is not regarded as an essential qualification for the position, and the Board will select a man with particular attention as to his executive ability as well as a disposition to be impartial and treat all sections and interests alike." McAllister did not disappoint. He knew nothing and did little, but one of his first acts was to move the warden's office from Astoria to the supposedly neutral turf of Portland.[60]

The moderating impulse continued with final rulings in the Hume lawsuits. As Hume's biographer has noted, it was "the jurist, not the vigilante," who ultimately shaped the social geographies of the Rogue River. In May the Oregon Supreme Court rejected Hume's protest against the state license fee. In August the court ruled that the state, not private citizens, retained ultimate authority over its waters. The decisions asserted state sovereignty in unequivocal terms and effectively ended Hume's thirty-year struggle to monopolize Rogue River salmon. Discussion of these cases has focused on antimonopoly sentiment and the shortcomings of Hume's legal arguments, but such interpretations abstract these cases from the vital context of Oregon's fish fights during the early twentieth century. Hume's legal defeats also need to be understood as part of a widespread retaliation by the state and the public against what was perceived as a greedy, irresponsible industry.[61]

Although moderates succeeded in removing Van Dusen and defeating Hume, their successes made blocking the fishing initiatives even more difficult. The replacement of Van Dusen in fact exacerbated matters. Having lost a key ally, gillnetters grew even more determined to destroy their competitors. Meanwhile trap and wheel owners tried to capitalize on the netters' loss by publishing caustic advertisements designed to carry the war home to the gillnetters. They concluded the campaign with a newspaper ad that mixed numbers and images to create a thoroughly alarming scenario. Crying "PROTECT OUR SALMON," wheel owners cited David Starr Jordan to prove that wheels were not dangerous to salmon. They then argued that gillnets and seines were the true villains, and that most of these were located in a highly congested area around Astoria. "In 10 miles by 5 miles," the ad claimed, "are 570 miles net, 80 miles seines, catching 95% of salmon." Wheels, on the other hand, were located "1 to 5 miles apart." In case the reader still did not get the picture, they drew one. The ad showed a lower river dotted with nets contrasted against a capacious, sparsely fished upper river. The wheel men implored Oregonians to "Vote Against the 'Astoria Hog-it-All' Bill."62

Gillnetters countered with their own inflammatory ads that claimed to be the "LAST WORD" on the election. Not surprisingly, gillnetters drew radically different conclusions about economics and conservation. They argued that shutting down the wheels "Means Bread and Butter for Five Thousand Hard-Working Fishermen." Claiming that salmon could not reach their spawning grounds because of the wheels, they too quoted Jordan to prove that "wheels and all stationary traps are especially pernicious . . . and should be everywhere prohibited." Gillnetters drew their own picture. They showed a constricted upper river riddled with fishwheels juxtaposed against a capacious lower river. "Fish must be protected above tide water," the caption warned, "or the industry is doomed."63

Against this backdrop the *Morning Oregonian* tried vainly to counsel restraint. In February the paper criticized both the gillnetter and fishwheel bills for being "silent on the most important element of salmon legislation—extension of closed season in months when fish need protection most and when greed of salmon men is keenest." But by May the *Morning Oregonian* had not offered its own solution. The paper characterized the entire campaign as a "fish scramble" between rivals trying "to shift the whole responsibility for a waning industry on their neighbors." They criticized the factions for offering bills, "not with a view to fair and reasonable regulation, but each attempting to serve a selfish interest." The *Morning Oregonian* recommended against both bills and offered a postelection image

PROTECT OUR SALMON

THIS LINE REPRESENTS THE GILLNET CATCH OF THE COLUMBIA RIVER

65 %

CATCH OF TRAPS AND SEINES **30 %**

CATCH OF WHEELS **5 %**

U. S. BUREAU OF FISHERIES, JAN. 10, 1907.

The Department sees no reason for advocating the elimination of fish wheels from the river, as there is no evidence to show that this form of apparatus is particularly destructive to salmon.

OSCAR S. STRAUS, Secretary.

VOTE A SQUARE DEAL--318 X--YES
ENACTMENT GOVERNMENT RECOMMENDATION

WHEELS 1 TO 5 MILES APART.

SNAKE RIVER

COLUMBIA R.

CELILO

1 MI. WIDE
WHEELS

THE DALLES

1½ MI. WIDE
WHEELS

CASCADE LOCKS
½ MI. WIDE

WASHINGTON

OREGON

C O L U M B I A   R I V E R

2 MI. WIDE

7 MI. WIDE
NETS

NETS

ASTORIA

WILLAMETTE RIVER

PORTLAND

FORT STEVENS

CAPE DISAPPOINTMENT

SAND I.

2 MI. WIDE
ENTRANCE

JETTY

IN 10 MILES BY
5 MILES ARE
570 MILES NET
80 SEINES
CATCHING 95%
OF SALMON

PACIFIC OCEAN

Vote Against the "Astoria Hog-it-All" Bill--Vote 333 X--No

of two trolls locked in a tug-of-war over a distressed-looking salmon, but they offered little in the way of alternatives.[64]

Gillnetters, wheel owners, and moderates all tried to wield the rhetoric of conservation to their advantage, but their arguments remained open to other interpretations and uses. As early as February the *Morning Oregonian* had noted presciently, "a great many people would take pleasure in enactment of both bills. . . . perhaps this is the opportunity." The paper probably inflamed voters antipathy in mid-May by noting that the fishing "season has been almost a failure to date." When Oregonians went to the polls on 1 June, they passed both measures, effectively shutting down the entire Columbia River fishery.[65]

The fallout from the campaign and election radically altered the political geography of Oregon's salmon fisheries. Major changes began when McAllister relocated his office from Astoria to Portland in May 1908, and then to Salem the following year. The moves contained a class bias that placed gillnetters at a logistical disadvantage. Gillnetting bound fishers to the river by the cycle of tides, and the distance from the lower Columbia to Portland and Salem, along with the costs of travel, discouraged fishers from making the long trek to meet legislators and administrators.[66]

Wealthier wheel owners experienced no similar hindrance, but they suffered their own setbacks as a result of the election. Passage of the rival bills initially hurt them more than gillnetters because the courts ruled that the new laws pertained only to Oregon waters. The division of the Columbia into separate state spaces allowed gillnetters to cross an imaginary line and fish under Washington licenses while Oregon fishwheels stood idle.[67]

Wheel owners' problems continued when the master fish warden announced plans to build a central hatchery at Bonneville. Frank Warren, who owned a nearby cannery, protested that the hatchery would impede his operations and sought a court injunction, but Warren only succeeded in delaying construction. When finished, the Central Hatchery stood as a triumph of organization. Capable of incubating sixty million eggs and nursing three million more in retaining ponds, it was billed by the *Morning Oregonian* as the largest hatchery in the world. When put into operation, however, it accelerated the concentration of salmon reproduction in the lower Columbia. Fish culturists imported salmon eggs from all over the

(*Facing page*) In 1908 fishwheel owners emphasized the threat that gillnetters posed by suggesting an alarmingly dense concentration of nets near the mouth of the Columbia compared with the few wheels located upstream. (*Oregonian*, 31 May 1908.)

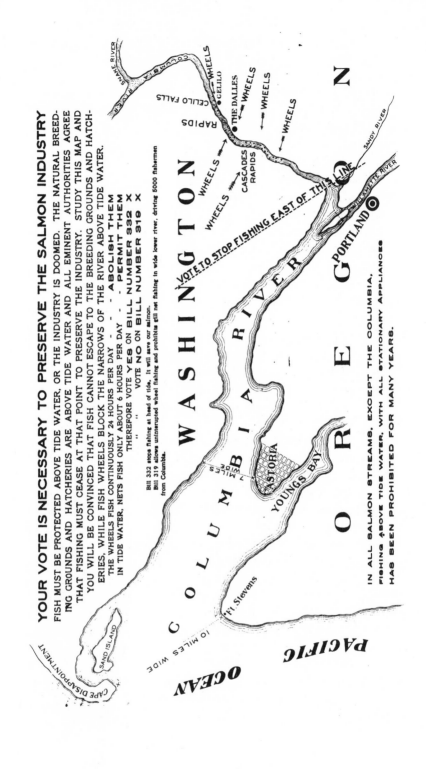

YOUR VOTE IS NECESSARY TO PRESERVE THE SALMON INDUSTRY

FISH MUST BE PROTECTED ABOVE TIDE WATER, OR THE INDUSTRY IS DOOMED. THE NATURAL BREED-
ING GROUNDS AND HATCHERIES ARE ABOVE TIDE WATER AND ALL EMINENT AUTHORITIES AGREE
THAT FISHING MUST CEASE AT THAT POINT TO PRESERVE THE INDUSTRY. STUDY THIS MAP AND
YOU WILL BE CONVINCED THAT FISH CANNOT ESCAPE TO THE BREEDING GROUNDS AND HATCH-
ERIES, WHILE FISH WHEELS BLOCK THE NARROWS OF THE RIVER ABOVE TIDE WATER.

THE WHEELS FISH CONTINUOUSLY 24 HOURS PER DAY - - ABOLISH THEM

IN TIDE WATER, NETS FISH ONLY ABOUT 6 HOURS PER DAY - - PERMIT THEM

THEREFORE VOTE YES ON BILL NUMBER 332 X

" " VOTE NO ON BILL NUMBER 319 X

Bill 332 stops fishing at head of tide. It will save our salmon.

Bill 319 allows uninterrupted wheel fishing and prohibits gill net fishing in wide lower river, driving 5000 fishermen
from Columbia.

VOTE TO STOP FISHING EAST OF THIS LINE

IN ALL SALMON STREAMS, EXCEPT THE COLUMBIA,
FISHING ABOVE TIDE WATER, WITH ALL STATIONARY APPLIANCES
HAS BEEN PROHIBITED FOR MANY YEARS.

WASHINGTON

OREGON

COLUMBIA RIVER

PACIFIC OCEAN

YOUNGS BAY

ASTORIA

7 MILES WIDE

10 MILES WIDE

SAND ISLAND

CAPE DISAPPOINTMENT

Ft. Stevens

PORTLAND

SANDY RIVER

WILLAMETTE RIVER

SNAKE RIVER

COLUMBIA RIVER

CELILO FALLS

RAPIDS

CELILO

THE DALLES

CASCADES RAPIDS

WHEELS

N

state but released juveniles at Bonneville instead of their original spawning beds. This altered the fishes' homing instincts, undermined upstream runs, and hurt wheel owners and Indian fishers alike.[68]

Throughout the summer wheel owners and gillnetters squabbled over which bill should take precedence. The state supreme court eventually ruled both laws unconstitutional, but the highly publicized battle only deepened public disgust. To break the management deadlock, some Pacific northwesterners turned to the federal government. In March the *Morning Oregonian* reported growing support among canners and the secretary of commerce for federal intervention. Following the June election, Miller Freeman, publisher of the influential *Pacific Fisherman,* wrote to the commissioner of the Bureau of Fisheries, "I am becoming more convinced than ever that the only solution of the problem in such districts as the Columbia is proper administration under a single control; namely, the United States Bureau of Fisheries." At this point Hume's battle against Oregon merged with the larger debate.[69]

Growing doubts about the ability of Oregon and Washington to manage salmon produced a political climate in which public and federal eclipsed private and state. In his December 1908 state of the union address, President Theodore Roosevelt suggested that the best course of action was to federalize all the Pacific fisheries. Even the *Morning Oregonian,* which adamantly opposed federalization, acknowledged the policy's wisdom:

> To stave off National control of Puget Sound and the Columbia River, it will be necessary for the conflicting Legislatures to agree right away on concurrent laws and afford needed salmon protection. They have tried this often enough in past years and just as often have failed, on account of the warring interests. It will hardly be disputed that it would be better to take fish control away from the States of Washington and Oregon and the Province of British Columbia, and place it in a higher authority, than to continue the destruction of salmon. It is, therefore, "up to" the lawmaking bodies of Oregon, Washington and British Columbia to "make good." This may be their last chance.[70]

In the next three months Oregon and Washington legislators did "make good." Ignoring appeals by gillnetters and wheel owners to eliminate their

(*Facing page*) The gillnetters' political flier simply reversed the election's spatial imagery by juxtaposing a capacious lower river with a constricted upper river choked with fishwheels. (Box 1/27, Frank M. Warren Papers, Oregon Historical Society.)

"A Little Tough on the Fish." This postelection cartoon by Harry Murphy portrayed the sentiment of most Oregon voters during the 1908 election by depicting an ugly contest among unsympathetic interests, all of whom were trying to have their salmon and consume them too. (*Oregonian*, 4 June 1908.)

opponents, legislators agreed in principle and then fact to concurrent jurisdiction of the fisheries. They coordinated closed seasons and gear regulations, and except for some last-minute shenanigans in the Oregon statehouse, the resulting agreement worked amazingly well. In 1915 the legislatures renewed the agreement and established a principle of mutual consent concerning fishery regulations. They then submitted the resulting "Columbia River Compact" to Congress, which extended its federal sanction in 1918. After forty-four years of federal urging and interstate feuding, Oregon and Washington finally had attained a measure of coordinated management, but peace came at considerable political cost to the industrial fishery. Fishers and canners had lost most of their political influence and nearly all of their ability to play one state against the other.[71]

The history of wildlife conservation is still a highly contested subject. The eminent historian Samuel Hays has argued that "conservation, above all, was a scientific movement," and A. Hunter Dupree insisted that it took the Pinchot-Ballinger dispute in 1910 to reduce conservation to "the very stuff of politics." Such arguments make Progressive conservation seem like a new and holy endeavor sullied by external forces, yet, as we already know from the history of fish culture, conservation was neither new nor apolitical in the 1900s. As early as the 1880s, fishers had expanded the content of salmon management far beyond a technical pursuit of fish culture. Early struggles over declining runs suggest that fishery management had also become a process of deciding who should benefit. Fish fights were really Spencerian struggles to divide society into haves and have-nots, to turn natural space into social space, and to claim exclusive use of resources for oneself and one's group.[72]

Every interest claimed to speak for citizens and salmon, but their rhetoric revealed that the core dispute was less about salmon than social legitimacy. Gillnetters portrayed themselves as hardworking family men, not unlike independent farmers. They contrasted the owners of traps, wheels, and seines as corpulent capitalists, who siphoned the wealth of labor and nature and employed too many Asians. The critique was as much about democratic work and race as about conservation. Their opponents defended themselves as decent citizens, property owners, and taxpayers. *They* were the honest farmers of streams, not gillnetters, who were rootless immigrant vandals. Definitions of "Americanism" were as much at stake as salmon in these debates. As the social struggle unfolded, northwesterners segregated the salmon fisheries by race, ethnicity, class, and geography, but dividing and redividing the natural spaces of streams and ocean did not help salmon. More often it deflected attention from the more germane issues of unbridled consumption and growing social complexity, and it always devastated marginal communities.[73]

6 / Urban Salmon

Sportsmen loom large in historical interpretations of modern conservation because some scholars have argued that conservation's roots were urban and elite and that hunters and anglers were the "spearheads" of reform after 1850. Sportsmen's love for nature thus prompted them to decry the despoliation of wilderness when few others cared, but sportsmen did more than criticize. They lobbied for change, and their efforts produced numerous state fish and game commissions to protect and regulate resources. Conservation entered its second, more recognizable phase about 1900, when Progressive social Brahmins such as Gifford Pinchot and Theodore Roosevelt blended the themes of efficiency, expertise, and equity into a timely campaign to save forests. But in elevating the influence of experts, they also created antidemocratic agencies run by elites.[1]

Anglers were central players in these developments. Sportfishing began as a nineteenth-century pastime of urbanites, but as enthusiasts organized clubs and articulated values, they extended their influence beyond the city. Although they exploited some areas to fuel urban growth, they set aside other areas as refuges. They also established rules to control behavior and employed fish culture to boost production. What began in the East in the 1830s had reached the Pacific Northwest by the 1870s. Anglers missionized their values through writings, exhibitions, and physical manipulations of the environment. They were not politically significant during the nineteenth century, but by 1910 urbanization and Progressive voting reforms had created the social and electoral conditions for a rapid reorganization of salmon fishing.

Prior historical interpretations help explain the rise of conservation and its dominance by particular social groups, but they do not satisfactorily explore the environmental and social consequences of this middle- and upper-class, urban movement. Sportfishers introduced exotic fish to "improve nature," but some of their efforts seriously compromised indigenous plants and animals. Following the 1908 election, northwestern anglers waged a relentless campaign against overfishing. By 1956 they had won control of most streams and imposed radically different rules for fishing, but their victories left a long trail of displaced peoples, devastated communities, and disrupted management. By 1960 sportfishers had successfully claimed the public mantle of "Most Worthy Protector," but during their reign salmon conservation remained as much about eliminating rivals as saving salmon.

American angling grew up in the cities. It gained popularity with middle- and upper-class urbanites as a pastoral retreat. Anglers sought more than fish, however; they moralized and gendered a landscape that they preserved and enhanced by appropriating space, controlling behavior, and reordering nature.

Sportfishing was a product of urban and elite tastes. Angling culture began among a middling class of merchants and courtiers in seventeenth-century London. This was the society of Izaak Walton, an upwardly mobile Anglican priest and author who used fishing to inculcate piety and befriend powerful bishops. Walton's *The Compleat Angler* languished in obscurity for more than a century before nineteenth-century Americans erected him as a sort of patron saint of sport. His upper-middle-class homilies evolved into the guiding principles of respectable recreation. By the 1830s Philadelphia, New York, and Boston professionals and businessmen were creating fishing clubs and pursuing their avocation on the outskirts of towns. By the 1870s Portland also had a "Sportsmen's Club." These clubs became rural retreats and social gathering spots. Members had to comport themselves like gentlemen in the lodge and on the water. To maintain civility and prevent depletion, they insisted on fishing by hook and line. This leveled competition between friends, elevated the challenge of capture, and heightened its significance while limiting the scope of mastering nature. Clubs became pastoral refuges where genteel urbanites could affirm their masculinity among peers.[2]

Urbanization forced anglers to move farther afield. Members of the Schuylkill Fishing Club had to move their location twice during the nineteenth century to escape the environmental changes that accompanied expanding Philadelphia. Growth also brought more anglers. Late-nineteenth-century transportation advances such as interurban railways allowed more people to escape the city. In Portland and Vancouver, British Columbia, anglers began to establish new clubs on the edge of town. Those in search of more rugged experiences ventured to more remote areas such as the Adirondacks in New York or the Rogue River in Oregon. Such excursions traversed rough country, yet participants remained genteel adventurers. Sportsmen and sportswomen spent one to several weeks touring through dense forests and steep terrain, all the while accompanied by an entourage of guides and porters who carried luggage, rowed boats, cleaned fish, and cooked meals.[3]

The development that drove sportsmen farther afield threatened them in other ways as well. Not only did industrialization and urban growth induce environmental changes that compromised habitat, they also brought anglers into greater contact with people who did not share their values. As game diminished, sportsmen began to compete with market hunters and fishers for animals and space. Such encounters threatened not only the material rewards of hunting and fishing but also the sporting aesthetic. Hunting and fishing for profit or subsistence seemed antithetical to the sporting life.[4]

To better control the actions of others, sportsmen tried to prescribe ethical behavior in the woods and on the water. Hunters and anglers proselytized a code of sportsmanship that was both altruistic and self-serving. They displayed rare foresight in promoting bag and creel limits; but they were also imposing genteel values on society as a whole. They also began to make proprietary claims to space, purchasing blocks of land as private reserves, lobbying strenuously for fish and game laws, and advocating the preservation of vast areas like the Adirondacks as pristine wilderness. Nineteenth-century sportsmen thus tried to reserve the bounty of the woods and waters for themselves by asserting the moral authority of their class and culture.[5]

Fish culturists and conservationists also participated in this elitist endeavor. In his report to Vermont, George Perkins Marsh declared, "The people of New-England are suffering, both physically and morally, from a too close and absorbing attention to pecuniary interests." Marsh's antidote was angling, "an innocent and healthful recreation," he argued, that deserved "to be promoted rather than discouraged by public and even legislative patronage." Seth Green and Livingston Stone were avid anglers, as were Robert Barnwell Roosevelt and his nephew Theodore Roosevelt, who insisted that the vigorous life of sport was necessary to maintain a manly, masterful people. Such arguments cast angling as a source of national virtue.[6]

Having wrapped themselves in the flag, anglers contrasted their self-image with a darker portrait of those who had no time or interest for sportsmanship. Canada's Samuel Wilmot decried whites and Indians who used torch lights and spears to victimize salmon. Such methods were "unlawful," "murderous," and "merciless." Oregon fish and game protector F. C. Reed railed against spear fishing as "the most barbarous, cruel, and destructive mode of taking fish that has yet been invented; in fact, this mode was never invented, but was handed down to the white race by the Indians, who never possessed any inventive power." Anglers denigrated bait, subsistence, and market fishers as "pot fishers." David Starr Jordan bemoaned the presence of the "trout hog" on the Pacific slope. Such sociopaths threatened anglers' Jeffersonian right to pursue happiness; to protect their rights, they demanded that these "un-American" fishers be excluded from their waters.[7]

Angling elitists traveled the country extolling the virtues of their avocation. Captain Cleveland Rockwell, Rudyard Kipling, and Zane Grey all fished and wrote about Oregon's salmon streams, erasing inconvenient marks of settlement and development to accentuate the sense of adventure. Settings were sublime, company was fraternal, and fish were noble. Kipling escaped the oppressive environment of Portland by going *mano a mano* with a "royal" chinook on the wild Clackamas, but he failed to mention that his fishing hole was less than a mile from the rack at the U.S. Fish Commission (USFC) hatchery. Similarly, Grey recounted the lower Rogue River as a "wilderness" despite passing numerous gold mines and guiding his boat around one rapid via a fish ladder.[8]

These travel narratives also served as morality plays. Authors peppered their tales with racially and occupationally marginal characters. Chinese workers, Indians, and bait fishers gave stories a contrapuntal moral edge; the authors' ability to transcend the moral turpitude that surrounded them made obvious the superiority of angling. Kipling endured Dantesque encounters with Chinese cannery workers who "looked like blood-besmirched yellow devils." Grey was a man among men who won over Indians with his mastery of the fly and mocked his Japanese cook's inability to pronounce English or capture steelhead. Rockwell was a missionary who converted the uncultivated to fly-fishing and then mocked their efforts to emulate him.[9]

Although angling grew in popularity, not everyone subscribed to the central tenets of genteel traditions. Middle- and upper-class sportsmen could write customs and laws for angling and hunting, but working-class fishers followed their own principles. They even turned elitist disdain into a badge of honor. Portland resident Frederick Bracher boasted that his friends "were all 'pot fishermen.'" They were not interested in "killing for killing's sake. . . . [but] usually caught only what we wanted to eat." Bracher mocked the pretensions of Zane Grey and private fishing clubs. He "wanted no part of such effete pastimes." Bracher's rejection of genteel traditions revealed tensions that transcended conservation. Being a "pot fisherman" or "poacher" was more often a sign of class identity than of predatory behavior.[10]

Anglers also imposed their values on nature, finding it suitable or not for their recreation. Sportfishers assessed landscapes according to their accommodation to pastoral imagery. On a trip into Washington's Northern Cascades, Zane Grey portrayed the transition from a logging clear-cut to an uncut forest as an escape from "a ghastly naked blot on the earth" to the "forest primeval!" But when the Douglas fir forest failed to produce "golden aspen glades, flaming maple thickets, where the elk bugled and deer rustled," it became "[m]elancholy, lonely, silent as a grave." Truly genteel angling required sylvan glades, and the Northern Cascades lacked these qualities. Nature was deficient.[11]

What was true for landscapes also applied to fish. In estimating the worth of a species, anglers considered its "character," which was shorthand for a fish's preference of bait, fighting ability, and taste. Those that passed muster were lionized; those that failed were labeled "coarse" or "rough." Charles Hallock argued, "Define me a gentleman, and I will define you a game fish; which the same is known by the company he keeps, and recognized by his dress and address, features, habits, intelligence, haunts, food, and manner of eating. . . . [O]ther coarse fish might 'pass in a crowd' as the shabby genteel frequently do."[12]

Urban anglers tried to turn their values into reality by creating pastoral middle grounds, places that were neither wholly wild nor completely denatured. They passed laws to constrain or exclude people from rivers and employed fish culture to reorder the ecological organization of streams.

One way of creating these middle landscapes was through technology. Beginning in 1870, Oregon anglers demanded the construction of a fishway at Willamette Falls to help salmon pass into the upper Willamette Valley. "There is no reason," one writer argued, "why every settler in Oregon should not be able to obtain, at a trifling cost, an abundant supply of the very best quality of this fish." Salmon would "distribute themselves throughout the waters of all the tributaries" and "thus supply the people of our largest and best valley in the most economical and convenient manner with a very valuable article of food." Two decades later the editor of the *Salem Daily Statesman* repeated the request. The upper Willamette *needed* a fishway, Clare Irvine complained, because it contained "no fish whatever," or at least "none worth mentioning."[13]

For Irvine and others, the Oregon country remained incomplete, but the problem was not so much an absence of fish as a deficiency of the right sort of fish. Yet what qualified as the right fish could be highly subjective. In

1857 George Perkins Marsh endorsed species that increased profit; in the 1870s Spencer Baird deplored "inferior fish," but his primary criterion was taste. Thus the scup was his candidate *par excellence.*" In 1892 a resort owner considered it "a shame that [a local lake] has not got different kinds of good fish," but in this case a "good fish" was one that put up a fight for anglers. Angling writer Ben Lampman argued that others saw "an aching void around and over them" because they were "lonely" for the fish of their youth.[14]

Oregonians had several ways of rectifying this inadequacy; each involved radically reorganizing the ecology of streams and lakes. Using poisons and dynamite, they eradicated undesirable fish and replaced them with exotic species. Through private efforts and petitions to the USFC, Oregonians transplanted carp, shad, whitefish, sunfish, bream, perch, crappie, calico, pickerel, pike, striped bass, tench, bullfrogs, eels, and several species each of trout, bass, and catfish. Many came to view the USFC as a kind of biological mail-order house, supplying not only fish but rice seed, water plants, and scientists as well.[15]

The vast majority of the petitioners of the USFC were urban businessmen and professionals. Merchants, doctors, lawyers, architects, and politicians made individual requests and petitioned as groups of "leading citizens," as Portland's Mazamas mountaineering club, and as rod and gun clubs. The largest and most persistent of these clubs was the Oregon Fish and Game Association (OFGA), a group led by Portland magnates Joseph Teal and A. E. Gebhard. The OFGA requested so many fish that it eventually took on proprietary airs. In 1903 and 1905 the OFGA suggested that the U.S. Bureau of Fisheries (USBF) send fish directly to them and they would decide where it would be best to plant the fish. The USBF declined the offer.[16]

Transplanting was not completely driven by urban demands, but even the exceptions highlight the class aspect of its appeal. A few farmers also requested fish, but these tended to be owners of very large operations near Portland, Salem, or Yakima. One of these farmers was also a state senator. A few industrial fishers also supported transplants, including Oregon fish commissioner F. C. Reed, Astoria lawyer J. Q. A. Bowlby, and canner and wheel owner Frank Warren Jr., who was also an active member of the OFGA.[17]

With time, however, transplants attracted increasing criticism for the ecological changes that they wrought. Trout, bass, pike, and catfish tended to prey on juvenile salmon and eggs. Once industrial fishers learned of these problems, they and a few anglers strenuously opposed further introductions of predatory species, and in 1886 Spencer Baird acknowledged these concerns. Baird explained to an Oregon congressman that he opposed shipping catfish: "It will . . . disturb the balance of nature, and if it thrives there, it will be to the disadvantage of native species." In 1888, Marshall McDonald made this formal policy. Later commissioners endorsed and extended the ban to include black bass and other species, and Oregon made it law in 1901.[18]

The USFC's opposition to black bass proved particularly contentious from the 1880s to the 1920s. Even though bass had devastated eastern salmon and trout streams, western anglers and resort promoters lobbied vigorously for exemptions. The Portland Rod and Gun Club countered the USFC by claiming that David Starr Jordan said bass would not harm salmon; when that tack failed they tried to ingratiate themselves by supplying technical information on runs and harvests. Clare Irvine used the *Statesman* to drum support for bass plantings in the Willamette, and Scott Morris sent petitions and hounded congressmen for three years because he thought that bass would lure tourists to Florence, Oregon. Irvine, Morris, and others simply regarded the USFC's decision as a "mistake."[19]

Angler pressure began to overwhelm government resistance. Resort communities in eastern Oregon and Washington demanded bass and insisted that the lakes and rivers they wanted to plant had no "natural outlets" or were above falls that salmon could not pass. When the USFC noted that some of these lakes did have outlets via flumes, and that bass could still descend over falls, advocates pressured state and congressional representatives. State commissioners buckled, and even federal administrators paused. George Bowers wrote to one applicant: "I cannot but admire the persistency of the sportsmen in your vicinity in attempting to secure [bass], but believe that if they understood the situation fully and viewed it from the point which I took they would not desire to have bass introduced there. As frequent letters of refusal do not seem satisfactory, I will say that when I [or my assistant] visit the Pacific Slope again, . . . you will be advised in order that a conference may be arranged." Although Bowers never altered his opposition, neither could he simply ignore the political influence of anglers and dismiss their requests out of hand.[20]

As in its struggle over regulation, the USFC ultimately could not enforce its will with respect to transplants. Bass policy was less a wall of opposition than a series of backfires. The USFC initially denied all requests, but when pressure persisted they granted applications for ponds or supposedly isolated lakes. In reality, these were convenient fictions. The USFC expected residents to plant other lakes once fish multiplied, and by 1896 William Ravenal admitted that "at different times bass have been introduced in so-called land-locked lakes in Washington, Oregon, and Idaho; and the Commission is now fearful that they have gotten into some of the tributaries of the Columbia River." Even when the USFC denied applications, its employees often advised people on where they could obtain such fish privately.[21]

In the end, there were too many actors and too much water to prevent introductions. Anglers made transplants under cover of darkness, and governments could not control their own employees. In 1892 the USFC shipped five hundred bass to Oregon fish commissioner E. P. Thompson to mollify Clare Irvine. Thompson maintained that the bass were for a private pond in Salem, but he instead dumped them directly into the Willamette. Oregon commissioners continued to ignore the USBF into the 1930s. Oregon game warden Matt Ryckman was famously defiant. One approving angler explained with a conspiratorial wink that "Uncle Matt . . . did not agree" with federal policy, so he made many "surreptitious" plants in the interests of constituent anglers.[22]

Anglers planted exotic fish in hopes of creating a more bountiful nature, but they could not control the results. Fish rarely stayed put. Ponded fish escaped into streams during floods or dam breaks, and fish planted in one stream often migrated elsewhere. In 1879 the USFC transplanted striped bass from the Chesapeake Bay to the Sacramento River, but the USFC halted the program after learning that bass preyed on salmon. The anadromous bass nevertheless had migrated up the coast to the Rogue River by 1899 and to Coos Bay by 1914. In another incident the USBF disposed of its display fish at the Lewis and Clark Fair by dumping them in the exposition lake. When the lake's dam later broke, a large school of bass, crappie, and perch washed into the Willamette River.[23]

Nor could humans predict the impact of exotic fish on indigenous plants and animals. As carp spread throughout the lower Columbia River, their feeding habits all but eliminated native wapato plants. Similarly, by the 1940s anglers were catching a "mixed creel" of exotic "spiny-rayed fishes" in coastal lakes, but the native salmon and trout had vanished. Exotic fish had little impact on Columbia salmon until the construction of dams along the main stem of the river, but then they multiplied rapidly in the resulting slack-water pools. By the 1990s the Columbia and Snake held fewer and fewer salmon but large stocks of carp, shad, bass, and walleye.[24]

These exotic fish were a crucial component of anglers' pastoral vision. Stanley Jewett insisted that the "men of foresight who brought [fish] from 'back home,' were the men who helped develop the West as a better place in which to live." Ben Lampman agreed that it was "their glad gift to us." This version of rural finishing reflected essentially urban interests, but such parochialism did not bother Jewett and Lampman. For them, Oregon was simply Portland writ large. "The general disposition of the Portland populace," Lampman argued, "will [doubtless] serve to reveal the opinion of the region." And that opinion, according to Lampman, was that exotic fish brought "true contentment . . . to town and farm house." Urban anglers had conflated city and country into a seamless image of a pastoral Oregon.[25]

Other Oregonians were less enthusiastic about these changes, but also less capable of opposing them. Industrial fishers feared exotic fish, which they called the "finny enemies" of salmon. They criticized the USBF for the "blunder" of "placing worthless fish in our streams for the edification of certain sportsmen." Commissioner Bowers sympathized but insisted that the states were responsible for allowing transplants. Anglers smugly accepted the changes as a fait accompli. According to Lampman, even if some fish did harm salmon, "there is nothing we can do about it, save to forgive the enthusiasm of" the transplanters and adjust. The heyday of the industrial fishery was fast waning, and Oregon was changing in ways that commercial fishers could neither control nor accommodate. Anglers owned the future.[26]

As urbanization and resource extraction accelerated after 1900, and as Progressive Era reforms reoriented the locus of political power in Oregon salmon management, salmon habitat and the social position of fishers went into free-fall decline.

Oregon shifted from a predominantly rural to a numerically urban society after 1900. Between 1900 and 1930 the state's population grew 131 percent to 953,000. The greatest gains occurred in the Willamette Valley, and cities grew faster than surrounding areas. Portland, Salem, Eugene, Medford, and Klamath Falls expanded rapidly because of immigration, natural increase, and annexation, while towns like Astoria stagnated. By 1930, 51.3 percent of the state's population lived in urban areas. The trend stalled during the Great Depression, but by 1950 the state's population had reached 1,521,000. Oregonians increasingly lived in concentrated areas along a corridor that ran from Medford through Grants Pass, Roseburg, Eugene, Corvallis, Albany, and Salem to the greater Portland area.[27]

As cities grew, they reshaped an ever-expanding area around them. Suburbanization extended the immediate impact of urban living in Portland, Salem, Eugene, and Medford, but cities reached beyond the suburban limits as well. Urban living demanded power generation and water. Beginning in the late 1880s, private companies and governments began to build

Dipnetting at obstacles such as shown in this 1890s photograph of the Wenatchee River required considerable balance, skill, and hard work, yet Indians were able to secure sizable supplies of salmon for winter use. (Special Collections Division, University of Washington Libraries, negative no. N A 1313.)

This drawing of the Willamette Falls fishery in 1841 reveals some of the changes that followed contact. Indians still fished for salmon, but in dress and modes of exchange they were increasingly being drawn into a Euro-American world. (Special Collections Division, University of Washington Libraries, negative no. N A 3995.)

Aboriginal fishing techniques such as the weir depicted in this 1841 drawing from the Wilkes expedition posed a potentially serious threat to salmon runs, but Indians removed these structures from streams once they had their winter stores. (Special Collections Division, University of Washington Libraries, negative no. NA 3991.)

Hydraulic mining ditches such as this one near Galice Creek in the early 1860s diverted streams and anything that swam in them, including juvenile and adult salmon, into artificial creeks that sometimes reached over 100 miles in length. (Oregon Historical Society, negative no. OrHi 13224.)

Hydraulic miners were still working claims as late as this 1910 operation near Galice Creek. Their water cannons washed untold tons of earth into streams all over the Pacific Northwest. The resulting silt clogged gills, suffocated fish, and buried spawning beds. (Oregon Historical Society, negative no. 99964.)

Mining dredges such as this one near Idaho City overturned riverbeds so thoroughly that a few streams, including the Yankee Fork of Salmon River, literally disappeared into the loosened gravel, making it impossible for salmon to reach spawning grounds, let alone spawn. (Special Collections Division, University of Washington Libraries, negative no. UW 277.)

Irrigators had already appropriated most of the Yakima River's summer flow, drying up the riverbed and making it impossible for fish to pass this diversion dam for the Sunnyside Canal. (U.S. Geological Survey, *Water-Supply Paper* 252 [1910]: pl. VI.)

This photo of dead salmon smolts was taken by USBF superintendent Dennis Winn in a Yakima Valley irrigation ditch during the early 1900s. Like hydraulic-mining canals, early irrigation ditches went unscreened and diverted huge numbers of juvenile and adult salmon to dead-end deaths. (John Nathan Cobb Papers, Special Collections Division, University of Washington Libraries, negative no. UW 18300.)

Grazing sheep cropped grasses, compacted soils, and changed plant communities in ways that made it more difficult for eastern Oregon and Washington watersheds to retain runoff. The result was streams that flooded more violently in winter and dried up more often in summer. (Oregon Historical Society, negative no. G: 221.)

Cow and cattle herds posed as serious a threat to salmon as sheep because their frequent visits to streams tended to erode banks, trample spawning beds, and turn creeks and streams into bovine toilets. (Oregon Historical Society, negative no. OrHi 96213.)

Loggers built structures like this Wind River splash dam to regulate the transportation of logs to mills. During logging operations they would alternate between stopping the river and unleashing violent flash floods that scoured streambeds and buried spawning grounds. (Oregon Historical Society, negative no. 60631.)

This log drive on the White Salmon River reveals the destructive torrents that resulted when loggers released water from behind splash dams to flush logs downstream. (U.S. Geological Survey, *Water-Supply Paper* 253 [1910].)

Although early dams were relatively small, they often blocked salmon entirely. Oregon passed laws as early as the 1840s requiring owners to build fishways such as this one on the John Day River, but the resulting ladders were ramshackle designs that usually failed to serve salmon. (*Biennial Report of the Fish and Game Commission of the State of Oregon* [1912]: 94.)

The massive dams of the twentieth century introduced problems of an entirely different scale. This is the experimental collection system at the base of Bonneville Dam. The entire structure was designed simply to attract migrating adult salmon *toward* fish ladders. (Harlan B. Holmes, "The Passage of Fish at Bonneville Dam," *Stanford Ichthyological Bulletin* 1 [May 1940]: 192.)

Even when logs reached lumber mills they could still threaten salmon by emitting natural toxins into stagnant backwaters, sink to the bottom and crush organisms, or, in the early days, smother bottoms and absorb oxygen as sawdust. (Oregon Historical Society, negative no. GI 509.)

Gillnets operated by ensnaring fish in the mesh by their gills or fins. The work was laborious and even dangerous, especially before the installation of internal combustion engines in the early 1900s to help navigate and retrieve nets. (Courtesy of the Columbia River Maritime Museum, Astoria, Oreg.)

Poundnets were large, expensive structures that diverted salmon into a trap called the heart. As this photo suggests, trap men portrayed themselves as upstanding property owners and family men, but opponents focused on the long weirs of meshing that deflected migrating salmon, blocked fishing areas, and occasionally trapped and drowned gillnetters during the night. (Courtesy of the Columbia River Maritime Museum, Astoria, Oreg., negative no. 1963.243.)

Seines were another fishing technology on the lower Columbia River. The cost of the huge, highly efficient nets limited their use to wealthy canners, who often hired the cheap labor of college-aged men looking for a summertime lark. (Special Collections Division, University of Washington Libraries, negative no. UW 5721.)

Similarly expensive to build and operate were the ingenious fishwheels that operated on the middle Columbia. These devices also monopolized fishing space and displaced Indians to less effective or more dangerous fishing sites. (Special Collections Division, University of Washington Libraries, negative no. NA 745.)

Hatchery workers often employed the same fishing tactics as Indians, but when they erected "racks" such as this one across the lower Clackamas River, they kept them in place for much longer. Most salmon injured themselves trying to escape upstream, and many instead spawned below racks on overcrowded redds. (National Archives.)

Hatchery workers used the same methods as industrial fishers to harvest salmon: seining, gillnetting, and even spearing adults (sometimes repeatedly) to find enough eggs and milt to fill hatchery quotas. (National Archives.)

This staged photo from around 1900 shows workers performing various steps in selecting, killing, and stripping salmon of their eggs and milt at the USFC's Battle Creek Station on the Sacramento River. (National Archives.)

The USFC frequently transferred salmon eggs from one Pacific Northwest stream to another. This staged photo shows hatchery workers packing fertilized eggs for shipment. Note also the ingenious organization of the hatchery interior. The troughs were designed to channel percolating water over baskets of eggs until alevins hatched, but the dense concentration of eggs created a ripe environment for diseases. (National Archives.)

By 1900 concerns about losses from predation inspired fish culturists to protect salmon fry in ponds such as these at Oregon's Central Hatchery near Bonneville. Although ponds did protect juveniles from predators, they also fostered endemic diseases and altered the evolution of salmon. (*Biennial Report of the Fish and Game Commission of the State of Oregon* [1912]: 65.)

The U S F C and U S B F used major fairs such as Portland's Lewis and Clark Exposition to promote their authority in fish culture. The Government Building housed aquariums that showed all the fish the government raised around the country, while the small shed at left was a working hatchery, officially titled the Willamette Station, which supposedly raised salmon for local streams. (National Archives.)

The ideal angling experience pitted man against fish in a solitary battle amid pastoral splendor quite similar to the conditions in this photo of a sportfisher bringing aboard a "Royal" chinook on the Willamette River in the early twentieth century. (Special Collections Division, University of Washington Libraries, negative no. UW 5741.)

The reality of modern sportfishing was increasing participation, overcrowded rivers, and group strategies such as "hoglines" just below the power plant at Willamette Falls. An individual angler stood less chance of hooking a migrating salmon than a tightly packed group simultaneously dangling hooks across the path of migrating salmon. (Oregon Historical Society, negative no. OrHi 52315.)

Read the opinions of the foremost authorities on the Rogue River fishing situation

BABE RUTH
Celebrities fish the Rogue and help to advertise It.

We ask you to VOTE YES on Ballot No. 308

A Bill Prohibiting Commercial Fishing on Rogue River

GRANTS PASS CHAMBER OF COMMERCE,
By H. L. Wilson, Vice President
By J. R. Harvey, Secretary.

ASHLAND CHAMBER OF COMMERCE,
By B. G. Barkwill, President,
By R. E. Detrick, Secretary.

MEDFORD CHAMBER OF COMMERCE,
By W. S. Bolger, President,
By C. T. Baker, Secretary.

VOTE 308 X YES

To expand fishing opportunities, anglers tried to evict nets from rivers. This 1932 brochure reveals the biases in these campaigns, as inland businesses aligned against downriver interests and then invoked the authority of everyone from U S B F commissioner Henry O'Malley (without permission) to Zane Grey and even Babe Ruth. Voters nevertheless rejected this initiative. (National Archives.)

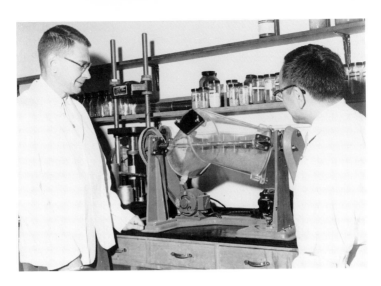

Although trained scientists had criticized fish culturists earlier in the century, by the 1940s dam building and habitat decline had forced a rapprochement between the two sides. Fish culturists adopted more rigorous methods for testing claims, and scientists developed drugs, vitamins, and feeds to improve hatchery productivity. (Oregon Historical Society, negative no. OrHi 99965.)

Although present-day hatcheries such as the rebuilt facility at Bonneville Dam appear very modern—complete with antiseptic fertilization facilities, marshaled rows of ponds, and university-trained scientists—the basic assumptions of the 1870s still prevail. Pacific northwesterners still spend huge sums of money in the hope that technology will fix social problems created by modern civilization. (Oregon Department of Fish and Wildlife.)

hydroelectric and storage dams (see table 3). By the early 1930s there were at least ninety-three sizable dams on regional rivers, including the Umpqua, Rogue, and Alsea along the coast. In 1937 the federal government counted a total of 174 dams in the Columbia River basin alone.[28]

Urban boosters were a central force in the damming of the Columbia and Snake Rivers. Rufus Woods promoted Grand Coulee with the hope that it would irrigate farms, provide cheap electricity, and transform Wenatchee into an industrial and market center. The Inland Empire Waterways Association (IEWA) waged a ninety-year battle to dam the lower Snake and turn Lewiston, Idaho, into a seaport. Portland boosters promoted a similar agenda in their own quest to dam the Columbia at the Cascade Rapids. Like Woods, Portland desired cheap electricity to increase its industrial base; like the IEWA, it aimed to boost business at the city's docks by improving upstream shipping conditions.[29]

Dam building fueled dramatic economic expansion, but it also eroded salmon habitat. Many early structures lacked adequate fish ladders, but state authorities tended to ignore infractions and to accommodate builders. Only rarely did they prosecute violators, and then only when public outrage forced the issue. By 1932 Oregon's director of fish culture Hugh Mitchell estimated that spawning grounds in the Columbia basin had already diminished by 50 percent. The construction of main-stem dams between 1933 and 1969 eliminated thousands more miles of habitat. Grand Coulee alone blocked over one thousand miles of river to one hundred thousand chinook, sockeye, and steelhead, and additional structures inundated almost all downstream habitat. Oregonians knew that dams harmed salmon, but most regarded them as engines of economic progress that were too important to stop. They mollified their concerns with the knowledge that hatcheries would make it "possible to have dams and salmon both."[30]

The construction of large dams introduced a new set of problems, but they did not negate the importance of such older activities as mining. Placer methods declined as mining companies invested in dredges that could work directly in the streambeds of southern and eastern Oregon and Idaho. Dredges could process far more material and produce far greater profits, but they also tore up spawning beds, and the loosened gravel was so porous that some streams submerged under the gravel. By the 1940s large sections of the Burnt, Grande Ronde, and Clearwater Rivers were judged "unsuitable for salmon." Mining for quicksilver boomed in 1927 and released untold amounts of mercury into streams. Sand and gravel mining also increased over time.[31]

By the 1930s many people understood the damage mining caused, but

TABLE 3. Hydroelectric, Diversion, and Storage Dams, 1888–1930

Year	Dam	Watershed	Year	Dam	Watershed
1888	T. M. Sullivan	Willamette	1915	Arrowrock	Boise
1894	Winchester	Umpqua	1915	[no name]	Okanogan
1895	Waterworks Dam	Bull Run	1917	Keechelus	Yakima
1896	Monroe Street	Spokane	1917	Wapato	Yakima
1898	Lower Bonnington	Kootenay	1918	Clear Creek	Tieton
1904	Gold Ray	Rogue	1919	Warm Springs	Malheur
1904	Ament	Rogue	1921	Savage Rapids	Rogue
1904	Kachess	Kachess	1921	Salmon Lake	Salmon Creek
1904	Keechelus	Yakima	1923	Powerdale	Hood River
1904	Leavenworth	Wenatchee	1924	Black Canyon	Payette
1904	Cazadero	Clackamas	1925	Rimrock	Tieton
1905	Enloe	Similkameen	1926	Glines Canyon	Elwha
1905	Rock Creek	Powder	1926	McKay	McKay Creek
1906	Naches	Naches	1927	Lewiston	Trinity
1906	Prosser	Yakima	1929	Dam #1	Bull Run
1906	Umatilla	Umatilla	1929	Easton	Yakima
1907	Tumwater Canyon	Wenatchee	1929	[no name]	Wallowa Lake
1907	Dryden	Wenatchee	c. 1920s	[hydroelectric]	Lemhi
1907	Cle Elum	Yakima	c. 1920s	[hydroelectric]	Powder (3 dams)
1907	Echo	Umatilla	c. 1920s	Eastern Oreg.	Grande Ronde
1909	Minidoka	Snake		P&L	(2 dams)
c. 1900s	Milton	Walla Walla	c. 1920s	Pacific P&L	Grande Ronde
c. 1900s	[no name]	Wallowa			(2 dams)
c. 1900s	Elk Creek	Rogue	c. 1920s	[hydroelectric]	Clearwater
c. 1900s	[no name]	Alsea			(5 dams)
c. 1900s	[no name]	Hood River	c. 1920s	Puget Sound	Entiat
1910	Swan Falls	Snake		P&L	
1910	Bumping Lake	Bumping	c. 1920s	Pacific P&L	Walla Walla
1910	Conconully	Salmon Creek	c. 1920s	Milton	Walla Walla
1911	River Mill	Clackamas	c. 1920s	Peacock Mill	Walla Walla
1912	Boise Diversion	Boise	c. 1920s	Eastern Oreg.	John Day
1912	Condit	White Salmon		L&P	
1912	Marmot	Bull Run	c. 1920s	[no name]	Herman Creek
1912	Pateros	Methow	c. 1920s	[no name]	Willamette
1912	Elwha	Elwha			(5 dams)
1913	Sunbeam	Clearwater	c. 1920s	[no name]	Santiam
1914	Three Mile	Umatilla			(11 dams)

ʾear	Dam	Watershed	Year	Dam	Watershed
1920s	[no name]	Willamina Creek	c. 1920s	[no name]	Washougal
1920s	[no name]	Tualatin	c. 1920s	[no name]	Kalama
1920s	[no name]	Baker Creek	1930	Leaburg	McKenzie
1920s	[no name]	Bridal Veil Creek	1930	[no name]	Metolius
1920s	[no name]	Sandy			

SOURCES: F. F. Henshaw and H. J. Dean, *Surface Water Supply of Oregon, 1878–1910*, U.S. Geological Survey, Jater-Supply Paper 370 (Washington: Government Printing Office, 1915), 217, 619, 631; Interior Department, *olumbia River Basin*, Project Planning Report no. 1–5.0–1 (Portland: Bureau of Reclamation—Region 1, 1946), 56, 157, 160, 164–72, 235, 277, 278, 284, 293, 334, 339–40, 349, 351, 389, 399; U. B. Gilroy, "Report on Status of Fish rotective Works on Certain Federal Irrigation Projects in the Northwest," 30 Mar. 1932, box 1, Records concern-g Fishways and Fish Protection Devices on Water Development Projects, 1919–35, RG 22, NA; John C. Page to rank Bell, 26 Mar. 1936, box 611, fldr. 826.53, General Classified Files, 1902–65, RG 22, NA; Robert C. Wissmar, anette E. Smith, Bruce A. McIntosh, Hiram W. Li, Gordon H. Reeves, and James R. Sedell, "A History of esource Use and Disturbance in Riverine Basins of Eastern Oregon and Washington (Early 1800s–1990s)," *orthwest Science* 68 (Special Issue 1994): 26; James W. Mullan, "Determinants of Sockeye Salmon Abundance in e Columbia River, 1880's–1982: A Review and Synthesis," *Biological Report* 86 (Sept. 1986): 3; NWPPC, "Compila-ɔn of Information on Salmon and Steelhead Losses in the Columbia River Basin" (Portland: Northwest Power lanning Council, 1985), 100; Frederick A. Davidson, "The Development of Irrigation in the Yakima River Basin d Its Effect on the Migratory Fish Populations in the River" (1965), Grant County Public Utilities District ɪbrary, Ephrata, Wash.; *Oregonian*, 20 May 1894, 5; 24 Oct. 1909, sec. 2, 12; Bowers to Superintendent, 30 Mar. ¹05, vol. 660, p. 9429; Bowers to P. M. Hall-Lewis, 5 Sept. 1905, vol. 673, p. 1481, Press Copies of Letters Sent, ʾ71–1906, RG 22, NA; Donald L. McKernan, Donald R. Johnson, and John I. Hodges, "Some Factors Influencing e Trends of Salmon Populations in Oregon," *Transactions of the Fifteenth North American Wildlife Conference* 15 ɪ950): 433; Lyman Griswold, "Ariel Dam on the Lewis River," *Civil Engineering* 1 (1931): 1115–17.

industry and government used science to blunt criticism. Oregon's Department of Geology and Mineral Industries hired Henry Baldwin Ward to defend placer mining on the Rogue. An expert on parasitology, fish migrations, and pollution, an officer in many prestigious scientific societies, and an active member of the National Wild Life Federation and the Izaak Walton League, Ward was the perfect choice, but his report revealed few of these talents. Ward's mission was to refute placer mining critics, so he focused solely on whether sediment killed migrating salmon.[32]

Ward dismissed the larger issue of habitat destruction with an odd assortment of inconsistent arguments. He deflected blame away from mining by attributing damage to other forms of development, but he then exonerated all resource users by arguing that "these changes are inevitable, but no one would wish it otherwise. Some modifications of natural condi-

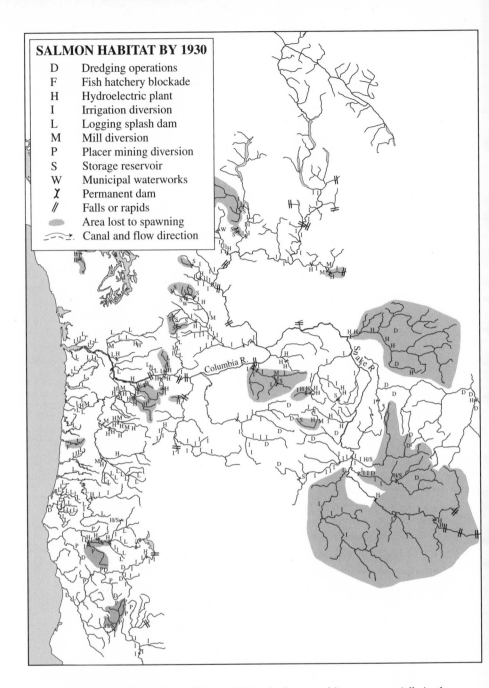

MAP 13. Significant loss of salmon habitat had occurred by 1930, especially in the Snake, Clearwater, Umatilla, Similkameen, Sandy, Clackamas, and Rogue River basins. Each incursion further concentrated reproduction, yet fishers continued to shoulder most of the blame for declining runs.

tions must be accepted if the land is ever to be made useful for human homes and the prosperous existence of man." Ward claimed that the river was in better shape than before white settlement—even though it carried much higher sediment loads. These heavy silt loads were actually good for fish, he argued, because they provided cover from anglers. The Oregon Department of Geology and Mineral Industries used Ward's apologia to discount all criticism of mining, then turned a deaf ear when other researchers criticized Ward for not considering the impact of sediment on incubating eggs.[33]

Other resource industries also continued to affect salmon. Congress created the Reclamation Service in 1902 and began to subsidize irrigation projects throughout the Pacific Northwest. Irrigated acreage expanded rapidly, but few farmers screened diversions until the federal government intervened in the 1930s. By the early 1940s parts of the Yakima River were dry, but the Bureau of Reclamation stifled criticism from Fish and Wildlife scientists at public meetings. Logging expanded as well. Improvements in steam donkey engines, high-lead yarding, saw blades, chain saws, splash dams, and log trucks allowed the industry to cut faster and deeper into forests, and this exacerbated problems with erosion, siltation, logjams, and fires. Deforestation also accelerated the snowmelt, which launched juvenile salmon on their seaward migration before they were ready to smoltify. By 1930, grazing had severely eroded large areas of eastern Oregon, and effluents from pulp and paper mills, heavy industry, and urban sewers threatened many western Oregon streams. Oxygen levels in the Willamette River dropped to less than three parts per million, making it a virtual dead zone.[34]

Most Portlanders enthusiastically supported these activities because of their economic benefits. The *Morning Oregonian,* civic boosters, labor unions, and legislators endorsed development of the region's natural resources in editorials, pamphlets, and memorials. Regional growth was portrayed as an unambiguous boon from which Portland would inevitably prosper. Growth would stimulate merchant trade with bustling communities; inland products would travel across its docks or through its train yards. The city thus profited from goods both entering and leaving its economic hinterland.[35]

But economic expansion cost the salmon fisheries dearly. Promoting logging, mining, dredging, irrigating, damming, *and* fishing made sense only in the abstract. In the real world these activities collided (see map 13). The combination of intensive harvests and habitat decline pulled the salmon fisheries into a downward spiral which the *Morning Oregonian* had clearly identified by 1910. "Development of our lumber, fruit, dairy and stock industries has proceeded on such an extensive scale that the salmon business no longer attracts the attention which was given it when its value as a trade factor was excelled only by the grain and stock industries."[36]

Urban anglers, many of whom depended on these changes for their livelihoods, were ambivalent about the reorganized Pacific Northwest. They welcomed urban economic prosperity, but they mourned the loss of nature in this supposedly unavoidable bargain. One writer eulogized that loss: "The wild beauty of Willamette Falls has been destroyed by the harness that civilization has placed upon its back, and one of its most romantic features, as witnessed in former years by the persistent efforts of salmon to jump the falls, on the brink of which Indians awaited them with ready spears, has now in its turn passed away, thus completing the triumph of use over the simplicity of Nature."[37]

Sportsmen regretted less the loss of actual Indians than the simplicity they signified in anglers' neo-Romantic critique of civilization. In real life anglers drove Indians relentlessly from desirable fishing spots. During the 1910s and 1920s Washington fish commissioner H. L. Darwin waged "a personal vendetta against Indian fishing," and both Oregon and Washington continued to persecute Indian fishers until 1976, when the Supreme Court upheld a lower court's recognition of treaty-guaranteed fishing rights.[38]

Industrial fishers also found themselves cornered by changing attitudes. Having initially justified their industry as economically more important than others, salmon fishers were increasingly vulnerable to accusations of insignificance based on their own criteria. The *Morning Oregonian* had once called the fishery an "important branch of industry," but after 1900 a new assessment emerged. Fishers were guilty of "murderous greed" and "reckless disregard for posterity's interests." Urbanites collapsed commercial fishers' complicated relationship with salmon into a simple tale of greed. Wanting salmon for themselves, urban anglers asked the state to reserve salmon in the name of the people, not special interests. Changing social and economic conditions had diminished the importance of industrial fishing in favor of recreational angling.[39]

As sportfishing grew dramatically during the twentieth century, anglers increasingly detached their interests from those of industrial fishers. To protect and ensure their pastoral vision, they created a government agency to serve them, claimed hatcheries and fish as prizes, and used their newfound power to alter the understanding of fish and the ecology of rivers.

Between 1900 and 1920 sportfishing grew increasingly popular. Anglers organized clubs and disseminated the values of light tackle and good sportsmanship to the broader public. The *Morning Oregonian* began regular coverage of sportfishing. In 1909 the paper avidly described four hundred anglers plying the Willamette River below its falls, "patiently in wait for the wary salmon." The paper treated weekend fishing as a social event. Reports highlighted notable guests and prize catches. Interest grew. By 1915 there were 1,200 fishers on the Willamette, and angling overshadowed even baseball. "From daylight to dark the boats are anchored in every available location. There are literally thousands of fishermen and they come from all parts of the United States and even some from England."[40]

But growth irrevocably altered the sport. Gone were the days of pastoral interludes on the bank. Anglers had to wake earlier and earlier to get a good spot on the river. As participation escalated, anglers began to form "hoglines" at productive spots, bunching their boats in tight rows so salmon had less chance of escape. Fishing space reached critical mass. To disperse the crowds, the *Morning Oregonian* promoted more distant streams. For the first time, sportfishing required regulating.[41]

To accommodate the growing power of sportsmen, the Oregon legislature reorganized the Fish Commission in 1911 as the Board of Fish and Game Commissioners. The new board was supposed to address the needs of both industrial fishers and sportfishers, but the split focus only deepened antagonism. Anglers wanted the master fish warden to devote more time and energy to law enforcement, and they wanted the state hatcheries to raise trout as well as salmon. They gained ground in 1915 when Governor James Withycombe appointed Carl D. Shoemaker as state game warden. Shoemaker was editor of the *Roseburg News* and a staunch supporter of outdoor sports. During his tenure, management swung sharply in favor of sportfishing. He surveyed streams to determine which should be angling havens, imposed fishing deadlines on rivers to restrict the spaces available to gillnetters and seiners, and encouraged stronger ties between the board and the Oregon Sportsmen's League, rod and gun clubs, and game protective associations. As a measure of his biases, commercial fishing received less than one page of discussion in a fifty-five-page annual report.[42]

Shoemaker shifted the focus of salmon management but did not divest it of politics. One of the complaints against Van Dusen had been his flagrant politicization of staff, but later wardens proved no different. In 1908 salmon canner and wheel owner Frank Seufert wrote to Secretary of State Frank Benson and expressed his hope that H. C. McAllister would become the spiritual successor to H. D. McGuire, who Seufert felt had been a wise and evenhanded administrator. Within a few months, however, Benson forced

McAllister to hire one of his cronies as deputy warden in order to pay off a political debt. Patronage only escalated over time. In 1914 Governor Oswald West purged the entire commission to pay political debts, and in 1915 Governor Withycombe purged both commissioners and wardens during his appointment of Shoemaker.[43]

By 1919 sportfishers had had enough. Despite Shoemaker's efforts, the Oregon Sportsmen's League accused the commission of favoring commercial interests by producing more salmon than trout at state hatcheries. League president Dr. A. K. Downs demanded an investigation of the commission and the resignation of its members. Board defenders called the accusations a Democratic ploy to purge the commission of Republicans. Governor Benjamin Olcott held a one-day hearing in June to resolve the issue. At the end of the session Olcott announced that "politics has no place in the work of the Commission or of any of its employees," but he meant this only in the narrow sense of political parties.[44]

In a broader sense the commission was hopelessly riven by fishery politics and Olcott knew it. In December he explained that "factional differences and strife" had led to a managerial equivalent of irreconcilable differences and he announced plans to divide the commission along interest lines. In January the legislature agreed. From 1920 to 1975 anglers and industrial fishers had separate game and fish commissions, respectively.[45]

Like many divorces, the estrangement only led to further complications. Property had to be divided. The Game Commission kept its home while the Fish Commission moved into separate quarters in a different Portland office. Hatcheries were the next item of business. The Fish Commission kept the stations on the Columbia, Alsea, Umpqua, Siuslaw, and Coos Rivers; the Game Commission kept the hatcheries at Tumalo, on Union Creek, and on the Klamath, Rogue, and McKenzie Rivers (see table 4). The commissions shared visiting rights to stations on the upper Willamette, Santiam, Nehalem, and Trask Rivers. Finally, there was custody of the children, and this was straightforward. The Fish Commission got salmon and the Game Commission got trout.[46]

One issue defied easy resolution. Since the 1880s steelhead had perplexed scientists and fishers alike. Ichthyologists noted that the fish's skeletal structure resembled that of rainbow trout, which inhabited the same streams, but an adult steelhead clearly looked much more like other salmon than trout. At one level the confusion revealed a problem of nomenclature. In 1894 David Starr Jordan reminded readers that both salmon and trout were European names that people applied indiscriminately to North America species. In reality, Pacific salmon (*Oncorhynchus*) were not even the same

TABLE 4.   Oregon Hatcheries by Commission and District, 1910–40

	Fish Commission			Game Commission
	District 1	District 2	Statewide	Statewide
1910	5	7	—	—
1915	10	10	—	—
1920	11	8	—	13
1925	11	11	—	8
1930	13	11	—	24
1935	—	—	22	14
1940	—	—	28	15

genus as Atlantic salmon (*Salmo*). According to Jordan, Pacific salmon were "therefore, in strictness, not salmon at all, but something more intensely salmon than the salmon of Europe itself is." The same would eventually be said about western trouts, which ichthyologists reclassified under *Oncorhynchus* in 1989.[47]

These were not simple errors of category but part of a deliberate contest to claim the use of steelhead. Indians, industrial fishers, and anglers all exploited steelhead. Indians consumed them fresh because the fish did not cure well. Canners initially ignored the fish for similar reasons, but the arrival of railroads allowed packers to ship steelhead fresh. By 1887 they were a popular and lucrative item in eastern markets. Anglers revered steelhead because they put up a wicked fight when hooked. Although many people pursued the same fish, they classified it very differently. Indians and netters knew it as salmon; anglers insisted even more fiercely that it was a trout. As Jordan noted, how one identified steelhead was "a matter of some importance, in view of the fact that the fishery laws . . . discriminate between trout and salmon, permitting the catching of the one when to take the other is forbidden." The contest was thus less about determining steelhead's true nature than about its true constituency.[48]

Anglers blended politics and science to restrict access to the fish. Arguing that steelhead was a trout and thus naturally a game fish, in 1925 they persuaded Washington legislators to stop the sale of steelhead; in 1928 Oregon legislators restricted commercial harvests of steelhead but did not outlaw its sale until 1975. Industrial fishers and Indians protested this arbitrary policy. Making steelhead a game fish deprived them of their means of living during winter. It also presented an untenable problem because nets could not discriminate legal from illegal fish. In 1935 Oregon anglers tried to naturalize this change by legislating a scientific classification as trout. Northern Willamette Valley representatives passed the measure in the House, but the Senate heeded ichthyologists' misgivings and refused the measure.[49]

The tug-of-war even extended to fish culturists. In 1892 Marshall Mc-Donald noted the interest in steelheads and began to propagate and distribute the fish in eastern waters. By 1900 William Ravenal considered steelhead propagation almost as important as salmon propagation. The USBF was even willing to pay a fifty-dollar fee to a property owner in order to harvest steelhead eggs at Willamette Falls. Fish culturists moved steelhead eggs around the region to create new runs or breed larger fish, and many eggs went to hatcheries operated by anglers. State hatcheries propagated a few steelhead until the creation of the Fish and Game Commission, when it began raising more steelhead than any other fish but chinook. After the breakup in 1920, the Game Commission hatched steelhead and other game fish, while the Fish Commission propagated any salmon species that would sell.[50]

By churning out only those fish people preferred, agencies eventually reshaped stream ecology. Coho runs dominated on coastal streams until the 1920s, but by the 1960s steelhead and chinook prevailed. The reasons for the shift were complex. Postwar logging harmed coho more than other species because coho spawned on smaller tributaries, which were more prone to damage. The Game Commission abetted this decline, however, by habitually neglecting coho in favor of the more popular steelhead and chinook.[51]

Once again politics and economy reshaped ecology and biology. The divorce of the commissions did not alleviate tensions between commercial and sporting interests; it institutionalized those differences in ways that divided people, rivers, and fish. The split made explicit the social constituencies of nature: on one side were industrial fishers and salmon; on the other, anglers and trout. Over time those alignments reshaped nature and knowledge. On "trout" or "salmon" hung the fate of people and nature.

Re-creating natural space was one aspect of the struggle between anglers and other fishers. Sportsmen also used their political leverage to rearrange the social spaces of fishing. Adopting Progressive Era tactics, they used voter initiatives to wage a relentless battle against industrial fishers in the name of conservation and the people. By 1956 they had closed almost all of Oregon's rivers to industrial fishers.

Social, economic, and environmental shifts had much to do with the reversal of fortunes in the fisheries, but political reforms also played a role. The Progressive Era lasted roughly from 1900 to 1920. Progressivism was a diffuse set of movements by a variety of groups interested in reforming American society, culture, and politics. Issues included everything from the eight-hour day to health and safety laws, temperance, and suffrage. Reform began in the cities and extended to the states and finally to the federal government during the presidencies of Theodore Roosevelt and Woodrow Wilson.[52]

The most important Progressive reforms affecting the salmon fisheries originated in Oregon in 1902: the voter initiative and referendum. These enabled voters for the first time to bypass the legislature and create or nullify laws through direct elections. This form of "direct democracy" had important implications for the angling movement. Until Oregon reapportioned political districts in the 1960s, legislatures were often inordinately biased toward rural interests. The initiative thus allowed urban interests to circumvent unsympathetic rural legislators.[53]

The initiative proved an ideal political tool for urban organizations. Unrestricted use of initiatives allowed labor unions and sportfishers "to take advantage of their organization and their generally urban location, where potential signers were conveniently concentrated." Anglers could mobilize their forces more easily than industrial fishers, and they had a base of voters. With voter participation declining throughout the period, strong factional support "enhanced tremendously the possibility for minority rule." This was especially pertinent during Oregon's special elections, when only "militant groups [tended to] appear." Demographic and economic shifts thus intersected with political reforms and changing voting patterns to create an unprecedented opportunity for anglers to seize control of fishing space.[54]

The June 1908 election between gillnetters and wheel owners revealed the political portent of demographic shifts. Gillnetters received over 7,000 more votes for their initiative than did the wheel owners for theirs, but both groups discovered that neither controlled the fate of the salmon fisheries. A seismic shift had occurred in Oregon's political landscape. In the realm of initiative politics, power shifted from the canneries, fishing halls, and legislature to Portland, Oregon City, Salem, Eugene, Roseburg, and Medford (see maps 14 and 15). Over half the votes in 1908 came from the counties of these urban centers. Multnomah County, home to Portland, accounted for more than a quarter of all returns. Urban votes now determined the fate of legislation, and urban voters' influence was about to thoroughly rearrange the balance of power in the fisheries.[55]

Anglers exploited continuing strife among fishers after 1908 to claim

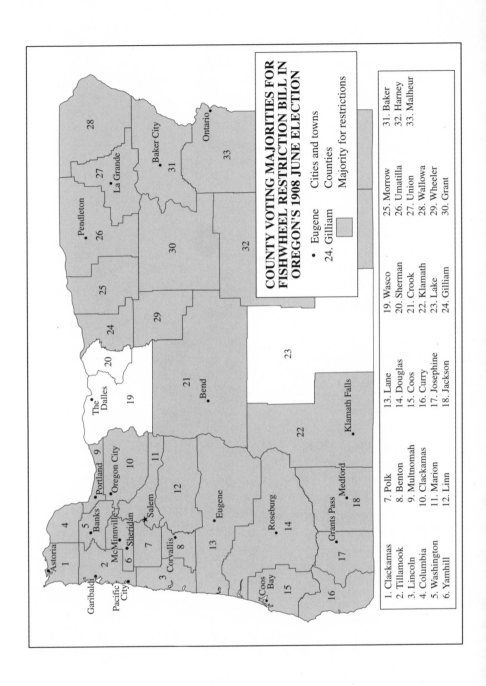

COUNTY VOTING MAJORITIES FOR FISHWHEEL RESTRICTION BILL IN OREGON'S 1908 JUNE ELECTION

- Eugene   Cities and towns
24. Gilliam   Counties

Majority for restrictions

1. Clackamas	7. Polk	13. Lane	19. Wasco	25. Morrow	31. Baker
2. Tillamook	8. Benton	14. Douglas	20. Sherman	26. Umatilla	32. Harney
3. Lincoln	9. Multnomah	15. Coos	21. Crook	27. Union	33. Malheur
4. Columbia	10. Clackamas	16. Curry	22. Klamath	28. Wallowa	
5. Washington	11. Marion	17. Josephine	23. Lake	29. Wheeler	
6. Yamhill	12. Linn	18. Jackson	24. Gilliam	30. Grant	

MAP 14. The 1908 election demonstrated voter disgust with industrial fishers.

186

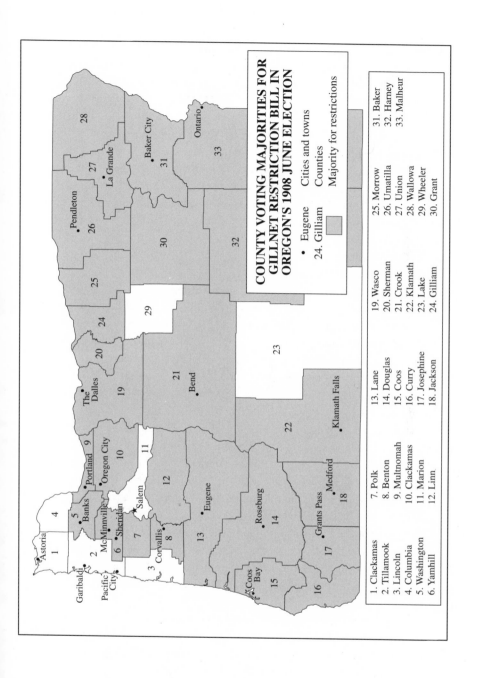

COUNTY VOTING MAJORITIES FOR GILLNET RESTRICTION BILL IN OREGON'S 1908 JUNE ELECTION

- Eugene · Cities and towns
- 24. Gilliam · Counties
- Majority for restrictions

1. Clackamas	7. Polk
2. Tillamook	8. Benton
3. Lincoln	9. Multnomah
4. Columbia	10. Clackamas
5. Washington	11. Marion
6. Yamhill	12. Linn

13. Lane	19. Wasco
14. Douglas	20. Sherman
15. Coos	21. Crook
16. Curry	22. Klamath
17. Josephine	23. Lake
18. Jackson	24. Gilliam

25. Morrow	31. Baker
26. Umatilla	32. Harney
27. Union	33. Malheur
28. Wallowa	
29. Wheeler	
30. Grant	

MAP 15. Gillnetters garnered more support, or perhaps less animosity, than wheel owners, but neither group had much support outside their local communities.

the moral high ground and appropriate the conservation banner for their own campaign to control fishing spaces. In 1910 Medford anglers played on public disgust to close the Rogue River to gillnets. The *Morning Oregonian* rejected the measure, but R. D. Hume's death in 1908 weakened opposition. Without Hume, lower Rogue fishers possessed neither the talent nor the resources to refute the misinformation coming from anglers and upstream merchants, and urban Oregonians voted the measure into law. The legislature reopened the Rogue three years later when strong runs confounded earlier claims of disaster, but they did so only after netters had conceded to a series of economically debilitating compromises concerning the times and spaces for fishing. Other fishers and fisheries would be less fortunate.[56]

The Willamette River was the next site of battle. Gillnetters on the Willamette and Clackamas had long clashed with anglers from Portland and Oregon City, but netters earned special enmity in 1909 and 1910 when state representatives from Clackamas County altered the language of the concurrent jurisdiction compromise between Oregon and Washington. By eliminating the word "tributaries" from the 1909 bill in the Oregon legislature, they exempted Willamette River gillnetters from restrictions valid elsewhere on the Columbia. Warden McAllister discovered the error too late, and netters won a court injunction when he tried to prevent fishing in March 1909.[57]

McAllister tried again in 1910. This time he blockaded rivers and roads to prevent the transportation of salmon to Portland packers, but the courts again favored netters after one of McAllister's deputies pulled a gun on a gillnetter and fled downstream with the confiscated catch. McAllister had instructed his deputy to sell the salmon to a Washington packer. McAllister did not want defiant netters and packers to profit from ill-gotten fish, but the owner of the Portland Fish Company enlisted sheriffs from two counties to pursue the deputy warden and salmon in an all-day chase. The fishmonger won the battle by recovering the fish, but the headlines so besmirched netters and packers that the local industrial fishery never recovered its reputation.[58]

This episode and others left commercial fishers increasingly vulnerable to attacks by anglers. As news accounts mounted of working-class and ethnic fishers arrested for fishing illegally, public distrust grew. Anglers used the opportunity to claim fishing space for themselves. In 1915 anglers gained the support of the *Morning Oregonian* in their campaign to restrict gillnetters from the area immediately around Willamette Falls. They extended their reach in 1918 when Oregonians voted to prohibit nets above

Oswego. This time Master Fish Warden R. E. Clanton (who was from Grants Pass), State Game Warden Shoemaker, and the *Morning Oregonian* all endorsed the closure, but it only passed on the strong support of Multnomah County voters. Rural areas continued to vote for gillnetters.[59]

Anglers tangled with industrial fishers repeatedly over the next few years, but sportfishers' only successes came by dividing their opposition. In 1919 Oregon City gillnetters tried to shift control of fishery management from the state to the counties. This would have neutralized the threat of initiative politics, but legislators refused to relinquish control of management. The legislature did vote to outlaw the use of purse seines on the Columbia, but this was largely because seiners were mostly Washington residents. In 1922 anglers tried to eliminate traps, seines, and wheels, but the initiative failed to make the ballot. In 1926 they tried again and succeeded by teaming with gillnetters. Washington anglers and gillnetters followed suit in 1934 when they passed Initiative 77. These measures did not conserve salmon, however. They simply eliminated some gear and shifted allocations to other users.[60]

The alliance with gillnetters ended abruptly when anglers began to covet coastal streams. In the early twentieth century Tillamook County drew many visitors from Portland and Salem. Situated on the Nestucca River, Pacific City was the closest coastal settlement to the Willamette Valley. The Nestucca boasted large salmon runs, and the town offered campgrounds and health spas. During the 1910s and 1920s, it was *the* place for tourists on the northern Oregon coast. Pacific City also enjoyed a vibrant commercial fishery, but visiting anglers had little love for gillnetters. Nets seemed to take too many fish and obstruct trolling. Banning an economic activity was a drastic move, however, and as anglers had learned on the Rogue, gillnetters could regain access if the evidence of destruction was less than totally persuasive. Thus anglers needed a crisis to proscribe gillnetting.[61]

That crisis began in 1925 with the return of El Niño. Late that year the Southern Oscillation reversed. By early 1926 strong surface winds were driving Kelvin waves of warm water eastward across the Pacific. Ocean levels rose dramatically from San Francisco to Ketchikan, and ocean temperatures increased significantly as far north as the west coast of Vancouver Island. By summer the warm water was causing abnormally high diversions of Fraser River sockeye through Johnstone Strait at the north end of Vancouver Island rather than through Puget Sound, and the Nestucca harvest plummeted from 605,578 pounds in 1925 to 385,863 pounds in 1926 (see table 5).[62]

TABLE 5. Nestucca River Salmon Catch, 1887–1927 (thousands of pounds)

Year	Chinook	Coho	Chum	Steelhead	Total
1887	—	—	—	—	292
1888	—	—	—	—	340
1889	—	—	—	—	456
1891	—	—	—	—	—
1899	75	206	35	—	316
1900	—	—	—	—	—
1901	18	242	27	—	287
1905	204	68	27	—	299
1906	178	168	11	—	357
1907	143	241	10	—	394
1908	136	204	7	—	347
1910	136	224	10	—	370
1911	242	484	44	—	770
1912	210	420	48	—	678
1913	9	17	—	—	26
1914	241	390	18	—	649
1915	14	267	54	—	335
1916	163	276	14	—	453
1917	136	258	18	—	412
1918	204	218	15	—	437
1919	129	163	31	—	323
1923	172	166	16	65	419
1924	263	272	21	66	622
1925	279	253	30	44	606
1926	164	173	5	44	386
1927	—	—	—	19	19

SOURCES: Figures from John N. Cobb, *The Pacific Salmon Fisheries,* Fisheries Document 1092 (Washington: Government Printing Office, 1930); Robert E. Mullen, *Oregon's Commercial Harvest of Coho Salmon, "Oncorhynchus kisutch"* (Walbaum), 1892–1960, Information Report Series, Fisheries 81–3 (Corvallis: Oregon Department of Fish and Wildlife, Fish Division, 1981); F. C. Cleaver, *Fisheries Statistics of Oregon,* Contribution 16 (Salem: Oregon Fish Commission, 1951).

As with earlier declines, anglers immediately assumed that gillnetters were at fault. Miscounting, they said the harvest had fallen 100,000 pounds and prophesied extinction. The actual drop was in fact far greater, but the 1925 run had been above recent averages. Furthermore, the El Niño affected

1926 runs from California to British Columbia. Harvests plummeted coastwide, yet, as with most El Niños, the effects did not last. By early 1927 runs had rebounded in most areas, but gillnetters never learned whether the Nestucca also recovered. Few people knew about El Niño, and no one suspected its far-reaching effects on ocean and terrestrial climate. Sir Gilbert Walker had yet to publish his definitive paper linking the Southern Oscillation to global weather patterns, and scientists lacked the tools to decipher these events. Not until the 1950s did California oceanographers perceive connections between El Niño and fluctuating salmon runs, and public recognition would wait even longer.[63]

Ignorance and misperception allowed fishers and politicians to fixate on fishing as the reason for the decline. State representatives Arthur McPhillips and Walter Russell responded to the dramatic decrease by introducing House Bill 282 to outlaw all gear on the Nestucca other than "hook and line, commonly called angling." Both representatives were from McMinnville, forty miles east of Pacific City, and one held extensive real estate holdings in and around Pacific City. Local campground owner Arthur Beals also supported the bill because "it might work to the benefit of [his] summer resort" by attracting more customers. In Salem, McPhillips spoke in the name of the people and for conservation, but H.B. 282 had more to do with land speculation and creating a sportsman's paradise.[64]

House Bill 282 quickly revealed a geography to statehouse politics. After a second reading, the speaker sent H.B. 282 to the Game Committee, which reported favorably eight days later. Next Nestucca representative George Winslow moved the bill to the Fisheries Committee. The contest over referrals illuminated a polarized power struggle. The Game Committee was the traditional stronghold of sportsmen's interests in the legislature, and its members were from interior communities like Arlington, Eugene, West Linn, Roseburg, Portland, Burns, and Helix. The Fisheries Committee advocated commercial interests, and most of its members came from the coastal and lower Columbia towns of Astoria, Rainier, Toledo, Myrtle Point, and Sixes.[65]

Thus, determining which committee would review H.B. 282 proved crucial to its fate. When the Game Committee recommended passage, Winslow tried to buy time while building opposition to the bill. Referral to Fisheries would at least delay passage and might even lead to a tabling. Russell knew this and recalled the bill before any damage could be done. Representative S. P. Pierce of Sixes made a last-ditch attempt to postpone the bill indefinitely, but he lost a procedural vote. These efforts now appear as a descending spiral of failure; each successive motion failed by a greater margin. The House passed H.B. 282, forty-one to seventeen. The six coastal representatives who voted against the measure were a drop in the bucket compared to the fourteen Portland representatives who voted for it.[66]

Events proceeded rapidly in the Senate. The president referred the bill to Fishing Industries, which only had two members from the coast: Senator Hall from Marshfield and Chairman Norblad from Astoria. The other five were from The Dalles, Grants Pass, Oregon City, and two from Portland. Most members had little connection to the industry, and the committee recommended passage the same day. Senator Norblad motioned the bill back to committee to lobby against it, but three days later the committee again recommended passage. The following day the Senate passed the bill, twenty-one to six, and eight days later the governor signed it into law.[67]

The anglers' power play threatened the livelihood of eighty fishermen, so Nestucca fishers and farmers began a grassroots effort to overturn the bill. Local farmers immediately barred anglers from crossing their land to fish the river, and some pressed trespass charges. The Nestucca local of the Tillamook County Fishermen's Union and the Cloverdale Grange also began a campaign to refer the bill to the June ballot so voters could reject it. Fishers H. W. Southmayd and John T. McLaughlin and farmers G. D. Sanders and Adella Jensen drafted the petition, organized the drive, and coordinated petition circulators.[68]

Because coastal populations were small, circulators gathered most signatures in the Willamette Valley. This meant working in opposition territory. Fishers did receive support from the Portland Central Labor Council and the State Council of Fishermen. Both organizations cited the loss of jobs and investments in equipment as reasons for opposing the closure. Circulators nevertheless had trouble filling petitions, and some fishermen spent more than a month away from home soliciting signatures in Salem, Oregon City, Portland, and elsewhere. Not until the end of May did they file petitions with the secretary of state and qualify for the ballot.[69]

Opponents of the closure concentrated their rhetorical efforts on the official pamphlet that the state distributed before elections. Both the Grange and unions drafted arguments. They highlighted the unemployment of eighty fishermen, whom they depicted as family men and small farmers; the destruction of a $100,000 industry; and the loss of revenue to the Fish Commission. They characterized the bill as "one of the freaks of the 1927 legislature" and attributed its passage to political horse trading. The pamphlet arguments were the only official response made by the coalition during the campaign, but a few opponents also wrote letters to newspapers.[70]

Foremost among these writers was fisherman Ernest Edmunds. Unlike most writers, Edmunds offered what turned out to be accurate information on the condition of runs and the costs of closure. Arguing that it was "ridiculous . . . to think that anglers can catch enough salmon . . . to justify the closing of [the Nestucca] to commercial fishing," Edmunds tried to defuse tensions by claiming there were enough fish for everyone, but his strategy was weak and the media ignored him. His patient explanations distinguished him, however, as the best-informed writer in the state.[71]

Sportfishers ignored the voter pamphlet in favor of a relentless media attack that quickly overshadowed their opponents. Sporting organizations inundated newspapers with letters and advertisements supporting the closure. They depicted the Nestucca gillnetters as "ruthless," as "greedy," as "a small coterie of commercial fishermen looking only to their own pecuniary interests." Anglers, on the other hand, were "loyal, patriotic citizens" who urged all "true and loyal citizen[s] to use their influence" to close the Nestucca. The editor of the *Klamath Falls Evening Herald* encouraged "every red blooded citizen who likes to catch a fish" to vote yes, while E. K. Plasec asked rhetorically, "Why should 50 commercial fishermen be allowed to take all the fish from the Nestucca river . . . for the purpose of barter and trade as against all the rest of the people of the state who have helped put them there?"[72]

Angling enthusiast R. B. Denny seemed to epitomize urban assumptions about gillnetting and rural labor. Under the *Oregon Journal* headline "Says fishermen few and that the income of those few is meagre; State better off with Nestucca a sportsmen's resort," Denny argued, "The average fisherman on Nestucca Bay did not make as a gross return to exceed $275." Denny insisted that such small wages would never be missed by the state as a whole. The paper's editors made similar points through doublespeak. Hailing the Multnomah Hunters and Anglers Club for its "devoted" efforts at conserving salmon, they argued that the Nestucca closure was "an instance where closing really means the opening of the river for all time. . . . How far may commercial fishing go before destroying the resource?"[73]

Such arguments were simple, simplistic, and deeply flawed. They misconstrued the complicated natural forces driving the "crisis," and they ignored the importance of seasonal work in the diversified rural economy. Unfortunately for gillnetters, many urban voters shared anglers' assumptions about "hicks."[74]

Anglers also used fish culture to justify closure. Oregon, they argued, should preserve the Nestucca as a "seed stream." It could then transplant excess eggs to restore other streams. The pseudonymous "Nestucca River

Farmer" asked rhetorically, "Do the people of Oregon want to adopt a constructive policy of conservation and protect this great brood stream, capable of producing nearly 100,000,000 salmon eggs annually, and thereby promote the best interest of commercial fishing as a whole and also protect the angling interest, or do they want to destroy these interests by the continuance of unbridled commercial fishing?" The Douglas County Sportsmen Association implored voters to sustain the ban so "one of Oregon's great natural resources may be conserved and perpetuated for the use of all our citizens."[75]

At the end of the campaign opponents challenged the anglers' arguments by turning the rhetoric of "the people" on its head.

> Persistent and effective effort on the part of organized sportsmen, operating through the state game commission and allied clubs, forced the passage of the bill. . . . It is argued that the interest of the entire people of the state, represented, we presume, by the interests of the sportsmen, is paramount in importance to the interests of the local fishermen. . . . So runs the argument, but we are not, in this case, much impressed by it. . . . The question may properly be raised as to just why the right of some people to make a legitimate living should be cramped by the desire of a relatively few men to flick a fly or cast a spoon.[76]

Opponents also pointed to contradictions in the "seed stream" scheme. The funds that supported state hatcheries, they noted, came from the license and poundage fees collected from local commercial fishers, so closing the river would undermine funding for the state hatchery. The *Oregon Voter* warned, "Anglers . . . if they prohibit commercial fishing, may spite themselves."[77]

Not all anglers ignored the social consequences of creating this "sportsmen's paradise." M. Sommer wrote to the *Oregon Journal* on behalf of the Oregon Sportsmen's Club of Waterloo, Oregon. Sommer regretted the effort to close the Nestucca, and his club publicly opposed the bill because of the hardship it would cause local residents. But Sommer's concern was less than completely altruistic. He worried about "hordes of 'wealthy sportsmen' from every state and corner of the world camping along the stream until the last fish is caught out." Sommer and his fellow club members were seemingly motivated as much by a fear of outsiders as by the fate of rural fishers.[78]

The newspaper campaign revealed geographic biases. Papers in Portland, Salem, McMinnville, Banks, and Roseburg ran front-page articles and editorials favoring closure and buried opponents in the letters section.

David Robinson, chair of the Oregon State Sportsmens Association, rallied angler support in Portland and Roseburg, and the *Portland Telegram* featured his letter at the top of page 1 under the large banner "Opponents of Nestucca Fish Bill are Flayed." The same paper published Plasec's letter at the top of page 3 under the headline "Who Owns Fish In Nestucca?" Ernest Edmunds's letter appeared the same day in the same paper, but on the bottom of page 12 under the small leader "Claims Commercial Fishing Doesn't Hurt Sport Fishing."[79]

Gillnetters faced an uphill struggle just to get their message published, but some newspapers did support them. Most of these papers were located in communities near the Nestucca or on the coast. Tillamook, Garibaldi, Sheridan, Coos Bay, and Eugene papers opposed closure, as did the *Oregon Voter*, which condemned anglers' heavy lobbying and the bill's economic harm. Eastern Oregon papers leaned toward closure, but they treated it as a political oddity. Bend editors favored the measure but admitted ignorance. The Baker paper deferred to the State Game Commission, "who had studied the matter," but it complained about having to vote on an issue so distant to eastern Oregon. The Dalles paper also backed closure but wondered whether there was a workable compromise that would preserve commercial fishing in Nestucca Bay. Distance limited familiarity, but it also seemed to foster the sort of detached consideration that was sorely missing in western Oregon.[80]

Anglers spent liberally, and their political investments paid great dividends. The Douglas County Sportsmens Association purchased large ads in the 24 and 25 June editions of the *Roseburg News Review*. In return the paper published a long report of the association's June meeting that featured the group's support of the closure. The Oregon State Sportsmens Association also published ads in the *News Review* and *Portland Telegram*. Willamette Valley papers gave favorable publicity to the Multnomah Hunters and Anglers Club and the Salem Rod and Gun Club but discredited organizations and individuals opposed to the measure. The *Portland Oregon Journal* attacked the Oregon Sportsmen's Club of Waterloo for publicly criticizing the closure. The Corvallis paper accused Grangers of ignorance for opposing closure, and the *Portland News* called a former game warden's support of the Nestucca fishermen "criminal."[81]

The 28 June special election exposed all the gillnetters' weaknesses. Turnout was light, and voters paid far more attention to the ten measures on property and income taxes than to the fate of a small coastal stream. The typically low interest in a special election also left gillnetters vulnerable to, as one political scientist noted, the concerted voting of "militant groups"

Protect Oregon's Interests

**Duty Demands We Conserve Our
Natural Resources .**

**VOTE "YES" TO SAVE OUR FISH
AND GAME**

VOTE | 322 X | YES

and close the Nestucca to Net Fishing.

*Douglas County Sportsmen's and Game
Protective Association*

In 1927 anglers transformed their interests into higher principle by framing the closure of the Nestucca as an effort to "Protect Oregon's Interests" from a supposedly "greedy" "coterie" of local gillnetters bent on destroying their own livelihood. (*Roseburg News*, 25 June 1927.)

like anglers. As with the petition drives, gillnetters needed support away from the coast. This time they did not get it. Oregonians voted fifty-three to forty-seven for closure (see map 16).[82]

The vote totals revealed several salient details. Twenty-four of Oregon's thirty-six counties opposed the closure, but seven of the twelve counties that favored the bill were located in the Willamette Valley. Overwhelming support came from Clackamas, Marion, Multnomah, Polk, Washington, and Yamhill Counties. Portland was decisive. Outside the Willamette Valley the referendum actually lost by 6,132 votes, but in Multnomah County alone it passed by 6,028 votes. The newspaper campaign had been crucial. Counties supporting closure correlated strongly with newspapers favoring

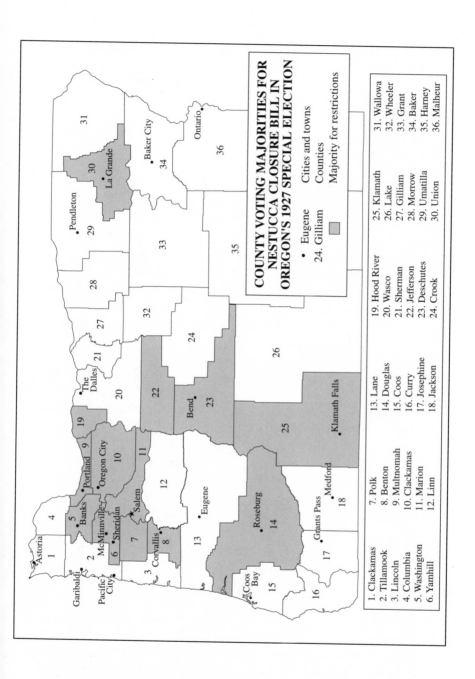

MAP 16. Unlike in 1908, the June referendum in 1927 demonstrated much narrower opposition to industrial fishers. Counties voting for the Nestucca closure correlated strongly with urban centers and newspapers opposed to gillnetting interests.

passage. Lane and Linn were the only valley counties opposing closure, and the *Eugene Register Guard* was the only valley paper that supported the gillnetters. Nestucca gillnetters lost because Willamette Valley papers opposed them. Northern Willamette precincts in particular broke the referendum effort.[83]

The Nestucca closure produced irony and tragedy. The state hatchery closed from lack of funds, and many fishers fled to other streams, exacerbating problems with overcrowding. A few stayed and fished illegally, experimented with trolling, and founded the town's famed dory fleet. Meanwhile anglers watched their sportsmen's paradise turn into a joke. They expected catches to rise, but without nets to harass the salmon, the fish tarried in tidewater until they were ready to spawn and thus were too rotten to eat. Catches declined, the Depression kept anglers away, and they stopped coming altogether once the Salmon River Highway diverted traffic to Lincoln City. In 1930 the state fish commissioner asked legislators to reauthorize gillnet fishing to help Nestucca farmers, and local representatives proposed several bills to that effect during the 1930s. None succeeded, and Pacific City's economy collapsed.[84]

After the Nestucca, anglers resumed their struggle for the Rogue. Between 1910 and 1935 they submitted six separate measures to close the river to nets. They championed conservation and advertised the support of everyone from USBF Commissioner Henry O'Malley (unauthorized), to zoologist and angler Henry Ward, the Grants Pass and Ashland Chambers of Commerce, Zane Grey, and Babe Ruth.[85]

Zane Grey was an interesting figure in the later campaigns. At the height of his literary career and liking to fish any exotic locale possible, during the 1920s Grey grew fond of the Rogue and built a rustic cabin on a rugged stretch of the lower river. He was a bit misanthropic in his yearning for unpeopled places, however, and by the end of the decade he had worn out his welcome and moved to the north fork of the Umpqua River. At least part of his heart remained with the Rogue, though, because in short stories and novels he continued to criticize gillnetters and lobby to save "his" stream.[86]

Grey's major contribution was published in 1929. *Rogue River Feud* is a potboiler that traces the adventures of Kevin as he descends the river to learn why steelhead are disappearing. Kevin arrives at the mouth to discover a "hard crowd" intent on exterminating steelhead. "It's a rotten, cruel, greedy business," he growls. The story pits moral farmers, townspeople, and anglers against a bloodthirsty assortment of cutthroats, drunks, and "half-breed" netters. There is murder, mayhem, and romance.[87]

There is also political science. Kevin asks the rhetorical question, "Are a few men to be allowed to kill the food value and sport value of this river?" His partner responds, "I suppose mine is the sportsman's point of view. It oughtn't have much weight with the legislature, though I think the steelhead should be preserved." "If [the steelhead] don't get stopped altogether [by nets] they've a chance to survive. An' the upriver folks ought to fight fer them." A more explicit prescription for an initiative campaign is hard to find. Grey was not a political Svengali, and *Rogue River Feud* was hardly his best work, but he did help popularize a political campaign on the rise.[88]

Unlike other fishing groups, anglers largely succeeded in claiming exclusive use of vast stretches of fishery space, but many of their later victories came as often from the legislature as from voter initiatives. The final closure on the Rogue in 1935 itself resulted less from conservation arguments than from the conversion of lower-river merchants to the business opportunities of tourism. In 1941 the legislature passed a bill to close most coastal streams to nets, but Oregon voters rejected the law as too extreme in a referendum election the following year. When the legislature closed streams again in 1945, voters approved the ensuing referendum. In 1948 anglers persuaded Oregon voters to eliminate the last traps and seines from the Columbia River, and in 1956 they eliminated gillnets from all remaining rivers except a small chum fishery on Tillamook Bay and the Columbia River below The Dalles Dam.[89]

Anglers justified closures as necessary to "save Oregon's salmon and steelhead before it is too late," but eliminating gear did not help salmon recover. As early as 1926 USBF Commissioner Henry O'Malley had worried that the emphasis on eliminating gear was a poor substitute for restricting total harvest. Later evidence substantiated O'Malley's fears. In 1950 researchers declared that "the elimination of commercial fishing . . . has by no means resulted in any phenomenal increase in the runs or improvement in the recreational fishery." Outlawing traps, wheels, and seines on the Columbia had only reallocated salmon to gillnets and dipnets, and proscribing gillnets on coastal streams simply gave more fish to sportfishers and ocean trollers. Researchers also worried that gear regulation would be fruitless if government did not also protect habitat from the effects of dams, irrigation, and logging.[90]

Neither did eliminating nets reduce industrial fishing; it simply moved harvesting to the ocean. The development of dependable engines in the early 1900s had allowed fishers and anglers to cross the dangerous Columbia bar and fish the ocean. Within a few years trollers were also working outside Tillamook Bay, Yaquina Bay, and Coos Bay, and by the 1930s

smaller ports existed at Pacific City, Depoe Bay, Winchester Bay, Port Orford, and Bandon. In 1936 there were 376 trollers serving limited fresh-fish and mild-cure markets, but river closures rapidly escalated the ocean fishery. In 1950 about 500 commercial trollers and a growing number of sport trollers caught 99,000 chinook and 167,000 coho. By 1957 those figures had climbed to 330,000 and 675,000 respectively. Modern conservationists did not reduce the harvest; they just displaced it to the ocean and increased expenses.[91]

The growth of trolling also raised a number of concerns. In 1914 the *Morning Oregonian* argued that "there seems to be only one way to conserve the salmon supply and that is to regulate freshwater fishing with considerable rigor and forbid entirely fishing in the deep sea." In 1926 Henry O'Malley criticized trollers for harvesting salmon prematurely, and biologist Charles Gilbert warned that "the continuation of trolling will spell the utter destruction of the chinook and coho runs . . . if not controlled." Canners feared the fresh-fish and mild-cure markets and called trolling "pernicious." In 1927 they tried to prohibit the sale of salmon caught outside state waters, but the very fact that trolling took place in federal and international waters made it impossible for states to regulate. In 1928 California sportfishers asked the USBF to regulate the oceans, but federal managers were powerless.[92]

By pushing the fishery onto the ocean, anglers inadvertently convoluted management, exacerbated waste, and altered evolution. Ocean fishing crippled the ability of managers to regulate harvests on individual runs. Trolling also induced incredible waste. Fish that escaped hooks or were undersized suffered mortality rates as high as 30–40 percent. A growing percentage of salmon runs vanished without even reaching the marketplace, let alone the spawning grounds. Ocean harvesting also put inordinate pressure on salmon that spent longer periods in the ocean, and over time chinook began to evolve downward in size and life span as a result.[93]

In the end, anglers did very little to protect or conserve salmon. Anglers lost interest in industrial fishers once they were out of sight. Trolling fleets grew tremendously between 1950 and 1978, and with no limits on participation and seasons that extended from early June to late October, trolling remained essentially unregulated until the late 1970s. Meanwhile, urban development fueled logging, agricultural, and damming booms that con-

(*Facing page*) This 1948 ad by Columbia River gillnetters reveals the increasing sophistication of fishers' campaigns to shape voter emotions, in this case rhetorically transforming poundnets into bear traps. (*Portland Oregon Voter*, 30 Oct. 1948.)

sumed ever more spawning habitat. Anglers did not intend to harm salmon, but their political agenda and economies nevertheless played a central, if unexamined, role in the escalating destruction of runs.[94]

Historian John Reiger has countered critics of hunting and fishing by pointing out that sportsmen were the vanguard of modern conservation, but he and other defenders have preferred to ignore the social and environmental consequences of the sort of conservation that sportsmen supported. Much of conservation has in fact been a process of segregating space along racial and class lines. In the South hunters used state agencies to bar African Americans from subsistence hunting; in the West hunters used federal agencies to exclude Indians, Hispanics, and poor whites. In the Pacific Northwest, anglers used similar tactics to reshape the social and natural spaces of streams. They reorganized landscapes so raw materials and energy flowed to cities, colonized rivers to create pastoral refuges, imposed their own rules of comportment on society, and deracinated any species or people which seemed to threaten their aesthetic and material pursuits.[95]

In the process anglers perfected a cannibalistic brand of conservation that consumed fishers to save salmon. Oregon's 1908 election was a watershed political event. The campaign allowed anglers to seize the moral high ground, and voter returns revealed a significant demographic shift in legislative power. Sportfishers blended these developments into a potent movement against all industrial fishers, but in their agendas, tactics, and results, anglers essentially emulated their opponents. They tapped into a public discourse already hyperfocused on fishing, marshaled public disgust and urban votes, and sustained a highly effective campaign to eliminate their rivals. Yet when we look closely at their actual accomplishments, we can see that they deployed the rhetoric of conservation with greater facility than fealty. Their efforts transformed the industrial fishery, but they did little to save salmon, a lot to harm salmon ecology, and a tremendous amount to hinder management. Anglers did not so much conserve as urbanize salmon. Their deeds merged with many more during the twentieth century to thoroughly remake this fish and crisis.[96]

7 / Remaking Salmon

Fish culturists and fishery scientists have debated hatchery practices since the 1870s. They have argued over the effect of predators on survival, whether to protect fry by retaining them in ponds, what to feed ponded fish, and when to release them. The language and conduct of these debates reveal much about the politics of hatchery policy. Convinced that ponds were a logical step in protecting young fish and increasing runs, fish culturists lobbied strenuously to change state and federal hatchery practices. Academically trained fishery scientists were more skeptical. Many of these boosterish claims seemed poorly documented at best, and a few ideas were downright absurd. Eventually their own studies disproved some of the original justifications for hatcheries, and fish culturists lost much of their prestige as practical scientists.

The debunking of many of fish culture's central tenets sparked a secondary debate over the relative merits of book knowledge versus practical experience in understanding and saving salmon. These arguments only widened the divide that separated the two groups. Although scientists tended to win the factual debates, pond-raising advocates ultimately prevailed in policy struggles. Their victory emerged less from the merits of their arguments than because development had precluded other options. The changed circumstances, mostly the result of habitat loss, opened new avenues for cooperation. In the 1940s a rapprochement occurred between the two groups. Fish culturists incorporated new science to solve old problems with malnutrition and disease, and scientists investigated new ways to increase hatchery productivity. By 1960 these cooperative trends had culminated in an apotheosis of pond-raising: Oregon's Smolt Program for coho.

In their efforts to make salmon, however, fish culturists and scientists unintentionally helped to remake salmon. By instituting ever more intensive interventions in the salmon's life cycles and environments, they deflected fish onto new evolutionary paths. But salmon responded poorly to domestication. Pond-raising altered the process of natural selection by imposing strange new pressures on early development and introducing endemic diseases not found in wild populations. By the 1950s scientists were noting significant changes in the behavior, size, and genetic diversity of salmon stocks. By the 1970s these changes were transforming the survival of wild stocks into a critical management issue. Hatcheries had remade salmon into creatures that threatened not only the remaining wild runs but also their own long-term interests.

Nineteenth-century fish culturists divided nature into the economically useful and useless, instituted practices to protect favored species, and reshaped the environmental pressures on fish. They argued the merits of these practices for decades, but their debates were largely deductive and inconclusive.

Salmon had evolved to survive in a complex, constantly changing world. Varying environmental and chemical compositions of natal streams, seasonal and random climatic shifts, fluctuating ocean conditions, and multiple predator and prey relationships constantly shaped their evolution. These pressures and their varied environments helped differentiate salmon in many ways. Sockeye specialized by spawning in lakes, while other species spawned in streams; pink and chum juveniles migrated to sea immediately after hatching, while chinook and sockeye waited up to three years before leaving. Evolution also created variations within species. Upper Columbia River chinook grew larger and had higher percentages of fat than lower-river chinook because they needed the extra energy to travel the one thousand or more miles to their spawning beds; they also matured at a variety of ages to guard against poor reproduction in any single year. In short, salmon evolved into incredibly complex creatures in very complicated environments.[1]

Fish culturists had a much simpler understanding of environmental interactions. Desiring to produce as many of a preferred species as possible, they reduced nature to binary categories of friends and "enemies." Europeans had long portrayed fish predators in these terms, and Americans adopted the perspective as well. In an 1883 questionnaire sent to carp recipients, the U.S. Fish Commission (USFC) asked respondents to list the "enemies of fish" in their area.[2]

Fish culturists and hatchery boosters, ignorant of complicated predator-prey relationships, described salmon in simple, culturally comprehensible terms. In 1872 Albert Hager complained about the "stupidity" of fry because of their seeming willingness to become prey. In 1880 Livingston Stone explained that alevins lived in "the honeycombed ground below their ene-

mies" because they were "persecuted by larger fish . . . like the Christians in
the catacombs." In 1897 Hollister McGuire worried, "The poor little salmon . . . at once becomes the prey of every fish that is large enough to
swallow it and active enough to catch it." The metaphors of observers
revealed the social values they read into nature; they portrayed economically
valuable species as dangerously victimized and in need of human protection
from their "enemies."[3]

This dichotomization of nature was, however, increasingly out of step
with modern science. By the end of the nineteenth century, European and
American scientists were emphasizing theoretical and experimental research,
and one of the new scientific fields was ecology. While ecologists were
heralding the complexity and interconnectedness of nature, fish culturists
were trying to simplify nature by abstracting salmon from their environments
and misperceiving or ignoring the role of adaptation in species development
and survival. In the process fish culturists propelled hatchery practices along
an economically logical, but scientifically skewed, path.[4]

Fish culturists and hatchery boosters hoped to make nature more efficient, more convenient, and more profitable. Albert Hager wanted to edu-
cate salmon into proper American individualists: "Before he [the fry] is
permitted to enter streams with other fish, he should be disciplined in a
stream by himself and taught the great and important lesson of *taking care of
himself* and become self supporting. When this course is pursued I think
success will follow the efforts of those trying to restock our streams with
salmon, but never will it do to put *uneducated* little fish with *crafty* large
ones." Hager's manipulative impulse was not unique. Spencer Baird wanted
to alter the time of hatching to accommodate distribution schedules, and
others tried to breed salmon like cattle, replace smaller fish with the eggs
from larger fish, or eradicate predators.[5]

Artificial-rearing ponds were central to nineteenth-century fish culture.
Ideally, such ponds allowed workers to segregate alevins and fry from
predators and raise them to "fingerling" length. Private fish culturists had
used ponds since the 1870s, but the USFC followed only hesitantly in 1887
because ponds introduced sticky technical and economic problems surrounding the question of what to feed fish. Supporters tried everything from
maggots to pureed meat, coagulated blood, offal, and infertile fish eggs and
milt. But others rejected these feeds, citing their high costs and unnatural
provenience. They also argued that protected fish would be unfit "to take
care of themselves."[6]

"Fry versus fingerling" developed into a vigorous but ultimately dead-end
debate. Both sides had enthusiastic partisans, but most arguments were

strictly deductive. Neither side possessed conclusive evidence, and the American Fisheries Society (AFS) eventually tabooed these inconclusive discussions at conferences. The USFC continued to retain a few salmon fry at its hatcheries until, as one reporter put it, "they are big enough to look out for themselves in the race to the season." In practice, however, the vast majority of hatchery salmon entered streams as alevins, and most fry followed a month or two later because of overcrowding, lack of funds, or epidemics.[7]

Although the effects of these practices would not be widely recognized until the mid-twentieth century, they immediately began to deflect salmon onto a new evolutionary path. In the wild, nature selected for fish that hid alone from predators and preyed on insects and small organisms. Hatcheries, on the other hand, selected for individuals that thrived on human-supplied feeds. Over time hatcheries preserved more of the less-fit, thus reducing the overall vitality of the gene pool. They also altered behavior by acclimating fry to live in schools and tolerate the presence of workers who fed them. But fish that thrived in ponds did not necessarily survive well in the wild. After release, hatchery fish remained in dense concentrations and outcompeted wild fish for food, but the dense concentrations also made them susceptible to heavy predation by birds and fish that they no longer avoided. A few contemporary critics had anticipated these effects, but they could not prove their fears. The rest embraced pond-raising and waited for production to increase.[8]

Oregon's most outspoken proponent of pond-raising was R. D. Hume. Hume enjoyed an unrivaled reputation as a salmon expert because of the results of his private hatchery on the Rogue River. Fishers had worked the Rogue successfully since 1870, but Hume's first year of canning coincided with the El Niño of 1877. When the runs failed that year, Hume thought he had been "caught for a sucker." But rather than admit defeat, Hume rode 125 miles to the USFC station at McCloud River to inspect their operations. He returned with an assistant of Stone's, built a hatchery, collected 215,000 eggs, and released about 100,000 fry. This was not a very significant number even when the *Morning Oregonian* stretched it to 250,000.[9]

In the next decade Hume used his hatchery to bolster his reputation as a salmon expert. He ran the hatchery himself and, as a sideline, marked spawned fish and returned them to the river. When cannery workers supposedly recaptured these fish as recovered adults, Hume announced he had proof that salmon did not die after spawning. When runs began to rebound from El Niño in 1881, Hume proclaimed fish culture victorious (see table 6). Oregonians crowned him an authority on salmon, the great "salmon king" of Oregon, and his proclamations became tacit proof of the success of fish culture. Both state and federal officials cited him to prove that salmon

TABLE 6. Rogue River Salmon Catch, 1877–1908 (thousands of pounds)

Year	Chinook	Coho	Total	Year	Chinook	Coho	Total
1877	—	—	531	1893	218	—	—
1878	—	—	580	1894*			
1879	—	—	583	1895	706	298	1,004
1880	—	—	528	1896	1,020	204	1,224
1881	—	—	838	1897	1,044	248	1,292
1882	—	—	1,305	1898	882	34	916
1883	—	—	1,099	1899	373	119	492
1884	—	—	842	1900	—	—	—
1885	—	—	633	1901	182	285	467
1886	—	—	825	1902	258	278	536
1887	—	—	1,170	1903	572	326	898
1888	—	—	1,432	1904	1,088	221	1,309
1889	—	—	1,496	1905	1,258	102	1,360
1890	—	—	1,632	1906	816	408	1,224
1891	—	—	1,428	1907	513	122	635
1892	680	612	1,292	1908	296	180	476

* Cannery not operated due to fire.

SOURCES: Figures from John N. Cobb, *The Pacific Salmon Fisheries*, Fisheries Document 1092 (Washington: Government Printing Office, 1930); Robert E. Mullen, *Oregon's Commercial Harvest of Coho Salmon, "Oncorhynchus kisutch" (Walbaum), 1892–1960*, Information Report Series, Fisheries 81–3 (Corvallis: Oregon Department of Fish and Wildlife, Fish Division, 1981).

did not die after spawning and that hatcheries worked. Hume even persuaded a stingy Oregon legislature to subsidize an expansion of his ponds in 1888.[10]

In 1893 Hume wrote a series of newspaper articles on fish culture which he then published as a booklet and distributed with every case of salmon he sold. *Salmon of the Pacific Coast* offered his peculiar understanding of fish. Hume repeated his claim that not all salmon died after spawning. For proof he cited the annual runs of jacks, which were immature but sexually precocious juvenile males that accompanied adults to the spawning grounds. "It is unreasonable to suppose that the Creator has so deviated from the law which he has established as to have created salmon with such an excess of the male species that millions could be thus cut off prior to maturity without damage to the perpetuation of the whole class." "I do not believe that Nature departs so far from her general economy as to produce any useless surplus." Like his contemporaries, Hume read his own values into nature and expected salmon to behave accordingly.[11]

The book's main goal was to "call attention of both producer and consumer to the danger of the total extinction of this most valuable of food fishes, and provide a simple method for their preservation." Hume repeated an apocryphal quotation that one acre of water could produce as much as seven acres of land, but he insisted that the truer figure was forty acres of land. He claimed that he had increased salmon runs "four fold" by raising fry to five or six inches in length. Self-promotion had its intended effect, and visitors to his hatchery seemed persuaded by his methods. The Washington fish commissioner emulated Hume by building a hatchery on the Chinook River near the mouth of the Columbia River, and the *Morning Oregonian* cited Hume as the reigning expert on salmon. "There is so much common sense, backed by so much practical accomplishment, in Mr. Hume's ideas, that they should command attention."[12]

Many Oregonians regarded Hume as an expert, but his reputation often exceeded his results. Hume's biographer called him an ichthyologist who "helped to guide the weak conservation forces of his day to ultimate triumph," but during the 1880s and 1890s the Rogue River hatchery ran only intermittently, experienced repeated disasters, and rarely produced adequate records. Hume was also credited with ensuring "a steady supply of salmon over the years at but a small cost," yet he depended heavily on government subsidies. The same year that he published his booklet, Hume asked the USFC to transplant salmon eggs from the McCloud to the Rogue. Thereafter he continually relied on state and federal assistance to maintain his hatchery.[13]

Hume's opinions carried less weight with federal officials. In 1896 Hume boldly wrote to Commissioner John Brice, "The result of my experiments at Rogue River during the past twenty years has shed much light upon the subject of propagation of salmon, and I should be glad if I could make plain some of the questions which are made quite a mystery of at present." When Brice failed to be impressed, Hume's ego deflated significantly. He began to humble himself in correspondence, request advice, and admit that "we may be rather old-fashioned in our ideas." After one argument with William Ravenal, Hume prostrated himself "in sack cloth and ashes, repenting [his] misdeeds." He admitted ignorance about USFC procedures and that he had only been "operating a hatchery in a moderate way on the lower Rogue River for more than twenty years."[14]

Despite the lack of respect, Hume did lure the U.S. Bureau of Fisheries

(USBF) briefly into pond-raising. In 1899 Hume planned to raise 2.5 million fingerlings and feed them spent salmon. When he broached his ideas to USBF administrators, they agreed to help, and Columbia River canners, who were intrigued by the proposal, promised to donate condemned canned salmon. At first the plan seemed to work. An enthusiastic William Ravenal remarked, "The office has no doubt as to the advantages of artificial propagation, especially the value of holding the fish until they reach a reasonable size." George Bowers added that spent salmon "has been very successfully used for the past year at several of our stations."[15]

But then things went awry. In January 1901 hatcheries had trouble getting a sufficient supply of salmon from canners, and in February the Clackamas hatchery experienced an "alarming mortality among fry." The canned salmon was inducing some sort of disease which workers only stemmed by switching to beef liver. Liver and other meats increased the cost of operations and fouled the water, but the salmon fry seemed to respond positively. Canned salmon, researchers would later discover, did not contain all the essential nutrients that fry needed. In 1902 a flood wrecked the federal station on the Rogue, canned salmon created more problems with disease, and budget woes forced the USFC to release fry sooner than desired. Federal administrators lost enthusiasm. J. W. Titcomb began to express doubts, and in 1905 the USBF recommended releasing alevins rather than fingerlings.[16]

Hume refused to admit defeat. When the USFC backed away from fingerlings, he gathered allies who shared his beliefs. Joining him were his hatchery assistant George Rickman and a disaffected federal employee named J. W. Berrian. In 1902 Rickman tried to persuade the USFC that Hume's methods were superior, but Titcomb ignored him. Hume then tried to get the like-minded Berrian promoted to hatchery superintendent. When Bowers refused, Berrian quit and went to work for Hume. The trio rejected federal policies, if not their subsidies, and expanded Hume's operation.[17]

Hume also took his battle to the newspapers. In article after article he derided alevin releases and suggested that the USBF "might better throw the money into the river." Deputy Fish Warden Herman Webster seconded Hume. "The betterment or even future maintenance of the industry depends entirely upon whether or not the various departments act upon and put into effect a system so plainly pointed out in [Hume's] statements." When hatchery production seemed to stagnate after the 1904 debacle, the *Morning Oregonian* followed suit. The paper warned "that something is wrong . . . with the hatchery system." It cited an 1895 experiment in which the USFC marked 5,000 fry before release from the Clackamas hatchery.

When fishers recovered only 497 tagged adults, the paper blamed the loss on "predatory fish," criticized alevin releases as "a big waste," and endorsed "longer retention of hatchery fry."[18]

Most fishery administrators rejected these arguments. Van Dusen acknowledged that Washington's state fish commissioner and many canners favored "nurseries" for salmon, but he dismissed pond-raising with lengthy quotations from Bowers and John P. Babcock, the commissioner of fisheries for British Columbia. Bowers defended the status quo by blaming decline on unrestricted fishing and habitat loss, not trout predation. Although he defended hatcheries, he discounted fingerling supporters. Babcock favored hatchery practices that mimicked "as closely as possible the footsteps of nature." He opposed fingerling programs because they relied on unnatural foods, created problems with gastric parasites, and made the fry miss the spring floods that carried them to sea.[19]

Fingerling advocates nevertheless persisted. In April 1907 the *Morning Oregonian* criticized the Oregon Fish Commission for locating hatcheries on the McKenzie and Snake Rivers, where trout would "devour many infant salmon." Meanwhile, Hume mailed fingerlings to the Oregon Fish Commission and USBF and invited them to visit his hatchery and view his methods. When nobody showed, Hume attacked the "preconceived notions to which some of the so-called authorities so fondly cling." He insisted that salmon did not die after spawning; that Oregon build hatcheries near the ocean so spawners could return to sea; and that ponded salmon grew faster and returned sooner. "If the Oregon Fish Commission will follow my advice," he argued, "they will make salmon so plentiful that you can walk across the Columbia River on their backs."[20]

Fingerling advocates elevated local and practical knowledge above the distant, bookish opinions of critics. Salmon canner and Washington State senator H. S. McGowan urged the public to "Protect Baby Fish." "It has been too long taken for granted that all public officers know and employ the best means to the fullest measure of success." Bowers and the USBF had failed because they lacked a proper "knowledge of local conditions." Hume, on the other hand, was a longtime observer of salmon and had "made notable experiments in salmon culture." McGowan and Hume invoked nature to make their case. McGowan argued, "The nursery partisan has the natural and obvious argument that all young life is menaced by predatory enemies." Hume insisted that spent salmon was the perfect hatchery feed because "like begets like."[21]

The debate reflected genuine differences of opinion about how to run hatcheries, but it also involved a series of personal, political, and industrial feuds. Hume accused Van Dusen of opposing his views to curry favor with gillnetters, while Van Dusen considered Hume and other canners so many greedy, lawbreaking capitalists. Webster wanted Van Dusen's job, so he endorsed Hume to get the support of Rogue River fishers. McGowan attacked Van Dusen to discredit gillnetters, and gillnetters dismissed Mc-Gowan as an apologist for seine, trap, and fishwheel operators. Hume only slightly overstated the case when he told Bowers, "Everything is subservient to politics in [Oregon] and the active movers would sell the whole country in order to get a pull at the public teat."[22]

Both fry and fingerling advocates wanted to increase production, but the underlying economic assumptions everyone shared inevitably favored fingerlings because all parties regarded juvenile predation as an irrational economic and biological loss. This was critical, because the debate ultimately turned on the weight of deductive logic, not empirical evidence. Fish culturists purported to experiment with and know nature, but few kept adequate records, maintained controls, or hypothesized results. There was, in short, no way to assess the claims people made, so most statements had to be taken at face value. Fishery science remained a discipline without fixed standards, less an objective discipline than a rhetorical means of legitimating policies.[23]

In the political arena of salmon management, policy bent to whichever side spoke loudest and longest, and Hume's relentless efforts eventually prevailed in the Oregon Fish Commission. In December 1907 he crowed, "I have at last convinced them that my methods are the correct ones and the future." Readers of Hume's proclamations began to seek his advice and endorse his methods, and state opposition collapsed after Van Dusen's dismissal in March 1908. Warden McAllister, who had been selected for the job because he knew so little about salmon and the fishing industry, hired several Hume supporters, and in July, when he visited the Rogue, he proclaimed Hume "the best-posted man in the Pacific Northwest in this work." McAllister quickly remodeled state operations to follow Hume's methods and sought Hume's advice on using spent salmon as feed. In return, Hume received secret shipments of Columbia River eggs to bolster his faltering hatchery program. When McAllister announced plans to build a central hatchery at Bonneville, he hired J. W. Berrian to operate it.[24]

Oregon initiated these programs with great enthusiasm. McAllister held a grand opening at Bonneville in November 1909. The *Morning Oregonian* proclaimed it the largest hatchery in the world, and perhaps sensitive to problems with disease, the paper assured readers that the water supply was

"FREE OF FUNGUS." The dedication also became an occasion to celebrate another new program. McAllister and Frank A. Seufert, a salmon canner and wheel owner from The Dalles, had pleaded for sockeye eggs all summer. The USBF eventually agreed to send two million eggs from Yes Bay, Alaska, each year for the next four years. The *Morning Oregonian* declared it "the greatest progressive step in the development of this immense industry that has ever been made."[25]

Such sentiments, and another fortuitously good run in 1914, fueled an era of confident expansion. Between 1910 and 1940 the number of state hatcheries mushroomed from twelve to forty-three (see table 4). State and federal agencies shared expenses, loaned trucks, and exchanged fish. Employees developed a strong sense of camaraderie, of being one of "the boys," while packers and merchants believed that "commercial fishing on the Columbia River would have been a thing of the past" without hatcheries. If it would help hatchery operations, packers gladly donated meat scraps, salmon offal, frozen smelt, cold-storage space, canning equipment, timber, and even funds for a school. Industry leaders worked in close conjunction with fishery agencies and coordinated lobbying efforts for best effect. In return, the Oregon Fish Commission supported tax breaks for the industry. Pond-raising had seemingly arrived.[26]

Although salmon hatcheries remained publicly popular until the 1980s, after 1900 a group of formally trained fishery scientists grew increasingly skeptical of fish culturists' claims. Their studies cast doubt on hatchery efficacy and produced a fissure between culturists and scientists that widened over time.

Far from saving salmon, it seemed, fish culture often exacerbated biological problems. Harvests fell precipitously from 1884 to 1890, fluctuated wildly until 1911, and then began a long period of decline. Fish culturists compensated for losses by trying to transfer eggs or breed bigger fish. These practices failed to restore stocks. Transfers reduced genetic diversity, relocated fish fared poorly, and crossbreeding usually failed. The more genetically homogeneous salmon became, the more susceptible they were to epizootics and inbreeding.[27]

Oregon's hatcheries also created fiscal problems. District 2, which included all streams south of the Columbia, never generated enough license revenues to fund hatchery operations on every stream. The Bonneville hatchery in district 1 also ran over budget. Deficits became a perennial concern, and emergency expenses due to fires, floods, and droughts further depleted funds. Even popularity became a burden. In 1909 the USBF had to erect a fence around the Rogue River Station to prevent the curious from overrunning the grounds.[28]

Such budget shortfalls compromised management. When money ran out, the master fish warden had to go begging to the canners. Packers made "voluntary" donations whenever asked, but in return they insisted on inspecting commission books and micromanaging hatchery operations. In 1915 they extended their meddling to personnel decisions; had one of their own, Frank Warren, appointed to the Fish and Game Commission; and tried to halt further transfers of eggs from one stream to another.[29]

Like other wildlife managers, fish culturists and administrators deflected the criticism of academics and canners by blaming nature. Fish culturists operated from a body of experiences and practical knowledge. Trained to improve nature through manipulation, and firmly believing in the efficacy of fish culture, their tacit knowledge led them to conclude that poor returns signaled a problem with nature or techniques. Thus when egg transfers showed poor results and massive fry plantings induced heavy predation, managers instituted bounties and encouraged Oregonians to "exterminate" such "pests" as seals, sea lions, cormorants, and even songbirds. Privately, however, U S B F employee Henry O'Malley considered egg transfers a "grievous mistake."[30]

While fish culturists and administrators soft-pedaled problems, fishery scientists became increasingly disillusioned with fish culture. In the years surrounding 1900, a growing number of American scientists began to emphasize the importance of quantification and experimentation. Given a growing body of contradictory evidence, these formally trained scientists were no longer willing to accept at face value the tacit claims of fish culturists.[31]

Evidence of persistent problems and inconsistent results had been around for decades. In 1897 William Ravenal asked Louis Bean to observe chinook fry after release from the Siuslaw hatchery. Bean visited two creeks at irregular intervals and made unsystematic observations. Bean noticed that the salmon had disappeared after an invasion of trout; he surmised that the trout had eaten the fry. Many fish culturists already knew about the damage done by trout, but Ravenal, who knew little about salmon, dismissed the idea and asked Bean to make more detailed observations the following year. When Bean reached the same conclusion under Ravenal's supervision, Ravenal reluctantly agreed to alter release practices.[32]

Evidence only mounted after 1900. In the late 1880s, F. C. Reed tried to gauge the effectiveness of hatcheries by marking juvenile salmon before release. By the late 1890s the U S F C was also clipping fins. The information from these experiments was problematic. Researchers depended on voluntary reporting, but they could never be certain whether fishers inflated figures. The way they marked fish also increased mortality. Nevertheless, by 1906 these experiments demonstrated that less than 3 percent of all hatchery fish returned as adults, a far cry from expectations. The results reinforced fingerling advocates' belief in ponds, but they also fed skepticism about the efficacy of fish culture.[33]

The fallout from these developments first appeared in 1907. R. D. Hume wanted the Oregon Fish Commission to refund his license fees to cover hatchery expenses, so he asked the USBF to endorse his request. Bowers asked Barton Warren Evermann to review Hume's records. Evermann, an ichthyologist trained at Indiana University, replied, "Mr. Hume may have knowledge which convinces him, and which ought to be convincing to the State authorities, that the increased catch in Rogue River is due to the hatchery operation on that stream; but the evidence as presented here does not seem conclusive. There may be other factors that enter."[34]

Bowers was more politic. "In regard to your statement as to the number of salmon taken and the wonderful results, the Bureau has not investigated other possible factors which may have entered into the case, and while there may not have been any, it is deemed only justice to all concerned that this statement should be made." Bowers tried to mediate, but he was less concerned with resolving differences than protecting the USBF, which by the early twentieth century had become fiscally dependent on fish culture.[35]

In 1910 a fundamental break between science and fish culture appeared at the annual meeting of the AFS. Three zoologists read papers on the role of limnology and ecology in fishery management: Stephen A. Forbes outlined a study of the impact of development on Illinois's Illinois River, and T. L. Hankinson and Roy Waldo Miner presented limnological studies of lake and marine environments. All stressed the need for comprehensive aquatic surveys, not just narrow inspections for economic species.[36]

They also stressed the complexity and interdependence of aquatic life. As Miner stated, "The deduction from all this is obvious. Life in the seas, as elsewhere, must be regarded not as sets of unrelated phenomena, but as a totality, a unit, composed of interlocking parts or associations. . . . From this point of view no species or group of species can be considered without reckoning in its entire environment." Forbes criticized fish culturists for releasing young fish into waters without understanding the larger environment. Such practices, he asserted, "can no longer be defended as either scientific or practical; it is simply ignorant." The audience of fish culturists responded enthusiastically to Forbes's call for surveying sources of pollution, but his emphasis on complexity and his criticisms met with cold silence.[37]

In the ensuing years the schism between culturists and scientists yawned ever wider. Fishers and fish culturists openly criticized scientists for not conducting more "practical investigations." They had to channel their complaints through politicians, however, because academic scientists now controlled the elected offices and editorial board of the AFS, which was the major organization for fish culturists. Fish culturists could no longer invoke the authority of science as freely as they once did.[38]

In Oregon, hatchery boosters began a counterattack. When David Starr Jordan endorsed natural reproduction and opposed poundnets and fishwheels, Frank Seufert accused Jordan of being a "Nature faker." Seufert not only wanted to protect his wheels but was also envious of Alaska and Fraser River sockeye because they commanded higher prices than Columbia River bluebacks. Thus he insisted that sockeye were not native to the Columbia and that they needed to be hatched artificially. Jordan calmly invoked his authority as a systematic ichthyologist. He dismissed Seufert's contentions by noting that bluebacks and sockeyes were the same species with different local names.[39]

As scientific criticism swelled, western fish culturists circled the wagons. In 1910, Master Fish Warden McAllister organized a meeting of federal and state administrators, hatchery superintendents, and supporters within the fishing industry. Participants heard lectures on hatchery practices, conservation problems, and the future of fish culture. They also formed the Pacific Coast Hatcherymen's Association (PCHA). The public announcement of the new organization illustrated the growing tension between academic science and craft knowledge: "The knowledge gained by the hatchery superintendents by years of experience and practical study of the habits of the salmon after entering fresh water, is certainly of far greater value to the public at large than is the opinion of some scientist who never had the real practical experience . . . that is enjoyed by the [hatchery] superintendents . . . of the Pacific coast."[40]

Having lost control of the AFS, and with it the *Transactions of the American Fisheries Society,* members of the PCHA sought more amenable organs for their views. They began to lodge complaints in regional newspapers and trade magazines, and in 1912 they gained an exception from the USBF to raise fingerlings in Oregon and Washington. With the help of Henry O'Malley, they had transformed the Clackamas River Station by

1919 into a showcase for "the great value of fingerlings over fry." In the 1920s some hatchery advocates even attempted to raise salmon in pens near the ocean.[41]

Without a national base, however, the PCHA lost momentum. In 1914 it changed its name to the Pacific Fisheries Society (PFS) and named Henry O'Malley as secretary. O'Malley was superintendent of the Clackamas River Station and a rising star in the USBF. He would be regional field agent by 1918 and commissioner by 1922. During O'Malley's tenure as president, he increased the organization's respectability and drive. The PFS even tried to displace the AFS on the Pacific slope by scheduling meetings at conflicting times, but it lost energy during World War I and never seriously threatened the AFS.[42]

Although fish culturists failed to undermine their critics, academic scientists were no more influential with fishery managers, and state administrators continued to endorse fish culture in the most confident tones. In 1911 a Washington State official assured readers of the *Pacific Fisherman* that "there need be no fear felt as to the future if the various state governments and the federal government will maintain the proper hatchery system." The Oregon Fish and Game Commission echoed these sentiments in 1915: "The success of the fishing industry in [the Columbia River] is dependent entirely on the success of hatchery work. . . . It is practically a foregone conclusion that if the hatcheries are run to their full capacity and the laws are permitted to remain as they now exist, a steady average increase in the output of the river can be looked for."[43]

Although absent from these remarks was the sort of scientific rhetoric that permeated earlier claims, fish culturists and administrators could not afford to dismiss the importance of science in their work. As one hatchery superintendent remarked, "If we wish to build up the fishing industry to a desired standard, it is self evident that we must call on science for assistance." "There are good practical men in the hatcheries but they need a man of science to consult at times. . . . Give us a teacher." Fish culturists desired a particular brand of Progressive science, one that would improve and legitimate their activities without threatening criticism. They sought to subordinate formal (scientific) knowledge to tacit (practical) knowledge, but fishery scientists resisted.[44]

In 1911 Barton Evermann tried to find a middle ground in the debate. Evermann criticized the "tendency to decry all hatchery work [that was] supplanting the former extreme optimism," but neither was he an apologist for fish culture. Although he too had once claimed that "the only way by which the preservation of the salmon fisheries can be effected is by means of artificial propagation," by 1911 he admitted, "It is not improbable that a general undervaluation of natural productivity and a corresponding overestimate of the results to be expected from hatchery work is responsible for the one time widely diffused belief that the presence of a few hatcheries would cure all the ills of an unremitting pursuit of salmon."[45]

Evermann brought a rare degree of candor and balance to this discussion. Fish culturists could hatch a higher percentage of eggs than wild fish, he noted, but "in all subsequent career [the hatchery fish] is at the most on a par with its naturally produced neighbor, granting it is equally as capable." Evermann did defend hatcheries after a fashion, but it was hardly the ringing endorsement offered by state and federal administrators.[46]

In the next two decades fishery scientists exposed additional problems with hatcheries. Fish-marking studies revealed not only consistently low returns but also a high number of hatchery fish straying into other streams. Although scientists did not know it at the time, these strays accelerated the homogenization of the gene pool. The marking studies themselves became another problem. Researchers initially relied on voluntary reporting, but after 1910 they paid bounties for recovered tags. The system worked fine in low-return years, but in 1926 returns exceeded expectations and began to siphon money from other programs. Studies of transplants and hatchery diseases further elaborated the problems of fish culture, while hatchery inspections revealed incompetence, poor record keeping, and endemic diseases.[47]

The more information they generated, the more scientists criticized hatcheries. Canadian researcher Harley White remarked, "It is . . . known well by those of us who are acquainted with the facts, that many of the plantings of [hatchery] fry are complete failures." Stanford zoologist and USBF researcher Willis Rich remarked that the practice of releasing alevins "probably inflicted as much, or more, damage to the salmon runs as they did service of value." This could have been a damaging statement, but like Evermann, Rich shaped his remarks so current managers could distance themselves from former practices. Criticism instead became proof of fish culture's ability to learn from the past and improve.[48]

In 1922 Rich delivered an even more devastating assessment. Using a technique that was still relatively new in American fishery management, Rich conducted a statistical analysis of hatchery releases and returns for Columbia River chinook. After a lengthy discussion of his results, Rich concluded, "There is no evidence obtainable . . . that artificial propagation has been an effective agent in conserving the supply of salmon." Although Rich qualified his findings by noting that abject record keeping limited the ability to prove anything, his work nevertheless eroded the claims of two generations of hatchery boosters.[49]

During the 1920s Canadian researchers offered additional critiques using methods that revealed an increasing level of rigor in science. In 1924, Harley White, an ichthyologist from Queen's University, demonstrated that hatching more eggs did not necessarily ensure greater production. White hypothesized that predation was a major agent of decline. To test this assumption he conducted a controlled experiment using two creeks. White seined as many fish as possible from one creek to reduce predation; the other he left unmolested. White then introduced 5,000 trout fry into confined sections of each creek, and for the next three months he recorded population levels and examined the stomachs of predators.[50]

By the end of the experiment almost 70 percent of the fry had disappeared from the extirpated creek, but this was a huge success compared to the 96 percent decline in the control creek. Stomach examinations linked attrition to predation by yearling trout, rock bass, mudminnows, sunfish, frogs, green herons, and snakes. White also noted, "The native fry were, on the average, more advanced than the hatchery fry," a condition he attributed to the power of natural selection in wild populations. Harley White's experiment was far more rigorous than Louis Bean's anecdotal and impressionistic observations of 1897 and 1898, yet their findings were identical. Scientific rigor counted for little in hatchery circles, however. Fish culturists vilified White, accused him of falsifying data, and shunned him for decades.[51]

The following year the Biological Board of Canada initiated a systematic examination of hatchery efficacy. Board director A. P. Knight encouraged Wilber Clemens and Russell Foerster to design a comprehensive study. Clemens and Foerster developed a twelve-year plan that covered three generations of sockeye and compared reproductive methods ranging from natural to intensively artificial propagation. Foerster conducted the research at Cultus Lake, a tributary to the lower Fraser River in southern British Columbia. The lake was an ideal location. It contained a discrete population of sockeye with a known history from previous research, and the outlet was narrow enough to erect a weir and monitor passage. Foerster's ability to count juvenile and adult migrants allowed him to make significant comparisons across generations and between modes of reproduction.[52]

Foerster's study was the most systematic and sophisticated analysis of fish culture and natural propagation yet attempted in North America. He compared methods at several stages of the life cycle, including reproductive efficiency, survival to migration, and adult returns. Superficially, his findings seemed to confirm fish culturists' assumptions. Natural reproduction had the lowest percentage of hatched eggs, artificially fertilized eggs planted in gravel had a higher hatch rate, and incubating eggs and releasing fry were most efficient. But the differences were far less than expected, and when the question shifted from reproduction to ocean migration, Foerster noted that comparison of data "indicates that no statistically significant difference existed" between artificial propagation and any of the less intrusive methods. Foerster concluded, "In comparing the efficiencies of natural and artificial propagation it is found that, when the variations between the several years' results are considered there is no statistically significant difference apparent." Retaining fry did improve survival, but the added cost of feeding for a marginal improvement in escapement proved economically unjustifiable.[53]

Here was the double edge of science. Fish culturists had long relied on the rhetoric of science to justify their craft, but political reliance seemed to backfire when research no longer confirmed rhetoric. In 1934, Foerster's work persuaded the Biological Board of Canada to recommend terminating Canada's hatchery program. By 1937 the Dominion had closed all its federal hatcheries despite intense opposition from fishers and fish culturists. The USBF responded similarly in Alaska. Early reports from investigations at Karluk Lake, on Kodiak Island, confirmed many of Foerster's conclusions about heavy predation before seaward migration. Hatcheries could not hold fish long enough to prevent such losses without incurring heavy costs, so Commissioner Frank Bell began to close USBF stations in 1933. By the end of 1936, the last USBF hatchery in Alaska had closed its doors.[54]

Historians have interpreted these closures as a triumph of science in Canada and Alaska and contrasted them with the absence of scientific guidance in Oregon and Washington. The relationship between fish culture and science, bureaucracies, and development suggests a different conclusion, however. The decision to terminate operations hinged less on science than on immediate fiscal concerns consistent with the larger political economy of fishery management.[55]

Science *was* important in these episodes, but it was hardly determinative. The triumphalist thesis fails to explain why state managers ignored research that was widely available. Rich, White, and Foerster published extensively in the major journals of fishery science, and in 1929 Foerster personally explained his work to the commissioner of the Bureau of Fisheries, state fish commissioners, and hatchery superintendents at a regional conference in Seattle. Yet no state followed the lead of Canada and Alaska.[56]

So why did the Biological Board and the USBF bow to science that state agencies resisted or ignored? The answer runs to the heart of the political reception of scientific criticism in fishery management. Rather than an explanation that rests on Canadian and Alaskan enlightenment, the critical element was the differing, and quite specific, contexts in which identical information was produced and presented. As historian Arthur McEvoy and others have shown, science has been mediated by any number of factors, and politicians have regularly embraced or ignored research depending on what best served their immediate purposes. In the evaluation of hatcheries, four factors seem most germane: the institutional structure of management, the economy, the environment, and bureaucratic politics. Together they circumscribed the influence of science on fishery management in Canada, Alaska, and the states.[57]

The structure of management in Canada and Alaska provides a starting point for comparison. In Canada, the Dominion controlled the salmon fisheries, and management was hierarchical in both the Department of Marine and Fisheries and the Biological Board. A few well-placed individuals thus had a great influence on policy. This was especially significant in the case of Biological Board chairman A. P. Knight and director Wilber Clemens, who had been skeptical of fish culture since the 1910s. The security of their positions allowed Knight and Clemens to develop research with relative impunity, and under their stewardship Harley White and Russell Foerster received important institutional protection while conducting sustained, highly unpopular research. The same conditions applied in Alaska, where the USBF had a virtual fiefdom over fishery management.[58]

The economy also shaped the influence of research. Foerster began his study in 1925, but he published his most important findings beginning in 1929. Thus economic depression and budget shortfalls shaped the political reception of his work. Canadian ministers reviewed cost-benefit estimates, realized salmon hatcheries were not making a significant contribution to the economy, and pulled the plug. Alaska hatcheries experienced a similar review. In 1924 Barton Evermann concluded that the decline of salmon was "not an artificial propagation problem . . . [but] a problem wherein a sufficient escapement should be provided to take care of the spawning bed because it would be too expensive to provide otherwise." When hatcheries began to seem a waste of money during the Depression, Commissioner Bell curtailed operations and cited a "limitation of funds."[59]

Nature also played a critical role by delimiting the options of managers. A retreat from hatcheries was possible in Canada and Alaska because spawning beds remained largely intact. Thus Foerster could argue that "where a natural run of sockeye occurred with a reasonable expectancy of successful spawning, artificial propagation . . . provided no advantage over natural spawning, as a means of maintaining the run." In the political economy for fishery science north of the forty-ninth parallel, federal administrators could investigate volatile questions; science could legitimate Depression era budget cuts; and the environment offered a reasonable alternative to hatcheries.[60]

No similar set of circumstances prevailed, or was likely to prevail, in Oregon and Washington. Fishery management was a highly fractured exercise in spatial politics. Federal, state, and private entities took turns cooperating and contesting each other's authority to manage natural and social space; conservation frequently took a back seat to jurisdictional turf wars; and politicians mediated almost all decisions. Between the 1870s and 1910 the federal government organized the vast majority of scientific research on fisheries in the West. Undependable funding kept Oregon and Washington from developing either the infrastructure or the will to pursue this work, and they regularly deferred to the USFC and USBF. This posed few problems as long as fishery scientists ignored fish culture, but when criticism continued into the 1930s, Oregon initiated its own, more utilitarian research program.[61]

Bureaucratic politics further complicated the production and reception of science. Willis Rich conducted his hatchery research while Hugh Smith was commissioner, but he completed his most critical report after Henry O'Malley assumed control of the bureau in 1922. Unlike Smith, a medical doctor by training who had directed the Division of Scientific Inquiry for many years before becoming commissioner in 1913, O'Malley was a fish culturist who had risen through bureau ranks by promoting fish culture and creating strong ties with Pacific coast salmon packers. Although O'Malley occasionally criticized hatchery workers for poor practices, he never undermined the validity of fish culture. Moreover, O'Malley's boss, Secretary of Commerce Herbert Hoover, was actively promoting a more utilitarian approach to management and science. As Hoover explained to a correspondent during his search to replace Smith, "The Bureau is in essence a business concern rather than one for the development of pure science." Rich thus submitted his critical evaluation of hatcheries at a particularly awkward moment. Not only were federal administrators rapidly redirecting bureau scientists away from the basic research conducted during Hugh Smith's tenure; they were also increasingly unwilling to challenge such a seemingly utilitarian program as fish culture.[62]

Economic development and dam building further shielded hatcheries from the consequences of scientific criticism by limiting the option of returning to a policy of natural reproduction. Although fish culturists preferred pristine rivers, they had long regarded development as a mixed blessing.

Workers at the Big White Salmon River Station feared that the Great Northern Railroad would block access to the river in 1905, yet they looked forward to regular mail deliveries and speedier egg shipments. Dams produced similarly ambivalent reactions. Dams blocked habitat, but fish culturists also viewed them as a way to increase their collection of salmon eggs. The USBF and the Oregon Fish Commission occasionally built permanent dams to halt runs, but these schemes often failed. Sometimes salmon could not find or negotiate poorly designed fishways; other times netters, anglers, and Indians sabotaged hatchery operations by diverting salmon to themselves.[63]

Over time the practice of mitigating the loss of habitat through hatcheries became official policy. State and federal agencies initially gave ground on an ad hoc basis when development impinged operations. This happened on the Clackamas River after the Gladstone Dam in 1890 and the Cazadero Dam in 1904 were erected, and on the Rogue River after the Gold Ray and Ament Dams were built in 1904. Developers encouraged cooperation by offering to pay for hatcheries or provide cheap electrical rates in lieu of fishways. Federal managers were skeptical of the trade-offs, but they had less influence on policy than the states, which had jurisdiction over habitat. Washington moved toward a formal "in lieu" policy in 1906, and Oregon followed three years later. Congress also enumerated mitigation responsibilities for water projects as part of the Federal Power Act in 1920.[64]

Mitigation fostered a symbiotic relationship between hatcheries and development (see map 17). State officials rarely enforced fishway and screen laws before the 1930s. Instead, they and developers trumpeted hatcheries as a way of having salmon and consuming them too. Each compromise meant a further reduction of spawning habitat, however, and by 1932 Hugh C. Mitchell, Oregon director of fish culture, estimated that the spawning grounds in the Columbia River basin had diminished by 50 percent. As the spaces of natural reproduction dwindled, hatcheries grew ever more essential and numerous. The more hatcheries there were, the less essential habitat seemed; the less important habitat became, the easier it was to justify development and hatcheries.[65]

Scientific studies had cast considerable doubt on the benefits of fish culture, but state managers interpreted research in the most positive light possible. In 1931, for example, Hugh Mitchell dismissed as insignificant fish-marking studies that reported low return rates for hatchery fish. The marked fish, he insisted, "represent not the total returns, but an unknown and varying proportion of the total." Mitchell nevertheless hailed the same studies for proving "beyond question the heritable quality" of home-stream rule

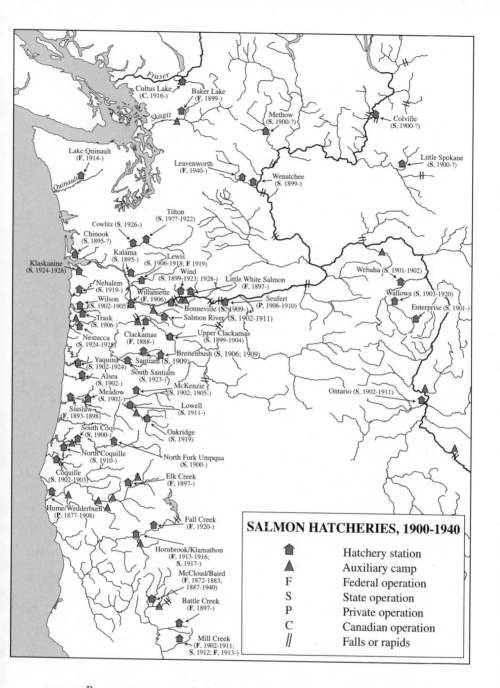

SALMON HATCHERIES, 1900-1940

🏠	Hatchery station
🔺	Auxiliary camp
F	Federal operation
S	State operation
P	Private operation
C	Canadian operation
//	Falls or rapids

Map labels:

Cultus Lake (C, 1916-)
Baker Lake (F, 1899-)
Methow (S, 1900-?)
Colville (S, 1900-?)
Little Spokane (S, 1900-?)
Lake Quinault (F, 1914-)
Leavenworth (F, 1940-)
Wenatchee (S, 1899-)
Tilton (S, 19??-1922)
Cowlitz (S, 1926-)
Chinook (S, 1895-?)
Kalama (S, 1895-)
Lewis (S, 1906-1918; F 1919)
Klaskanine (S, 1924-1928)
Webaha (S, 1901-1902)
Wallowa (S, 1903-1920)
Enterprise (S, 1901-)
Nehalem (S, 1919-)
Wind (S, 1899-1923; 1928-)
Little White Salmon (F, 1897-)
Wilson (S, 1902-1905)
Willamette (F, 1906)
Bonneville (S, 1909-)
Seufert (P, 1906-1910)
Salmon River (S, 1902-1911)
Trask (S, 1906-)
Nestucca (S, 1924-1928)
Clackamas (F, 1888-)
Upper Clackamas (S, 1899-1904)
Breitenbush (S, 1906; 1909)
Yaquina (S, 1902-1924)
Santiam (S, 1909)
Ontario (S, 1902-1911)
Alsea (S, 1902-)
South Santiam (S, 1923-)
Meadow (S, 1902-)
McKenzie (S, 1902; 1905-)
Siuslaw (F, 1893-1898)
Lowell (S, 1911-)
South Coos (S, 1900-)
Oakridge (S, 1919)
North Coquille (S, 1910-)
North Fork Umpqua (S, 1900-)
Coquille (S, 1902-1903)
Elk Creek (F, 1897-)
Hume/Wedderburn (P, 1877-1908)
Fall Creek (F, 1920-)
Hornbrook/Klamathon (F, 1913-1916; S, 1917-)
McCloud/Baird (F, 1872-1883; 1887-1940)
Battle Creek (F, 1897-)
Mill Creek (F, 1902-1911; S, 1912; F, 1913-)

MAP 17. By 1940, most streams had at least one state or federal hatchery despite the hatcheries' inability to restore even one declining fishery. Note the continued tendency to sacrifice inland habitat by locating stations in the lower portions of watersheds and west of the Cascades.

and seasonal runs. "The experiments," he concluded, "substantiate the plans and policies [that Oregon's] Department of Fish Culture adopted in 1924." The way Mitchell read reports for best effect on his agency suggests the role politics played in the interpretation of science. The more scientists saw of this behavior, the more they disdained administrators. By the 1940s some simply did not trust Oregon officials.[66]

The tendency to stifle criticism occasionally infected the USBF as well. American scientists did not duplicate Foerster's research because of an international agreement that delegated to Foerster all research on hatchery efficacy, but Willis Rich's statistical analysis from 1921–22 did remain influential despite nonpublication. As late as 1934, Stanford ichthyologist Paul Needham requested a copy of the report from Elmer Higgins, chief of the Division of Scientific Inquiry. Higgins knew nothing about it, so he asked Rich for information. Rich replied that the report was, "naturally, somewhat out of date now but I think that the main conclusions would not be materially changed even if it were brought up to date." Higgins conveyed the study to Needham, but he added an explicit proviso at the bottom of the cover letter: "This report has not been released for publication and no additional copies should be made or distributed."[67]

The exchange, some twelve years after Rich submitted his study, suggests several possible reasons for the report's limited circulation. Higgins and others might have lacked confidence in Rich's findings, but Rich seemed better versed than Higgins on methodology and steadfastly confident of his conclusions. Another possible explanation is that Rich's findings were too volatile for public consumption, but such caution seems unwarranted in the light of the broad publication of the Canadian studies and concurrent policy changes in British Columbia and Alaska.[68]

Rich continued to criticize fish culture into the late 1930s. In a 1939 address to ichthyologists at Stanford, Rich noted: "Biologists in general are skeptical of the claims made for artificial propagation . . . because these claims have often been extravagant and the proof is entirely inadequate. Indeed, many conservationalists feel that the complacent confidence felt by fishermen, laymen, and administrators in the ability of artificial propagation to counterbalance any inroads that man may make . . . is a serious stumbling block in the way of the development of proper conservation programs."[69]

There was irony in Rich's words. Although the separation between biologists and fish culturists was explicit, Willis Rich was himself no longer simply a scientist. The preceding year the Oregon Fish Commission had hired him to direct its new Research Division. As an administrator, Rich could not undermine the fundamental policy of the institution he served, so he qualified himself. "The possibilities of developing methods of artificial propagation that will produce satisfactory returns in terms of fish of commercial size is too great to be passed over lightly or with prejudice."[70]

With Bonneville Dam in operation and Grand Coulee nearly complete, Rich resigned himself to accommodation. He saw opposition to development as "futile . . . particularly those [such as] water power and agriculture. In general they are potentially more valuable to the community as a whole than are the fishery resources, and the laws of economics will be served." Managers should instead work within the system and rely on technological solutions because "it seems not unreasonable to believe that general principles may eventually be developed that will be of general application and that may point the way to the development of our water resources in such a manner as to leave the supply of migratory fishes more or less intact."[71]

Like fish culturists, Rich had not rejected science. Instead, he deferred questions of efficacy until "general principles" magically developed. A century after Jules Haime had prophesied that fish culture would soon "be naturalized among the useful sciences," administrators were still pining for a Progressive science that would support them. Ironically, it was development, and not science, that ensured the place of artificial propagation by precluding alternative strategies that relied on nature. This was the political, economic, and environmental context of fish culture and fishery science in the states of the American Northwest.[72]

The three decades between 1930 and 1960 witnessed a massive reengineering of the environment and biology of salmon. Dam building completed the concentration of reproduction; fish culturists relocated and retained salmon for ever longer periods; and scientists tried to solve problems stemming from these activities. Action culminated in 1960 with Oregon's shift to a smolt release program, but each change further altered the biology of salmon.

Bonneville, Grand Coulee, and other dams (see table 7) made many people fear for salmon, but the political economy of development increasingly worked against the fish. Rich warned that damming the Columbia "may well result in the extermination of a large part of the remaining runs of both chinooks and bluebacks." Even if Bonneville's fishways worked, the cumulative effect of many dams could still modify "the entire ecological organization" of the Columbia "to the detriment of the native fishes." Fishers, managers, and scientists tried to moderate damage, but their combined numbers and strongest arguments paled before the bureaucratic might, popular appeal, and Progressive ideology of the Bureau of Reclama-

TABLE 7. Hydroelectric, Diversion, and Storage Dams, 1931–59

Year	Dam	Watershed	Year	Dam	Watershed
1931	Ariel	Lewis	1952	Hungry Horse	Flathead
1931	Merwin	Lewis	1953	McNary	Columbia
1931	Deadwood	Payette	1953	Yale	Lewis
1932	Owyhee	Owyhee	1953	Detroit	Santiam
1932	Thief Valley	Powder	1954	Big Cliff	Santiam
1933	Rock Island	Columbia	1954	Lookout Point	Willamette
1933	Cle Elum	Yakima	1955	Chief Joseph	Columbia
1935	Agency Valley	Malheur	1955	Albeni Falls	Pend Oreille
1937	Bonneville	Columbia	1955	Dexter	Willamette
1937	Unity	Burnt	1956	Chandler	Yakima
1939	Kerr	Flathead	1957	The Dalles	Columbia
1942	Grand Coulee	Columbia	1957	Palisades	Snake
1945	Shasta	Sacramento	1957	Pelton	Deschutes
1949	Bliss	Snake	1958	Brownlee	Snake
1949	Dorena	Willamette	1958	Roza	Yakima
1950	Anderson Ranch	Boise	1958	Swift #1	Lewis
1950	Keswick	Sacramento	1959	Priest Rapids	Columbia
1952	C. J. Strike	Snake	1959	Moxon Rapids	Clark Fork
1952	Cabinet Gorge	Clark Fork			

SOURCES: U.S. Department of Energy, *Multipurpose Dams of the Pacific Northwest* (Portland: Bonneville Power Administration, 1978); U.S. Army Corps of Engineers and Federal Emergency Management Agency, *National Inventory of Dams* (Washington, 1995–96, computer file).

tion, Corps of Engineers, and Bonneville Power Administration. Salmon fishing was simply less profitable than other industries. Rich resurrected the idea of protecting salmon by ceding control to federal managers, but although Oregon wanted the federal government to bear the cost of protection, it still refused to yield jurisdiction.[73]

Congress instead tried to mitigate damage through technology. In 1938 it passed the Mitchell Act, which instructed the Bureau of Reclamation

(*Facing page*) Well into the twentieth century, Americans still believed that technology would save salmon from the new dams on the Columbia, yet as this cartoon suggests, most still thought narrowly in terms of adults migrating upstream. Few considered the threats to juveniles swimming over spillways or through turbines. (*Nature Magazine* 28 [Aug. 1936].)

TOO BAD THE POOR FISH CAN'T DO THIS!

If dams could have fishways, there would be
no objection to them

and Corps of Engineers to work with the USBF and, after 1940, the Fish and Wildlife Service (FWS), to save salmon. Dam builders received carte blanche to impound rivers, and fishery agencies relied on the time-honored solutions of fishways, irrigation screens, and hatcheries to ameliorate change. This time, however, they also adopted more radical measures. Grand Coulee was going to block over 1,000 miles of spawning habitat, and additional dams would inundate or obstruct many more miles. Administrators decided to offset the loss of habitat by actively transplanting upper-river stocks into streams closer to the Pacific.[74]

The salvage program involved three daunting tasks: identifying or "creating" streams suitable for fish production, constructing a much larger hatchery system, and developing techniques for relocating fish. It translated a century's worth of environmental and managerial trends into a formal policy that systematically completed the spatial concentration of salmon reproduction. The USBF began a comprehensive survey of Columbia tributaries in 1934. They started with streams near Grand Coulee because of the pressing problem of that dam, but eventually canvassed every river in the basin. They located logging dams, logjams, beaver dams, irrigation ditches, and pollution sources. The USBF and FWS then used Works Progress Administration labor to clear streams, build fishways, and screen ditches. The result was a complicated transformation of salmon habitat that was neither wholly successful nor a complete failure. Although development did obstruct many miles of spawning grounds, government programs did re-open important areas that previously had been blocked off, including the upper reaches of the Clackamas, Clearwater, and Rogue Rivers.[75]

Phase 2 called for a sizable increase in hatcheries. The Bureau of Reclamation briefly proposed reserving "some streams as fish refuges on which no conflicting development would be made," but it had neither the power nor the will to enforce the suggestion. The federal government instead invested the majority of its resources in developing and testing "techniques with the end of attaining greater efficiency" from fish culture. The Oregon Fish Commission and the USBF had to relocate the Central and Big White Salmon hatcheries before Bonneville Dam inundated these facilities. The USBF also dug additional ponds at other hatcheries and built a new hatchery on Icicle Creek at Leavenworth, Washington. Since Icicle Creek went dry in summer, the government created an artificial river by digging a 2,500-foot tunnel to Snow Lake.[76]

The final phase involved the physical relocation of salmon to new streams. Salvage operations began in 1939 as Grand Coulee neared completion. The Bureau of Reclamation supplied eight customized tank trucks, and in May state and federal workers began to trap salmon at Rock Island Dam. The first year they transported 36,000 adult salmon to the Wenatchee, Methow, Okanogan, and Entiat Rivers. In 1940 the FWS transferred salmon directly to the holding ponds at Leavenworth. The FWS also planted upper Columbia sockeye in a number of downstream watersheds (see map 18).[77]

Federal administrators quickly declared victory in saving salmon. Harlan Holmes, director of salmon passage operations at Bonneville Dam, noted in 1940 that "from the standpoint of the passage of fish, hydraulic turbines differ all the way from literal sausage grinders to a very satisfactory route for the passage of fish." He insisted that Bonneville's turbines were "at the latter end of this range." There was "little to worry about. Consideration of screening therefore was discontinued." Holmes also dismissed worries about spillways harming fish, and in 1943 dam boosters and the Bureau of Reclamation heralded Grand Coulee's salmon transplant program a success. A liaison for the FWS told a *Reader's Digest* editor that the program was "highly satisfactory." Officials rushed to reassure the public and thus bolster their reputation, but their declarations were premature and overly optimistic.[78]

Bureau of Fisheries researchers were more dubious. A 1938 study warned, "Under present conditions it is questionable if it will be practicable to compensate by purely artificial means for the extensive spawning and rearing grounds which will no longer be available." The authors criticized an important study on methods for holding adult salmon. "The few fish used in the experiment were held under much more favorable conditions than will be possible when some 20,000 to 25,000 are confined in the same area. Such crowding will probably result in greatly increased mortality and may also have an adverse effect on the developing eggs and sperm." The report also cast doubts about lower-river habitat. "All of these streams at one time supported large runs of salmon and steelhead," but "the fact that these runs are practically extinct is sufficient evidence that something is radically wrong."[79]

There were numerous other worries with the salvage program. Trapping activities at Rock Island interfered with habitat surveys almost immediately, and many adults died from handling and from transport in the tank trucks. More fish died before workers could spawn the fish; freezes and droughts killed numerous adults and fry at Leavenworth; and an insufficient water supply plagued the station despite the Snow Lake tunnel. In addition, World War II interrupted the ditch screening and pollution abatement programs unless they related directly to wartime production.[80]

Restoration and development created more subtle problems. Fishery workers removed logs and beaver dams from streams under the assumption that these obstacles threatened salmon. They succeeded in opening vast areas for spawning, but they also simplified rivers in detrimental ways. Eliminating blockages depleted critical habitat and increased streamflow. Juvenile salmon had fewer refuges during floods. By 1945 researchers knew that turbines did destroy many young salmon, that infectious diseases such as columnaris were endemic in Columbia River runs, that many of these fish died from stress induced by injuries during handling or by warm water, and that an unidentified toxicity in the impounded lakes behind dams also killed salmon.[81]

Although fishery administrators rejected complete reliance on fish culture, they nevertheless believed it was the central tool of recovery. By 1945 Paul Needham was director of fisheries for the Oregon Game Commission. In correspondence with the director of North Pacific Fishery Investigations, he noted, "While the Game Commission looks with favor upon artificial propagation as promising beneficial results, it regards placing entire reliance on that remedy alone as inadvisable." Joseph Barnaby probably agreed when he wrote, "At the present time, a reasonable doubt exists whether artificial propagation of certain races and species of salmon can be defended, either biologically or economically." But development left few alternatives, so Barnaby hastily added, "It is believed, however, that many of the apparent inadequacies of artificial propagation do not stem from an inherent inadequacy but from failure to develop and apply efficient fish-cultural techniques and practices."[82]

The tendency of administrators to define social conflicts as technical problems was in fact *the* central failing of salmon management. From artificial insemination to pond-raising to feeding fry, fish culturists and fishery managers had tried to maintain runs through ever more intensive intrusions into the lives of salmon. By the late 1930s, Russell Foerster and William Ricker were studying the efficacy of eliminating predators to increase production; Lauren Donaldson and Fred Foster were manipulating water temperatures and feed to determine optimal conditions for growing salmon; and the USBF was chlorinating hatchery water to prevent diseases. In each case they defined the problem as essentially technical, forgetting or ignoring the role development played in the decline of salmon. Culturists and managers were treating symptoms. They had been layering technology on technology for so long that they lost sight of the underlying social roots of the problem.[83]

Thus when hatcheries continued to run short of expectations, administrators gravitated toward more technology. In 1940 fish culturists had yet to find a suitable fish feed or to solve problems with diseases, so the FWS set

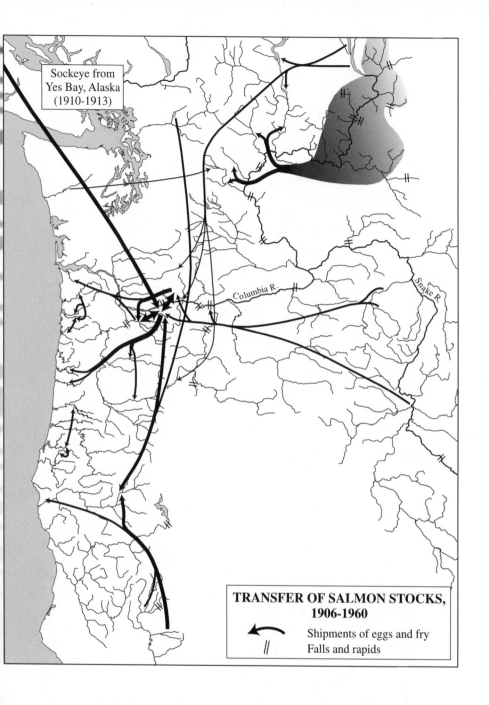

Sockeye from
Yes Bay, Alaska
(1910-1913)

Columbia R.

Snake R.

**TRANSFER OF SALMON STOCKS,
1906-1960**

Shipments of eggs and fry
Falls and rapids

MAP 18. Salmon managers continued the practice of transferring eggs and fry
between streams well into the twentieth century. By 1960, few, if any, streams had
not been affected by this process.

up a series of labs to study nutrition, diseases, toxicology, and genetics. Researchers developed techniques for using antibiotics, antibacterial agents, and antifungals to counter diseases. They also incorporated vitamin supplements into fish feeds. These "prophylactic measures" signaled a sharp break from previous approaches, yet they remained essentially conservative efforts to reform existing practices. The federal labs became sites for a rapprochement between fish culture and science, but it was a reunion wholly on fish culturists' terms.[84]

The more scientists looked, however, the more problems they discovered. By the mid-1940s Russell Foerster noted that sockeye egg transfers had failed to establish new runs, a lesson Oregon fish culturists steadfastly ignored. He also found an inverse correlation between brood populations and the size of individuals, suggesting that making more salmon undermined survival. Concentrating juvenile salmon in hatchery ponds also increased the frequency and impact of disease. In 1949 an outbreak at Leavenworth produced a "virtually 100 percent" mortality, and additional losses occurred at substations during the next two years. Coastal stocks of coho declined despite increased hatchery work, and hatchery survival fell measurably. Between 1940 and the early 1960s, attrition rates *in the hatcheries* approached 50 percent.[85]

Researchers also discovered problems with the new dams. In 1955 the Oregon Fish Commission documented an increase in mortality at dams during periods of high runoff. In the late 1960s scientists linked these dieoffs to supersaturated levels of nitrogen in the water. Researchers found other problems as well. By 1956 they had documented a delay in migration because of dams; by 1959 they knew that squawfish, which thrived in the slack-water pools behind dams, were preying heavily on juvenile salmon; by 1962 they noted that dam-induced changes in temperatures influenced migration patterns; and by 1964 they identified problems with adult salmon falling back over dams after passage. Mortality climbed with each additional dam. The sum of these studies made Willis Rich's warnings about ecological change appear prescient.[86]

Fish culture practices and environmental changes accelerated the process of remaking salmon. Some salmon streams seemed stable, but close inspection revealed marked changes. The Wenatchee had once harbored large runs of sockeye, steelhead, and chinook and small runs of coho. It still had many salmon, but species composition had "shifted significantly" toward chinook, with few sockeye and no coho. Fish culturists also replaced the indigenous race of sockeye with Quinault River stocks to compensate for migration problems induced by the Dryden Dam. They replaced other sockeye stocks with fish from the Arrow Lakes in Canada. Dams began to displace runs to noninundated areas, and fishways selected against large salmon, which suffered more injuries during passage (see map 19). Salmon responded by growing smaller and maturing sooner.[87]

In the 1950s fishery agencies were only beginning to grasp the evolutionary effect of these changes. In 1956 genetics and evolution were still new concepts in management when Peter Larkin explained to administrators why hatchery fish were "less hardy" and more prone to disease than wild salmon. "A hatchery will bypass the high natural mortality on eggs and young fish, but in so doing will largely protect a number of 'weaklings' that die soon after liberation, and/or may condition the fish by diet, water flow—in many ways so that they are less viable. The net result is very little better and often not as good as the natural production."[88]

But fish culturists continued to believe in technology, and advances in fish feeds seemed to confirm their faith. For some time they had wanted to replace liver and culled salmon with a drier substance that would prevent the spread of disease, but no one had yet perfected a feed that was simultaneously nutritious, inexpensive, and capable of delivering antibiotics and vitamin supplements. In the early 1950s researchers with the Cortland Lab at Gracie Swamp, New York, the Fish Nutrition Lab at Cook, Washington, and the Seafood Lab in Astoria, Oregon, turned their attention to the problem. Through a series of developments in which each group improved on the work of the others, the three labs began to create recipes that were steadily drier and more nutritious. The final step came in 1959 when the Seafood Lab adapted a commercial noodle machine to chop material into pellets for salmon.[89]

The Oregon Fish Commission hailed the resulting "semimoist" feed as a breakthrough. Named the Oregon Moist Pellet, it allowed fish culturists to push pond-raising to its logical conclusion. In 1960 Oregon announced a new policy of retaining fry in ponds until they were ready to migrate to sea. Only after they underwent a series of biochemical and physiological changes, called smoltification, would hatcheries release juvenile salmon into streams. The resulting Smolt Program represented the ultimate development in making salmon. Fish culturists would at last be able to segregate salmon from their enemies throughout early life. Ecologically, however, the new policy simply exacerbated the evolutionary problems Peter Larkin had already identified.[90]

During the next fifteen years the Smolt Program produced seemingly wondrous results. Coho production rose from 7.5 million smolts in 1960 to 24 million in 1982, and salmon runs increased substantially on many

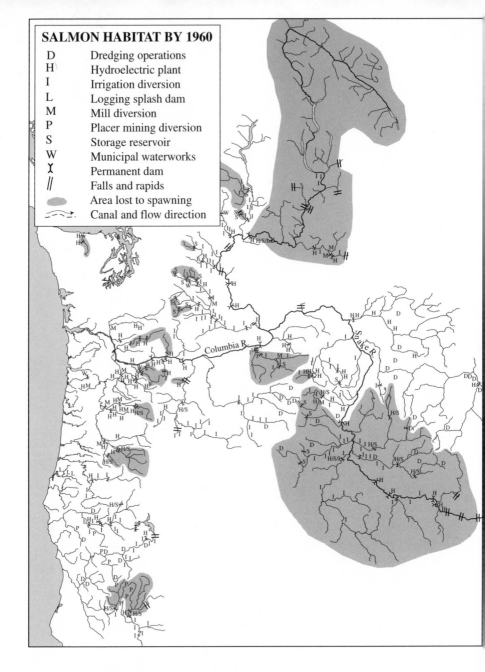

MAP 19. Although improvements to fishways and irrigation ditches reopened some downstream areas between 1930 and 1960, dams had eliminated far more habitat upstream. Main-stem dams had blocked salmon from huge portions of the upper Columbia and Snake River basins. These dams also slowed the current in areas still accessible to salmon, inundating much of the remaining spawning grounds with silt.

Oregon streams despite continued loss of habitat. The popularity of fish culture reached new heights. At the University of Washington, fisheries professor Lauren Donaldson was called a "wizard" for his work on salmon and trout culture. Donaldson used his fame to declare war against " 'fuddy-duddyism'—the broken record that says everything new 'can't work.' " He demanded that America "apply 'mass production' techniques to its fisheries." The Oregon Fish Commission dutifully followed suit, bravely declaring, "Artificial propagation, pursued for more than 80 years, is only now becoming an exact science." Even Canada returned to fish culture by building artificial spawning channels to offset habitat loss.[91]

But impressions of success had again tarnished by the 1980s. By the early 1970s fishery scientists began to worry about plummeting populations of nonhatchery, or "wild," runs of salmon. The downturn raised "the distressing question of whether hatcheries enhanced or hurt" salmon overall. Researchers and fishers also noticed that many hatchery releases were not making it to sea but were instead feeding growing populations of cormorants in estuaries and squawfish in reservoirs behind new dams. Then in the late 1970s all of Oregon's salmon runs experienced sudden and very sharp declines, bottoming out during the intense El Niño of 1983–84. The widespread failure turned scientists' attention to the ocean. Ocean trawlers were harvesting large numbers of salmon as an "incidental bycatch," but physical oceanographers and atmospheric scientists also began to correlate run variations with decades-long, widespread fluctuations in ocean climates. Scientists noticed that hatchery successes neatly coincided with periods of congenial ocean conditions for salmon in the early century and again from 1947 to 1976. This research increasingly challenged the basic premises of artificial propagation. Fish culturists had long believed that they could make salmon more efficiently than nature. As late as 1991, Lauren Donaldson still insisted, "The technology is there—just tell us how many fish you want," but the history of salmon management and recent scientific research on salmon biology and salmon environments suggest a different conclusion.[92]

Fish culturists approached their craft with a peculiar mind-set. They divided nature into categories of friends and enemies and then tried to husband those categories to produce marketable species. This approach worked well with many domesticated animals, but *Oncorhynchus* were less malleable. Ecologists and fishery scientists warned fish culturists that there were potential problems with this approach, but fish culturists' habit of thinking in binary terms propelled them down a different path. They appropriated those scientific ideas which they could assimilate into their agenda and condemned or ignored the rest. To protect juvenile salmon from enemy predators, hatchery operators switched to pond-raising schemes. But retaining fry deflected salmon onto new evolutionary paths. Pond environments selected for individuals that could tolerate dense concentrations of fish. Ponds also harbored endemic diseases and produced fish that, on average, were smaller, weaker, and genetically more similar over time. Researchers anticipated these consequences, but fish culturists and fishery administrators deflected criticism to protect their authority and programs.[93]

The entire history of fish culture has been shaped by political economy. Salmon hatcheries gained and maintained their popularity because they appeared to resolve problems within economic development. Material conflicts between rival interests raised all sorts of nasty political questions about who should benefit from finite resources, but fish culturists redefined these social and political issues as technical problems. This was fortuitous for politicians and fish culturists alike. Fish culture offered legislators a politically appealing panacea, and fish culturists gained continuing governmental support. When problems arose, fishery administrators blandished their expertise before critics and used production figures to bolster popular support for agencies. Ultimately and ironically, it was not science but development that legitimated hatcheries. Euro-American settlement had so thoroughly reorganized the Oregon country that natural reproduction no longer seemed like a viable alternative. The sweeping changes of development made Pacific salmon a stranger in its own natal streams, yet for economic and cultural reasons Pacific northwesterners tried to save these runs almost regardless of cost. The result has been a sort of ecological Ponzi scheme requiring ever greater infusions of money and genetic material to keep hatcheries afloat. Making salmon has been a political success story but a fiscal and ecological disaster.

8 / Taking Responsibility

The way we remember the past shapes the way we understand the present and prepare for the future. Thus the stories we tell about the past are critical. This is why history matters and why Americans contest its content so bitterly. History *is* political. Its ability to legitimate or condemn activities of the state, society, and markets makes it a force in public debates, which is, in part, why Pacific northwesterners have argued so vehemently about *Who Was To Blame* for the decline of salmon. Every explanation has rested on a rendition of the past, and each version holds profound social, cultural, and environmental consequences. Some stories have had greater currency than others, however, and the preferred ones ultimately have done both humans and salmon a grave disservice. Thus we should step back for a moment and examine how and why people remember, portray, and respond to the past the way they do.[1]

The stories northwesterners have told about salmon reveal crucial tensions between the complexity of the past and the simplifying tendencies of storytelling in general and history in particular. Constructing any narrative requires an author to make decisions about what information to include and how to order it. The alternative is a seemingly random list of details with no apparent beginning, middle, end, or plot. These are basic rules for all storytellers, including historians, but history is a special form of narrative. Historians must not only document their evidence but be bound by extra constraints. Like any storyteller, they must select among details and subjects as they form and focus their narratives, but they cannot ignore inconvenient facts or reorder events that seem messy or aesthetically unsatisfying. Historians instead have to struggle with this tension between the simplifying tendencies of narrative and the complexity of the past. Since no single history can contain all details or encompass all viewpoints, all historians can expect challenges as to what information is extraneous. By its very nature then, history is incomplete, and its rules open the way for numerous competing versions of the past.[2]

Some of the variability in histories stems from the contingency of experience. We do not all view the world through a common lens. Identity, culture, and location affect how we understand the present and remember the past. Though Tillamooks, Klickitats, and Paiutes had different explanations for the return of salmon, they had more in common with each other than with the traders, trappers, ministers, miners, and farmers who entered the Oregon country after 1800. Culture takes us only so far, however. Space and class could also separate. Gillnetters, trap men, wheel men, and anglers all pursued salmon, but location, work, and access to capital shaped one's views on the legitimacy of technology, markets, and occupations. These factors produced a cacophony of explanations and accusations about the decline of salmon in the nineteenth and twentieth centuries. No one viewpoint dominated because no single experience encompassed all people or reconciled all interests.[3]

Nothing illustrated the way interest could shape stories better than how resource users explained the roots of the salmon crisis. Everybody invoked the lapsarian narrative of salmon's fall from grace, but each interest group tweaked the story to bolster their particular agenda. Fishers focused on changes to the land and waters and challenged the social legitimacy of rivals; nonfishers concentrated on the sins of overfishing and rationalized decline as sad but unavoidable. Managers were more willing to discuss the broad sweep of environmental change, if only to justify their own technological preferences, but they were less candid about their own role in the crisis. Ironically, all tales were Progressive in that they portrayed change as, on balance, having produced more good than ill. In the process most Oregonians absolved the consumptive engine of capitalism of its central role in the accelerated exploitation of the region. By tacitly accepting the commodification and widespread consumption of nature as inherently just, observers had to adopt other explanations to understand why salmon, and so many other species, diminished rapidly after 1800. Unwilling to critique the marketplace, they pitted resource user against resource user in a Spencerian struggle. Salmon politics devolved into a zero-sum endgame that only exacerbated the simplifying and fracturing tendencies of narrative and experience.[4]

The way Americans managed the fisheries also encouraged people to assign blame rather than assume responsibility, but to cast blame effectively, contestants had to shape their explanations of the crisis so rivals appeared as unambiguous villains. The key to political success, in other words, lay in thinking simplistically, and Pacific northwesterners have done this with amazing facility. As different interests scrambled to maintain their access to resources, history fissioned into severely distorted partisan visions. Each group cultivated a highly selective memory, scapegoated opponents, and marginalized the weak through violence or legislation. Complexity and contingency evaporated in this superheated atmosphere through deliberate acts of amnesia. Political myopia infected every group in the debate.

What was true in the past continues today. Concerned with the plight of salmon, urban environmentalists have taken to reinventing the past to save the future. One author has hazily romanticized subsistence fishing as filled with "virtues worthy of . . . reflection." Others have blended aboriginal ceremony and consumerism into didactic tools. The first-salmon ceremony has reemerged as a New Age rendezvous where Indians and whites meet to exchange stories, food, and goods in the form of books, smoked salmon, and t-shirts. Perhaps the ultimate distortion is that of writer Tom Jay, who heralds the ceremony as a way to "get back in sync with the salmon cycle."

> Imagine a Thanksgiving dinner of your great-great-grandchildren 100 years from now. In the center of the table is a bright silver salmon locally caught and cooked in the practiced way of long enjoyment and reverence. At the end of the feast there will be a simple ceremony—a long walk to the creek with neighboring families, each with a wooden bowl of salmon bones, to return the remains to the waters of their creation in gratitude and respect. Perhaps there will be mention of the ancestors, if that is who we decide to be—the old ones who stayed put, who gave the salmon shelter in their hearts and who found their own way home.[5]

Reimbuing salmon with spiritual qualities seems appealing, but it tends to mystify rather than enlighten the connections between fish, environments, and people (see map 20). In portraying the aboriginal relationship to salmon as essentially benign, Jay misconstrues both the intent and the effect of aboriginal practices. He obscures crucial questions about material relationships with nature by resorting to magical solutions. But Jay's errors are hardly unique. Like other resource users, environmentalists don the garb of *Most Worthy Protector* in order to speak for salmon and The People. In neither case have they been broadly persuasive. Although angler Bill Bakke has vigorously led both Oregon Trout and the Native Fish Society in an effort "to bring about public support for the region's native fish," and environmental spokesman Andy Kerr has boasted that "environmentalists

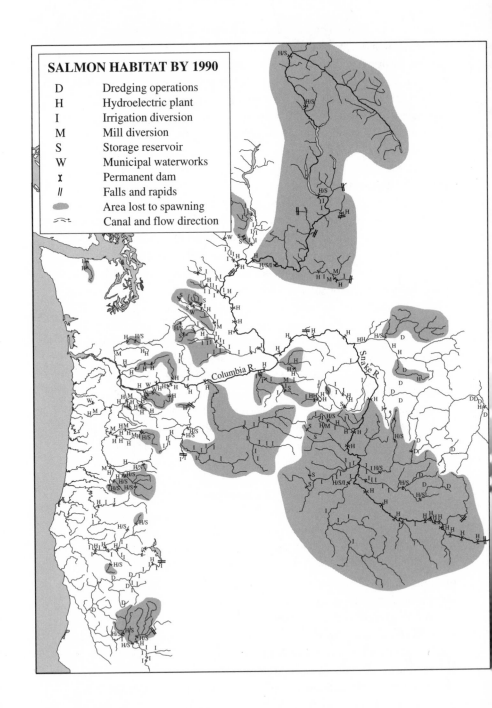

SALMON HABITAT BY 1990

D	Dredging operations
H	Hydroelectric plant
I	Irrigation diversion
M	Mill diversion
S	Storage reservoir
W	Municipal waterworks
✗	Permanent dam
∥	Falls and rapids
	Area lost to spawning
～	Canal and flow direction

Columbia R.

Snake R.

are hell to live with but make great ancestors," one needs to ask: which public and whose ancestors?[6]

In decrying the excesses of other resource users and management agencies, environmentalists have artfully converted self-interest into principle. Their demonization of rivals has conveniently obscured their own material interests in nature as consumed experience, yet those interests are no less tangible and no less biased by class, race, and location. Scenic consumption is big business among the urban middle class, and they have donated billions of dollars to environmental organizations to maintain access to their preferred environmental experiences. Those organizations have, in turn, assumed the mantle of *Most Worthy Protector* and worked to exclude other user groups from coveted spaces. Environmentalism heralded the dawn of a new era in the 1960s and 1970s, but historians have noted repeatedly that "it never entirely shed its privileged-class origins." "Nature appreciation [remains] a 'full stomach' phenomenon that is [largely] confined to the rich, urban, sophisticated."[7]

Thus modern solutions to the salmon crisis only serve to illustrate further the persistent gap between rhetorical and material interests in nature. Concerned about disappearing salmon runs, salmon advocates restore creeks and streams in hopes of luring salmon back to urban and suburban watersheds. Such efforts not only revive salmon but enhance real-estate investments, and while such profits are not necessarily wrong, self-interest again suggests the limits of concern. Restoration activities possess potent symbolism, but they also seem to be small and futile gestures. "Restoring" Ravenna Creek near the University of Washington or tearing down dams on a few minor streams pales before the mounting problems on the Snake, Columbia, Fraser, Sacramento, and most coastal streams. As one fishery administrator remarked, environmentalists may be "winning battles but losing the war."[8]

Although urbanites have applied considerable energy to cleaning up degraded habitat, they have resisted limits on their broader destructive impulse. In 1973, Oregon established the Land Conservation and Development Commission. The LCDC's stated intention was to govern urban

MAP 20 (*facing page*). By 1990, development had eliminated all but a small fraction of salmon's former habitat. Main-stem dams block huge portions of the upper Columbia and Snake River basins, inundate much of the rest with lakes and silt, and impede the seaward and spawning migrations of salmon. Mining, logging, grazing, irrigation, fishing, and urbanization in areas without dams continue to pressure habitat in other ways.

growth and to protect rural and scenic values, yet developers and politicians have pierced those boundaries repeatedly to fuel their local economies. Urbanization has displaced many natural-resource activities during this growth, yet cities have not diminished their consumption of those resources. As historian William Cronon notes, "Although we too easily tend to forget this fact, every urban culture also farms." He might have added that they also graze, fish, log, and mine. Despite land use planners' intentions, continued development inside boundaries nevertheless escalates the demand for resources elsewhere in the region. Any jump in home construction increases the consumption of food, water, and electricity, reduces forest and wetland cover, and exacerbates the problem of winter flooding and summer "drought." Circumscribing growth spatially has not stemmed the decline of habitat, because it does not address the problem of consumption. Growth boundaries only say where consumption will occur; they do little or nothing to limit its intensification in those areas.[9]

Lenient with their own demands, urbanites have been less hesitant to restrict the activities of rural neighbors. Portland environmentalists have formed several trusts to save salmon by leasing water rights in rural areas. Other groups deploy salmon in the courts to halt logging and grazing on public lands. Both approaches share an important and by now familiar strategy: they displace the burden of conservation onto more marginal groups and away from home. One pays ruralites not to farm; the other litigates them not to log. University of Oregon economist Ed Whitelaw has rationalized this asymmetric approach to environmental regulation as new rules for a new society. According to Whitelaw, as the Pacific Northwest's economy shifts from natural resources to the service sector, it makes sense to manage nature as an amenity for its urban, white-collar future rather than its rural, blue-collar past. Lost in Whitelaw's analysis, though, is the Pacific Northwest's diversity. Although the I-5 corridor running from Seattle to Medford is increasingly urban and postindustrial, most of the rest of the region and many of its citizens still engage in such supposedly moribund activities as fishing, farming, logging, and grazing. Moreover, they do so because urban consumers demand their products.[10]

"Environmental amenities" is a recent rationale that, as much as any argument, signifies how modern our contests over salmon have become; but special claims to salmon have been around for centuries, and none has proved more bitter, long-lasting, and significant than the treaty-guaranteed rights of Indians. By the late 1950s, Indians were taking less than 5 percent of the harvest, yet whites resented even this much and blamed Indians for declining runs. Anglers, who saw Indians as taking "their" steelhead, encouraged state officials to rein in tribal fishers, and Oregon and Washington fish and game managers began to ignore standing agreements between the states and tribes and systematically coerce Indians from the rivers of Puget Sound and the Columbia. In the early 1960s, Indians responded by emulating the civil rights movement and conducting a series of "fish-ins." When Indians openly defied state fishing regulations, enforcement agencies responded with sometimes violent arrests and equipment seizures. The confrontations inflamed public opinion, and people on both sides demagogued the issue in the media. While much was in dispute, all parties agreed that the cases should be used to test the validity and scope of the Indians' treaty rights to salmon.[11]

As the cases moved through the courts, and decisions became increasingly decisive in Indians' favor, events revealed lingering social and cultural fissures. In Oregon, state officials tried three cases involving Umatilla and Yakima Indians. They lost all, and in 1969, Judge Robert Belloni handed down decisions reaffirming Indian treaty rights, independent access to waters on or off reservations, and "a fair and equitable share of all fish." Oregonians reacted virulently to Belloni's decisions, but state officials conceded the issue and agreed to manage salmon runs equitably with the tribes. Under the leadership of State Attorney General Slade Gorton, contests in Washington were long, spiteful, and destructive. Gorton, who had family ties to the New England industrial fishery, claimed that the treaties had made Indians into "supercitizens." During the 1960s and 1970s he pursued cases against Puget Sound and Columbia River Indians with great vigor but incredible incompetence, and by the late 1970s he had unintentionally guaranteed Indians the right to 50 percent of the harvest; the right to catch all species of salmon, wild or hatchery, and on or off reservations; the right to participate in fishery management; and an implicit right to protect habitat to sustain those runs.[12]

The Washington rulings, now known as the "Boldt decisions" for presiding judge George Boldt, stunned the region and transformed salmon management. Public bitterness over the outcome stemmed partly from ignorance of previous court decisions and misunderstandings about Indians' constitutional standing, but there were also very real injuries. To accommodate court-ordered harvest reallocations, managers drastically curtailed non-Indian fishing. Trollers and netters struggled to make loan payments during shorter seasons and adverse conditions, while Indians built up their fleets with government subsidies. In retaliation, some non-Indians and Washington state officials openly defied the law, but that only resulted in greater intrusion by the federal courts in state management. Others used the Boldt decisions as springboards to power and influence. Gorton became a study in upward failure. Having orchestrated a litigious disaster, he used Indian success to incite conservative anger and ran for the U.S. Senate in 1980. Meanwhile the Nez Perce, Umatilla, Warm Springs, and Yakima Confederated Tribes formed the Columbia River Intertribal Fish Commission in 1976 and began to invoke their court-affirmed right to participate as equals in fishery and habitat management.[13]

Although treaty rights remain unpopular among non-Indians, dam removal has supplanted them in recent years as an even more contentious issue. In 1994 the Oregon Water Resources Commission voted to tear down Savage Rapids Dam on the Rogue River. The commission made its decision reluctantly and only after investigations revealed that the installation of irrigation pumps would be far less expensive than building new fish ladders. The vote to tear down the dam was only the first salvo in a longer and deeper battle. Local residents resisted removal, claiming that pumping water would raise their expenses and put them out of business. They persuaded legislators not only to overturn the decision but to *increase* their water allocation. Environmentalists fumed at the reversal but had little sway in Salem. Ultimately it took a carrot and stick approach by the U.S. Fish and Wildlife Service, offering economic incentives with one hand while threatening litigation and withdrawal of funds with the other, to persuade the local water board to accept removal. Voters promptly recalled the board and, when the new board again voted for removal, recalled that one too. Similarly, plans to tear down two dams on the Elwha River in Washington State have turned on the will of a fiscally conservative Congress to fund demolition and, for a while at least, the ability of a Port Angeles paper mill to find cheap electricity elsewhere. Such episodes reveal how recovery continues to hinge on economic issues more than sympathy for salmon.[14]

Like many facets of this history, the problems of power and interest have been most pronounced in the Columbia River basin. Dam building continued into the mid-1970s (see table 8) as power companies and the Army Corps of Engineers erected one large dam after another to generate electricity, facilitate barging, and control flooding. With the completion of Lower Granite Dam in 1975, the Inland Empire Waterways Association and Army Corps of Engineers had at last succeeded in constructing a 350-mile river highway from the Pacific to the Clearwater. Lewiston, Idaho, had become a seaport, and Snake River salmon had to pass eight dams on their way to sea or to spawn.[15]

The transformation of the Columbia and Snake into a modern transportation corridor was both a victory for inland resource users and a disaster for salmon. Gas bubble disease, turbines, predation, and delayed migration

TABLE 8. Hydroelectric, Diversion, and Storage Dams, 1961–84

Year	Dam	River	Year	Dam	River
1961	Rocky Reach	Columbia	1967	Duncan	Duncan
1961	Ice Harbor	Snake	1967	Boundary	Pend Oreille
1961	Oxbow	Snake	1967	Green Peter	Santiam
1961	Foster	Santiam	1968	John Day	Columbia
1962	Hills Creek	Willamette	1968	Keenleyside	Columbia
1962	Dam #2	Bull Run	1968	Lower Monumental	Snake
1962	Trinity	Trinity	1968	Mossy Rock	Cowlitz
1962	Iron Gate	Klamath	1970	Little Goose	Snake
1963	Wanapum	Columbia	1973	Mica	Columbia
1963	Mayfield	Cowlitz	1973	Lost Creek	Rogue
1963	Whiskeytown	Sacramento	1974	Dworshak	Clearwater
1964	Round Butte	Deschutes	1975	Lower Granite	Snake
1964	Cougar	McKenzie	1975	Libby	Kootenai
1965	Fall Creek	Willamette	1980	Applegate	Applegate
1967	Wells	Columbia	1984	Revelstroke	Columbia
1967	Hells Canyon	Snake			

SOURCES: U.S. Department of Energy, *Multipurpose Dams of the Pacific Northwest* (Portland: Bonneville Power Administration, 1978); U.S. Army Corps of Engineers and Federal Emergency Management Agency, *National Inventory of Dams* (Washington, 1995–96, computer file).

took an increasing toll on juvenile salmon, much as Willis Rich had predicted in 1938. By the late 1960s the Corps of Engineers acknowledged these problems and began experiments to ameliorate conditions by transporting fish past dams using trucks, airplanes, and barges. Preliminary tests were ambiguous, but the temporary program proved so popular with people east of the Cascades that it became a permanent fixture in the annual budget of the Corps. A fleet of specially designed barges now transports between 15 and 20 million juvenile salmon downstream each year, but observers hotly contest barging's impact. Some studies show that juvenile salmon survive far better when barged around dams, but they also suggest that barged salmon do not survive in the ocean as well as nonbarged and wild runs. Barged fish also tend to stray more frequently as adults, and barging clearly has not stemmed the decline of Snake River runs. Like fish culture before it, barging continues not because science has proved that it works but because it helps politicians ameliorate disputes between the river's many users.[16]

The continued decline of Pacific salmon has drawn Congress's attention more constantly than at any time since the 1930s. In 1980, Congress created the Northwest Power Planning Council (NWPPC) to ensure that dam operators gave equal consideration to salmon in managing rivers. Fiscal and ecological matters surrounding recovery kept Congress's attention riveted on the Columbia for more than a decade, and in 1994 it appointed an independent scientific team to survey the management of Columbia and Snake River runs. Like so many before them, Congress wanted to know what was harming salmon and why recovery had cost so much yet produced so little. The Independent Scientific Group (ISG) reported that environmental and social issues were too complex and research too incomplete to answer many questions, but they did address the issue of dams in emphatic terms. Noting that the only healthy population of salmon resided in the one remaining undammed stretch of the middle Columbia River, the so-called Hanford Reach, the ISG argued that the surest strategy for restoring salmon was to return the Columbia and Snake to the "normative ecosystem conditions" that prevailed before dams and development. The ISG recommendations put dam and power agencies in an awkward position. Having previously praised the ISG's expertise, the Corps and Bonneville Power Administration were unable to dismiss this scientific criticism of river management. Concrete monoliths and an industrial infrastructure that have controlled the Columbia and Snake for sixty years with impunity now suddenly seem vulnerable.[17]

The ISG recommendations have unleashed a telling debate about the future of the Columbia basin. On one side stand environmentalists, Indians, and fishers in favor of breaching four dams on the lower Snake and draining the reservoir behind John Day Dam on the Columbia. They want to accelerate river flows and emulate conditions before the 1920s, so they criticize the "sacred cows of barging to Lewiston, corporate farming and aluminum subsidies" and call for a return to the aboriginal river. In an ironic inversion of earlier values, some now regard progress as an acceptable sacrifice in order to save salmon. Those with a vested interest in the harnessed river think otherwise. Dam and power agencies, irrigators, electric companies, barge operators, and aluminum smelters claim dam removal is a "selfish" attempt to place fish above people. They forecast a bleak future of floods, polluted air, and economic depression and prefer a continuation of large hatcheries, salmon barging, and restricted fishing—in other words, business as usual. As in the 1908 election, a politic middle has tried to depolarize the debate by blaming more distant threats, including foreign fishing fleets, ocean climates, and natural predators. They demand federal subsidies, stronger treaties, and vigorous elimination of seals, sea lions, and birds. As usual, each perspective sees the problem lying elsewhere.[18]

These centrifugal forces are tearing apart the governing structure of salmon recovery. In 1980 salmon advocates celebrated the creation of the NWPPC as marking the dawn of a new era and declared an end to power interests riding "roughshod over the public interest," but they were too optimistic. The NWPPC spent ten long years lobbying for salmon, yet in 1990 the federal government had to list Snake River sockeye and chinook runs under the Endangered Species Act. Only, then, after disaster had struck, did the NWPPC gain significant political leverage. The council finally forced dam operators to manage the rivers for migrating salmon, and land users to restore habitat for spawning fish. By 1997, however, these efforts had cost more than $3 billion, and salmon were still declining. Critics of salmon recovery complained about the expense and tried to undermine the council's authority. Slade Gorton, now a U.S. senator and strong advocate for irrigation, barging, and power generation, demanded a fiscal accounting of recovery and insisted that there was "a cost above which, regrettably, you let species disappear." Then, to ensure this outcome, he helped pass federal legislation that limited the amount of money which could be spent on salmon recovery.[19]

Soon after, the NWPPC began to disintegrate. In early 1997 the council approved the release of water from upstream dams as part of an experiment to see if accelerated river flows would flush juvenile salmon to sea faster and increase downstream survival. The state of Montana objected to lowering its western reservoirs to save runs in other states, so it quit the council in protest. One month later Indians withdrew their support as well, citing a persistent unwillingness by the council to consult with treaty tribes over salmon policy. As the infrastructure of salmon recovery fractured and shattered, one close observer framed the problem succinctly by noting that "nobody is in charge."[20]

The debate over the Columbia River's future has dramatically qualified claims about salmon's regional importance. Advocates have recently asserted salmon as a regional symbol in order to justify huge government expenditures and dramatic environmental transformations, but in doing so, defenders of salmon mark themselves not simply as northwesterners but also as urban and residing west of the Cascades. Seattle writer Tim Egan has argued that the Pacific Northwest is "wherever the salmon can get to," while others insist that "salmon symbolize nature in the Pacific Northwest" and "are sacred to most Northwesterners." People living elsewhere in the region feel remarkably different. Residents east of the Cascades depend on rivers for irrigation and power. They regard salmon advocates as "outsiders" and are frank about their loyalties. The manager of an inn near Grand Coulee Dam told one journalist that he did not "give a good goddamn about salmon," and a retiree in Redmond, Oregon, told the *Portland Oregonian* that he "would rather have a light in my cold refrigerator than a warm salmon on the shelf."[21]

Salmon is not the tie that binds. Fish advocates claim that salmon signify profound cultural values worth preserving, but opponents reject this argument. Salmon may be fun to catch and good to eat, but they hardly constitute a transcendent symbol when so many people reject them out of hand. Contestants often talk past each other about their divergent concerns, and debates painfully reveal that there is no such thing as a homogeneous regional culture. In everyday life, there is not one Northwest but many Northwests—not one region but many places—and the residents of each place value their environments in remarkably different ways. Salmon does bring people together after a fashion, but these contests revolve less around symbolism than such material issues as access to water, power, and habitat.

This lack of consensus highlights a modern paradox surrounding salmon, symbolism, and regionalism. As much as any species, salmon do map a region. Their genetically coded movements through lakes, rivers, and oceans limn a series of spaces that humans long ago learned to recognize and exploit. This part of the regional argument is undeniable, but salmon advocates err when they ignore the issue of social fragmentation. Salmon migrations define a biologically coherent region, but human culture is not conterminous with those movements. Many residents no longer care about salmon, and some openly resent the fish. Valuation persists in compressed form, surviving contentiously only in those cities, towns, and reservations that still pursue salmon as a way of life or whose economies are not threatened by salmon's presence. The paradox of salmon is that they inscribe a natural region even as they bare their cultural irrelevance over much of it. Advocates who invoke symbolism testify to their concerns, but when they insist that their concerns are, or should be, universal, they simply expose the social and cultural fissures that underlie these environmental contests. This is one example of how simple stories can fail humans and nature, yet the way Americans use the state to resolve such conflicts empowers just this sort of simplistic thinking.

Government is an exercise in social power that usually marginalizes the needs of nature. Representatives serve the interests of abstract bodies called "states" and "districts." They speak for communities, political parties, and backers—not salmon. Their power is gauged by the ability to realize constituents' interests, and success is measured in votes. But salmon do not vote, they are not a constituency, and despite protestations to the contrary, they are not represented in American politics. Yet any attempt to restore salmon must pass through legislative bodies in the Northwest and Congress because nineteenth-century politicians asserted their jurisdiction over the fisheries. Then and now, politicians have desired big salmon runs, but they also have needed to keep constituents happy, especially those with an economic interest in salmon or their habitats. Legislators and administrators have accommodated these interests by managing nature to serve economic and political allies—not salmon. When conflict erupted over declining runs, fishery management became a political exercise in apportioning blame.[22]

And the best way to cast blame has been to tell simple stories. Keeping things simple is an axiom of politics. Legislators and lawyers like to reduce complicated issues to binary choices. Yes or no; guilty or innocent: these are the preferred verdicts. The perpetual grayness of the past can cripple an advocate in the courtroom or legislative hall, so contestants make issues as simple and straightforward as possible. Simplicity also strengthens the moral of the story, whether it be the sins of nets, dams, or chain saws, or the superiority of race, hook and line, or environmentalism. Thus experience has shaped the *way* people have understood the salmon crisis, and the American political system has influenced *how* they have explained it. The result has been an adversarial approach to social memory. Advocates pleaded their strongest, if simplified, cases, exposed them to criticism from opponents, and legislators, voters, and jurors assessed the relative merits of each story. In idealized form, a larger truth should have emerged from these partial representations, but such outcomes have been rare at best.[23]

People's resistance to acknowledging a more complex history has stemmed from their inability to set aside their interests in the matter, which is in turn intrinsically connected to the way we govern ourselves. The salmon crisis is so complicated that it implicates everyone. No voter, juror, or legislator has stood outside the problem, because everybody has had a material interest in the outcome. This does not mean voters and jurors were, or are, incapable of acknowledging their role in the crisis—just that it has not been the case to date. Legislators have been no less compromised by interest, but they suffer additional burdens as well. As both advocates arguing for the interests of constituents and jurors voting on the merits of those arguments, elected officials inhabit dual roles that hopelessly compromise objectivity.

And because legislative power hinges on the ability to stay in office, representatives have had little incentive to counter the interests of their constituents. Elections are popularity contests, after all, and going against the interests of voters is a sure way to become unpopular and unemployed. Contentious, tangled issues like salmon are the sort of occupational hazard most elected officials wish to avoid, yet since the 1870s they have insisted on jurisdiction over fishery issues—which have historically been some of the most entangling problems to solve. In the process, they have become the weak link in the chain of social responsibility. Though far from alone in blame, politicians' shortcomings loom particularly large because they had more power and greater ability to rectify problems than anybody else in the region.

The compromised position of legislators was a critical factor because they also set the terms upon which science and management would meet in the nineteenth century to save salmon. Scientists at the time had much to say about fish and the fisheries, but like other actors in this story, they were not of one mind. Some insisted that there were limits to how much people could exploit nature, while others claimed that there were, or would soon be, methods for producing as many fish as society needed. Legislators heard all these messages, but some were clearly more appealing than others. Unwilling to restrict their constituents, politicians instead pursued technological solutions, and scientists, some of whom were politicians in their own right, became willing partners in order to secure needed government funding.

Fish culture was the spawn of these mutual interests. Founded on the premise that humans could produce salmon better than nature, fish culturists such as Livingston Stone, Samuel Wilmot, R. D. Hume, and Henry O'Malley, science entrepreneurs such as Spencer Baird, Hugh Smith, and Lauren Donaldson, and political hacks such as Hollister McGuire, F. C. Reed, Hustler Van Dusen, and Herman McAllister promised to make endless supplies of salmon efficiently and scientifically. Although a few observers understood that technology would never wholly solve the problem of decline, most Americans believed in fish culture with a faith bordering on fanaticism. During the next century politicians and the public spent huge sums of money in the hope that science would find a panacea, and administrators and scientists happily received these funds and continued their work. Fish culture began its long service as the foundation of fishery management. Resting on a set of assumptions that appealed to most Americans, it provided a politically stable philosophy of management for all concerned: making salmon.

If everything had worked out as planned, we would now frame these events as a great success story, and in fact, for a long time Americans did regard fish culture as a triumph. But not anymore. Fish culture helped politicians ameliorate a host of social tensions, but it hurt salmon. Hatcheries helped rationalize the loss of habitat, the narrowing of genetic pools, and the alteration of biology. Bureaucracies grew and administrators proclaimed success, but salmon runs plummeted, fisheries died, and communities dissolved. Making salmon was a bureaucratic success story but an ecological and social nightmare. Its failure unleashed a series of virulent contests as rivals struggled over a shrinking pie and legislators rejected more sweeping changes.

Eager to avoid entanglement in these controversies, and worried about their own interests, fishery administrators and scientists have also tended to suppress the complexity of the salmon crisis. Despite huge amounts of historical data, fishery agencies have woeful institutional memories. Research on the consequences of environmental change is a case in point. Although George Perkins Marsh and Spencer Fullerton Baird offered sophisticated explanations of the perils of environmental change during the 1850s and 1870s, researchers have had to document the impact of fishing, mining, logging, irrigating, and pollution repeatedly during the twentieth century. Successive studies have offered increasingly precise explanations of the material effects of human and natural activities, but the basic insights of Marsh and Baird remain intact.

But these issues have been relatively open to inquiry compared to the subject of fish culture. From the beginning, salmon politics has been embedded in a series of highly volatile spatial, racial, cultural, and class tensions. Politicians and fishery administrators avoided these conflicts like week-old fish. They instead relied on technology to solve social problems, science to cultivate an impression of technical mastery, and public faith to sustain support. The more technologically dependent salmon management became, the more reluctant administrators were to examine their raison d'être. And even when individuals such as Barton Evermann and Willis Rich did criticize practices, they framed their remarks in ways that insulated present policies from past mistakes. Such tendencies persist. As late as 1979, an Oregon Department of Fish and Wildlife biologist insisted that "although hatchery records are available prior to the 1960 brood, they are not reported [because] the impacts of introductions made prior to 1960 are probably negligible." Oregon salmon managers thus dismissed the relevance of events before the Smolt Program. By fiat, a century of human intervention, genetic tinkering, and egg transfers ceased to be germane. History now begins in 1960.[24]

This lack of historical sensitivity has multiple roots. The fisheries have always focused on the future. Managers have been primarily concerned with production and prediction because this is what industry and politicians have wanted. There have also been few institutional incentives or mechanisms for inspecting the past, and the history of salmon politics has consistently warned managers away from certain issues. Many administrators have wanted to restrain fishing and protect habitat, but they have understood quite clearly the political and constitutional obstacles to restricting human activities. The experiences of Spencer Baird and H. G. Van Dusen served as object lessons of the political consequences of such attempts. History offers many lessons, and sometimes we think it says, "Don't look too closely at the past!"

But this is a short-sighted attitude, and many instances of historical ignorance are simply indefensible. Scientific truth is a case in point. Some groups have tried to shape scientific research so as to insulate themselves from criticism or forestall corrective actions. Insisting that it would be unfair for regulators to restrict their livelihoods on the basis of findings that were less than absolutely certain—a standard most scientists admit is impossible to attain—fishers, miners, loggers, irrigators, dam operators, manufacturers, and fish culturists have demanded that additional studies be conducted. Research has become a way of deflecting criticism by mystifying the process of learning, but retrospection casts doubt on such claims. We know all too well that technological solutions failed to redress social problems and that political consensus is a laudable but chimeric goal.[25]

Thus scientific fishery management has been dysfunctional. Instituted to save salmon, it has instead abetted decline. Politicians and managers avoided controversy by rejecting social restrictions in favor of technological solutions and by treating symptoms rather than causes. The public approved this scientific approach and rationalized results as a function of progress. The paradoxical result was a series of seemingly logical policy choices that, in the end, produced a thoroughly crazed result. Many observers have criticized salmon management during the last 125 years, but probably the most succinct summary was leveled by Canadian biologist Peter Larkin in a 1979 article titled "Maybe You Can't Get There from Here." Larkin argued that trying to manage salmon to accommodate human needs has consistently undermined the long-term interests of the fish. Salmon, Larkin insisted, must come first. Indians understood and accepted this principle, and most modern observers concede its wisdom as well—at least in the abstract.[26]

The problem with principles, though, is that when implemented in real time and real space, conflicts between resource users have proven unavoidable. There were many reasons for these struggles, but at the center was always the hard reality that resources were finite. Rivers may have seemed limitless commodities, but when farmers and fishers went about their business, each soon realized that there was not enough water to go around. Although both produced food, their interests in water placed them at odds: one needed water clear, cold, and abundant to sustain fish; the other had to extract it for crops and return it warmer and dirtier. Similar antagonisms characterized relationships among rival groups of fishers and between fishers and a host of resource users including miners, loggers, grazers, and urbanites. All exploited nature in ways that, to some extent, were inimical to the activities of others, and each developed a unique social and cultural relationship with nature that has made it more difficult to communicate with other groups. Making salmon was a way to negotiate these impasses, but it has not worked.

If we are to preserve both salmon and ways of life, then the histories we tell will matter greatly. We need to understand what went wrong. We need to know how our predecessors erred and what we can learn from their mistakes. Simple histories have failed to save salmon, so I have complicated matters in hopes of undermining the legitimacy of simple explanations. The past was too messy, too uncertain, and too ambiguous. There was not one villain but many contributing forces—as many as there were people and stories—and there is not one answer but many. Ignoring such insights can only lead us back into the morass we wish to escape. We need to eschew simple stories. Though they have long dominated debates about salmon, their myopic perspectives have only served to deflect blame and encourage solutions that were commensurably inadequate. Simple stories will remain valid only so long as people tolerate historical myopia. They will end only when salmon go extinct or people embrace more complicated renditions of the past.

We know we can tell simple stories. We have turned them into a perverse form of art. We tell simple stories portraying vanishing salmon as a Hobson's choice between a chaotic wilderness ruled by Indians and a civilization of order and prosperity. Declining runs become a sad inevitability in such tales, and we only need to decide who should benefit. To resolve that issue we tell other simple stories which delineate the worthy from the unworthy by pitting *The People* against *Special Interests*. Fishers, anglers, industrialists, and environmentalists have all claimed that their interests were synonymous with the majority, and that their rivals have threatened public opportunity. In each case social legitimacy has hinged on identity. Race, ethnicity, class, and technology gain moral and political connotations, and legislators and voters have shunted aside those groups who have not appeared white or wealthy enough to deserve the fruits of salmon.

When these social distinctions grow murky, we tell another set of simple stories about the power and promise of technology to ameliorate tensions. But with so many runs extinct, more listed under the Endangered Species Act every year, and everyone affected by this disaster, isn't it time to admit that simple stories fail us?

When we stand back from these simple stories, when we take in the grand sweep of events, we see far more complicated relationships between cause and effect. Consider Oregon's 1992 fall election. Sportsmen told voters that the only way to save salmon was by passing Measure 8, which would have eliminated gillnetters and tightly restricted ocean trollers. Anglers disseminated their message through newspaper and television ads. The newspapers were made out of wood from clear-cut forests, transported on roads that increased flooding and erosion, and recycled using a water-intensive process that increased stream consumption. The television ads were broadcast with electricity generated by regional dams, consumed in homes built from regional timber, and discussed over meals raised on regional farms. The very production, distribution, and consumption of this political campaign not only illuminated the many threats to salmon but exacerbated the problem it claimed it could solve. When we take a broad perspective, simple explanations seem simplistic, self-righteous, and self-serving. Complicated stories may undermine scapegoating, but they are far more accurate and, ultimately, far more useful.

But usefulness comes at a cost because complexity can threaten our comfortable self-assurance. Americans have inculcated themselves in a theology of Progressive individualism. We believe that we are the architects of our own fate and that our prosperity or failure ultimately rests in our hands. But the salmon crisis casts doubt on these assumptions. Americans have made tremendous improvements to the standard of living during the last 150 years, but progress has come at an increasingly dear cost to nature and people. Resource depletion, habitat destruction, species extinction, pollution, and poverty are not abberations of this progress but its intrinsic products. Such insights underscore an unsettling reality: the American Dream has collided with the material limits of nature. And while some insist that our way out of this mess is a technological innovation away, salmon belie that argument. Mine too many hills, log too many trees, graze too many plants, take too many fish, dam too many streams, irrigate too many fields, build too many homes, and we undermine other people's lives and the nature we covet. Every opportunity has a cost, and increasingly the prosperity of some comes from the deprivation of others.

This is the reality of our present condition. We have built a world that no longer comfortably harbors salmon or the people who depend upon them, and now we must decide what to do about it. Some judge these changes just and moralize their view using numbers. They stress cheap electricity and the relatively greater economic contributions of manufacturing, logging, and farming to suggest that the majority is happy with the status quo. Selfish fishers, supercitizen Indians, and elitist environmentalists are simply unworthy of consideration. Salmon advocates call declining runs unjust, but they too moralize through numbers. They like to emphasize the economic value of environmental amenities in a postindustrial society. Welfare-loggers, -grazers, and -irrigators, greedy industrialists, and atavistic dam agencies are equally unworthy of consideration. The argument is circular: everybody blames somebody, and nobody perceives the scene's underlying absurdity.

Recognizing the fruitlessness of this debate is crucially important, because the very structure of the argument perpetuates the problem. To date, Americans have embraced two contradictory but integrated strategies to resolve fishery problems: one has been to deny the existence of limits and pour tremendous resources into technological panaceas; the other, paradoxically, has been to acknowledge limits and withdraw resources from the powerless. These were conscious choices made for the sake of expediency. Both alleviated social tensions temporarily. Neither saved salmon. The old ways have failed. The old values need refining. We vigorously defend our access to water, wood, grass, fish, electricity, and scenery. We wax eloquent about individual and property rights but say little about social responsibility and almost nothing about limits. We need to face these environmental and social problems squarely, to acknowledge the limits of natural resources and individual opportunity, and to embrace a more equitable and honest approach.

What would happen if such changes occurred? What would they look and sound like? Perhaps it is deliberate naiveté to project such a future, but suspend for a moment your knowledge of how resource politics has operated to date. Imagine a roundtable discussion of the salmon crisis. Everyone is there, but before anyone can speak, they must first say a mea culpa for their contribution to the problem, acknowledge the legitimacy of their neighbors' relationships with nature, and agree to detach salmon's needs from the social pressures that warp salmon policy. How different the ensuing conversation would sound if we eliminated the blame game by admitting culpability. Debate could begin not with accusations and recriminations but with suggestions of how each group could limit their impact on salmon and salmon habitat, and the tired shibboleth of "sustained growth" would evaporate of its own airy hypocrisy. How different the solutions

"Finding a scapegoat is killing the salmon." This editorial cartoon by Jack Ohman captures the hopelessly simplistic and circular arguments that still shape debates about the salmon crisis. (*Oregonian*, 5 Sept. 1994.)

would look if we agreed to eschew technological panaceas. Resources sunk in a failed hatchery system could be freed to restore habitat, relocate dams, restructure fishing, and compensate property losses. Regardless of the specifics, the outcome would *have* to look different because the old divide-and-conquer strategies will have lost their social and political legitimacy.

These changes are imperative because the old strategies are still alive and festering. A case in point is a 1998 letter to the *Oregonian* that defended dams by incriminating foreign dragnetters, exploding seal populations, and rapacious fishers. "Man has interfered with nature's food chain all the way down the line," the writer argued. "How would dynamiting the dams solve this problem?" The author begins with the sort of complex perspective I am calling for but then exempts dams from criticism. Dams are instead an unambiguous good which provide flood control, "pollution-free, renewable energy," drinking and irrigation water, recreation, property values, oil conservation, ozone protection, national security, and "funds to run the fish hatcheries that breed the millions of salmon to more than make up for any problems presented to the fish on their way to the sea." Problem and solution flow from a story that is ultimately simple, clear, traditional, and thoroughly flawed.[27]

Complicated histories propel us past such reasoning. The broader our perspective, the less patience we have with snap answers. Nobody and nothing stand outside this problem, and technology cannot produce salmon better than nature can produce them. We can no longer wrap ourselves in simple explanations of the past. They are neither accurate nor useful. They only perpetuate problems. The fate of salmon and people depends on our being more sophisticated about the tangled issues that salmon recovery presents. We need to understand the complicated history of making salmon, recognize the tensions between individual rights and social responsibility, and acknowledge the complex connections between nature and social prosperity.

And then we must act. This is not a problem that will solve itself, except in a negative way—with continued extinctions. But contrary to what opponents of recovery may think, letting salmon decline into oblivion will only elevate the economic and environmental costs that their downward spiral poses for society. This is as much a human crisis as a salmon crisis. We must commit ourselves to restoring a balance between the interests of humans and of salmon, and we must do so soon. We used to ask how we could save salmon without hurting people, but that compromised nature far too often. The Endangered Species Act reversed the equation by blocking all development that threatened salmon, but that raised protests because the law ignored important human interests. Neither way has worked. What we need to do is reverse the original question and ask how we can help people without hurting salmon. This moves us away from the fallacy of trying to control nature and toward the more realistic goal of trying to govern ourselves. We need to stop making salmon and to stop blaming other people. Both the problems and the solutions are, and have always been, our collective responsibility.

Citation Abbreviations

ARCIA   *Annual Report of the Commissioner of Indian Affairs.* U.S. Congress, Washington.

AROFC   Annual reports of the Oregon Fish Commission, under various titles, including *Report of the State Board of Fish Commissioners* (1887–92); *Annual Reports of the Fish and Game Protector to the Governor* (1893–97); *Annual Report of the Department of Fisheries* (1899–1910); *Biennial Report of the Fish and Game Commission of the State of Oregon* (1911–19); *Biennial Report of the Fish Commission* (1920–72); *Biennial Report of the Game Commission* (1920–72).

ARUSCF   *Annual Report of the Commissioner of Fisheries.* Washington: Government Printing Office, 1872–1940.

ARWDFG   Annual reports of the Washington Department of Fish and Game.

BECMNAA   Bureau of Ethnology Catalogue of Manuscripts. National Anthropological Archives, Washington.

Benson Papers   Frank William Benson Papers. Oregon Historical Society, Portland.

Bulletin   Annual research publication of U.S. Fish Commission under various titles, including *Bulletin of the United States Fish Commission* (1881–1903); *Bulletin of the Bureau of Fisheries* (1904–11); *Bulletin of the United States Bureau of Fisheries* (1912–40); *Fishery Bulletin of the Fish and Wildlife Service* (also known as *Fishery Bulletin*) (1941–70).

Cobb Papers   John N. Cobb Papers. Manuscripts and University Archives, University of Washington Libraries, Seattle.

CPHHPL   Commerce Papers. Herbert Hoover Presidential Library, West Branch, Iowa.

CRMM   Columbia River Maritime Museum, Astoria, Oreg.

CRPAPCRMM   Columbia River Packers Association Papers. Columbia River Maritime Museum, Astoria, Oreg.

CRPAPOHS   Columbia River Packers Association Papers. Oregon Historical Society, Portland.

CUCA   Columbia University Contributions to Anthropology.

EFCC   Everding and Farrell Company Collection. Special Collections, Knight Library, University of Oregon, Eugene.

Failing Papers Henry Failing Papers. Oregon Historical Society, Portland.

HNAI, GB   *Handbook of North American Indians.* Vol. 7, *Great Basin.* Ed. Warren L. D'azevedo. Washington: Smithsonian Institution, 1986.

HNAI, HIWR   *Handbook of North American Indians.* Vol. 4, *History of Indian-White Relations.* Ed. Wilcomb Washburn. Washington: Smithsonian Institution, 1988.

HNAI, NWC   *Handbook of North American Indians.* Vol. 11, *Northwest Coast.* Ed. Wayne Suttles. Washington: Smithsonian Institution, 1990.

Hume Papers   R. D. Hume Papers. Special Collections, Knight Library, University of Oregon, Eugene.

Kyle Papers   William Kyle Manuscripts. Lane County Historical Society, Eugene, Oreg.

MRGC   Papers Multnomah Rod and Gun Club Papers. Oregon Historical Society, Portland.

NAJFM   *North American Journal of Fisheries Management.*

NWFSCL   Northwest Fisheries Science Center Library. National Marine Fisheries Service, Seattle.

NWPPC   Northwest Power Planning Council, Portland, Oregon.

ODFW   Papers Records of the Department of Fish and Wildlife. 92A-19. Oregon State Archives, Salem.

Oregonian   *Portland Morning Oregonian* and *Portland Oregonian.*

PMFCB   *Pacific Marine Fisheries Commission Bulletin.*

RG 22, NA   Record Group 22. Fish and Wildlife Service Records. National Archives, College Park, Md.

RU 26   Record Unit 26. Incoming Correspondence, 1863–69. SIA.

RU 30   Record Unit 30. Office of the Secretary. Incoming Correspondence, 1882–90. SIA.

RU 33	Record Unit 33. Office of the Secretary. Outgoing Correspondence, 1865–91. SIA.
RU 52	Record Unit 52. Incoming Correspondence, 1850–77. SIA.
RU 54	Record Unit 54. Assistant Secretary in Charge of the United States Natural Museum, 1877–96. Series 3. Incoming Correspondence, Mostly concerning the USCFF [U.S. Commission on Fish and Fisheries], 1877–95. SIA.
RU 213	Record Unit 213. Division of Fishes Records, 1852, 1865–1941. Correspondence, 1865–1941. SIA.
RU 7050	Record Unit 7050. George Brown Goode Collection. SIA.
SBCCP	Seufert Brothers Canning Company Papers. Oregon Historical Society, Portland.
SIA	Smithsonian Institution Archives. Science and Industry Building, Smithsonian Institution, Washington.
SIBEB	Smithsonian Institution Bureau of Ethnology Bulletin.
SSPOSA	Secretary of State Papers. Oregon State Archives, Salem.
TAFS	*Transactions of the American Fisheries Society.*
UCPAAE	University of California Publications in American Archaeology and Ethnography.
UCPAR	University of California Publications in Anthropological Records.
UOAP	University of Oregon Anthropological Papers.
UWPA	*University of Washington Publications in Anthropology.*
Warren Papers	Frank M. Warren Papers. Oregon Historical Society, Portland.

Notes

INTRODUCTION: A DURABLE CRISIS

1. *New York Times,* 15 Nov. 1994, B7, B13; *Oregonian,* 14 July 1997, E1, E10; 27 July 1997, A1, A16; *Northwest Salmon Recovery Report,* 22 Aug. 1997, 1–12.

2. *Oregonian,* 21 May 1875, 3; 3 Oct. 1876, 1; 21 Sept. 1878, 2; 20 July 1894, 4; 1 Apr. 1905, 8; Marshall McDonald to Sylvester Pennoyer, 30 Oct. 1893, vol. 360, pp. 399–410, Press Copies of Letters Sent, 1871–1906, RG 22, NA; Willis H. Rich, "The Present State of the Columbia River Salmon Resources," in *Proceedings of the Sixth Pacific Science Congress* 3 (1939): 426; Ed Chaney, *A Question of Balance: Water/ Energy—Salmon and Steelhead Production in the Upper Columbia River Basin* (Portland: Northwest Resource Information Center, 1978), 28; Willa Nehlsen, Jack E. Williams, and James A. Lichatowich, "Pacific Salmon at the Crossroads: Stocks at Risk from California, Oregon, Idaho, and Washington," *Fisheries* 16 (Mar.–Apr. 1991): 4.

3. Rich, "Present State," 429; Philip Johnson, "Historical Assessment of Elwha River Fisheries," draft report on file, Olympic National Park, May 1994, 74.

4. Lisa Mighetto and Wesley J. Ebel, *Saving the Salmon: A History of the U.S. Army Corps of Engineers' Efforts to Protect Anadromous Fish on the Columbia and Snake Rivers,* prepared for U.S. Army Corps of Engineers, North Pacific Division, Portland and Walla Walla Districts (Seattle: Historical Research Associates, 1994), 195.

5. J. D. McPhail, "The Origin and Speciation of *Oncorhynchus* Revisited," in *Pacific Salmon and Their Ecosystems: Status and Future Options,* ed. Deanna J. Stouder, Peter A. Bisson, and Robert J. Naiman (New York: Chapman and Hall, 1997), 29–38.

6. C. Groot and L. Margolis, *Pacific Salmon Life Histories* (Vancouver: University of British Columbia Press, 1991); Robin S. Waples, "Pacific Salmon and the Definition of 'Species' under the Endangered Species Act," *Marine Fisheries Review* 53 (1991); Michael J. Bradford, "Comparative Review of Pacific Salmon Survival Rates," *Canadian Journal of Fisheries and Aquatic Sciences* 52 (1995): 1327–38.

7. Arthur McEvoy, *The Fisherman's Problem: Ecology and Law in the California*

Fisheries, 1850–1980 (New York: Cambridge University Press, 1986). For a treatment of the fisheries and conservation that accords nature little agency, see Richard Judd, *Common Lands, Common People: The Origins of Conservation in Northern New England* (Cambridge: Harvard University Press, 1997).

8. The term "Oregon country" came into use following the settlement of the War of 1812, when the Treaty of Ghent awarded joint custody of the area between Spanish California and Russian Alaska to Britain and the United States. See Carlos A. Schwantes, *The Pacific Northwest: An Interpretive History* (Lincoln: University of Nebraska Press, 1989), 59; Frederick Merk, *The Oregon Question: Essays in Anglo-American Diplomacy and Politics* (Cambridge: Belknap Press of Harvard University Press, 1967), 102–3.

9. Dianne Newell, *Tangled Webs of History: Indians and the Law in Canada's Pacific Coast Fisheries* (Toronto: University of Toronto Press, 1993), 24.

10. Joseph Cone and Sandy Ridlington, eds., *The Northwest Salmon Crisis: A Document History* (Corvallis: Oregon State University Press, 1996).

11. Robert V. Bruce, *The Launching of Modern American Science, 1846–1876* (New York: Alfred A. Knopf, 1987); Charles E. Rosenberg, *No Other Gods: On Science and American Social Thought* (Baltimore: Johns Hopkins University Press, 1976); Donna Haraway, "Situated Knowledges: The Science Question in Feminism as a Site of Discourse on the Privilege of Partial Perspective," *Feminist Studies* 14 (1988): 575–99; N. Katherine Hayles, "Constrained Constructivism: Locating Scientific Inquiry in the Theater of Representation," *New Orleans Review* (1991): 76–85.

12. Garrett Hardin, "The Tragedy of the Commons," *Science* 162 (13 Dec. 1968): 1243–48; McEvoy, *Fisherman's Problem,* 72; Bonnie J. McCay, "The Culture of the Commoners: Historical Observations on Old and New World Fisheries," in *The Question of the Commons: The Culture and Ecology of Communal Resources,* ed. Bonnie J. McCay and James M. Acheson (Tucson: University of Arizona Press, 1987), 201–15; Joseph E. Taylor III, " 'Politics Is at the Bottom of the Whole Thing': Spatial Relations of Power in Oregon Salmon Management," in *Power and Place in the North American West,* ed. Richard White and John M. Findlay (Seattle: University of Washington Press, 1999), 233–63.

13. Edward W. Soja, *Postmodern Geographies: The Reassertion of Space in Critical Social Theory* (London: Verso, 1989), 11, 32; Allan Pred, *Making Histories and Constructing Human Geographies: The Social Transformation of Practice, Power Relations, and Consciousness* (Boulder: Westview Press, 1990), 12.

1 / DEPENDENCE, RESPECT, AND MODERATION

1. Richard White, "Native Americans and the Environment," in *Scholars and the Indian Experience,* ed. W. R. Swagerty (Bloomington: Indiana University Press,

1984), 180; Jack M. Van Hyning, "Factors Affecting the Abundance of Fall Chinook Salmon in the Columbia River," *Research Reports of the Fish Commission of Oregon* 4 (Mar. 1973): 40; Kirk T. Beiningen, "Apportionment of Columbia River Salmon and Steelhead," Investigative Reports of Columbia River Fisheries Project (Portland: Pacific Northwest Regional Commission, 1976), R1; Richard A. Cooley, *Politics and Conservation: The Decline of the Alaska Salmon* (New York: Harper and Row, 1963), 20–21.

2. Eugene S. Hunn and Nancy M. Williams, introduction to *Resource Managers: North American and Australian Hunter-Gatherers,* ed. Eugene S. Hunn and Nancy M. Williams (Boulder: Westview Press, 1982), 1. I largely ignore Great Basin and Klamath Lakes groups because salmon were relatively unimportant in these areas; Ruth Lisa Greenspan, "Fish and Fishing in Northern Great Basin Prehistory" (Ph.D. diss., University of Oregon, 1985), 17; Peter B. Moyle, *Inland Fishes of California* (Berkeley: University of California Press, 1976), 37; K. G. Davies and A. M. Johnson, eds., *Peter Skene Ogden's Snake Country Journal, 1826–27* (London: Hudson's Bay Record Society, 1961), 57; Gordon W. Hewes, "Aboriginal Use of Fishery Resources in Northwestern North America" (Ph.D. diss., University of California, Berkeley, 1947), 97.

3. Reuben Gold Thwaites, ed., *Original Journals of the Lewis and Clark Expedition, 1804–1806,* 7 vols. (New York: Antiquarian Press, 1959), 4:133; Erna Gunther, "Indian Life of the Pacific Northwest," in *The Pacific Northwest: A Regional, Human, and Economic Survey of Resources and Development,* ed. Otis W. Freeman and Howard H. Martin (New York: John Wiley, 1942), 7; Robert Suphan, "An Ethnographical Report on the Identity and Localization of Certain Native Peoples of Northwestern Oregon," in *Oregon Indians 1,* ed. David Agee Horr (1953; reprint, New York: Garland, 1974), 192–93, 199–200; Herbert C. Taylor Jr., "Anthropological Investigation of the Chinook Indians Relative to Tribal Identity and Aboriginal Possession of Lands," in *Oregon Indians 1,* ed. David Agee Horr (1953; reprint, New York: Garland, 1974), 125; David H. French, "Ethnobotany of the Pacific Northwest Indians," *Economic Botany* 19 (Oct. 1965): 381; Robert T. Boyd and Yvonne P. Hajda, "Seasonal Population Movement along the Lower Columbia River: The Social and Ecological Context," *American Ethnologist* 14 (May 1987): 316.

4. Boyd and Hajda, "Seasonal Population Movement," 318; Rick Minor, Stephen Dow Beckham, Phyllis E. Lancefield-Steeves, and Kathryn Anne Toepel, *Culture Resource Overview of the BLM Salem District, Northwestern Oregon: Archaeology, Ethnography, History,* UOAP 20 (Eugene: University of Oregon, 1980), 67, 75; Calvin Martin, *Keepers of the Game: Indian-Animal Relationships and the Fur Trade* (Berkeley: University of California Press, 1978), 154; Randall F. Schalk, "The Structure of an Anadromous Fish Resource," in *For Theory Building in Archaeology: Essays on Faunal Remains, Aquatic Resources, Spatial Analysis, and Systemic Modeling,*

ed. Lewis R. Binford (New York: Academic Press, 1977), 213, 214, 217, 225, 226, 228, 237, 240, 242; Randall F. Schalk, pers. comm. with author, 10 Feb. 1992.

5. Joseph G. Jorgensen, *Western Indians: Comparative Environments, Languages, and Cultures of 172 Western Indians* (San Francisco: W. H. Freeman, 1980), 39; Roberta L. Hall, *The Coquille Indians: Yesterday, Today, and Tomorrow* (Lake Oswego: Smith, Smith, and Smith, 1984), 2; Clara Pearson and Elizabeth Derr Jacobs, *Nehalem Tillamook Tales*, ed. Melville Jacobs (Corvallis: Oregon State University Press, 1990), 159; Eugene S. Hunn, *Nch'i-Wána, "The Big River": Mid-Columbia Indians and Their Land* (Seattle: University of Washington Press, 1990), 151; Franz Boas, *Chinook Texts*, SIBEB 20 (Washington: Smithsonian Institute, 1894), 188; Jacobs, "Clackamas Chinook Texts," 321; Rick Minor, "Aboriginal Settlement and Subsistence at the Mouth of the Columbia River" (Ph.D. diss., University of Oregon, 1983), 38, 60, 74; A. L. Kroeber, *Cultural and Natural Areas of Native North America*, UCPAAE 38 (Berkeley: University of California Press, 1939), 55–59.

6. For fishing sites see Charles Wilkes, *The Narrative of the United States Exploring Expedition, During the Years 1838, 1839, 1840, 1841, and 1842*, 5 vols. (Philadelphia: Lea and Blanchard, 1845), 4:282–84; Hunn, *Nch'i-Wána*, 206–11; H. G. Barnett, *Culture Element Distributions: Oregon Coast*, UCPAR 1 (Berkeley: University of California, 1937), 164; Hall, *Coquille Indians*, 60–61; Philip Drucker, *Contributions to Alsea Ethnography*, UCPAAE 35 (Berkeley: University of California Press, 1939), 85, 86; Omer C. Stewart, *Culture Element Distributions: Northern Paiute*, UCPAR 4 (Berkeley: University of California, 1939), 406; Beatrice Blyth Whiting, *Paiute Sorcery*, Viking Fund Publications in Anthropology 15 (New York: Viking Fund, 1950), 17–20, 75; Erminie Voegelin, *Culture Element Distributions: Northeast California*, UCPAR 7 (Berkeley: University of California, 1942), 62–63; Judith K. Brown, "A Note on the Division of Labor by Sex," *American Anthropologist* 72 (Oct. 1970): 1075, 1076; Marshall Sahlins, *Stone Age Economics* (Chicago: Aldine-Atherton, 1972), 79, 87; John Sauter and Bruce Johnson, *Tillamook Indians of the Oregon Coast* (Portland: Binfords and Mort, 1974), 59–62; Stephen Dow Beckham, Kathryn Anne Toepel, and Rick Minor, *Cultural Resource Overview of the Siuslaw National Forest, Western Oregon* (Portland: U.S. Department of Agriculture, Forest Service, Pacific Northwest Region, 1982), 95; Eugene Heflin, *The Pistol River Site of Southwest Oregon*, Reports of the University of California Archaeology Survey 67 (Berkeley: University of California Press, 1966), 157, 175.

7. John A. Woodward, "Salmon, Slaves, and Grizzly Bears: The Prehistoric Antecedents and Ethnohistory of Clackamas Indian Culture" (Ph.D. diss., University of Oregon, 1974), 203–4, 218; Beckham et al., *Culture Resource Overview*, 81–82; Edward Sapir, *Wishram Texts*, Publications of the American Ethnological Society 2 (Leyden: E. J. Brill, 1909), 240; Leslie Spier and Edward Sapir, "Wishram Ethnography," *UWPA* 3 (1930): 168; David French, "Wasco-Wishram," in *Perspec-*

tives in American Indian Culture Change, ed. Edward H. Spicer (Chicago: University of Chicago Press, 1961), 341; Leslie M. Scott, "Indian Women as Food Providers and Tribal Counselors," *Oregon Historical Quarterly* 42 (Sept. 1941): 211–13; French, "Ethnobotany," 378–81; Verne F. Ray, "Lower Chinook Ethnographic Notes," *UWPA* 7 (1938): 107–10; Washington Irving, *Astoria, or Anecdotes of an Enterprize Beyond the Rocky Mountains,* ed. Richard Dilworth Rust (1836; reprint, Boston: Twayne Publishers, 1976), 56; Jorgensen, *Western Indians,* 329; Robert H. Ruby and John A. Brown, *The Chinook Indians: Traders of the Lower Columbia River* (Norman: University of Oklahoma Press, 1976), 13; William Lee Wuerch, "History of the Middle Chinooks to the Reservation Era" (M.A. thesis, University of Oregon, 1979), 8; Hubert Howe Bancroft, *The Native Races of the Pacific States of North America,* vol. 1, *Wild Tribes* (New York: D. Appleton and Co., 1875), 234.

8. Deward E. Walker Jr., *American Indians of Idaho,* vol. 1, *Aboriginal Cultures,* Anthropological Monographs of the University of Idaho 2 (Moscow: University of Idaho, 1973), 9; Rick Minor and Audrey Frances Pecor, *Cultural Resource Overview or the Willamette National Forest, Western Oregon,* UOAP 12 (Eugene: University of Oregon, 1977), 86; Hewes, "Aboriginal Use of Fishery Resources," 104–5, 115–16; Irving, *Astoria,* 227; Thwaites, *Lewis and Clark Journals,* 3:122, and 4:152, 154–55; Verne Ray, *Culture Element Distributions,* no. 22, *Plateau,* UCPAR 8 (Berkeley: University of California, 1942), 104, 387; Whiting, *Paiute Sorcery,* 16–18; Beckham et al., *Siuslaw National Forest,* 121; Gray, *The Takelma and Their Athapaskan Neighbors: A New Ethnographic Synthesis for the Upper Rogue River Area of Southwestern Oregon,* UOAP 37 (Eugene: University of Oregon, 1987), 51, 56; Edward Sapir, "Notes on the Takelma Indians of Southwestern Oregon," *American Anthropologist* 9 (Apr. 1907): 253; Luther S. Cressman, *The Sandal and the Cave: The Indians of Oregon* (1962; reprint, Corvallis: Oregon State University, 1981), 39; George Peter Murdock, "Notes on the Tenino, Molala, and Paiute of Oregon," *American Anthropologist* 40 (July 1938): 396; Daniel S. Meatte, *Prehistory of the Western Snake River Basin,* Occasional Papers of the Idaho Museum of Natural History 35 (Pocatello: Idaho Museum of Natural History, 1990), 13–14, 17, 65–70; Julian H. Steward, *Basin-Plateau Aboriginal Sociopolitical Groups,* SIBEB 120 (Washington: Smithsonian Institution Press, 1938), 42; Glyndwr Williams, ed., *Peter Skene Ogden's Snake Country Journals, 1827–28* (London: Hudson's Bay Record Society, 1971), 164 n. 3; Mark G. Plew, *Archaeological Investigations in the Southcentral Owyhee Uplands, Idaho,* Archaeological Reports 7 (Boise: Boise State University, 1980), 72, 81–82; Deward E. Walker Jr., *Mutual Cross-Utilization of Economic Resources in the Plateau, an Example from Aboriginal Nez Perce Fishing Practices,* Washington State University Laboratory of Anthropology Report of Investigations 41 (Pullman: Washington State University Press, 1967), 81; Marilyn Dunlap Couture, "Recent and Contemporary Foraging Practices of the Harney Valley Paiute" (M.A. thesis, Portland

State University, 1978), 34; Donald Jackson and Mary Lee Spence, eds., *The Expeditions of John Charles Frémont*, vol. 1, *Travels from 1833 to 1844* (Urbana: University of Illinois Press, 1970), 530; E. S. Lohse and D. Sammons Lohse, "Sedentism on the Columbia: A Matter of Degree Related to the Easy and Efficient Procurement of Resources," *Northwest Anthropology Research Notes* 20 (fall 1986): 115; Hunn, *Nch'i-Wána*, 91–93, 98–105, 119–34; Jeff Zucker, Kay Hummel, and Bob Høgfoss, *Oregon Indians: Culture, History, and Current Affairs* (Portland: Western Imprints, 1983), 31; Eugene S. Hunn, "Mobility as a Factor Limiting Resource Use in the Columbia Plateau of North America," in *Resource Managers: North American and Australian Hunter-Gatherers*, ed. Eugene S. Hunn and Nancy M. Williams (Boulder: Westview Press, 1982), 23, 36.

9. Schalk, "Structure," 218–19, 224, 230, 239; Hewes, "Aboriginal Use of Fishery Resources," 116.

10. F. Ann McKinney, "Kalapuyan Subsistence: Reexamining the Willamette Falls Salmon Barrier," *Northwest Anthropology Research Notes* 18 (spring 1984): 26; Erhard Rostlund, *Freshwater Fish and Fishing in Native North America*, University of California Publications in Geography 9 (Berkeley: University of California Press, 1952), 20–21; Stephen Dow Beckham, *The Indians of Western Oregon: This Land Was Theirs* (Coos Bay: Arago Books, 1977), 48; Thomas J. Connolly, "Terrestrial and Riverine Economies in Southwest Oregon: A View from Camas Valley," in *Contributions to the Archaeology of Oregon, 1983–1986* (Portland: Portland State University, 1986), 191, 197, 210; Lloyd R. Collins, "The Cultural Position of the Kalapuya in the Pacific Northwest" (M.S. thesis, University of Oregon, 1951), 146; Kroeber, *Cultural and Natural Areas*, 155; Minor et al., *Culture Resource Overview*, 56–57; Melville Jacobs, "Santiam Kalapuya Ethnologic Texts," *UWPA* 11 (1945): 6–7; Dennis J. Gray, *Takelma and Their Athapaskan Neighbors*, 39, 65; Jeffery LaLande, *First over the Siskiyous: Peter Skene Ogden's 1826–1827 Journey through the Oregon-California Borderlands* (Portland: Oregon Historical Society Press, 1987), 61; Sapir, "Notes on Takelma," 257–60; Alex Dony Krieger, "Environment, Population, and Prehistory in the Northwestern United States" (M.A. thesis, University of Oregon, 1939), 7–12; Drucker, *Northwest Coast*, 192; Gunther, "Indian Life," 5; Kenneth M. Ames and Alan G. Marshall, "Villages, Demography, and Subsistence Intensification on the Southern Columbia Plateau," *North American Archaeologist* 2 (1980–81): 31–32; Randall F. Schalk and Gregory C. Cleveland, "A Chronological Perspective on Hunter-Gatherer Land Use Strategies in the Columbia Plateau," in *Project Report* 8 (Pullman: Washington State University, 1983), 33–34, 37–38; Philip Drucker, *The Tolowa and Their Southwest Oregon Kin*, UCPAAE 36 (1937), 227–28; Whiting, *Paiute Sorcery*, 405 n. 65, 407. Access to salmon was so coveted that a band of Teninos drove a group of Molallas west across the Cascade Range in 1810 or 1811 in order to claim the valued fishing sites at Sherars Falls on the Deschutes

River; Murdock, "Notes on the Tenino," 396, 398–99. Ames and Marshall suggest that location of food plants during late winter and early spring may have been another important factor in determining the location of winter villages; Ames and Marshall, "Villages, Demography, and Subsistence Intensification."

11. James F. O'Connell, Kevin T. Jones, and Steven R. Simms, "Some Thoughts on Prehistoric Archaeology in the Great Basin," in *Man and Environment in the Great Basin*, ed. David B. Madsen and James F. O'Connell (Washington: Society for American Archaeology, 1982), 233–35; Brian Hayden, "The Carrying Capacity Dilemma: An Alternative Approach," in *Population Studies in Archaeology and Biological Anthropology: A Symposium*, ed. Alan C. Swedlund (Washington: Society for American Archaeology, 1975), 11–12; Hunn, "Mobility," 20; Martin A. Baumhoff, *Ecological Determinants of Aboriginal California Populations*, UCPAAE 49 (Berkeley: University of California Press, 1963), 185; Leland Donald and Donald H. Mitchell, "Some Correlates of Local Group Rank among the Southern Kwakiutl," *Ethnology* 14 (Oct. 1975): 334–35, 338–39; Krieger, "Environment, Population, and Prehistory," 35; Paul G. Sneed, "Of Salmon and Men: An Investigation of Ecological Determinants and Aboriginal Man in the Canadian Plateau," in *Aboriginal Man and Environments on the Plateau of Northwest America*, ed. Arnoud H. Stryd and Rachel A. Smith (Calgary: Students' Press, 1971), 235–36.

12. Drucker, *Alsea Ethnography*, 82–83; Wilkes, *United States Exploring Expedition*, 4:344–46; Hewes, "Aboriginal Use of Fishery Resources," 82–83; Minor, "Aboriginal Settlement and Subsistence," 61–62; Patricia Ann Berringer, "Northwest Coast Traditional Salmon Fisheries: Systems of Resource Utilization," (M.A. thesis, University of British Columbia, 1982), 112–28; Barnett, *Culture Element Distributions*, 163–64; Ray, *Culture Element Distributions*, 109–110; Stewart, *Culture Element Distributions*, 370–71; Drucker, *Tolowa*, 294; Sapir, "Notes on Takelma," 259–60; Voegelin, *Culture Element Distributions*, 55–56; Woodward, "Salmon, Slaves, and Grizzly Bears," 199; Davies and Johnson, *Ogden's Snake Country Journal, 1826–27*, 5–6; Beckham et al., *Siuslaw National Forest*, 96; James G. Swan, *The Northwest Coast; or, Three Years' Residence in Washington Territory* (New York: Harper and Brothers, 1857), 103; Joseph A. Craig and Robert L. Hacker, *The History and Development of the Columbia River*, Bulletin of the Bureau of Fisheries 32 (Washington: Government Printing Office, 1940), 135–37; Sapir, *Wishram Texts*, 184–85.

13. Drucker, *Tolowa*, 283, 294; Robert F. Heizer, *Aboriginal Fish Poisons*, SIBEB 51 (Washington: Smithsonian Institution Press, 1953), 250–51; Jorgensen, *Western Indians*, 38; Rostlund, *Freshwater Fish*, 81; A. L. Kroeber and S. A. Barrett, *Fishing among the Indians of Northwest California*, UCPAAE 21 (Berkeley: University of California Press, 1960), 50–53; Wayne Suttles, "Coping with Abundance: Subsistence on the Northwest Coast," in *Man the Hunter*, ed. Richard B. Lee and Irven

DeVore (Chicago: Aldine Publishing, 1968), 62; Richard M. Pettigrew, *A Prehistoric Culture Sequence in the Portland Basin of the Lower Columbia Valley*, UOAP 22 (Eugene: University of Oregon, 1981), 136; Barnett, *Culture Element Distributions*, 164; Pearson and Jacobs, *Nehalem Tillamook Tales*, 35; Sauter and Johnson, *Tillamook Indians*, 54–59; Stephen Dow Beckham, "Cascade Head and the Salmon River Estuary: A History of Indian and White Settlement" (University of Oregon Library, 1975, typed MS), 4; Heflin, *Pistol River Site*, 168, 188; Ray, *Culture Element Distributions*, 108–9; Herbert Joseph Spinden, *The Nez Percé Indians*, Memoirs of the American Anthropological Association 2 (Lancaster: American Anthropological Association, 1907–15), 208; Meatte, *Western Snake River Basin*, 67; Gray, *Takelma and Their Athapaskan Neighbors*, 32–33; Voegelin, *Culture Element Distributions*, 55–56; Beckham et al., *Siuslaw National Forest*, 107; Thwaites, *Lewis and Clark Journals*, 3:350; Hunn, *Nch'i-Wána*, 189; Hilary Stewart, *Indian Artifacts of the Northwest Coast* (Seattle: University of Washington Press, 1973), 78.

14. Swan, *Northwest Coast*, 104–7; Kroeber and Barrett, "Fishing among the Indians," 49–51; Hunn, *Nch'i-Wána*, 156.

15. Kroeber and Barrett, "Fishing among the Indians," 50–53; Berringer, "Northwest Coast Traditional Salmon Fisheries," 60–66.

16. Barnett, *Culture Element Distributions*, 163–64; Berringer, "Northwest Coast Traditional Salmon Fisheries, 67–100; Ray, *Culture Element Distributions*, 15–16, 104–5, 107; Walker, *Mutual Cross-Utilization*, 27–28; Stewart, *Culture Element Distributions*, 370–71; Meatte, *Western Snake River Basin*, 67; Hewes, "Aboriginal Use of Fishery Resources," 100; Gray, *Takelma and Their Athapaskan Neighbors*, 32–33; Jeffery LaLande, "The Indians of Southwestern Oregon: An Ethnohistorical Review" (paper given at the symposium "Living with the Land: The Indians of Southwest Oregon," Ashland, Oregon, 1989), 15; Voegelin, *Culture Element Distributions*, 55–56, 173–74; Kroeber and Barrett, "Fishing among the Indians," 10–11, 24–25; Spinden, *Nez Percé*, 208.

17. Kroeber and Barrett, "Fishing among the Indians," 10–11; Beckham et al., *Siuslaw National Forest*, 100–102; Drucker, *Alsea Ethnography*, 82; Walker, *Mutual Cross-Utilization*, 26.

18. Hewes, "Aboriginal Use of Fishery Resources," 149; Hunn, *Nch'i-Wána*, 136; Alexander Ross, *The Fur Hunters of the Far West*, ed. Kenneth A. Spaulding (1855; reprint, Norman: University of Oklahoma Press, 1856), 178–79; Craig and Hacker, *History and Development*, 143–44; Walker, *Mutual Cross-Utilization*, 25; Gray, *Takelma and Their Athapaskan Neighbors*, 33.

19. Randall F. Schalk, "Estimating Salmon and Steelhead Usage in the Columbia Basin before 1850: The Anthropological Perspective," *Northwest Environmental Journal* 2 (1986): 14–20.

20. John Minto, "The Number and Condition of the Native Race in Oregon

When First Seen by White Men," *Oregon Historical Quarterly* 1 (Sept. 1900): 305; James Mooney, *The Aboriginal Population of America North of Mexico*, Smithsonian Miscellaneous Collections 80 (Washington: Smithsonian Institution Press, 1928), 13–14; Kroeber, *Cultural and Natural Areas*, 138; Leslie M. Scott, "Indian Diseases as Aids to Pacific Northwest Settlement," *Oregon Historical Quarterly* 29 (June 1928): 149–50; Craig and Hacker, *History and Development*, 142; Jack M. Van Hyning, "Factors Affecting the Abundance of Fall Chinook Salmon in the Columbia River," *Research Reports of the Fish Commission of Oregon* 4 (Mar. 1973): 40.

21. Edward Swindell, "Report on Source, Nature, and Extent of the Fishing, Hunting, and Miscellaneous Related Rights of Certain Indian Tribes in Washington and Oregon Together with Affidavits Showing Location of a Number of Usual and Accustomed Fishing Grounds and Stations" (Los Angeles: U.S. Department of the Interior, Office of Indian Affairs, Division of Forestry and Grazing, 1942), 13; Hewes, "Aboriginal Use of Fishery Resources," 103 n. 167; Schalk, "Estimating Salmon and Steelhead Usage," 16; Gordon W. Hewes, "Indian Fisheries Productivity in Pre-contact Times in the Pacific Salmon Area," *Northwest Anthropology Research Notes* 7 (fall 1973): 133–55.

22. Krieger, "Environment, Population, and Prehistory," 14.

23. Robert T. Boyd, "The Introduction of Infectious Diseases among the Indians of the Pacific Northwest, 1774–1874" (Ph.D. diss., University of Washington, 1985); Robert T. Boyd, "Demographic History, 1774–1874," in *HNAI, NWC*, 135–38; Walker, *Mutual Cross-Utilization*, 19, 23; Schalk, "Estimating Salmon and Steelhead Usage," 15–20; Boyd and Hajda, "Seasonal Population Movement," 312–13, 320; Whiting, *Paiute Sorcery*, 17; Gillett Griswold, *Aboriginal Patterns of Trade between the Columbia Basin and the Northern Plains*, Archaeology in Montana 11 (Missoula: Montana Archaeological Society, 1970), 36–37; William D. Honey and Thomas C. Hogg, eds., *Cultural Resource Overview: Umpqua National Forest and Bureau of Land Management, Roseburg District* (Corvallis: Oregon State University, 1980), 69.

24. Schalk, "Estimating Salmon and Steelhead Usage," 19–21; Swindell, "Report," 14; Gabriel Franchere, *Narrative of a Voyage to the Northwest Coast of America in the Years 1811, 1812, 1813, and 1814, or the First American Settlement on the Pacific*, trans. and ed. J. V. Huntington (New York: Redfield, 1854), 265–66; Craig and Hacker, *History and Development*, 201. Schalk used the same population figures as Hewes because Robert Boyd's data was not yet available. Thus 41 million pounds may still be a conservative figure. Schalk, pers. comm. with author, 10 Feb. 1992; Boyd, "Demographic History," 135–38.

25. Schalk, "Estimating Salmon and Steelhead Usage," 21; Rostlund, *Freshwater Fish*, 17; Ray Hilborn, "The Frequency and Severity of Fish Stock Declines and Increases," in *Developing and Sustaining World Fisheries Resources: The State of Science*

and Management, ed. D. A. Hancock, D. C. Smith, A. Grant, and J. P. Beumer (Victoria, Australia: CSIRO Publishing, 1997), 36–38.

26. Schalk and Cleveland, "Chronological Perspective," 31–32, 40; Schalk, "Structure," 231; Meatte, *Western Snake River Basin,* 71; Couture, "Foraging Practices," 20–21; Hunn and Williams, introduction to *Resource Managers,* 7; Stewart, *Culture Element Distributions,* 376, 429; Barnett, *Culture Element Distributions,* 165; Gray, *Takelma and Their Athapaskan Neighbors,* 32; Swindell, "Report," 13; Suttles, "Coping," 63; Thwaites, *Lewis and Clark Journals,* 4:122.

27. Robert Boyd, *People of The Dalles: The Indians of Wascopam Mission* (Nebraska: University of Nebraska Press, 1996), 52–55; Walker, *Mutual Cross-Utilization,* 13; Thwaites, *Lewis and Clark Journals,* 4:147–48; Wilkes, *United States Exploring Expedition,* 4:384; Spier and Sapir, "Wishram Ethnography," 179; Swindell, "Report," 153, 165.

28. Spier and Sapir, "Wishram Ethnography," 224–25, 228–29. Discovery of Pacific coast sea shells in Atlantic coast middens suggests a continental aboriginal trade network as early as 7,000 years ago; Griswold, *Aboriginal Patterns of Trade,* 7, 10, 14–17, 23–25, 84–85; Raymond W. Wood, *Contrastive Features of Native North American Trade Systems,* UOAP 4 (Eugene: University of Oregon, 1972), 160–61; Irving, *Astoria,* 70; Thwaites, *Lewis and Clark Journals,* 3:148, 155, 288, 343, 362–63, and 4:289; Alexander Ross, *Adventures of the First Settlers on the Oregon or Columbia River, 1810–1813* (1904; reprint, Lincoln: University of Nebraska Press, 1986), 129, 229. Smaller centers of trade developed at Willamette Falls, Champoeg, Camas Prairie, and other major root-harvesting sites across the Plateau; Wood, *Contrastive Features,* 154, 158–59, 161; Minor et al., *Culture Resource Overview,* 54; Meatte, *Western Snake River Basin,* 20; Walker, *Mutual Cross-Utilization,* 16; Kevin Erickson, "Marine Shell Utilization in the Plateau Culture Area," *Northwest Anthropological Research Notes* 24 (1990): 105–15, 129; Robert F. Heizer, "The Introduction of Monterey Shells to the Indians of the Northwest Coast," *Pacific Northwest Quarterly* 31 (Oct. 1940): 401–2; Ray, *Culture Element Distributions,* 395; Wood, *Contrastive Features,* 158, 163; E. E. Rich, "Trade Habits and Economic Motivation among the Indians of North America," *Canadian Journal of Economics and Political Science* 26 (Feb. 1960): 50; Spier and Sapir, "Wishram Ethnography," 228; Bill Brunton, "Ceremonial Integration in the Plateau of Northwestern North America," *Northwest Anthropology Research Notes* 2 (spring 1968): 13. The widespread diffusion of similar myths underscores the breadth of cultural exchanges accompanying economic exchange and marriage in the Oregon country; Jarold Ramsey, ed., *Coyote Was Going There: Indian Literature of the Oregon Country* (Seattle: University of Washington Press, 1977), xxviii.

29. Boyd and Hadja, "Seasonal Population Movement," 318; Wood, *Contrastive Features,* 164–65; Wayne Suttles, "Affinal Ties, Subsistence, and Prestige among

the Coast Salish," *American Anthropologist* 62 (Apr. 1960): 299; Suttles, "Coping," 60; Gray, *Takelma and Their Athapaskan Neighbors*, 34; Walker, *Mutual Cross-Utilization*, 9–11, 39; Couture, "Foraging Practices," 20–21; Leslie Spier, *Klamath Ethnography*, UCPAAE 30 (Berkeley: University of California, 1930), 234; W. W. Elmendorf, "The Structure of Twana Culture," *Coast Salish and Western Washington Indians*, vol. 4, ed. David Agee Horr (1960; reprint, New York: Garland, 1974), 328–29, 335, 337; Drucker, *Northwest Coast*, 129–33; Albert S. Gatschet, "Various Ethnographic Notes," *Journal of American Folklore* 12 (July 1899): 214; Ray, *Culture Element Distributions*, 208; Drucker, *Alsea Ethnography*, 94; Barnett, *Culture Element Distributions*, 176–77; Spinden, *Nez Percé*, 250; Spier and Sapir, "Wishram Ethnography," 220–21; Stewart, *Culture Element Distributions*, 404; Franz Boas, "Traditions of the Tillamook, II," *Journal of American Folklore* 11 (Apr. 1898): 146.

30. Suttles, "Affinal Ties," 297–301, 303; Suttles, "Coping," 60.

31. Minor et al., *Culture Resource Overview*, 84; Richard A. Gould, "To Have and Have Not: The Ecology of Sharing among Hunter-Gatherers," in *Resource Managers: North American and Australian Hunter-Gatherers*, ed. Eugene S. Hunn and Nancy M. Williams (Boulder: Westview Press, 1982), 76; Boyd and Hajda, "Seasonal Population Movement," 310; Drucker, *Tolowa*, 246–47, 252–53; Beckham et al., *Siuslaw National Forest*, 47, 125, 139–40; Albert S. Gatschet, Leo J. Frachtenberg, and Melville Jacobs, "Kalapuya Texts," UWPA 11 (1945): 160–63; Walker, *Mutual Cross-Utilization*, 17–18, 24, 26; Drucker, *Alsea Ethnography*, 94; Beckham, "Cascade Head," 5; Livingston Farrand, "Notes on the Alsea Indians of Oregon," *American Anthropologist* 3 (Apr. 1901): 242–43; Verne Ray, "The Historical Position of the Lower Chinook in the Native Culture of the Northwest," *Pacific Northwest Quarterly* 28 (Oct. 1937): 63–67; Spier and Sapir, "Wishram Ethnography," 217; Spinden, *Nez Percé*, 250; Edward Sapir, *Takelma Texts*, Anthropological Publications of the University Museum 2 (Philadelphia: University of Pennsylvania, 1909), 177–79; Spier, *Klamath Ethnography*, 304–5; Ray, "Historical Position," 63–67; Voegelin, *Culture Element Distributions*, 131, 133, 226; Ray, *Culture Element Distributions*, 212–13; Sapir, "Notes on Takelma," 267–68, 274–75; Barnett, *Culture Element Distributions*, 176–77; Spier and Sapir, "Wishram Ethnography," 220–21; Stewart, *Culture Element Distributions*, 404; Collins, "Cultural Position of the Kalapuya," 50.

32. Thwaites, *Lewis and Clark Journals*, 3:325; Davies and Johnson, *Ogden's Snake Country Journal, 1826–27*, 174, 185; Minor et al., *Culture Resource Overview*, 58, 73, 75, 83; Beckham et al., *Siuslaw National Forest*, 97; Ruby and Brown, *Chinook Indians*, 21; Suphan, "Ethnographical Report," 193–94, 237; Collins, "Cultural Position of the Kalapuya," 21; Griswold, *Aboriginal Patterns of Trade*, 54, 68–69; Gray, *Takelma and Their Athapaskan Neighbors*, 34; Ray, *Culture Element Distributions*, 395.

33. Franchere, *Voyage to the Northwest Coast*, 236–37, 245–46; Schalk, "Structure," 232–33, 236; Randall Schalk, pers. comm. with author, 10 Feb. 1992; Mark G.

Plew, "Implications of Nutritional Potential of Anadromous Fish Resources of the Western Snake River Plain," *Journal of California and Great Basin Anthropology* 5 (summer and winter 1983): 61–63; Jorgensen, *Western Indians,* 128. For a different interpretation of nutrition see Wayne Suttles, "Coping with Abundance," 63.

34. Walker, *Mutual Cross-Utilization,* 9; Suphan, "Ethnographical Report," 210–12; Thwaites, *Lewis and Clark Journals,* 4:228; E. E. Rich and M. M. Johnson, eds., *Ogden's Snake Country Journals, 1824–26* (London: Hudson's Bay Record Society, 1950), 133; Davies and Johnson, *Ogden's Snake Country Journal, 1826–27,* 78; LaLande, *First over the Siskiyous,* 53–59; Franchere, *Voyage to the Northwest Coast,* 279; Swan, *Northwest Coast,* 87; Ames and Marshall, "Villages, Demography, and Subsistence," 31–32; Boyd and Hajda, "Seasonal Population Movement," 317; Drucker, *Tolowa,* 232; Spier, *Klamath Ethnography,* 147; Boyd, *People of The Dalles,* 58–59; Boas, "Traditions of Tillamook, II," 143–44; Leo J. Frachtenberg, *Coos Texts,* CUCA 1 (New York: Columbia University, 1913), 135; Boas, *Chinook Texts,* 232; Franz Boas, *Kathlamet Texts,* SIBEB 26 (Washington: Smithsonian Institution Press, 1901), 50, 216–20; Melville Jacobs, *The People Are Coming Soon: Analyses of Clackamas Chinook Myths and Tales* (Seattle: University of Washington Press, 1960), 331–32; Sapir, *Wishram Texts,* 226–29, 226 n. 1, 244–45; Gatschet et al., "Kalapuya Texts," 356; Boyd, "Demographic History," 136; Minto, "Native Race in Oregon," 308.

35. Suttles, "Affinal Ties," 302; Wood, *Contrastive Features,* 164.

36. William Christie MacLeod, "Conservation among Primitive Hunting Peoples," *Scientific Monthly* 43 (Dec. 1939): 562; Cressman, *Sandal,* 74; Martin, *Keepers of the Game,* 156; Hunn, *Nch'i-Wána,* 230, 236; Spier and Sapir, "Wishram Ethnography," 236.

37. Schalk and Cleveland, "Chronological Perspective," 30, 35.

38. Boyd and Hadja, "Seasonal Population Movement," 318.

39. Melville Jacobs, *The Content and Style of an Oral Literature: Clackamas Chinook Myths and Tales* (Chicago: University of Chicago, 1959), 196; Jacobs, *People Are Coming Soon,* ix; Farrand, "Notes on the Alsea," 241; Dell Hymes, "Language, Memory, and Selective Performance: Cultee's 'Salmon Myth' as Twice Told to Boas," *Journal of American Folklore* 98 (Oct. 1985): 422; Gatschet et al., "Kalapuya Texts," 175.

40. Boas, "Kathlamet Texts," 5–6; Gray, *Takelma and Their Athapaskan Neighbors,* 13; Sherburne Cook, *The Epidemic of 1830–1833 in California and Oregon,* UCPAAE 43 (Berkeley: University of California Press, 1955), 307–8, 315–16; McKinney, "Kalapuyan Subsistence," 31; Hall, *Coquille Indians,* 130–31; Jacobs, *Content and Style,* 249; Ray, "Lower Chinook Ethnographic Notes," 111.

41. Despite these complications and shortcomings, myths remain invaluable resources for their information on values, attitudes, and customs of different groups;

Hall, *Coquille Indians*, 24–25; Ramsey, *Coyote Was Going There*, xxv; Jacobs, *Content and Style*, 197–98; Jacobs, *People Are Coming Soon*, x.

42. Boas, "Kathlamet Texts," 56; Livingston Farrand and Leo J. Frachtenberg, "Shasta and Athapascan Myths from Oregon," *Journal of American Folklore* 28 (July 1915): 237, 238; Franz Boas, *Notes on the Tillamook*, UCPAAE 20 (Berkeley: University of California Press, 1923), 10, 12; Archie Phinney, *Nez Perce Texts*, CUCA 25 (New York: Columbia University, 1934), 227; Boas, "Traditions of Tillamook, II," 145–46; Pearson and Jacobs, *Nehalem Tillamook Tales*, 5, 130; Leo J. Frachtenberg, *Alsea Texts and Myths*, SIBEB 67 (Washington: Smithsonian Institution, 1920), 83, 113; Farrand, "Notes on the Alsea," 241–42, 246; Beckham, *Western Oregon Indians*, 9–10; Frachtenberg, *Coos Texts*, 9; Franchere, *Voyage to the Northwest Coast*, 258; Gatschet et al., "Kalapuya Texts," 359; Ramsey, *Coyote Was Going There*, 93; Clarence Orvel Bunnell, *Legends of the Klickitats* (Portland: Metropolitan Press, 1935), 20–41.

43. Ake Hultkrantz, *The Religions of the American Indians*, trans. Monica Setterwall (1967; reprint, Berkeley: University of California Press, 1979), 32–36; Edward Sapir, "Preliminary Report on the Language and Mythology of the Upper Chinook," *American Anthropologist* 9 (July 1907): 542–43; Dell Hymes, "Mythology," in *HNAI, NWC*, 594; Erna Gunther, "A Further Analysis of the First Salmon Ceremony," *UWPA* 2 (1928): 163; A. L. Kroeber and E. W. Gifford, *World Renewal: A Cult System of Native Northwest California*, UCPAAE 13 (Berkeley: University of California Press, 1949), 116–17, 120–22, 123–24; Sapir, *Wishram Texts*, 3–7, 28–29, 266–67; Ramsey, *Coyote Was Going There*, 9, 47–49; James A. Teit, Livingston Farrand, Marian K. Gould, and Herbert J. Spinden, *Folk-Tales of Salishan and Sahaptin Tribes*, Memoirs of the American Folk-Lore Society 11 (Lancaster: American Folk-Lore Society, 1917), 139–44; Herbert J. Spinden, "Myths of the Nez Perce," *Journal of American Folklore* 21 (Jan. 1908): 15–16; Phinney, *Nez Perce Texts*, 380–81; Gatschet et al., "Kalapuya Texts," 237; Frachtenberg, *Alsea Texts*, 105–7; Jacobs, "Clackamas Chinook Texts," 101–2; Jacobs, *People Are Coming Soon*, 92; Gatschet et al., "Kalapuya Texts," 223–24; Jacobs, *Content and Style*, 150–51.

44. Sapir, "Preliminary Report," 543; Hymes, "Language, Memory, and Selective Performance," 422, 427; Boas, "Kathlamet Texts," 50–53, 56.

45. Boas, *Chinook Texts*, 78–79; Jacobs, *Clackamas Chinook Texts*, 42–51.

46. Thwaites, *Lewis and Clark Journals*, 4:302.

47. Courtland Smith, *Salmon Fishers of the Columbia* (Corvallis: Oregon State University, 1979), 7; Rostlund, *Freshwater Fish*, 15; Drucker, *Northwest Coast*, 140–41.

48. Melville Jacobs, "Northwest Sahaptin Texts, I," *UWPA* 2 (1929): 196–200; Farrand and Frachtenberg, "Shasta and Athapascan Myths," 228; Frachtenberg, *Alsea Texts*, 217; Franz Boas, "Traditions of the Tillamook Indians, I," *Journal of*

American Folklore 11 (Jan. 1891), 24; Melville Jacobs, "Coos Narrative and Ethnological Texts," *UWPA* 8 (1939): 52–53.

49. Boas, "Kathlamet Texts," 98; Boas, "Traditions of Tillamook, II," 142; Teit et al., *Folk-Tales,* 168–69; Phinney, *Nez Perce Texts,* 301; Sapir, *Wishram Texts,* 26–27; Ramsey, *Coyote Was Going There,* 93; Frachtenberg, *Coos Texts,* 35–37; Pearson and Jacobs, *Nehalem Tillamook Tales,* 143.

50. Phinney, *Nez Perce Texts,* 205–27.

51. Jacobs, *Coos Myths,* 184; Boas, "Traditions of Tillamook, I," 25.

52. Boas, "Traditions of Tillamook, I," 26; Frachtenberg, *Alsea Texts,* 85, 107.

53. Boas, *Chinook Texts,* 106, 101–6; Boas, "Kathlamet Texts," 45–49.

54. Jorgensen, "Salish," 143, 152; Sapir, "Religious Ideas of the Takelma Indians of Southwestern Oregon," *Journal of American Folklore* 20 (Jan. 1907): 33; Gunther, "Further Analysis," 148, 150–51; Richard Bryant, David Eisler, and John Nelson, *Report of the Cultural Resource Survey: Northeastern Klamath Marsh Study Area,* vol. 1 (Eugene: Pro-Lysts, 1978), 54–55.

55. Boas, "Notes on the Tillamook," 9; Gunther, "Further Analysis," 148, 150–51.

56. Boas, "Notes on the Tillamook," 9–10; Gunther, "Further Analysis," 147–leaf; Gray, *Takelma and Their Athapaskan Neighbors,* 61; Drucker, *Tolowa,* 225, 276, 296; Beckham, *Western Oregon Indians,* 82; Erna Gunther, "An Analysis of the First Salmon Ceremony," *American Anthropologist* 28 (Oct. 1926): 610; Ray, "Lower Chinook Ethnographic Notes," 110–11; Spier and Sapir, "Wishram Ethnography," 248–49; Sapir, *Wishram Texts,* 182–83; Murdock, "Notes on the Tenino," 401; Kathryn Anne Toepel, William F. Willingham, and Rick Minor, *Cultural Resource Overview of BLM Lands in North-Central Oregon: Archaeology, Ethnography, History,* UOAP 17 (Eugene: University of Oregon, 1980), 40–41, 61; Ray, *Culture Element Distributions,* 115; Ruby and Brown, *Chinook Indians,* 13; Stephen Dow Beckham, Kathryn Anne Toepel, and Rick Minor, *Native American Religious Practices and Uses, Siuslaw National Forest* (Portland: U.S. Department of Agriculture, Forest Service, Pacific Northwest Region, 1982), 16; Frachtenberg, *Alsea Texts,* 83.

57. Spinden, *Nez Percé,* 260; Gunther, "Analysis," 611; Beckham et al., *Native American Religious Practices,* 66; Spier, *Klamath Ethnography,* 14, 140, 148; Voegelin, *Culture Element Distributions,* 56–57, 173–74; Stewart, *Culture Element Distributions,* 374, 427.

58. Jacobs, "Coos Narrative," 41; Gunther, "Further Analysis," 148, 150–51; Hall, *Coquille Indians,* 30; Boas, "Kathlamet Texts," 207–15; Gunther, "Analysis," 615; Barnett, *Culture Element Distributions,* 165; Drucker, *Alsea Ethnography,* 85, 97; Frachtenberg, *Coos Texts,* 37; Gray, *Takelma and Their Athapaskan Neighbors,* 49; Boas, *Chinook Texts,* 233; Hunn, *Nch'i-Wána,* 153; Ray, *Culture Element Distributions,* 116, 129, 135; Spier, *Klamath Ethnography,* 149–50; Boyd, *People of The Dalles,* 127–29.

59. Gunther, "Further Analysis," 166, 148–49, 151–52; Beckham et al., *Native American Religious Practices*, 18–19, 45–46; Barnett, *Culture Element Distributions*, 167, 179, 180, 181, 183; Boas, *Chinook Texts*, 102; Boas, "Kathlamet Texts," 49; Spier and Sapir, "Wishram Ethnography," 249; Ray, *Culture Element Distributions*, 104, 116, 127, 221; Stewart, *Culture Element Distributions*, 411; Sapir, "Notes on Takelma," 275; Voegelin, *Culture Element Distributions*, 117, 128, 129, 139, 140; Boas, "Notes on the Tillamook," 10; Beckham, *Western Oregon Indians*, 87; Drucker, *Alsea Ethnography*, 100; Phinney, *Nez Perce Texts*, 346.

60. Drucker, *Tolowa*, 277; Gunther, "Analysis," 614; Gunther, "Further Analysis," 144, 151; Ray, "Lower Chinook Ethnographic Notes," 111; Warren D. Vaughn, "Early Settlement of Tillamook County, Oregon, 1851–1858" (Tillamook Pioneer Museum, Tillamook, Oreg., typed MS), 26; Davies and Johnson, *Ogden's Snake Country Journal, 1826–27*, 173; Boas, *Chinook Texts*, 103–5; Hunn, *Nch'i-Wâna*, 154. Sean L. Swezey and Robert F. Heizer make a similar argument for rivers in California ("Ritual Regulation of Anadromous Fish Resources in Native California," in *The Fishing Culture of the World: Studies in Ethnology, Cultural Ecology, and Folklore*, ed. Béla Gunda, 2 vols. [Budapest: Akadémiai Kiadó, 1984], 967–89).

61. Franchere, *Voyage to the Northwest Coast*, 260; Swan, *Northwest Coast*, 107–9; Ross, *Adventures*, 111; Wilkes, *United States Exploring Expedition*, 4:324; Vaughn, "Early Settlement," 26; Davies and Johnson, *Ogden's Snake Country Journal, 1826–27*, 173; Ruby and Brown, *Chinook Indians*, 68.

62. Walker, *Mutual Cross-Utilization*, 10–11; Thwaites, *Lewis and Clark Journals*, 4:228, 302; Gunther, "Analysis," 614; Hultkranz, *Religions*, 104–6, 142–43; Martin, *Keepers of the Game*, 186.

63. Beckham, *Western Oregon Indians*, 83–86; Spier and Sapir, "Wishram Ethnography," 237.

64. Spinden, *Nez Percé*, 249; Spier and Sapir, "Wishram Ethnography," 238–40; Spier, *Klamath Ethnography*, 103, 111–12; Barnett, *Culture Element Distributions*, 190; Ray, "Lower Chinook Ethnographic Notes," 79–80; Ray, *Culture Element Distributions*, 234; Whiting, *Paiute Sorcery*, 27–30; Sapir, "Notes on Takelma," 267; Beckham et al., *Native American Religious Practices*, 17, 69; Boas, *Chinook Texts*, 230; Sapir, *Wishram Texts*, 260–63. A strong caveat must of course be stated, because the correlation between spirituality and dependence is based on an absence of evidence from what are admittedly incomplete lists of personal spirits (Spier and Sapir, "Wishram Ethnography," 237). The coincidental evidence nevertheless suggests that economic factors may have influenced the adoption of certain spirits.

65. Ruby and Brown, *Chinook Indians*, 13; Frachtenberg, *Alsea Texts*, 184; Hunn, *Nch'i-Wâna*, 153–54.

66. Nellie B. Pipes, ed., "Journal of John H. Frost, 1840–43," *Oregon Historical Quarterly* 35 (Mar. 1934): 71–72, and ibid. (Dec. 1934): 366–67. For a different

argument see Barbara Lane, "Background of Treaty Making in Western Washington," *American Indian Journal* 3 (Apr. 1977): 4–5.

67. Frachtenberg, *Coos Texts,* 135; Sapir, *Wishram Texts,* 7, 267; Sapir, *Takelma Texts,* 42, 114; Gatschet et al., "Kalapuya Texts," 356, 360; Jacobs, "Clackamas Chinook Texts," 102.

68. Rada Dyson-Hudson and Eric Alden Smith, "Human Territoriality: An Ecological Reassessment," *American Anthropologist* 8 (Mar. 1978): 36–37; Alan Richardson, "The Control of Productive Resources on the Northwest Coast of North America," in *Resource Managers: North American and Australian Hunter-Gatherers,* ed. Eugene S. Hunn and Nancy M. Williams (Boulder: Westview Press, 1982), 95–99; Hunn, "Mobility," 35–36; Hewes, "Aboriginal Use of Fishery Resources," 21; Michael Silverstein, "Chinookans of the Lower Columbia," in *HNAI, NWC,* 536; Hunn, *Nch'i-Wána,* 93–94, 148, 153–54; Boyd and Hajda, "Seasonal Population Movement," 318; Drucker, *Tolowa,* 223–24; Jorgensen, *Western Indians,* 130–31.

69. Barnett, *Culture Element Distributions,* 186; Beckham, *Western Oregon Indians,* 6; Drucker, *Tolowa,* 240–45, 250, 273, 280; Sapir, *Wishram Texts,* 186–87; Spier and Sapir, "Wishram Ethnography," 175; Hunn, *Nch'i-Wána,* 290; Cressman, *Sandal,* 73; Gray, *Takelma and Their Athapaskan Neighbors,* 50, 57–58; Suphan, "Ethnographical Report," 241; Phinney, *Nez Perce Texts,* 279. Ownership of smokehouses was important in coastal areas that experienced heavy rainfall; Suttles, "Coping," 63; Jorgensen, "Salish," 135, 150; Thwaites, *Lewis and Clark Journals,* 3:360; Silverstein, "Chinookans," 536; Drucker, *Northwest Coast,* 121; Hunn, "Mobility," 34; Ray, *Culture Element Distributions,* 229; Spinden, *Nez Percé,* 242, 245–46; Henry B. Zenk, "Contributions to Tualatin Ethnography: Subsistence and Ethnobiology" (M.A. thesis, Portland State University, 1976), 50–51; Gatschet et al., "Kalapuya Texts," 185; Richardson, "Control of Productive Resources," 100–101; Whiting, *Paiute Sorcery,* 76; Meatte, *Western Snake River Basin,* 19; Stewart, *Culture Element Distributions,* 407. The Klamath Lakes Indians were perhaps the sole exception to this rule of usufruct rights. Spier (*Klamath Ethnography,* 149) claims that fishing sites were open to all, but Voegelin (*Culture Element Distributions,* 62, 104) reports village group ownership.

70. Minor et al., *Culture Resource Overview,* 61, 72; Franchere, *Voyage to the Northwest Coast,* 251; Ray, "Historical Position," 367; Cressman, *Sandal,* 57, 63, 68, 70; Krieger, "Environment, Population, and Prehistory," 40; Catherine S. Fowler, "Food-Named Groups among Northern Paiute in North America's Great Basin: An Ecological Interpretation," in *Resource Managers: North American and Australian Hunter-Gatherers,* ed. Eugene S. Hunn and Nancy M. Williams (Boulder: Westview Press, 1982), 117, 125; Barnett, *Culture Element Distributions,* 185, 196; Ray, "Lower Chinook Ethnographic Notes," 55, 73; Sapir, "Notes on Takelma," 267–68;

Bryant et al., *Report of Cultural Resource Survey,* 53; Drucker, *Northwest Coast,* 118; Boyd, "Infectious Diseases," 317.

71. Barnett, *Culture Element Distributions,* 165, 186; Ray, "Lower Chinook Ethnographic Notes," 56, 111; Drucker, *Tolowa,* 240–45, 254, 295; Spinden, *Nez Percé,* 245–46; Walker, *Mutual Cross-Utilization,* 39; Gray, *Takelma and Their Athapaskan Neighbors,* 57–58; Pearson and Jacobs, *Nehalem Tillamook Tales,* 88–90; Melville Jacobs, "Texts in Chinook Jargon," *UWPA* 7 (1936): 6–12; Gatschet et al., "Kalapuya Texts," 356; Melville Jacobs, "Santiam Myth Texts," *UWPA* 11 (1945): 92–96; Beckham et al., *Native American Religious Practices,* 16; Beckham, *Western Oregon Indians,* 82; Drucker, *Alsea Ethnography,* 96; Jacobs, "Coos Narrative," 66–67; Ray, *Culture Element Distributions,* 134; Stewart, *Culture Element Distributions,* 411; Whiting, *Paiute Sorcery,* 106; Ramsey, *Coyote Was Going There,* 257; Voegelin, *Culture Element Distributions,* 54; Hunn, *Nch'i-Wána,* 209; Sahlins, *Stone Age Economics,* 212.

72. Walker, *Mutual Cross-Utilization,* 14; Sahlins, *Stone Age Economics,* 92, 128, 214; MacLeod, "Conservation among Primitive Hunting Peoples," 565. This situation contrasts sharply with Garrett Hardin's scenario in "The Tragedy of the Commons," *Science* 162 (13 Dec. 1968): 1244–45.

73. Minor et al., *Culture Resource Overview,* 45; T. T. Waterman and A. L. Kroeber, *The Kepel Fish Dam,* UCPAAE 35 (Berkeley: University of California Press, 1938), 50–51.

74. Krieger, "Environment, Population, and Prehistory," 4.

2 / HISTORICIZING OVERFISHING

1. Candace Slater, "Amazonia as Edenic Narrative," in *Uncommon Ground: Toward Reinventing Nature,* ed. William Cronon (New York: W. W. Norton, 1995), 114–31; Carolyn Merchant, "Reinventing Eden: Western Culture as a Recovery Narrative," in *Uncommon Ground,* ed. Cronon, 132–59; Donna Haraway, "The Promises of Monsters: A Regenerative Politics for Inappropriate/d Others," in *Cultural Studies,* ed. Lawrence Grossberg, Cary Nelson, and Paula A. Treichler (London: Routledge, 1992), 311–15. For versions of this fall-from-grace narrative see Samuel Wilmot, "Report on Fish Breeding in the Dominion of Canada, 1881," in *Fourteenth Annual Report of the Department of Marine and Fisheries, Being for the Fiscal Year Ended 30th June, 1881,* suppl. 2 (Ottawa: MacLean, Roger and Co., 1882), 38; Anthony Netboy, *Salmon of the Pacific Northwest: Fish vs. Dams* (Portland: Binfords and Mort, 1958); Alan Thein Durning, "The Six Floods," *World Watch* (Nov.–Dec. 1996), 28–36; D. W. Chapman, "Salmon and Steelhead Abundance in the Columbia River in the Nineteenth Century," *TAFS* 115 (1986): 666; Joseph

Cone, *A Common Fate: Endangered Salmon and the People of the Pacific Northwest* (New York: Henry Holt, 1995).

2. Robert T. Boyd, "The Introduction of Infectious Diseases among the Indians of the Pacific Northwest, 1774–1874" (Ph.D. diss., University of Washington, 1985), 72; Francis L. Black, "Why Did They Die?" *Science* 258 (11 Dec. 1992): 1739–40.

3. Alfred W. Crosby, "Virgin Soil Epidemics as a Factor in the Aboriginal Depopulation in America," *William and Mary Quarterly* 33 (1976): 293–97; Wilbur R. Jacobs, "The Tip of the Iceberg: Pre-Columbian Indian Demography and Some Implications for Revisionism," *William and Mary Quarterly* 31 (Jan. 1974): 123–32; Ann F. Ramenofsky, *Vectors of Death* (Albuquerque: University of New Mexico Press, 1987), 161; Frederick Merk, ed., *Fur Trade and Empire: George Simpson's Journal . . . 1825–25,* rev. ed. (Cambridge: Belknap Press of Harvard University Press, 1968), 94; Gillett Griswold, *Aboriginal Patterns of Trade between the Columbia Basin and the Northern Plains,* Archaeology in Montana 11 (Missoula: Montana Archaeological Society, 1970).

4. George I. Quimby Jr., "Culture Contact on the Northwest Coast, 1785–1795," *American Anthropologist* 50 (Apr. 1948): 247; George Gibbs, "Tribes of Western Washington and Northwestern Oregon," *Contributions to North American Ethnology* 1 (1877): 236–37; Sarah K. Campbell, *Post-Columbian Culture History in the Northern Columbia Plateau,* A.D. 1500–1900 (New York: Garland Publishing, 1990), 186–87.

5. Boyd, "Infectious Diseases," 71, 90, 105; Robert T. Boyd, "Demographic History, 1774–1874," in *HNAI, NWC,* 137–38; Cole Harris, "Voices of Disaster: Smallpox around the Strait of Georgia in 1792," *Ethnohistory* 41 (fall 1994): 591–626; Gibbs, "Tribes," 238–39.

6. Boyd, "Demographic History," 138–42; Sherbourne F. Cook, "The Epidemic of 1830–1833 in California and Oregon," *UCPAAE* 43 (1955): 303–26; Robert Boyd, "Another Look at the 'Fever and Ague' of Western Oregon," *Ethnohistory* 22 (spring 1975): 125–74; E. E. Rich, ed., *McLoughlin's Fort Vancouver Letters: First Series, 1825–38* (London: Champlain Society, 1941), 88.

7. Cook, "The Epidemic of 1830–1833," 306; Boyd, "Demographic History," 139–40; David Lee and J. H. Frost, *Ten Years in Oregon* (New York: Collord, 1844), 132.

8. Boyd, "Demographic History," 138–42, 146–47; Boyd, "Infectious Diseases," 386, 371; Joy Leland, "Population," in *HNAI,* GB, 608–19.

9. Crosby, "Virgin Soil Epidemics"; Boyd, "Demographic History," 147; Andrew P. Vayda, "A Re-examination of Northwest Coast Economic Systems," *Transactions of the New York Academy of Sciences* 23 (May 1961): 622.

10. Stephen J. Pyne, *Fire in America* (Princeton: Princeton University Press, 1982), 336–39; Robert Boyd, "Strategies of Indian Burning in the Willamette Val-

ley," *Canadian Journal of Anthropology* 5 (fall 1986): 65–86; Lee and Frost, *Ten Years in Oregon*, 88–89; Thomas J. Connolly, "Terrestrial and Riverine Economies in Southwest Oregon: A View from Camas Valley," in *Contributions to the Archaeology of Oregon, 1983–1986* (Portland: Portland State University, 1986), 193; Nancy Langston, *Forest Dreams, Forest Nightmares: The Paradox of Old Growth in the Inland West* (Seattle: University of Washington Press, 1995), 29–41; Joseph A. Craig and Robert L. Hacker, *The History and Development of the Fisheries of the Columbia River*, Bulletin of the Bureau of Fisheries 32 (Washington: Government Printing Office, 1940), 150; Gordon W. Hewes, "Aboriginal Use of Fishery Resources in Northwestern North America" (Ph.D. diss, University of California, Berkeley, 1947), 237; Erhard Rostlund, *Fresh Water Fish and Fishing in Native North America*, University of California Publications in Geography 9 (Berkeley: University of California Press, 1952), 17; Randall Schalk, "The Structure of an Anadromous Fish Resource," in *For Theory Building in Archaeology: Essays on Faunal Remains, Aquatic Resources, Spatial Analysis, and Systemic Modeling*, ed. Lewis R. Binford (New York: Academic Press, 1977), 207–49; Ray Hilborn, "The Frequency and Severity of Fish Stock Declines and Increases," in *Developing and Sustaining World Fisheries Resources: Proceedings of the Second World Fisheries Congress*, ed. D. A. Hancock, D. C. Smith, A. Grant, and J. P. Beumer (Victoria, Australia: CSIRO, 1997), 36–38. Schalk disagrees with this argument about declining aboriginal harvests for the Columbia, but his assertion that dependence on salmon increased among surviving groups and that distant groups migrated to take advantage of open fisheries fails to account for the huge decline in human population. While trade may have somewhat boosted declining salmon consumption, Indians could not have compensated completely for the region's overall population reduction; Randall F. Schalk, "Estimating Salmon and Steelhead Usage in the Columbia Basin Before 1850: The Anthropological Perspective," *Northwest Environmental Journal* 2 (1986): 22–23 n. 5.

11. Boyd, "Demographic History," 146–47; Stephen Dow Beckham, *Requiem for a People* (Norman: University of Oklahoma Press, 1971), 69; Henry B. Zenk, "Kalapuyans," in *HNAI, NWC,* 551–52; Peter Boag, "The Calapooian Matrix: Landscape and Experience on a Western Frontier" (Ph.D. diss., University of Oregon, 1988), 35–36 n. 41; William R. Seaburg and Jay Miller, "Tillamook," in *HNAI, NWC,* 561; Michael E. Kraus, "Kwalhioqua and Clatskanie," in *HNAI, NWC,* 531–32; Henry B. Zenk, "Alseans," in *HNAI, NWC,* 570; Henry B. Zenk, "Siuslawans and Coosans," in *HNAI, NWC,* 578; and Daythal L. Kendall, "Takelma," in *HNAI, NWC,* 592; Henry B. Zenk, "Chinook Jargon and Native Cultural Persistence in the Grand Ronde Indian Community, 1856–1907: A Special Case of Creolization" (Ph.D. diss., University of Oregon, 1984); Michael Silverstein, "Chinookans of the Lower Columbia," in *HNAI, NWC,* 536.

12. Melville Jacobs, "Coos Myth Texts," *UWPA* 8 (1940): 240; Gustavus Hines,

Wild Life in Oregon (New York: Hurst and Co., 1881), 117–18; Rich, *McLoughlin's Letters, 1825–38*, 88, 104, 233; Peter Boag, *Environment and Experience: Settlement Culture in Nineteenth-Century Oregon* (Berkeley: University of California Press, 1992), 58.

13. Samuel N. Dicken and Emily F. Dicken, *The Making of Oregon: A Study in Historical Geography* (Portland: Oregon Historical Society, 1979), 64–83.

14. *ARCIA* (1850) S. Exec. Doc. 1 (31–2) 587:146; Alban W. Hoopes, *Indian Affairs and Their Administration, with Special Reference to the Far West, 1849–1860* (Philadelphia: Temple University Press, 1932), 77–78; Francis Paul Prucha, *The Great Father: The United States Government and the American Indians* (Lincoln: University of Nebraska Press, 1984), 398. Settlers claimed another 300,000 acres in Washington Territory; James M. Bergquist, "The Oregon Donation Act and the National Land Policy," *Oregon Historical Quarterly* 58 (Mar. 1957): 17–35; William G. Robbins, "The Indian Question in Western Oregon: The Making of a Colonial People," in *Experiences in a Promised Land: Essays in Pacific Northwest History*, ed. G. Thomas Edwards and Carlos A. Schwantes (Seattle: University of Washington Press, 1986), 53–57; William A. Bowen, *The Willamette Valley: Migration and Settlement on the Oregon Frontier* (Seattle: University of Washington Press, 1978); Francis Paul Prucha, "United States Indian Policies, 1815–1860," in *HNAI, HIWR*, 40; C. F. Coan, "The First Stage of the Federal Indian Policy in the Pacific in the Pacific Northwest, 1849–1852," *Oregon Historical Quarterly* 22 (Mar. 1921): 46–89.

15. Beckham, *Requiem for a People*, 116; E. A. Schwartz, *The Rogue River Indian War and Its Aftermath, 1850–1980* (Norman: University of Oklahoma Press, 1997), 44–147; Robert M. Utley and Wilcomb E. Washburn, *The American Heritage History of the Indian Wars* (New York: American Heritage, 1977), 201.

16. Clifford E. Trafzer, ed., *Indians, Superintendents, and Councils* (Lanham, Md.: University Press of America, 1986); Jeff Zucker, Day Hummel, and Bob Høgfoss, *Oregon Indians: Culture, History and Current Affairs* (Portland: Western Imprints, 1983); Beckham, *Requiem for a People*, 47–191; Utley and Washburn, *Indian Wars*, 201–5; Kent D. Richards, *Isaac I. Stevens: Young Man in a Hurry* (Provo: Brigham Young University Press, 1979), 235–56.

17. Dicken and Dicken, *Making of Oregon*, 84, 105–8; U.S. Department of the Interior, Census Office, *Abstract of the Twelfth Census of the United States, 1900* (Washington: Government Printing Office, 1904), lxxxii–lxxxvi, 32, 40.

18. Lorne Hammond, "Marketing Wildlife: The Hudson's Bay Company and the Pacific Northwest, 1821–49," *Forest and Conservation History* 37 (Jan. 1993): 14–25; John F. Due and Giles French, *Rails to the Mid-Columbia Wheatlands: The Columbia Southern and Great Southern Railroads and the Development of Sherman and Wasco Counties, Oregon* (Washington, D.C.: University Press of America, 1979);

Michael Williams, *Americans and Their Forests: A Historical Geography* (New York: Cambridge University Press, 1989), 292, 294, 298; Daniel B. Deloach, *The Salmon Canning Industry* (Corvallis: Oregon State College, 1939), 61–67, 70, 77–79.

19. Thomas R. Dunlap, *Saving America's Wildlife: Ecology and the American Mind, 1850–1990* (Princeton: Princeton University Press, 1988); William Cronon, *Nature's Metropolis: Chicago and the Great West* (New York: W. W. Norton, 1991), 266–67; Richard White, "Animals and Enterprise," in *The Oxford History of the American West,* ed. Clyde A. Milner II, Carol A. O'Connor, and Martha A. Sandweiss (New York: Oxford University Press, 1994), 236–73; Robert Bunting, *The Pacific Raincoast: Environment and Culture in an American Eden, 1778–1900* (Lawrence: University Press of Kansas, 1997).

20. Bunting, *Pacific Raincoast,* 22–35; James R. Gibson, *Otter Skins, Boston Ships, and China Goods: The Maritime Fur Trade of the Northwest Coast, 1785–1841* (Seattle: University of Washington Press, 1992); Douglas Cole and David Darling, "History of the Early Period," in *HNAI, NWC,* 125, 128–29; T. C. Elliot, "The Fur Trade in the Columbia River Basin prior to 1811," *Washington Historical Quarterly* 6 (Jan. 1915): 3–10; Marion O'Neil, "The Maritime Activities of the North West Company, 1813–1821," *Washington Historical Quarterly* 21 (Oct. 1930): 243–44; Merk, *Fur Trade and Empire,* 98; Alexander Ross, *Adventures of the First Settlers on the Oregon or Columbia River* (1849; reprint, New York: Citadel Press, 1969), 84; Robert H. Ruby and John A. Brown, *Chinook Indians: Traders of the Lower Columbia River* (Norman: University of Oklahoma Press, 1976), 122, 133; James Ronda, *Astoria and Empire* (Lincoln: University of Nebraska Press, 1990).

21. Merk, *Fur Trade and Empire,* xxi, 94; Cole and Darling, "History of the Early Period," 130; Gibbs, "Tribes," 234–35; Neil M. Howison, "Military Posts— Council Bluffs to the Pacific Ocean," H.R. Rep. 31 (27–3) 426:57.

22. Theodore Stern, *Chiefs and Chief Traders: Indian Relations at Fort Nez Percés, 1818–1855* (Corvallis: Oregon State University Press, 1993), 18–33.

23. Karen Leidholt-Bruner, David E. Hibbs, and William C. McComb, "Beaver Dam Locations and Their Effects on Distribution and Abundance of Coho Salmon in Two Coastal Oregon Streams," *Northwest Science* 66 (Nov. 1992): 218–23; David J. Wishart, *The Fur Trade of the American West, 1807–1840* (Lincoln: University of Nebraska Press, 1979), 32, 131; Langston, *Forest Dreams,* 58–59; Steven L. Johnson, *Freshwater Environmental Problems and Coho Production in Oregon,* Informational Reports 84–11 (Corvallis: Oregon Department of Fish and Wildlife, Fish Division, 1984), 3.

24. Alfred Crosby, *Ecological Imperialism: The Biological Expansion of Europe, 900–1900* (New York: Cambridge University Press, 1986); Richard White, *Land Use, Environment, and Social Change* (Seattle: University of Washington Press,

1980); Langston, *Forest Dreams;* Donald W. Meinig, *The Great Columbian Plain: A Historical Geography, 1805–1910* (Seattle: University of Washington Press, 1968), 223–26; Dicken and Dicken, *Making of Oregon,* 75–77, 79, 92–93.

25. Dicken and Dicken, *Making of Oregon,* 84–88; Howard C. Brooks and Len Ramp, *Gold and Silver in Oregon,* Oregon Department of Geology and Mineral Industries Bulletin 61 (Portland: Oregon Department of Geology and Mineral Industries, 1968), 43, 167; J. S. Diller, *Mineral Resources of Southwestern Oregon,* U.S. Geological Survey Bulletin 546 (Washington: Government Printing Office, 1914), 30–34, 38–39, 45–47, 51, 58, 90, 114; Rodman Wilson Paul, *Mining Frontiers of the Far West, 1848–1880* (New York: Holt, Rinehart, and Winston, 1963), 149; Langston, *Forest Dreams,* 69–70; Randall Rohe, "The Impact of Placer Mining in the American West, 1848–1974" (Ph.D. diss., University of Colorado, 1978), 90, 326–31. For a sampling of strikes and mining figures see *Oregonian* for 21 Mar. 1870, 3; 25 Apr. 1871, 1; 8 Nov. 1871, 1; 20 May 1874, 1; 16 Mar. 1875, 1; 24 May 1875, 1; 14 June 1875, 1; 28 June 1875, 1; 22 Feb. 1876, 3; 23 Mar. 1876, 1; 17 May 1877, 1; 22 Sept. 1877, 1; 5 Dec. 1878, 1; 16 Mar. 1879, 1; 25 Nov. 1879, 1.

26. Robert C. Wissmar, Jeanette E. Smith, Bruce A. McIntosh, Hiram W. Li, Gordon H. Reeves, and James R. Sedell, "A History of Resource Use and Disturbance in Riverine Basins of Eastern Oregon and Washington (Early 1800s–1990s)," *Northwest Science* 68 (Special Issue 1994): 3–6; Brooks and Ramp, *Gold and Silver,* 282, 286, 292, 301; Diller, *Mineral Resources,* 28–29, 120–29; J. T. Pardee, *Beach Placers of the Oregon Coast,* U.S. Geological Survey Circular 8 (Washington: Government Printing Office, 1934), 38, 39; *Oregonian,* 18 Feb. 1870, 2; 1 Nov. 1873, 3; 3 Dec. 1873, 3; 31 Mar. 1875, 1; 9 Dec. 1886, 2, 3; N W P P C, "Compilation of Information on Salmon and Steelhead Losses in the Columbia River Basin" (Portland: Northwest Power Planning Council, 1985), 134–35; Paul, *Mining Frontiers,* 138–40; Kenneth Thompson, "Columbia Basin Fisheries Past, Present, and Future," in *Investigative Reports of Columbia River Fisheries Project* (Portland: Pacific Northwest Regional Commission, 1976), A19.

27. Bruce A. McIntosh, James R. Sedell, Jeanette E. Smith, Robert C. Wissmar, Sharon E. Clarke, Gordon H. Reeves, and Lisa A. Brown, "Historical Changes in Fish Habitat for Select River Basins of Eastern Oregon and Washington," *Northwest Science* 68 (Special Issue 1994): 47; Brooks and Ramp, *Gold and Silver;* F. W. Libbey, *Progress Report on Coos Bay Coal Field,* Oregon Department of Geology and Mineral Industries Bulletin 2 (Portland: Oregon Department of Geology and Mineral Industries, 1938), 2; Diller, *Mineral Resources,* 130–33; and John C. Shideler, *Coal Towns in the Cascades: A Centennial History of Roslyn and Cle Elum, Washington* (Spokane: Melior, 1986), 77–89. One flask contained 76 pounds of mercury; C. N. Schuette, *Quicksilver in Oregon,* Oregon Department of Geology and Mineral Industries Bulletin 4 (Portland: Oregon Department of Geology and

Mineral Industries, 1938), 47, 81, 111, 145, 170; Francis G. Wells and Aaron C. Waters, *Quicksilver Deposits of Southwestern Oregon,* U.S. Geological Survey Bulletin 850 (Washington: Government Printing Office, 1934), 3, 28–29, 34, 38, 40; *Oregonian,* 16 Feb. 1875, 1; 20 Apr. 1875, 1.

28. *Oregonian,* 7 June 1876, 2.

29. Randall E. Rohe, "After the Gold Rush: Chinese Mining in the Far West, 1850–1890," *Montana, the Magazine of Western History* 32 (autumn 1982): 9–10.

30. *Oregonian,* 23 May 1877, 3; 1 Apr. 1878, 1; Randall E. Rohe, "Hydraulicking in the American West: The Development and Diffusion of a Mining Technique," *Montana, the Magazine of Western History* 35 (spring 1985): 28–31; Rohe, "Geographical Impact of Placer Mining," 150–54; Brooks and Ramp, *Gold and Silver,* 167–68; Randall Rohe, "Environment and Mining in the Mountainous West," in *The Mountainous West: Explorations in Historical Geography,* ed. William Wyckoff and Lary M. Dilsaver (Lincoln: University of Nebraska Press, 1995), 175.

31. Brooks and Ramp, *Gold and Silver,* 43, 167–68; *Boise News* quoted in Rohe, "Geographical Impact of Placer Mining," 153, 251; Diller, *Mineral Resources,* 109; Cole M. River, "Rough Draft, Rogue River Report" (reprint file, NWFSCL, typed MS copy), 19–20; *Oregonian,* 27 Mar. 1873, 1; 29 May 1876, 3; 13 Nov. 1876, 1; 24 Apr. 1877, 4; 23 May 1877, 3; 13 Aug. 1877, 3; 17 Sept. 1877, 1; 28 Sept. 1877, 3; 24 Oct. 1877, 3; 7 May 1878, 1; 26 Nov. 1878, 1; 16 Mar. 1879, 1; Thompson, "Columbia Basin Fisheries," A19.

32. Henry Baldwin Ward, *Placer Mining on the Rogue River, Oregon, in Its Relation to the Fish and Fishing in That Stream* (Portland: Oregon Department of Geology and Mineral Industries, 1938), 6, 8; Charles H. Gilbert and Barton W. Evermann, "A Report upon Investigations in the Columbia River Basin, with Descriptions of Four New Species of Fishes," *Bulletin* 14 (1894): 179; NWPPC, "Salmon and Steelhead Losses," 132–36; *Oregonian,* 11 Feb. 1879, 3; 27 Dec. 1888, 8; Rohe, "Geographical Impact of Placer Mining," 251–52, 256, 263, 269; Thompson, "Columbia Basin Fisheries," A19; Wissmar et al., "History of Resource Use," 6, 17, 27; L. Nelson, M. L. McHenry, and W. S. Platts, "Mining," in *Influences of Forest and Rangeland Management,* ed. William R. Meehan, American Fisheries Society Special Publication 19 (Bethesda: American Fisheries Society, 1991), 425–58; R. D. Hume to Robert McLean (1 June 1896), vol. 84, pp. 582–91, Hume Papers; Livingston Stone to Spencer F. Baird, 4 Sept. 1880, box 10, Letters Received, 1878–81, RG 22, NA; U.S. Department of the Interior, *Columbia River Basin: Development of Water and Other Resources Present and Potential of the Columbia River Basin in Washington, Oregon, Idaho, Montana, Wyoming, Nevada, and Utah,* Project Planning Report no. 1–5.0–1 (Washington: Bureau of Reclamation, 1946), 314; AROFC (1888): 18 and (1890): 19; Barton Warren Evermann and Seth Eugene Meek, "A Report upon Salmon Investigations in the Columbia River Basin and Elsewhere on

the Pacific Coast in 1896," *Bulletin* 17 (1897): 32; Marshall McDonald to James Crawford, 29 Sept. 1890, vol. 280, pp. 183–86, Press Copies of Letters Sent, 1871–1906, R G 22, N A.

33. *Oregonian,* 1 Aug. 1871, 2; 2 Aug. 1875, 1; 19 Mar. 1879, 3; 30 Apr. 1879, 3; 8 July 1879, 3; 12 Aug. 1879, 1; 25 Aug. 1879, 3; Thompson, "Columbia Basin Fisheries," A21; Ward, *Placer Mining,* 9; Gilbert and Evermann, "Report upon Investigations," 179.

34. William G. Robbins, *Landscapes of Promise: The Oregon Story, 1800–1940* (Seattle: University of Washington Press, 1997), 142–45, 150–57; Carlos A. Schwantes, *The Pacific Northwest: An Interpretive History* (Lincoln: University of Nebraska Press, 1989), 92; Joseph R. Conlin, *Bacon, Beans, and Galantines: Food and Foodways on the Western Mining Frontier* (Reno: University of Nevada Press, 1986); Dicken and Dicken, *Making of Oregon,* 79, 92–93; *Oregonian,* 11 Mar. 1886, 4; 8 Nov. 1908, sec. 1, 10; Ward, *Placer Mining,* 9; John T. Gharrett and John I. Hodges, *Salmon Fisheries of the Coastal Rivers of Oregon South of the Columbia,* Oregon Fish Commission Contribution 13 (Portland: Oregon Fish Commission, 1950), 20–21; James R. Sedell and Karen J. Luchessa, "Using the Historical Record as an Aid to Salmonid Habitat Enhancement," in *Acquisition and Utilization of Aquatic Habitat Inventory Information,* ed. Neil B. Armantrout (Portland: American Fisheries Society, 1982), 216.

35. Department of Interior, *Columbia River Basin,* 155, 160, 164–66, 283, 333, 339, 349; Wissmar et al., "History of Resource Use," 7, 8; Frederick A. Davidson, "The Development of Irrigation in the Yakima River Basin and Its Effect on the Migratory Fish Populations in the River," Grant County [Wash.] Public Utilities District Library, 1965, 3, 5; Kirk Bryan, "Geology of the Owyhee Irrigation Project, Oregon," in *Contributions to the Hydrology of the United States, 1928,* U.S. Geological Survey Water-Supply Paper 597 (Washington: Government Printing Office, 1929), 39; N W P P C, "Salmon and Steelhead Losses," 156; Langston, *Forest Dreams,* 70; *Oregonian,* 2 Dec. 1878, 8; Bunting, *Pacific Raincoast,* 78–80.

36. Petition from I. L. Reese et al., vol. 21, fldr. 135, Henry Villard Papers, Baker Library, Harvard Business School, Boston; Richard White, *It's Your Misfortune and None of My Own: A History of the American West* (Norman: University of Oklahoma Press, 1991), 257–58; Cronon, *Nature's Metropolis,* 97; Davidson, "Development of Irrigation," 3–4; Wissmar et al., "History of Resource Use," 6; Dicken and Dicken, *Making of Oregon,* 105–22; U.S. Census Office, *Twelfth Census,* 6:855–57.

37. N W P P C, "Salmon and Steelhead Losses," 146; Gilbert and Evermann, "Report upon Investigations," 178–79; Peter Nelson and Frank Graham to Commissioner, 23 Feb. 1897, box 271, no. 10530, Letters Received, 1882–1900, R G 22, N A; Thompson, "Columbia Basin Fisheries," A26; Wissmar et al., "History of Resource

Use," 26; Department of Interior, *Columbia River Basin,* 165–66; Marshall Mc-Donald, "The Salmon Fisheries of the Columbia River Basin," *Bulletin* 14 (1894): 155; *Oregonian,* 9 Sept. 1904, 4.

38. Davidson, "Development of Irrigation," 1–4; J. W. Titcomb to Superintendent, 4 Feb. 1903, vol. 603, p. 6835; George M. Bowers to A. W. Anthony, 4 Feb. 1903, vol. 602, p. 6370, Press Copies of Letters Sent, 1871–1906, RG 22, NA; B. E. Stoutemyer to Henry O'Malley, 28 Jan. 1931, box 1, Records concerning Fishways and Fish Protection Devices on Water Development Projects, 1919–35, RG 22, NA; Livingston Stone, "Report of Operations at the Salmon-Hatching Station on the Clackamas River, Oregon, in 1877," *ARUSCF* (1877): 784–85; Evermann and Meek, "Report upon Salmon Investigations," 33; *AROFC* (1888): 16; Gilbert and Evermann, "Report upon Investigations," 186; *Oregonian,* 14 Dec. 1901, 4; James W. Mullan, "Determinants of Sockeye Salmon Abundance in the Columbia River, 1880's–1982: A Review and Synthesis," *Biological Report* 86 (Sept. 1986): 47, 115–16.

39. Dicken and Dicken, *Making of Oregon,* 94–95, 127–30; Gilbert and Evermann, "Report upon Investigations," 199–200; *Oregonian,* 5 Jan. 1874, 1; 6 Oct. 1875, 3; 26 Aug. 1878, 1; 15 Aug. 1879, 1; 3 Nov. 1879, 3; 14 June 1893, 2; L. T. Barin to J. W. Cook, 26 Dec. 1885, box 95, no. 55656; Thomas Day to Spencer F. Baird, 22 Jan. 1886, box 97, no. 56762; S. N. Gibson to Baird, 11 Feb. 1885, box 75, no. 43613; F. C. Reed to Marshall McDonald, 30 Mar. 1889, box 144, no. 104711; C. A. Wright to Commissioner, 8 Sept. 1890, box 159, no. 115118; J. C. Cowgill to Commissioner, 23 Apr. 1890, box 156, no. 112441; A. F. Padgett to U.S. Fish Commission, 24 Sept. 1891, box 172, no. 124464; Hollister D. McGuire to McDonald, 17 Feb. 1894, box 215, no. 9615, Letters Received, 1882–1900, RG 22, NA; McDonald to Governor of California, 2 Oct. 1889, vol. 258, pp. 187–91, Press Copies of Letters Sent, 1871–1906, RG 22, NA; *AROFC* (1890): 7.

40. Meinig, *Great Columbia Plain,* 220–23, 291–93; J. Orin Oliphant, *On the Cattle Ranges of the Oregon Country* (Seattle: University of Washington Press, 1968), 39–114; Wissmar et al., "History of Resource Use," 6, 7, 17; Langston, *Forest Dreams,* 70, 74; *Oregonian,* 28 Jan. 1878, 3; Dicken and Dicken, *Making of Oregon,* 93, 122–25; Robbins, *Landscapes of Promise,* 152–53.

41. Meinig, *Great Columbia Plain,* 292–93; McIntosh et al., "Historical Changes," 47.

42. Langston, *Forest Dreams,* 48–49; Francis D. Haines Jr., "The Northward Spread of Horses among the Plains Indians," *American Anthropologist* 40 (July 1938): 429–37; W. S. Platts, "Livestock Grazing," in *Influences of Forest and Rangeland Management,* ed. Meehan, 389–423.

43. McIntosh et al., "Historical Changes," 44, 47; Wissmar et al., "History of Resource Use," 8; Langston, *Forest Dreams,* 75; NWPPC, "Salmon and Steelhead

Losses," 138; Platts, "Livestock Grazing"; J. L. Peterson, "Ecological Survey of Brush Areas, Applegate Division, Crater National Forest" (Forestry Libary, University of Washington, Seattle, Nov. 1916, typed MS).

44. Langston, *Forest Dreams*, 81–82; Williams, *Americans and Their Forests*, 289–309; Dicken and Dicken, *Making of Oregon*, 128, 193–94; *Oregonian*, 31 July 1871, 1; 17 Sept. 1872, 1; 24 Dec. 1873, 1.

45. Williams, *Americans and Their Forests*, 291; Sedell and Luchessa, "Using the Historical Record," 216; McIntosh et al., "Historical Changes," 44; Pyne, *Fire in America*, 336–39; William G. Morris, "Forest Fires in Western Oregon and Western Washington," *Oregon Historical Quarterly* 35 (Dec. 1934): 313–39; Thornton T. Munger, "Out of the Ashes of the Nestucca," *American Forests* 50 (July 1944): 342–44; Boyd, "Strategies of Indian Burning," 65–86; Peter G. Boag, "The World Fire Created," *Columbia* 5 (summer 1991): 5–11; Wissmar et al., "History of Resource Use," 8–9; Langston, *Forest Dreams*, 315–16 n. 75; *Oregonian*, 24 Aug. 1871, 3; 28 May 1873, 3; 3 Nov. 1874, 3; 28 Sept. 1875, 3; 17 July 1877, 3; 14 Aug. 1878, 1; 25 Aug. 1879, 3.

46. D. W. Chapman, "Effects of Logging upon Fish Resources of the West Coast," *Journal of Forestry* 60 (Aug. 1962): 533; Sedell and Luchessa, "Using the Historical Record," 212, 216; NWPPC, "Salmon and Steelhead Losses," 123–24; Henry O. Wendler and Gene Deschamps, *Logging Dams on Coastal Washington Streams*, Fisheries Research Papers 1 (Olympia: State Printing Office, 1953), 27–38; Langston, *Forest Dreams*, 82.

47. Wendler and Deschamps, *Logging Dams*, 30–33; Chapman, "Effects of Logging," 534; Sedell and Luchessa, "Using the Historical Record," 215; Rollin R. Geppert, Charles W. Lorenz, and Arthur G. Larson, eds., *Cumulative Effects of Forest Practices on the Environment: A State of Knowledge* (Olympia: Ecosystems, 1984), 155; J. R. Sedell, F. N. Leone, and W. S. Duval, "Water Transportation and Storage of Logs," in *Influences of Forest and Rangeland Management*, ed. Meehan, 335.

48. Dicken and Dicken, *Making of Oregon*, 93–94; U.S. Census Office, *Twelfth Census*, 9:894, 895, 897; Wissmar et al., "History of Resource Use," 17; Sedell et al., "Water Transportation and Storage," 335, 351–52, 359–64.

49. T. M. Smith to Marshall McDonald, 16 Aug. 1889, box 147, no. 106290; J. C. Cowgill to Commissioner, 23 Apr. 1890, box 156, no. 112441; C. A. Wright to Commissioner, 8 Sept. 1890, no. 115118, box 159; A. F. Padgett to U.S. Fish Commission, 24 Sept. 1891, box 172, no. 124464; J. G. Anderson to McDonald, 28 May 1894, box 222, no. 14426; George W. Milhan to Commissioner, 10 June 1895, box 241, no. 14770; N. E. Linsley to John J. Brice, 29 Sept. 1897, box 281, no. 3381, Letters Received, 1882–1900, RG 22, NA; *Oregonian*, 14 Jan. 1887, 3; *AROFC* (1892):

4; W. de C. Ravenal to J. N. Wisner, 25 Aug. 1899, vol. 520, p. 1786, Press Copies of Letters Sent, 1871–1906, R G 22, N A; Bunting, *Pacific Raincoast*, 145–47.

50. *Oregonian*, 31 Aug. 1874, 2; U.S. Census Office, *Twelfth Census*, lxxxii–lxxxv, 432–33; Lawrence H. Larsen, *The Urban West at the End of the Frontier* (Lawrence: Regents Press of Kansas, 1978), 14, 22–29; Dicken and Dicken, *Making of Oregon*, 81–83, 91–92, 135–37.

51. White, *It's Your Misfortune*, 246–57; Peter J. Lewty, *To the Columbia Gateway: The Oregon Railway and the Northern Pacific, 1879–1884* (Pullman: Washington State University Press, 1987); Dicken and Dicken, *Making of Oregon*, 95–99, 108–17; *Oregonian*, 19 Jan. 1870, 1; 19 Mar. 1871, 2; 17 Aug. 1872, 3; 14 Nov. 1872, 2; 5 Mar. 1874, 3; Sedell and Luchessa, "Using the Historical Record," 214, 216; Rick Harmon, "The Bull Run Watershed: Portland's Enduring Jewel," *Oregon Historical Quarterly* 96 (summer–fall 1995): 242–48; Craig Wollner, *Electrifying Eden: Portland General Electric, 1889–1965* (Portland: Oregon Historical Society, 1990); N W P P C, "Salmon and Steelhead Losses," 100.

52. Craig and Hacker, *History and Development*, 195.

53. Frederic W. Howay, ed., *Voyages of the "Columbia" to the Northwest Coast, 1787–1790 and 1790–1793* (Portland: Oregon Historical Society Press, 1990), 398; Ronda, *Astoria and Empire*, 207, 220.

54. Rich, *McLoughlin's Letters, 1825–38*, lxxiii, lxxxi, xcii, 37, 77, 88, 92, 95; Merk, *Fur Trade and Empire*, 121 n. 173, 240, 252.

55. Samuel Elliot Morison, "New England and the Opening of the Columbia River Salmon Trade, 1830," *Oregon Historical Quarterly* 28 (June 1927): 112 n. 4, 114–15, 131, 132; F. W. Howay, "Brig Owhyhee in the Columbia, 1827," *Oregon Historical Quarterly* 34 (Dec. 1933): 324–29; F. W. Howay, "The Brig Owhyhee in the Columbia, 1829–30," *Oregon Historical Quarterly* 35 (Mar. 1934): 14, 18; Rich, *McLoughlin's Letters, 1825–38*, 95, 120, 120 n. 1.

56. For recent treatments of imperialism that do accord Indian agency, see Ronda, *Astoria and Empire;* Gibson, *Otter Skins;* Alexandra Harmon, "Lines in Sand: Shifting Boundaries between Indians and Non-Indians in the Puget Sound Region," *Western Historical Quarterly* 26 (winter 1995): 429–53; F. G. Young, ed., *The Correspondence and Journals of Captain Nathaniel Wyeth, 1831–6* (Eugene: University Press, 1899), 60; Morison, "New England," 130; Ruby and Brown, *Chinook Indians*, 193; Craig and Hacker, *History and Development*, 147.

57. Morison, "New England," 132; Rich, *McLoughlin's Letters, 1825–38*, 108–9, 141; Ruby and Brown, *Chinook Indians*, 193; Oscar O. Winther, "Commercial Routes from 1792 to 1843 by Sea and Overland," *Oregon Historical Quarterly* 42 (Sept. 1941): 233.

58. Rich, *McLoughlin's Letters, 1825–38*, 170, 267; E. E. Rich, ed., *McLoughlin's*

Fort Vancouver Letters: Second Series, 1839–44, Publications of the Hudson's Bay Record Society 6 (London: Champlain Society, 1943), xx, 5, 25, 35, 37, 41, 56–57, 63, 82, 85, 92–93, 96, 101, 136, 144, 159, 178, 194, 227–28, 230, 264–65, 268, 272, 274–75, 305; Merk, *Fur Trade and Empire,* 120–21; Craig and Hacker, *History and Development,* 148.

59. Arthur F. McEvoy, *The Fisherman's Problem: Ecology and Law in the California Fisheries, 1850–1980* (New York: Cambridge University Press, 1986); R. D. Hume, "The First Salmon Cannery," *Pacific Fisherman Yearbook* (Seattle, 1903), 19; Ruby and Brown, *Chinook Indians,* 240; R. D. Hume, *Salmon of the Pacific Coast* (San Francisco, 1893), 10; Sister Mary de Sales McLellan, "William Hume, 1830–1902," *Oregon Historical Quarterly* 35 (Sept. 1934): 272 n. 4; Craig and Hacker, *History and Development,* 149–50; Hubert Howe Bancroft, *History of Washington, Idaho, and Montana, 1845–1889* (San Francisco: History Co., 1890), 348–49.

60. Courtland L. Smith, *Salmon Fishers of the Columbia* (Corvallis: Oregon State University Press, 1979), 15–22; Deloach, *Salmon Canning Industry,* 13; Clark Patrick Spurlock, "A History of the Salmon Industry in the Pacific Northwest" (M.A. thesis, University of Oregon, 1940), 115–17; Patrick W. O'Bannon, "Waves of Change: Mechanization in the Pacific Coast Canned Salmon Industry, 1864–1914," *Technology and Culture* 28 (July 1987): 558–57; McEvoy, *Fisherman's Problem,* 73; Dean C. Allard Jr., *Spencer Fullerton Baird and the U.S. Fish Commission* (New York: Arno, 1978), 118; Irene Martin, *Legacy and Testament: The Story of Columbia River Gillnetters* (Pullman: Washington State University Press, 1994), 18–22; Bruce Brown, *Mountain in the Clouds: A Search for the Wild Salmon* (New York: Simon and Schuster, 1982), 25, 233; *Oregonian,* 2 Apr. 1873, 3.

61. Smith, *Salmon Fishers,* 108–12.

62. *Oregonian,* 16 July 1874, 1; 1 Jan. 1880, 7; Schalk, "Estimating Salmon and Steelhead Usage," 6; Dianne Newell, "Dispersal and Concentration: The Slowly Changing Spatial Pattern of the British Columbia Salmon Canning Industry," *Journal of Historical Geography* 14 (Jan. 1988): 25–26; Dianne Newell, "The Rationality of Mechanization in the Pacific Salmon-Canning Industry before the Second World War," *Business History Review* 62 (winter 1988): 626–55.

63. *Oregonian,* 2 July 1875, 4; Smith, *Salmon Fishers,* 15–22, 30–38; Craig and Hacker, *History and Development,* 164–79; Karen Johnson, *A History of Coho Fisheries and Management in Oregon through 1982,* Information Reports 83–12 (Corvallis: Oregon Department of Fish and Wildlife Research Section, 1983), 11; Joseph A. Craig, "Memorandum regarding Fishing in the Columbia River above and below Bonneville Dam, 1938" (reprint file, NWFSCL, typed MS), 3; Ivan J. Donaldson and Frederick K. Cramer, *Fishwheels of the Columbia* (Portland: Binfords and Mort, 1971), 120–23; W. A. Jones, "The Salmon Fisheries of the Columbia River," S. Exec. Doc. 123 (50–1) 2510:48.

64. Seufert Bros. to Everding and Farrell, 21 Dec. 1892, 21 Jan. 1893, 14 Apr. 1893, E F P; Deloach, *Salmon Canning Industry,* 14, 61–67, 70, 77–79; *Oregonian,* 16 July 1873, 3; 21 Feb. 1874, 3; 16 Mar. 1874, 2; W. A. Wilcox to H. M. Smith, 9 Dec. 1900, box 2, Correspondence of Hugh Smith relating to the Bureau of Fisheries, 1885–1910, R G 22, N A.

65. M. J. Kinney to W. de C. Ravenal, 22 Aug. 1896, box 261, no. 2526, Letters Received, 1882–1900, R G 22, N A; M. Patricia Marchak, "What Happens When Common Property Becomes Uncommon," *BC Studies* 80 (winter 1988–89): 14; McEvoy, *Fisherman's Problem,* 72; *Oregonian,* 27 May 1892, 12; 8 Oct. 1894, 5; 3 Nov. 1904, 6; 1 Apr. 1905, 8; 12 Sept. 1906, 8; Thomas Van Pelt to R. D. Hume, 11 Nov. 1895, box 1, Hume Papers; *A R O F C* (1892): 12; Dianne Newell, *Tangled Webs of History: Indians and the Law in Canada's Pacific Coast Fisheries* (Toronto: University of Toronto Press, 1993), 50; Dianne Newell, ed., *The Development of the Pacific Salmon-Canning Industry: A Grown Man's Game* (Montreal: McGill-Queen's University Press, 1989), 12–13; Cicely Lyons, *Salmon, Our Heritage: The Story of a Province and an Industry* (Vancouver: British Columbia Packers, 1969), 210; Smith, *Salmon Fishers,* 30–31, 84; Anthony Netboy, *The Columbia River Salmon and Steelhead Trout* (Seattle: University of Washington Press, 1980), 25, 143; Timothy Egan, *The Good Rain: Across Time and Terrain in the Pacific Northwest* (New York: Alfred A. Knopf, 1990), 187.

66. *Oregonian,* 17 Jan. 1878, 1; 25 Nov. 1886, 3; 27 July 1893, 3; and L. Wilzinski to Walter C. Newberry, 4 June 1892, box 184, no. 132301–3, Letters Received, 1882–1900, R G 22, N A; Kirk T. Beiningen, "Apportionment of Columbia River Salmon and Steelhead," in *Investigative Reports of Columbia River Fisheries Project* (Portland: Pacific Northwest Regional Commission, 1976), R8; Jones, "Salmon Fisheries," 47; Smith, *Salmon Fishers,* 53, 108, 110; Deloach, *Salmon Canning Industry,* 16; Spurlock, "History of the Salmon Industry," 124, 130–31; John N. Cobb, *Pacific Salmon Fisheries,* Bureau of Fisheries Document 1092 (Washington: Government Printing Office, 1930), 427, 434–37, 441–43; Lyons, *Salmon, Our Heritage,* 187; *A R O F C* (1890): 37.

67. W. A. Wilcox to A. W. Reed, 7 Apr. 1894, vol. 412, p. 30, Press Copies of Letters Sent, 1871–1906, R G 22, N A; *Oregonian* 2 July 1873, 3; 16 July 1874, 1; 12 May 1879, 1; 10 Jan. 1887, 5; 2 Jan. 1905, 18; *A R O F C* (1892): 35; Willis H. Rich, "The Present State of the Columbia River Salmon Resources," *Proceedings of the Sixth Pacific Science Congress* 3 (1939): 425; Willis H. Rich, "A Statistical Analysis of the Results of the Artificial Propagation of Chinook Salmon, 1921–1922" (reprint file, N W F S C L, typed MS), 4; "Meeting of International Pacific Salmon Investigation Federation, Executive Committee, Seattle, Washington, Dec. 2, 1926," p. 4, fldr. 1 of 4, box 4, Records concerning Societies, Councils, Conferences, and Other Groups, 1904–37, R G 22, N A; Craig, "Memorandum regarding Fishing in the Co-

lumbia," 3; Craig and Hacker, *History and Development*, 197; Jack M. Van Hyning, *Factors Affecting the Abundance of Fall Chinook Salmon in the Columbia River*, Research Reports of the Fish Commission of Oregon 4 (Salem: Oregon Fish Commission, 1973), 37; William A. Wilcox, *The Commercial Fisheries of the Pacific Coast States in 1904*, Bureau of Fisheries Document 612 (Washington: Government Printing Office, 1905), 10; Lyons, *Salmon, Our Heritage*, 274; Chapman, "Salmon and Steelhead Abundance," 665; Barton W. Evermann, "A Preliminary Report upon Salmon Investigations in Idaho in 1894," *Bulletin* 15 (1895): 262–76; Evermann and Meek, "Report upon Salmon Investigations," 53; Johnson, "History of Coho Fisheries," 9; Adam Eckert to Agricultural Department, 12 Mar. 1895, box 237, no. 11299, Letters Received, 1882–1900, RG 22, NA; *AROFC* (1890): 12–13; Wissmar et al., "History of Resource Use," 5; Jones, "Salmon Fisheries," 28–29.

68. Personal communications with Nathan Mantua and James Anderson, School of Fisheries, University of Washington; M. D. Brands, *Flood Runoff in the Willamette Valley, Oregon*, U.S. Geological Survey Water-Supply Paper 968-A (Washington: Government Printing Office, 1947); *Oregonian*, 15 Feb. 1878, 1; 12 Dec. 1879, 3; Donaldson and Cramer, *Fishwheels of the Columbia*, 83; Richard White, *The Organic Machine: The Remaking of the Columbia River* (New York: Hill and Wang, 1995), 30–31; Lisa J. Graumlich, "Precipitation Variation in the Pacific Northwest (1675–1975) as Reconstructed from Tree Rings," *Annals of the Association of American Geographers* 77 (Mar. 1987): 19–29; *AROFC* (1890): 3; L. E. Bean to W. de C. Ravenal, 16 Oct. 1897, box 4, Siuslaw Bundles, Records concerning Abandoned Stations, 1879–1931, RG 22, NA; Ravenal to E. N. Carter, 7 Nov. 1900, vol. 549, p. 3533, Press Copies of Letters Sent, 1871–1906, RG 22, NA; *Pacific Fisherman Yearbook* (1910), 36.

69. Robert C. Francis and Steven R. Hare, "Decadal-Scale Regime Shifts in the Large Marine Ecosystems of the North-East Pacific: A Case for Historical Science," *Fisheries Oceanography* 3 (1994): 279–91; Gunnar I. Roden, "Low-Frequency Sea Level Oscillations along the Pacific Coast of North America," *Journal of Geophysical Research* 71 (15 Oct. 1966): 4755–76; George N. Kiladis and Henry F. Diaz, "An Analysis of the 1877–78 ENSO Episode and Comparison with 1982–83," *Monthly Weather Review* 114 (June 1986): 1035–47.

70. John Cleghorn, "On Fluctuations in the Herring Fisheries," *Report of the British Association for the Advancement of Science* 24 (1854): 134; C. H. Joh. Petersen, "What Is Over-Fishing?" *Journal of the Marine Biological Association* 6 (1900–1903): 587–94; Tim D. Smith, *Scaling Fisheries: The Science of Measuring the Effects of Fishing, 1855–1955* (New York: Cambridge University Press, 1994), 9; Hume, *Salmon of the Pacific Coast*, 17; Courtland L. Smith, "Resource Scarcity and Inequality in the Distribution of Catch," *NAJFM* 10 (summer 1990): 272; Marchak, "What Happens," 12; Smith, *Salmon Fishers*, 1.

3 / INVENTING A PANACEA

1. Brad Matsen cited Genesis 1:26–28 during a seminar at the School of Fisheries, University of Washington, 24 Oct. 1995; see also Joseph Cone, *A Common Fate: Endangered Salmon and the People of the Pacific Northwest* (New York: Henry Holt, 1995), 52, 76; Lynn White Jr., "The Historical Roots of Our Ecological Crisis," *Science* 155 (10 Mar. 1967): 1203–7; Jeanne Kay, "Human Dominion over Nature in the Hebrew Bible," *Annals of the Association of American Geographers* 79 (June 1989): 214–32; J. Baird Callicott, "Genesis Revisited: Murian Musings on the Lynne White, Jr. Debate," *Environmental History Review* 14 (spring–summer 1990): 65–90; Brad Matsen, "Barging Down the River," in *Reaching Home: Pacific Salmon, Pacific People*, ed. Natalie Fobes, Tom Jay, and Brad Matsen (Anchorage: Alaska Northwest Books, 1994), 83; Bruce Brown, *Mountain in the Clouds: A Search for the Wild Salmon* (New York: Simon and Schuster, 1982), 146.

2. Theodore Steinberg, *Nature Incorporated: Industrialization and the Waters of New England* (New York: Cambridge University Press, 1991), 169–75; J. T. Bowen, "A History of Fish Culture as Related to the Development of Fishery Programs," in *A Century of Fisheries in North America*, ed. Norman G. Benson, American Fisheries Society Special Publication no. 7 (Washington: American Fisheries Society, 1970), 71–77; G. Brown Goode, "Epochs in the History of Fish Culture," *TAFS* 10 (1881): 34–57; James W. Milner, "The Progress of Fish-Culture in the United States," *ARUSCF* (1873): 523–58; Charles E. Rosenberg, *No Other Gods: On Science and American Social Thought* (Baltimore: Johns Hopkins University Press, 1976), 109–22; George P. Marsh, *Report Made Under Authority of the Legislature of Vermont, on the Artificial Propagation of Fish* (Burlington: Free Press, 1857), appendix, 46–47.

3. Samuel Wilmot, "Fish Culture and Fish Protection," *TAFS* 4 (1875): 25, 28–29.

4. Marsh, *Report*, 13–16; David Lowenthal, *George Perkins Marsh: Versatile Vermonter* (New York: Columbia University Press, 1958), 185–86.

5. Marsh, *Report*, 9, 15–16.

6. Marsh, *Report*, 9; Steinberg, *Nature Incorporated*, 175–202; Gary Kulik, "Dams, Fish, and Farmers: Defense of Public Rights in Eighteenth-Century Rhode Island," in *The Countryside in the Age of Capitalist Transformation: Essays in the Social History of Rural America*, ed. Steven Hahn and Jonathan Prude (Chapel Hill: University of North Carolina Press, 1985); John T. Cumbler, "The Early Making of an Environmental Consciousness: Fish, Fisheries Commissions, and the Connecticut River," *Environmental History Review* 15 (winter 1991): 73–91; J. Willard Hurst, *Law and the Conditions of Freedom in the Nineteenth-Century United States* (Madison: University of Wisconsin Press, 1956), chap. 1; Bonnie J. McKay, "The Culture of the Commoners: Historical Observations on Old and New World Fisheries," in

The Question of the Commons: The Culture and Ecology of Communal Resources, ed. Bonnie J. McCay and James M. Acheson (Tucson: University of Arizona Press, 1987), 195–216. An apparent exception would be the incipient national parks system, but as Alfred Runte and others point out, parks were also linked to the development of tourism and cities; Alfred Runte, *National Parks: The American Experience* (Lincoln: University of Nebraska Press, 1981); Philip G. Terrie, " 'Imperishable Freshness': Culture, Conservation, and the Adirondack Park," *Forest and Conservation History* 37 (July 1993): 132–41.

7. Marsh, *Report,* 35, 43; and appendix, 39, 58–61.

8. Marsh, *Report,* 5, 11.

9. Marsh, *Report,* 2, 5, 51; and appendix, 10, 12, 30, 46, 49.

10. I am indebted to Richard White for pointing out the connections between Marsh's ideas and Jeffersonian and republican ideology; Marsh, *Report,* 4, 16–17, 20, 50; and appendix, 59–60.

11. George Perkins Marsh, *Man and Nature,* ed. David Lowenthal (Cambridge: Belknap Press of Harvard University Press, 1965), 11–12; Lowenthal, *George Perkins Marsh,* 186; Livingston Stone, "Some Brief Reminiscences of the Early Days of Fish-Culture in the United States," *Bulletin* 17 (1897): 337–43; M. C. Edmunds, "The Introduction of Salmon into American Waters," *TAFS* 1 (1872): 32–39; Hugh MacCrimmon, "The Beginning of Salmon Culture in Canada," *Canadian Geographical Journal* 71 (July 1965): 96–103.

12. Tim Smith, *Scaling Fisheries: The Science of Measuring the Effects of Fishing, 1855–1955* (New York: Cambridge University Press, 1994), 39–43; Dean Conrad Allard Jr., *Spencer Fullerton Baird and the U.S. Fish Commission* (New York: Arno Press, 1978), 60–86; George Brown Goode, "The First Decade of the United States Fish Commission: Its Plan of Work and Accomplished Results, Scientific and Economical," *Bulletin* 2 (1882): 169. For a detailed account of these events in Buzzard's Bay see Richard Judd, *Common Lands, Common People: The Origins of Conservation in Northern New England* (Cambridge: Harvard University Press, 1997), 234–40.

13. Smith, *Scaling Fisheries,* 43–47; Allard, *Spencer Fullerton Baird,* 115–22; Stephen Skowronek, *Building a New American State: The Expansion of National Administrative Capacities, 1877–1920* (New York: Cambridge University Press, 1982), 45–46; Jeanne Nienaber Clarke and Daniel McCool, *Staking Out the Terrain: Power Differentials among Natural Resources Management Agencies* (Albany: SUNY Press, 1985), 89.

14. Allard, *Spencer Fullerton Baird,* 25–59; E. F. Rivinus and E. M. Youssef, *Spencer Baird of the Smithsonian* (Washington: Smithsonian Institution Press, 1992), 42–43, 120–21; William Healy Dall, *Spencer Fullerton Baird: A Biography* (Philadelphia: J. B. Lippincott, 1915), 164–69, 418–19; Lowenthal, *George Perkins Marsh,*

186; Spencer Baird to Livingston Stone, 31 May 1873, vol. 5, pp. 108–9, Press Copies of Letters Sent, 1871–1906, R G 22, N A.

15. *A R U S C F* (1872): xxxviii–xxxix; Allard, *Spencer Fullerton Baird,* 87–94; Smith, *Scaling Fisheries,* 47–51.

16. Samuel Powel to Baird, 26 Mar. 1872, fldr. 3, Letters Received, 1871–72, R G 22, N A; *A R U S C F* (1872): 33–36; Allard, *Spencer Fullerton Baird,* 93–101; Smith, *Scaling Fisheries,* 49.

17. *A R U S C F* (1873): 35; Dean C. Allard Jr., "Spencer Fullerton Baird and the Foundations of American Marine Science," *Marine Fisheries Review* 50, no. 4 (1988): 125–26.

18. Allard, *Spencer Fullerton Baird,* 124 n. 36, 121–25.

19. Ibid., 125; 42d Cong., 2d sess., *Congressional Globe, Appendix,* 626–30.

20. Stone to Baird, 21 July 1872, fldr. 4, Letters Received, 1871–72, R G 22, N A; Allard, *Spencer Fullerton Baird,* 127.

21. Samuel P. Hays, *The Response to Industrialism, 1885–1914* (Chicago: University of Chicago Press, 1957); Robert H. Wiebe, *The Search for Order, 1877–1920* (New York: Hill and Wang, 1967); Alan Trachtenberg, *The Incorporation of America: Culture and Society in the Gilded Age* (New York: Hill and Wang, 1982); Ann Fabian, *Card Sharps, Dream Books, and Bucket Shops: Gambling in 19th Century America* (Ithaca: Cornell University Press, 1990).

22. Rosenberg, *No Other Gods,* 150–51, 159, 165; Allard, "Foundations of American Marine Science," 127; Theodore Whaley Cart, "The Federal Fisheries Service, 1871–1940" (M.A. thesis, University of North Carolina, 1968), 7.

23. Allard, *Spencer Fullerton Baird,* 157–61; Allard, "Foundations of American Marine Science," 124–26.

24. Baird to Seth Greene [*sic*], 2 July 1872, vol. 2, pp. 382–85, Press Copies of Letters Sent, 1871–1906, R G 22, N A; Allard, *Spencer Fullerton Baird,* 160.

25. Stone to Baird, 18 June 1872, vol. 7, p. 98, Letters Received, 1871–74, R G 22, N A; Stone to Baird, 2 Mar. 1872 and 18 Oct. 1872, fldr. 4, Letters Received, 1871–72, R G 22, N A; Joel W. Hedgpeth, "Livingston Stone and Fish Culture in California," *California Fish and Game* 27 (July 1941): 126–48.

26. Stone to Baird, 18 June 1872, vol. 7, p. 98, Letters Received, 1871–74, R G 22, N A; Stone to Baird, 28 Dec. 1872, fldr. 4, Letters Received, 1871–72, R G 22, N A; *Oregonian,* 21 May 1875, 3.

27. Baird to Stone, 6 July 1872, vol. 2, pp. 408–11; Baird to Stone, 26 July 1872, vol. 3, p. 18; Baird to Stone, 21 Nov. 1873, vol. 6, pp. 316–17; Baird to Stone, 18 Mar. 1878, vol. 25, p. 252, Press Copies of Letters Sent, 1871–1906, R G 22, N A; Spencer F. Baird, *A R U S C F* (1873–74 and 1874–75): xxiv; Rufus Saxton to General M. C. Meigs, 20 June 1872, fldr. 3; Stone to Baird, 13 Oct. 1872, 4 Oct. 1872, and 20 Dec. 1872, fldr. 4, Letters Received, 1871–72, R G 22, N A.

28. Stone to Baird (c. 15 Apr. 1875), Letters Received, 1871–74, R G 22, N A; *Oregonian,* 18 Nov. 1875, 1; W. A. Jones, "The Salmon Fisheries of the Columbia River," S. Exec. Doc. 123 (50–1) 2510:30; Baird to Stone, 9 Jan. 1873, vol. 4, pp. 8–9, Press Copies of Letters Sent, 1871–1906, R G 22, N A.

29. Stone to Baird, 16 Sept. 1872, 1 Oct. 1872, 7 Oct. 1872, and 15 Oct. 1872, fldr. 4, Letters Received, 1871–72, R G 22, N A; Jones, "Salmon Fisheries," 31–32. The sight of dying salmon had stymied William Clark almost seventy years earlier; he remarked in his journal that "I can't account for it." Gary E. Moulton, ed., *The Journals of Lewis and Clark,* 13 vols. (Lincoln: University of Nebraska Press, 1983–), 5:286.

30. Horace D. Dunn to Baird, 26 Sept. 1876; and Stone to Baird, 26 Sept. 1876, box 2, fldr. D B F, Letters Received, 1878–81, R G 22, N A; Livingston Stone, "Artificial Propagation of Salmon in the Columbia Basin," *T A F S* 13 (1884): 21–22; Leo Marx, *The Machine in the Garden: Technology and the Pastoral Ideal in America* (New York: Oxford University Press, 1964).

31. M. C. Edmunds, "The Introduction of Salmon into American Waters," *T A F S* 1 (1872): 38.

32. Ibid., 38–39.

33. George Brown Goode, "The Status of the US Fish Commission in 1884," *A R U S C F* (1884): 65; Edmunds, "Introduction of Salmon," 382.

34. Samuel P. Hays, *Conservation and the Gospel of Efficiency: The Progressive Conservation Movement, 1890–1920* (Cambridge: Harvard University Press), 1959; Wiebe, *Search for Order;* A. Hunter Dupree, *Science in the Federal Government: A History of Policies and Activities to 1940* (New York: Harper and Row, 1957), 246.

35. I am indebted to Richard White and Kathy Morse for help in refining these ideas.

36. Stone to Baird, 19 Oct. 1872, 2 Nov. 1872, and 16 Nov. 1872, fldr. 4, Letters Received, 1871–72, R G 22, N A; Jones, "Salmon Fisheries," 29, 33; "Evening Session," *T A F S* 18 (1889): 31–36.

37. Box 1, Correspondence of Hugh Smith Relating to the Bureau of Fisheries, 1885–1910, R G 22, N A; "A Salmon Caught in the Sacramento River, 1894–1895," box 1, Correspondence concerning Fishery Expeditions, Experiments, and Research, 1885–1908, Letters Received, 1871–74, R G 22, N A; George W. Hume to Baird, 22 Mar. 1881, box 5, R U 54, S I A; McDonald to Stone, 27 Dec. 1887, vol. 215, p. 405; McDonald to Stone, 24 Feb. 1888, vol. 218, p. 13; Herbert A. Gill to Bowlby, 7 May 1895, vol. 408, p. 145, Press Copies of Letters Sent, 1871–1906, R G 22, N A. Similar battles erupted between Columbia River and Alaska canners over the brand name of chinook, and between Puget Sound and Alaska canners over the identity of sockeye; Frank M. Warren to Smith, 8 Jan. 1916, box 3, Smith to Warren, 17 Jan. 1916, box 3, Letters Received, 1871–74, R G 22, N A; Herbert Knox to George M.

Bowers, 12 July 1907, and Charles Early Smith, "Memorandum," 11 July 1907, box 3, fldr. 4, Cobb Papers; B. B. Redding to Baird, 9 Sept. 1880, box 10, fldr. QBR, Letters Received, 1878–81, RG 22, NA; *Oregonian*, 31 July 1883, 2; 26 Sept. 1883, 2; 28 Sept. 1883, 4; 23 Nov. 1887, 4; 14 Mar. 1904, 11; 3 May 1909, 4; Jones, "Salmon Fisheries," 16–19, 21, 45–46; J. Q. A. Bowlby to Commission, 30 Apr. 1895, box 239, no. 13122; Bowlby to Acting Commissioner, 14 May 1895, box 240, no. 13759, Letters Received, 1882–1900, RG 22, NA; *AROFC* (1902): 68–78. Canners did seem to understand the phenomena of separate runs and races of fish much better than the USFC; Stone to Baird, 17 Sept. 1877, Letters Received, 1871–74, RG 22, NA.

38. David Starr Jordan, "Story of a Salmon," *Popular Science Monthly* 19 (May 1881): 1–6; David Starr Jordan and Charles H. Gilbert, "Observations on the Salmon of the Pacific," *American Naturalist* 15 (Mar. 1881): 177–86; Jones, "Salmon Fisheries," 22; Keith R. Benson, "From Museum Research to Laboratory Research: The Transformation of Natural History into Academic Biology," in *The American Development of Biology*, ed. Ronald Rainger, Keith R. Benson, and Jane Maienschein (New Brunswick: Rutgers University Press, 1988), 49–83; Stone to Baird, 11 May 1875, box 58, vol. 206, p. 245, and 30 Sept. 1875, box 58, vol. 206, p. 292, RU 52, SIA; Watson to Baird, 23 Oct. 1880, box 5, RU 54, SIA; Livingston Stone, "The Salmon Fisheries of the Columbia River," *ARUSCF* (1875–76): 819–20; Stone to Baird, 11 Oct. 1877, box 11, RU 213, SIA; Stone to Baird, 23 Nov. 1877, box 13, no. 6131, Letters Received, 1882–1900, RG 22, NA; David Starr Jordan, "Salmon and Trout of the Pacific Coast," in *Thirteenth Biennial Report of the State Board of Fish Commissioners of the State of California* (Sacramento: California State Printer, 1894), 129–30; David Starr Jordan, "Notes on a Collection of Fishes from Clackamas River, Oregon," *Proceedings of the United States National Museum* 1 (1878): 69–85; Charles J. Smith to Baird, 13 Aug. 1880, box 10, fldr. S, Letters Received, 1878–81, RG 22, NA.

39. Jordan, "Salmon and Trout," 131–36; Smith, *Scaling Fisheries*, 28–30. Jordan was also occasionally stumped, admitting at one point: "The only thing as yet which I can not understand is, how do they get rid of the hooked nose and the hump after going back to the salt-water? They surely can not all die after spawning" (Jones, "Salmon Fisheries," 29, 31).

40. Jordan, "Salmon and Trout," 136; James Crawford to McDonald, 24 May 1895, box 240, no. 14081, Letters Received, 1882–1900, RG 22, NA; McDonald to Crawford, 4 June 1895, vol. 411, pp. 145–46, Press Copies of Letters Sent, 1871–1906, RG 22, NA.

41. A. H. Sturtevant, *A History of Genetics* (New York: Harper and Row, 1965); Oregon, *AROFC* (1931): 30–31; Willis H. Rich, "The Biology of the Columbia River Salmon," *Northwest Science* 9 (Feb. 1935): 3–14; Willis H. Rich, "Local Popula-

tions and Migration in Relation to the Conservation of Pacific Salmon in the Western States and Alaska," in *The Migration and Conservation of Salmon*, ed. Forest Ray Moulton (Lancaster: Science Press, 1939), 47.

42. Samuel Wilmot, "Report on Fish Breeding in the Dominion of Canada, 1881," in *Fourteenth Annual Report of the Department of Marine and Fisheries, Being for the Fiscal Year Ended 30th June, 1881*, suppl. no. 2 (Ottawa: MacLean, Roger and Co., 1882), 34, 46; Baird to John H. Mitchell, 23 Apr. 1877, vol. 19, pp. 279–87, Press Copies of Letters Sent, 1871–1906, RG 22, NA; *Oregonian*, 24 May 1877, 3.

43. *ARUSCF* (1874): xxix; Baird to Newton Booth, 28 Mar. 1880, box 12, no. 5900, Letters Received, 1882–1900, RG 22, NA; Wilmot, "Report on Fish Breeding," 32; James W. Milner, "The Progress of Fish-Culture in the United States," *ARUSCF* (1872–73): 523–58; Livingston Stone, "Operations on the McCloud River in Salmon Breeding, in 1875," *ARUSCF* (1875–76): 921–33; Charles W. Smiley, "What Fish Culture Has First to Accomplish," *Bulletin* 4 (1884): 65–68; William F. Page, "The Most Recent Methods of Hatching Fish Eggs," *Bulletin* 8 (1888): 207–18; Jules Haime, "The History of Fish-Culture in Europe from Its Earlier Records to 1854," *ARUSCF* (1872–73): 465–92; Baron de la Valette St. George, "The Enemies of Fish," *ARUSCF* (1878): 509–16; E. von Reichardt, "The Purification of Refuse Water," *ARUSCF* (1878): 519–24; Christian Wagner, "What Does a Fish Cost?" *ARUSCF* (1878): 531–36; "Extracts from the First Annual Report of the Fishery Board of Scotland for the Year Ending December 31, 1882," *ARUSCF* (1882): 229–36; Baird to Stone, 20 Nov. 1873, vol. 6, pp. 303–6, Press Copies of Letters Sent, 1871–1906, RG 22, NA.

44. Wilmot, "Report on Fish Breeding," 29, 31; Robert J. Stevens to Baird, 20 Sept. 1879, box 6, fldr. RBS, Letters Received, 1878–81, RG 22, NA; *Oregonian*, 4 Mar. 1875, 1; 20 Jan. 1876, 4; "American Salmon, Stocking Our Rivers and Lakes: Prospect of an Abundance of This Delicious Fish," no. 5867, box 12, Letters Received, 1882–1900, RG 22, NA; clippings in box 11, fldr. 1, RU 7050, SIA; Allard, *Spencer Fullerton Baird*, 148–52.

45. Cart, "Federal Fisheries Service," 114, 116; Allard, "Foundations of American Marine Science," 126; Goode, "First Decade," 170.

46. Baird to Stone, 27 Feb. 1883, vol. 94, pp. 97–102; Baird to Stone, 15 Apr. 1885, vol. 150, pp. 273–74; and Baird to John H. Mitchell, 25 Jan. 1886, vol. 170, pp. 115–17, Press Copies of Letters Sent, 1871–1906, RG 22, NA; J. W. Collins, "Report on the Fisheries of the Pacific Coast of the United States," *ARUSCF* (1888–89): 10–11; Allard, *Spencer Fullerton Baird*, 143, 157–58, 266–68; "Evening Discussion," *TAFS* 18 (1889): 31–36; Jno. T. McDonnell to Commissioner, 28 Oct. 1887, box 125, no. 86847, Letters Received, 1882–1900, RG 22, NA.

47. Goode, "First Decade," 172; Wilmot, "Report on Fish Breeding," 25, 36, 47; Marshall McDonald, "Some Objective Points in Fish-Culture," *TAFS* 14 (1885): 72–

73; Livingston Stone, "Brief Reminiscences," 339. Baird was a master at using the USFC to further Smithsonian agendas; see Rivinus and Youssef, *Spencer Baird of the Smithsonian*, 146; Baird to Stone, 7 Mar. 1871, vol. 1, p. 1; Baird to Stone, 8 Aug. 1877, vol. 21, pp. 398–99, Press Copies of Letters Sent, 1871–1906, RG 22, NA; G. Brown Goode to Baird, 25 June 1885, box 5, p. 178, RU 30, SIA.

48. Cart, "Federal Fisheries Service," 18–19.

49. Stone, "Brief Reminiscences," 340–43; Stone to Baird, 27 Feb. 1875, box 58, vol. 206, p. 233; 16 Nov. 1875, box 58, vol. 206, pp. 310–11, RU 52, SIA; Baird to Stone, 17 Nov. 1873, vol. 6, pp. 286–90; Marshall McDonald to C. E. Gorham, 16 Oct. 1890, vol. 281, pp. 453–55, Press Copies of Letters Sent, 1871–1906, RG 22, NA; William C. Kendall, "Marshall McDonald, 1835–1895," *Progressive Fish Culturist* 43 (1939): 19–30; J. Percy Moore, "Marshall McDonald," *American Naturalist* 29 (1895): 1042–43; "Marshall McDonald," in *Appleton's Cyclopaedia of American Biography*, vol. 7 (New York: D. Appleton and Co., 1900), 173; "Marshall McDonald," in *National Cyclopaedia of American Biography*, vol. 13 (New York: James T. White, 1906), 321; Robert H. Connery, *Governmental Problems in Wild Life Conservation* (New York: Columbia University Press, 1935), 121; Cart, "Federal Fisheries Service," 19–20; Seymour Bower to McDonald, 24 May 1890, box 3, fldr. B (2 of 2), Letters Received by Marshall McDonald, 1879–95, RG 22, NA.

50. Stone to McDonald, 19 Nov. 1888, box 137, no. 100230; Stone to McDonald, 19 Dec. 1888, box 138, no. 100719; F. C. Reed to McDonald, 27 Apr. 1889, box 143, no. 103665, Letters Received, 1882–1900, RG 22, NA; McDonald to Stone, 16 Nov. 1889, vol. 260, p. 130; McDonald to Hon. J. N. Dolph, 22 Nov. 1887, vol. 215, p. 140; McDonald to Stone, 22 Jan. 1889, vol. 243, pp. 96–97; McDonald to F. C. Reed, 2 Apr. 1889, vol. 247, pp. 156–59, Press Copies of Letters Sent, 1871–1906, RG 22, NA.

51. McDonald to Stone, 24 Apr. 1889, vol. 248, pp. 408–10; McDonald to Stone, 4 June 1889, vol. 250, pp. 412–15; McDonald to Stone, 2 Oct. 1889, vol. 258, pp. 197–202; McDonald to Waldo F. Hubbard, 28 Oct. 1889, vol. 259, p. 17; McDonald to Stone, 11 Nov. 1889, vol. 259, p. 164; McDonald to Stone, 16 Dec. 1889, vol. 262, p. 112; McDonald to Stone, 17 Dec. 1889, vol. 262, pp. 181–88, Press Copies of Letters Sent, 1871–1906, RG 22, NA; Stone to McDonald, 15 Oct. 1889, box 153, no. 110433; John Gay to McDonald, 23 Dec. 1889, box 151, no. 108828, Letters Received, 1882–1900, RG 22, NA.

52. Stone to McDonald, 1 Mar. 1890, box 154, no. 111123; Stone to McDonald, 13 Sept. 1890, box 159, no. 115097; Edward Hayes to Stone, 29 Sept. 1890, box 162, no. 116596; Stone to McDonald, 8 Oct. 1890, box 160, no. 115608; Stone to McDonald, 14 Nov. 1890, box 162, no. 116596; Stone to McDonald, 5 Jan. 1891, box 164, no. 118105; Stone to McDonald, 21 Feb. 1891, box 166, no. 119493; Stone to McDonald, 29 May 1891, box 169, no. 122095; Stone to McDonald, 18 July

1891, box 170, no. 123176; Stone to Officer, 15 Aug. 1891, box 171, no. 123616; Stone to McDonald, 22 Apr. 1892, box 184, no. 132790, Letters Received, 1882–1900, R G 22, N A; McDonald to Stone, 13 Jan. 1891, vol. 287, pp. 432–38; McDonald to Stone, 19 May 1891, vol. 295, pp. 227–28; McDonald to Stone, 13 Aug. 1891, vol. 301, p. 279; J. J. O'Connor to Stone, 19 Aug. 1891, vol. 301, p. 397; McDonald to Stone, 23 Mar. 1892, vol. 313, pp. 155–56; McDonald to Stone, 13 July 1892, vol. 320, pp. 457–60, Press Copies of Letters Sent, 1871–1906, R G 22, N A. Ironically, Stone had lobbied vigorously in favor of McDonald's appointment as commissioner, and the U S F C eventually resurrected the position of field superintendent for Stone's successor at the Clackamas Station; F. C. Reed to J. N. Dolph, 18 Feb. 1888, box 129, no. 89315–16; Reed to John H. Mitchell, 18 Feb. 1888, box 129, no. 89828–29, Letters Received, 1882–1900, R G 22, N A; W. Dec. Ravenal to W. F. Hubbard, 27 Jan. 1898, vol. 482, p. 448, Press Copies of Letters Sent, 1871–1906, R G 22, N A.

53. Stone to Baird, 26 Apr. 1877, Letters Received, 1871–74, R G 22, N A; John F. Miller, 2 June 1882, box 14, no. 6733; F. C. Reed to J. F. Ellis, 11 Mar. 1889, box 141, no. 102722; F. C. Reed to McDonald, 13 Feb. 1891, box 165, no. 119351; McBride to J. J. Brice, 21 Sept. 1897, box 280, no. 2884; McBride to Brice, 21 Sept. 1897, box 281, no. 3183, Letters Received, 1882–1900, R G 22, N A; McDonald to J. H. Mitchell, 24 Feb. 1891, vol. 290, pp. 235–38; Herbert A. Gill to Stone, 12 Aug. 1893, vol. 355, pp. 258–60; McDonald to Mitchell, 5 Jan. 1894, vol. 367, p. 72; McDonald to Hubbard, 8 Oct. 1894, vol. 392, pp. 296–97; Ravenal to Hubbard, 10 Oct. 1896, vol. 450, pp. 221–22; Ravenal to Hubbard, 10 Nov. 1896, vol. 453, p. 81; Ravenal to Waldo F. Hubbard, 24 Aug. 1897, vol. 472, p. 388; Ravenal to Thomas Tongue, 6 Jan. 1900, vol. 529, p. 5608; Bowers to Mitchell, 19 Apr. 1901, vol. 560, p. 8123; Bowers to Mitchell, 19 Nov. 1901, vol. 574, p. 3706; Bowers to C. W. Fulton, 20 Apr. 1903, vol. 609, p. 9463, Press Copies of Letters Sent, 1871–1906, R G 22, N A; vol. 52, entry 2682, Registers of Letters Received, 1882–1917, R G 22, N A. Neither Brice nor Bowers was above patronage politics; Brice to George McBride, 5 Aug. 1897, vol. 471, p. 455; Bowers to Superintendent, 15 Dec. 1904, vol. 650, p. 5225, Press Copies of Letters Sent, 1871–1906, R G 22, N A. Centralization continued when the U S B F concentrated its Oregon operations at a new office in Oregon City; J. N. Wisner to Commissioner, 9 Aug. 1905, vol. 675, p. 2645; Wisner to Commissioner, 12 Sept. 1905, vol. 675, p. 2675; and Bowers to Superintendent, 18 Sept. 1905, vol. 675, p. 2645, Press Copies of Letters Sent, 1871–1906, R G 22, N A.

54. Collins's views are hard to gauge because of the paucity of letters by him in the files. McDonald to J. W. Collins, 28 Sept. 1892 and 11 Oct. 1892, box 2, fldr. 3, Letters Received by Marshall McDonald, 1879–95, R G 22, N A; and letters in vol. 2, pp. 75–76, 81–87, 125–54, 179–81, 188, 194–95, Press Copies of Confidential Letters Sent by Commissioner Marshall McDonald, 1888–95, R G 22, N A.

55. McDonald to Alexander Agassiz, 20 Oct. 1892, vol. 2, pp. 135–37; Mc-

Donald to Judge Long, 14 Nov. 1892, vol. 2, pp. 179–91; McDonald to W. K. Brooks, 26 Oct. 1892, vol. 2, pp. 138–40, Press Copies of Confidential Letters Sent by Commissioner Marshall McDonald, 1888–95, R G 22, N A.

56. H. Wayne Morgan, *From Hayes to McKinley: National Party Politics, 1877–1896* (Syracuse: Syracuse University Press, 1969), 331–33, 395–435; McDonald to Collins, 11 Oct. 1892; McDonald to W. C. Titcomb, 22 Sept. 1892; McDonald to Hugh Smith, no date, box 2, fldr. 3, Letters Received by Marshall McDonald, 1879–95, R G 22, N A; McDonald to President, 7 Apr. 1893, vol. 2, pp. 292–94; and 22 May 1893, vol. 3, pp. 11–14, Press Copies of Confidential Letters Sent by Commissioner Marshall McDonald, 1888–95, R G 22, N A.

57. McDonald to Hubbard, 7 Feb. 1890, vol. 266, pp. 54–57; Ravenel to Hubbard, 20 July 1894, vol. 387, p. 83; Ravenel to Hubbard, 29 June 1894, vol. 387, pp. 177–78; Ravenel to Hubbard, 7 Aug. 1894, vol. 388, p. 183; Ravenel to Hubbard, 10 Aug. 1894, vol. 388, pp. 216–17; Ravenel to Hubbard, 10 Apr. 1896, vol. 435, p. 224; Ravenel to H. M. Smith, 7 July 1896, vol. 446, pp. 97–98; Commissioner, 6 July 1896, vol. 446, pp. 74–75; Ravenel to Hubbard, 11 Aug. 1896, vol. 448, p. 54; Ravenel to L. E. Bean, 2 Jan. 1897, vol. 456, p. 93; Ravenel to Hubbard, 27 Dec. 1898, vol. 503, p. 11, Press Copies of Letters Sent, 1871–1906, R G 22, N A.

58. McDonald to Stone, 3 Oct. 1888, vol. 232, pp. 113–14; McDonald to F. B. Stockbridge, 5 Mar. 1892, vol. 311, pp. 422–26; McDonald to I. H. Taffe, 22 June 1895, vol. 411, pp. 466–67, Press Copies of Letters Sent, 1871–1906, R G 22, N A; Fishery Address (c. 1893), vol. 3, pp. 62–64, Press Copies of Confidential Letters Sent by Commissioner Marshall McDonald, 1888–95, R G 22, N A; *Oregonian*, 27 July 1889, 3. For complaints see J. C. Cowgill to Commissioner, 23 Apr. 1890, box 156, no. 112441; James W. Tomb to Board of Fish Commissioners, 21 Oct. 1892, box 192, no. 3289; J. G. Anderson to McDonald, 28 May 1894, box 222, no. 14426; George W. Milhan to Commissioner, 10 June 1895, box 241, no. 14770; Peter Nelson and Frank Graham to Commissioner, 23 Feb. 1897, box 271, no. 10530; N. E. Linsley to John J. Brice, 29 Sept. 1897, box 281, no. 3381, Letters Received, 1882–1900, R G 22, N A. For U S F C responses see McDonald to Fowle and West, 14 May 1889, vol. 249, pp. 345–46; McDonald to T. M. Smith, 20 Aug. 1889, vol. 256, p. 34; McDonald to Cowgill, 15 May 1890, vol. 273, p. 307; J. J. O'Connor to C. A. Wright, 19 Sept. 1890, vol. 279, p. 194; McDonald to A. F. Padgett, 5 Oct. 1891, vol. 303, p. 29; McDonald to Tomb, 1 Nov. 1892, vol. 327, p. 346; McDonald to Anderson, 3 Oct. 1894, vol. 392, pp. 216–17; McDonald to Milhan, 19 June 1895, vol. 411, p. 401, Press Copies of Letters Sent, 1871–1906, R G 22, N A; McDonald to Governor of California, 22 Dec. 1892, box 1, fldr. 1, Letters Received by Marshall McDonald, 1879–95, R G 22, N A.

59. Fishery Address (c. 1893), vol. 3, pp. 62–64, Press Copies of Confidential Letters Sent by Commissioner Marshall McDonald, 1888–1895, R G 22, N A.

60. Allard, *Spencer Fullerton Baird,* 153–56; Charles Hallock, "Laws for the Preservation of Fish," *TAFS* 3 (1874): 45–46; B. B. Redding to Baird, 30 Mar. 1880, box 10, fldr. QBR, Letters Received, 1878–81, RG 22, NA; Baird to Stone, 14 Aug. 1883, vol. 108, pp. 330–33; Ravenal to Ewing Cockrell, 26 May 1896, vol. 437, pp. 424–31, Press Copies of Letters Sent, 1871–1906, RG 22, NA; Marsh, *Report,* 12–15; Baird to Zachary Chandler, 25 Jan. 1875, box 12, no. 5887, Letters Received, 1882–1900, RG 22, NA.

61. Barton W. Evermann, "The Investigation of Rivers and Lakes with Reference to the Fish Environment," *Bulletin* 13 (1893): 69; Allard, *Spencer Fullerton Baird,* 166–79, 252–53, 296–341. Even when Baird doubted he had funding or authority, he still found ways to further research; Baird to Stone, 29 Oct. 1872, vol. 3, pp. 231–32, Press Copies of Letters Sent, 1871–1906, RG 22, NA; Dean Conrad Allard Jr., "The Fish Commission Laboratory and Its Influence on the Founding of the Marine Biological Laboratory," *Journal of the History of Biology* 23 (summer 1990): 251–70; Keith R. Benson, "Why American Marine Stations? The Teaching Argument," *American Zoologist* 28, no. 1 (1988): 7–14; Kurt Dunbar and Chris Friday, "Salmon, Seals, and Science: The *Albatross* and Conservation in Alaska, 1888–1914," *Journal of the West* 38 (Oct. 1994): 6–13; McDonald, "Some Objective Points in Fish-Culture," 72–76; Marshall McDonald, "The Salmon Fisheries of the Columbia River Basin," *Bulletin* 14 (1894): 153–68.

62. McDonald to Charles E. Gorham, 4 Sept. 1892, vol. 323, pp. 337–49; Memorandum to Barton A. Bean, 1892, vol. 324, pp. 56–57; McDonald to B. W. Evermann, 23 May 1893, vol. 340, pp. 403–8, Press Copies of Letters Sent, 1871–1906, RG 22, NA; Charles H. Gilbert and Barton W. Evermann, "A Report upon Investigations in the Columbia River Basin, with Descriptions of Four New Species of Fishes," *Bulletin* 14 (1894): 185.

63. McDonald to Johnston McCormac, 30 Jan. 1894, vol. 367, pp. 477–80; McDonald to Adlai E. Stevenson, 31 May 1894, vol. 379, pp. 37–39, Press Copies of Letters Sent, 1871–1906, RG 22, NA; Marshall McDonald, "The Salmon Fisheries of the Columbia River Basin," *Bulletin* 14 (1894): 165, 168.

64. Gilbert and Evermann, "Report upon Investigations," 200.

65. McDonald to Evermann, 16 Apr. 1891, vol. 293, pp. 225–27; McDonald to Evermann, 6 July 1891, vol. 298, pp. 156–58, Press Copies of Letters Sent, 1871–1906, RG 22, NA; Cart, "Federal Fisheries Service," 18, 116; Ronald Kline, "Construing 'Technology' as 'Applied Science': Public Rhetoric of Scientists and Engineers in the United States, 1880–1945," *Isis* 86 (June 1995): 194–221.

66. McDonald to Charles H. Gilbert, 1 May 1894, vol. 375, pp. 478–79, Press Copies of Letters Sent, 1871–1906, RG 22, NA.

67. "John J. Brice," in *National Cyclopaedia of American Biography,* vol. 5 (New York: James T. White, 1891), 362; Ravenal to Hubbard, 18 Sept. 1895, vol. 421, p.

331; Ravenal to L. E. Bean, 2 Dec. 1896, vol. 453, pp. 320–21, Press Copies of Letters Sent, 1871–1906, RG 22, NA; J. J. Brice, "A Manual of Fish Culture, Based on the Methods of the United States Commission of Fish and Fisheries," *ARUSCF* 23 (1898): appendix, 1–340; Smith, *Scaling Fisheries*, 66; Goode, "First Decade," 171; Benson, "From Museum Research to Laboratory Research," 77; Fred R. Mather, "Remarkable Development of Embryo Salmon," *TAFS* 11 (1881): 7–15; John A. Ryder, "On the Forces Which Determine the Survival of Fish Embryos," *TAFS* 13 (1883): 195–200; Ravenal to Hubbard, 16 Oct. 1896, vol. 450, p. 314; Ravenal to Hubbard, 26 Jan. 1897, vol. 456, p. 413; Ravenal to Hubbard, 2 Nov. 1896, vol. 478, pp. 76, 85; Ravenal to Hubbard, 27 Mar. 1897, vol. 462, p. 83, Press Copies of Letters Sent, 1871–1906, RG 22, NA; Claudius Wallich, "A Method of Recording Egg Development for Use of Fish-Culturists," *ARUSCF* (1900): 185–94.

68. Moore, "Marshall McDonald," 1042–43; Stone to Baird, 29 Oct. 1872, vol. 3, pp. 231–32; Baird to Stone, 29 May 1874, vol. 8, pp. 346–47; Ravenal to Hubbard, c. 18 June 1896, vol. 440, p. 380; Ravenal to Hubbard, 7 July 1896, vol. 446, p. 85; J. J. Brice to Hubbard, 5 Sept. 1896, vol. 448, p. 340, Press Copies of Letters Sent, 1871–1906, RG 22, NA; Barton Warren Evermann and Seth Eugene Meek, "A Report upon Salmon Investigations in the Columbia River Basin and Elsewhere on the Pacific Coast in 1896," *Bulletin* 17 (1897): 15–84; Cloudsley Rutter, "Natural History of the Quinnat Salmon: A Report of Investigations in the Sacramento River, 1896–1901," *Bulletin* 22 (1902): 65–141.

69. Seymour Bower, "Fish Protection and Fish Production," *TAFS* 26 (1897): 60; Seymour Bower, "Natural versus Assisted Reproduction of Certain Kinds of Fishes," *TAFS* 27 (1898): 46–56; Ravenal to Hubbard, 21 Sept. 1896, vol. 448, pp. 499–501; Ravenal to Hubbard, 18 Jan. 1898, vol. 503, p. 263, Press Copies of Letters Sent, 1871–1906, RG 22, NA.

70. A. Hunter Dupree, *Science in the Federal Government: A History of Policies and Activities to 1940* (New York: Harper and Row, 1957), 238; Connery, *Governmental Problems*, 121; Arthur W. MacMahon, "Selection and Tenure of Bureau Chiefs in the National Administration of the United States," *American Political Science Review* 20 (Nov. 1926): 780–81. The same argument can be made about Hugh Smith's appointment by the Democrat Woodrow Wilson in 1913; see MacMahon's timeline (p. 807) for party affiliations and tenures.

71. Jordan, "Salmon and Trout," 136; Stone, "Brief Reminiscences," 339.

72. Wilmot, "Report on Fish Breeding," 29; R. D. Hume to George M. Bowers, 12 Feb. 1900, no. 9057, box 314, Letters Received, 1882–1900, RG 22, NA; A. J. Malmgren, "A Verdict Against Artificial Fish-Culture, and an Answer Thereto," *Bulletin* 3 (1883): 382–87; Chamberlain von Polenz, "An Opinion Regarding the Answer of R. Eckerdt to Professor Malmgren," *Bulletin* 3 (1883): 387–88.

73. Wilmot, "Report on Fish Breeding," 29, 44; Wilmot, "Fish Culture and Fish

Protection," 25–26; Bill Parenteau, "Creating a 'Sportsmen's Paradise': Salmon Fishing Regulation and Social Conflict in New Brunswick, 1868–1900" (paper presented at the American Society for Environmental History Conference, Las Vegas, Mar. 1995, paper in possession of author); John H. Bissell, "Fish Culture—A Practical Art," *TAFS* 15 (1886): 36–50; Stone to Baird, 11 Mar. 1880, box 10, fldr. S; Samuel N. Norton to Baird, 26 Feb. 1880, box 9, fldr. MBN, Letters Received, 1878–81, RG 22, NA.

74. Tarleton Bean to H. D. McGuire, 27 Sept. 1894, p. 412, vol. 390; Brice to John H. Mitchell, 15 Dec. 1896, vol. 454, pp. 387–88, Press Copies of Letters Sent, 1871–1906, RG 22, NA; *Oregonian,* 3 Oct. 1894, 3; 1 Jan. 1877, 3; *ARCIA* (1897) H. Doc. 5 (55–2) 3641:299.

75. Ravenal to S. W. Downing, 24 Oct. 1899, p. 3288, vol. 523; Bowers to E. N. Carter, 29 May 1900, p. 10286, vol. 538; Bowers to F. C. Reed, 7 Nov. 1899, vol. 524, p. 3768; Bowers to F. C. Reed, 1 Dec. 1899, vol. 526, p. 4567; Bowers to Thomas H. Tongue, 24 Mar. 1900, vol. 533, p. 7627, Press Copies of Letters Sent, 1871–1906, RG 22, NA; *ARUSCF* (1900): 5.

76. Rosenberg, *No Other Gods,* 195.

77. Bowers to Superintendent, 30 Mar. 1903, vol. 608, p. 8827; Bowers to Superintendent, 16 Dec. 1903, vol. 628, p. 5849; Bowers to Superintendent, 21 Dec. 1904, vol. 650, p. 5340; H. M. Smith to Leighton Kelly, 8 Mar. 1906, vol. 687, p. 8103; Ravenal to Hubbard, 27 Sept. 1898, vol. 498, p. 85; Bowers to Stone, 8 May 1899, vol. 511, p. 345; Bowers to Superintendent, 14 Nov. 1905, vol. 682, 5437; Bowers to Superintendent, 21 Nov. 1905, vol. 682, p. 5548; H. M. Smith to Superintendent, 1 Mar. 1906, vol. 687, p. 8032, Press Copies of Letters Sent, 1871–1906, RG 22, NA; *ARUSCF* (1905): 2; Cart, "Federal Fisheries Service," 116.

78. Bowers to Secretary of Commerce and Labor, 21 Dec. 1904, vol. 650, p. 5346; Bowers to Superintendent, 27 Jan. 1906, vol. 683, p. 6248; Bowers to R. D. Hume, 25 Aug. 1902, vol. 591, p. 1141; Barton W. Evermann to Commissioner, 2 Oct. 1903, vol. 638, p. 10565; Bowers to Superintendent, 21 Aug. 1905, vol. 671, p. 779, Press Copies of Letters Sent, 1871–1906, RG 22, NA; Richard A. Cooley, *Politics and Conservation: The Decline of the Alaska Salmon* (New York: Harper and Row, 1963), 76–77.

79. Marsh, *Report,* 51–52; Robert W. Rydell, *All the World's a Fair: Visions of Empire at American International Expositions, 1876–1916* (Chicago: University of Chicago Press, 1984); Cart, "Federal Fisheries Service," 119–20; G. Brown Goode, *Exhibit of the Fisheries and Fish Culture of the United States of America, Made at Berlin in 1880,* Bulletin of the United States National Museum no. 21 (Washington: Government Printing Office, 1880); *AROFC* (1890): 11; McDonald to Hubbard, 19 July 1892, vol. 321, pp. 122–24, Press Copies of Letters Sent, 1871–1906, RG 22, NA.

80. McDonald to Tarleton H. Bean, 2 Oct. 1893, box 9, RU 213, SIA; Mc-

Donald to Hubbard, 24 Feb. 1892, vol. 310, pp. 488–91, 312; S. G. Worth to Hubbard, 31 Aug. 1893, vol. 356, p. 196; Worth to Hubbard, 26 Sept. 1893, vol. 358, p. 86, Press Copies of Letters Sent, 1871–1906, RG 22, NA.

81. Memorandum to A. H. Balwin, 30 Jan. 1905, vol. 658, p. 8310; Memorandum to the Commissioner, 10 Feb. 1905, vol. 658, p. 8416; Titcomb to A. H. Baldwin, 10 Feb. 1905, vol. 658, p. 8417; Bowers to Superintendent, 10 Mar. 1905, vol. 659, p. 8758; I. H. Dunlop to Superintendent, 13 Mar. 1905, vol. 659, p. 8813; J. Ward Ellis to Superintendent, 22 Mar. 1905, vol. 659, p. 8902; J. W. Titcomb to A. H. Baldwin, 10 June 1905, vol. 667, p. 13334, Press Copies of Letters Sent, 1871–1906, RG 22, NA.

82. Bowers to Acting Superintendent, 23 May 1905, vol. 665, p. 11669; Bowers to Superintendent, 20 June 1905, vol. 669, p. 13567; Bowers to Superintendent, 24 May 1905, vol. 665, p. 11691; J. Ward Ellis to Superintendent, 24 June 1905, vol. 669, p. 13620; Bowers to Superintendent, 28 June 1905, vol. 669, p. 13633; Bowers to Superintendent, 20 June 1905, vol. 669, p. 13596; H. M. Smith to Superintendent, 4 Apr. 1906, vol. 690, p. 9365; Bowers to A. H. Baldwin, 28 June 1905, vol. 667, p. 12667; Bowers to Superintendent, 15 June 1905, vol. 669, p. 13447; Titcomb to Superintendent, 1 June 1905, vol. 665, p. 11773; Bowers to Baldwin, 14 Sept. 1905, vol. 673, p. 1668, Press Copies of Letters Sent, 1871-1906, RG 22, NA.

83. H. M. Smith to Superintendent, 7 Aug. 1905, vol. 671, p. 547; J. W. Titcomb to Superintendent, 17 July 1905, vol. 672, p. 1022; H. M. Smith to T. R. Kershaw, 7 Aug. 1905, vol. 671, p. 548; J. W. Titcomb to Superintendent, 12 Aug. 1905, vol. 672, p. 1327; Bowers to J. N. Wisner, 12 Sept. 1905, vol. 673, p. 1638, Press Copies of Letters Sent, 1871–1906, RG 22, NA.

4 / MAKING SALMON

1. *Oregonian*, 12 Aug. 1870, 2; 24 Sept. 1873, 3; 29 Oct. 1873, 3; 25 Aug. 1874, 2; 18 Sept. 1874, 4. Some modern observers still argue that decline was rooted in a belief in the inexhaustibility of nature; Joseph Cone, *A Common Fate: Endangered Salmon and the People of the Pacific Northwest* (New York: Henry Holt, 1995), 116.

2. *Oregonian*, 3 Oct. 1876, 1; 19 Aug. 1874, 2; 18 Sept. 1874, 4.

3. *Oregonian*, 19 Aug. 1874, 1; 20 Aug. 1874, 1; 25 Aug. 1874, 1; 1 July 1874, 2; 19 Aug. 1874, 2; Courtland L. Smith, *Salmon Fishers of the Columbia* (Corvallis: Oregon State University Press, 1979), 110.

4. Steven L. Johnson, *Freshwater Environmental Problems and Coho Production in Oregon*, Informational Reports 84–11 (Corvallis: Oregon Department of Fish and Wildlife, Fish Division, 1984), 13; *Oregonian*, 12 Aug. 1870, 2; 3 Sept. 1874, 2; 18 Sept. 1874, 4; George S. Turnbull, *Governors of Oregon* (Portland: Binfords and Mort, 1959), 37–39.

5. *Oregonian*, 6 Feb. 1872, 1; 12 Dec. 1872, 2; 18 Sept. 1874, 4; 26 Jan. 1875, 1.

6. Livingston Stone to Spencer Baird, 10 Oct. 1877, Letters Received from Livingston Stone, 1874–77, RG 22, NA; *Oregonian*, 20 Oct. 1874, 1.

7. *Oregonian*, 21 Oct. 1874, 1; "Resolution of the Legislature of Oregon," 43d Cong., 2d sess., 1874, S. Misc. Doc. 33.

8. *Oregonian*, 17 Sept. 1877, 2; 22 Sept. 1877, 4; Richard White, *It's Your Misfortune and None of My Own: A History of the American West* (Norman: University of Oklahoma Press, 1991), 57–59.

9. "Letter of Professor Spencer F. Baird to the Chairman of the Committee on Commerce," 43d Cong., 2d sess., 1874, S. Misc. Doc. 79; Baird to Hon. Z. Chandler, 25 Jan. 1875, box 12, no. 5887, Letters Received, 1882–1900, RG 22, NA; R. D. Hume, *Salmon of the Pacific Coast* (San Francisco, 1893), 17.

10. "Letter of Professor Spencer F. Baird."

11. Ibid.

12. *Oregonian*, 3 Mar. 1875, 1; Baird to Stone, 29 Aug. 1872, vol. 3, pp. 88–90; Baird to Stone, 26 Oct. 1872, vol. 3, pp. 193–99; Baird to Stone, 23 May 1873, vol. 5, pp. 73–75; Baird to Stone, 22 Mar. 1875, vol. 11, pp. 381–83, Press Copies of Letters Sent, 1871–1906, RG 22, NA; Stone to Baird, 28 Dec. 1872, fldr. 4, Letters Received, 1871–72, RG 22, NA; Stone to Baird, 8 Sept. 1873, vol. 7, p. 137, Letters Received, 1871–74, RG 22, NA.

13. Livingston Stone, "The Salmon Fisheries of the Columbia River," *ARUSCF* (1875–76): 801–23; *Oregonian*, 21 May 1875, 3.

14. *For the Protection and Preservation of the Salmon-Fisheries of the Columbia River*, 44th Cong., 2d sess., 1876, S.B. 1076; *Oregonian*, 18 Jan. 1877, 3; 22 Jan. 1877, 3. As the recent development of watershed councils illustrates, the assertion of local wisdom in environmental management remains a staple of the modern political landscape. See Joseph E. Taylor III, "History, Memory, and Salmon: Reconciling the Past in Natural Resource Management" (paper given at the Seventh International Symposium on Society and Resource Management, Columbia, Mo., May 1998).

15. *Oregonian*, 18 Jan. 1877, 3; 22 Jan. 1877, 3; *Congressional Record*, 44th Cong., 2d sess., 1876, vol. 5, 154.

16. *Oregonian*, 17 Aug. 1876, 3; 13 Sept. 1876, 4; 2 Oct. 1876; 3 Oct. 1876, 1; Smith, *Salmon Fishers*, 74; Stone to Baird, 23 Sept. 1876, Letters Received from Livingston Stone, 1874–77, RG 22, NA.

17. Smith, *Salmon Fishers*, 110.

18. John D. Horel and John M. Wallace, "Planetary-Scale Atmospheric Phenomena Associated with the Southern Oscillation," *Monthly Weather Review* 109 (Apr. 1981): 813–29; Eugene M. Rasmusson and John M. Wallace, "Meteorological Aspects of the El Niño/Southern Oscillation," *Science* 222 (16 Dec. 1983): 1195–1202; Harry Van Loon and Roland A. Madden, "The Southern Oscillation. Part I:

Global Associations with Pressure and Temperature in Northern Winter," *Monthly Weather Review* 109 (June 1981): 1150–62; Sir Gilbert T. Walker and E. W. Bliss, "World Weather V," *Memoirs of the Royal Meteorological Society* 4 (1932): 53–84.

19. For El Niño's physical mechanics see Kathleen A. Miller and David L. Fluharty, "El Niño and Variability in the Northeastern Pacific Salmon Fishery: Implications for Coping with Climate Change," in *Climate Variability, Climate Change, and Fisheries*, ed. Michael H. Glantz (New York: Cambridge University Press, 1992), 49–88; Lawrence A. Mysak, "El Niño, Interannual Variability and Fisheries in the Northeast Pacific Ocean," *Canadian Journal of Fisheries and Aquatic Science* 43 (Feb. 1986): 464–97; William H. Quinn, David O. Zopf, Kent S. Short, and Richard T. W. Kuo Yang, "Historical Trends and Statistics of the Southern Oscillation, El Niño, and Indonesian Droughts," *Fishery Bulletin* 76 (July 1979): 663–78; William H. Quinn, Victor T. Neal, and Santiago E. Antunez de Mayolo, "El Niño Occurrences over the Past Four and a Half Centuries," *Journal of Geophysical Research* 92 (15 Dec. 1987): 14449–61; William H. Quinn and Victor T. Neal, "The Historical Record of El Niño Events," in *Climate since* A.D. 1500, ed. Raymond S. Bradley and Philip D. Jones (London: Routledge, 1992), 623–48; Richard E. Thomson, Howard J. Freeland, and Laurence F. Giovando, "Long-Term Sea Surface Temperature Variations along the British Columbia Coast," *Tropical Ocean-Atmosphere Newsletter* (July 1984): 9–11; Lisa E. Wells, "Holocene History of the El Niño Phenomenon as Recorded in Flood Sediments of Northern Coastal Peru," *Geology* 18 (1990): 1134–37; William J. Emery and Kevin Hamilton, "Atmospheric Forcing of Interannual Variability in the Northeast Pacific Ocean: Connections with El Niño," *Journal of Geophysical Research* 90 (20 Jan. 1985): 857–68; Harry van Loon and Jeffery C. Rogers, "The Southern Oscillation. Part II: Associations with Changes in the Middle Troposphere in the Northern Winter," *Monthly Weather Review* 109 (June 1981): 1163–68.

For biological reactions see William G. Pearcy, *Ocean Ecology of North Pacific Salmonids* (Seattle: Washington Sea Grant Program, 1992), 43, 54, 70–72; Allan C. Hartt, "Juvenile Salmonids in the Oceanic Ecosystem—The Critical First Summer," in *Salmonid Ecosystems of the North Pacific*, ed. William J. McNeill and Daniel C. Himsworth (Corvallis: Oregon State University Press, 1980), 25–57; Thomas E. Nickelson, "Influences of Upwelling, Ocean Temperature, and Smolt Abundance on Marine Survival of Coho Salmon (*Oncorhynchus kisutch*) in the Oregon Production Area," *Canadian Journal of Fisheries and Aquatic Sciences* 43 (Mar. 1986): 527–35; T. E. Nickelson and J. A. Lichatowich, "The Influence of the Marine Environment on the Interannual Variation in Coho Salmon Abundance: An Overview," in *The Influence of Ocean Conditions on the Production of Salmonids in the North Pacific*, ed. William G. Pearcy (Corvallis: Oregon State University, 1984), 24–36; W. Pearcy, J. Fisher, R. Brodeur, and S. Johnson, "Effects of the 1983 El Niño on Coastal

Nekton off Oregon and Washington," in *El Niño North: Niño Effects in the Eastern Subarctic Pacific Ocean*, ed. Warren S. Wooster and David L. Fluharty (Seattle: Washington Sea Grant Program, 1985), 188–204.

20. Steven L. Johnson, "The Effects of the 1983 El Niño on Oregon's Coho (*Oncorhynchus kisutch*) and Chinook (*O. tshawytscha*) Salmon," *Fisheries Research* 6 (1988): 105–23; Gary D. Sharp, "Fishery Catch Records, El Niño/Southern Oscillation, and Longer-Term Climate Change as Inferred from Fish Remains in Marine Sediments," in *El Niño: Historical and Paleoclimatic Aspects of the Southern Oscillation*, ed. Henry F. Diaz and Vera Markgraf (New York: Cambridge University Press, 1992), 388–89. According to oceanographer Warren Wooster, the tendency toward anthropocentric assessments of causation still consumes many fishery managers and lay observers (conversation with author, 12 July 1996).

21. For weather see George N. Kiladis and Henry F. Diaz, "An Analysis of the 1877–78 ENSO Episode and Comparison with 1982–83," *Monthly Weather Review* 114 (June 1986): 1035–47; *Oregonian*, 17 Jan. 1877, 3; 5 Feb. 1877, 3; 13 Feb. 1877, 1; 20 July 1877, 1. In 1997, El Niño revisited the Pacific Northwest with waters warm enough to induce the tropical mahimahi fish (*Coryphaena hippurus*) as far north as Florence, Oregon; *Oregonian*, 20 Aug. 1997, C9. For fishing season see *Oregonian*, 26 Feb. 1877, 3; 12 May 1877, 4; 17 May 1877, 4; 29 May 1877, 1; 26 June 1877, 1; 4 July 1877, 3; 3 Aug. 1877, 4; 18 Aug. 1877, 3; 14 Sept. 1877, 3; Stone to Baird, 14 June 1877, Letters Received from Livingston Stone, 1874–77, RG 22, NA; Robert Deniston Hume, *A Pygmy Monopolist*, ed. Gordon B. Dodds (Madison: University of Wisconsin Press, 1961), 50.

22. *Oregonian*, 4 Aug. 1877, 1; 17 Sept. 1877, 2; 17 May 1877, 4; *Astorian* is quoted in *Oregonian*, 28 May 1877, 3.

23. J. W. Cook to Baird, 5 Jan. 1876, box 42, vol. 188, p. 156–58, RU 52, SIA; Stone to Baird, 9 Mar. 1877, Letters Received from Livingston Stone, 1874–77, RG 22, NA; *Oregonian*, 11 Apr. 1877, 2; 12 Apr. 1877, 2; 13 Apr. 1877, 1.

24. Sen. John H. Mitchell to Baird, 21 Apr. 1877, box 52, pp. 300–301, RU 52, SIA; Baird to Mitchell, 23 Apr. 1877, vol. 19, pp. 279–87; Baird to Stone, 23 Apr. 1877, vol. 19, pp. 288–89; Baird to Stone, 28 Apr. 1877, vol. 19, pp. 324–25, Press Copies of Letters Sent, 1871–1906, RG 22, NA; Baird to Stone, 15 May 1877, Letters Received from Livingston Stone, 1874–77, RG 22, NA; Livingston Stone, "Report of Operations at the Salmon-Hatching Station on the Clackamas River, Oregon, in 1877," *ARUSCF* (1877): 783–96; Oregon and Washington Fish Propagating Company papers, box 2, Failing Papers.

25. Stone to Baird, 16 May 1877; Stone to Baird, 30 July 1877; Stone to Baird, 14 June 1877, Letters Received from Livingston Stone, 1874–77, RG 22, NA.

26. Ravenal to Hubbard, 8 July 1896, vol. 446, pp. 114–15; Ravenal to Hubbard, 20 Nov. 1896, vol. 453, p. 191, Press Copies of Letters Sent, 1871–1906, RG 22, NA;

Willis H. Rich, "Local Populations and Migration in Relation to the Conservation of Pacific Salmon in the Western States and Alaska," in *The Migration and Conservation of Salmon*, ed. Forest Ray Moulton (Lancaster: Science Press, 1939), 45–50.

27. *Oregonian*, 2 July 1877, 1; 20 July 1877, 3; 23 Aug. 1877, 3; Stone to Baird, 5 July 1877, 10 July 1877, 18 July 1877, Letters Received from Livingston Stone, 1874–77, RG 22, NA; George W. McCrory to Baird, 20 Apr. 1878, box 178, RU 26, SIA.

28. Stone to Baird, 18 Aug. 1877, Letters Received from Livingston Stone, 1874–77, RG 22, NA; Stone, "Report on Operations on the Clackamas," 787, 790–91; *Oregonian*, 27 Dec. 1888, 8; 30 July 1895, 8; 5 Aug. 1895, 8; 29 Aug. 1895, 10.

29. *Oregonian*, 16 Aug. 1877, 3; 12 July 1877, 3; 28 July 1877, 3; 30 July 1877, 3; 14 Sept. 1877, 3; Stone to Baird, 31 Aug. 1877, Letters Received from Livingston Stone, 1874–77, RG 22, NA.

30. Baird to Stone, 8 Mar. 1877, vol. 19, pp. 33–34; Baird to Stone, 5 July 1877, vol. 20, pp. 436–39; Baird to Stone, 17 Sept. 1877, vol. 22, pp. 304–5, Press Copies of Letters Sent, 1871–1906, RG 22, NA; *Oregonian*, 24 May 1877, 3; 13 Oct. 1877, 1; 3 Nov. 1877, 4; 6 Nov. 1877, 1; 10 Nov. 1877, 8; 17 Nov. 1877, 5; Stone to Baird, 10 Oct. 1877, Letters Received from Livingston Stone, 1874–77, RG 22, NA.

31. *Oregonian*, 27 Aug. 1888, 8; McDonald to Hubbard, 7 Nov. 1890, vol. 282, pp. 190–93; Ravenal to Commissioner, 2 Sept. 1897, vol. 475, pp. 20–21, Press Copies of Letters Sent, 1871–1906, RG 22, NA.

32. Stone, "Report of Operations on the Clackamas," 787–89; Myron Green to Baird, 24 Sept. 1877, box 45, vol. 192, pp. 369–70, RU 52, SIA; *Oregonian*, 4 Oct. 1877, 1. For similar floods and solutions see Ravenal to S. W. Downing, 26 Oct. 1899, vol. 527, p. 4635, Press Copies of Letters Sent, 1871–1906, RG 22, NA; T. H. Hill to Frank Benson, 17 Apr. 1907, Benson Papers; Stone to Baird, 1 July 1878, box 3, fldr. S, Letters Received, 1878–81, RG 22, NA; Stone to Baird, 23 Oct. 1877, Letters Received from Livingston Stone, 1874–77, RG 22, NA; *Oregonian*, 6 Oct. 1877, 3; 26 Oct. 1877, 3; 29 Oct. 1877, 3.

33. Stone, "Report of Operations on the Clackamas," 790; Stone to Baird, 26 Aug. 1875, box 58, vol. 206, p. 277, RU 52, SIA; Stone to Baird, 9 Apr. 1881, box 16, fldr. S (5 of 5), Letters Received, 1878–81, RG 22, NA; *Oregonian*, 20 Oct. 1877, 5.

34. *For the Protection of Salmon in the Columbia River*, 45th Cong., 1st sess., 1877, H.R. 1168; *Congressional Record*, 45th Cong., 1st sess., 1877, vol. 6, 251; *For the protection of the salmon-fisheries of the Columbia River*, 45th Cong., 2d sess., 1878, S.B. 492; *Congressional Record*, 45th Cong., 2d sess., 1878, vol. 7, 303.

35. For discussion of the Mitchell bill see box 2, fldr. H–K, and Stone to Baird, 29 Jan. 1878, Feb. 1878, and 20 Feb. 1878, box 3, fldr. R–S, Letters Received, 1878–81, RG 22, NA; Baird to Stone, 30 Nov. 1877, vol. 23, pp. 370–72; Baird to Mitchell, 17 Jan. 1878, vol. 24, p. 328; Baird to Mitchell, 10 Apr. 1878, vol. 26, pp. 139–40; Baird to Stone, 27 Apr. 1878, vol. 26, pp. 467–69, Press Copies of Letters Sent,

1871–1906, RG 22, NA. George Bowers accomplished the same end with Oregon senator Joseph Simon in 1900; Joseph Simon to George M. Bowers, 8 May 1900, box 318, no. 12600, Letters Received, 1882–1900, RG 22, NA.

36. *Oregonian,* 18 June 1878, 2; 18 July 1878, 1; 21 Sept. 1878, 2; 12 Sept. 1878, 1, 4.

37. Karen Johnson, *A History of Coho Fisheries and Management in Oregon through 1982,* Information Reports 84–12 (Corvallis: Oregon Department of Fish and Wildlife Research Section, 1983), 36, 38, 42, 43; Steven Johnson, "Freshwater Environmental Problems," 13; John T. Gharrett and John I. Hodges, *Salmon Fisheries of the Coastal Rivers of Oregon South of the Columbia,* Oregon Fish Commission Contribution 13 (Portland: Oregon Fish Commission, 1950), 5; *Oregonian,* 26 Oct. 1878, 4; 21 Feb. 1879, 1; 24 Feb. 1879, 1; 3 Mar. 1879, 3; 18 Mar. 1879, 3; 25 Mar. 1879, 1; 1 Apr. 1879, 1; 18 Apr. 1879, 3; 6 Mar. 1880, 2; 8 Apr. 1880, 3.

38. *Oregonian,* 4 Apr. 1878, 3; Stone to Baird, 25 Oct. 1877; Stone to Baird, 10 Nov. 1877, Letters Received from Livingston Stone, 1874–77, RG 22, NA; Stone to Baird, 4 Jan. 1878, box 3, fldr. R–S; John Adair Jr. to Baird, 10 Mar. 1878, box 1, fldr. A; Stone to Baird, 31 Mar. 1878, box 3, fldr. R–S; Stone to Baird, 26 Apr. 1878, box 3, fldr. S; Stone to Baird, 30 Apr. 1878 and 3 May 1878, box 3, fldr. S; Stone to Baird, 22 June 1878, box 3, fldr. S, Letters Received, 1878–81, RG 22, NA; Baird to Stone, 13 June 1878, vol. 28, pp. 117–18; Baird to Stone, 17 Aug. 1878, vol. 29, pp. 291–92; Baird to Stone, 6 July 1872, vol. 2, pp. 408–11; Baird to Stone, 29 May 1875, vol. 12, pp. 395, Press Copies of Letters Sent, 1871–1906, RG 22, NA.

39. Kiladis and Diaz, "Analysis of 1877–78 ENSO Episode," 1040–46; *Oregonian,* 14 Feb. 1878, 1; 20 Feb. 1878, 1; 27 Feb. 1878, 1; 30 Mar. 1878, 1; 30 Apr. 1878, 3; 6 May 1878, 1; 20 July 1878, 3; 9 Sept. 1878, 3; 12 Oct. 1878, 5; Smith, *Salmon Fishers,* 110; W. F. Hubbard, "Report of Salmon-Hatching Operations in 1878, at the Clackamas Hatchery," *ARUSCF* (1878): 771–72.

40. For funding negotiations see Stone to Baird, 20 Nov. 1878, box 3, fldr. S, Letters Received, 1878–81, RG 22, NA; Baird to Stone, 9 Nov. 1878, vol. 31, pp. 236–37; Baird to Stone, 11 Nov. 1878, vol. 31, pp. 246–47; Baird to Stone, 15 Nov. 1878, vol. 31, pp. 310–11; Baird to Stone, 25 Nov. 1878, vol. 31, pp. 378; Baird to J. G. Megler, 5 Dec. 1878, vol. 31, pp. 461–64; Baird to Stone, 5 Dec. 1878, vol. 31, pp. 467–68; Baird to Megler, 3 Jan. 1879, vol. 32, p. 254; Baird to Stone, 2 Apr. 1879, vol. 34, p. 212; Baird to Stone, 9 Apr. 1879, vol. 34, p. 235; Baird to Megler, 28 Apr. 1879, vol. 34, pp. 400–401; Baird to Megler, 29 Apr. 1879, vol. 34, p. 412; Baird to Stone, 8 May 1879, vol. 34, p. 497; Baird to Megler, 28 July 1879, vol. 37, pp. 32–33, Press Copies of Letters Sent, 1871–1906, RG 22, NA; Stone to Baird, 1 Dec. 1878, box 2, Clackamas fldr., Records concerning Abandoned Stations, 1879–1931, RG 22, NA.

For repairs and consequences see *Oregonian,* 8 Sept. 1879, 3; Theodore Wygant to Baird, 10 Feb. 1880, box 10, fldr. W–Z; Stone to Baird, 27 Feb. 1880, box 10, fldr. S, Letters Received, 1878–81, RG 22, NA; Baird to J. W. Cook, 12 Mar. 1881, vol. 56, pp.

295–96; Baird to Stone, 25 Feb. 1880, vol. 42, pp. 331–32; Baird to Stone, 14 Mar. 1881, vol. 56, p. 281, Press Copies of Letters Sent, 1871–1906, RG 22, NA; *Oregonian*, 7 Apr. 1880, 3; 8 Apr. 1880, 3; 12 Apr. 1881, 3; J. W. Cook to Baird, 9 Feb. 1881, box 45, no. 25452, Letters Received, 1882–1900, RG 22, NA; Livingston Stone, "Artificial Propagation of Salmon in the Columbia Basin," *TAFS* 13 (1884): 26.

41. David Starr Jordan and Charles H. Gilbert, "Observations on the Salmon of the Pacific," *American Naturalist* 15 (Mar. 1881): 177–86; *Oregonian*, 21 July 1883, 1; 1 Aug. 1883, 2.

42. Quinn et al., "El Niño Occurrences," 14450–51; R. C. Francis, S. R. Hare, A. B. Hollowed, and W. S. Wooster, "Effects of Interdecadal Climate Variability on the Oceanic Ecosystems of the Northeast Pacific," *Fisheries Oceanography* (in press); F. A. Seufert to George Bowers, 15 July 1899, box 306, no. 956, Letters Received, 1882–1900, RG 22, NA; Ravenal to Hubbard, 8 Aug. 1898, vol. 494, p. 154; Ravenal to S. W. Downing, 25 Sept. 1899, vol. 523, p. 3000; Bowers to R. D. Hume, 2 Oct. 1899, vol. 522, p. 2728; Ravenal to Downing, 24 Oct. 1899, vol. 523, p. 3288; Bowers to F. C. Reed, 1 Dec. 1899, vol. 526, p. 4567; Bowers to J. N. Wisner, 16 July 1900, vol. 543, p. 239; Bowers to Wisner, 28 Sept. 1900, vol. 549, p. 3199; Bowers to R. D. Hume, 5 Dec. 1900, vol. 551, p. 4104, Press Copies of Letters Sent, 1871–1906, RG 22, NA.

43. W. A. Jones, "The Salmon Fisheries of the Columbia River," S. Exec. Doc. 123 (50–1) 2510:42, 54–55, 58.

44. M. C. George to Baird, 20 Dec. 1882, box 24, no. 12527; Astoria Chamber of Commerce to Baird, 29 Dec. 1882, box 25, no. 13371; George to Baird, 28 Feb. 1883, box 29, no. 15594, Letters Received, 1882–1900, RG 22, NA; Baird to Stone, 7 Mar. 1883, vol. 95, pp. 67–71; Baird to George, 27 Feb. 1883, vol. 94, pp. 95–96; Baird to James H. Slater, 20 Jan. 1883, vol. 90, pp. 245–47, Press Copies of Letters Sent, 1871–1906, RG 22, NA; E. C. Holden, "The Columbia River Salmon—A Hatchery Needed," *Bulletin* 4 (1884): 305; C. H. Walker, "Location of a Salmon Hatchery in Oregon," *Bulletin* 5 (1885): 309–10; E. L. Smith, "Hood River, Oregon, as a Place For Salmon Breeding," *Bulletin* 6 (1886): 87–88; L. T. Barin, "Salmon in the Clackamas," *Bulletin* 6 (1886): 111–12; A. S. Abernethy, "Salmon in the Clackamas River," *Bulletin* 6 (1886): 332; B. S. Huntington to Baird, 19 July 1886, box 106, no. 77041, Letters Received, 1882–1900, RG 22, NA.

45. Stone to Baird, 3 Mar. 1883 and 10 Mar. 1883, box 2, Clackamas fldr., Records concerning Abandoned Stations, 1879–1931, RG 22, NA; Baird to M. C. George, 27 June 1883, vol. 105, pp. 76–77, Press Copies of Letters Sent, 1871–1906, RG 22, NA; Baird to Stone, 8 Sept. 1883, vol. 110, pp. 102–3; Baird to J. N. Dolph, 18 Dec. 1884, vol. 140, pp. 213–14; Baird to Stone, 5 Jan. 1884, vol. 117, pp. 109–10; Baird to J. N. Dolph, 26 Dec. 1884, vol. 140, pp. 358–59, Press Copies of Letters Sent, 1871–1906, RG 22, NA; Stone to Baird, 5 Oct. 1883, box 146, no. 105417,

Letters Received, 1882–1900, RG 22, NA; Livingston Stone, "Explorations on the Columbia River from the Head of Clarke's Fork to the Pacific Ocean, Made in the Summer of 1883, with Reference to the Selection of a Suitable Place for Establishing a Salmon-Breeding Station," *ARUSCF* (1885): 237–58.

46. For crisis see Jones, "Salmon Fisheries," 29; *Oregonian,* 22 Nov. 1886, 1; 25 Nov. 1886, 3; 1 Jan. 1887, 16; 2 Jan. 1887, 4; 12 Jan. 1887, 3; 13 Jan. 1887, 2, 3, 4; 21 Jan. 1887, 3; 24 Jan. 1887, 4; 21 Jan. 1887, 3; 23 Nov. 1887, 4; 8 Dec. 1887, 6; 16 Dec. 1887, 4; J. H. Kidder to Sylvester Pennoyer, 6 Jan. 1888, vol. 233, pp. 304–5, Press Copies of Letters Sent, 1871–1906, RG 22, NA. For blaming nature see *Oregonian,* 30 Dec. 1886, 4; 12 Jan. 1887, 3; *AROFC* (1892): 38–39; W. Woodson to McDonald, 23 Jan. 1890, box 153, no. 110386; George McBride to George Bowers, 26 Nov. 1899, box 311, no. 6428, Letters Received, 1882–1900, RG 22, NA; Bowers to R. D. Hume, 4 June 1901, vol. 562, p. 9501, Press Copies of Letters Sent, 1871–1906, RG 22, NA; R. D. Hume to Bowers, 23 Aug. 1901, box 26, Rogue River fldr., Records concerning Fish Culture Stations, 1875–1929, RG 22, NA; Range D. Bayer, *The Cormorant/Fisherman Conflict in Tillamook County, Oregon,* Studies in Oregon Ornithology no. 6 (Newport: Gahmken Press, 1989), 9–10.

47. For the transfer of the Clackamas hatchery to the state, see *AROFC* (1887); *AROFC* (1888): 14; Livingston Stone, "The Artificial Propagation of Salmon on the Pacific Coast of the United States, with Notes on the Natural History of the Quinnat Salmon," *Bulletin* 16 (1896): 217; John H. Mitchell to Baird, 15 Jan. 1886, box 6, no. 55990; J. N. Dolph to Baird, 7 May 1886, box 103, no. 75044, Letters Received, 1882–1900, RG 22, NA; Baird to J. N. Dolph, 11 May 1886, vol. 178, pp. 105–7; Baird to Stone, 25 May 1886, vol. 178, pp. 312–14; Baird to Dolph, 2 July 1886, vol. 181, pp. 298–400; Baird to Stone, 26 July 1886, vol. 186, pp. 324–25, Press Copies of Letters Sent, 1871–1906, RG 22, NA; Stone to Baird, 26 July 1886, box 2, Clackamas fldr., Records concerning Abandoned Stations, 1879–1931, RG 22, NA; *Oregonian,* 8 Dec. 1886, 4; 16 Dec. 1886, 4; 24 Dec. 1886, 4; 16 Apr. 1888, 8; 1 Feb. 1889, 3. For legislation see Dolph to Baird, 3 Jan. 1887, box 115, no. 82019; A. S. Abernethy to Dolph, 29 Nov. 1886, box 115, no. 82020; Dolph to Baird, 9 Jan. 1887, box 115, no. 82134; Dolph to Baird, 2 Feb. 1887, box 116, no. 82923, Letters Received, 1882–1900, RG 22, NA; Baird to Dolph, 8 Jan. 1887, vol. 195, pp. 76–77; Marshall McDonald to Stone, 21 Feb. 1887, vol. 217, pp. 378–79, Press Copies of Letters Sent, 1871–1906, RG 22, NA. For the railroad see Baird to F. C. Reed, 23 Apr. 1887, vol. 197, pp. 373–74; McDonald to Dolph, 25 Apr. 1887, vol. 198, pp. 443–44, Press Copies of Letters Sent, 1871–1906, RG 22, NA; John H. Mitchell to Baird, 15 Jan. 1886, box 6, no. 55990; J. N. Dolph to Baird, 7 May 1886, box 103, no. 75044, Letters Received, 1882–1900, RG 22, NA; Stone to Baird, 26 July 1886, box 2, Clackamas fldr., Records concerning Abandoned Stations, 1879–1931, RG 22, NA.

48. Baird to J. N. Dolph, 10 Feb. 1887, vol. 195, pp. 333–34, Press Copies of

Letters Sent, 1871–1906, RG 22, NA; *Sundry Civil Appropriations Bill*, 49th Cong., 2d sess., 1887, H.R. 10072; *Congressional Record*, 49th Cong., 1st sess., 1886, vol. 17, 6553; *Congressional Record*, 49th Cong., 2d sess., 1887, vol. 18, 697, 1241; Baird to Stone, 7 Aug. 1886, vol. 187, pp. 69–70; W. W. Bretherton to Baird, 5 Mar. 1887, vol. 195, p. 485; Baird to Bretherton, 1 Apr. 1887, vol. 197, p. 227, Press Copies of Letters Sent, 1871–1906, RG 22, NA.

49. Stone to F. C. Reed, 13 Oct. 1887, vol. 214, pp. 174–75, Press Copies of Letters Sent, 1871–1906, RG 22, NA; G. Brown Goode to Dolph, 19 Oct. 1887, vol. 1, pp. 228–29, Press Copies of Confidential Letters Sent by Commissioner G. Brown Goode, RG 22, NA; John N. Cobb, *The Salmon Fisheries of the Pacific Coast*, Bureau of Fisheries Document 751 (Washington: Government Printing Office, 1910), 164–65; *Oregonian*, 12 Jan. 1888, 3; Stone, "Artificial Propagation of Salmon on the Pacific Coast," 217–18.

50. McDonald to Stone, 21 May 1888, vol. 224, p. 10; McDonald to Stone, 9 Mar. 1889, vol. 245, p. 440, Press Copies of Letters Sent, 1871–1906, RG 22, NA; *Oregonian*, 30 July 1888, 3.

51. McDonald to F. C. Reed, 22 Jan. 1889, vol. 243, pp. 98–101, Press Copies of Letters Sent, 1871–1906, RG 22, NA; J. W. Collins, "Report on the Fisheries of the Pacific Coast of the United States," *ARUSCF* (1889): 222 n.; *Oregonian*, 15 Oct. 1889, 3; 19 Nov. 1895, 4; 18 June 1898, 4.

52. *Oregonian*, 19 Nov. 1895, 4; 9 Nov. 1896, 7; 21 July 1907, 6; Hugh M. Smith, "Notes on a Reconnaissance of the Fisheries of the Pacific Coast of the United States in 1894," *Bulletin* 14 (1894): 226.

53. David Starr Jordan, "Salmon and Trout of the Pacific Coast," in *Thirteenth Biennial Report of the State Board of Fish Commissioners of the State of California* (Sacramento: California State Printer, 1894), 136; *Oregonian*, 2 Jan. 1888, 15; 29 July 1893, 4; 12 Sept. 1894, 8; 3 Oct. 1894, 8; 19 Nov. 1895, 4; 22 June 1897, 5; 24 July 1898, 4, 11; 6 July 1907, 6; *AROFC* (1891): 5–6; William A. Wilcox, "The Fisheries of the Pacific Coast," *AROFC* (1893): 231–32; J. W. Titcomb to Superintendent, 11 Nov. 1902, vol. 597, p. 3978; Bowers to Superintendent, 16 Feb. 1905, vol. 658, p. 8462, Press Copies of Letters Sent, 1871–1906, RG 22, NA.

54. McDonald to Stone, 27 Sept. 1888, vol. 232, pp. 32–34, Press Copies of Letters Sent, 1871–1906, RG 22, NA; Joseph A. Craig and Robert L. Hacker, *The History and Development of the Fisheries of the Columbia River*, Bulletin of the Bureau of Fisheries 32 (Washington: Government Printing Office, 1940), 152.

55. For Reed and McGuire see *Oregonian*, 16 Apr. 1888, 8; 1 Oct. 1893, 12; F. C. Reed to McDonald, 30 Mar. 1889, box 144, no. 104711; Reed to McDonald, 13 Feb. 1891, box 165, no. 119351; Hollister D. McGuire to McDonald, 27 Apr. 1895, box 239, no. 12940, Letters Received, 1882–1900, RG 22, NA. For Hubbard see *Oregonian*, 25 May 1895, 10; McDonald to James Crawford, 1 May 1891, vol. 294,

p. 237; Herbert A. Gill to W. F. Hubbard, 13 May 1895, vol. 408, p. 269; McDonald to J. N. McGraw, 30 May 1895, vol. 409, p. 331; Ravenal to Hubbard, 5 July 1895, vol. 417, p. 274, Press Copies of Letters Sent, 1871–1906, RG 22, NA; Brice to Hubbard, 24 Dec. 1897, vol. 480, p. 265; Bower to McGuire, 27 Mar. 1899, vol. 507, p. 385, Press Copies of Letters Sent, 1871–1906, RG 22, NA; Evermann to Richard Rathbun, 8 Aug. 1896, box 4, Siuslaw Bundles, Records concerning Abandoned Stations, 1879–1931, RG 22, NA. Hubbard's advice was often disastrous; Ravenal to Hubbard, 26 June 1895, vol. 417, pp. 179–81; Ravenal to Hubbard, 17 Aug. 1896, vol. 448, p. 112; Ravenal to W. F. Hubbard, 19 Aug. 1896, vol. 448, pp. 152–53; Ravenal to Evermann, 19 Aug. 1896, vol. 447, p. 74, Press Copies of Letters Sent, 1871–1906, RG 22, NA. Ravenal's ignorance was just as profound. On one occasion Hubbard recommended locating a rack next to an irrigation ditch, and Ravenal approved; Ravenal to Commissioner, 6 July 1896, vol. 446, pp. 74–75; Ravenal to Hubbard, 24 May 1897, vol. 464, pp. 231–32, Press Copies of Letters Sent, 1871–1906, RG 22, NA; Hubbard to Ravenal, 2 June 1897, box 26, Rogue River fldr., Records concerning Fish Culture Stations, 1875–1929, RG 22, NA.

56. McDonald to Stone, 17 Dec. 1887, vol. 215, pp. 338–40; Ravenal to Hubbard, 30 July 1896, vol. 446, pp. 427–28; Bowers to Superintendent, 21 Dec. 1904, vol. 650, p. 5342; H. M. Smith to H. G. Van Dusen, 5 Oct. 1905, vol. 674, p. 2172, Press Copies of Letters Sent, 1871–1906, RG 22, NA.

57. McDonald to James Crawford, 29 July 1890, vol. 277, pp. 99–102; Hollister McGuire to McDonald, 17 Feb. 1894, box 215, no. 9615, Press Copies of Letters Sent, 1871–1906, RG 22, NA; *Morning Oregonian*, 2 Jan. 1888, 15; 4 Mar. 1897, 4; 29 Mar. 1901, 4; Oregon, *AROFC* (1887): 8; Barton Warren Evermann and Seth Eugene Meek, "A Report upon Salmon Investigations in the Columbia River Basin and Elsewhere on the Pacific Coast in 1896," *Bulletin* 17 (1897): 50; *AROFC* (1892): 6, 29–30, 38; Johnson, "History of Coho Fisheries and Management," 36, 42; Johnson, "Freshwater Environmental Problems," 14–15.

58. *Oregonian*, 30 July 1888, 3. Settlers tore down racks repeatedly when they interfered with subsistence fishing; L. L. McArthur to Hubbard, 25 May 1889, box 144, no. 104326, Letters Received, 1882–1900, RG 22, NA; R. D. Hume to George Bowers, 11 June 1900, box 26, Rogue River fldr., Records concerning Fish Culture Stations, 1875–1929, RG 22, NA; *Oregonian*, 10 Dec. 1904, 14. For egg wars see McDonald to Stone, 4 Dec. 1888, vol. 237, pp. 190–95; McDonald to E. P. Thompson, 4 Dec. 1888, vol. 237, pp. 198–99; McDonald to F. C. Reed, 10 Dec. 1888, vol. 237, pp. 332–35; McDonald to Stone, 10 Dec. 1888, vol. 237, pp. 336–38; McDonald to F. C. Reed, 30 Aug. 1889, vol. 256, pp. 39–41; McDonald to Reed, 19 Nov. 1889, vol. 260, pp. 298–303; McDonald to Hubbard, 24 Sept. 1890, vol. 280, pp. 280–81; McDonald to Hubbard, 5 Sept. 1891, vol. 302, pp. 88–89, Press Copies of Letters Sent, 1871–1906, RG 22, NA; Reed to McDonald, 7 Dec. 1889,

box 151, no. 108828, Letters Received, 1882–1900, R G 22, N A; *Oregonian*, 27 Dec. 1888, 8; Livingston Stone, "A National Salmon Park," *T A F S* 21 (1892): 149–62.

59. *Oregonian*, 1 Mar. 1890, 9; *A R O F C* (1889): 22; *A R O F C* (1892): 31; McDonald to Hubbard, 16 Sept. 1892, vol. 324, p. 104; McDonald to Hubbard, 10 Nov. 1891, vol. 304, pp. 367–68; McDonald to Sylvester Pennoyer, 2 Dec. 1891, vol. 305, pp. 454–58; Ravenal to Binger Hermann, 18 Feb. 1896, vol. 431, pp. 6–7, Press Copies of Letters Sent, 1871–1906, R G 22, N A; F. C. Reed to McDonald, 9 Apr. 1892, box 182, no. 130782, Letters Received, 1882–1900, R G 22, N A.

60. McDonald to Hubbard, 12 Jan. 1893, vol. 329, p. 431; McDonald to Evermann, 5 Aug. 1893, vol. 359, p. 48; S. G. Worth to W. F. Hubbard, 4 Nov. 1893, vol. 361, p. 317, Press Copies of Letters Sent, 1871–1906, R G 22, N A; *Oregonian*, 1 Oct. 1893, 12; 3 Oct. 1893, 6. Thirteen years later George M. Bowers threatened to suspend hatchery work on the Rogue if Oregon continued to ignore illegal fishing below fishways on the river; Bowers to Superintendent, 21 Feb. 1906, vol. 687, p. 7932, Press Copies of Letters Sent, 1871–1906, R G 22, N A; *A R O F C* (1894): 4.

61. McDonald to Sylvester Pennoyer, 30 Oct. 1893, vol. 360, pp. 399–401; McDonald to E. C. Holden, 18 Oct. 1893, vol. 360, pp. 213–15, Press Copies of Letters Sent, 1871–1906, R G 22, N A; Marshall McDonald, "Inspection of Clackamas Hatchery," 25 Nov. 1893, box 2, fldr. 4, Letters Received by Marshall McDonald, 1879–95, R G 22, N A; Dolph to McDonald, 1 Feb. 1894, box 214, no. 8755, Letters Received, 1882–1900, R G 22, N A; *A R O F C* (1894): 3–4; *Oregonian*, 29 Mar. 1895, 9.

62. McDonald to Hubbard, 12 May 1894, vol. 377, pp. 187–88; Tarleton Bean to Hubbard, 6 June 1894, vol. 378, pp. 389–90; McDonald to Dolph, 2 July 1894, vol. 385, pp. 181–83; McDonald to John H. Mitchell, 7 July 1894, vol. 385, pp. 246–48; McDonald to Charles Gilbert, 6 Aug. 1894, vol. 391, pp. 46–47, Press Copies of Letters Sent, 1871–1906, R G 22, N A; *Oregonian*, 14 July 1894, 6; *A R O F C* (1894): 12. For reaction to McDonald's ultimatum see George T. Myers, Hollister D. McGuire, J. McCraken, Frank Motter, and G. P. Frank to Marshall McDonald, 26 July 1894, box 225, no. 987, Letters Received, 1882–1900, R G 22, N A; McDonald to Myers et al., 7 Aug. 1894, vol. 391, pp. 33–34; McDonald to L. T. Barin, 3 Oct. 1894, vol. 392, pp. 220–21; H. M. Smith to Frank M. Warren, 12 Nov. 1894, vol. 413, p. 114; McDonald to Binger Hermann, 4 Dec. 1894, vol. 394, pp. 190–92; Herbert A. Gill to L. T. Barin, 15 Jan. 1895, vol. 399, p. 466; McDonald to Barin, 18 Jan. 1895, vol. 402, p. 47, Press Copies of Letters Sent, 1871–1906, R G 22, N A; Marshall McDonald, "The Salmon Fisheries of the Columbia River Basin," *Bulletin* 14 (1894): 168.

63. H. M. Smith to M. J. Kinney, 21 Mar. 1895, vol. 413, p. 434; Ravenal to Hubbard, 3 Feb. 1896, vol. 430, pp. 73–74, Press Copies of Letters Sent, 1871–1906,

RG 22, NA; *Oregonian*, 29 Mar. 1895, 9; 12 May 1895, 8; 24 July 1895, 4; 22 Sept. 1895, 10. For retaliation see Ravenal to Hubbard, 24 Jan. 1896, vol. 428, p. 434; Ravenal to Hubbard, 24 Apr. 1896, vol. 435, p. 492; Ravenal to Hubbard, 12 May 1896, vol. 437, p. 255; Ravenal to Hubbard, 15 May 1896, vol. 437, p. 284; Ravenal to Hubbard, 9 June 1896, vol. 440, p. 107; J. J. Brice to Hubbard, 18 June 1896, vol. 441, p. 202, Press Copies of Letters Sent, 1871–1906, RG 22, NA. Hubbard eventually built a gate in the racks to pass logs through, but this required an extra hand to attend the gate; Ravenal to Hubbard, 1 Sept. 1896, vol. 448, p. 299, Press Copies of Letters Sent, 1871–1906, RG 22, NA.

64. McDonald to McGuire, 17 May 1895, vol. 408, p. 365, Press Copies of Letters Sent, 1871–1906, RG 22, NA; "Board Minutes of the Oregon Fish Commission," pp. 58, 60, 63–64, and 66–67, ODFW Papers.

65. *Oregonian*, 14 Apr. 1877, 1; 21 June 1908, sec. 2, 1; J. Q. A. Bowlby to Dolph, 23 June 1894, box 224, no. 18; and Thomas H. Tongue to John J. Brice, 28 Dec. 1897, box 285, no. 6570; McGuire to Ravenal, 7 Feb. 1899, box 299, no. 7601, Letters Received, 1882–1900, RG 22, NA; Cobb, *Salmon Fisheries of the Pacific Coast*, 164–65; J. J. Brice to R. D. Hume, 5 Jan. 1897, vol. 455, pp. 224–25; George M. Bower to Judge Wm. S. Crowell, 19 Jan. 1900, vol. 529, p. 5798; Bowers to H. G. Van Dusen, 9 May 1901, vol. 560, p. 8497; Bowers to F. A. Seufert, 10 Dec. 1903, vol. 625, p. 4342; Bowers to Wallich, 28 Nov. 1904, vol. 653, p. 6152, Press Copies of Letters Sent, 1871–1906, RG 22, NA; "Board Minutes of the Oregon Fish Commission," p. 8, ODFW Papers. Washington accomplished a similar exchange at Baker Lake in 1899 and on the Klickitat River in 1901; Bowers to A. C. Little, 24 May 1899, vol. 512, pp. 56–57; Ravenal to J. N. Wisner, 16 Dec. 1901, vol. 575, p. 4065, Press Copies of Letters Sent, 1871–1906, RG 22, NA.

66. *AROFC* (1893): 4; McDonald to McGuire, 15 Nov. 1893, vol. 362, pp. 172, 175–76; McDonald to Dolph, 12 May 1894, vol. 377, pp. 190; McDonald to McGuire, 12 May 1894, vol. 377, pp. 191–92; McGuire to McDonald, 4 May 1894, box 220, no. 13138; McDonald to McGuire, 22 June 1894, vol. 385, p. 3, Press Copies of Letters Sent, 1871–1906, RG 22, NA; McGuire to McDonald, 11 June 1894, box 222, no. 14673; McGuire to John H. Mitchell, 11 June 1894, box 223, no. 14970; Mitchell to McDonald, 29 June 1894, box 223, no. 14969; B. F. Alley to J. N. Dolph, 5 May 1894, box 220, no. 13186, Letters Received, 1882–1900, RG 22, NA; *Oregonian*, 22 Jan. 1894, 5; 13 Feb. 1894, 6; 4 May 1894; 20 May 1894, 5.

67. Evermann and Meek, "Report upon Salmon Investigations," 38; Tarleton Bean to W. F. Hubbard, 5 Sept. 1894, vol. 390, p. 65; T. Bean to Hubbard, 14 Sept. 1894, vol. 390, p. 216; T. Bean to McGuire, 14 Sept. 1894, vol. 390, p. 200; T. Bean to McGuire, 27 Sept. 1894, vol. 390, p. 412; T. Bean to Hubbard, 27 Sept. 1894, vol. 390, p. 413; McDonald to Hubbard, 3 Oct. 1894, vol. 395, p. 4; Ravenal to Hubbard, 23 Oct. 1894, vol. 396, p. 49; Ravenal to George H. Tolbert, 23 Oct. 1894, vol. 396,

p. 50; Ravenal to J. W. Berrian, 14 Jan. 1895, vol. 399, p. 438, Press Copies of Letters Sent, 1871–1906, R G 22, N A; McGuire to T. Bean, 20 Sept. 1894, box 228, no. 3521, Letters Received, 1882–1900, R G 22, N A; *Oregonian*, 3 Oct. 1894, 8.

68. Johnson, "History of Coho Fisheries and Management," 21.

69. Louis E. Bean to Binger Hermann, 5 Feb. 1896, box 251, no. 8581; Binger Hermann to Commissioner, 15 Feb. 1896, box 251, no. 8580, Letters Received, 1882–1900, R G 22, N A; L. E. Bean to Ravenal, 21 Nov. 1896, box 4; L. E. Bean to Hermann, 12 July 1896, box 4, Siuslaw Bundles, Records concerning Abandoned Stations, 1879–1931, R G 22, N A; Ravenal to Hermann, 22 July 1896, vol. 445, p. 189, Press Copies of Letters Sent, 1871–1906, R G 22, N A.

70. "Meek, Seth Eugene," in *Who Was Who in America*, vol. 1, *1897–1942* (Chicago: A. N. Marquis Co., 1943), 827; Evermann and Meek, "Report upon Salmon Investigations in the Columbia," 54–56; Meek to Ravenal, 27 Oct. 1896; Meek to Evermann, 21 Sept. 1896; Meek to Rathbun, 26 Oct. 1896; Meek to Evermann, 21 Sept. 1896, box 4, Siuslaw Bundles, Records concerning Abandoned Stations, 1879–1931, R G 22, N A; Ravenal to Meek, 13 Oct. 1896, vol. 450, p. 251; Richard Rathbun to S. E. Meek, 6 Oct. 1897, vol. 468, pp. 262–63, Press Copies of Letters Sent, 1871–1906, R G 22, N A.

71. *Oregonian*, 1 Oct. 1893, 12; 6 Oct. 1894, 9; 12 Dec. 1894, 3; E. N. Carter to Commissioner, 18 Mar. 1907; S. W. Downing to Commissioner, 19 Mar. 1907; Hubbard to Commissioner, 19 Mar. 1907, box 4, Upper Clackamas fldr., Records concerning Abandoned Stations, 1879–1931, R G 22, N A; William R. Nelson and Jack Bodle, "Ninety Years of Salmon Culture at Little White Salmon National Fish Hatchery," *Biological Report* 90 (Dec. 1990); H. M. Smith to M. J. Kinney, 2 Jan. 1895, vol. 413, pp. 214–15, Press Copies of Letters Sent, 1871–1906, R G 22, N A; A. E. Houchen to McDonald, 15 Jan. 1895, box 234, no. 8759, Letters Received, 1882–1900, R G 22, N A; Meek to Rathbun, 26 Oct. 1896; Meek to Commission, 30 Sept. 1896; L. E. Bean to Ravenal, 2 Nov. 1896; L. E. Bean to Ravenal, 2 Nov. 1896; L. E. Bean to Ravenal, 15 Nov. 1896, box 4, Siuslaw Bundles, Records concerning Abandoned Stations, 1879–1931, R G 22, N A.

72. Meek to Ravenal, 21 Nov. 1896; L. E. Bean to Ravenal, 26 Nov. 1896, box 4, Siuslaw Bundles, Records concerning Abandoned Stations, 1879–1931, R G 22, N A; Ravenal to L. E. Bean, vol. 453, p. 279; Ravenal to Hubbard, 20 May 1895, vol. 408, pp. 426–27; Ravenal to Hubbard, 26 June 1895, vol. 417, pp. 179–81; Ravenal to Hubbard, 30 Sept. 1895, vol. 421, p. 458; Ravenal to Hubbard, 2 Oct. 1895, vol. 421, p. 493; Ravenal to Hubbard, 17 Nov. 1895, vol. 423, pp. 168–69; Ravenal to Hubbard, 17 Oct. 1896, vol. 450, pp. 331–32; Ravenal to Hubbard, 24 Nov. 1896, vol. 453, p. 240; Ravenal to Hubbard, 27 Nov. 1896, vol. 453, p. 264; Ravenal to Hubbard, 5 Dec. 1896, vol. 453, p. 355; Brice to Hubbard, 21 Dec. 1896, vol. 456, p. 31; Ravenal to Hubbard, 28 Dec. 1896, vol. 456, p. 61; Ravenal to Hubbard, 2 Jan. 1897, vol. 456,

p. 95; Ravenal to Hubbard, 1 Feb. 1897, vol. 456, p. 489; Ravenal to Hubbard, 15 Feb. 1897, vol. 460, p. 180; Ravenal to Hubbard, 18 Feb. 1897, vol. 460, p. 212; Ravenal to Hubbard, 30 Mar. 1897, vol. 462, p. 97; Ravenal to Hubbard, 26 Apr. 1897, vol. 462, pp. 371–72, Press Copies of Letters Sent, 1871–1906, R G 22, N A. The U S B F had more troubles in 1904, when a neighbor tried to extort money from the federal government by withholding water; Bowers to Superintendent, 12 Dec. 1904, vol. 650, p. 5613, Press Copies of Letters Sent, 1871–1906, R G 22, N A.

73. L. E. Bean to Ravenal, 10 Dec. 1896; L. E. Bean to Ravenal, 22 Feb. 1896; L. E. Bean to Ravenal, 22 Feb. 1896; Bean to unknown, c. 6 Jan. 1897, box 4, Siuslaw Bundles, Records concerning Abandoned Stations, 1879–1931, R G 22, N A; Ravenal to Hubbard, 7 Nov. 1894, vol. 396, p. 349; Ravenal to Hubbard, 26 Nov. 1894, vol. 397, p. 165; Brice to Binger Hermann, 5 Jan. 1897, vol. 455, pp. 222–23; Ravenal to L. E. Bean, 3 Feb. 1897, vol. 460, pp. 38–39; Ravenal to L. E. Bean, 3 Mar. 1897, vol. 460, p. 324, Press Copies of Letters Sent, 1871–1906, R G 22, N A.

74. L. E. Bean to Ravenal, 6 Feb. 1897; Ravenal to Brice, 3 July 1897; L. E. Bean to Ravenal, 14 July 1896; Hermann to Commissioner, 15 July 1896; George W. McBride to Brice, 22 July 1897, box 4, Siuslaw Bundles, Records concerning Abandoned Stations, 1879–1931, R G 22, N A; McGuire to Brice, 2 Mar. 1897, box 271, no. 10606; William Kyle to Thomas H. Tongue, 14 July 1897, box 278, no. 870; Thomas H. Tongue to Brice, 22 July 1897, box 278, no. 869, Letters Received, 1882–1900, R G 22, N A; Brice to L. E. Bean, 6 July 1897, vol. 496, p. 321; Brice to Hubbard, 2 July 1897, vol. 469, p. 245; Richard Rathbun to B. W. Evermann, 22 July 1897, vol. 468, p. 163; Brice to Tongue, 24 July 1897, vol. 471, pp. 215–16; Brice to McBride, 28 July 1897, vol. 471, pp. 289–90; Brice to Tongue, 30 July 1897, vol. 471, pp. 359–60, Press Copies of Letters Sent, 1871–1906, R G 22, N A.

75. Ravenal to L. E. Bean, 30 July 1897, vol. 472, pp. 222–23, Press Copies of Letters Sent, 1871–1906, R G 22, N A; L. E. Bean to Ravenal, 12 Sept. 1897 and 26 Sept. 1897, box 4, Siuslaw Bundles, Records concerning Abandoned Stations, 1879–1931, R G 22, N A.

76. L. E. Bean to Ravenal, 26 Sept. 1897, 27 Oct. 1897, 8 Nov. 1896, 8 Nov. 1897; L. E. Bean to Commissioner, 22 Nov. 1897, 31 Dec. 1897, 28 Feb. 1898, box 4, Siuslaw Bundles, Records concerning Abandoned Stations, 1879–1931, R G 22, N A; Fred W. Allendorf, Nils Ryman, and Fred M. Utter, "Genetics and Fishery Management," in *Population Genetics and Fishery Management,* ed. Nils Ryman and Fred Utter (Seattle: Washington Sea Grant, 1987), 1–19; Fred W. Allendorf and Nils Ryman, "Genetic Management of Hatchery Stocks," in *Population Genetics and Fishery Management,* 141–59; Ravenal to L. E. Bean, 29 Nov. 1897, vol. 478, p. 422, Press Copies of Letters Sent, 1871–1906, R G 22, N A. The U S F C and U S B F endured similar pressures on the Rogue over lobbying for various hatchery sites and moving stations due to land use politics and the patronage of R. D. Hume; Ravenal to

Hubbard, 18 June 1897, vol. 470, p. 66; Ravenal to Hubbard, 22 June 1897, vol. 470, pp. 106–8; Brice to Hubbard, 2 July 1897, vol. 469, p. 245; Bowers to Superintendent, 12 Feb. 1903, vol. 607, p. 8374; Bowers to Superintendent, 17 Feb. 1903, vol. 607, p. 8442, Press Copies of Letters Sent, 1871–1906, RG 22, NA.

77. *AROFC* (1889): 3 and (1890): 36; McGuire to Brice, 14 Feb. 1897, box 8, Little White Salmon fldr., Records concerning Fish Culture Stations, 1875–1929, RG 22, NA; *Oregonian*, 22 June 1897, 5; 28 Nov. 1897, 10; 24 July 1898, 11; John H. Mitchell to McDonald, 7 July 1894, box 224, no. 216, Letters Received, 1882–1900, RG 22, NA.

78. Ravenal to Hubbard, 11 Apr. 1899, vol. 510, p. 45, Press Copies of Letters Sent, 1871–1906, RG 22, NA; *Oregonian*, 13 Apr. 1899, 6; Cobb, *Salmon Fisheries of the Pacific Coast*, 160–66; Harry Bultman to William Kyle, 4 July 1901; H. G. Van Dusen to William Kyle, 7 Aug. 1901, box 2/45; H. A. Webster to William Kyle, 1 Sept. 1906, box 3/86, Kyle Papers; J. W. Berrian to R. D. Hume, 6 July 1902, box 3; H. A. Webster to R. D. Hume, 22 Nov. 1906, box 6, Hume Papers; Ravenal to J. N. Wisner, 2 Nov. 1901, vol. 572, p. 3092; Bowers to Van Dusen, 12 Feb. 1902, vol. 578, p. 5508; H. M. Smith to Van Dusen, 10 Mar. 1902, vol. 578, p. 5896; Bowers to Thomas H. Tongue, 2 June 1902, vol. 582, p. 8869; I. H. Dunlop to Van Dusen, 5 Sept. 1902, vol. 591, p. 1307; J. W. Titcomb to J. N. Wisner, 11 Dec. 1902, vol. 599, p. 4909, Press Copies of Letters Sent, 1871–1906, RG 22, NA.

79. Herbert A. Gill to Adam Eckert, 22 Mar. 1895, vol. 404, pp. 448–49; Ravenal to John H. Mitchell, 29 June 1896, vol. 441, pp. 386–88; Bowers to Van Dusen, 16 Feb. 1899, vol. 505, p. 124; Bowers to Hubbard, 16 Mar. 1899, vol. 508, p. 243, Press Copies of Letters Sent, 1871–1906, RG 22, NA; Knott C. Egbert to Smithsonian, 2 Mar. 1900, box 315, no. 9865, Letters Received, 1882–1900, RG 22, NA. For egg transfers see Ravenal to Hubbard, 22 Mar. 1898, vol. 484, p. 377; Ravenal to Hubbard, 27 Sept. 1898, vol. 498, p. 74; Ravenal to Hubbard, 26 Oct. 1898, vol. 498, p. 383; Bowers to F. C. Reed, 7 Nov. 1899, vol. 524, p. 3768, Press Copies of Letters Sent, 1871–1906, RG 22, NA; *Oregonian*, 6 July 1907, 6; "The United States Fisheries Bureau: An Outline of the Department's Work on the Pacific," *Pacific Fisherman* 8 (1910): 12. For quotas see McDonald to Hubbard, 28 June 1894, vol. 385, p. 91; Ravenal to Hubbard, 14 May 1896, vol. 437, p. 271; Ravenal to Commissioner, 2 Sept. 1897, vol. 475, pp. 20–21; Ravenal to Hubbard, 29 Sept. 1898 and 3 Oct. 1898, vol. 498, pp. 110, 145; Ravenal to S. W. Downing, 1 Aug. 1899, vol. 520, p. 1561; Bowers to Superintendent, 10 Jan. 1905, vol. 657, p. 8068, Press Copies of Letters Sent, 1871–1906, RG 22, NA; Stone to McDonald, 12 Apr. 1889, box 142, no. 103364, Letters Received, 1882–1900, RG 22, NA; vol. 53, entry 5716, Registers of Letters Received, 1882–1917, RG 22, NA. For centralization see Stone, "Artificial Propagation of Salmon on the Pacific Coast," 218; Ravenal to Hubbard, 10 Nov. 1896, vol. 453, p. 81; Ravenal to Hubbard, 26 Oct. 1897, vol. 475,

pp. 483–84; Ravenal to Hubbard, 20 June 1898, vol. 491, p. 313; Ravenal to Hubbard, 30 Jan. 1899, vol. 503, pp. 347–48; Ravenal to J. N. Wisner, 31 Aug. 1899, vol. 520, p. 1810; Bowers to J. N. Wisner, 28 Sept. 1900, vol. 549, p. 3199, Press Copies of Letters Sent, 1871–1906, RG 22, NA; F. C. Reed to Bowers, 22 Feb. 1900, box 314, no. 9346, Letters Received, 1882–1900, RG 22, NA; Bowers to E. N. Carter, 29 May 1900, Upper Clackamas fldr., Records concerning Abandoned Stations, 1879–1931, RG 22, NA.

80. Francis et al., "Effects of Interdecadal Climate Variability"; S. R. Hare, N. J. Mantua, and R. C. Francis, "Inverse Production Regimes: Alaska and West Coast Pacific Salmon," *Fisheries* (in press); W. A. Wilcox to H. M. Smith, 31 Aug. 1894, box 2, Correspondence of Hugh Smith relating to the Bureau of Fisheries, 1885–1910, RG 22, NA; Ravenal to J. N. Wisner, 7 Oct. 1901, vol. 569, p. 1888; Bowers to Knute Nelson, 15 Feb. 1905, vol. 655, p. 7081, Press Copies of Letters Sent, 1871–1906, RG 22, NA; *AROFC* (1902): 64; *Oregonian,* 19 June 1904, 4; 2 Jan. 1905, 18.

81. *AROFC* (1902): 79–82, 85; *Oregonian,* 25 Dec. 1902, 7. For similar attitudes in Washington State see "Salmon Hatcheries and Their Maintenance," Seattle, 23 May 1901, in vol. 1, clipping files, Warren Papers.

82. *Oregonian,* 9 Sept. 1904, 4; 13 Sept. 1904, 5; 18 Oct. 1904, 4; 6 Nov. 1904, 13; 15 Nov. 1904, 1; 20 Nov. 1904, 6; 2 Jan. 1905, 18; 11 Aug. 1905, 6; *AROFC* (1904): 109–11, 119–22, 134–35; *ARWDFG* (1904), 9–10.

83. *Oregonian,* 3 Nov. 1904, 6, 8; 4 Nov. 1904, 6, 8; 30 Jan. 1905, 6; 1 Apr. 1905, 8; Bowers to Claudius Wallich, 6 Dec. 1904, vol. 650, p. 5032; Bowers to C. W. Fulton, 16 Jan. 1905, vol. 654, p. 6454; Bowers to H. G. Van Dusen, 16 Jan. 1905, vol. 654, p. 6455; Bowers to Governor of Oregon, 16 Jan. 1905, vol. 654, p. 6456; Bowers to Wallich, 27 Jan. 1905, vol. 654, p. 6571; H. M. Smith to Superintendent, 28 Jan. 1905, vol. 658, p. 8303, Press Copies of Letters Sent, 1871–1906, RG 22, NA.

84. Willis H. Rich, "Early History and Seaward Migration of Chinook Salmon in the Columbia and Sacramento Rivers," *Bulletin* 37 (1919–20): 68.

5 / TAKING SALMON

1. Courtland L. Smith, *Oregon Fish Fights* (Corvallis: Oregon State University Sea Grant College Program, 1974). For exceptions see Gordon B. Dodds, "The Fight to Close the Rogue," *Oregon Historical Quarterly* 60 (Dec. 1959): 461–74; Joseph E. Taylor III, "For the Love of It: A Short History of Commercial Fishing in Pacific City, Oregon," *Pacific Northwest Quarterly* 82 (Jan. 1991): 22–32.

2. Robert M. Utley, "Indian–United States Military Situation, 1848–1891," in *HNAI, HIWR,* 166–67; Jane Marie Harger, "The History of the Siletz Reservation, 1856–1877" (M.A. thesis, University of Oregon, 1972), 12–41; E. A. Shwartz, *The*

Rogue River Indian War and Its Aftermath, 1850–1980 (Norman: University of Oklahoma Press, 1996), 148–84.

3. *ARCIA* (1860) S. Doc. 1 (36–2) 1078:441; *ARCIA* (1862) H. Exec. Doc. 1 (37–3) 1157:398–99, 428–29; *ARCIA* (1863) H. Exec. Doc. (38–1) 1182:201; *ARCIA* (1865) H. Exec. Doc. 1 (39–1) 1248:647.

4. E. A. Shwartz, "Sick Hearts: Indian Removal on the Oregon Coast, 1875–1881," *Oregon Historical Quarterly* 92 (fall 1991): 229–64; Shwartz, *Rogue River Indian War; Oregonian*, 8 Oct. 1875, 3; Alexandria Rock, "A Short History of the Little Nestucca River Valley and Its Early Pioneers" (University of Oregon Library, 1949, typed MS), 45–46.

5. Charles J. Kappler, comp., *Indian Affairs: Laws and Treaties*, 5 vols. (1904–41; reprint, New York: AMS Press, 1971), 2:714–19, 908–9; Bruce H. Wendt, "The Dalles Treaty Council," in *Indians, Superintendents, and Councils*, ed. Clifford E. Trafzer (Lanham: University Press of America, 1986), 85–98; "Purchase of Land for Indians upon Warm Springs Indian Reservation, for Fishing Privileges," H. Exec. Doc. 183 (50–1) 2558:8; *ARCIA* (1869) H. Exec. Doc. 1 (41–2) 1414:303, 603; *ARCIA* (1873) H. Exec. Doc. 1 (43–1) 1601:688; *ARCIA* (1901) H. Doc. 5 (57–1) 4290:357; Joseph E. Taylor III, "Who's in Charge Here Anyway? Contested Federal Authority on the Warm Spring Reservation during the Late Nineteenth Century" (paper presented at the Pacific Northwest History Association, Eugene, Oreg., Mar. 1993); Confederated Tribes of Warm Springs Reservation, *The People of Warm Springs* (n.p., 1984), 26. The Huntington Treaty is one of the most fraudulent documents in U.S. history, and although most agents ignored it in practice, it nevertheless precluded treaty Indians from claiming compensation when Bonneville Dam flooded ancestral fishing sites in the late 1930s; Edward Swindell, "Report on Source, Nature, and Extent of the Fishing, Hunting, and Miscellaneous Related Rights of Certain Indian Tribes in Washington and Oregon Together with Affidavits Showing Location of a Number of Usual and Accustomed Fishing Grounds and Stations" (Los Angeles: U.S. Department of the Interior, Office of Indian Affairs, Division of Forestry and Grazing, 1942), 113–15, 323.

6. By the early 1870s the Warm Springs agent was paying a white settler $60 annually so Indians could fish their ancestral sites at The Dalles; *ARCIA* (1868) H. Exec. Doc. 1 (40–3) 1366:577; *ARCIA* (1871) H. Exec. Doc. 1 (42–2) 1505: 545, 725–26; *ARCIA* (1872) H. Exec. Doc. 1 (42–3) 1560:751; *ARCIA* (1873) H. Exec. Doc. 1 (43–1) 1601:688; *ARCIA* (1878) H. Exec. Doc. 1 (45–3) 1850:617; *ARCIA* (1887) H. Exec. Doc. 1 (50–1) 2542:273; *ARCIA* (1888) H. Exec. Doc. 1 (50–2) 2637:210; *ARCIA* (1896) H. Doc. 5 (54–2) 3489:277; *ARCIA* (1897) H. Doc. 5 (55–2) 3641:254; *ARCIA* (1898) H. Doc. 5 (55–3) 3757:259; *ARCIA* (1899) H. Doc. 5 (56–1) 3915:282, 318; *ARCIA* (1901) H. Doc. 5 (57–1) 4290:350; John N. Cobb, *The Pacific Salmon*

Fisheries, Bureau of Fisheries Bulletin Doc. 1092 (Washington: Government Printing Office, 1930), 566.

7. *ARCIA* (1859) S. Doc. 1 (36–1) 1023:802; *ARCIA* (1871) H. Exec. Doc. 1 (42–2) 1505:714; *ARCIA* (1887) H. Exec. Doc. 1 (50–1) 2542:277–78; *ARCIA* (1894) H. Exec. Doc. 1 (53–3) 3306:23, 326; *ARCIA* (1895) H. Doc. 5 (54–1) 3382:108; "Indian Fishing Privileges," H. Exec. Doc. 183 (50–1) 2558:4–5; W. A. Jones, "The Salmon Fisheries of the Columbia River," Sen. Exec. Doc. 123 (50–1) (1887) 2510:47.

8. Jones, "Salmon Fisheries," 47; Barton Eugene Evermann and Seth Eugene Meek, "A Report upon Salmon Investigations in the Columbia River Basin and Elsewhere on the Pacific Coast in 1896," *Bulletin* 17 (1897): 30–31.

9. *ARCIA* (1887) H. Exec. Doc. 1 (50–1) 2542:80; *ARCIA* (1901) H. Doc. 5 (57–1) 4290:357; "Indian Fishing Privileges." For court cases see *United States v. Taylor, Pacific Reporter* 13 (1887): 333–36; *Eels et al. v. Ross, Federal Reporter* 64 (1894): 417–21; *United States v. Winans,* 198 U.S. 1088 (1905); *Seufert Brothers v. United States,* 249 U.S. 555 (1919). For the land grant near Celilo Falls, see *U.S. Statutes at Large* 39 (1917): 986.

10. Chris Friday, *Organizing Asian American Labor: The Pacific Coast Canned-Salmon Industry, 1870–1942* (Philadelphia: Temple University Press, 1994), 68; *Oregonian,* 2 Jan. 1905, 18.

11. Friday, *Organizing Asian American Labor,* 68, 116–18; *Oregonian,* 13 Mar. 1886, 4.

12. Courtland L. Smith, *Salmon Fishers of the Columbia* (Corvallis: Oregon State University Press, 1978), 48–49, 108, 110; *Oregonian,* 16 July 1874, 1; Courtland L. Smith, "Resource Scarcity and Inequality in the Distribution of Catch," *NAJFM* 10 (summer 1990): 271.

13. Joseph A. Craig and Robert L. Hacker, *The History and Development of the Fisheries of the Columbia River,* Bulletin of the Bureau of Fisheries 32 (Washington: Government Printing Office, 1940), 166–67; Irene Martin, *Legacy and Testament: The Story of Columbia River Gillnetters* (Pullman: Washington State University Press, 1994), 70; *Oregonian,* 8 July 1879, 1; 23 May 1895, 5; Smith, *Salmon Fishers,* 28–30, 53–54; Friday, *Organizing Asian American Labor,* 45–46, 68; J. J. Reynolds to Hugh M. Smith, 12 Apr. 1915, box 3, Correspondence of U.S. Fish Commissioner Hugh Smith, 1913–22, RG 22, NA.

14. Martin, *Legacy and Testament,* 89–93, 94.

15. Ibid., 73, 83–99; Taylor, "For the Love of It," 25–30; Paul George Hummasti, *Finnish Radicals in Astoria, Oregon, 1904–1940: A Study in Immigrant Socialism* (New York: Arno Press, 1979).

16. Charlene J. Allison, Sue-Ellen Jacobs, and Mary A. Porter, eds., *Winds of Change: Women in Northwest Commercial Fishing* (Seattle: University of Washington

Press, 1989); Ray Fadich, *Last of the Rivermen* (Entiat: Riba Publishing, 1993); Lawrence D. Jackson, "Reminiscence: Lawrence D. Jackson on Sand Island Fishing," *Oregon Historical Quarterly* 89 (spring 1988): 30–69; Lawrence Johnson, producer, *Work Is Our Joy: The Story of the Columbia River Gillnetter,* videorecording (Corvallis: Oregon State University, 1989); Martin, *Legacy and Testament;* Richard White, *The Organic Machine: The Remaking of the Columbia River* (New York: Hill and Wang, 1995), 40–46.

17. Martin, *Legacy and Testament,* 70–71, 89–90; Smith, *Salmon Fishers,* 91–93; *Oregonian,* 27 June 1874, 3; Evermann and Meek, "Report upon Salmon Investigations," 51.

18. Karen Johnson, *A History of Coho Fisheries and Management in Oregon through 1982,* Information Reports 84–12 (Corvallis: Oregon Department of Fish and Wildlife Research Section, 1983), 11; Smith, *Salmon Fishers,* 30–32; Jones, "Salmon Fisheries," 48; I. J. Donaldson and F. K. Cramer, *Fishwheels of the Columbia* (Portland: Binfords and Mort, 1971), 7–8.

19. Jones, "Salmon Fisheries," 3, 6, 50; *Oregonian,* 15 Mar. 1876, 2; 21 Jan. 1887, 3. The rivalry had existed since at least 1877, when the Portland Board of Trade proposed eliminating traps to prevent overfishing; *Oregonian,* 20 Oct. 1877, 5; 11 Mar. 1886, 4; A. Sutton to Spencer F. Baird, 30 Sept. 1886, box 109, no. 78807, Letters Received, 1882–1900, RG 22, NA.

20. Baird to A. Sutton, 16 Oct. 1886, vol. 200, pp. 158–60, RU 33, SIA; Jones, "Salmon Fisheries." In 1882 the *Morning Oregonian* tried to blame gillnets for causing the shoaling, but the charge did not stick; *Oregonian,* 27 June 1882, 2; 25 Nov. 1886, 3; 13 Dec. 1886, 2; 24 Jan. 1887, 4; Smith, *Salmon Fishers,* 30, 91–93.

21. *Oregonian,* 10 Dec. 1886, 1; 23 Dec. 1886, 3; 30 Dec. 1886, 4; 10 Jan. 1887, 4, 8. Gillnetters were equally cavalier about the murder of a poundnet owner by gillnetters; *Oregonian,* 30 Dec. 1883, 3.

22. A. Sutton to Baird, 30 Sept. 1886, box 109, no. 78807; H. S. McGowan to Baird, 7 Dec. 1886, box 114, no. 81443; McGowan to Baird, 2 Jan. 1887, box 114, no. 81443, Letters Received, 1882–1900, RG 22, NA; *Oregonian,* 25 Nov. 1886, 3; 10 Dec. 1886, 1; 13 Dec. 1886, 2; 23 Dec. 1886, 3; 25 Dec. 1886, 2; 30 Dec. 1886, 4; 10 Jan. 1887, 8.

23. David Starr Jordan, "Salmon and Trout of the Pacific Coast," in *Thirteenth Biennial Report of the State Board of Fish Commissioners of the State of California* (Sacramento: California State Printer, 1894), 128. G. W. Williams, who was cited as an expert in the army engineer's report, spoke of "little samlets" and claimed there were twelve species of salmon in the Columbia; another writer insisted that salmon were eighteen inches long by the time they entered the ocean; Jones, "Salmon Fisheries," 18–21; *Oregonian,* 12 Jan. 1887, 3; 2 Jan. 1887, 4.

24. Jones, "Salmon Fisheries," 7; Oregon Legislature, *Report of Special Com-*

mittee to Examine into and Investigate the Fishing Industry of this State (Salem: State Printer, 1893), 4; *Oregonian,* 18 Jan. 1887, 1; 20 Jan. 1887, 2; 21 Jan. 1887, 3; 8 Dec. 1887, 6.

25. Jones, "Salmon Fisheries," 50–51.

26. Ibid., 17, 58.

27. *AROFC* (1889): 4; Smith, *Salmon Fishers,* 83–85.

28. *Oregonian,* 9 Apr. 1880, 3; 13 Apr. 1880, 5; 19 Apr. 1880, 3; 22 Apr. 1880, 1; 23 Apr. 1880, 1; 22 Nov. 1886, 1; 28 Nov. 1886, 2; 23 May 1895, 5; "A Salmon Caught in the Sacramento River," 1894–95, box 1, Correspondence concerning Fishery Expeditions, Experiments, and Research, 1885–1908, RG 22, NA; Seufert Bros. to Everding and Farrell, 21 Dec. 1892, 21 Jan. 1893, 14 Apr. 1893, EFP.

29. Johnston McCormac to McDonald, 15 Dec. 1893, box 212, no. 6952, Letters Received, 1882–1900, RG 22, NA.

30. *Oregonian,* 20 Oct. 1892, 8; Johnston McCormac to McDonald, 15 Dec. 1893, box 212, no. 6952; E. C. Holden to John H. Mitchell, 23 June 1894, box 224, no. 113; C. F. Lester to McDonald, 6 Sept. 1894, box 227, no. 2969; George T. Myers to McDonald, 10 Sept. 1894, box 227, no. 3109; Sofus Jensen to T. H. Bean, 6 Nov. 1894, box 230, no. 5722; M. J. Kinney to H. Smith, 16 Mar. 1896, box 253, no. 9855; Charles C. Rosenberg to William McKinley, 8 Mar. 1897, box 275, no. 13981, Letters Received, 1882–1900, RG 22, NA. For closing hatchery streams see J. Q. A. Bowlby to Commissioner, 11 Dec. 1895, box 249, no. 6525; E. C. Holden to John H. Mitchell, 29 May 1896, box 258, no. 14150; John H. Mitchell to Hoke Smith, 19 June 1896, box 258, no. 14149; Hoke Smith to Commissioner, 26 June 1896, box 258, no. 14148, Letters Received, 1882–1900, RG 22, NA; George E. Perkins to John J. Brice, 17 Dec. 1896, box 8, Records concerning Fish Culture Stations, 1875–1929, RG 22, NA.

31. Donaldson and Cramer, *Fishwheels of the Columbia,* 109; I. H. Taffe to McDonald, 30 July 1892, box 189, no. 801, Letters Received, 1882–1900, RG 22, NA; McDonald to Taffe, 11 Aug. 1892, vol. 322, p. 141, Press Copies of Letters Sent, 1871–1906, RG 22, NA.

32. Taffe to McDonald, 8 Oct. 1893, box 209, no. 4111, Letters Received, 1882–1900, RG 22, NA; *Oregonian,* 27 June 1895, 7.

33. Frank M. Warren to Assistant Commissioner, 21 Jan. 1895, box 234, no. 8835; Taffe to McDonald, 10 Mar. 1895, box 237, no. 11057; D. C. Ireland to Taffe, 7 Mar. 1895, box 237, no. 11057, Letters Received, 1882–1900, RG 22, NA.

34. H. M. Smith, "Memorandum to Professor Evermann," 24 Apr. 1894, vol. 412, pp. 60–61, Press Copies of Letters Sent, 1871–1906, RG 22, NA; Richard Rathbun to Acting Commissioner, 4 Apr. 1895, box 237, no. 11057, Letters Received, 1882–1900, RG 22, NA; Marshall McDonald, "The Salmon Fisheries of the

Columbia River Basin," *Bulletin* 14 (1894): 167–68; William A. Wilcox, "Notes on the Fisheries of the Pacific Coast in 1899," *ARUSCF* (1900): 503, 505, 537.

35. McDonald to Taffe, 11 Aug. 1892, vol. 322, p. 141; McDonald to Holden, 18 Oct. 1893, vol. 360, pp. 213–15; McDonald to Taffe, 27 Nov. 1893, vol. 362, pp. 410–13, Press Copies of Letters Sent, 1871–1906, RG 22, NA; McDonald, "Salmon Fisheries of the Columbia," 167–68.

36. McDonald to Taffe, 27 Nov. 1893, vol. 362, pp. 410–13, Press Copies of Letters Sent, 1871–1906, RG 22, NA.

37. Oregon, Senate Bill no. 183 (18th sess., 1895); *Journal of the Senate of the Legislative Assembly of the State of Oregon* (Salem: State Printer, 1895), 213, 214, 308; McGuire to McDonald, 27 Mar. 1895, box 237, no. 11724; A. F. Stearns to Binger Hermann, 20 Nov. 1894, box 232, no. 6728, Letters Received, 1882–1900, RG 22, NA; *Oregonian*, 27 June 1895, 4.

38. *Oregonian*, 1 Mar. 1901, 4; 5 Mar. 1901, 4; 29 Mar. 1908, 8; Ravenal to Hubbard, 14 June 1897, vol. 464, pp. 500–501, Press Copies of Letters Sent, 1871–1906, RG 22, NA; Claudius Wallich to Commissioner, 14 May 1904; J. N. Wisner to Commissioner, 1 Aug. 1904, box 4, Upper Clackamas fldr., Records concerning Abandoned Stations, 1879–1931, RG 22, NA.

39. Washington, Washington House Bill 357 (7th sess., 1901); *House Journal of the Seventh Legislature of the State of Washington* (Olympia: State Printer, 1901), 284, 393, 490–92, 493–95; *Senate Journal of the Seventh Legislature of the State of Washington* (Olympia: State Printer, 1901), 525, 549.

40. *AROFC* (1902): 88–91; *AROFC* (1904): 105; *Oregonian*, 27 June 1895, 4; 12 Sept. 1906, 8.

41. *AROFC* (1905): 9; *Pacific Fisherman* (June 1905): 19; *Oregonian*, 27 June 1895, 4; 12 Sept. 1906, 8.

42. *AROFC* (1902): 88–91.

43. *Washington v. Oregon*, 211 U.S. 127–36 (1908) and 214 U.S. 205–18 (1909); *AROFC* (1908): 138–39; *Oregonian*, 5 Oct. 1904, 4; 17 Nov. 1908, 4; *Pacific Fisherman*, Apr. 1905, 10; Dec. 1908, 17; Jackson, "Reminiscence," 30.

44. *Pacific Fisherman*, June 1905, 18–19; Dec. 1908, 17.

45. Gordon B. Dodds, *The Salmon King of Oregon: R. D. Hume and the Pacific Fisheries* (Chapel Hill: University of North Carolina Press, 1959); R. D. Hume, *A Pygmy Monopolist: The Life and Doings of R. D. Hume, Written by Himself and Dedicated to His Neighbors*, ed. G. B. Dodds (Madison: State Historical Society of Wisconsin, 1961); R. D. Hume to George M. Bowers, 17 Feb. 1900, no. 9193, box 314; Hume to Bowers, 5 Mar. 1900, box 315, no. 9819, Letters Received, 1882–1900, RG 22, NA; W. de C. Ravenal to S. W. Downing, 28 Feb. 1900, vol. 532, p. 7188; Ravenal to E. N. Carter, 2 July 1900, vol. 544, p. 682, Press Copies of Letters Sent,

1871–1906, RG 22, NA; R. D. Hume to George M. Bowers, 11 June 1900, box 26, Rogue River fldr., Records concerning Fish Culture Stations, 1875–1929, RG 22, NA.

46. R. D. Hume, *Salmon of the Pacific Coast* (San Francisco, 1893), 17–20; Arthur F. McEvoy, *The Fisherman's Problem: Ecology and Law in the California Fisheries, 1850–1980* (New York: Cambridge University Press, 1986), 73.

47. Hume, *Pygmy Monopolist*, 45–50; Dodds, *Salmon King*, 131; Patrick Spurlock, "A History of the Salmon Industry in the Pacific Northwest" (M.A. thesis, University of Oregon, 1940), 124.

48. *Oregonian*, 27 July 1877, 3; Hume, *Pygmy Monopolist*, 46–48; Dodds, *Salmon King*, 81, 107–9, 111–12; R. D. Hume to Robert McLean, 1 June 1896, vol. 84, pp. 582–91; R. D. Hume to Herbert Hume, 24 Aug. 1906, box 6, Hume Papers; "Fish and Game Commission minutes," box 1, folder 1, p. 67, ODFW Papers; George M. Bowers to R. D. Hume, 25 Aug. 1902, vol. 591, p. 1141, Press Copies of Letters Sent, 1871–1906, RG 22, NA.

49. Dodds, *Salmon King*, chap. 6.

50. Richard A. Cooley, *Politics and Conservation: The Decline of the Alaska Salmon* (New York: Harper and Row, 1963); George M. Bower to Judge Wm. S. Crowell, 19 Jan. 1900, vol. 529, p. 5798; Bowers to R. D. Hume, 29 Jan. 1900, vol. 529, p. 5945; Bowers to Hume, 2 July 1900, vol. 542, p. 33, Press Copies of Letters Sent, 1871–1906, RG 22, NA; Hume to Bowers, 17 Feb. 1900, box 314, no. 9193; Hume to Bowers, 12 Feb. 1900, box 314, no. 9057, Letters Received, 1882–1900, RG 22, NA; Hume to Bowers, 21 Mar. 1900, box 26, Rogue River fldr., Records concerning Fish Culture Stations, 1875–1929, RG 22, NA.

51. *Oregonian*, 6 Aug. 1907, 11; H. C. McAllister to R. D. Hume, 11 Sept. 1908; Henry O'Malley to R. D. Hume, 12 Sept. 1908, box 7, Hume Papers. Hume strenuously opposed exporting Rogue River eggs but had no qualms about importing eggs; Ravenal to S. W. Downing, 13 Dec. 1899, vol. 530, p. 6065, Press Copies of Letters Sent, 1871–1906, RG 22, NA; R. D. Hume to Ravenal, 4 Dec. 1899, box 312, no. 6759, Letters Received, 1882–1900, RG 22, NA; P. A. Larkin, "Management of Pacific Salmon of North America," in *A Century of Fisheries in North America*, ed. Norman G. Benson, American Fisheries Society Special Publication no. 7 (Washington: American Fisheries Society, 1970), 233.

52. R. D. Hume to Herbert Hume, 18 June 1906, box 4, Hume Papers.

53. Gordon B. Dodds, "Rogue River Monopoly," *Pacific Historical Review* 27 (Aug. 1958): 267, 271–72, 278–79; Livingston Stone to Spencer F. Baird, 17 Mar. 1879, box 6, fldr. R–S, Letters Received, 1878–81, RG 22, NA; *AROFC* (1906): 152; Dodds, *Salmon King*, 150–52.

54. W. C. Hale to R. D. Hume, 28 May 1906; J. O. Hawthorn to R. D. Hume, 29 May 1906, box 4; R. D. Hume to Herbert Hume, 20 Dec. 1907, box 7, Hume

Papers; R. D. Hume to Bowers, 26 Dec. 1907, box 26, Rogue River fldr., Records concerning Fish Culture Stations, 1875–1929, RG 22, NA.

55. Smith, *Salmon Fishers,* 31, 54; "Board Minutes of the Oregon Fish Commission," 1/1, p. 5, ODFW Papers.

56. *AROFC* (1904): 115, 132; *AROFC* (1907): 6–7.

57. *Oregonian,* 23 July 1900, 10; 29 June 1907, 12; 30 Sept. 1907, 4; 2 Jan. 1908, 15; *San Francisco Coast Seamen's Journal,* 15 Jan. 1908, 1, 2, 6, 10, 11; 1 July 1908, 2; 9 Dec. 1908, 1, 10; CRFPU, "Your Vote Is Necessary to Preserve the Salmon Industry"; H. M. Lorntsen, "Read Carefully, Act Conscientiously"; and "Shall the Salmon Industry Be Turned Over To Corporate Greed and Grab????" box 1/27, Warren Papers.

58. *Oregonian,* 24 June 1907, 4; 4 July 1907, 7; 3 Feb. 1908, 10, 15; 5 Feb. 1908, 7; 20 Feb. 1908, 6; 22 Feb. 1908, 6; 10 May 1908, 8; *AROFC* (1908): 129–33; political handbills in box 1/27, Warren Papers.

59. *Oregonian,* 4 July 1907, 8.

60. Van Dusen's problems had been simmering for years and extended to all corners of the fishery; "Fish and Game Commission minutes," 5 Jan. 1905, box 1/1, p. 100, ODFW papers; H. A. Webster to R. D. Hume, 26 July 1906, 10 Aug. 1906, 25 Jan. 1907; F. W. Benson to Hume, 30 Jan. 1907; George Chamberlain to Hume, 1 Mar. 1907; Henry L. Benson to Hume, 7 Mar. 1907, box 6; Samuel Elmore to Hume, 14 Aug. 1907, box 8, Hume Papers; I. H. Bingham to William Kyle, 2 Aug. 1906, box 3/65, Kyle Papers; *Oregonian,* 21 Jan. 1907, 6; 3 Aug. 1907, 14; W. W. Ridehalgh to Frank Benson, 16 Mar. 1908, Benson Papers. For defense of Van Dusen see "Fish and Game Commission minutes," box 1/2, p. 116, ODFW Papers; *Oregonian,* 16 Feb. 1908, 7; Alma D. Katz to Frank Benson, 7 Feb. 1907, Benson Papers. On replacing him, see J. L. Kruse to Frank Benson, 17 Feb. 1907; W. P. Andrus to Benson, 20 Feb. 1907; Van Dusen to Benson, 23 Feb. 1908; [Frank Benson] to Van Dusen, 26 Feb. 1908; "Fish Commissioner Office Change," *Portland Telegraph,* 4 Mar. 1908; John C. McCue to Benson, 7 Mar. 1908; Benson to McCue, 12 Mar. 1908; W. M. Cake to Benson, 13 Mar. 1908; Van Dusen to Benson, 17 Mar. 1908; Frank Seufert to Benson, 6 Apr. 1908; Benson to Seufert, 4 May 1908, Benson Papers; "Fish and Game Commission minutes," box 1/2, pp. 118–20, ODFW Papers; *Oregonian,* 11 Mar. 1908, 6; 26 Mar. 1908, 6; 27 Mar. 1908, 7; 31 Mar. 1908, 8. McAllister was not impartial, and he was soon vexed by the same patronage issues as his predecessors; H. C. McAllister to Frank Benson, 4 Aug. 1908, Benson Papers; *Oregonian,* 29 Mar. 1908, 8.

61. Dodds, "Rogue River Monopoly," 278–80; Dodds, *Salmon King,* 151–54; *Oregonian,* 18 Dec. 1907, 8.

62. "Defense of Poundnet Fishermen," box 1/27, Warren Papers; *Oregonian,* 28 May 1908, 4; 31 May 1908, 11.

63. *Oregonian,* 31 May 1908, sec. 2, 11, 12; 1 June 1908, 6; "Your Vote Is Necessary to Pressure the Salmon Industry," box 1/27, Warren Papers. Jordan hastily disassociated himself from both sides; *Oregonian,* 28 May 1908, 8; 29 May 1908, 10; *Pacific Fisherman* 7 (Apr. 1909): 26. For the campaign see *Oregonian,* 16 Jan. 1908, 7; 17 Jan. 1908, 10; 25 Jan. 1908, 10; 27 Jan. 1908, 4; 22 Feb. 1908, 6; 1 Mar. 1908, Magazine Section, 9; 9 Mar. 1908, 4; 21 May 1908, 16; 23 May 1908, 4; 25 May 1908, 3; 30 May 1908, 3; 31 May 1908, sec. 4, 11.

64. *Oregonian,* 25 Feb. 1908, 8; 1 Mar. 1908, Magazine Section, 9; 9 Mar. 1908, 6; 22 May 1908, 8; 29 May 1908, 10; 30 May 1908, 8. For newspaper commentary see *Oregonian,* 14 May 1908, 8; 25 May 1908, 8; 30 May 1908, 3; 31 May 1908, 9; 1 June 1908, 4; 4 June 1908, 1.

65. *Oregonian,* 25 Feb. 1908, 8; 13 May 1908, 17; "County voter abstracts for the Special election of June 1, 1908," box 3, Abstracts of Votes, Accession 70A-61/8, SSPOSA.

66. *AROFC* (1908): 130–33; *AROFC* (1909): 6.

67. *Oregonian,* 9 Oct. 1908, 18.

68. *AROFC* (1907): 30–31; *AROFC* (1908): 128–29; *Oregonian,* 21 Sept. 1907, 16; 13 Feb. 1908, 7; 2 Sept. 1908, 14; 3 Feb. 1909, 18; 8 July 1909, 11; 9 Nov. 1909, 6; 15 Nov. 1909, 9; Leonard A. Fulton, *Spawning Areas and Abundance of Chinook Salmon ("Oncorhynchus tshawytscha") in the Columbia River Basin—Past and Present,* U.S. Fish and Wildlife Service Special Scientific Report—Fisheries no. 571 (Washington: Government Printing Office, 1968), 23; Leonard A. Fulton, *Spawning Areas and Abundance of Steelhead Trout and Coho, Sockeye, and Chum Salmon—Past and Present,* Special Scientific Report—Fisheries no. 618 (Washington: Government Printing Office, 1970), 32–34.

69. *Oregonian,* 20 Mar. 1908, 10; 5 June 1908, 8; 30 June 1908, 7; 2 July 1908, 3; 7 Sept. 1908, 14; 12 Sept. 1908, 7; 13 Sept. 1908, A8; 16 Sept. 1908, 12; Miller Freeman to David Starr Jordan, 7 Feb. 1907; Freeman to Oscar Strauss, 9 Nov. 1907; Strauss to Freeman, 26 Nov. 1907; Freeman to Strauss, 12 Dec. 1907; Freeman to George M. Bowers, 18 June 1908, box 1, Correspondence with Publishers of *Pacific Fisherman,* 1903–17, RG 22, NA.

70. *Congressional Record,* 60th Cong., 2d sess., 1908, vol. 43, 26; *Oregonian,* 7 Dec. 1908, 6; Johnson, "History of Coho Fisheries and Management," 39.

71. CRFPU, "To the Members of the 27th Legislative Assembly of the State of Oregon," box 1/27, Warren Papers; *AROFC* (1909): 10–12; *Oregonian,* 25 May 1908, 8; 13 June 1908, 2; 13 Sept. 1908, A1, A8; 12 Nov. 1908, 4; 15 Dec. 1908, 8; 6 Jan. 1909, 10; 29 Jan. 1909, 10; 31 Jan. 1909, sec. 1, 6; 1 Feb. 1909, 1, 2, 3; 29 June 1909, 10; *Pacific Fisherman* 8 (1910): 17–18. For the Columbia River Compact see *Colum-*

bia River and Its Tributaries, 65th Cong., 2d sess., H.R. 360. The federal courts reinforced this agreement almost immediately by ruling against Oregon's claim of unilateral jurisdiction; *Oregonian*, 24 Feb. 1909, 3.

72. Samuel Hays, *Conservation and the Gospel of Efficiency: The Progressive Conservation Movement, 1890–1920* (Cambridge: Harvard University Press, 1959), 2; A. Hunter Dupree, *Science in the Federal Government: A History of Policies and Activities to 1940* (New York: Harper and Row, 1957), 251; *Oregonian*, 20 Jan. 1876, 4; Patricia M. Limerick, *The Legacy of Conquest: The Unbroken Past of the American West* (New York: Norton, 1987), 27 (I have paraphrased Limerick in the last sentence of my paragraph).

73. *Oregonian*, 22 Jan. 1877, 3; 14 Aug. 1877, 1; 18 Mar. 1879, 3; 31 July 1879, 1; 1 Feb. 1889, 3; 27 June 1895, 7; I. H. Taffe to Marshall McDonald, 8 Oct. 1893, box 209, no. 4111; Taffe to McDonald, 10 Mar. 1895, box 237, no. 11057, Letters Received, 1882–1900, RG 22, NA.

6 / URBAN SALMON

1. John F. Reiger, *American Sportsmen and the Origins of Conservation*, rev. ed. (Norman: University of Oklahoma Press, 1986), 21; Samuel P. Hays, *Conservation and the Gospel of Efficiency: The Progressive Conservation Movement, 1890–1920* (Cambridge: Harvard University Press, 1959); James A. Tober, *Who Owns the Wildlife? The Political Economy of Conservation in Nineteenth-Century America* (Westport: Greenwood Press, 1981); Michael McCarthy, *Hour of Trial: The Conservation Conflict in Colorado and the West, 1891–1907* (Norman: University of Oklahoma Press, 1977); Clayton Koppes, "Efficiency/Equity/Esthetics: Towards a Reinterpretation of American Conservation," *Environmental Review* 11 (summer 1987): 127–46.

2. Jonquil Bevan, ed., *Izaak Walton: "The Compleat Angler," 1653–1676* (Oxford: Clarendon Press, 1983), 1–8, 15, 27–28; Jonquil Bevan, *The Compleat Angler: The Art of Recreation* (Brighton: Harvester Press, 1988); Colleen J. Sheehy, "American Angling: The Rise of Urbanism and the Romance of the Rod and Reel," in *Hard at Play: Leisure in America, 1840–1940*, ed. Kathryn Grover (Amherst: University of Massachusetts Press, 1992), 78–92; Thomas R. Dunlap, "Sport Hunting and Conservation, 1880–1920," *Environmental Review* 12 (spring 1988): 52–53; Thomas L. Altherr, "The American Hunter-Naturalist and the Development of the Code of Sportsmanship," *Journal of Sport History* 5 (spring 1978): 7–22; Reiger, *American Sportsmen*, 25–49; Philip G. Terrie, "Urban Man Confronts the Wilderness: The Nineteenth-Century Sportsman in the Adirondacks," *Journal of Sports History* 5 (winter 1978): 7–20; *Oregonian*, 31 Aug. 1872, 3; 24 July 1874, 3; 3 July 1878, 3; 24 Nov. 1879, 1; 3 Oct. 1893, 5; "Constitution and By-Laws of the Multnomah Rod and Gun Club," 5 Jan. 1883, Associations, Institutions, etc. file, MRGC Papers.

3. Sheehy, "American Angling," 79; Terrie, "Urban Man," 8, 11, 15; Richard Slotkin, *The Fatal Environment: The Myth of the Frontier in the Age of Industrialization, 1800–1890* (New York: Atheneum, 1985); *Oregonian*, 26 Feb. 1909, 14; Barbara Schrodt, " 'Taking The Tram': Traveling to Sport and Recreation Activities on Greater Vancouver's Interurban Railway—1890s to 1920s," *Canadian Journal of History of Sport* 19 (May 1988): 52–62; Zane Grey, *Zane Grey's Adventures in Fishing*, ed. Ed Zern (New York: Harper and Brothers, 1952), 47. Private fishing reserves have grown in popularity in the American West in recent decades; *Oregonian*, 10 May 1998, E3.

4. Reiger, *American Sportsmen*, 26.

5. Altherr, "American Hunter-Naturalist," 8–9; Sheehy, "American Angling," 79, 83–85; Reiger, *American Sportsmen*, 56–72; *Oregonian*, 15 Jan. 1873, 3; 6 Feb. 1887, 7; Terrie, "Urban Man," 15; Philip G. Terrie, " 'Imperishable Freshness': Culture, Conservation, and the Adirondack Park," *Forest and Conservation History* 37 (July 1993): 132–41; Karl Jacoby, "Class and Environmental History: Lessons from 'The War in the Adirondacks,' " *Environmental History* 2 (July 1997): 324–42; F. E. Hare, "Headwaters," *TAFS* 53 (1923): 106–9.

6. Reiger, *American Sportsmen*, 43–49; Livingston Stone, "Some Brief Reminiscences of the Early Days of Fish-Culture in the United States," *Bulletin* 17 (1897): 340; Bill Parenteau, "Creating a 'Sportsmen's Paradise': Salmon Fishing Regulation and Social Conflict in New Brunswick, 1868–1900" (paper presented at the American Society for Environmental History Conference, Mar. 1995, Las Vegas, Nev.); George Perkins Marsh, *Report Made Under Authority of the Legislature of Vermont, on the Artificial Propagation of Fish* (Burlington: Free Press, 1857), 8–9; Altherr, "American Hunter-Naturalist," 14–16; H. Wheeler Perce, "Some General Remarks on Fishing for Sport," *TAFS* 40 (1910): 397–403.

7. Samuel Wilmot, "Report on Fish Breeding in the Dominion of Canada, 1881," in *Fourteenth Annual Report of the Department of Marine and Fisheries, Being for the Fiscal Year Ended 30th June, 1881*, suppl. 2 (Ottawa: MacLean, Roger, and Co., 1882), 43; *AROFC* (1890): 21; Altherr, "American Hunter-Naturalist," 8; David Starr Jordan, "Salmon and Trout of the Pacific Coast," in *Thirteenth Biennial Report of the State Board of Fish Commissioners of the State of California* (Sacramento: State Printer, 1894), 141; Perce, "Some General Remarks"; S. L. Hulen to Commissioner, 4 Nov. 1890, box 163, no. 117392, Letters Received, 1882–1900, Entry 8, RG 22, NA. Anglers later portrayed Indians in more kindly, if equally inaccurate and self-serving, terms. By 1923 an Iowan was willing to call Indians the "true American sportsman," but since Indians had supposedly vanished into history, anglers were now the true spiritual heirs of American sportsmanship. For similar reasons Zane Grey emphasized a pseudo-Indian heritage; Hare, "Headwaters"; Grey, *Zane Grey's*

Adventures, 20, 135; Robert F. Berkhofer Jr., *The White Man's Indian: Images of the American Indian from Columbus to the Present* (New York: Alfred A. Knopf, 1978).

8. Captain Cleveland Rockwell, "The First Columbia River Salmon Ever Caught with a Fly," *Pacific Monthly* 10 (1903): 202–3; Rudyard Kipling, *American Notes* (Boston: Brown, 1899), 57–79; Grey, *Zane Grey's Adventures,* 41–57; Lisa Mighetto, "Sport Fishing on the Columbia River," *Pacific Northwest Quarterly* 87 (winter 1995–96): 6–7; Richard White, *The Organic Machine: The Remaking of the Columbia River* (New York: Hill and Wang, 1995), 32–34.

9. Kipling, *American Notes,* 58–59; Grey, *Zane Grey's Adventures,* 53, 106–8, 132–44; Rockwell, "First Columbia River Salmon."

10. Frederick Bracher, "Reminiscence: Fishing in Untroubled Waters," *Oregon Historical Quarterly* 93 (fall 1992): 295, 302; E. Marray Arenschield, "Progress Comes to Bear Valley," *Harpers Magazine* 174 (Mar. 1937): 440; Louis S. Warren, *The Hunter's Game: Poachers and Conservationists in Twentieth-Century America* (New Haven: Yale University Press, 1997).

11. Grey, *Zane Grey's Adventures,* 18–19.

12. Sheehy, "American Angling," 83–84; S. P. Bartlett, "The Decrease of Coarse Fish and Some of Its Causes," *TAFS* 41 (1911): 195–206; J. P. Snyder, "Black Bass vs. Netting Coarse Fish," *TAFS* 53 (1923): 201–6.

13. *Oregonian,* 12 Aug. 1870, 2; Clare B. Irvine to Marshall McDonald, 28 Apr. 1892, box 182, no. 131244; Irvine to J. N. Dolph, 28 Apr. 1892, box 182, no. 131268–69; F. C. Reid to Irvine, 11 June 1892, box 184, no. 132749; Irvine to McDonald, 27 Jan. 1893, box 197, no. 7406; Irvine to Dolph, 23 Apr. 1892, box 182, no. 131269–69; James Odgers to Watson B. Squire, 2 July 1894, box 224, no. 392, Letters Received, 1882–1900, RG 22, NA; *Salem Daily Statesman,* 13 Apr. 1892, 4.

14. Marsh, *Report,* 45; Baird to Stone, 5 Dec. 1872, vol. 3, pp. 364–67; Baird to Stone, 13 Apr. 1874, vol. 7, pp. 463–65, Press Copies of Letters Sent, 1871–1906, RG 22, NA; John A. Egan to Commission, 7 Aug. 1892, box 189, no. 931, Letters Received, 1882–1900, RG 22, NA; Ben Hur Lampman, *The Coming of the Pond Fishes: An Account of the Introduction of Certain Spiny-Rayed Fishes, and Other Exotic Species, into the Waters of the Lower Columbia River Region and the Pacific Coast States* (Portland: Binfords and Mort, 1946), 1, 22, 137.

15. B. F. Dowell to Dolph, 20 Aug. 1884, box 64, no. 36991; L. Seaman to McDonald, 18 Nov. 1891, box 175, no. 125952; Reed to McDonald, 9 Apr. 1892, box 182, no. 130782; J. L. Dahlin to Commission, 12 Mar. 1893, box 200, no. 9596; T. C. Farrell to Smithsonian Institute [*sic*], 29 June 1895, box 242, no. 288; letters to Bowers, May 1899, box 304, no. 11906–8, Letters Received, 1882–1900, RG 22, NA; Bowers to Captain Joseph J. Dawson, 11 Jan. 1906, vol. 683, p. 5853; Bowers to A. E. Reames, 31 May 1906, vol. 694, p. 11106, Press Copies of Letters Sent, 1871–

1906, RG 22, NA; *Oregonian,* 28 Jan. 1889, 3; 16 May 1886, 5; Hugh M. Smith, "A Review of the History and Results of the Attempts to Acclimatize Fish and Other Water Animals in the Pacific States," *Bulletin* 15 (1895): 379–472; Lampman, *Coming of Pond Fishes;* Cole M. River, "Rough Draft, Rogue River Report" (Oregon Game Commission, 1961, copy of typed MS in the reprint file, NWFSCL), 7–13; Robert Stickney, *Aquaculture in the United States: A Historical Survey* (New York: John Wiley and Sons, 1996), 39–47; "Carp Applicants from Oregon, 1882," box 1, Correspondence of U.S. Fish Commissioner Spencer F. Baird, 1872–86, RG 22, NA; S. G. Wingard to Baird, 14 Feb. 1873, vol. 10, pp. 298–99, Letters Received, 1871–74, RG 22, NA.

16. Lampman, *Coming of Pond Fishes,* 12–13, 88–89, 144; John H. Mitchell to McDonald, 15 Sept. 1890, box 160, no. 115129; G. S. Allison to Jon. L. Wilson, 22 Apr. 1892, box 182, no. 131139–40; D. L. Williams to Goode, 27 Jan. 1893, box 198, no. 7692; S. H. Greene to Commission, 11 Apr. 1893, box 201, no. 10401; Norris R. Cox to Dolph, 15 Sept. 1893, box 207, no. 2667; J. A. Richardson to McDonald, 16 July 1896, box 260, no. 919; Dave Vinyard to Commission, 3 Feb. 1899, box 299, no. 7416, Letters Received, 1882–1900, RG 22, NA; Baird to Dolph, 1 Apr. 1885, vol. 148, pp. 428–29; Smith to C. W. Fulton, 20 Jan. 1905, vol. 654, p. 6408, Press Copies of Letters Sent, 1871–1906, RG 22, NA. For public pressure see Milan Still to Commissioner, 19 July 1894, box 224, no. 703; Charles McDonald et al. to John L. Wilson, 10 Aug. 1890, box 159, no. 114690–91; E. P. Thompson to Commissioner, 1 June 1891, box 169, no. 122188; W. A Gowan to McDonald, 6 July 1894, box 224, no. 446; R. R. Parrish et al. to John H. Mitchell, 11 May 1896, box 256, no. 12444; Robert Ryan et al. to Francis Whishman, 15 May 1900, box 310, no. 13416, Letters Received, 1882–1900, RG 22, NA; *Oregonian,* 6 Nov. 1896, 8; Baird to Mitchell, 25 Feb. 1878), vol. 25, p. 129, Press Copies of Letters Sent, 1871–1906, RG 22, NA.

For rod and gun clubs see L. D. Wolford to George Turner, 8 Apr. 1897, box 273, no. 12160; F. C. Reed to George M. Bowers, 28 June 1899, box 306, no. 57; Reed to Bowers, 24 Nov. 1899, box 311, no. 6290, Letters Received, 1882–1900, RG 22, NA; McDonald to Dolph, 1 Mar. 1888, vol. 218, pp. 285–86; Smith to C. W. Fulton, 17 Oct. 1904, vol. 646, p. 3592; Smith to George L. Cleaver, 20 Mar. 1905, vol. 660, p. 9196; Bowers to A. F. Wieseman, 19 Sept. 1905, vol. 673, p. 1779, Press Copies of Letters Sent, 1871–1906, RG 22, NA; "Fish and Game Commission minutes," box 1/2, p. 62, ODFW Papers. For OFGA see A. C. Ware to Commissioner, 18 June 1897, box 277, no. 15368, Letters Received, 1882–1900, RG 22, NA; Bowers to J. N. Teal, 22 Apr. 1902, vol. 581, p. 7159; Bowers to Teal, 2 Jan. 1903, vol. 600, p. 5323; Bowers to Mitchell, 3 Jan. 1903, vol. 600, p. 5342; Bowers to Joseph Simon, 9 Jan. 1903, vol. 600, p. 5458; J. M. Smith to Thomas H. Tongue, 3 Jan. 1903, vol. 600, p. 5341; Bowers to H. G. Van Dusen, 20 Jan. 1903, vol. 602, p. 6061;

Bowers to A. E. Gebhardt, 20 Mar. 1903, vol. 606, p. 7832; Bowers to Gebhardt, 3 Apr. 1903, vol. 606, p. 8181; Bowers to Teal, 25 Apr. 1903, vol. 609, p. 9616; and Bowers to Superintendent, 10 Apr. 1905, vol. 659, p. 9064, Press Copies of Letters Sent, 1871–1906, R G 22, N A.

17. J. N. Dolph to G. Brown Goode, 9 Feb. 1888, box 128, no. 89257; F. C. Reed to McDonald, 26 May 1890, box 157, no. 113300; P. E. Peterson to Fish Commission, 10 Aug. 1891, box 171, no. 123639; B. H. Bowman to F. H. Page, 22 Jan. 1892, box 178, no. 128368; George Weikel to Commission, 15 Aug. 1893, box 206, no. 1408; Benjamin Hayden to Binger Hermann, 22 Oct. 1893, no. 5037, box 210; F. M. Warren Jr. to Hugh M. Smith, 24 Feb. 1900, box 314, no. 9467; Warren to W. de C. Ravenal, 6 Mar. 1900, box 315, no. 9794; Warren to Bowers, 16 Apr. 1900, box 317, no. 11686, Letters Received, 1882–1900, R G 22, N A.

18. Dahlin to Commission, 12 Mar. 1893, box 200, no. 9596; K. O. Walders to Watson Squire, 24 Jan. 1895, box 251, no. 8191; McGuire to Brice, 25 July 1896, box 260, no. 1218; John B. Sloan to Squire, 25 Jan. 1896, box 251, no. 8192; McGuire to Brice, 2 Mar. 1897, box 271, no. 10606; Reed to Bowers, 28 June 1899, box 306, no. 57, Letters Received, 1882–1900, R G 22, N A; Bowers to Miller T. Freeman, 6 Jan. 1906, box 1, Correspondence with Publishers of *Pacific Fisherman*, 1903–17, R G 22, N A; Baird to Dolph, 17 Nov. 1884, vol. 138, p. 414; Baird to Binger Hermann, 29 Jan. 1886, vol. 181, p. 331; McDonald to Mitchell, 6 Mar. 1888, vol. 218, pp. 391–92; McDonald to Mitchell, 25 Apr. 1888, vol. 222, pp. 268–69; Brice to McGuire, 10 Mar. 1897, vol. 459, pp. 327–28; Ravenal to E. N. Carter, 8 May 1901, vol. 561, p. 9020; Bowers to State Board of Fish Commissioners, 5 June 1901, vol. 562, p. 9542; Bowers to T. R. Kershaw, 4 Apr. 1902, vol. 580, p. 6791; Bowers to T. T. Gear, 13 Nov. 1902, vol. 596, p. 2546; Bowers to S. E. Thayer, 15 Feb. 1906, vol. 685, p. 6785, Press Copies of Letters Sent, 1871–1906, R G 22, N A; J. J. Brice, "Establishment of Stations for the Propagation of Salmon on the Pacific Coast," *A R U S C F* (1892): 388.

19. *Oregonian,* 2 Apr. 1893, 20; 15 Apr. 1909, 9; Lampman, *Coming of Pond Fish,* 101–4; Irvine to Dolph, 28 Apr. 1892, box 182, no. 131268; S. H. Greene to Commission, 11 Apr. 1893, box 201, no. 10401; Greene to Herbert A. Gill, 26 Apr. 1893, box 202, no. 10929; James McCann to McDonald, 22 Nov. 1894, box 231, no. 6471; Irvine to McDonald, 6 Apr. 1895, box 238, no. 12228; Scott Morris to Binger Hermann, 21 Feb. 1896, box 252, no. 9122; Hermann to Commissioner, 3 Mar. 1896, box 252, no. 9123; Morris and H. H. Lawton to Commissioner, 4 Sept. 1896, box 263, no. 3516; Morris to Thomas Tongue, 31 Jan. 1898, box 286, no. 7902, Letters Received, 1882–1900, R G 22, N A; Ravenal to Morris, 12 Sept. 1896, vol. 447, p. 413, Press Copies of Letters Sent, 1871–1906, R G 22, N A.

20. McDonald to Charles McDougall, 19 Aug. 1890, vol. 278, pp. 40–41; McDonald to T. C. Little and A. H. Fisher, 25 May 1892, vol. 317, pp. 408–9; McDonald to Wallace Baldwin, 25 May 1892, vol. 317, pp. 270–71; McDonald to

Irvine, 9 July 1892, vol. 320, pp. 371–72; Tarleton Bean to F. M. Caldwell, 20 Apr. 1894, vol. 374, pp. 173–74; Bowers to W. F. Sheard, 3 Apr. 1902, vol. 580, p. 6740; Bowers to T. R. Kershaw, 8 Dec. 1902, vol. 598, p. 4493; Bowers to Kershaw, 11 Sept. 1905, vol. 673, p. 1580, Press Copies of Letters Sent, 1871–1906, RG 22, NA; D. C. Corbin to Wilson, 8 Aug. 1890, box 159, no. 114477; Milan Still to Commissioner, 19 July 1894, box 224, no. 703; Still to Commission, 29 July 1894, box 225, no. 1119; Thomas Riggs Jr. to Ravenal, c. Oct. 1895, box 246, no. 4235; Still et al. to Commission, c. Nov. 1895, box 248, no. 5869, Letters Received, 1882–1900, RG 22, NA; "Board Minutes of the Oregon Fish Commission," box 1/1, pp. 54–55, ODFW Papers.

21. McDonald to F. W. Hilgert, 14 Feb. 1891, vol. 290, pp. 22–23; McDonald to John M. Phy, 8 June 1891, vol. 296, p. 260; S. G. Worth to D. L. Williams, 9 Feb. 1893, vol. 334, p. 369; Worth to Norris R. Cox, 29 Sept. 1893, vol. 358, p. 148; Ravenal to G. A. Douglas, 19 Oct. 1895, vol. 423, p. 266; Ravenal to J. N. T. Goss, 30 Jan. 1896, vol. 430, p. 25; Smith to John G. Peters, 12 Oct. 1905, vol. 674, p. 2299, Press Copies of Letters Sent, 1871–1906, RG 22, NA.

22. Lampman, *Coming of Pond Fishes*, 71, 74–75, 82, 88, 91–92, 94, 96, 97, 102, 130, 140; *Oregonian*, 3 May 1893, 3; E. P. Thompson to Commissioner, 1 June 1891, box 169, no. 122188, Letters Received, 1882–1900, RG 22, NA; McDonald to Thompson, 16 Apr. 1891, vol. 292, pp. 254–55; Tarleton H. Bean to Binger Hermann, 15 Dec. 1892, vol. 331, p. 4721; McDonald to Greene, 10 May 1893, vol. 340, pp. 126–27, Press Copies of Letters Sent, 1871–1906, RG 22, NA. Exotic plantings have continually plagued fishery agencies up to the present; *Oregonian*, 27 Oct. 1997, E2.

23. Lampman, *Coming of Pond Fishes*, 14, 70, 117–20, 143, 146; R. D. Hume to Brice, 18 May 1899, box 26, Rogue River fldr., Records concerning Fish Culture Stations, 1875–1929, RG 22, NA; Titcomb to Superintendent, 27 Sept. 1905, vol. 675, p. 2713, Press Copies of Letters Sent, 1871–1906, RG 22, NA. Despite clear evidence of predation, the Oregon Department of Fish and Wildlife continued to plant striped bass in Coos Bay until 1997. When they terminated this program, however, anglers protested. The president of the Oregon Striped Bass Association declared, "At a time when we have trouble with all our other fisheries, I think it's unconscionable [that ODFW is stopping the plantings]"; *Oregonian*, 12 Nov. 1997, E2.

24. Lampman, *Coming of Pond Fishes*, 124, 160; Francis P. Griffiths, "Considerations of the Introduction and Distribution of Exotic Fishes in Oregon," *TAFS* 69 (1939): 240–43; White, *Organic Machine*, 90.

25. Stanley Jewett, introduction to Lampman, *Coming of Pond Fish*, ix, 56–57, 100–101, 120, 164, 167.

26. *Oregonian*, 31 Jan. 1909, A8; Commissioner to Editor of *Pacific Fisherman*, 21 May 1909, box 1, Correspondence with Publishers of *Pacific Fisherman*, 1903–17, RG 22, NA.

27. Samuel N. Dicken and Emily F. Dicken, *The Making of Oregon: A Study in Historical Geography* (Portland: Oregon Historical Society, 1979), 135–37, 158–60, 171–73.

28. F. F. Henshaw and H. J. Dean, *Surface Water Supply of Oregon, 1878–1910*, U.S. Geological Survey, Water-Supply Paper 370 (Washington: Government Printing Office, 1915), 217, 619, 631; U.S. Department of the Interior, *Columbia River Basin: Development of Water and Other Resources Present and Potential of the Columbia River Basin in Washington, Oregon, Idaho, Montana, Wyoming, Nevada, and Utah*, Project Planning Report no. 1–5.0–1 (Portland: Bureau of Reclamation—Region 1, 1946), 156, 157, 160, 164–72, 235, 277, 278, 284, 293, 334, 339–40, 349, 351, 389, 399; U. B. Gilroy, "Report on Status of Fish Protective Works on Certain Federal Irrigation Projects in the Northwest," 30 Mar. 1932, box 1, Records concerning Fishways and Fish Protection Devices on Water Development Projects, 1919–35, RG 22, NA; "Fishery Protection and the Development of Water Power and Irrigation," box 611, fldr. 826.53; John C. Page to Frank Bell, 26 Mar. 1936, box 611, fldr. 826.53, General Classified Files, 1902–65, RG 22, NA; Robert C. Wissmar, Jeanette E. Smith, Bruce A. McIntosh, Hiram W. Li, Gordon H. Reeves, and James R. Sedell, "A History of Resource Use and Disturbance in Riverine Basins of Eastern Oregon and Washington (Early 1800s–1990s)," *Northwest Science* 68 (Special Issue 1994): 26; James W. Mullan, "Determinants of Sockeye Salmon Abundance in the Columbia River, 1880's–1982: A Review and Synthesis," *Biological Report* 86 (Sept. 1986): 3; NWPPC, "Compilation of Information on Salmon and Steelhead Losses in the Columbia River Basin" (Portland: Northwest Power Planning Council, 1985), 100; Frederick A. Davidson, "The Development of Irrigation in the Yakima River Basin and Its Effect on the Migratory Fish Populations in the River" (1965), copy on file in Grant County Public Utilities District Library, Ephrata, Wash.; *Oregonian*, 20 May 1894, 5; 24 Oct. 1909, sec. 2, 12; Bowers to Superintendent, 30 Mar. 1905, vol. 660, p. 9429; Bowers to P. M. Hall-Lewis, 5 Sept. 1905, vol. 673, p. 1481, Press Copies of Letters Sent, 1871–1906, RG 22, NA; Donald L. McKernan, Donald R. Johnson, and John I. Hodges, "Some Factors Influencing the Trends of Salmon Populations in Oregon," *Transactions of the Fifteenth North American Wildlife Conference* 15 (1950): 433; Lyman Griswold, "Ariel Dam on the Lewis River," *Civil Engineering* 1 (Sept. 1931): 1115–17.

29. Robert E. Ficken, *Rufus Woods, the Columbia River, and the Building of Modern Washington* (Pullman: Washington State University Press, 1995); Paul C. Pitzer, *Grand Coulee: Harnessing a Dream* (Pullman: Washington State University Press, 1994), 9–59; Keith C. Petersen, *River of Life, Channel of Death: Fish and Dams on the Lower Snake* (Lewiston: Confluence Press, 1995), 73–148; Lisa Mighetto and Wesley J. Ebel, *Saving the Salmon: A History of the U.S. Army Corps of Engineers' Efforts to Protect Anadromous Fish on the Columbia and Snake Rivers*

(Seattle: Historical Research Associates, 1994), 60; William G. Robbins, *Landscapes of Promise: The Oregon Story, 1800–1940* (Seattle: University of Washington Press, 1997), 188–200; *Oregonian*, 1 Jan. 1934, sec. 3.

30. John D. Wilson to H. G. Van Dusen, 5 July 1907 and 29 July 1907, box 8, Hume Papers; Charles R. Pollock and S. F. Rathbun to J. R. Russell, 11 Feb. 1931, box 1, Records concerning Fishways and Fish Protection Devices on Water Development Projects, 1919–35, R G 22, N A; "Hearing Before the Bureau of Fisheries on Ways and Means of Providing Adequate Fishways over the Clearwater Dam," 12 Apr. 1938, box 710, fldr. 876.1; Daniel C. Roper to Secretary of Interior, 25 Nov. 1938, box 713, fldr. 876.8; F. A. Davidson to Acting Commissioner, 9 Apr. 1940, box 605, fldr. 826.1, General Classified Files, 1902–65, R G 22, N A; Interior Department, *Columbia River Basin*, 85–86, 99, 110, 151, 157, 169, 197, 251, 284, 334, 339–40, 350, 396–97; River, "Rough Draft," 20–21; Mullan, "Determinants," 41; Kenneth Thompson, "Columbia Basin Fisheries Past, Present and Future," in *Investigative Reports of Columbia River Fisheries Project* (Portland: Pacific Northwest Regional Commission, 1976), A36–37.

For poor enforcement of fishway requirements, see Steven L. Johnson, *Freshwater Environmental Problems and Coho Production in Oregon*, Information Reports 84–11 (Corvallis: Oregon Department of Fish and Wildlife, Fish Division, 1984), 14, 16; Williams, Wood, and Linthicum to R. D. Hume, 24 June 1902, box 3; John D. Wilson to Van Dusen, 5 July 1907 and 29 July 1907, box 8, Hume Papers; Van Dusen to Frank Benson, 9 Mar. 1907; Benson to Van Dusen, 9 Mar 1907; J. L. Kendall to Benson, 20 Mar. 1907, Benson Papers; *Oregonian*, 23 May 1914, 7; *A R O F C* (1932): 15; Howard L. Raymond, "Effects of Hydroelectric Development and Fisheries Enhancement on Spring and Summer Chinook Salmon and Steelhead in the Columbia River Basin," *N A J F M* 8 (winter 1988): 7; Ralph Cowgill, "A Report concerning the Sport vs. Commercial Fishing on the Rogue, with Pertinent Information on Phases of Fish Conservation throughout the River" (Oregon Game Commission, 1927–28, copy of typed MS in the reprint file, N W F S C L), 88; Wesley Arden Dick, "When Dams Weren't Damned: The Public Power Crusade and Vision of the Good Life in the Pacific Northwest in the 1930s," *Environmental Review* 13 (fall/winter 1989): 113–53; Alvin Anderson, "Shall We Have Salmon, Dams, or Both?" *Transactions of the Fifteenth North American Wildlife Conference* 15 (1950): 451; Carl L. Hubbs, H. L. Shantz, J. N. Darling, A. H. Wiebe, Elmer Higgins, Kenneth A. Reid, Frank B. Wire, James R. Simon, and A. D. Aldrich, "The Place of Fish Production in a Program of Multiple Water Use," *T A F S* 71 (1941): 309.

31. J. S. Diller, *Mineral Resources of Southwestern Oregon*, U.S. Geological Survey Bulletin 546 (Washington: Government Printing Office, 1914), 30–34, 81–88, 102–14; Henry Baldwin Ward, *Placer Mining on the Rogue River, Oregon, in Its*

Relation to the Fish and Fishing in That Stream (Portland: Oregon Department of Geology and Mineral Industries, 1938), 16; Howard C. Brooks and Len Ramp, *Gold and Silver in Oregon,* Oregon Department of Geology and Mineral Industries Bulletin 61 (Portland: Department of Geology and Mineral Industries, 1968), 45, 168–69; Randall Rohe, "The Geographical Impact of Placer Mining in the American West, 1848–1974" (Ph.D. diss., University of Colorado, 1978), 161, 164, 170, 269; Wissmar et al., "History of Resource Use," 17; Bruce A. McIntosh, James R. Sedell, Jeanette E. Smith, Robert C. Wissmar, Sharon E. Clarke, Gordon H. Reeves, and Lisa A. Brown, "Historical Changes in Fish Habitat for Select River Basins of Eastern Oregon and Washington," *Northwest Science* 68 (Special Issue 1994): 43–44; Nancy Langston, *Forest Dreams, Forest Nightmares: The Paradox of Old Growth in the Inland West* (Seattle: University of Washington Press, 1995), 70; Interior Department, *Columbia River Basin,* 134, 197; C. N. Schuette, *Quicksilver in Oregon,* Oregon Department of Geology and Mineral Industries Bulletin 4 (Portland: State Printer, 1938), 83–84, 170; Francis G. Wells and Aaron C. Waters, *Quicksilver Deposits of Southwestern Oregon,* U.S. Geological Survey Bulletin 850 (Washington: Government Printing Office, 1934), 3, 28–29; NWPPC, "Compilation," 133, 135.

32. Cowgill, "Report concerning the Sport vs. Commercial Fishing," 75–78; M. M. Ellis, "Measuring Pollution in Fresh Water Streams," *TAFS* 65 (1935): 240–45; "Ward, Henry Baldwin," in *Dictionary of American Biography,* suppl. 3 (New York: Scribners, 1941–45), 802–3; "Ward, Henry Baldwin," *The National Cyclopedia of American Biography,* vol. 35 (New York: J. T. White, 1949), 174–75; Hugh Hawkins, "Transatlantic Discipleship: Two American Biologists and Their German Mentor," *Isis* 71 (June 1980): 197–210; Ward, *Placer Mining on the Rogue River,* 13.

33. Ward, *Placer Mining on the Rogue River,* 7, 9–10, 19; Osgood R. Smith, "Placer Mining Silt and Its Relation to Salmon and Trout on the Pacific Coast," *TAFS* 69 (1939): 225–30; Johnson, *Freshwater,* 11.

34. For irrigation see Carlos A. Schwantes, *The Pacific Northwest: An Interpretive History* (Lincoln: University of Nebraska Press, 1989), 203–6; NWPPC, "Compilation," 145–46, 150–61; Henshaw and Dean, *Surface Water Supply,* 147–49, 2–3, 217, 276, 280–84, 641, 646; Interior Department, *Columbia River Basin,* 133–34; Cole M. River, "Third Progress Report of Fishery Investigation of the Rogue River and Its Tributaries" (copy of typed MS in the reprint file, NWFSCL), 27–28; Wissmar et al., "History of Resource Use," 8–9; Johnson, *Freshwater,* 16, 26; "Columbia River Salmon Situation," *San Francisco Trade Journal,* p. 5, news clipping file, Warren Papers; John N. Cobb, "Protecting Migrating Pacific Salmon," *TAFS* 52 (1922): 146–52; E. E. Prince, "Irrigation Canals as an Aid to Fisheries Development in the West," *TAFS* 52 (1922): 157–65; S. F. Rathbun, Charles R. Pollock, and Charles R. Maybury to Charles J. Bartholet, 21 Jan. 1931; B. E. Stoutemeyer to

O'Malley, 28 Jan. 1931, box 1, Records concerning Fishways and Fish Protection Devices on Water Development Projects, 1919–35, RG 22, NA; George W. Field, "Biology as the Panacea for Some National Problems," *TAFS* 62 (1932): 369–76; Ward, *Placer Mining on the Rogue River,* 9; Joseph A. Craig, "Memorandum regarding Fishing in the Columbia River above and below Bonneville Dam, 1938" (photocopy of typed MS in reprint file, NWFSCL); Charles E. Jackson to Craig, 16 Oct. 1939, box 611, fldr. 826.51; Craig to Director, 19 June 1941, box 611, fldr. 826.51; "Department of Fisheries, State of Washington, Application for P.W.A. Funds," c. 1934, and "Memorandum on Federal Emergency Administrations of Public Works Projects to the Bureau of Fisheries," 24 Nov. 1933, box 375; Joseph A. Craig to Elmer Higgins, 19 June 1941, box 611, fldr. 826.51; Edward W. Bailey to Higgins, 20 Apr. 1945, box 451, fldr. 660.1, General Classified Files, 1902–65, RG 22, NA.

For logging see Michael Williams, *Americans and Their Forests: A Historical Geography* (New York: Cambridge University Press, 1989), 309–30; Brian R. Wall, *Log Production in Washington and Oregon: An Historical Perspective,* USDA Forest Service Resource Bulletin PNW-42 (Portland: Pacific Northwest Forest and Range Experiment Station, 1972); Langston, *Forest Dreams,* 83–84; Interior Department, *Columbia River Basin,* 370; Oliver Harry Heintzelman, "The Dairy Economy of Tillamook County, Oregon" (Ph.D. diss., University of Washington, 1952), 52–54; James R. Sedell and Karen J. Luchessa, "Using the Historical Record as an Aid to Salmonid Habitat Enhancement," in *Acquisition and Utilization of Aquatic Habitat Inventory Information,* ed. Neil B. Armantrout (Portland: American Fisheries Society, Western Division, 1982), 210–23; Rollin R. Geppert, Charles W. Lorenz, and Arthur G. Larson, *Cumulative Effects of Forest Practices on the Environment: A State of Knowledge* (Olympia: Ecosystems, 1984), 155; Wissmar et al., "History of Resource Use," 15, 25; McIntosh et al., "Historical Changes," 44; Henry O. Wendler and Gene Deschamps, *Logging Dams on Coastal Washington Streams,* Fisheries Research Papers 1 (Olympia: State Printing Office, 1953), 32; Johnson, *Freshwater,* 16; *Oregonian,* 4 Jan. 1914, sec. 1, 10; 6 Oct. 1905, 6; Master Fish Warden Diary, box 1/1, pp. 15–17; "Fish and Game Commission minutes," box 1/2, p. 18, ODFW Papers; Berrian to Hume, 28 Apr. 1902, box 3, Hume Papers; Forest Supervisor to District Forester, 16 June 1909, box 3, fldr. 4, Cobb Papers; Mullan, "Determinants," 65; NWPPC, "Compilation," 123, 129; John T. Gharrett and John I. Hodges, *Salmon Fisheries of the Coastal Rivers of Oregon South of the Columbia,* Oregon Fish Commission Contribution 13 (Portland: Oregon Fish Commission, 1950), 20–21; McKernan et al., "Some Factors," 427–54; Henry W. Anderson, "Suspended Sediment Discharge as Related to Streamflow," *Transactions, American Geophysical Union* 35 (Apr. 1954): 268–81; D. W. Chapman, "Effects of Logging upon Fish Resources of the West Coast," *Journal of Forestry* 60 (Aug. 1962): 533–37.

For grazing see Wissmar et al., "History of Resource Use," 8, 11, 15, 20; Mc-

Intosh et al., "Historical Changes," 47, 49; NWPPC, "Compilation," 138; Langston, *Forest Dreams*, 206, 221, 227, 232–33, 236–37. For pollution see Cowgill, "Report concerning the Sport vs. Commercial Fishing," 69–75; Harlan B. Holmes to Higgins, 23 June 1942, and Holmes to Director, 24 June 1942, box 611, fldr. 826.5, General Classified Files, 1902–65, RG 22, NA; Interior Department, *Columbia River Basin*, 369–70; McKernan et al., "Some Factors," 435; NWPPC, "Compilation," 169; *Oregonian*, 5 Sept. 1906, 6; William G. Robbins, "The World of Columbia River Salmon: Nature, Culture, and the Great River of the West," in *The Northwest Salmon Crisis: A Documentary History*, ed. Joseph Cone and Sandy Ridlington (Corvallis: Oregon State University Press, 1996), 13.

35. *Oregonian*, 19 Dec. 1896; 4 Sept. 1901, 7; 1 Jan. 1903, 20; 1 Jan. 1906, 4; 2 July 1910, 10; 22 Jan. 1915, 8; 7 Mar. 1915, 8; 20 Apr. 1915, 1; 7 May 1915, 10; Jane Jacobs, *Cities and the Wealth of Nations: Principles of Economic Life* (New York: Random House, 1984), 45–71; Carl Abbott, "Regional and Network City: Portland and Seattle in the Twentieth Century," *Western Historical Quarterly* 23 (Aug. 1992): 293–319; Donald W. Meinig, *The Great Columbian Plain: A Historical Geography* (Seattle: University of Washington Press, 1805–1910), 270–71, 509.

36. Warren D. Smith, ed., *Physical and Economic Geography of Oregon* (Salem: Oregon State Board of Higher Education, 1940); *Oregonian*, 29 Aug. 1910, 6.

37. *Oregonian*, 2 Sept. 1904, 8.

38. Daniel L. Boxberger, *To Fish in Common: The Ethnohistory of Lummi Indian Salmon Fishing* (Lincoln: University of Nebraska Press, 1989), 90; Donald L. Parman, "Inconstant Advocacy: The Erosion of Indian Fishing Rights in the Pacific Northwest, 1933–1956," *Pacific Historical Review* 53 (May 1984): 163–89; Shannon Bentley, "Indians' Right to Fish: The Background, Impact, and Legacy of *United States v. Washington*," *American Indian Law Review* 17 (1992): 1–36; Russel L. Barsh, "Backfire from Boldt: The Judicial Transformation of Coast Salish Proprietary Fisheries into a Commons," *Western Legal History* 4 (winter–spring 1991): 96; Jeff Zucker, Day Hummel, and Bob Høgfoss, *Oregon Indians; Culture, History, and Current Affairs* (Portland: Western Imprints, 1983), 162.

39. *Oregonian*, 24 Sept. 1873, 3; 30 Jan. 1905, 6; 1 Apr. 1905, 8; White, *Organic Machine*, 93–94.

40. *Oregonian*, 26 Apr. 1909, 5; 1 May 1910, sec. 1, 2; 22 Mar. 1914, sec. 2, 6; 3 May 1914, 5; 16 Apr. 1915, 15; 19 Apr. 1915, 11; 3 May 1915, 15; H. L. Kelly to H. M. Smith, 13 Apr. 1915, box 2, Correspondence of U.S. Fish Commissioner Hugh Smith, 1913–22, RG 22, NA. Newspapers still perform these functions for anglers; *Oregonian*, 23 Jan. 1997, E7.

41. *Oregonian*, 16 May 1909, sec. 4, 4; 5 Apr. 1914, sec. 4, 6; 3 May 1914, sec. 2, 5; 10 May 1914, sec. 2, 4; 17 May 1914, sec. 2, 5; 19 Apr. 1915, 10.

42. Morris S. Isseks, "History of State Administrative Agencies in Oregon,

1843–1937," Report on Projects O.P. 65–94–823 and O.P. 165–94–6052 under Auspices of the Works Progress Administration (1939, copy of typed MS on file at Oregon State Library, Salem, Oreg.), 236. Anglers had hatched trout privately since the 1870s, but government did not participate until anglers gained political power; *Oregonian*, 22 Oct. 1877, 2; 2 Jan. 1905, 28; 17 June 1915, 11; 24 June 1915, 5; 25 June 1915, 7; George E. Chamberlain to Bureau of Fisheries, 6 Feb. 1911, box 26; Smith to Chamberlain, 8 Feb. 1911, box 26, Records concerning Fish Culture Stations, 1875–1929, RG 22, NA; *AROFC* (1913): 58–60, 107–11; *AROFC* (1917): 29–34, 36–38, 49–50.

43. Frank Seufert to Frank Benson, 6 Apr. 1908; McAllister to Frank Benson, 4 Aug. 1908, Benson Papers; *Oregonian*, 9 Jan. 1914, 16; 8 Feb. 1914, 1, 4; 9 Feb. 1914, 1, 3; 10 Feb. 1914, 5; 12 Feb. 1914, 1, 5, 8; 27 Feb. 1915, 12; 14 May 1915, 9; 27 May 1915, 1, 3; 25 June 1915, 7.

44. *Oregonian*, 15 Mar. 1919, 12; 20 Mar. 1919, 7; 1 Apr. 1919, 14; 4 Apr. 1919, 17; 19 Apr. 1919, 15; 14 May 1919, 15; 21 May 1919, 4; 7 June 1919, 1, 7.

45. *Oregonian*, 21 Dec. 1919, sec. 1, 22; 17 Jan. 1920, 1.

46. *AROFC* (1921): 3–4.

47. David Starr Jordan, "Salmon and Trout of the Pacific Coast," *Thirteenth Biennial Report of the State Board of Fish Commissioners of the State of California* (Sacramento: California State Printer, 1894), 128, 139; Tarleton Bean to Hubbard, 5 Aug. 1892, vol. 325, p. 125, Press Copies of Letters Sent, 1871–1906, RG 22, NA; "Taxonomic Changes in North American Trout Names," *TAFS* 117 (July 1988): 321; Gerald R. Smith and Ralph F. Stearley, "The Classification and Scientific Names of Rainbow and Cutthroat Trouts," *Fisheries* 14 (Jan.–Feb. 1989): 4–10.

48. Phillip Drucker, "Athapascan notes," vol. 3, pp. 2–4, and "Clackamas Notes," vol. 6, MS 4516 (78), BECMNAA; *Oregonian*, 12 Jan. 1887, 3; 14 Jan. 1887, 3; 28 Nov. 1897, 10; 14 Aug. 1904, 7; 5 Jan. 1906, 6; 2 Jan. 1908, 15; Smith to M. J. Kinney, 2 Jan. 1895, vol. 413, p. 218, Press Copies of Letters Sent, 1871–1906, RG 22, NA; McGuire to Brice, 16 Dec. 1897, box 285, no. 6415, Letters Received, 1882–1900, RG 22, NA; W. A. Jones, "The Salmon Fisheries of the Columbia River," S. Exec. Doc. 123 (50–1) 2510:21; Grey, *Zane Grey's Adventures*, 22, 111, 132; Jordan, "Salmon and Trout," 129.

49. Craig, "Memorandum regarding Fishing," 3; Gharrett and Hodges, *Salmon Fisheries of Coastal Rivers*, 17; Karen Johnson, *A History of Coho Fisheries and Management in Oregon through 1982*, Information Reports 84–12 (Corvallis: Oregon Department of Fish and Wildlife Research Section, 1983), 60; Courtland L. Smith, *Fish or Cut Bait* (Corvallis: Oregon State University Sea Grant College Program, 1977), 17; Boxberger, *To Fish in Common*, 96; *Portland Oregon Voter*, 9 Mar. 1935, 17–18; 16 Mar. 1935, 16. During the summer of 1997, Oregon reversed a long-

standing policy to allow Indian fishers to retail Columbia River steelhead, which anglers immediately criticized based on arguments strikingly similar to those used seventy-five years earlier; *Oregonian,* 8 Aug. 1997, C1, C7; 26 Aug. 1997, B8; 13 Sept. 1997; 15 Sept. 1997.

50. For McDonald see McDonald to Hubbard, 31 May 1892, vol. 318, p. 6, Press Copies of Letters Sent, 1871–1906, RG 22, NA. For demand by eastern anglers see, e.g., Ravenal to Hubbard, 22 Jan. 1899, vol. 503, p. 292, Press Copies of Letters Sent, 1871–1906, RG 22, NA. For almost as important as chinook, see Ravenal to S. W. Downing, 14 Mar. 1900, vol. 534, p. 7821, Press Copies of Letters Sent, 1871–1906, RG 22, NA. For the $50 paid to a property owner, see Titcomb to Superintendent, 8 Apr. 1905, vol. 659, p. 9026, Press Copies of Letters Sent, 1871–1906, RG 22, NA; John N. Cobb, *The Salmon Fisheries of the Pacific Coast,* Bureau of Fisheries Document 751 (Washington: Government Printing Office, 1910), 165. For private propagating efforts, see Albion Gile, "Notes on Columbia River Salmon," *Oregon Historical Quarterly* 56 (June 1955): 148; *Oregonian,* 11 Sept. 1904, 6; Ravenal to E. N. Carter, 26 May 1900, vol. 540, p. 11124; Titcomb to Superintendent, 9 June 1900, vol. 614, p. 11814; Ravenal to Hubbard, 12 Apr. 1899, vol. 510, p. 57; Bowers to Carter, 29 May 1900, vol. 540, p. 11154; Bowers to Carter, 23 May 1901, vol. 561, p. 9251; Bowers to Superintendent, 20 Mar. 1903, vol. 607, p. 8701; Titcomb to Superintendent, 15 Aug. 1905, vol. 672, p. 1362; Titcomb to Superintendent, 9 Sept. 1905, vol. 675, p. 2494; Titcomb to Superintendent, 20 Sept. 1905, vol. 675, p. 2662, Press Copies of Letters Sent, 1871–1906, RG 22, NA; C. K. Cranston, "The Fish and Game Laws of Oregon," *TAFS* 42 (1912): 78; *AROFC* (1926): 42–54; *AROFC* (1927): 37.

51. Craig, "Memorandum regarding Fishing," 2–3; McKernan et al., "Some Factors," 433, 435–37, 449; Robert E. Mullen, *Oregon's Commercial Harvest of Coho Salmon, "Oncorhynchus kisutch" (Walbaum), 1892–1960,* Information Report Series, Fisheries 81–3 (Corvallis: Oregon Department of Fish and Wildlife, Fish Division, 1981); Johnson, *History of Coho,* 21, 23; Wall, *Log Production;* William Robbins, *Hard Times in Paradise: Coos Bay, Oregon, 1850–1986* (Seattle: University of Washington Press, 1988); T. W. Chamberlain, R. D. Harr, and F. H. Everest, "Timber Harvesting, Silviculture, and Watershed Processes," in *Influences of Forest and Rangeland Management on Salmonid Fishes and Their Habitats,* ed. William R. Meehan, American Fisheries Society Special Publication 19 (Bethesda: American Fisheries Society, 1991), 183–84, 194; Anderson, "Suspended Sediment Discharge"; Geppert et al., *Cumulative Effects of Forest Practices,* 155, 157.

52. Steven J. Diner, *A Very Different Age: Americans of the Progressive Era* (New York: Hill and Wang, 1998); Samuel P. Hays, *The Response to Industrialism, 1885–1914* (Chicago: University of Chicago Press, 1957); Arthur S. Link and Richard L. McCormick, *Progressivism* (Arlington Heights: Harlan Davidson, 1983); Robert H.

Wiebe, *The Search for Order, 1877–1920* (New York: Hill and Wang, 1967); Daniel T. Rodgers, "In Search of Progressivism," *Reviews in American History* 10 (Dec. 1982): 113–32.

53. Lloyd Sponholtz, "The Initiative and Referendum: Direct Democracy in Perspective, 1898–1920," *American Studies* 14 (fall 1973): 60; Gordon B. Dodds, *The American Northwest: A History of Oregon and Washington* (Arlington Heights: Forum, 1986), 185; Waldo Schumacher, "Thirty Years of People's Rule in Oregon: An Analysis," *Political Science Quarterly* 47 (June 1932): 242–58; George H. Haynes, " 'People's Rule' in Oregon, 1910," *Political Science Quarterly* 26 (Mar. 1911): 32–62; Gordon E. Baker, *Reapportionment Revolution: Representation, Political Power, and the Supreme Court* (New York: Random House, 1966), 35.

54. Sponholtz, "Initiative and Referendum," 58; Schumacher, "Thirty Years," 254.

55. "Abstracts of elections," SSPOSA.

56. Upriver interests had been trying to close sections of the Rogue as early as 1902; J. W. Berrian to R. D. Hume, 16 May 1902, box 3, Hume papers; *Oregonian*, 22 June 1907, 7; 3 Nov. 1910, 12; 7 Nov. 1910, 10; Gordon B. Dodds, "The Fight to Close the Rogue," *Oregon Historical Quarterly* 60 (Dec. 1959): 461–66, 470–74; Smith, *Fish or Cut Bait,* 29; Haynes, " 'People's Rule' in Oregon," 51–52.

57. *Oregonian,* 7 Apr. 1909, 18; 17 Apr. 1909, 16; 24 Apr. 1909, 11; 26 Apr. 1909, 5; 27 Apr. 1909, 11.

58. *Oregonian,* 13 Jan. 1910, sec. 4, 5; 23 Jan. 1910, sec. 3, 12; 31 Jan. 1910, 4; 1 Mar. 1910, 10; 6 Mar. 1910, 10; 13 Apr. 1910, 7; 23 Apr. 1910, 7; 24 Apr. 1910, sec. 1, 10; 25 Apr. 1910, 1, 5; 26 Apr. 1910, 10, 12; 27 Apr. 1910, 10; 1 May 1910, sec. 1, 14.

59. *Oregonian,* 3 May.1914, sec. 2, 5; 7 May 1914, 6; 18 Dec. 1914, 15; 29 Dec. 1914, 12; 19 Jan. 1915, 6; 20 Jan. 1915, 7; 14 Feb. 1915, sec. 2, 1; 17 Feb. 1915, 12; 2 May 1915; 9 May 1915, sec. 2, 16; 3 Nov. 1918, 11; 4 Nov. 1918, 6; 5 Nov. 1918, 10; 7 Nov. 1918, 18; 10 Aug. 1919, 11.

60. *Oregonian,* 3 June 1919, 15; Johnson, *History of Coho,* 11; "Initiative Petition filed with the Secretary of State, June 22, 1922," box 24, Initiative Petition Records, Accession 58–10, SSPOSA; Courtland L. Smith, *Oregon Fish Fights* (Corvallis: Oregon State University Sea Grant College Program, 1974), 3; Courtland L. Smith, *Salmon Fishers of the Columbia* (Corvallis: Oregon State University Press, 1979), 95–99.

61. Joseph E. Taylor III, "For the Love of It: A Short History of Commercial Fishing in Pacific City, Oregon," *Pacific Northwest Quarterly* 82 (Jan. 1991): 22–32; *Oregonian,* 29 June 1907, 10; Bert Webber, *Bayocean: The Oregon Town that Fell into the Sea* (Medford, Oreg.: Webb Research Group, 1989).

62. Warren S. Wooster, "Early Observations and Investigations of El Niño: The Event of 1925," in *Oceanography: The Past,* ed. Mary Sears and Daniel Merriman

(New York: Springer-Verlag, 1980), 629–41; Clara Deser and John M. Wallace, "El Niño Events and Their Relation to the Southern Oscillation: 1925–1986," *Journal of Geophysical Research* 92 (15 Dec. 1987): 14189–96; William H. Quinn and Victor T. Neal, "The Historical Record of El Niño Events," in *Climate since A.D. 1500*, ed. Raymond S. Bradley and Philip D. Jones (London: Routledge, 1992), 624; Gunnar I. Roden, "Analysis and Interpretation of Long-Term Climatic Variability along the West Coast of North America," in *Aspects of Climate Variability in the Pacific and the Western Americas*, ed. David H. Peterson, Geophysical Monograph 55 (Washington: American Geophysical Union, 1989), 106; Lawrence A. Mysak, "El Niño, Interannual Variability and Fisheries in the Northeast Pacific Ocean," *Canadian Journal of Fisheries and Aquatic Science* 43 (Feb. 1986): 465; Richard E. Thomson, Howard J. Freeland, and Laurence F. Giovando, "Long-Term Sea Surface Temperature Variations along the British Columbia Coast," *Tropical Ocean-Atmosphere Newsletter* (July 1984): 10–11; F. Heyward Bell and Alonzo T. Pruter, "Climatic Temperature Changes and Commercial Yields of Some Marine Fisheries," *Journal of the Fisheries Research Board of Canada* 15 (July 1958): 630; Kevin Hamilton, "A Study of the Variability of the Return Migration Route of Fraser River Sockeye Salmon (*Oncorhynchus nerka*)," *Canadian Journal of Zoology* 63 (Aug. 1985): 1934, 1940; John N. Cobb, *The Pacific Salmon Fisheries*, Fisheries Document 1092 (Washington: Government Printing Office, 1930), 554–55, 566; Mullen, *Oregon's Commercial Harvest*, B-47. Harvest figures after 1923 appear inflated because Oregon began a far more detailed reporting system in that year. Earlier figures normally represented only cannery consumption, but S. Elmore and Company closed its Nestucca cannery after 1919. Thus there were no official records for the years 1920–22, yet as the figures for 1923–25 demonstrate (a small cannery operated on the river in 1926), a vibrant fishery continued in the cannery's absence. Most of these fish went to the fresh-fish market in the Willamette Valley.

63. *Portland Oregon Journal*, 25 June 1927, 4; Mullen, *Oregon's Commercial Harvest*, B-47; Cobb, *Pacific Salmon Fisheries*, 554–55; Craig to Higgins, 18 Apr. 1938, box 611, file 826.51, General Classified Files, 1902–65, RG 22, NA; Gary D. Sharp, "Fishery Catch Records, El Niño/Southern Oscillation, and Longer-Term Climate Change as Inferred from Fish Remains in Marine Sediments," in *El Niño: Historical and Paleoclimatic Aspects of the Southern Oscillation*, ed. Henry F. Diaz and Vera Markgraf (New York: Cambridge University Press, 1992), 388–89; Myrl C. Hendershott, "The Role of Instruments in the Development of Physical Oceanography," in *Oceanography*, ed. Sears and Merriman, 195–203; Kern E. Kenyon, "North Pacific Sea Surface Temperature Observations: A History," in *Oceanography*, ed. Sears and Merriman, 267–79; Sir Gilbert T. Walker and E. W. Bliss, "World Weather V," *Memoirs of the Royal Meteorological Society* 4, no. 36 (1932): 53–84;

Oscar E. Sette, "The Long Term Historical Record of Meteorological, Oceano-graphic, and Biological Data," *California Marine Research Committee, California Cooperative Oceanic Fisheries Investigations Reports* 7 (1960): 192.

64. Oregon, *House and Senate Journals* (1927), 61, 369; *General Laws of Oregon, 1927,* 219–20; Tillamook County Deedbook D, 295, 298; Deedbook J, 172, 174; Probate Journal of Yamhill County, vol. 21, 546, Tillamook County Courthouse, Tillamook, Oreg.; *Garibaldi (Oreg.) News,* 17 June 1927, 2.

65. Oregon, *House and Senate Journals* (1927), 4–5, 7–8, 377, 443.

66. Ibid., 454.

67. Ibid., 3, 7, 183, 194, 196, 201, 214, 227, 615.

68. *The Oregon Voter's Pamphlet for the Special Election, Tuesday, June 28, 1927,* Oregon State Library, 52–53; *Tillamook Herald,* 31 Mar. 1927, 1; "The Nestucca Bay Fish Closing Bill," filed 27 May 1927, box 24, Initiative Petition Records, Accession 58–10, SSPOSA.

69. *Tillamook Herald,* 14 Apr. 1927, 1; 26 May 1927, 7.

70. *Oregon Voter's Pamphlet for the Special Election, June 28, 1927,* 52–53.

71. *Portland Telegram,* 27 June 1927, 12.

72. *Portland Oregon Journal,* 27 June 1927, 3; *Oregonian,* 25 June 1927, 5; *Portland News,* 20 June 1927, 1; *Roseburg News Review,* 25 June 1927, 1; *Klamath Falls Evening Herald,* 25 June 1927, 4; *Portland Telegram,* 27 June 1927, 3.

73. *Portland Oregon Journal,* 24 June 1927, 12; *McMinnville News-Reporter,* 23 June 1927, 1; *Portland Oregon Journal,* 16 June 1927, 10.

74. Taylor, "For the Love of It," 25–30.

75. The "unbridled" letter was published in three different newspapers under slightly different pseudonyms: *Portland Oregon Journal,* 25 June 1927, 4; *Oregonian,* 25 June 1927, 5; *Portland News,* 20 June 1927, 1. The Douglas County Sportsmen Association is quoted from *Roseburg News Review,* 25 June 1927, 1.

76. *Portland Oregon Voter,* 18 June 1927, 310.

77. *AROFC* (1901): 25; *AROFC* (1909): 32; *AROFC* (1926): 36–37; *Portland Oregon Voter,* 18 June 1927, 310; *Portland Telegram,* 27 June 1927, 12; *Oregonian,* 27 June 1927, 12.

78. *Portland Oregon Journal,* 18 June 1927, 4.

79. For pro-sportfishing editorials see *Portland Telegram,* 23 June 1927, 1, 15; 27 June 1927, 1, 3; *Portland News,* 20 June 1927, 1; *Salem Oregon Statesman,* 20 June 1927, 1; *McMinnville News Reporter,* 16 June 1927, 1; *Banks Herald,* 23 June 1927, 1; *Roseburg News Review,* 24 June 1927, 4; 25 June 1927, 1, 4, 6. For Robinson see *Portland Telegram,* 23 June 1927, 1, 15. For Plasec and Edmunds see *Portland Telegram,* 27 June 1927, 3, 12; *Oregonian,* 27 June 1927, 12.

80. For anticlosure editorials see *Tillamook Herald,* 23 June 1927, 8; *Garibaldi News,* 17 June 1927, 2; 24 June 1927, 1; *Sheridan Sun,* 23 June 1927, 2; *Coos Bay*

Times, 16 June 1927, 1; *Eugene Register Guard,* 23 June 1927, 4; *Portland Oregon Voter,* 25 June 1927, 28–29. An exception to this general trend was the *Marshfield Southwestern Oregon Daily News,* 27 June 1927, 4. For eastern Oregon see *Bend Bulletin,* 27 June 1927, 4; *Baker Herald,* 27 June 1927, 4; *The Dalles Weekly Chronicle,* 23 June 1927, 4.

81. *Roseburg News Review,* 24 June 1927, 4; 25 June 1927, 4, 6; *Portland Telegram,* 23 June 1927, 1, 15; *Portland Oregon Journal,* 16 June 1927, 10; 24 June 1927, 12; *Salem Capital Journal,* 22 June 1927, 6; *Salem Oregon Statesman,* 22 June 1927, 1; *Corvallis Gazette Times,* 25 June 1927, 2; *Portland News,* 25 June 1927, 2.

82. Schumacher, "Thirty Years," 254.

83. "County Voter Abstracts for the Special Election of June 28, 1927," box 3, Abstracts of Votes, Accession 70A-61/8, SSPOSA.

84. *AROFC* (1927–28): 21, 23; *AROFC* (1930): 15; Taylor, "For the Love of It," 26–29; Oregon, *General Laws of Oregon* (1931), 516; Oregon, *House and Senate Journals* (1931), 255, 257, 284, 290, 311; "Senate Bill 170" (1933), Oregon State Library, Salem; Oregon, *House and Senate Journals* (1933), 182, 183, 236; "House Bill 191" (1935), Oregon State Library, Salem; Oregon, *House and Senate Journals* (1935), 54, 365, 370, 390, 395, 398, 399, 428, 435; *Portland Oregon Voter,* 11 Mar. 1933, 17–18; 9 Mar. 1935, 17; Ole B. Redberg to Ray W. Gill, State Grange Master, 7 Feb. 1935, letter in possession of author; *Oregonian,* 7 Feb. 1935, 8.

85. Schumacher, "Thirty Years," 248; "Referendum Bill of Oregon Senate Bill no. 1 (Thirty-sixth Legislative Assembly) for the Oregon General Election of Nov. 8, 1932"; "Voter Abstracts for the Oregon General Election of Nov. 8, 1932," box 3, Abstracts of Votes, Accession 70A-61/8, SSPOSA; M. Kerlin to Arthur I. Moulton, 14 Nov. 1932; J. R. Russell to P. B. Hawley, 9 Feb. 1933; "Read the Opinions of the Foremost Authorities on the Rogue River Fishing Situation," box 1, Records concerning Fishways and Fish Protection Devices on Water Development Projects, 1919–35, RG 22, NA.

86. Mary Korbulic, "Romancing the Rogue: Zane Grey's Fickle Love Affair with the Rogue River," *Table Rock Sentinel* 12 (Nov.–Dec. 1992): 2–11; Stephen J. May, *Zane Grey: Romancing the West* (Athens: Ohio University Press, 1997), 83–86; Zane Grey, *Tales of Fresh-Water Fishing* (New York: Harper and Brothers, 1928), 108–22; Grey, *Zane Grey's Adventures in Fishing.*

87. Zane Grey, *Rogue River Feud* (New York: Curtis, 1929), 21, 45, 58.

88. Ibid., 58, 85–86.

89. Dodds, "Fight to Close the Rogue," 470–74; "Referendum Bill of Oregon Senate Bill no. 53 (Forty-first Legislative Assembly) for the Oregon General Election of Nov. 3, 1942"; "Voter Abstracts for the Oregon General Election of Nov. 3, 1942"; "Referendum Bill of Oregon House Bill no. 378 (Forty-third Legislative Assembly) for the Oregon General Election of Nov. 5, 1946"; Voter Abstracts for

the Oregon General Election of Nov. 5, 1946"; list of payments made to the Oregon Secretary of State for arguments for and against measures on the Oregon General Election ballot of 5 Nov. 1946, box 24, Initiative Petition Records, Accession 58–10, SSPOSA; Smith, *Oregon Fish Fights*; Smith, *Fish or Cut Bait*, 29; Smith, *Salmon Fishers*, 96–100.

90. Smith, *Salmon Fishers*, 96–100; Jack M. Van Hyning, *Factors Affecting the Abundance of Fall Chinook Salmon in the Columbia River*, Research Reports of the Fish Commission of Oregon 4 (Salem: Oregon Fish Commission, 1973), 38; Henry O'Malley to Hugh C. Mitchell, 18 May 1926, box 85, fldr. 55, CRPAPCRMM; Willis H. Rich, "The Present State of the Columbia River Salmon Resources," *Proceedings of the Sixth Pacific Science Congress* 3 (1939): 427; Willis H. Rich, "The Future of the Columbia River Salmon Fisheries," *Stanford Ichthyological Bulletin* 2 (Dec. 1940): 39, 45; Gharrett and Hodges, *Salmon Fisheries of Coastal Rivers*, 11–12, 19–30; McKernan et al., "Some Factors," 429–30, 448.

91. John Earnest Damron, "The Emergence of Salmon Trolling on the American Northwest Coast: A Maritime Historical Geography" (Ph.D. diss., University of Oregon, 1975), 134; Clark Patrick Spurlock, "A History of the Salmon Industry in the Pacific Northwest" (M.S. thesis, University of Oregon, 1940), 32–48; Donald H. Fry Jr. and Eldon P. Hughes, "The California Salmon Troll Fishery," *PMFCB* 2 (1951): 7–42; Jack Van Hyning, "The Ocean Salmon Troll Fishery of Oregon," *PMFCB* 2 (1951): 43–76; Donald E. Kauffman, "Research Report on the Washington State Offshore Troll Fishery," *PMFCB* 2 (1951): 77–92; Robert R. Parker and Walter Kirkness, *King Salmon and the Ocean Troll Fishery of Southeastern Alaska*, Research Report of the Alaska Department of Fisheries 1 (Juneau: Alaska Department of Fisheries, 1956); Henry O. Wendler, "The Importance of the Ocean Sport Fishery to the Ocean Catch of Salmon in the States of Washington, Oregon, and California," *California Fish and Game* 46 (1960): 291–300; D. J. Milne and H. Godfrey, *The Chinook and Coho Salmon Fisheries of British Columbia*, Bulletin 142 (Ottawa: Fisheries Research Board of Canada, 1964), 30; Kenneth A. Henry, "Ocean Distribution, Growth, and Effects of the Troll Fishery on Yield of Fall Chinook Salmon from Columbia River Hatcheries," *Bulletin* 70 (1972): 431–45; Johnson, *History of Coho*, 36, 46–47; *Oregonian*, 4 Apr. 1915, sec. 3, 12; Taylor, "For the Love of It," 25–32; Van Hyning, *Factors Affecting Salmon*, 31–32.

92. *Oregonian*, 3 Jan. 1914, 6; 2 Jan. 1914, 1; O'Malley to Mitchell, 18 May 1926, box 85, fldr. 55; Phil McDonough to N. H. Weber, 22 Jan. 1927, box 85, fldr. 55, CRPAPCRMM; "Meeting of International Pacific Salmon Investigation Federation, Executive Committee, Seattle, Washington, Dec. 2, 1926," box 4, fldr. 1 of 4, pp. 38–40; Willis H. Rich to O'Malley, 2 Apr. 1930, box 4, fldr. 3 of 4, Records concerning Societies, Councils, Conferences, and Other Groups, 1904–1937, RG 22, NA; Rich, "Present State of Columbia River Salmon," 429; Commissioner to H. O.

Preston, 12 Sept. 1928, box 1; Preston to O'Malley, 7 Sept. 1928, box 1; Salmon Packers of the Columbia to O'Malley, 8 Sept. 1927, box 10; "Transcript of the Meeting of the International Pacific Salmon Investigation Federation, Executive Committee, . . . Seattle, Washington, Nov. 24, 1925," box 10, pp. 104–5; H. G. Smith to O'Malley, 30 Sept. 1927, box 10, General Correspondence of the Division of Scientific Inquiry, 1880–1935, R G 22, N A; Washington House Bill 162 (20th sess., 1927), copy in Suzzallo Library, University of Washington, Seattle; *Oregonian*, 27 Dec. 1919, 11.

93. Van Hyning, *Factors Affecting Salmon*, 30–33; Rich, "Present State of Columbia River Salmon," 429; Frederick Charles Cleaver, "The Effects of Ocean Fishing upon the Columbia River Hatchery Stocks of Fall Chinook Salmon" (Ph.D. diss., University of Washington, 1967), 122–28, 139; James A. Crutchfield and Giulio Pontecorvo, *The Pacific Salmon Fisheries: A Study of Irrational Conservation* (Baltimore: Johns Hopkins Press, 1969).

94. Willa Nehlsen, Jack E. Williams, and James A. Lichatowich, "Pacific Salmon at the Crossroads: Stocks at Risk from California, Oregon, Idaho, and Washington," *Fisheries* 16 (Mar.–Apr. 1991): 4–21.

95. Reiger, *American Sportsmen*, 11–24; Thomas L. Altherr and John F. Reiger, "Academic Historians and Hunting: A Call for More and Better Scholarship," *Environmental History Review* 19 (fall 1995): 39–56; Tober, *Who Owns the Wildlife?* 251; Dunlap, "Sport Hunting and Conservation," 51–60; *Portland Oregon Voter*, 2 Nov. 1928, 34.

96. Donald Pisani argues that Gifford Pinchot and other conservationists did not so much revolutionize environmental policy as become "better salesmen" of existing ideas. The same can be said for anglers. They did not so much innovate as adapt. They attached a new identity to time-worn strategies, and persuaded a new polity, better than their competitors. Donald J. Pisani, *Water, Land, and Law in the West: The Limits of Public Policy, 1850–1920* (Lawrence: University Press of Kansas, 1996), 195.

7 / REMAKING SALMON

1. Stuart L. Pimm, *The Balance of Nature? Ecological Issues in the Conservation of Species and Communities* (Chicago: University of Chicago Press, 1991); Jonathon Weiner, *The Beak of the Finch* (New York: Vintage, 1994); C. Groot and L. Margolis, *Pacific Salmon Life Histories* (Vancouver: University of British Columbia Press, 1991).

2. Baron de la Valette St. George, "The Enemies of Fish," A R U S C F (1878): 509–16; George Perkins Marsh, *Report Made Under Authority of the Legislature of Vermont, on the Artificial Propagation of Fish* (Burlington: Free Press, 1857), 35,

appendix 25; Livingston Stone, "The Salmon Fisheries of the Columbia River," *ARUSCF* (1875–76): 807; Robert R. Stickney, *Aquaculture in the United States: A Historical Survey* (New York: John Wiley and Sons, 1996), 45–46.

3. Albert D. Hager to Spencer Baird, 8 Nov. 1872, fldr. 3, Letters Received, 1871–72, RG 22, NA; Livingston Stone to Baird, 5 Apr. 1880, box 13, no. 6466, Letters Received, 1882–1900, RG 22, NA; *Oregonian*, 28 Nov. 1897, 10.

4. Marshall McDonald to Waldo Hubbard, 24 Feb. 1892, vol. 310, pp. 488–91, Press Copies of Letters Sent, 1871–1906, RG 22, NA; W. A. Jones, "The Salmon Fisheries of the Columbia River," S. Exec. Doc. 123 (50–1) 25102:9; Cloudsley Rutter, "Natural History of the Quinnat Salmon: A Report of Investigations in the Sacramento River, 1896–1901," *Bulletin* 22 (1902): 65–141; *Oregonian*, 25 Dec. 1902, 7; C. K. Cranston, "The Fish and Game Laws of Oregon," *TAFS* 42 (1912): 77.

5. Hager to Baird, 8 Nov. 1872, fldr. 3, Letters Received, 1871–72, RG 22, NA; Baird to Stone, 13 Mar. 1875, vol. 11, p. 309, Press Copies of Letters Sent, 1871–1906, RG 22, NA; *Oregonian*, 16 Apr. 1888, 8; 23 July 1900, 10; 25 Dec. 1902, 7; 10 Dec. 1904, 14.

6. M. C. Edmunds, "The Introduction of Salmon into American Waters," *TAFS* 1 (1872): 32–39; Marsh, *Report*, app., 31, 42; "The Best Food For Young Salmonoids and for Larger Salmonoids in Ponds," *ARUSCF* (1877): 779–82; John J. Brice, "A Manual of Fish Culture, Based on the Methods of the United States Commission of Fish and Fisheries," *ARUSCF* (1897): 7–26; Hugh MacCrimmon, "The Beginning of Salmon Culture in Canada," *Canadian Geographical Journal* 71 (July 1965): 99; Baird to Stone, 7 May 1887, vol. 197, pp. 462–64; Acting Commissioner to Claudius Wallich, 3 Oct. 1904, vol. 646, p. 3255; J. W. Titcomb to Superintendent, 21 Feb. 1906, vol. 687, p. 7918; H. M. Smith to Superintendent, 6 Mar. 1906, vol. 687, p. 8081, Press Copies of Letters Sent, 1871–1906, RG 22, NA; M. E. O'Brien, "The Propagation of Natural Food for Fish, With Special Reference to Fish-Culture," *TAFS* 17 (1888): 29–33; Charles G. Atkins, "Salmon Breeding at Bucksport," *TAFS* 2 (1873): 30.

7. A. Nelson Cheney, "Food For Fishes," *TAFS* 21 (1892): 22–32; Frank N. Clark, "Rearing Fish for Distribution," *TAFS* 21 (1892): 78–81; James Nevin, "Planting Fry vs. Planting Fingerlings," *TAFS* 21 (1892): 81–86; Fred Mather, "Planting Trout as Fry or Yearlings," *TAFS* 21 (1892): 86–90; Herschell Whitaker, "Fry vs. Fingerlings," *TAFS* 21 (1892): 94–98; William F. Page, "Plant Yearlings Where Needed," *TAFS* 22 (1893): 71–93; John L. Leary, "Planting Fish vs. Fry," *TAFS* 36 (1907): 142; Bowers to Editor of the *Pacific Fisherman*, 3 Oct. 1907, box 1, Correspondence with Publishers of *Pacific Fisherman*, 1903–17, RG 22, NA; *Oregonian*, 2 Nov. 1890, 7; Stickney, *Aquaculture*, 112; W. de C. Ravenal to Hubbard, 12 Nov. 1897, vol. 478, p. 224; George M. Bowers to J. N. Wisner, 4 Apr. 1902, vol. 579, p.

6402; Titcomb to Superintendent, 21 Jan. 1903, vol. 603, p. 6786, Press Copies of Letters Sent, 1871–1906, RG 22, NA.

8. Fred W. Allendorf, Nils Ryman, and Fred M. Utter, "Genetics and Fishery Management," in *Population Genetics and Fishery Management*, ed. Nils Ryman and Fred Utter (Seattle: Washington Sea Grant, 1987), 14; Fred W. Allendorf and Nils Ryman, "Genetic Management of Hatchery Stocks," in *Population Genetics and Fishery Management*, 143, 151, 153; Michael L. Goodman, "Preserving the Genetic Diversity of Salmonid Stocks: A Call for Federal Regulation of Hatchery Programs," *Environmental Law* 20, no. 1 (1990): 111–66.

9. *Oregonian*, 15 Dec. 1870, 2; 5 May 1871, 1; 8 Apr. 1873, 1; 18 Feb. 1875, 1; 11 Mar. 1878, 3; Robert Deniston Hume, *A Pygmy Monopolist*, ed. Gordon B. Dodds (Madison: State Historical Society of Wisconsin, 1961), 50–53; R. D. Hume, *Salmon of the Pacific Coast* (San Francisco, 1893), 38; Gordon B. Dodds, *The Salmon King of Oregon: R. D. Hume and the Pacific Fisheries* (Chapel Hill: University of North Carolina Press, 1959), 130–57; Kirby B. Pratt, "Report of Salmon-Hatching Operations on Rogue River, Oregon, 1877–'78," *ARUSCF* (1878): 773–74.

10. Baird to Hume, vol. 35, pp. 165–67, Press Copies of Letters Sent, 1871–1906, RG 22, NA; Dodds, *Salmon King*, 135–36 n. 16; Jones, *Salmon Fisheries*, 16; *AROFC* (1888): 12–13; *AROFC* (1891): 27–31; J. W. Collins, "Report on the Fisheries of the Pacific Coast of the United States," *ARUSCF* (1888–89): 11; John N. Cobb, *The Salmon Fisheries of the Pacific Coast*, Bureau of Fisheries Document 751 (Washington: Government Printing Office, 1910), 159–60.

11. Dodds, *Salmon King*, 137–38 n. 18; Hume, *Salmon of the Pacific Coast*, 21, 30; *Oregonian*, 8 Dec. 1893, 4; Hume to Ravenal, 24 Dec. 1899, box 312, no. 7396, Letters Received, 1882–1900, RG 22, NA.

12. Hume, *Salmon of the Pacific Coast*, preface, 22–23, 48–51, 52; Hume to Bowers, 17 May 1900, box 319, no. 13332, Letters Received, 1882–1900, RG 22, NA; Titcomb to H. L. Kelly, 13 Mar. 1906, vol. 690, p. 9062, Press Copies of Letters Sent, 1871–1906, RG 22, NA; *Oregonian*, 8 Dec. 1893, 4; 21 Oct. 1894, 16.

13. Dodds, *Salmon King*, 132, 135–36, 155–57; Charles I. Finely, "Shad in Oregon Waters—A New Salmon Hatchery," *Bulletin* 4 (1884): 88; Charles I. Finely, "Further Report of R. D. Hume's Salmon Hatchery, Oregon," *Bulletin* 4 (1884): 174; *AROFC* (1892): 40–41; Cobb, *Salmon Fisheries of the Pacific Coast*, 161–64; Hume to J. J. Brice, 26 Dec. 1896, box 268, no. 7724; R. D. Hume to Bowers, 3 July 1900, box 320, no. 14948, Letters Received, 1882–1900, RG 22, NA; McDonald to Hume, 21 Nov. 1893, vol. 362, p. 258; Bowers to Hubbard, 15 Sept. 1898, vol. 494, p. 458; Ravenal to Hume, 24 June 1899, vol. 514, p. 286, Press Copies of Letters Sent, 1871–1906, RG 22, NA; *Oregonian*, 12 July 1908, 10.

14. Hume to Brice, 26 Dec. 1896, box 268, no. 7724; Hume to Bowers, 4 Apr.

1900, box 316, no. 11171; Hume to Bowers, 5 Mar. 1900, box 315, no. 9819, Letters Received, 1882–1900, R G 22, N A; Hume to Brice, 21 June 1897, box 26, Records concerning Fish Culture Stations, 1875–1929, R G 22, N A.

15. Hume to Bowers, 27 Nov. 1899, box 311, no. 6429; Hume to Ravenal, 4 Dec. 1899, box 312, no. 6759; Hume to Ravenal, 24 Dec. 1899, box 312, no. 7396; Hume to Bowers, 3 Feb. 1900, box 314, no. 8723; Hume to Bowers, 12 Feb. 1900, box 314, no. 9057, Letters Received, 1882–1900, R G 22, N A; Hume to Bowers, 22 Jan. 1900; Hume to Bowers, 21 Mar. 1900, box 26, Rogue River fldr., Records concerning Fish Culture Stations, 1875–1929, R G 22, N A. For U S F C pond-raising see Ravenal to S. W. Downing, 30 Dec. 1899, vol. 530, p. 6212; Bowers to Hume, 19 Feb. 1900, vol. 531, p. 6745; Bowers to Hume, 2 July 1900, vol. 542, p. 33; Ravenal to E. N. Carter, 14 Nov. 1900, vol. 549, p. 3567; *Oregonian,* 28 Oct. 1901, 9. For salmon feed see Bowers to Hume, 12 Feb. 1900, vol. 531, p. 6624; Bowers to Carter, 3 Oct. 1900, vol. 549, p. 3246; Ravenal to Carter, 14 Nov. 1900, vol. 549, p. 3582; Ravenal to Hume, 29 Aug. 1901, vol. 568, p. 1117; Bowers to G. H. Tolbert, 16 Jan. 1901, vol. 552, p. 5004; Titcomb to Superintendent, 19 Aug. 1902, vol. 594, p. 2292, Press Copies of Letters Sent, 1871–1906, R G 22, N A.

16. For insufficient supply of salmon and diseases see vol. 53, entries 7174, 8674, 9847, Registers of Letters Received, 1882–1917, R G 22, N A; Bowers to Carter, 5 Mar. 1901, vol. 557, p. 7120; Ravenal to Carter, 16 Mar. 1901, vol. 557, p. 7233; Bowers to Carter, 29 Mar. 1901, vol. 557, p. 7329; Titcomb to Superintendent, 23 Mar. 1903, vol. 608, p. 8727; Titcomb to Wisner, 20 May 1902, vol. 586, p. 9245, Press Copies of Letters Sent, 1871–1906, R G 22, N A; Ronald W. Hardy, "Diet Preparation," in *Fish Nutrition,* ed. John E. Halver (San Diego: Academic Press, 1989), 477, 478. I am indebted to Ron Hardy for information on problems with early feeding practices. Disease was nothing new to Hume. Long before the 1901 outbreak, he had devised an elaborate feeding system to avoid foul water; Hume to Bowers, 5 Feb. 1900, box 314, no. 8826, Letters Received, 1882–1900, R G 22, N A; and memos between George Rickman, Arthur Duncan, and R. D. Hume from Mar. and May 1902, box 3, Hume Papers.

For the 1902 flood see Titcomb to Superintendent, 29 Jan. 1903, vol. 603, p. 6767, Press Copies of Letters Sent, 1871–1906, R G 22, N A. For fingerlings, budget, and records see George M. Bowers to J. N. Wisner, 4 Apr. 1902, vol. 579, p. 6402; Titcomb to Wisner, 7 May 1902, vol. 582, p. 7659; Titcomb to Wisner, 8 May 1902, vol. 582, p. 7671; Titcomb to Superintendent, 20 Aug. 1903, vol. 622, p. 2873; J. Ward Ellis to Superintendent, 27 Aug. 1903, vol. 622, p. 2915, Press Copies of Letters Sent, 1871–1906, R G 22, N A. For loss of enthusiasm see Smith to Superintendent, 5 Aug. 1904, vol. 641, p. 1343; Bowers to Hume, 10 Sept. 1904, vol. 643, p. 2375; Titcomb to Superintendent, 14 Sept. 1905, vol. 659, p. 8809; Titcomb to

Cloudsley Rutter, 4 Sept. 1902, vol. 594, p. 2454, Press Copies of Letters Sent, 1871–1906, RG 22, NA. For alevins see H. M. Smith to Superintendent, 21 Oct. 1905, vol. 681, p. 5173; Bowers to Charles W. Fulton, 9 Jan. 1905, vol. 652, p. 5641, Press Copies of Letters Sent, 1871–1906, RG 22, NA; Smith to Superintendent, 27 Nov. 1908, box 8, Records concerning Fish Culture Stations, 1875–1929, RG 22, NA.

17. J. W. Berrian to Hume, 6 July 1902, box 3, Berrian to Hume, 13 July 1904, box 5; R. D. Hume to Herbert Hume, 12 Nov. 1906 and 29 Oct. 1906, box 6, Hume Papers; Herbert A. Gill to Hubbard, 4 Sept. 1894, vol. 389, pp. 233–34; I. H. Dunlop to Rickman, 29 July 1902, vol. 589, p. 248; Titcomb to Wisner, 29 July 1902, vol. 590, p. 724; Titcomb to Superintendent, 12 Aug. 1902, vol. 590, p. 836; Bowers to Hume, 21 Nov. 1902, vol. 598, p. 4172; Bowers to Rickman, 8 Dec. 1902, vol. 598, p. 4494; Dunlop to Berrian, 26 May 1904, vol. 634, p. 8457; Bowers to Hume, 10 Aug. 1904, vol. 640, p. 830, Press Copies of Letters Sent, 1871–1906, RG 22, NA.

18. *Oregonian,* 17 Dec. 1905, 8; 4 Nov. 1906, 8; 5 Nov. 1906, 6; 12 Feb. 1907, 5.

19. *Oregonian,* 19 Dec. 1906, 7; 16 July 1907, 10; Bowers to Miller Freeman, 19 Mar. 1907, box 1, Correspondence with Publishers of *Pacific Fisherman,* 1903–17, RG 22, NA.

20. *Oregonian,* 22 Apr. 1907, 6; 19 May 1907, 45; 22 June 1907, 5, 7; "Fish and Game Commission Minutes," box 1/2, pp. 69–72, 75–76, ODFW Papers; G. W. A. Chamberlain to Hume, 7 May 1907, box 5; H. G. Van Dusen to Hume, 15 Apr. 1907, box 6; Henry L. Benson to Hume, 1 May 1907, box 7; Van Dusen to Hume, 15 June 1907, 5 July 1907, and 24 July 1907, box 8; Van Dusen to Henry O'Malley, 5 July 1907, box 8; G. Kerr to Hume, 23 Feb. 1907, vol. 90, Hume Papers.

21. *Oregonian,* 22 June 1907, 7; 24 June 1907, 4; 21 July 1907, 5; 6 Aug. 1907, 11.

22. Van Dusen to George M. Bowers, 24 Dec. 1903, box 2, Correspondence of Hugh Smith Relating to the Bureau of Fisheries, 1885–1910, RG 22, NA; Dodds, *Salmon King,* 145–46, 151; Hume to Bowers, 25 Nov. 1907, box 26, Records concerning Fish Culture Stations, 1875–1929, RG 22, NA; Webster to Hume, 26 July 1906 and 23 Nov. 1906; Webster to Hume, 10 Aug. 1906, box 6, Hume Papers; *Oregonian,* 19 May 1907, 45; 24 June 1907, 4; 29 June 1907, 12; Hume to Bowers, 14 Jan. 1908, box 26, Rogue River fldr., Records concerning Fish Culture Stations, 1875–1929, RG 22, NA.

23. W. O. Buck, "Some Details of Salmon Culture," *TAFS* 39 (1909): 120–23.

24. John H. Whyte to Hume, 15 May 1907; Henry E. Dosch to Hume, 20 Nov. 1908; R. D. Hume to Herbert Hume, 21 Dec. 1907, box 7; E. R. Pipes to Hume, 1 Aug. 1907; James Withycombe to Hume, 3 Aug. 1907; Freeman to Hume, 4 Oct. 1907, box 8, Hume Papers; Miller Freeman to Bowers, 12 Sept. 1907, box 1, Correspondence with Publishers of *Pacific Fisherman,* 1903–17, RG 22, NA; *Oregonian,* 24 May 1908, B1; 12 July 1908, 10. For Hume's influence see McAllister to

Hume, 4 Sept. 1908, 11 Sept. 1908, 3 Nov. 1908; O'Malley to Hume, 12 Sept. 1908, Hume Papers; Dodds, *Salmon King*, 155–56; *Oregonian*, 13 Feb. 1908, 7; 2 Sept. 1908, 14.

25. *Oregonian*, 21 Sept. 1907, 16; 8 July 1909, 11; 15 Aug. 1909, sec. 1, 8; 24 Oct. 1909, sec. 2, 12; 9 Nov. 1909, 6; 15 Nov. 1909, 9.

26. *Oregonian*, 11 Jan. 1914, sec. 1, 11; 18 Oct. 1914, sec. 2, 16; Steven L. Johnson, *Freshwater Environmental Problems and Coho Production in Oregon,* Informational Reports 84–11 (Corvallis: Oregon Department of Fish and Wildlife, 1984), 19; Hugh C. Mitchell to R. E. Clanton, 5 Nov. 1912; O'Malley to Clanton, 2 Dec. 1913, box 7/1; "Phone, Roy Beamer, Salem (7/9/19)," box 7/28, ODFW Papers; Ravenal to Carter, 18 Sept. 1901, vol. 569, p. 1762, Press Copies of Letters Sent, 1871–1906, RG 22, NA; Fred Barker to Clanton, 19 Nov. 1914; Clanton to Barker, 30 Nov. 1914; McAllister to Elmore, 12 Mar. 1910; O'Malley to Clanton, 8 Feb. 1912; Clanton to CRPA, 20 Feb. 1912; George H. George to Clanton, 23 Feb. 1912; Clanton to CRPA, 4 Apr. 1912, box 14/15; Fred Barker to Clanton, 15 May 1915 and 7 Feb. 1918; S. G. Galbraith, Perry Katzmiller, and A. L. Fisher to CRPA, 23 Sept. 1918; CRPA to Galbraith, 5 Oct. 1918, CRPAPOHS.

For the various feeds see correspondence between Department and Swift and Company of North Portland, box 8/19; Smith to Clanton, 9 Dec. 1913, box 7/1, ODFW Papers. For industry influence see Miller Freeman to Bureau, 13 Apr. 1904; Freeman to Smith, 17 Nov. 1913, 26 Nov. 1913, and 4 Dec. 1913, box 1, Correspondence with Publishers of *Pacific Fisherman,* 1903–17, RG 22, NA; George H. George to Clanton, 1 Aug. 1910, box 14/15, CRPAPOHS; J. J. Reynolds to William Redfield, 10 July 1914, Records concerning Societies, Councils, Conferences, and Other Groups, 1904–37, RG 22, NA; Smith to Seufert, 19 Sept. 1914 and 22 Mar. 1916; correspondence between Hugh Smith and Frank M. Warren, 2 May 1916, 12 Mar. 1917, 30 Apr. 1917, 4 May 1917, 15 May 1917, 24 Jan. 1919, 8 Feb. 1919, and 9 May 1919; William Redfield to Smith, 28 Apr. 1917; Smith to Frank Wright, 25 Sept. 1918, box 3, Correspondence of U.S. Fish Commissioner Hugh Smith, 1913–22, RG 22, NA. For tax breaks see correspondence between Clanton and Union Fishermen's Co-Operative Packing Co., 23 Nov. 1917 to 28 Jan. 1918, box 7/50, ODFW Papers.

27. Joseph A. Craig and Robert L. Hacker, *The History and Development of the Fisheries of the Columbia River,* U.S. Bureau of Fisheries Bulletin 32 (Washington: Government Printing Office, 1940), 152–53, 196–97; Robert E. Mullen, *Oregon's Commercial Harvest of Coho Salmon, Oncorhynchus kisutch (Walbaum), 1892–1960,* Informational Report Series, Fisheries 81–3 (Corvallis: Oregon Department of Fish and Wildlife, 1981); R. D. Hume to McDonald, 11 Nov. 1893, box 210, no. 4916; A. C. Little to Bowers, 24 Dec. 1898, box 298, no. 6094, Letters Received, 1882–1900, RG 22, NA; Ravenal to Hubbard, 21 June 1897, vol. 470, p. 97; Bowers to F. C.

Reed, 20 Oct. 1900, vol. 548, p. 2848; Titcomb to Superintendent, 20 Aug. 1903, vol. 622, p. 2871, Press Copies of Letters Sent, 1871–1906, RG 22, NA; W. Kuykendall to William Kyle, 18 Oct. 1898, Kyle Papers; "Board Minutes of the Oregon Fish Commission," box 1/1; O'Malley to Clanton, 14 Nov. 1913 and 29 Nov. 1913, box 7/1; memos in miscellaneous file, box 7, ODFW Papers; AROFC (1888): 11; AROFC (1920): 20–23; AROFC (1926): 31, 33; Oregonian, 10 Dec. 1904, 14; 5 Apr. 1905, 6; Edwin H. Duncan to F. P. Kendall, 4 Mar. 1909, box 5; Berrian to Hume, 31 Dec. 1906 and 25 Jan. 1907, box 6; Herbert Hume to O'Malley, 24 Jan. 1908, vol. 90, Hume Papers; Arthur Sykes, "Inbreeding Pond-Reared Trout," TAFS 31 (1902): 116–24; Allendorf and Ryman, "Genetic Management," 144, 149, 151; John L. Dentler and David V. Buchanan, *Are Wild Salmonid Stocks Worth Saving?* Information Reports 86–7 (Corvallis: Oregon Department of Fish and Wildlife, Fish Division, 1986).

28. *Oregonian*, 9 Sept. 1906, 4; 3 Feb. 1909, 18; 7 Sept. 1910, 6; "Fish and Game Commission minutes," box 1/2, p. 71, ODFW Papers; Stephen J. Pyne, *Fire in America: A Cultural History of Wildland and Rural Fire* (Princeton: Princeton University Press, 1982), 322–45; M. D. Brands, *Flood Runoff in the Willamette Valley, Oreg.*, U.S. Geological Survey Water-Supply Paper 968-A (Washington: Government Printing Office, 1947); U.S. Department of the Interior, *Columbia River Basin: Development of Water and Other Resources Present and Potential of the Columbia River Basin in Washington, Oregon, Idaho, Montana, Wyoming, Nevada, and Utah*, Project Planning Report no. 1–5.0–1 (Portland: Bureau of Reclamation—Region 1, 1946), 334, 338, 385, 399; Donald L. McKernan, Donald R. Johnson, and John I. Hodges, "Some Factors Influencing the Trends of Salmon Populations in Oregon," *Transactions of the Fifteenth North American Wildlife Conference* 15 (1950): 438–39, 449; Kelly to C. H. Warner, 22 Apr. 1909, box 5, Hume Papers.

29. Clanton to Seufert, 25 July 1910, SBCCP; Clanton to George H. George, 5 July 1910, 23 Dec. 1912, 31 Jan. 1913; George to Clanton, 8 Sept. 1910, 12 Sept. 1910, 7 Jan. 1913; Clanton to Barker, 22 Jan. 1914, 6 Apr. 1914; Barker to Clanton, 9 Apr. 1914, 21 Apr. 1914, 11 Dec. 1914, 19 Apr. 1918; Clanton to CRPA, 7 Sept. 1910, 24 Feb. 1911, 23 Nov. 1914; Board of Fish and Game Commissioners to "Fishermen, Canners, Packers and Others Interested in the Fishing Industry," 16 Nov. 1914; Telegram to James Withycombe, 6 Mar. 1915; "copy of petition to James Withycombe," c. 1915; "Copy of report by the State Fish Commission on fiscal problems in the hatchery program," 1 Mar. 1917, box 14, CRPAPOHS; "Resolution of the Salmon Protective Association," 2 Oct. 1926, box 85:55, 1172, CRPAPCRMM; Hume to Bowers, 21 Nov. 1899, box 311, no. 6147, Letters Received, 1882–1900, RG 22, NA; *Oregonian*, 26 Apr. 1914, sec. 2, 4.

30. AROFC (1888): 7; AROFC (1925): 24–25; Titcomb to Superintendent, 24 Feb. 1906, vol. 687, p. 7953, Press Copies of Letters Sent, 1871–1906, RG 22, NA; *Ore-*

gonian, 5 Feb. 1910, 13; Range D. Bayer, *The Cormorant/Fisherman Conflict in Tillamook County, Oregon,* Studies in Oregon Ornithology no. 6 (Newport: Gahmken Press, 1989); *Pacific Fisherman* 3 (1905): 9; O'Malley to Smith, 21 Feb. 1916, box 2, Correspondence of U.S. Fish Commissioner Hugh Smith, 1913–22, RG 22, NA; Francis P. Griffiths, "Considerations of the Introduction and Distribution of Exotic Fishes in Oregon," *TAFS* 69 (1939): 240–43.

31. H. M. Collins, "The Structure of Knowledge," *Social Research* 60 (spring 1993): 95–116; Bruce E. Seely, "The Scientific Mystique of Engineering: Highway Research at the Bureau of Pubic Roads, 1918–1940," *Technology and Culture* 25 (Oct. 1984): 798–831. For changes in research emphases see Charles Wilson Greene, "Physiological Studies of the Chinook Salmon," *Bulletin* 24 (1904): 429–56; John Otterbien Snyder, "The Fishes of the Coastal Streams of Oregon and Northern California," *Bulletin* 27 (1907): 153–89; Charles W. Greene, "Anatomy and Histology of the Alimentary Tract of the King Salmon," *Bulletin* 32 (1912): 73–100; Charles Wilson Greene, "The Skeletal Musculature of the King Salmon," *Bulletin* 33 (1913): 21–60; Charles Wilson Greene, "The Storage of Fat in the Muscular Tissue of the King Salmon and Its Resorption during the Fast of the Spawning Migration," *Bulletin* 33 (1913): 69–138; Charles Wilson Greene, "The Fat-Absorbing Function of the Alimentary Tract of the King Salmon," *Bulletin* 33 (1913): 149–76.

32. Tarleton Bean to H. D. McGuire, 27 Sept. 1894, vol. 390, p. 412; Ravenal to L. E. Bean, 28 Apr. 1897, vol. 463, p. 145; Ravenal to L. E. Bean, 9 Feb. 1898, vol. 484, p. 45, Press Copies of Letters Sent, 1871–1906, RG 22, NA; L. E. Bean to Ravenal, 19 Apr. 1897; L. E. Bean to Commissioner, 31 Jan. 1898, box 4, Siuslaw Bundles, Records concerning Abandoned Stations, 1879–1931, RG 22, NA; *Oregonian,* 3 Oct. 1894, 3; S. W. Downing, "Propagation of the Pacific Salmon," *TAFS* 29 (1900): 154–63.

33. *Oregonian,* 16 Apr. 1888, 8; 4 Nov. 1906, 8; 5 Nov. 1906, 6; 17 Aug. 1908, 13; 1 July 1910, 2; Commission to Columbia River Canners, 8 July 1899, vol. 517, pp. 163–64; J. G. Megler to S. W. Downing, 14 Feb. 1900, vol. 532, p. 7067; Bowers to Superintendent, 26 Feb. 1903, vol. 607, p. 8514; J. Ward Ellis to Superintendent, 16 Mar. 1904, vol. 633, p. 8111; Bowers to Superintendent, 6 July 1904, vol. 641, p. 1108; Bowers to Columbia River canners, 5 Jan. 1905, vol. 652, pp. 5566–77; Smith to Superintendent, 19 Jan. 1905, vol. 652, p. 5894, Press Copies of Letters Sent, 1871–1906, RG 22, NA; Frederick Charles Cleaver, "The Effects of Ocean Fishing upon the Columbia River Hatchery Stocks of Fall Chinook Salmon" (Ph.D. diss., University of Washington, 1967), 44–65; Charles W. Greene, "The Migration of Salmon in the Columbia River," *Bulletin* 29 (1909): 129–48.

34. Hume to George M. Bowers, 25 Nov. 1907; "Chinook Salmon Only," box 26; Evermann to Chief Clerk, 23 Dec. 1907; Commissioner to Hume, 20 Dec. 1907,

box 26, Rogue River fldr., Records concerning Fish Culture Stations, 1875–1929, RG 22, NA.

35. Commissioner to R. D. Hume, 20 Dec. 1907, box 26, Rogue River fldr., Records concerning Fish Culture Stations, 1875–1929, RG 22, NA; Max Weber, *From Max Weber: Essays in Sociology*, ed. and trans. H. H. Gerth and C. Wright Mills (New York: Oxford University Press, 1946), 228–29, 233; Charles E. Rosenberg, *No Other Gods: On Science and American Social Thought* (Baltimore: Johns Hopkins University Press, 1976); Dean Conrad Allard, "The Fish Commission Laboratory and Its Influence on the Founding of the Marine Biological Laboratory," *Journal of the History of Biology* 23 (summer 1990): 251–70.

36. Stephen A. Forbes, "The Investigation of a River System in the Interest of Its Fisheries," *TAFS* 40 (1910): 179–93; T. L. Hankinson, "Ecological Notes on the Fishes of Walnut Lake, Michigan," *TAFS* 40 (1910): 195–206; Roy Waldo Miner, "The Study of Marine Ecology and Its Importance to the Fisheries," *TAFS* 40 (1910): 207–17; Francis B. Sumner, "An Intensive Study of the Fauna and Flora of a Restricted Area of Sea Bottom," *Bulletin* 28 (1908): 1225–64; Edward A. Birge, "A Limnological Study of the Finger Lakes of New York," *Bulletin* 32 (1912): 525–610.

37. Miner, "Study of Marine Ecology," 215; Forbes, "Investigation," 182. For audience response see discussion in *TAFS* 40 (1910): 189–93, 217.

38. "Fish and Game Minutes," box 1/2, pp. 106–7, ODFW Papers; Miller Freeman to Charles Nagel, 2 Aug. 1912, box 1, Correspondence with Publishers of *Pacific Fisherman*, 1903–17, RG 22, NA; Robert V. Bruce, *The Launching of Modern American Science, 1846–1876* (New York: Alfred A. Knopf, 1987), 353; Norman G. Benson, "The American Fisheries Society, 1920–1970," in *A Century of Fisheries in North America*, ed. Norman B. Benson (Washington: American Fisheries Society, 1970), 13.

39. *Oregonian*, 22 June 1907, 7; 24 June 1907, 4; 21 July 1907, 5; 15 Aug. 1909, sec. 1, 8; 17 Aug. 1909, 10.

40. McAllister to Sam Elmore, 12 Mar. 1910; McAllister to Elmore, 25 Mar. 1910, box 14, CRPAPOHS; *Oregonian*, 5 Apr. 1910, 8; 6 Apr. 1910, 6; *Pacific Fisherman* 8 (May 1910): 15; *Pacific Fisherman* 20 (Nov. 1922): 12–13.

41. *ARUSCF* (1912): 43; *ARUSCF* (1914): 47; John N. Cobb to H. M. Smith, 14 Mar. 1914; Smith to Cobb, 27 Mar. 1914, box 1, Correspondence with Publishers of *Pacific Fisherman*, 1903–17, RG 22, NA; O'Malley to Commissioner, 15 Dec. 1916, box 371, fldr. 603.3, General Classified Files, 1902–65, RG 22, NA; Henry O'Malley, "Artificial Propagation of the Salmons of the Pacific Coast," *ARUSCF* (1919): 29; "copy of speech by Henry O'Malley to the Salmon Day Banquet, held at the Arctic Club, Seattle, Washington," 10 Mar. 1916, box 2, Correspondence of U.S. Fish Commissioner Hugh Smith, 1913–22, RG 22, NA; Arthur S. Einarsen, "Economic Factors in the Salt-Water Rearing of Salmon," *TAFS* 57 (1927): 288–93.

42. Carl Westerfield to Hugh Smith, 27 Apr. 1914; Westerfield to Smith, 17 July 1915, box 3, fldr. "W," Correspondence of U.S. Fish Commissioner Hugh Smith, 1913–22, RG 22, NA; John Cobb to Smith, 7 May 1915; Cobb to Smith, 15 Apr. 1917, box 4, Records concerning Societies, Councils, Conferences, and Other Groups, 1904–37, RG 22, NA; John N. Cobb, "The Pacific Salmon Fisheries Society," *TAFS* 44 (1915): 65–66; *Pacific Fisherman* 20 (Sept. 1922): 16–17.

43. *Pacific Fisherman* 9 (Nov. 1911): 11; *ARWDFG* (1917): 8–9, 38; *AROFC* (1915): 17–18; Cranston, "Fish and Game Laws of Oregon," 77.

44. Frank G. Young to Committee of Fisheries, Washington State Legislature, 31 Mar. 1908, box 3, fldr. 4, Cobb Papers; *ARWDFG* (1904): 45–46; *Oregonian*, 29 Mar. 1894, 4. For discussions of tacit and formal knowledge in science, see Collins, "Structure of Knowledge," 95–116; Seely, "Scientific Mystique," 798–831; Thomas R. Dunlap, *Saving America's Wildlife* (Princeton: Princeton University Press, 1988).

45. Carl L. Hubbs, "History of Ichthyology in the United States after 1850," *Copeia* (Mar. 1964): 52–54; Barton Warren Evermann, *Alaska Fisheries and Fur Industries in 1911*, Bureau of Fisheries Document 766 (Washington: Government Printing Office, 1912), 10; Evermann to Commissioner, 2 Oct. 1903, vol. 638, p. 10565, Press Copies of Letters Sent, 1871–1906, RG 22, NA.

46. Evermann, *Alaska Fisheries*, 10.

47. For straying and transplants see "Meeting of International Pacific Salmon Investigation Federation, Executive Committee, Seattle, Washington, Dec. 2, 1926," pp. 7–8, 72–76, 80–81; Harlan Holmes, "Transplanting of Salmon," Annual Meeting, International Pacific Salmon Investigation Federation, box 4, fldr. 1 of 4, pp. 26–28, Records concerning Societies, Councils, Conferences, and Other Groups, 1904–37, RG 22, NA; Harlan Holmes to Henry B. Ward, 3 Feb. 1932, box 1, General Correspondence of the Division of Scientific Inquiry, 1880–1935; Andrew L. Pritchard, "A Study of the Natural Propagation of the Pink Salmon, *Oncorhynchus Gorbuscha*, in British Columbia," *TAFS* 69 (1939): 237–39; Francis P. Griffiths, Willard Jarvis, Andrew B. Smith, and Charles A. Lockwood, "Measurement of Fish for Liberation by Weighing," *TAFS* 70 (1940): 275–81; Jay W. Nicholas, Lisa Van Dyke, Robert C. Buckman, *Straying by Hatchery-Reared Coho Salmon Released in Yaquina Bay, Oregon*, Informational Reports 82–6 (Corvallis: Oregon Department of Fish and Wildlife, Fish Division, 1982), 19–20.

For tag bounties see Harlan Holmes, "Memorandum: On rewards for Columbia River marked salmon, for season of 1926"; Rich to O'Malley, 1 Dec. 1927, box 10, General Correspondence (of the Division of Scientific Inquiry), 1880–1935. For disease see A. B. Stirling, "Notes on the Fungus Disease Affecting Salmon," *ARUSCF* (1878): 525–29; A. B. Stirling, "Additional Observations on the Fungus Disease Affecting Salmon and Other Fish," *ARUSCF* (1878): 531–36; Eugene Vincent, "Causes of Disease in Young Salmonids," *Bulletin* 28 (1908): 907–16; Harvey

R. Gaylord and Millard C. Marsh, "Carcinoma of the Thyroid in the Salmonid Fishes," *Bulletin* 32 (1912): 363–524; H. S. Davis, "Schizamoeba Salmonis, a New Ameba Parasitic in Salmonid Fishes," *Bulletin* 42 (1926): 1–8; *Oregonian,* 4 Jan. 1914, sec. 1, 16.

For studies on salmon in the ocean see Charles H. Gilbert, "Age at Maturity of the Pacific Coast Salmon of the Genus *Oncorhynchus,*" *Bulletin* 32 (1912): 1–22; Willis H. Rich, "Early History and Seaward Migration of Chinook Salmon in the Columbia and Sacramento Rivers," *Bulletin* 37 (1919–20): 1–74; Willis H. Rich, "Growth and Degree of Maturity of Chinook Salmon in the Ocean," *Bulletin* 41 (1925): 15–90; Willis H. Rich, "Salmon-Tagging Experiments in Alaska, 1924 and 1925," *Bulletin* 42 (1926): 109–46; Willis H. Rich and Harlan B. Holmes, "Experiments in Marking Young Chinook Salmon on the Columbia River, 1916 to 1927," *Bulletin* 44 (1928): 215–64. For hatchery inspections see Fred J. Foster, "Report of Inspections of Bozeman, Ennis and Pacific Coast Stations," 9 Feb. 1934, box 369, fldr. 603.3; G. C. Leach, "Inspection of the Clackamas Station," 6 July 1939; Alphonse Kemmerich, "Report of Inspection of Fisheries Stations Located at Carson, Little White, Big White, Leavenworth, Winthrop and Entiat, Washington," 22 Aug. 1941, box 372, fldr. 603.3, General Classified Files, 1902–65, RG 22, NA.

48. H. C. White, "A Quantitative Determination of the Number of Survivors from Planting 5,000 Trout Fry in Each of Two Streams," *Contributions to Canadian Biology* 2 (Dec. 1924): 137; Rich, "Early History," 68.

49. Tim D. Smith, *Scaling Fisheries: The Science of Measuring the Effects of Fishing, 1855–1955* (New York: Cambridge University Press, 1994), 195; Willis H. Rich, "A Statistical Analysis of the Results of the Artificial Propagation of Chinook Salmon" (Seattle, 1921–22; copy of typed MS in reprint file, NWFSCL), 8.

50. Kenneth Johnstone, *The Aquatic Explorers: A History of the Fisheries Research Board of Canada* (Toronto: University of Toronto Press, 1977), 121; White, "Quantitative Determination," 138–49.

51. White, "Quantitative Determination," 144–45; Johnstone, *Aquatic Explorers,* 121, 126–27; J. A. Rodd, "Sketch of the Development of Fish Culture in Canada," *TAFS* 54 (1924): 159.

52. Johnstone, *Aquatic Explorers,* 109–12, 121, 126–27; J. A. Paulhus, "Consumption, Not Production—Industry's Chief Problem," *TAFS* 54 (1924): 138–47. The Biological Board initiated a similar study in eastern Canada a few years later; A. G. Huntsman, "Attack on the Fishery Problem," *TAFS* 60 (1930): 172–77. When Foerster explained his study to Oregon managers in 1925, they tried to alter his work to include fingerling methods; "Transcript of the Meeting of the International Pacific Salmon Investigation Federation, Executive committee, . . . Seattle, Washington, Nov. 24, 1925," box 10, General Correspondence of the Division of Scientific Inquiry, 1880–1935, RG 22, NA.

53. R. E. Foerster, "A Comparison of the Natural and Artificial Propagation of Salmon," *TAFS* 61 (1931): 121–30; R. E. Foerster and W. E. Ricker, "A Synopsis of the Investigations at Cultus Lake, British Columbia, Conducted by the Biological Board of Canada into the Life History and Propagation of Sockeye Salmon, 1924–1937," (Pacific Biological Station, Nanaimo, B.C., Dec. 1937; copy of typed MS in Fisheries Library, University of Washington, Seattle), 4–6; R. E. Foerster, "An Investigation of the Relative Efficiencies of Natural and Artificial Propagation of Sockeye Salmon (*Oncorhynchus nerka*) at Cultus Lake, British Columbia," *Journal of the Fisheries Research Board of Canada* 4 (Dec. 1938): 161.

54. Anthony Barker and B. Guy Peters, "Introduction," in *The Politics of Expert Advice: Creating, Using and Manipulating Scientific Knowledge for Public Policy*, ed. Anthony Barker and B. Guy Peters (Pittsburgh: University of Pittsburgh Press, 1993), 1–16; Richard Topf, "Conclusion: Science, Public Policy and the Authoritativeness of the Governmental Process," in *Politics of Expert Advice*, 104; Arthur W. Cooper, "Why Doesn't Anyone Listen to Ecologists—And What Can ESA Do about It?" *Bulletin of the Ecological Society of America* 63 (Dec. 1982): 350; Richard A. Cooley, *Politics and Conservation: The Decline of the Alaska Salmon* (New York: Harper and Row, 1963), 137, 165; Johnstone, *Aquatic Explorers*, 126–27; Cicely Lyons, *Salmon, Our Heritage: The Story of a Province and an Industry* (Vancouver: British Columbia Packers, 1969), 409; Charles H. Gilbert and Willis H. Rich, "Investigations concerning the Red-Salmon Runs to the Karluk River, Alaska," *Bulletin* 43 (1927): 1–69; Joseph T. Barnaby, "Fluctuations in Abundance of Red Salmon, *Oncorhynchus nerka*, (Walbaum) of the Karluk River, Alaska," *Bulletin* 39 (1944): 237–95; Ward T. Bower, "Alaska Fishery and Fur Industries in 1933," *ARUSCF* (1934): app. 2, 264; Ward T. Bower, "Alaska Fishery and Fur Industries in 1936," *ARUSCF* (1937): app. 2, 298.

55. Lyons, *Salmon, Our Heritage*, 409; Johnstone, *Aquatic Explorers*, 126–27; Smith, *Scaling Fisheries*, 278–69, 349 n. 3; R. J. Childerhose and Marj Trim, *Pacific Salmon and Steelhead Trout* (Seattle: University of Washington Press, 1979), 29; Theodore Whaley Cart, "The Federal Fisheries Service, 1871–1940" (M.A. thesis, University of North Carolina, 1968), 91–93.

56. H. C. White, "Some Observations on the Eastern Brook Trout (*S. Fontinalis*) of Prince Edward Island," *TAFS* 60 (1930): 101–8; H. C. White, "Some Facts and Theories concerning the Atlantic Salmon," *TAFS* 64 (1934): 360–62; R. E. Foerster, "Fry Production from Eyed-Egg Planting," *TAFS* 64 (1934): 379–81; R. E. Foerster, "An Investigation of the Life History and Propagation of the Sockeye Salmon (*Oncorhynchus nerka*) at Cultus Lake, British Columbia, no. 5, The Life History Cycle of the 1926 Year Class with Artificial Propagation Involving the Liberation of Free-Swimming Fry," *Journal of the Biological Board of Canada* 2 (May 1936): 311–33; "Transcript of the meeting of the executive committee of the International Pacific

Salmon Investigation Federation, held at Vancouver, British Columbia (5 Apr. 1929)," pp. 55–65, 73, box 4, Records concerning Societies, Councils, Conferences, and Other Groups, 1904–37, RG 22, NA.

57. Arthur F. McEvoy, *The Fisherman's Problem: Law and Ecology in the California Fisheries, 1850–1980* (New York: Cambridge University Press, 1986), 187–206; Nancy Langston, *Forest Dreams, Forest Nightmares: The Paradox of Old Growth in the Inland West* (Seattle: University of Washington Press, 1995), 211, 221.

58. *Oregonian,* 15 Dec. 1908, 8; Dianne Newell, *Tangled Webs of History: Indians and the Law in Canada's Pacific Coast Fisheries* (Toronto: University of Toronto Press, 1993), 10–11; Johnstone, *Aquatic Explorers,* 109–12, 121, 126–27; Bill Parenteau, "Creating a 'Sportsmen's Paradise': Salmon Fishing Regulation and Social Conflict in New Brunswick, 1868–1900" (paper presented at the American Society for Environmental History Conference, Las Vegas, Nev., Mar. 1995), paper in author's possession; Cooley, *Politics and Conservation,* 96–127.

59. R. E. Foerster, "An Investigation of the Life History of the Sockeye Salmon (*Oncorhynchus nerka*) at Cultus Lake, British Columbia. I. Introduction and Run of 1925," *Contributions to Canadian Biology and Fisheries* 5 (Sept. 1929): 1–35; R. E. Foerster, "An Investigation of the Life History of the Sockeye Salmon (*Oncorhynchus nerka*) at Cultus Lake, British Columbia. II. The Run of 1926," *Contributions to Canadian Biology and Fisheries* 5 (Sept. 1929): 37–53; R. E. Foerster, "An Investigation of the Life History of the Sockeye Salmon (*Oncorhynchus nerka*) at Cultus Lake, British Columbia. III. The Downstream Migration of the Young in 1926 and 1927," *Contributions to Canadian Biology and Fisheries* 5 (Oct. 1929): 55–82. I'm indebted to William Ricker for pointing out the role of budgetary concerns in the termination of Canada's hatchery program; pers. correspondence, William E. Ricker to author, 16 Mar. 1995; Cooley, *Politics and Conservation,* 86–87, 137; Bower, "Alaska Fishery and Fur Industries in 1933," 239–40, 264; Bower, "Alaska Fishery and Fur Industries in 1936," 298.

60. Foerster, "Investigation of Relative Efficiencies," 151.

61. Joseph E. Taylor III, " 'Politics Is at the Bottom of the Whole Thing': Spatial Relations of Power in Oregon Salmon Management," in *Power and Place in the North American West,* ed. Richard White and John M. Findlay (Seattle: University of Washington Press, 1999), 233–63; William H. Goetzmann, *Exploration and Empire: The Explorer and the Scientist in the Winning of the American West* (New York: Alfred A. Knopf, 1966); Larry T. Spencer, "Naturalists and Natural History Institutions of the American West," *American Zoologist* 26, no. 2 (1986): 295–384; A. G. Foster to George M. Bowers, 12 June 1899, box 305, no. 13117; Thomas H. Tongue to Bowers, 20 May 1899, box 304, no. 11824; Francis W. Cushman to Bowers, 21 May 1899, box 304, no. 11906; W. G. Steel to Bowers, 19 May 1899, box 304, no. 11907; George W. McBride to Bowers, 25 May 1899, box 304, no.

11908; Joseph Simon to Bowers, 24 May 1899, box 304, no. 11909; W. L. Jones to Bowers, 22 May 1899, box 304, no. 11910, Letters Received, 1882–1900, RG 22, NA; Smith to Van Dusen, 12 Jan. 1905, vol. 652, p. 5759, Press Copies of Letters Sent, 1871–1906, RG 22, NA; Hugh C. Mitchell to Harlan Holmes, 20 Apr. 1929, box 1, General Correspondence of the Division of Scientific Inquiry, 1880–1935, RG 22, NA; *AROFC* (1932): 16; John Veatch, Foreword to *Local Populations and Migration in Relation to the Conservation of Pacific Salmon in the Western States and Alaska,* by Willis H. Rich, Department of Research, Fish Commission of the State of Oregon, Contribution no. 1 (Salem: State Printing Department, 1939).

62. Allard, *Spencer Fullerton Baird;* Robert H. Connery, *Governmental Problems in Wild Life Conservation* (New York: Columbia University Press, 1935), 121–24; Arthur W. MacMahon, "Selection and Tenure of Bureau Chiefs in the National Administration of the United States," *American Political Science Review* 20 (Nov. 1926): 780–81 and n. 21; Samuel F. Hildebrand, "Hugh McCormick Smith," *Progressive Fish Culturist* 55 (Nov. 1941): 23–24; *Pacific Fisherman* 20 (June 1922): 16–18; O'Malley to Commissioner, 1 July 1899, box 307, no. 1190, Letters Received, 1882–1900, RG 22, NA; O'Malley to Smith, 21 Sept. 1915, box 2; O'Malley to Smith, 11 Mar. 1916; J. J. Reynolds to Smith, 14 June 1915, box 3, Correspondence of U.S. Fish Commissioner Hugh Smith, 1913–22, RG 22, NA; "Transcript of the meeting of the executive committee . . . 5 Apr. 1929," 64–65, box 4, Records concerning Societies, Councils, Conferences, and Other Groups, 1904–37, RG 22, NA; Hoover to J. M. Wadsworth Jr., 23 Dec. 1921, Commerce Department, Bureau of Fisheries, 1921, box 130, CPHHPL; Joseph E. Taylor III, "Rationalizing the Western Fisheries: Secretary Hoover and the Bureau of Fisheries" (paper presented at Hoover Symposium XI, 4 Oct. 1997, George Fox University, Newberg, Oreg.).

63. Wisner to Commissioner, 30 Oct. 1905, box 8, Big White Salmon fldr., Records concerning Fish Culture Stations, 1875–1929, RG 22, NA; Livingston Stone, "Explorations on the Columbia River from the Head of Clarke's Fork to the Pacific Ocean, Made in the Summer of 1883, with Reference to the Selection of a Suitable Place for Establishing a Salmon-Breeding Station," *ARUSCF* (1884): 252; Bowers to Carter, 12 Mar. 1901, vol. 556, p. 6675; Wisner to Commissioner, 1 Aug. 1904, vol. 641, p. 1287; Smith to Superintendent, 29 Aug. 1904, vol. 645, p. 2962; "Memorandum to the Deputy Commissioner," vol. 657, p. 8118, Press Copies of Letters Sent, 1871–1906, RG 22, NA; Berrian to Hume, 5 May 1904, box 5, Hume Papers; Wallich to Commissioner, 14 May 1904, box 4, Upper Clackamas fldr., Records concerning Abandoned Stations, 1879–1931, RG 22, NA; O'Malley to Commissioner, 27 July 1907, box 26, Records concerning Fish Culture Stations, 1875–1929, RG 22, NA; "Copy of report by the State Fish Commission on fiscal problems in the hatchery program," 1 Mar. 1917, CRPAPOHS; letters between R. E. Clanton and James R. Wheeler, 1921, box 8, ODFW Papers. For dams see Bowers to Carter, 21

Aug. 1901, vol. 569, p. 1498; Bowers to Superintendent, 27 Sept. 1904, vol. 648, p. 4121; Bowers to Superintendent, 21 Feb. 1905, vol. 658, p. 8551; Titcomb to Superintendent, 15 Aug. 1905, vol. 672, p. 1365, Press Copies of Letters Sent, 1871–1906, RG 22, NA; "Master Fish Warden Diary, 1901–1904," box 8/29, p. 11, ODFW Papers; *Oregonian*, 9 Sept. 1904, 4; 24 July 1906, 6; O'Malley to Commissioner, 19 Nov. 1908, box 8, Records concerning Fish Culture Stations, 1875–1929, RG 22, NA; H. A. Webster to Hume, 21 May 1906, box 4; John Wilson to Van Dusen, 2 Aug. 1907, box 8, Hume Papers; W. F. Gillam to Frank Benson, 6 Feb. 1907; Benson to Gillam, 9 Feb. 1907, Benson Papers.

64. For the Clackamas River see Ravenal to Hubbard, 26 Nov. 1897, vol. 478, p. 414; Titcomb to Superintendent, 26 Dec. 1902, vol. 599, p. 5041, Press Copies of Letters Sent, 1871–1906, RG 22, NA; O'Malley to Commissioner, 9 Apr. 1909; O'Malley to Commissioner, 13 Aug. 1909, Dedman Property fldr.; Bowers to Secretary of Commerce and Labor, 25 Feb. 1911, box 8, Records concerning Fish Culture Stations, 1875–1929, RG 22, NA.

For the Rogue River see Ravenal to Carter, 19 June 1900, vol. 540, p. 11399; Smith to Superintendent, 11 June 1904, vol. 639, p. 238; Bowers to Superintendent, 14 Dec. 1904, vol. 657, p. 7771; Titcomb to Superintendent, 10 Oct. 1905, vol. 681, p. 5009; Bowers to Superintendent, 20 Oct. 1905, vol. 681, p. 5153; Bowers to Superintendent, 27 Jan. 1906, vol. 683, p. 6248; Bowers to Superintendent, 8 Feb. 1906, vol. 687, p. 7760; Bowers to Superintendent, 17 Mar. 1906, vol. 690, p. 9131, Press Copies of Letters Sent, 1871–1906, RG 22, NA; Wisner to Hume, 6 Sept. 1906, box 6, Hume Papers; Kelly to Commissioner, 19 July 1910, box 26, Rogue River fldr., Records concerning Fish Culture Stations, 1875–1929, RG 22, NA; O'Malley to Commissioner, 11 Oct. 1917, box 370, fldr. 603.3, General Classified Files, 1902–65, RG 22, NA. For inducement and disenchantment concerning dams see A. McCalman to George E. Chamberlain, 15 Mar. 1909; Bowers to Chamberlain, 27 Mar. 1909; Chamberlain to Bowers, 19 July 1909, box 4, Upper Clackamas fldr.; Smith to Superintendent, 22 Aug. 1912, box 8; Records concerning Abandoned Stations, 1879–1931, RG 22, NA; O'Malley to Commissioner, 12 Aug. 191[2], box 8, Records concerning Fish Culture Stations, 1875–1929, RG 22, NA; G. C. Leach to Commissioner, 29 Nov. 1933, box 374, General Classified Files, 1902–65, RG 22, NA; O'Malley to Mitchell, 18 May 1926, 85, 55, 1178, CRPAPCRMM; Bowers to Superintendent, 27 Jan. 1906, vol. 683, p. 6248, Press Copies of Letters Sent, 1871–1906, RG 22, NA.

For in lieu policy see *ARWDFG* (1906): 35–36; "Proposal of the Joint Committees on Fisheries," 30 Jan. 1909, box 1.27, Warren Papers; Lane and Lane Associates, "The Elwha River and Indian Fisheries," prepared for the Bureau of Indian Affairs (1981), p. 55, copy on file at Suzzallo Library, University of Washington, Seattle; Charles W. Maib, "A Historical Note on the Elwha River, Its Power

Development, and Its Industrial Diversion" (Olympia: Stream Improvement Division, Department of Fisheries, 1952), 20; O'Malley to J. R. Russell, 19 Feb. 1932, box 1, Records concerning Fishways and Fish Protection Devices on Water Development Projects, 1919–35, R G 22, N A; Johnson, *Freshwater*, 15.

65. *A R O F C* (1932): 15.

66. *A R O F C* (1931): 30–31; Langston, *Forest Dreams*, 148; Rich to O'Malley, 23 Apr. 1929; O'Malley to Rich, 29 Apr. 1929; Rich to O'Malley, 7 May 1929, box 1, General Correspondence of the Division of Scientific Inquiry, 1880–1935, R G 22, N A; Frank B. Wire, "*Confidential* Memo for Mr. Craig and Mr. Holmes," 1 Nov. 1939, box 611, fldr. 826.51; Rich to Higgins, 23 May 1945, box 606, fldr. 826.1, General Classified Files, 1902–65, R G 22, N A.

67. "Meeting of International Pacific Salmon Investigation Federation . . . 1926," pp. 7–8; Rich to O'Malley, 1 Mar. 1930, box 4, fldr. 3 of 4, Records concerning Societies, Councils, Conferences, and Other Groups, 1904–37, R G 22, N A; Chief of the Division of Scientific Inquiry to Willis H. Rich, 23 Jan. 1934; Rich to Elmer Higgins, 30 Jan. 1934, box 609, fldr. 826.3; Chief, Division of Scientific Inquiry to Dr. Needham, 10 Mar. 1934, box 611, fldr. 826.53, General Classified Files, 1902–65, R G 22, N A. The U S B F archival records are extremely thin for the years 1921–34. The letters pertaining to Needham's request in 1934 were the only references I found to Rich's report, and N W F S C L is the only place possessing a copy of the report.

68. I'm indebted to Keith Benson, Matt Klingle, and Chris Young for helping flesh out a range of possible explanations for the report's obscurity.

69. Willis H. Rich, "The Present State of the Columbia River Salmon Resources," *Proceedings of the Sixth Pacific Science Congress* 3 (1939): 429; W. J. Calderwood, "Hydroelectricity and Salmon Fisheries," *T A F S* 58 (1928): 159–60; Bower, "Alaska Fishery and Fur Industries in 1933," 239–40, 264; Bower, "Alaska Fishery and Fur Industries in 1936," 298; Johnstone, *Aquatic Explorers*, 109–12, 121, 126–27; R. E. Foerster and W. E. Ricker, "Synopsis of Investigations."

70. Rich, "Present State," 429.

71. Willis H. Rich, "Fishery Problems Raised by the Development of Water Resources," *Stanford Ichthyological Bulletin* 1 (May 1940): 177–78.

72. Marsh, *Report*, app., 39.

73. Rich, "Present State," 426; John N. Cobb, "High Dams and Fish," *T A F S* 58 (1928): 114–16; Cobb to F. P. Kendall, 17 Jan. 1929, box 4, fldr. 3, Cobb Papers; "Biologist's Report: Summary of Stream Surveys, State of Washington, to Feb. 20, 1931," box 2, General Correspondence of the Division of Scientific Inquiry, 1880–1935, R G 22, N A; George B. Kelez, "The Silver Salmon of Puget Sound" (1935), box 609, file 826.3; Rich to Higgins, 6 Feb. 1941 and 25 Feb. 1941, box 611, fldr. 826.53, General Classified Files, 1902–65, R G 22, N A; James H. Cellars, "Save the Salmon,"

[Astoria] Bumble Bee 1 (Jan. 1945): 2; James H. Cellars, "Now the Cowlitz," *Bumble Bee* 4 (Nov. 1950): 2, in research library, CRMM; John T. Gharrett and John I. Hodges, *Salmon Fisheries of the Coastal Rivers of Oregon South of the Columbia*, Oregon Fish Commission Contribution 13 (Portland: Oregon Fish Commission, 1950), 10; Rich, "Fishery Problems," 177, 179–81; Richard White, *The Organic Machine: The Remaking of the Columbia River* (New York: Hill and Wang, 1995), 92–94.

74. Mitchell Act, 52 Stat. 345 75th Cong., 3d sess. (11 May 1938); Daniel C. Roper to Secretary of War, 6 Nov. 1934; Roper to Robert Smith, 25 Feb. 1936, vol. 1, Copies of Letters Sent by the Secretary of Commerce, Daniel C. Roper, 1934–36, RG 22, NA; F. A. Davidson, "Fishery Protection and the Development of Water Power and Irrigation," 14 Jan. 1937; Frank T. Bell to B. M. Brennan, 7 Feb. 1937; Joseph A. Craig, "Notes on Columbia River Investigation"; Joseph A. Craig, "Memorandum regarding Time of Run and Location of Spawning Grounds of the Columbia River Salmon and Steelhead Trout," c. June 1937; Fred J. Foster, "Outline of Artificial Propagation of Fish on the Lower Columbia River," c. July 1937, box 611, fldr. 826.53, General Classified Files, 1902–65, RG 22, NA; Interior Department, *Columbia River Basin*, 502–6; Leo L. Laythe, "The Fishery Development Program in the Lower Columbia River," *TAFS* 78 (1948): 42–55.

For mitigation see John N. Cobb, "Protecting Migrating Pacific Salmon," *TAFS* 52 (1922): 146–56; L. E. Mayhall, "Propagation Work and the Problems of Perpetuating the Salmon Fisheries of Washington," *TAFS* 57 (1927): 165–70; John N. Cobb, "Preliminary Report of Fishway Work," *TAFS* 57 (1927): 181–201; Shirley Baker, "Fish Screens in Irrigation Ditches," *TAFS* 58 (1928): 80–82; F. O. McMillan, "Electric Fish Screens," *Bulletin* 44 (1928): 215–64; U. B. Gilroy to J. R. Russell, 31 Mar. 1932, box 1, Records concerning Fishways and Fish Protection Devices on Water Development Projects, 1919–35, RG 22, NA; Paul R. Needham, Osgood R. Smith, and Harry A. Hanson, "Salmon Salvage Problems in Relation to Shasta Dam, California, and Notes on the Biology of the Sacramento River Salmon," *TAFS* 70 (1940): 55–69; Carl L. Hubbs, H. L. Shantz, J. N. Darling, A. H. Wiebe, Elmer Higgins, Kenneth A. Reid, Frank B. Wire, James R. Simon, and A. D. Aldrich, "The Place of Fish Production in a Program of Multiple Water Use," *TAFS* 71 (1941): 297–314; Interior Department, *Columbia River Basin*, 462–63, 504.

75. "Fishery Protection and the Development of Water Power and Irrigation," 14 Jan. 1937, file 826.53, box 611; Joseph T. Barnaby, "Development of the Salmon Fisheries of the Lower Columbia River," 25 May 1945, fldr. 660.1, box 451; Joseph T. Barnaby, "Dams That Should Be Removed or Provided with Fishways," Oct. 1945, fldr. 826.1, box 606; Holmes to Higgins, 23 June 1942, file 826.5, box 611, General Classified Files, 1902–65, RG 22, NA; James R. Sedell and Karen J. Luchessa, "Using the Historical Record as an Aid to Salmonid Habitat Enhancement," in *Acquisition and Utilization of Aquatic Habitat Inventory Information*, ed.

Neil B. Armantrout (Portland: American Fisheries Society, Western Division, 1982), 216, 219; Howard L. Raymond, "Effects of Hydroelectric Development and Fisheries Enhancement on Spring and Summer Chinook Salmon and Steelhead in the Columbia River Basin," *NAJFM* 8 (winter 1988): 8. Oregon had been trying to open streams to barges since the 1870s; *Oregonian*, 12 Aug. 1870, 2; 30 Oct. 1910, sec. 1, 5; 15 Nov. 1910, 7.

76. Interior Department, *Columbia River Basin*, 314, 504, 506; "Development of the Salmon Fisheries of the Lower Columbia River," 25 May 1945; Milo Moore, "Memorandum: Relation of Fisheries Administration in the State of Washington to the Federal Agencies," 2 May 1945; Robert S. Dreimer to Bureau of Fisheries, 27 May 1945, box 451, fldr. 660.1, General Classified Files, 1902–65, RG 22, NA; *AROFC* (1935): 14–16; Paul C. Pitzer, "Grand Coulee—The Dam" (Ph.D. diss., University of Oregon, 1990), 2:432.

77. Interior Department, *Columbia River Basin*, 313, 369, 370; Paul Pitzer, *Grand Coulee: Harnessing A Dream* (Pullman: Washington State University Press, 1994), 226–27; Barnaby to Chief, Division of Scientific Inquiry, "Report on Operations and Accomplishments," Oct. 1945, box 606, fldr. 826.1, General Classified Files, 1902–65, RG 22, NA.

78. Harlan B. Holmes, "The Passage of Fish at Bonneville Dam," *Stanford Ichthyological Bulletin* 1 (May 1940): 183, 185; John R. Gardner to Burt MacBride, 27 Apr. 1944; McBride to Dr. Gabrielson, 17 Apr. 1944; McBride to Gardner, 2 May 1944, box 452, fldr. 660.1, General Classified Files, 1902–65, RG 22, NA; Pitzer, *Grand Coulee*, 228–29; Rosenberg, *No Other Gods*, 194.

79. "Report of Investigations on Methods of Preserving Columbia River Salmon," 7 Feb. 1938; F. A. Davidson, "Memorandum of Report of Preliminary Investigations into the Possible Methods of Preserving the Columbia River Salmon and Steelhead at the Grand Coulee Dam, by B. M. Brennan, Washington State Department of Fisheries," c. Jan. 1938, box 611, fldr. 826.53, General Classified Files, 1902–65, RG 22, NA.

80. Chief, Division of Scientific Inquiry, to F. A. Davidson, 21 June 1939, box 605, fldr. 826.1; Holmes to S. O. Harper, 11 Apr. 1942; Harlan Holmes to Director, 24 June 1942, box 611, fldr. 826.5, General Classified Files, 1902–65, RG 22, NA; Pitzer, *Grand Coulee*, 227–28; James W. Mullan, "Determinants of Sockeye Salmon Abundance in the Columbia River, 1880's–1982: A Review and Synthesis," *Biological Report* 86 (Sept. 1986): 102.

81. Sedell and Luchessa, "Using the Historical Record," 219; Karen Leidholt-Bruner, David E. Hibbs, and William C. McComb, "Beaver Dam Locations and Their Effects on Distribution and Abundance of Coho Salmon in Two Coastal Oregon Streams," *Northwest Science* 66 (Nov. 1992): 220–22. While fishery agencies were clearing streams in western Oregon, the U.S. Forest Service was reintroducing

beaver to save watersheds in eastern Oregon; Langston, *Forest Dreams,* 229; Harlan Holmes, "Program for Fish Salvage Work in Connection with Grand Coulee Fish Salvage for Period July 1, 1942 to June 30, 1943," 20 May 1942, box 611, fldr. 826.5; Barnaby, "Report on Operations and Accomplishments," General Classified Files, 1902–65, RG 22, NA.

82. Needham to Frederick F. Fish, 14 June 1945, box 451, fldr. 660.1; Barnaby, "Report on Operations and Accomplishments."

83. Johnstone, *Aquatic Explorers,* 149–50; R. E. Foerster and W. E. Ricker, "The Effect of Reduction of Predaceous Fish on Survival of Young Sockeye Salmon at Cultus Lake," *Journal of the Fisheries Research Board of Canada* 5 (Dec. 1941): 315–36; Lauren R. Donaldson and Fred J. Foster, "A Summary Table of Some Experimental Tests in Feeding Young Salmon and Trout," *TAFS* 67 (1937): 262–70; Lauren R. Donaldson and Fred J. Foster, "Experimental Study of the Effect of Various Water Temperatures on the Growth, Food Utilization, and Mortality Rates of Fingerling Sockeye Salmon," *TAFS* 70 (1940): 339–46; Fred J. Foster, "Inspection of Clackamas, Oregon, Carson, Washington, Little White and Big White Salmon Stations," 19 Dec. 1939, box 372, file 603.3, General Classified Files, 1902–65, RG 22, NA.

84. H. S. Davis, "Laying the Foundations of Fishery Management: A Review of the Aquacultural Investigations of the Bureau of Fisheries," *Progressive Fish Culturist* 50 (May/June 1940): 1; Elmer Higgins, "Can the Fisheries Supply More Food during a National Emergency?" *TAFS* 71 (1941): 61–73; Barnaby, "Report on Operations and Accomplishments." I am indebted to John Halver for information on the broad sweep of research by the U.S. Fish and Wildlife Service during this period; John E. Halver, "The Vitamins," in *Fish Nutrition,* ed. John E. Halver, 32–35; Robert P. Wilson, "Amino Acids and Proteins," in *Fish Nutrition,* 112–17; James C. Simpson, "Report of the Chairman of the Western Division," *TAFS* 81 (1951): 319–20; Holmes, "Program for Fish Salvage Work"; Stickney, *Aquaculture,* 169–71, 190–92.

85. R. E. Foerster, "Restocking Depleted Sockeye Salmon Areas by Transfer of Eggs," *Journal of the Fisheries Research Board of Canada* 6 (Oct. 1946): 489–90; Gharrett and Hodges, *Salmon Fisheries of Coastal Rivers,* 29; R. E. Foerster, "On the Relation of Adult Sockeye Salmon (*Oncorhynchus nerka*) Returns to Known Smolt Seaward Migrations," *Journal of the Fisheries Research Board of Canada* 11 (July 1954): 349–50; R. R. Rucker, W. J. Whipple, J. R. Parvin, and C. A. Evans, "A Contagious Disease of Salmon Possibly of Virus Origin," *Bulletin* 76 (1953): 35–46; Anthony Netboy, *Salmon of the Pacific Northwest: Fish vs. Dams* (Portland: Binfords and Mort, 1958), 96–98; McKernan et al., "Some Factors," 435, 446; Jack M. Van Hyning, *Factors Affecting the Abundance of Fall Chinook Salmon in the Columbia River,* Research Reports of the Fish Commission of Oregon 4 (Salem: Oregon Fish Commission,

1973), 23; Mullan, "Determinants of Sockeye Abundance," iii; Holmes, "Program for Fish Salvage Work"; Roger E. Burrows, "Environmental Factors in Rearing Ponds," in *Ninth Annual Northwest Fish Culture Conference* (Seattle, 1958), 58–62, in research library, CRMM.

86. Theodore R. Merrell Jr., Melvin D. Collins, and Joseph W. Greenough, "An Estimate of Mortality of Chinook Salmon in the Columbia River near Bonneville Dam during the Summer Run of 1955," *Bulletin* 68 (1971): 461–92; Wesley J. Ebel, "Supersaturation of Nitrogen in the Columbia River and Its Effect on Salmon and Steelhead Trout," *Bulletin* 68 (1969): 1–11; Robert W. Schoning and Donald R. Johnson, *A Measured Delay in the Migration of Adult Chinook Salmon at Bonneville Dam on the Columbia River,* Oregon Fish Commission Contribution no. 23 (Portland: Oregon Fish Commission, 1956); Richard B. Thompson, "Food of the Squawfish *Ptychocheilus oregonensis* (Richardson) of the Lower Columbia River," *Bulletin* 60 (1959): 58; Mullan, "Determinants of Sockeye Abundance," 99; Richard L. Major and Gerald J. Paulik, "Effect of Encroachment of Wanapum Dam Reservoir on Fish Passage over Rock Island Dam, Columbia River," *Bulletin* 70 (1972): 132; Richard L. Major and James L. Mighell, "Influence of Rocky Reach Dam and the Temperature of the Okanogan River on the Upstream Migration of Sockeye Salmon," *Bulletin* 66 (1967): 136, 145–46; Van Hyning, *Factors,* 47.

87. Bruce A. McIntosh, James R. Sedell, Jeanette E. Smith, Robert C. Wissmar, Sharon E. Clarke, Gordon H. Reeves, and Lisa A. Brown, "Historical Changes in Fish Habitat for Select River Basins of Eastern Oregon and Washington," *Northwest Science* 68 (Special Issue 1994): 40; Mullan, "Determinants of Sockeye Abundance," 21, 41; Van Hyning, *Factors,* 45, 49, 54; Frederick Charles Cleaver, "The Effects of Ocean Fishing upon the Columbia River Hatchery Stocks of Fall Chinook Salmon" (Ph.D. diss., University of Washington, 1967), 140–41; Sedell and Luchessa, "Using the Historical Record," 220; William G. Pearcy, *Ocean Ecology of North Pacific Salmonids* (Seattle: University of Washington Press, 1992), 49.

88. William F. Royce, "An Interpretation of Salmon Production Trends," in *Salmon Production, Management, and Allocation: Biological, Economic, and Policy Issues,* ed. William J. McNeill (Corvallis: Oregon State University Press, 1988), 16; P. A. Larkin, "Power Development and Fish Conservation on the Fraser River," c. 1956; Loyd A. Royal to Commissioners, 24 May 1956, box 1, Research Reports Issued by the International Pacific Salmon Fisheries Commission, 1945–56, RG 22, NA.

89. I am indebted to John Halver for his insights into the history of fish feed development; Hardy, "Diet Preparation," 476–79; Stickney, *Aquaculture,* 188–89.

90. Johnson, *Freshwater,* 21; Hardy, "Diet Preparation," 478–79; Netboy, *Salmon of the Pacific Northwest,* 107–8; Anthony Netboy, *Columbia River Salmon and Steelhead Trout: Their Fight for Survival* (Seattle: University of Washington Press, 1980), 107; Groot and Margolis, *Pacific Salmon Life Histories,* 60–61.

91. Alan M. Mcgie, "Commentary: Evidence for Density Dependence among Coho Salmon Stocks in the Oregon Production Index Area," in *The Influence of Ocean Conditions on the Production of Salmonids in the North Pacific,* ed. William G. Pearcy (Corvallis: Oregon State University, 1984), 37; Robert C. Wissmar, Jeanette E. Smith, Bruce A. McIntosh, Hiram W. Li, Gordon H. Reeves, and James R. Sedell, "A History of Resource Use and Disturbance in Riverine Basins of Eastern Oregon and Washington (Early 1800s–1990s)," *Northwest Science* 68 (Special Issue 1994): 26; *Seattle Times,* 10 Jan. 1960, 14; Max Savelle, "Of Fish and the River," *Pacific Northwest Quarterly* 50 (Jan. 1959): 26–27; Netboy, *Salmon of the Pacific Northwest,* 114; Cicely Lyons, *Salmon, Our Heritage,* 628–33; Ray Hilborn and John Winton, "Learning to Enhance Salmon Production: Lessons from the Salmonid Enhancement Program," *Canadian Journal of Fisheries and Aquatic Sciences* 50 (Sept. 1993): 2043–56; John Winton and Ray Hilborn, "Lessons from Supplementation of Chinook Salmon in British Columbia," *NAJFM* 14 (winter 1994): 1–13.

92. McGie, "Commentary," 37; Carl J. Walters, "Mixed-Stock Fisheries and the Sustainability of Enhancement Production for Chinook and Coho Salmon," in *Salmon Production, Management, and Allocation,* ed. McNeill, 110–12; Winton and Hilborn, "Lessons from Supplementation," 1–13; Mark Herrmann and Joshua A. Greenberg, "A Revenue Analysis of the Alaska Pink Salmon Fishery," *NAJFM* 14 (Aug. 1994): 537–49; Ken Collis, Roy E. Beaty, and Bradford R. Crain, "Changes in Catch Rate and Diet of Northern Squawfish Associated with the Release of Hatchery-Reared Juvenile Salmonids in a Columbia Reservoir," *NAJFM* 15 (May 1995): 346–57; Ray Hilborn, "The Economic Performance of Marine Stock Enhancement Projects," *Bulletin of Marine Sciences* (in press); Pearcy, *Ocean Ecology,* 45–54; Johnson, *Freshwater,* 25; R. C. Francis, S. R. Hare, A. B. Hollowed, and W. S. Wooster, "Effects of Interdecadal Climate Variability on the Oceanic Ecosystems of the Northeast Pacific," *Fisheries Oceanography* 7 (Mar. 1998): 1–21; S. R. Hare, N. J. Mantua, and R. C. Francis, "Inverse Production Regimes: Alaska and West Coast Pacific Salmon," *Fisheries* 24 (Jan.–Feb. 1999): 6–14; Daniel L. Erickson and Ellen K. Pikitch, "Incidental Catch of Chinook Salmon in Commercial Bottom Trawls off the U.S. West Coast," *NAJFM* 14 (Aug. 1994): 550–63; Sandra Hines, "Born to be Wild?" *Columns* (Dec. 1991): 21; "Commissioner Schlip Speaks Out," *Tagline: The Newsletter of the Oregon Salmon Commission* 6 (Oct. 1992): 4–5.

93. Langston, *Forest Dreams,* 148.

8 / TAKING RESPONSIBILITY

1. Martin Anderson, *Impostors in the Temple* (New York: Simon and Schuster, 1992); William J. Bennett, *The De-valuing of America: The Fight for Our Culture and Our Children* (New York: Summit Books, 1992); Lynne V. Cheney, *Telling the*

Truth: Why Our Culture and Our Country Have Stopped Making Sense—And What We Can Do about It (New York: Simon and Schuster, 1995); John Clive, *Not by Fact Alone: Essays on the Writing and Reading of History* (New York: Houghton Mifflin, 1989); Gary B. Nash, Charlotte Crabtree, and Ross E. Dunn, *History on Trial: Culture Wars and the Teaching of the Past* (New York: A. A. Knopf, 1997); Peter Novick, *That Noble Dream: The "Objectivity Question" and the American Historical Profession* (New York: Cambridge University Press, 1988); Arthur M. Schlesinger Jr., *The Disuniting of America* (New York: Norton, 1992).

2. William Cronon, "A Place for Stories: Nature, History, and Narrative," *Journal of American History* 78 (Mar. 1992): 1347–76; Lawrence B. Slobodkin, *Simplicity and Complexity in Games of the Intellect* (Cambridge: Harvard University Press, 1992), 26, 65, 79, 150, 224–27.

3. Sidney W. Mintz, *Sweetness and Power: The Place of Sugar in Modern History* (New York: Viking, 1985), 157–58.

4. In recent decades industrialists have joined sportsmen to demonize gillnetters, and although they have enjoyed little political success since the 1960s, they have maintained a steady parade of laws and ballot measures. As late as 1992 in Oregon and 1995 in Washington, voters and legislators were still presented with these tactics; Bob Woods, *Kilowatts and Salmon: A Look at the Cost and Benefits of Preserving the Spawning Grounds and Habits of Commercial Salmon in the Upper Columbia River* (reprint, *Wenatchee Daily World*, 27 Feb.–10 Mar. 1958); Richard White, *The Organic Machine: The Remaking of the Columbia River* (New York: Hill and Wang, 1995), 105; Courtland L. Smith, *Salmon Fishers of the Columbia* (Corvallis: Oregon State University Press, 1979), 99; Joseph Cone, *A Common Fate: Endangered Salmon and the People of the Pacific Northwest* (New York: Henry Holt, 1995).

5. Bruce Brown, *Mountain in the Clouds: A Search for the Wild Salmon* (New York: Simon and Schuster, 1982), 239; Tom Jay, "Homecoming," in *Reaching Home: Pacific Salmon, Pacific People*, ed. Natalie Fobes, Tom Jay, and Brad Matsen (Anchorage: Alaska Northwest Books, 1994), 125–26, 128.

6. Cone, *Common Fate*, 61, 310.

7. Hal Rothman, *The Greening of a Nation? Environmentalism in the United States since 1945* (Fort Worth: Harcourt Brace, 1998), 209; Roderick Nash, *Wilderness and the American Mind*, 3d ed. (New Haven: Yale University Press, 1982), 343; Hal Rothman, *Devil's Bargains: Tourism in the Twentieth-Century American West* (Lawrence: University Press of Kansas, 1998); Ronald Bailey, *Ecoscam: The False Prophets of Ecological Apocalypse* (New York: St. Martin's, 1993); Alston Chase, *In a Dark Wood: The Fight over Forests and the Rising Tyranny of Ecology* (Boston: Houghton Mifflin, 1995); William Cronon, ed., *Uncommon Ground: Toward Reinventing Nature* (New York: W. W. Norton, 1995); Robert Gottlieb, *Forcing the Spring: The Transformation of the American Environmental Movement* (Washington,

D.C.: Island Press, 1993); Samuel P. Hays, *Beauty, Health, and Permanence: Environmental Politics in the United States, 1955–1985* (New York: Cambridge University Press, 1987); John C. Miles, *Guardians of the Parks: A History of the National Parks and Conservation Association* (Washington, D.C.: Taylor and Francis, 1995); Donald Worster, *The Wealth of Nature: Environmental History and the Ecological Imagination* (New York: Oxford University Press, 1993), 184–202.

8. Phone conversation with Rich Kolb, 20 Dec. 1994; Ravenna Creek Alliance, "Help Us Bring Ravenna Creek Back to Light," (Seattle, 1995).

9. William Cronon, "Kennecott Journey: The Paths Out of Town," in *Under an Open Sky: Rethinking America's Western Past*, ed. William Cronon, George Miles, and Jay Gitlin (New York: Norton, 1992), 39; *Oregonian*, 12 June 1996, B1, B7; 8 Aug. 1997, C1, C4; 28 Aug. 1997, C11; 10 Sept. 1997, B9; 28 Oct. 1997, B7; 17 Jan. 1998, D1, D3; Carl Abbott, Debra Howe, and Sy Adler, eds., *Planning the Oregon Way: A Twenty-Year Evaluation* (Corvallis: Oregon State University Press, 1994).

10. *Oregonian*, 4 Dec. 1994, B14; 8 Dec. 1994, C3; 4 Oct. 1996, B9; 14 Feb. 1997, C9; 11 Mar. 1997, D11; 27 Mar. 1997, D11; 21 May 1997, A11; 28 May 1997, B2; 7 June 1997, D1; 13 June 1997, C9; 29 June 1997, E5; 23 Sept. 1997, C11; Terry L. Anderson and Donald R. Leal, "The Rise of the Enviro-Capitalists," *Wall Street Journal*, 26 Aug. 1997; Carl Abbott, Sy Adler, and Margery Post Abbott, *Planning a New West: The Columbia River Gorge National Scenic Area* (Corvallis: Oregon State University Press, 1997), 133, 154, 166, 178; Richard White, " 'Are You an Environmentalist or Do You Work for a Living?' Work and Nature," in *Uncommon Ground*, ed. Cronon, 171–85; Ed Whitelaw, "Oregon's Real Economy," *Old Oregon* 72 (winter 1992): 30–33; Dave Frohnmayer, "Oregon's New Future," *Oregon Quarterly* 74 (autumn 1994): 14–17; Ed Whitelaw, "Rich Oregonian, Poor Oregonian," *Oregon Quarterly* 74 (summer 1995): 28–30; Jeff Kuechle, "Portland vs. Everybody: Why Does the Rest of the State Resent the Rose City?" *Oregon Quarterly* 74 (winter 1994): 21–23.

11. Donald L. Parman, "Inconstant Advocacy: The Erosion of Indian Fishing Rights in the Pacific Northwest, 1933–1956," *Pacific Historical Review* 53 (May 1984): 163–89; American Friends Service Committee (AFSC), *Uncommon Controversy: Fishing Rights of the Muckleshoot, Puyallup, and Nisqually Indians* (Seattle: University of Washington Press, 1970), 107–46; Fay G. Cohen, *Treaties on Trial: The Continuing Controversy over Northwest Indian Fishing Rights* (Seattle: University of Washington Press, 1986), 67–82; Daniel L. Boxberger, *To Fish in Common: The Ethnohistory of Lummi Indian Salmon Fishing* (Lincoln: University of Nebraska Press, 1989), 127–53.

12. AFSC, *Uncommon Controversy*, 201; *Maison v. Confederated Tribes of the Umatilla Indian Reservation*, 314 F. 2d 169 (CA 9, 1963). For Oregon cases see *Sohappy v. Smith*, USDC D, Oregon, no. 68–409 (1969); and *United States v. Oregon*,

USDC D, Oregon, no. 68–513 (1969); Cohen, *Treaties on Trial*, 90–91, 109, 115, 120; Brown, *Mountain in the Clouds*, 161. For Washington cases see *Puyallup Tribe v. Department of Game*, 391 U.S. 392, 20 L. Ed 689 (1968); *Puyallup Tribe v. Department of Game*, 414 U.S. 44 (1973); *U.S. v. Washington*, 384 F. Supp. 312 (1974); *U.S. v. Washington*, Phase II, 506 F. Supp. 187 (1980).

13. Cohen, *Treaties on Trial*, 115, 83–153; AFSC, *Uncommon Controversy*, 200–208; Lisa Mighetto and Wesley J. Ebel, *Saving the Salmon: A History of the U.S. Army Corps of Engineers' Efforts to Protect Anadromous Fish on the Columbia and Snake Rivers* (Seattle: Historical Research Associates, 1994), 159–61; Dianne Newell, *Tangled Webs of History: Indians and the Law in Canada's Pacific Coast Fisheries* (Toronto: University of Toronto Press, 1993).

14 For Savage Rapids Dam see *Oregonian*, 29 Oct. 1994, C1, C6; 29 Dec. 1994, F10; 16 June 1997, E6; 23 July 1997, C7; 6 Aug. 1997, C7; 11 May 1998, A1, A8. For the Elwha dams see *Seattle Times*, 19 May 1994, A1; 9 Aug. 1994, B5; 18 Aug. 1994, B8; *Newsweek*, 17 Nov. 1997, 70; *Oregonian*, 4 Apr. 1997, B6; 16 Nov. 1997, E3; 17 Nov. 1997, E8.

15. Cone, *Common Fate*, 133–34, 208–9; Blaine Harden, *A River Lost: The Life and Death of the Columbia* (New York: Norton, 1996), 25–27; Keith C. Petersen, *River of Life, Channel of Death: Fish and Dams on the Lower Snake* (Lewiston: Confluence Press, 1995), 140–41, 184–85.

16. A. E. Giorgi, T. W. Hillman, J. R. Stevenson, S. G. Hays, and C. M. Peven, "Factors That Influence the Downstream Migration Rates of Juvenile Salmon and Steelhead through the Hydroelectric System in the Mid–Columbia River Basin," *NAJFM* 17 (May 1997): 268–82; David L. Ward, Raymond R. Boyce, Franklin R. Young, and Frederick E. Olney, "A Review and Assessment of Transportation Studies for Juvenile Chinook Salmon in the Snake River," *NAJFM* 17 (Aug. 1997): 652–62; D. Chapman, C. Carlson, D. Weitkamp, G. Matthews, J. Stevenson, and M. Miller, "Homing in Sockeye and Chinook Salmon Transported around Part of Their Smolt Migration Route in the Columbia River," *NAJFM* 17 (Feb. 1997): 101–13; Robert M. Bugert, Glen W. Mendel, and Paul R. Seidel, "Adult Returns of Subyearling and Yearling Fall Chinook Salmon Released from a Snake River Hatchery or Transported Downstream," *NAJFM* 17 (Aug. 1997): 638–51; *Northwest Salmon Recovery Report* (Pendelton), 9 May 1997; Brad Matsen, "Barging down the River," in *Reaching Home*, ed. Fobes et al., 61–90.

17. D. D. Dauble and D. G. Watson, "Status of Fall Chinook Salmon Populations in the Mid–Columbia River, 1948–1992," *NAJFM* 17 (May 1997): 283–300; Independent Scientific Group, *Return to the River: Restoration of Salmonid Fishes in the Columbia River Ecosystem* (Portland: Northwest Power Planning Council, 1996), xxiv.

18. *Oregonian*, 9 Nov. 1996, A1, A11; 13 Dec. 1997, B1, B13; *Northwest Salmon*

Recovery Report, 7 Mar. 1997, 1, 12; 11 July 1997, 1, 3–8; "New Plan for Rescuing the Salmon," *New York Times,* 21 Apr. 1997; "The Big One" and "Damned If You Do," *Economist* 344 (29 Mar. 1997): 27–28. For support for breaching the dams see *Oregonian,* 4 Aug. 1997, B13; 8 Aug. 1997, C13; 3 Sept. 1997, E9; 8 Sept. 1997, E9; 18 Sept. 1997, B9; 20 Sept. 1997, C7. For opposition see *Oregonian,* 19 July 1996; 2 June 1997, B9; 8 Aug. 1997, C13; 23 Sept. 1997, C11; 2 Dec. 1997. For blaming others see *Oregonian,* 22 Aug. 1996, E8; 22 May 1997, D13; 5 Oct. 1997, A1, A16–17; 10 Jan. 1998, D11; 31 May 1998, E5; *Las Vegas Review-Journal* and *Las Vegas Sun,* 30 Mar. 1997, 6B.

19. Harden, *A River Lost,* 216–17, 228–29, 235–38; Cone, *Common Fate,* 30–39, 155–56; Petersen, *River of Life,* 225–26; *Oregonian,* 27 July 1997, A1, A16–17; 28 July 1997, A1, A6–7; 4 Aug. 1997, B13; 5 Oct. 1997, A1, A16–17; 10 Dec. 1997, D1.

20. *Northwest Salmon Recovery Report,* 28 Mar. 1997, 2; 9 May 1997, 1, 8–11; 30 May 1997, 1, 10–12.

21. Timothy Egan, *The Good Rain: Across Time and Terrain in the Pacific Northwest* (New York: Alfred A. Knopf, 1990), 22; White, *Organic Machine,* 90–91; Cone, *Common Fate,* 71; Brown, *Mountain in the Clouds;* Natalie Fobes, "Initiation," in *Reaching Home,* ed. Fobes et al., 17; Jay, "Homecoming"; Anthony Netboy, *The Columbia River Salmon and Steelhead Trout: Their Fight for Survival* (Seattle: University of Washington Press, 1980); Petersen, *River of Life,* 13–14; William G. Robbins, "The World of Columbia River Salmon: Nature, Culture, and the Great River of the West," in *The Northwest Salmon Crisis: A Documentary History,* ed. Joseph Cone and Sandy Ridlington (Corvallis: Oregon State University Press, 1996), 21; William G. Robbins, *Landscapes of Promise: The Oregon Story, 1800–1940* (Seattle: University of Washington Press, 1997), 305; Harden, *A River Lost,* 16, 18, 130, 140, 183–84, 106–7; *Oregonian,* 13 Aug. 1997, B9; 30 Nov. 1997, E5; 9 Dec. 1997, B8. For regionalism see John Findlay, "A Fishy Proposition: Regional Identity in the Pacific Northwest," in *Many Wests: Place, Culture, and Regional Identity,* ed. David M. Wrobel and Michael R. Steiner (Lawrence: University Press of Kansas, 1997), 37–70; William L. Lang, "River of Change: Salmon, Time, and Crisis on the Columbia River," in *Northwest Salmon Crisis,* ed. Cone and Ridlington, 355. The battle of symbolism is far from over. While residents battle over salmon's importance, gourmet merchants have begun marketing the fish to generate restoration funding. Thus they want us to consume salmon to save salmon; *Oregonian,* 2 May 1997, D14; 9 June 1997, B9; 12 Oct. 1997, E1, E2.

22. Christopher D. Stone, *Should Trees Have Standing? Toward Legal Rights for Natural Objects* (Los Altos: Kaufmann, 1974).

23. Sheila Jasanoff, *Science at the Bar: Law, Science, and Technology in America* (Cambridge: Harvard University Press, 1995), 42–49.

24. Mitchell J. Willis, *Out-System Transfers of Coho Salmon Stocks in Coastal*

River Systems, Information Report Series, Fisheries no. 79–9 (Corvallis: Oregon Department of Fish and Wildlife, Fish Division, 1979), 1; *Tagline: The Newsletter of the Oregon Salmon Commission* 6 (Oct. 1992): 4–5; Arthur F. McEvoy, *The Fisherman's Problem: Law and Ecology in the California Fisheries, 1850 to 1980* (New York: Cambridge University Press, 1980), 198–203; Tim D. Smith, *Scaling Fisheries: The Science of Measuring the Effects of Fishing, 1855–1955* (New York: Cambridge University Press, 1994), 2; Carl J. Walters and Jeremy S. Collie, "Is Research on Environmental Factors Useful to Fisheries Management?" *Canadian Journal of Fisheries and Aquatic Science* 45 (1988): 1848–54. For repeating science see D. W. Chapman, "Effects of Logging upon Fish Resources of the West Coast," *Journal of Forestry* 60 (Aug. 1962): 533; Jack M. Van Hyning, *Factors Affecting the Abundance of Fall Chinook Salmon in the Columbia River*, Research Reports of the Fish Commission of Oregon 4 (Salem: Oregon Fish Commission, 1973), 4; Dennis L. Scarnecchia, "Effects of Streamflow and Upwelling on Yield of Wild Coho Salmon (*Oncorhynchus kisutch*) in Oregon," *Canadian Journal of Fisheries and Aquatic Science* 38 (Apr. 1981): 474; S. B. Mathews, "Variability of Marine Survival of Pacific Salmonids: A Review," in *The Influence of Ocean Conditions on the Production of Salmonids in the North Pacific*, ed. William G. Pearcy (Corvallis: Oregon State University Press, 1984), 180; Kevin Hamilton, "A Study of the Variability of the Return Migration Route of Fraser River Sockeye Salmon (*Oncorhynchus nerka*)," *Canadian Journal of Zoology* 63 (Aug. 1985): 1932.

25. Ray Hilborn, "Institutional Learning and Spawning Channels for Sockeye Salmon (*Oncorhynchus nerka*)," *Canadian Journal of Fisheries and Aquatic Sciences* 49 (June 1992): 1126–36; Ray Hilborn, "Can Fisheries Agencies Learn from Experience?" *Fisheries* 17 (July–Aug. 1992): 6–14; Ray Hilborn, "Statistical Hypothesis Testing and Decision Theory in Fisheries Science," *Fisheries* 22 (Oct. 1997): 19–20; McEvoy, *Fisherman's Problem*, 202; Nancy Langston, *Forest Dreams, Forest Nightmares: The Paradox of Old Growth in the Inland West* (Seattle: University of Washington Press, 1995), 211, 221, 286; Ray Hilborn and John Winton, "Learning to Enhance Salmon Production: Lessons from the Salmonid Enhancement Program," *Canadian Journal of Fisheries and Aquatic Sciences* 50 (Sept. 1993): 2054; *Seattle Times*, 8 June 1997, B5; *Oregonian*, 4 Aug. 1997, B13; 29 Nov. 1997, E6; 8 Dec. 1997, A1, A10.

26. White, *Organic Machine*, 48, 90; Peter A. Larkin, "Maybe You Can't Get There from Here: A Foreshortened History of Research in Relation to Management of Pacific Salmon," *Journal of the Fisheries Research Board of Canada* 36 (Jan. 1979): 98–106.

27. *Oregonian*, 31 May 1998, E5. See also Mighetto and Ebel, *Saving the Salmon*.

SOURCE NOTES FOR MAPS

Map 1. Leonard A. Fulton, *Spawning Areas and Abundance of Chinook Salmon* *("Oncorhynchus tshawytscha")* *in the Columbia River Basin—Past and Present*, U.S. Fish and Wildlife Service Special Scientific Report—Fisheries no. 571 (Washington: Government Printing Office, 1968); Leonard A. Fulton, *Spawning Areas and Abundance of Steelhead Trout and Coho, Sockeye, and Chum Salmon—Past and Present*, U.S. Fish and Wildlife Service Special Scientific Report—Fisheries no. 618 (Washington: Government Printing Office, 1970).

Map 2. Leonard A. Fulton, *Spawning Areas and Abundance of Chinook Salmon* *("Oncorhynchus tshawytscha")* *in the Columbia River Basin—Past and Present*, U.S. Fish and Wildlife Service Special Scientific Report—Fisheries no. 571 (Washington: Government Printing Office, 1968); Leonard A. Fulton, *Spawning Areas and Abundance of Steelhead Trout and Coho, Sockeye, and Chum Salmon—Past and Present*, U.S. Fish and Wildlife Service Special Scientific Report—Fisheries no. 618 (Washington: Government Printing Office, 1970).

Map 3. *HNAI, NWC*; Gordon W. Hewes, "Aboriginal Use of Fishery Resources in Northwestern North America" (Ph.D. diss., University of California, Berkeley, 1947).

Map 4. Rodman W. Paul, *Mining Frontiers of the Far West, 1848–1880* (New York: Holt, Rinehart, and Winston, 1963); Randall Rohe, "The Geographical Impact of Placer Mining in the American West, 1848–1974" (Ph.D. diss., University of Colorado, 1978).

Map 5. Frederick A. Davidson, "The Development of Irrigation in the Yakima River Basin and Its Effect on the Migratory Fish Populations in the River" (1965; copy on file at the Grant County Public Utilities District Library, Ephrata, Wash.); Samuel N. Dicken and Emily F. Dicken, *The Making of Oregon: A Study in Historical Geography* (Portland: Oregon Historical Society, 1979); Carl H. Eigenmann, "Results of Explorations in Western Canada and the Northwestern United States," *Bulletin* 16 (1894): 101–32; Charles H. Gilbert and Barton W. Evermann, "A Report upon Investigations in the Columbia River Basin, with Descriptions of Four New Species of Fishes," *Bulletin* 14 (1894): 169–207; Fred F. Henshaw and H. J. Dean, *Surface Water Supply of Oregon, 1878–1910*, U.S. Geological Survey Water-Supply Paper 370 (Washington: Government Printing Office, 1915); R. B. Marshall, *Profile Surveys in Wenatchee River Basin, Washington*, U.S. Geological Survey Water-Supply Paper 368 (Washington: Government Printing Office, 1914); Bruce A. McIntosh, James R. Sedell, Jeanette E. Smith, Robert C. Wissmar, Sharon E. Clarke, Gordon H. Reeves, and Lisa A. Brown, "Historical Changes in Fish Habitat for Select River Basins of Eastern Oregon and Washington," *Northwest Science*

68 (Special Issue 1994): 36–53; Israel Cook Russell, *A Reconnaisance in Southeastern Washington*, U.S. Geological Survey Water-Supply Paper 4 (Washington: Government Printing Office, 1897); James R. Sedell and Karen J. Luchessa, "Using the Historical Record as an Aid to Salmonid Habitat Enhancement," ed. Neil B. Armantrout (Portland: American Fisheries Society, 1982), 210–23; Robert C. Wissmar, Jeanette E. Smith, Bruce A. McIntosh, Hiram W. Li, Gordon H. Reeves, and James R. Sedell, "A History of Resource Use and Disturbance in Riverine Basins of Eastern Oregon and Washington (Early 1800s–1990s)," *Northwest Science* 68 (Special Issue 1994): 1–35.

Map 6. John N. Cobb, *Pacific Salmon Fisheries*, Bureau of Fisheries Document 839 (Washington: Government Printing Office, 1917); and annual reports by the Oregon Fish Commission.

Map 7. Operational orders between hatchery superintendents and the commissioner of fisheries and chief assistants in Washington, D.C., in Letters Received, 1882–1900, and Press Copies of Letters Sent, 1871–1906, RG 22, NA; see also annual reports of the U.S. Fish Commission and the Oregon Fish Commission.

Map 8. Operational orders between hatchery superintendents in the Pacific Northwest and the commissioner of fisheries and chief assistants in Washington, D.C., in Letters Received, 1882–1900, and Press Copies of Letters Sent, 1871–1906, RG 22, NA; John N. Cobb, *Pacific Salmon Fisheries*, Bureau of Fisheries Document 839 (Washington: Government Printing Office, 1917).

Map 9. Operational orders between hatchery superintendents and the commissioner of fisheries and chief assistants in Washington, D.C., in Letters Received, 1882–1900, and Press Copies of Letters Sent, 1871–1906, RG 22, NA; John N. Cobb, *Pacific Salmon Fisheries*, Bureau of Fisheries Document 839 (Washington: Government Printing Office, 1917).

Map 10. Marshall McDonald, "The Salmon Fisheries of the Columbia River Basin," *Bulletin* 14 (1894): 153–68; U.S. Supreme Court, *Washington v. Oregon*, 211 U.S. (1908): 127–36.

Map 11. Marshall McDonald, "The Salmon Fisheries of the Columbia River Basin," *Bulletin* 14 (1894): 153–68; Ivan J. Donaldson and Frederick K. Cramer, *Fishwheels of the Columbia* (Portland: Binfords and Mort, 1971).

Map 12. Operational orders between hatchery superintendents and the commissioner of fisheries and chief assistants in Washington, D.C., in Letters Received, 1882–1900, and Press Copies of Letters Sent, 1871–1906, RG 22, NA; John N. Cobb, *Pacific Salmon Fisheries*, Bureau of Fisheries Document 839 (Washington: Government Printing Office, 1917); Cole M. Rivers, "Draft Report of Rogue River Investigations for the Oregon Fish Commission (1961; copy on file in the reprint files, NWFSCL).

Map 13. Randall Rohe, "The Geographical Impact of Placer Mining in the

American West, 1848–1974" (Ph.D. diss., University of Colorado, 1978); Leonard A. Fulton, *Spawning Areas and Abundance of Chinook Salmon ("Oncorhynchus tshawytscha") in the Columbia River Basin—Past and Present,* U.S. Fish and Wildlife Service Special Scientific Report—Fisheries no. 571 (Washington: Government Printing Office, 1968); Leonard A. Fulton, *Spawning Areas and Abundance of Steelhead Trout and Coho, Sockeye, and Chum Salmon—Past and Present,* U.S. Fish and Wildlife Service Special Scientific Report—Fisheries no. 618 (Washington: Government Printing Office, 1970); Donald L. McKernan, Donald R. Johnson, and John I. Hodges, "Some Factors Influencing the Trends of Salmon Populations in Oregon," *Transactions of the Fifteenth North American Wildlife Conference* 15 (1950): 427–49; Cole M. Rivers, "Draft Report of Rogue River Investigations for the Oregon Fish Commission (1961; copy on file in the reprint files, N W F S C L); Nathan C. Grover, H. D. McGlashan, and G. H. Canfield, *Surface Water Supply of the United States, 1930,* part 11, *Pacific Slope Basins in California,* U.S. Geological Survey Water-Supply Paper 706 (Washington: Government Printing Office, 1932); Nathan C. Grover, G. L. Parker, W. A. Lamb, and C. G. Paulsen, *Surface Water Supply of the United States, 1930,* part 12, *North Pacific Slope Drainage Basins, A. Washington and Upper Columbia River Basins,* U.S. Geological Survey Water-Supply Paper 707 (Washington: Government Printing Office, 1932); Nathan C. Grover, G. C. Baldwin, Lynn Crandall, G. L. Parker, C. G. Paulsen, A. B. Purton, and G. H. Canfield, *Surface Water Supply of the United States, 1930,* part 12, *North Pacific Slope Drainage Basins, B. Snake River Basin,* U.S. Geological Survey Water-Supply Paper 708 (Washington: Government Printing Office, 1932); Nathan C. Grover, G. H. Canfield, and G. L. Parker, *Surface Water Supply of the United States, 1930,* part 12, *North Pacific Slope Drainage Basins, C. Oregon and Lower Columbia River Basin,* U.S. Geological Survey Water-Supply Paper 709 (Washington: Government Printing Office, 1932); Fred F. Henshaw, John H. Lewis, and E. J. McCaustland, *Deschutes River, Oregon, and Its Utilization,* U.S. Geological Survey Water-Supply Paper 344 (Washington: Government Printing Office, 1914); Fred F. Henshaw and Glenn L. Parker, *Water Powers of the Cascade Range,* part 2, *Cowlitz, Nisqually, Puyallup, White, Green, and Cedar Drainage Basins,* U.S. Geological Survey Water-Supply Paper 313 (Washington: Government Printing Office, 1913); R. B. Marshall, *Profile Surveys in Snake River Basin, Idaho,* U.S. Geological Survey Water-Supply Paper 347 (Washington: Government Printing Office, 1914); R. B. Marshall, *Profile Surveys in Hood and Sandy River Basins, Oregon,* U.S. Geological Survey Water-Supply Paper 348 (Washington: Government Printing Office, 1914); R. B. Marshall, *Profile Surveys in Willamette River Basin, Oregon,* U.S. Geological Survey Water-Supply Paper 349 (Washington: Government Printing Office, 1914); R. B. Marshall, *Profile Surveys in Wenatchee River Basin, Washington,* U.S. Geological Survey Water-Supply Paper 368 (Washington: Government

Printing Office, 1914); R. B. Marshall, *Profile Surveys in Chelan and Methow River Basins, Washington*, U.S. Geological Survey Water-Supply Paper 376 (Washington: Government Printing Office, 1915); R. B. Marshall, *Profile Surveys in Spokane River Basin, Washington, and John Day River Basin, Oregon*, U.S. Geological Survey Water-Supply Paper 377 (Washington: Government Printing Office, 1915); R. B. Marshall, *Profile Surveys in 1914 on Middle Fork of Willamette River and White River, Oregon*, U.S. Geological Survey Water-Supply Paper 378 (Washington: Government Printing Office, 1915); R. B. Marshall, *Profile Surveys in 1914 in Umpqua River Basin, Oregon*, U.S. Geological Survey Water-Supply Paper 379 (Washington: Government Printing Office, 1915); Glenn L. Parker and Lasley Lee, *Water Powers of the Cascade Range*, part 4, *Wenatchee and Entiat Basins*, U.S. Geological Survey Water-Supply Paper 486 (Washington: Government Printing Office, 1922); Glenn L. Parker and Frank B. Storey, *Water Powers of the Cascade Range*, part 3, *Yakima River Basin*, U.S. Geological Survey Water-Supply Paper 369 (Washington: Government Printing Office, 1916); John C. Stevens, *Water Powers of the Cascade Range*, part 1, *Southern Washington*, U.S. Geological Survey Water-Supply Paper 253 (Washington: Government Printing Office, 1910).

Map 14. County voter abstracts for the special election of 1 June 1908, box 3, Abstracts of Votes, accession 70A-61/8, SSPOSA.

Map 15. County voter abstracts for the special election of 1 June 1908, box 3, Abstracts of Votes, accession 70A-61/8, SSPOSA.

Map 16. County voter abstracts for the special election of 27 June 1927, box 3, Abstracts of Votes, accession 70A-61/8, SSPOSA.

Map 17. John N. Cobb, *Pacific Salmon Fisheries*, Bureau of Fisheries Document 1092 (Washington: Government Printing Office, 1930); and annual reports of the U.S. Fish Commission, the Oregon Fish Commission, and the Oregon Game Commission.

Map 18. Jack M. Van Hyning, *Factors Affecting the Abundance of Fall Chinook Salmon in the Columbia River*, Research Reports of the Fish Commission of Oregon 4 (Salem: Oregon Fish Commission, 1973); and the annual reports of the U.S. Fish Commission, the Oregon Fish Commission, and the Oregon Game Commission.

Map 19. Leonard A. Fulton, *Spawning Areas and Abundance of Chinook Salmon ("Oncorhynchus tshawytscha") in the Columbia River Basin—Past and Present*, U.S. Fish and Wildlife Service Special Scientific Report—Fisheries no. 571 (Washington: Government Printing Office, 1968); Leonard A. Fulton, *Spawning Areas and Abundance of Steelhead Trout and Coho, Sockeye, and Chum Salmon—Past and Present*, U.S. Fish and Wildlife Service Special Scientific Report—Fisheries no. 618 (Washington: Government Printing Office, 1970); Cole M. Rivers, "Draft Report of Rogue River Investigations for the Oregon Fish Commission (1961; copy on file in the reprint files, NWFSCL); U.S. Department of the Interior, *Columbia River*

Basin: Development of Water and Other Resources Present and Potential of the Columbia River Basin in Washington, Oregon, Idaho, Montana, Wyoming, Nevada, and Utah, Project Planning Report no. 1–5.0–1 (Portland: Bureau of Reclamation, Region 1, 1946); Randall Rohe, "The Geographical Impact of Placer Mining in the American West, 1848–1974" (Ph.D. diss., University of Colorado, 1978).

Map 20. Leonard A. Fulton, *Spawning Areas and Abundance of Chinook Salmon ("Oncorhynchus tshawytscha") in the Columbia River Basin—Past and Present*, U.S. Fish and Wildlife Service Special Scientific Report—Fisheries no. 571 (Washington: Government Printing Office, 1968); Leonard A. Fulton, *Spawning Areas and Abundance of Steelhead Trout and Coho, Sockeye, and Chum Salmon—Past and Present*, U.S. Fish and Wildlife Service Special Scientific Report—Fisheries no. 618 (Washington: Government Printing Office, 1970); Willa Nehlsen, Jack E. Williams, and James A. Lichatowich, "Pacific Salmon at the Crossroads: Stocks at Risk from California, Oregon, Idaho, and Washington," *Fisheries* 16 (Mar.–Apr. 1991): 4–21.

Bibliographical Essay

Commercial fishing and maritime shipping are modern paradoxes. Although fishers and sailors still play crucial roles in feeding and supplying society, most consumers are oblivious to their labors. The market system that moves goods around the world so efficiently has effectively separated products from the identity of their producers. Thus a shopper in Iowa can buy a fillet of salmon and never know its species—let alone whether the fish was wild or hatchery bred, ocean or pen raised, commercial or farm harvested. Modern capitalism has erased the fish's history. A similar condition of ignorance pervades most products, but as long as stores have fish in the case, shoes on the shelves, clothes on the racks, and cars in the showroom, few shoppers seem to care where products come from, let alone how they got there.

These blinders have constrained scholars as well. Although Atlantic cod kept colonial New England solvent into the eighteenth century, and Pacific salmon enriched the Northwest until the 1970s, most researchers relegate these activities to footnotes. The academy seems filled with landlubbers, but not exclusively so. A few historians, anthropologists, folklorists, geographers, political scientists, and sociologists do investigate our maritime activities. Unfortunately, they, like their subjects, remain marginal figures in academia. Their obscurity stems in part from an absence of professional organs dedicated to fishery and maritime subjects, including the history of oceanography. This vacuum needs filling—and soon. In the meantime, I have compiled a brief guide of selected works on the fisheries to increase awareness; and to assist people interested in writing environmental histories of fishery and maritime subjects, I have also included a discussion of important problems and sources.

When it comes to fishery history, each fishery is unique enough that no single topical or chronological organization covers all cases. A chronology of studies on Pacific Northwest salmon, for example, does not even serve well for the California salmon fisheries, let alone Gulf Coast shrimp or Atlantic cod. Rather than try to invent a new topology, I will use the standard temporal and geographic categories of American history with the hope that readers will see how these studies mesh with broader historical themes. For useful bibliographies see "Selected References on the History of Marine Fisheries," *Marine Fisheries Review* 50, no. 4 (1988): 228–38; N. G. Benson, ed., *A Century of Fisheries in North America* (Washington: American Fisheries Society, 1970); A. F. McEvoy, *The Fisherman's Problem: Law and Ecology in the California Fisheries, 1850–1980* (New York: Cambridge University Press, 1986); and W. M. O'Leary, *Maine Sea Fisheries: The Rise of a Native Industry, 1830–1890* (Boston: Northeastern University Press, 1996).

Scholars have researched Indian fisheries extensively. Among the most significant, if dated works, are G. W. Hewes, "Aboriginal Use of Fishery Resources in Northwestern North America" (Ph.D. diss., University of California, Berkeley, 1947); C. Rau, *Prehistoric Fishing in Europe and North America* (Washington: Smithsonian Institution, 1884); and E. Rostlund, *Fresh Water Fish and Fishing in Native North America,* University of California Publications in Geography no. 9 (Berkeley: University of California Press, 1952). For cultural aspects see B. Gunda, ed., *The Fishing Culture of the World: Studies in Ethnology, Cultural Ecology, and Folklore,* 2 vols. (Budapest: Akadémiai Kiadó, 1984).

Among the more important works on Indian fishers are D. F. Arnold, " 'Putting Up Fish': Environment, Work, and Culture in Tlingit Society" (Ph.D. diss., University of California, Los Angeles, 1997); F. M. Atton, "Fish Resources and the Fisheries Industry of the Canadian Plains," *Prairie Forum* 9, no. 2 (1984): 315–25; D. R. M. Beck, "Return to Nam'O Uskitwmit: The Importance of Sturgeon in Menominee Indian History," *Wisconsin Magazine of History* 70 (Jan. 1995): 32–48; F. Berkes, "Fishery Resource Use in a Subarctic Indian Community," *Human Ecology* 5 (1977): 290–307; C. E. Cleland, "The Inland Shore Fishery of the Northern Great Lakes: Its Development and Importance in Prehistory," *American Antiquity* 47 (Oct. 1982): 761–84; B. Hayden and J. M. Ryder, "Prehistoric Cultural Collapse in the Lillooet Area," *American Antiquity* 56 (Jan. 1991): 50–65; C. Junker-Andersen, "The Eel Fisheries of the St. Lawrence Iroquoians," *North American Archaeologist* 9 (summer 1988): 97–121; A. L. Kroeber and S. A. Barrett, *Fishing among the Indians of Northwest California,* University of California Publications in American Archaeology and Ethnography no. 21 (Berkeley: University of California Press, 1960); I. La Rivers, *The Fishes and Fisheries of Nevada* (Reno: University of Nevada Press, 1994); and S. R. Martin, "Models of Change in the Woodland Settlement of the Northern Great Lakes Region" (Ph.D. diss., Michigan State University, 1985). For aboriginal fishing technology see Rau, *Prehistoric Fishing;* H. Stewart, *Indian Fishing: Early Methods on the Northwest Coast* (Seattle: University of Washington Press, 1977); and D. E. Walker Jr., *Mutual Cross-Utilization of Economic Resources in the Plateau: An Example from Aboriginal Nez Perce Fishing Practices,* Washington State University Laboratory of Anthropology Report of Investigations no. 41 (Pullman: Washington State University, 1967).

Studies of Indian treaty rights constitute their own subdiscipline. See especially M. R. Anderson, "Law and the Protection of Cultural Communities: The Case of Native American Fishing Rights," *Law and Policy* 9 (Apr. 1987): 125–42; R. L. Barsh, "The Economics of a Traditional Coastal Indian Salmon Fishery," *Human Organization* 41 (summer 1982): 170–76; R. L. Barsh, "Backfire from Boldt: The Judicial Transformation of Coast Salish Proprietary Fisheries into a Commons," *Western Legal History* 4 (winter–spring 1991): 85–102; D. L. Boxberger, *To Fish in Common: The Ethnohistory of Lummi Indian Salmon Fishing* (Lincoln: University of Nebraska Press, 1989); D. L. Boxberger, "Lightning Boldts and Sparrow Wings: A Comparison of Coast Salish Fishing Rights in British Columbia and Washington State," *Native Studies Review* 9, no. 1 (1993–94): 1–13; C. Broches, "Fish, Politics, and Treaty Rights: Who Protects Salmon Resources in Washington State," *BC Studies* 57 (1983): 86–98; F. G. Cohen, *Treaties on Trial: The Continuing Controversy over Northwest Indian Fishing Rights* (Seattle: University of Washington Press, 1986); R. Doherty, *Disputed Waters: Native Americans and the Great Lakes Fishery* (Lexington: University Press of Kentucky, 1990); A. G. Gulig, "In Whose Interest? Government-Indian Relations in Northern Saskatchewan and Wisconsin, 1900–1940" (Ph.D. diss., University of Saskatchewan, 1997); B. Miller, "The Press, the Boldt Decision, and Indian-White Relations," *American Indian Culture and Research Journal* 17 (summer 1993): 75–97; D. Newell, *Tangled Webs of History: Indians and the Law in Canada's Pacific Coast Fisheries* (Toronto: University of Toronto Press, 1993); and D. L. Parman, "Inconstant Advocacy: The Erosion of Indian Fishing Rights in the Pacific Northwest, 1933–1956," *Pacific Historical Review* 53 (1984): 163–89.

Colonial subjects have received considerable attention. The best works on oceangoing laborers are D. Vickers, *Farmers and Fishermen: Two Centuries of Work in Essex County, Massachusetts, 1630–1850* (Chapel Hill: University of North Carolina Press, 1994), and M. Rediker, *Between the Devil and* the Deep Blue Sea: Merchant Seamen, Pirates, and the Anglo-American Maritime World, 1700–1750 (New York: Cambridge University Press, 1987). For other studies see The Fisheries of Gloucester from the first catch by the English in 1623, to the centennial year, 1876 (Gloucester: Procter Brothers, 1876); B. Bailyn, The New England Merchants in the Seventeenth Century (New York: Harper and Row, 1955); B. A. Balcom, The Cod Fishery of Isle Royale, 1713–58 (Ottawa: Parks Canada, 1984); J. A. Goldenberg, Shipbuilding in Colonial America (Charlottesville: University Press of Virginia, 1976); C. L. Heyrman, Commerce and Culture: The Maritime Communities of Colonial Massachusetts, 1690–1750 (New York: W. W. Norton, 1984); O. U. Jazen, "The American Threat to Newfoundland Fisheries, 1776–1777," American Neptune 48 (fall 1988): 154–64; R. McFarland, A History of the New England Fisheries (New York: D. Appleton, 1911); S. E. Morison, The Maritime History of Massachusetts, 1783–1860 (Boston: Houghton-Mifflin, 1979); and V. R. Taylor, The Early Atlantic Salmon Fishery in Newfoundland and Labrador, Canadian Special Publication of Fisheries and Aquatic Sciences 76 (Ottawa: Department of Fisheries and Oceans, 1985).

The Newfoundland cod fisheries deserve separate mention. The standard text is still H. A. Innis, The Cod Fisheries: The History of an International Economy, rev. ed. (Toronto: University of Toronto Press, 1954), but see also M. Kurlansky, Cod: A Biography of the Fish That Changed the World (London: Jonathan Cape, 1997). Other important works include S. T. Cadigan, "Merchant Capital, the State, and Labour in a British Colony: Servant-Master Relations and Capital Accumulation in Newfoundland's Northeast-Coast Fishery, 1775–1799," Journal of the Canadian Historical Association 2 (1991): 17–42; G. T. Cell, English Enterprise in Newfoundland (Toronto: University of Toronto Press, 1969); D. D. Irvine, "The Newfoundland Fishery: A French Objective in the War of American Independence," Canadian Historical Review 13 (1932): 268–84; R. G. Lounsbury, The British Fishery at Newfoundland, 1634–1763 (New Haven: Yale University Press, 1934); K. Matthews, "A History of the West of England–Newfoundland Fishery" (D.Phil. diss., Oxford University, 1968); R. E. Ommer, From Outpost to Outport: A Structural Analysis of the Jersey-Gaspé Cod Fishery, 1786–1886 (Montreal: McGill-Queen's University Press, 1991); R. E. Ommer, ed., Merchant Credit and Labour Strategies in Historical Perspective (Fredericton: Acadiensis Press, 1990); P. E. Pope, "Scavengers and Caretakers: Beothuk/European Settlement Dynamics in Seventeenth-Century Newfoundland," Newfoundland Studies 9 (summer 1993): 279–93; G. M. Sider, Culture and Class in Anthropology and History: A Newfoundland Illustration (Cambridge: Cambridge University Press, 1986); and W. Whitely, "Governor Hugh Palliser and the

Newfoundland and Labrador Fishery, 1764–1768," *Canadian Historical Review* 50 (June 1969): 141–63.

For other colonial topics see J.-F. Brire, "The Port of Granville and the North American Fisheries in the 18th Century," *Acadiensis* 14 (summer 1985): 93–107; J.-F. Brire, "The French Codfishing Industry in North America and the Crisis of the Pre-Revolutionary Years, 1783–1792," *Proceedings of the Annual Meeting of the French Colonial Historical Society* 15 (1992): 201–10; A. Faulkner, "Archaeology of the Cod Fishery: Damariscove Island," *Historical Archaeology* 19 (1985): 57–86; T. Gray, "Devon's Coastal and Overseas Fisheries and New England Migration, 1597–1642" (D.Phil. diss., University of Exeter, 1988); E. A. Hammond, "The Spanish Fisheries of Charlotte Harbor," *Florida Historical Quarterly* 52 (Apr. 1973): 355–80; F. Harrington, "Sea Tenure in Seventeenth-Century New Hampshire: Native Americans and Englishmen in the Sphere of Coastal Resources," *Historical New Hampshire* 40 (spring–summer 1985): 18–33; A. J. B. Johnston, "The Early Days of the Lobster Fishery in Atlantic Canada," *Material History Review* 33 (1991): 56–60; W. Neitzey et al., "Fishing the Potomac: The Neitzey Family Fisheries at Ferry Landing and Stony Point," *Yearbook: The Historical Society of Fairfax County, Virginia* 23 (1991–92): 45–59; M. T. Taylor, "Seiners and Tongers: North Carolina Fisheries in the Old and New South," *North Carolina Historical Review* 69 (spring 1992): 1–36; D. Vickers, " 'A Knowen and Staple Commoditie': Codfish Prices in Essex County, Massachusetts, 1640–1775," *Essex Institute Historical Collections* 124, no. 3 (1988): 186–203; and J. Wharton, *The Bounty of the Chesapeake: Fishing in Colonial Virginia* (Williamsburg, Virginia, 350th Anniversary Celebration, 1957).

The best way to address later periods is through a regional approach, but two important, if dated, general studies are L. Sabine, *Report on the Principal Fisheries of the American Seas* (Washington: Government Printing Office, 1856) (see also W. L. Welch, "Lorenzo Sabine's History of the Fisheries," *American Neptune* 48 [fall 1988]: 165–72) and G. B. Goode, ed., *The Fisheries and Fishery Industries of the United States*, 5 sections in 8 parts (Washington: Government Printing Office, 1884–87). Although both works suffer from the biases of their times, they remain valuable sources on American fishers and fisheries. For the nineteenth-century Northeast see E. A. Ackerman, *New England's Fishing Industry* (Chicago: University of Chicago Press, 1941); B. A. Balcom, *History of the Lunenburg Fishing Industry* (Lunenburg, N.S.: Lunenburg Marine Museum Society, 1977); H. Beck, *Folklore of the Sea* (Middletown, Conn.: Wesleyan University Press, 1973); J. Gwyn, " 'A Little Province Like This': The Economy of

Nova Scotia under Stress, 1812–1853," *Canadian Papers in Rural History* 6 (1988): 192–225; S. J. Hornsby, "Staple Trades, Subsistence Agriculture, and Nineteenth-Century Cape Breton Island," *Annals of the Association of American Geographers* 79 (Sept. 1989): 411–34; Morison, *The Maritime History of Massachusetts;* B. J. McCay, "A Footnote to the History of New Jersey Fisheries: Menhaden as Food and Fertilizer," *New Jersey History* 98 (fall–winter 1980): 212–20; McFarland, *History of New England Fisheries;* O'Leary, *Maine Sea Fisheries;* and Vickers, *Farmers and Fishermen.*

For subtle but important changes in nineteenth-century Newfoundland see L. Little, "Collective Action in Outport Newfoundland: A Case Study from the 1830s," *Labour* 26 (1990): 7–35; J. Mannion, "Irish Merchants Abroad: The Newfoundland Experience, 1750–1850," *Newfoundland Studies* 2 (summer 1986): 127–90; D. A. McDonald, " 'Really No Merchant': An Ethnohistorical Account of Newman and Company and the Supplying System in the Newfoundland Fishery at Harbour Breton, 1850–1900" (Ph.D. diss., Simon Fraser University, 1992); S. Ryan, *Fish out of Water: The Newfoundland Saltfish Trade, 1814–1914* (St. John's: Breakwater Books, 1986); P. Thornton, "The Transition from the Migratory to the Resident Fishery in the Strait of Belle Isle," *Acadiensis* 19 (summer 1990): 92–120; F. A. Winsor, "The Newfoundland Bank Fishery: Government Policies and the Struggle to Improve Bank Fishing Crews' Working, Health, and Safety Conditions, 1876–1920" (Ph.D. diss., Memorial University of Newfoundland, 1997).

Researchers have neglected the nineteenth-century southern fisheries. For the Chesapeake see C. Ellis, *Fisher Folk: Two Communities on Chesapeake Bay* (Lexington: University Press of Kentucky, 1986); P. J. Johnson, ed., *Working the Water: The Commercial Fisheries of Maryland's Patuxent River* (Charlottesville: University Press of Virginia, 1988); Neitzey et al., "Fishing the Potomac"; and C. L. Quittmeyer, *The Seafood Industry of the Chesapeake Bay States of Maryland and Virginia: A Study in Private Management and Public Policy* (Richmond: Advisory Council on the Virginia Economy, 1957). For other southern fisheries see R. W. Doughty, "Sea Turtles in Texas: A Forgotten Commerce," *Southwestern Historical Quarterly* 88 (Jan. 1984): 43–70; W. C. Hamilton, "The Warren Fish Company of Pensacola," *Pensacola History Illustrated* 4 (summer 1992): 3–9; and Taylor, "Seiners and Tongers," *North Carolina Historical Review* 69 (1992).

Even rarer are studies of inland fisheries. For the Great Lakes see W. Ashworth, *The Late, Great Lakes: An Environmental History* (New York: Knopf, 1986); M. B. Bogue, "To Save the Fish: Canada, United States, the Great Lakes, and the Joint Commission of 1892," *Journal of American*

History 79 (Mar. 1993): 1429–54; Cleland, "Inland Shore Fishery of the Northern Great Lakes," *American Antiquity* 47 (Oct. 1982); J. L. Goodier, "Fishermen on Canadian Lake Superior: One Hundred Years," *Inland Seas* 45 (fall 1989): 284–306; S. Peters, "Working for a Living," *Michigan History* 76 (June 1992): 47–49; R. E. Rohe, "The Upper Great Lakes Lumber Era," *Inland Seas* 40 (spring 1984): 16–29. For other regions see Atton, "Fish Resources and the Fisheries Industry of the Canadian Plains," *Prairie Forum* 9, no. 2 (1984); La Rivers, *Fishes and Fisheries of Nevada;* K. Magnusson, "Icelandic Fisheries on Lake Winnipeg," *Beaver* 312 (Apr. 1982): 47–51; and F. Tough, "The Establishment of a Commercial Fishing Industry and the Demise of Native Fisheries in Northern Manitoba," *Canadian Journal of Native Studies* 4 (fall 1984): 303–19.

Unlike southern and inland areas, the nineteenth-century Pacific coast has received considerable attention. The most influential of these works is McEvoy, *Fisherman's Problem,* an incisive critique of the way economy, law, and environment shaped fishery management. For studies on salmon see J. A. Craig and R. L. Hacker, *The History and Development of the Fisheries of the Columbia River* (Washington: Government Printing Office, 1940); J. Cone and S. Ridlington, eds., *The Northwest Salmon Crisis: A Documentary History* (Corvallis: Oregon State University Press, 1996); G. B. Dodds, *The Salmon King of Oregon: R. D. Hume and the Pacific Fisheries* (Chapel Hill: University of North Carolina Press, 1959); C. Lyons, *Salmon, Our Heritage: The Story of a Province and an Industry* (Vancouver: Mitchell Press, 1969); McEvoy, *Fisherman's Problem;* and C. L. Smith, *Salmon Fishers of the Columbia* (Corvallis: Oregon State University Press, 1979). On ethnicity in the fisheries see S. Arestad, "Norwegians in the Pacific Coast Fisheries," *Norwegian-American Studies* 30 (1985): 96–129; L. E. Armentrout-Ma, "Chinese in California's Fishing Industry, 1850–1941," *California History* 60 (summer 1981): 142–57; D. L. Boxberger, "Ethnicity and Labor in the Puget Sound Fishing Industry, 1880–1935," *Ethnology* 33 (summer 1994): 179–91; D. Collins, "Emerging Archaeological Evidence of the Chinese Market Fisheries of Early California," *Pacific Coast Archaeological Society Quarterly* 23 (summer 1987): 63–68; A. F. McEvoy, "In Places Men Reject: The Chinese Fishermen at San Diego, 1870–1893," *Journal of San Diego History* 23 (1977): 12–24; and M. Postel, "A Lost Resource: Shellfish in San Francisco Bay," *California History* 67 (spring 1988): 26–41.

Literature on the twentieth-century is sprawling and uneven. The most significant works are C. J. Allison, S.-E. Jacobs, and M. A. Porter, eds., *Winds of Change: Women in Northwest Commercial Fishing* (Seattle: University of Washington Press, 1989); L. L. Fields, *The Entangling Net: Alaska's Commercial Fishing Women Tell Their Tales* (Urbana: University of Illinois Press, 1997); Gunda, *Fishing Culture of the World;* Bonnie J. McCay, *Oyster Wars and the Public Trust: Property, Law, and Ecology in New Jersey History* (Tucson: University of Arizona Press, 1998); McEvoy, *Fisherman's Problem;* P. Matthiessen, *Men's Lives: The Surfmen and Baymen of the South Fork* (New York: Random House, 1986); and R. E. Ommer, "What's Wrong with Canadian Fish?" *Journal of Canadian Studies* 20 (fall 1986): 122–42.

On northern Atlantic subjects see Ackerman, *New England's Fishing Industry;* M. E. Dewar, *Industry in Trouble: The Federal Government and the New England Fisheries* (Philadelphia: Temple University Press, 1983); A. Davis and L. Kasdan, "Bankrupt Government Policies and Belligerent Fishermen Responses: Dependency and Conflict in the Southwest Nova Scotia Small Boat Fisheries," *Journal of Canadian Studies* 19 (spring 1984): 108–24; R. W. Judd, "Grass-Roots Conservation in Eastern Coastal Maine: Monopoly and the Moral Economy of Weir Fishing, 1893–1911," *Environmental Review* 12 (summer 1988): 80–103; Matthiessen, *Men's Lives;* and G. W. Mescher, "Fisheries Industrialization and the Consequences for Small-Scale Fishermen: The Weir Fishermen of New Brunswick's Bay of Fundy Shore" (Ph.D. diss., Columbia University, 1993). For Newfoundland see P. Chantraine, *The Last Cod Fish: Life and Death of the Newfoundland Way of Life* (St. John's: Jesperson, 1993); B. L. L. Neis, "From Cod Block to Fish Food: The Crisis and Restructuring in the Newfoundland Fishing Industry, 1968–1986" (Ph.D. diss., University of Toronto, 1988); R. Ommer, "One Hundred Years of Fishery Crises in Newfoundland," *Acadiensis* 23 (summer 1994): 5–20; P. A. Pross and S. McCorquodale, *Economic Resurgence and the Constitutional Agenda: The Case of the East Coast Fisheries* (Montreal: McGill-Queen's University Press, 1987).

Researchers have given greater attention to the modern southern and Gulf fisheries. For the Chesapeake see Ellis, *Fisher Folk;* Johnson, *Working the Water;* R. S. Peffer, *Watermen* (Baltimore: Johns Hopkins University Press, 1979); L. S. Tyler, "The Blue Crab Industry of Chesapeake Bay: Technological Developments from 1873 to 1983" (Ed.D., University of Maryland, 1983); W. W. Warner, *Beautiful Swimmers: Watermen, Crabs, and the Chesapeake Bay* (New York: Penguin Books, 1987). For southeastern subjects see V. Singleton, "Hilton Head Island Fishing Co-Op: A Venture into Shrimp," *Southern Exposure* 11 (June 1983): 48–49; and W. N. Still Jr., "A Nickel a Bucket: A History of the North Carolina Shrimping Industry," *American Neptune* 47 (winter 1987): 257–74. For the Gulf of Mexico see I. T.

Joyce, "The Fisheries of the Cuban Insular Shelf: Culture, History, and Revolutionary Performance" (Ph.D. diss., Simon Fraser University, 1996); R. L. Maril, *Texas Shrimpers: Community, Capitalism, and the Sea* (College Station: Texas A & M University Press, 1983); and R. L. Maril, *The Bay Shrimpers of Texas: Rural Fishermen in a Global Economy* (Lawrence: University Press of Kansas, 1995).

Twentieth-century inland fisheries, as in earlier eras, are understudied. For the Great Lakes see Ashworth, *The Late, Great Lakes;* J. L. Goodier, "Fish Species in Canadian Lake Superior," *Inland Seas* 51 (spring 1995): 32–48; C. E. Herdendorff, "Our Changing Fish Species History," *Inland Seas* 39 (winter 1983): 276–86; R. W. Johnson, "The Rise and Fall of an Apostle Island Fishing Camp: A Great Lakes Subsistence Lifestyle," *Inland Seas* 41 (spring 1985): 20–27; A. B. McCullough, *The Commercial Fishery of the Canadian Great Lakes* (Hull: Canada Government Publication Center, 1989); and J. J. Van West, "Ecological and Economic Dependence in a Great Lakes Community-Based Fishery: Fishermen in the Smelt Fisheries of Port Dover, Ontario," *Journal of Canadian Studies* 24 (summer 1989): 95–115. For other areas see Atton, "Fish Resources and the Fisheries Industry of the Canadian Plains," *Prairie Forum* 9, no. 2 (1984); G. S. Gislason, J. A. MacMillan, and J. W. Craven, *The Manitoba Commercial Freshwater Fishery: An Economic Analysis* (Winnipeg: University of Manitoba Press, 1982); A. S. Gullig, "Sizing up the Catch: Native-Newcomer Resource Competition and the Early Years of Saskatchewan's Northern Commercial Fishery," *Saskatchewan History* 47 (summer 1995): 3–11; La Rivers, *Fishes and Fisheries of Nevada;* and J. Lund, *Flatheads and Spooneys: Fishing for a Living in the Ohio River Valley* (Lexington: University Press of Kentucky, 1995).

There is a vast literature on the Pacific fisheries. For salmon see Cone and Ridlington, *Northwest Salmon Crisis;* Craig and Hacker, *History and Development of the Fisheries of the Columbia River;* J. E. Damron, "The Emergence of Salmon Trolling on the American Northwest Coast: A Maritime Historical Geography" (Ph.D. diss., University of Oregon, 1975); B. B. Deloach, *The Salmon Canning Industry* (Corvallis: Oregon State College, 1939); O. W. Freeman, "Salmon Industry of the Pacific Coast," *Economic Geography* 11 (Apr. 1935): 109–29; Lyons, *Salmon, Our Heritage;* G. Meggs, *Salmon: The Decline of the British Columbia Fishery* (Vancouver: Douglas and McIntyre, 1991); G. Meggs and Stacey Duncan, *Cork Lines and Canning Lines: The Glory Years of Fishing on the West Coast* (Vancouver: Douglas and McIntyre, 1992); D. Newell, ed., *The Development of the Pacific Salmon-Canning Industry: A Grown Man's Game* (Montreal. McGill-Queen's University Press, 1989); P. Spurlock, "A History of the Salmon Industry in the Pacific Northwest" (M.A. thesis, University of Oregon, 1940); and R. White, *The Organic Machine: The Remaking of the Columbia River* (New York: Hill and Wang, 1995).

For Pacific deep-sea fisheries see J. L. McMullen, "State, Capital, and Debt in the British Columbia Fishing Fleet, 1970–1982," *Journal of Canadian Studies* 19 (spring 1984): 65–88; and J. Wade, "The 'Gigantic Scheme': Crofter Immigration and Deep-Sea Fisheries Development for British Columbia (1887–1893)," *BC Studies* 53 (1982): 28–44. For sardines see McEvoy, *Fisherman's Problem;* and S. M. Payne, "Unheeded Warnings: A History of Monterey's Sardine Fishery" (Ph.D. diss., University of California, Santa Barbara, 1987). For tuna see D. H. Estes, " 'Offensive Stupidity,' and the Struggle of Abe Tokunosuke," *Journal of San Diego History* 28 (winter 1982): 249–68; P. F. Fardner, "Tuna Poaching and Nuclear Testing in the South Pacific," *Orbis* 32 (summer 1988): 249–62; and E. C. Gallick, "Exclusive Dealing, Specialized Assets, and Joint Ownership: A Study of the Tuna Industry" (Ph.D. diss., University of California, Los Angeles, 1984). For halibut see D. Caldwell and F. Caldwell, *The Ebb and the Flood: A History of the Halibut Producers Cooperative* (Seattle: Waterfront Press, 1980); and F. H. Bell, *The Pacific Halibut, the Resource, and the Fishery* (Anchorage: Alaska Northwest, 1981). For Alaska see R. A. Cooley, *Politics and Conservation: The Decline of the Alaska Salmon* (New York: Harper and Row, 1963); Fields, *Entangling Net;* M. Kirchhoff, "When Alexander Was Great: The Story of a Southeast Fishing Town," *Alaska Journal* 13 (summer 1983): 26–32; J. T. Payne, "The Effects of the 1964 Alaska Earthquake on the Cordova, Alaska, Commercial Salmon Fishery: An Anthropological Perspective" (Ph.D. diss., Washington State University, 1983); and P. Roppel, *Salmon from Kodiak: An History of the Salmon Fishery of Kodiak Island, Alaska,* Studies in History no. 216 (Anchorage: Alaska Historical Commission, 1986).

For West Coast fishers see Allison et al., *Winds of Change;* M. De Santis, *Neptune's Apprentice: Adventures of a Commercial Fisherwoman* (Novato, CA: Presidio, 1984); Dodds, *Salmon King;* R. Fadich, *Last of the Rivermen* (Entiat: Riba Publishing, 1993); G. W. Ferrington, "Erick Enquist: An Immigrant's Story," *Oregon Historical Quarterly* 94 (summer–fall 1993): 225–45; Fields, *Entangling Net;* R. D. Hume, *A Pygmy Monopolist: The Life and Doings of R. D. Hume, Written by Himself and Dedicated to His Neighbors,* ed. G. B. Dodds (Madison: State Historical Society of Wisconsin, 1961); L. D. Jackson, "Reminiscence: Lawrence D. Jackson on Sand Island Fishing," *Oregon Historical Quarterly* 89 (spring 1988): 30–69; L. Johnson, producer, *Work Is Our Joy: The Story of the Columbia River Gillnetter,* videorecording (Corvallis: Oregon State University, 1989); I. Martin, *Legacy and Testament:*

The Story of Columbia River Gillnetters (Pullman: Washington State University Press, 1994); E. W. Pinkerton, "Resilience on the Margin: Local Culture in a Small Town" (Ph.D. diss., Brandeis University, 1981); F. Seufert, *Wheels of Fortune* (Portland: Oregon Historical Society, 1980); Smith, *Salmon Fishers of the Columbia;* J. E. Taylor III, "For the Love of It: A Short History of Commercial Fishing in Pacific City, Oregon," *Pacific Northwest Quarterly* 82 (Jan. 1991): 22–32; R. T. Tetlow and G. J. Barbey, *Barbey: The Story of a Pioneer Columbia River Salmon Canner* (Portland: Binford and Mort, 1990); J. G. Utley, "Japanese Exclusion from American Fisheries, 1936–1939: The Department of State and the Public Interest," *Pacific Northwest Quarterly* 65 (Jan. 1974): 8–16; and White, *Organic Machine.*

Some topics require separate thematic treatment. Whaling is a popular subject for historians, but much of the literature is antiquarian and nonanalytical. The best description of a whaling operation is still H. Melville, *Moby-Dick; or, The Whale* (New York: Oxford University Press, 1998). The best industry study is L. E. Davis, R. E. Gallman, and K. Gleiter, *In Pursuit of Leviathan: Technology, Institutions, Productivity, and Profits in American Whaling* (Chicago: University of Chicago Press, 1997). Also useful are R. Ellis, *Men and Whales* (New York: Knopf, 1991); A. Starbuck, *History of the American Whale Fishery, from Its Earliest Inception to the Year 1876* (New York: Argosy-Antiquarian, 1964); and W. Tower, *A History of the American Whale Fishery* (Philadelphia: University of Pennsylvania, 1907). For informative essays see L. E. Davis, R. E. Gallman, and T. D. Hutchins, "Call Me Ishmael—Not Domingo Floresta: The Rise and Fall of the American Whaling Industry," *Research in Economic History,* suppl. 6 (1991): 191–233; L. E. Davis, R. E. Gallman, and T. D. Hutchins, "The Decline of U.S. Whaling: Was the Stock of Whales Running Out?" *Business History Review* 62 (winter 1988): 569–95; N. Philbruck, " 'Every Wave Is a Fortune': Nantucket Island and the Making of an American Icon," *New England Quarterly* 66 (fall 1993): 434–47; and R. Reeves and E. Mitchell, "How Many Humpbacks—Then and Now?" *Log of Mystic Seaport* 34 (fall 1982): 71–83.

There are many topical and regional studies of whaling. For Indians and whaling see L. T. Black, "Whaling in the Aleutians," *Etudes/Inuit/Studies* 11 (summer 1987): 7–50; D. Boeri, *People of the Ice Whale: Eskimos, White Men, and Whales* (New York: Dutton, 1984); C. C. Collins, "Subsistence and Survival: The Makah Indian Reservation, 1855–1933," *Pacific Northwest Quarterly* 87 (Oct. 1996): 180–93; D. R. Huelsbeck, "Whaling in the Precontact Economy of the Central Northwest Coast," *Arctic Anthropology* 25 (Jan. 1988): 1–15; B. Leibhardt, "Among the Bowheads: Legal and

Cultural Change on Alaska's North Slope Coast to 1985," *Environmental Review* 10 (winter 1985): 277–301; J. Strong, "Shinnecock and Montauk Whalemen," *Long Island Historical Journal* 2 (spring 1989): 29–40; D. Vickers, "The First Whalemen of Nantucket," *William and Mary Quarterly* 40 (Oct. 1983): 560–83; and M. J. Villano, "Whaling: A Central Part of Long Island Indian Life," *Long Island Historical Journal* 5 (spring 1992): 112–17. For social and cultural aspects of whaling see B. C. Busch, *"Whaling Will Never Do for Me": The American Whaleman in the Nineteenth Century* (Lexington: University Press of Kentucky, 1994); M. S. Creighton, *Rites and Passages: The Experience of American Whaling, 1830–1870* (New York: Cambridge University Press, 1995); and M. L. Vose, "Identification of the Origins and Sources of Selected Scrimshaw Motifs in 18th and 19th Century Contemporary Culture" (Ph.D. diss., New York University, 1992). Though dated, E. P. Hohman, *The American Whaleman: A Study of Life and Labor in the Whaling Industry* (New York: Longmans, Green and Co., 1928), is still useful. For whaling towns see B. J. Logue, "In Pursuit of Prosperity: Disease and Death in a Massachusetts Commercial Port, 1660–1850," *Journal of Social History* 25 (summer 1991): 309–43; and L. Norling, "Contrary Dependencies: Whaling Agents and Whalemen's Families, 1830–1870," *Log of Mystic Seaport* 42 (spring 1990): 3–12. For crew composition see B. C. Busch, "Cape Verdeans in the American Whaling and Sealing Industry, 1850–1900," *American Neptune* 45 (summer 1985): 104–16; J. Farr, "A Slow Boat to Nowhere: The Multi-racial Crews of the American Whaling Industry," *Journal of Negro History* 68 (summer 1983): 159–70; H. M. McFerson, " 'Part-Black Americans' in the South Pacific," *Phylon* 43 (summer 1982): 177–80; M. S. Putney, *Black Sailors: Afro-American Merchant Seamen and Whalemen prior to the Civil War* (Westport: Greenwood, 1987); K. S. Reilly, "Slavers in Disguise: American Whaling and the African Slave Trade, 1845–1862," *American Neptune* 53 (fall 1993): 177–89; and D. Vickers, "Nantucket Whalemen in the Deep-Sea Fishery: The Changing Anatomy of an Early American Labor Force," *Journal of American History* 72 (Sept. 1985): 277–96.

For whaling in the Atlantic see S. H. Barkham, "The Basque Whaling Establishments in Labrador, 1536–1632—A Summary," *Arctic* 37 (winter 1984): 515–19; E. Byers, *The Nation of Nantucket: Society and Politics in an Early American Commercial Center* (Boston: Northeastern University Press, 1986); and M. B. Simpson Jr. and S. W. Simpson, "The Pursuit of Leviathan: A History of Whaling on the North Carolina Coast," *North Carolina Historical Review* 65 (spring 1988): 1–51. For Pacific whaling see B. C. Busch, "Whalemen, Missionaries, and the Practice of Christianity in the

Nineteenth-Century Pacific," *Hawaiian Journal of History* 27 (1993): 91–118; A. M. Gibson and J. S. Whitehead, *Yankees in Paradise: The Pacific Basin Frontier* (Albuquerque: University of New Mexico Press, 1993); W. A. Hagelund, *Whalers No More: A History of Whaling on the West Coast* (Madeira Park, B.C.: Harbour, 1987); E. C. Starks, *A History of California Shore Whaling*, California Fish Bulletin no. 6 (Sacramento: State Printer, 1922); and R. L. Webb, *On the Northwest: Commercial Whaling in the Pacific Northwest, 1790–1967* (Vancouver: University of British Columbia Press, 1988). For Arctic whaling see J. Bockstoce, *Whales, Ice, and Men: The History of Whaling in the Western Arctic* (Seattle: University of Washington Press, 1986); J. Bockstoce, "The Arctic Whaling Disaster of 1897," *Prologue* 26 (Special Issue 1994): 100–111; R. W. Gillies, *Arctic Whalers, Icy Seas* (Toronto: Irwin, 1985); and J. W. VanStone, "Commercial Whaling in the Arctic Ocean," *Pacific Northwest Quarterly* 49 (Jan. 1958): 1–10.

For twentieth-century whaling see S. G. Brown, "Some Developments in Whaling, 1975–81," *Polar Record* 21, no. 131 (1982): 165–70; A. Dickinson and C. Sanger, "Modern Shore-Based Whaling in Newfoundland and Labrador: Expansion and Consolidation, 1898–1902," *International Journal of Maritime History* 2 (spring 1990): 83–116; A. Dickinson and C. Sanger, "Modern Shore-Station Whaling in Newfoundland and Labrador: The Peak Season, 1904," *International Journal of Maritime History* 5 (spring 1993): 127–54; J. M. Goddard, "Life on a Whaling Station," *Canadian West* 8 (spring 1992): 12–18, and 8 (summer 1992): 52–58; J. M. Goddard, "The Rissmller Factor in North American Shore Whaling, 1900–1912," *International Journal of Maritime History* 5 (summer 1993): 135–55; R. Reeves and E. Mitchell, "Hunting Whales in the St. Lawrence," *Beaver* 67 (winter 1987): 35–40; C. Sanger and A. Dickinson, "The Origins of Modern Shore Based Whaling in Newfoundland and Labrador: The Cabot Steam Whaling Co. Ltd., 1896–98," *International Journal of Maritime History* 1 (spring 1989): 129–57; C. Sanger and A. Dickinson, "Renewal of Newfoundland and Labrador Shore-Station Whaling, 1918–1936," *International Journal of Maritime History* 7 (spring 1995): 83–103; and Webb, *On the Northwest*.

Like whaling, sealing has strong affinities with other fisheries despite its mammalian prey. The most comprehensive study of the industry is B. C. Busch, *The War against the Seals: A History of the North American Seal Fishery* (Kingston: McGill-Queen's University Press, 1985). For Indian sealing see E. Y. Arima, "Notes on Nootkan Sea Mammal Hunting," *Arctic Anthropology* 25 (spring 1988): 16–27; A. Fienup-Riordan, "The Bird and the Bladder: The Cosmology of Central Yup'ik Seal Hunting," *Etudes/ Inuit/Studies* 14 (spring–summer 1990): 23–38; B. Richling, "Not by Seals

Alone," *Beaver* 68 (spring 1988): 29–36; and G. Sabo III and D. R. Sabo, "Belief Systems and the Ecology of Sea Mammal Hunting among the Baffinland Eskimo," *Arctic Anthropology* 22 (summer 1985): 77–86. For Atlantic sealing see J. E. Candow, *Of Men and Seals: A History of the Newfoundland Seal Hunt* (Ottawa: Environment Canada, 1989); S. Ryan, "The Industrial Revolution and the Newfoundland Seal Fishery," *International Journal of Maritime History* 4 (summer 1992): 1–43; S. Ryan, *The Ice Hunters: A History of Newfoundland Sealing to 1914* (St. John's: Breakwater Books, 1994); C. W. Sanger, "The 19th Century Newfoundland Seal Fishery and the Influence of Scottish Whalemen," *Polar Record* 20, no. 126 (1980): 231–51; C. W. Sanger, "The Dundee–St. John's Connection: Nineteenth Century Interlinkages between Scottish Arctic Whaling and the Newfoundland Seal Fishery," *Newfoundland Studies* 4 (spring 1988): 1–26. For the Pacific see M. Sherwood, "Seal Poaching in the North Pacific: Japanese Raids on the Pribilofs, 1906," *Alaska History* 1 (spring 1984): 45–51; and O. R. Young, "The Pribilof Islands: A View from the Periphery," *Anthropologica* 29 (summer 1987): 149–67.

Like whalers, sealers ventured across the globe. For sealing below the equator see A. B. Dickinson, "Southern Hemisphere Fur Sealing from Atlantic Canada," *American Neptune* 49 (winter 1989): 278–90; B. M. Gough, "American Sealers, the United States Navy, and the Falklands, 1830–32," *Polar Record* 28, no. 166 (1992): 219–28; R. Richards, "An American Sealing Explorer: Captain Isaac Percival's Search for the Nimrod Islands, 1828–1830," *Log of Mystic Seaport* 44 (summer 1992): 59–63; and R. Waterhouse, "The Beginning of Hegemony or a Confluence of Interests? The Australian-American Relationship, 1788–1908," *Australasian Journal of American Studies* 9 (summer 1990): 12–19. For international diplomacy and sealing see K. Dorsey, "Putting a Ceiling on Sealing: Conservation and Cooperation in the International Arena, 1909–1911," *Environmental History Review* 15 (fall 1991): 27–45; J. T. Gay, *American Fur Seal Diplomacy: The Alaska Fur Seal Controversy* (New York: Peter Lang, 1987); A. C. Gluek Jr., "Canada's Splendid Bargain: The North Pacific Fur Seal Convention of 1911," *Canadian Historical Review* 63 (summer 1982): 179–201; G. O. Williams, *The Bering Sea Fur Seal Dispute, 1885–1911: A Monograph on the Maritime History of Alaska* (Eugene: Alaska Maritime, 1984).

For modern sealing see T. Bjorndal, J. M. Conrad, and K. G. Salvanes, "Stock Size, Harvesting Costs, and the Potential for Extinction: The Case of Sealing," *Land Economics* 69 (May 1993): 156–67; B. Richling, "Recent Trends in the Northern Labrador Seal Hunt," *Etudes/Inuit/Studies* 13 (1989): 61–74. For protest movements see C. Lamson, *"Bloody Decks and a*

Bumper Crop": The Rhetoric of Sealing Counter-protest (St. John's: Memorial University of Newfoundland, 1979); G. Wenzel, " 'I Was Once Independent': The Southern Seal Protest and Inuit," *Anthropologica* 29 (summer 1987): 195–210; G. Wenzel, *Animal Rights, Human Rights: Ecology, Economy, and Ideology in the Canadian Arctic* (Toronto: University of Toronto Press, 1991).

The literature on fishery management is huge. For a dated but still useful overview of the law of the sea see T. W. Fulton, *The Sovereignty of the Sea* (London: Blackwood and Sons, 1911). For regulation histories see M. B. Bogue, "In the Shadow of the Union Jack: British Legacies and Great Lakes Fishery Policy," *Environmental Review* 11 (spring 1987): 19–34; Bogue, "To Save the Fish," *Journal of American History* 79 (Mar. 1993); K. Dorsey, *The Dawn of Conservation Diplomacy: U.S.-Canadian Wildlife Protection Treaties in the Progressive Era* (Seattle: University of Washington Press, 1998); G. Ireland, "The North Pacific Fisheries," *American Journal of International Law* 36 (July 1942): 400–424; R. Judd, *Common Lands, Common People: The Origins of Conservation in Northern New England* (Cambridge: Harvard University Press, 1997); McEvoy, *Fisherman's Problem;* J. Tomasevich, *International Agreements on Conservation of Marine Resources, with Special Reference to the North Pacific* (Stanford: Food Research Institute, 1943); M. C. Wright, "Newfoundland and Canada: The Evolution of Fisheries Development Policies, 1940–1966" (Ph.D. diss., Memorial University of Newfoundland, 1997). For salmon see J. Cone, *A Common Fate: Endangered Salmon and the People of the Pacific Northwest* (New York: Henry Holt, 1995); Cooley, *Politics and Conservation;* J. A. Crutchfield and G. Pontecorvo, *The Pacific Salmon Fisheries: A Study in Irrational Conservation* (Baltimore: Resources for the Future, 1969).

There are many important works on class and labor in fisheries. For book-length studies see J. M. Acheson, *The Lobster Gangs of Maine* (Hanover, N.H.: University Press of New England, 1988); L. W. Casady, "Labor Unrest and the Labor Movement in the Salmon Industry of the Pacific Coast" (Ph.D. diss., University of California, Berkeley, 1938); W. Clement, *The Struggle to Organize: Resistance in Canada's Fishery* (Toronto: McClelland and Stewart, 1986); P. G. Hummasti, *Finnish Radicals in Astoria, Oregon, 1904–1940: A Study in Immigrant Socialism* (New York: Arno Press, 1979); and C. Friday, *Organizing Asian American Labor: The Pacific Coast Canned-Salmon Industry, 1870–1942* (Philadelphia: Temple University Press, 1994).

For influential articles see P. Barber, "Culture, Capital, and Class Conflicts in the Political Economy of Cape Breton," *Journal of Historical Sociol-*

ogy 3 (winter 1990): 362–78; S. Cadigan, "Battle Harbour in Transition: Merchants, Fishermen, and the State in the Struggle for Relief in a Labrador Community during the 1930s," *Labour* 26 (1990): 125–50; W. Clement, "Canada's Coastal Fisheries: Formation of Unions, Cooperatives, and Associations," *Journal of Canadian Studies* 19 (spring 1984): 5–33; E. P. Durrenberger, "The History of Shrimpers' Unions in Mississippi, 1915–1955," *Labor's Heritage* 5 (fall 1994): 66–76; B. Hayward, "The Co-op Strategy," *Journal of Canadian Studies* 19 (spring 1984): 48–64; M. Moberg and J. S. Thomas, "Class Segmentation and Divided Labor: Asian Workers in the Gulf of Mexico Seafood Industry," *Ethnology* 32 (spring 1993): 87–99; A. Muszynski, "The Organization of Women and Ethnic Minorities in a Resource Industry: A Case Study of the Unionization of Shoreworkers in the British Columbia Fishing Industry, 1937–1949," *Journal of Canadian Studies* 19 (spring 1984): 89–107; C. A. Scontras, "Maine Lobstermen and the Labor Movement: The Lobster Fishermen's International Protective Association, 1907," *Maine Historical Society Quarterly* 29 (spring 1989): 30–51; P. R. Sinclair, "Fishermen Divided: The Impact of Limited Entry Licensing in Northwest Newfoundland," *Human Organization* 42 (winter 1983): 307–13; and P. R. Sinclair, "Fishermen of Northwest Newfoundland: Domestic Commodity Production in Advanced Capitalism," *Journal of Canadian Studies* 19 (spring 1984): 37–47.

For conflicts between fishers and industrialization see J. Cumbler, "The Early Making of an Environmental Consciousness: Fish, Fisheries Commissions, and the Connecticut River," *Environmental History Review* 15 (winter 1991): 73–91; Judd, *Common Lands;* G. Kulik, "Dams, Fish, and Farmers: Defense of Public Rights in Eighteenth-Century Rhode Island," in *The Countryside in the Age of Capitalist Transformation: Essays in the Social History of Rural America,* ed. S. Hahn and J. Prude (Chapel Hill: University of North Carolina Press, 1985), 25–50; D. J. Pisani, "Fish Culture and the Dawn of Concern over Water Pollution in the United States," *Environmental Review* 8 (1984): 117–31; and T. Steinberg, *Nature Incorporated: Industrialization and the Waters of New England* (New York: Cambridge University Press, 1991).

There are a number of works on gender and maritime activities. For studies that consider both men and women see E. P. Antler, "Fisherman, Fisherwoman, Rural Proletariat: Capitalist Commodity Production in the Newfoundland Fishery" (Ph.D. diss., University of Connecticut, 1982); M. P. Connelly and M. McDonald, "State Policy, the Household, and Women's Work in the Atlantic Fishery," *Journal of Canadian Studies* 26 (winter 1991–92): 18–32; M. S. Creighton, " 'Women' and Men in American Whaling, 1830–1870," *International Journal of Maritime History* 4 (spring 1992): 195–218; J. Druett, "More Decency and Order: Women and Whalemen in the Pacific," *Log of Mystic Seaport* 39 (summer 1987): 65–74; B. J. Logue, "The Whaling Industry and Fertility Decline: Nantucket, Massachusetts, 1660–1860," *Social Science History* 7 (winter 1983): 427–56; B. J. Logue, "The Case for Birth Control before 1850: Nantucket Reexamined," *Journal of Interdisciplinary History* 15 (fall 1985): 371–91; and M. Porter, " 'She Was Skipper of the Shore Crew': Notes on the History of the Sexual Division of Labour in Newfoundland," *Labour/Le Travail* 15 (1985): 105–23.

Single-sex studies are more numerous, but few focus on men. For studies of men see P. R. Knutson, " 'You Take Serious What's Said in Play!': A Systematic Distortion of Communication on a Fishing Boat" (Ph.D. diss., University of Washington, 1987); and Rediker, *Between the Devil and the Deep Blue Sea*. For women see Allison et al., *Winds of Change;* De Santis, *Neptune's Apprentice;* J. Druett, "Those Female Journals," *Log of Mystic Seaport* 40 (winter 1989): 115–25; Fields, *Entangling Net;* C. A. Fournier, "Navigating Women: Exploring the Roles of Nineteenth-Century New England Sailing Wives," *Maine History* 35 (spring–summer 1995): 46–61; E. J. Gorn, "Seafaring Engendered: Comment on Gender and Seafaring," *International Journal of Maritime History* 4 (spring 1992): 219–25; E. A. Little, "The Female Sailor on the *Christopher Mitchell:* Fact and Fantasy," *American Neptune* 54 (fall 1994): 252–58; L. A. Norling, "Captain Ahab Had a Wife: Ideology and Experience in the Lives of New England Maritime Women" (Ph.D. diss., Rutgers University, 1992); J. E. Reddin, "Making Ends Meet: The Way of the Prince Edward Island Fisherman's Wife," *Canadian Folklore* 13 (fall 1991): 85–98; S. J. Stark, "The Adventures of Two Women Whalers," *American Neptune* 44 (spring 1984): 22–24; K. Young, " 'Sauf les Perils et Fortunes de la Mer': Merchant Women in New France and the French Transatlantic Trade, 1713–46," *Canadian Historical Review* 77 (fall 1996): 388–407.

There is a lot of uneven scholarship on anglers and angling. The best analyses of Izaak Walton are J. Bevan, ed., *Izaak Walton: "The Compleat Angler," 1653–1676* (Oxford: Clarendon Press, 1983); and J. Bevan, *The Compleat Angler: The Art of Recreation* (Brighton: Harvester Press, 1988). For the development of American angling see D. V. Giacobbe, "A History of the Saltwater Sport Fishing Industry in Florida" (M.A. thesis, Florida Atlantic University, 1996); L. Mighetto, "Sport Fishing on the Columbia River," *Pacific Northwest Quarterly* 87 (Jan. 1995–96): 5–15; and C. J. Sheehy, "American Angling: The Rise of Urbanism and the Romance of the Rod and Reel," in *Hard at Play: Leisure in America, 1840–1940*, ed. K. Grover (Amherst: University of Massachusetts Press, 1992), 78–92. For links between sportfishing and conservation see T. L. Altherr, "The American Hunter-Naturalist and the Development of the Code of Sportsmanship," *Journal of Sport History* 5 (spring 1978): 7–22; K. A. Clements, "Herbert Hoover and Conservation, 1921–33," *American Historical Review* 89 (Feb. 1984): 67–88; G. W. Colpitts, "Fish and Game Associations in Southern Alberta, 1907–1928," *Alberta History* 42 (winter 1994): 16–26; T. R. Dunlap, "Sport Hunting and Conservation, 1880–1920," *Environmental Review* 12 (spring 1988): 52–53; J. F. Reiger, *American Sportsmen and the Origins of Conservation*, rev. ed. (Norman: University of Oklahoma Press, 1986); and P. G. Terrie, "Urban Man Confronts the Wilderness: The Nineteenth-Century Sportsman in the Adirondacks," *Journal of Sports History* 5 (winter 1978): 7–20.

Sporting-inspired conservation was often volatile and violent. For conflicts involving sportsmen see N. S. Forkey, "Anglers, Fishers, and the St. Croix River: Conflict in a Canadian-American Borderland, 1867–1900," *Forest and Conservation History* 37 (Oct. 1993): 179–87; S. Hahn, "Hunting, Fishing, and Foraging: Common Rights and Class Relations in the Postbellum South," *Radical History Review* 26 (1982): 37–64; K. H. Jacoby, "Class and Environmental History: Lessons from 'The War in the Adirondacks,' " *Environmental History* 2 (July 1997): 324–42; K. H. Jacoby, "The Recreation of Nature: A Social and Environmental History of American Conservation, 1872–1919" (Ph.D. diss., Yale University, 1997); P. Johnson, "Fish Free or Die: The Marlboro South Pond Case of 1896," *Vermont History News* 43 (fall 1992): 43–46; S. A. Marks, *Southern Hunting in Black and White: Nature, History, and Ritual in a Carolina Community* (Princeton: Princeton University Press, 1991); L. S. Warren, *The Hunter's Game: Poachers and Conservationists in Twentieth-Century America* (New Haven: Yale University Press, 1997); and W. Wiltzius, "William Radcliffe and the Grand Mesa Lakes Feud," *American Fly Fisher* 13 (Jan. 1986): 23–26.

Even a casual glance at this book's notes reveals the extensive reliance on archival documents and research from other disciplines. As a service to those interested in pursuing research in the environmental history of fishery or maritime subjects, the following is a selective guide to issues and sources for interdisciplinary research in the fisheries.

There is no simple definition for environmental history. Scholars attempting answers have struggled to find a common denominator or chronology.

Invariably, they organize studies in shifting temporal or thematic categories that never quite work. My own admittedly vague explanation of the field is that it is less a temporal narrative such as colonial history, or a topical tale such as constitutional history, than a way of thinking about the past that integrates nature as a crucial factor in human experience. For overviews of the field see W. Cronon, "A Place for Stories: Nature, History, and Narrative," *Journal of American History* 78 (Mar. 1992): 1347–76; W. Cronon, "Kennecott Journey: The Paths Out of Town," in *Under an Open Sky: Rethinking America's Past*, ed. W. Cronon, G. Miles, and J. Gitlin (New York: Norton, 1992), 28–51; M. Melosi, "The Place of the City in Environmental History," *Environmental History Review* 17 (spring 1993): 1–23; C. M. Rosen and J. A. Tarr, "The Importance of an Urban Perspective in Environmental History," *Journal of Urban History* 20 (1994): 299–310; M. A. Stewart, "Environmental History: Profile of a Developing Field," *History Teacher* 31 (May 1998): 351–68; P. G. Terrie, "Recent Work in Environmental History," *American Studies International* 27 (Oct. 1989): 42–65; R. White, "American Environmental History: The Development of a New Historical Field," *Pacific Historical Review* 54 (1985): 297–335; D. Worster, "History as Natural History: An Essay on Theory and Method," *Pacific Historical Review* 53 (spring 1984): 1–19; D. Worster, ed., *The Ends of the Earth: Perspectives on Modern Environmental History* (New York: Cambridge University Press, 1988); and D. Worster et al., "A Round Table: Environmental History," *Journal of American History* 76 (Mar. 1990): 1087–147.

Historians normally attend to temporal change, but stories about nature require equal attention to spatial change. For introductions to geographical analysis see D. Cosgrove, *Social Formation and Symbolic Landscape* (London: Croom Helm, 1984); M. Foucault, *Power/Knowledge: Selected Interviews and Other Writings*, ed. and trans. C. Gordon (New York: Pantheon, 1980); C. Harris, "Power, Modernity, and Historical Geography," *Annals of the Association of American Geographers* 81 (winter 1991): 671–83; H. Lefebvre, *The Production of Space*, trans. D. Nicholson-Smith (Oxford: Blackwell, 1991); A. Pred, *Making Histories and Constructing Human Geographies: The Social Transformation of Practice, Power Relations, and Consciousness* (Boulder: Westview Press, 1990); E. W. Soja, *Postmodern Geographies: The Reassertion of Space in Critical Social Theory* (London: Verso, 1989); and M. Williams, "The Relations of Environmental History and Historical Geography," *Journal of Historical Geography* 20 (1994): 3–21. For spatial analyses of fisheries see D. Newell, "Dispersal and Concentration: The Slowly Changing Spatial Pattern of the British Columbia Salmon Canning Industry,"

Journal of Historical Geography 14 (Jan. 1988): 22–36; and D. W. Schneider, "Enclosing the Floodplain: Resource Conflict on the Illinois River, 1880–1920," *Environmental History* 1 (Apr. 1996): 70–96.

One of the principal challenges of environmental history is documenting alterations to nature. I initially tried to find a normative salmon run to gauge later changes, but I soon realized that this was hopeless because the assumption of balance in nature, which pervades environmentalist thought and many environmental histories, was a cultural expectation I was wishfully imposing upon the world, not an a priori reality. For useful discussions of this problem see F. N. Egerton, "Changing Concepts of the Balance of Nature," *Quarterly Review of Biology* 48 (1973): 322–50; R. White, "Discovering Nature in North America," *Journal of American History* 79 (Dec. 1992): 874–91; R. Williams, "Ideas of Nature," in *Problems in Materialism and Culture* (London: Verso, 1980), 67–85; and D. Worster, *Nature's Economy: A History of Ecological Ideas*, 2d ed (New York: Cambridge University Press, 1994).

A troubling consequence of these insights has been the erosion of scientific certainty. Belief in the balance of nature gained power in part because it was a guiding assumption among life scientists—especially those in the field of ecology, which profoundly influenced modern ideas about nature—yet scientists are no more immune to culture than the rest of society. For studies of this see E. Cittadino, *Nature as the Laboratory: Darwinian Plant Ecology in the German Empire, 1880–1900* (New York: Cambridge University Press, 1990); S. G. Cook, *Cowles Bog, Indiana, and Henry Chandler Cowles* (Chesterson: Indiana Dunes National Lakeshore, 1980); R. P. McIntosh, *The Background of Ecology: Concept and Theory* (New York: Cambridge University Press, 1985), 1–68; J. Hagen, *An Entangled Bank: The Origins of Ecosystem Ecology* (New Brunswick: Rutgers University Press, 1992); S. Kingsland, *Modeling Nature: Episodes in the History of Population Ecology* (Chicago: University of Chicago Press, 1985); G. Mitman, *The State of Nature: Ecology, Community, and American Social Thought, 1900–1950* (Chicago: University of Chicago Press, 1992); and R. C. Tobey, *Saving the Prairies: The Life Cycle of the Founding School of American Plant Ecology, 1895–1955* (Berkeley: University of California Press, 1981).

For general histories of American science see R. V. Bruce, *The Launching of Modern American Science, 1846–1876* (New York: Alfred A. Knopf, 1987); and A. H. Dupree, *Science in the Federal Government: A History of Policies and Activities to 1940* (New York: Harpers, 1957). For life sciences see G. E. Allen, "Naturalists and Experimentalists: The Genotype and the Phenotype," *Studies in the History of Biology* 3 (1970): 179–209; K. R.

Benson, J. Maienschein, and R. Rainger, eds., *The Expansion of American Biology* (New Brunswick: Rutgers University Press, 1991); J. Maienschein, *Transforming Traditions in American Biology, 1880–1915* (Baltimore: Johns Hopkins University Press, 1991); R. Rainger, K. R. Benson, and J. Maienschein, eds., *The American Development of Biology* (Philadelphia: University of Philadelphia Press, 1988); C. E. Rosenberg, *No Other Gods: On Science and American Social Thought* (Baltimore: Johns Hopkins University Press, 1976); M. L. Smith, *Pacific Visions: California Scientists and the Environment, 1850–1925* (New Haven: Yale University Press, 1987). For divisions in science see H. M. Collins, "The Structure of Knowledge," *Social Research* 60 (spring 1993): 95–116; R. Kline, "Construing 'Technology' as 'Applied Science': Public Rhetoric of Scientists and Engineers in the United States, 1880–1945," *ISIS* 86 (June 1995): 194–221; and B. E. Seely, "The Scientific Mystique of Engineering: Highway Research at the Bureau of Pubic Roads, 1918–1940," *Technology and Culture* 25 (1984): 798–831.

The realization that science and balance in nature were culturally constructed has transformed the way historians talk about past environments. For this impact see W. Cronon, ed., *Uncommon Ground: Toward Reinventing Nature* (New York: Norton, 1995); and R. White, "Indian Peoples and the Natural World: Asking the Right Questions," in *Rethinking American Indian History*, ed. D. L. Fixico (Albuquerque: University of New Mexico Press, 1997), 96–98. For overviews of recent changes in scientific constructions of nature see D. B. Botkin, *Discordant Harmonies: A New Ecology for the Twenty-first Century* (New York: Oxford University Press, 1990); and S. L. Pimm, *The Balance of Nature? Ecological Issues in the Conservation of Species and Communities* (Chicago: University of Chicago Press, 1991). For a cautionary assessment of these events see D. Worster, "The Ecology of Order and Chaos," in *The Wealth of Nature: Environmental History and the Ecological Imagination* (New York: Oxford University Press, 1993), 156–70.

For fishery historians, the two issues that these developments affect most directly are historical understandings of fish and of habitat. Although scientific ideas about fish have changed, no source addresses these changes systematically. For studies of ichthyologists and fishery science see D. Allard, "Spencer Fullerton Baird and the Foundations of American Marine Science," *Marine Fisheries Review* 50, no. 4 (1988): 124–29; D. Allard, "The Fish Commission Laboratory and Its Influence on the Founding of the Marine Biological Laboratory," *Journal of the History of Biology* 23 (summer 1990): 251–70; K. R. Benson, "From Museum Research to Laboratory Research: The Transformation of Natural History into Academic Biology," in *The American Development of Biology*, ed.

Rainger, Benson, and Maienschein, 49–83; K. R. Benson, "Why American Marine Stations? The Teaching Argument," *American Zoologist* 28
(1980): 7–14; Benson, *A Century of Fisheries in North America;* S. Bocking,
"Stephen Forbes, Jacob Reighard, and the Emergence of Aquatic Ecology
in the Great Lakes Region," *Journal of the History of Biology* 23 (fall 1990):
461–98; J. P. Brosco, "Henry Bryant Bigelow, the U.S. Bureau of Fisheries, and Intensive Area Study," *Social Studies of Science* 19 (summer 1989):
239–64; R. Dexter, "A Century of Fishery Biology at Cape Ann, Massachusetts," *American Neptune* 45 (summer 1985): 81–85; J. M. Hubbard,
"An Independent Progress: The Development of Marine Biology on the
Atlantic Coast of Canada" (Ph.D. diss., University of Toronto, 1993); C.
L. Hubbs, "History of Ichthyology in the United States after 1850," *Copeia*
(Mar. 1964): 42–60; K. Johnstone, *The Aquatic Explorers: A History of the
Fisheries Research Board of Canada* (Toronto: University of Toronto Press,
1977); P. J. Pauly, "Summer Resort and Scientific Discipline: Woods Hole
and the Structure of American Biology, 1882–1925," in *The American
Development of Biology,* ed. Rainger, Benson, and Maienschein, 121–50.

For relationships between science and management see D. C. Allard Jr.,
Spencer Fullerton Baird and the U.S. Fish Commission (New York: Arno,
1978); D. H. Cushing, "A History of Some of the International Fishery
Commissions," *Proceedings, Royal Society Edinburgh (B)* 73 (1972): 361–90;
K. Dunbar and C. Friday, "Salmon, Seals, and Science: The Albatross and
Conservation in Alaska, 1888–1914," *Journal of the West* 38 (Oct. 1994): 6–
13; F. N. Egerton, "Missed Opportunities: U.S. Fishery Biologists and
Productivity of Fish in Green Bay, Saginaw Bay, and Western Lake Erie,"
Environmental Review 13 (summer 1989): 33–63; B. Engholm, "Fishery
Conservation in the Atlantic Ocean," in *Atlantic Ocean Fisheries,* ed. G.
Borgstrom and A. J. Heighway (London: Fishing News, 1961), 40–48; A.
C. Finlayson, *Fishing for Truth: A Sociological Analysis of Northern Cod Stock
Assessments from 1977 to 1990* (St. John's: Memorial University of New-
foundland, 1994); E. C. Herber, *Correspondence between Spencer Fullerton
Baird and Louis Agassiz—Two Pioneer American Naturalists* (Hartford: Con-
necticut Printers, 1963); Judd, *Common Lands;* S. E. Kingsland, *Modeling
Nature: Episodes in the History of Population Ecology,* 2d ed. (Chicago: Univer-
sity of Chicago Press, 1995); M. W. Klingle, "Plying Atomic Waters:
Lauren Donaldson and the 'Fern Lake Concept' of Fisheries Management," *Journal of the History of Biology* 31 (spring 1998): 1–32; A. F.
McEvoy, "Science, Culture, and Politics in U.S. Natural Resources Management," *Journal of the History of Biology* 25 (winter 1992): 469–86; McEvoy,
Fisherman's Problem; A. F. McEvoy and H. N. Scheiber, "Scientists, Entre-

preneurs, and the Policy Process: A Study of the Post-1945 California Sardine Depletion," *Journal of Economic History* 44 (summer 1984): 393–406; J. F. Roos, *Restoring Fraser River Salmon: A History of the International Pacific Salmon Fisheries Commission, 1937–1985* (Vancouver: Pacific Salmon Commission, 1991); T. D. Smith, *Scaling Fisheries: The Science of Measuring the Effects of Fishing, 1855–1955* (Cambridge: Cambridge University Press, 1994); T. D. Smith, " 'Simultaneous and Complementary Advances': Mid-century Expectations of the Interaction of Fisheries Science and Management," *Reviews in Fish Biology and Fisheries* 8 (Sept. 1998): 335–48; and J. E. Taylor III, "Making Salmon: The Political Economy of Science and the Road Not Taken," *Journal of the History of Biology* 31 (spring 1998): 33–59.

For fish culture and hatcheries see J. W. Hedgpeth, "Livingston Stone and Fish Culture in California," *California Fish and Game* 27 (July 1941): 126–48; W. Hunt, *History of the Marine Hatcheries of Alaska* (Anchorage: Alaska Sea Grant Program, 1976); E. Leitritz, *A History of California's Fish Hatcheries, 1870–1960* (Sacramento: Department of Fish and Game, 1970); G. P. Marsh, *Report Made under the Authority of the Legislature of Vermont on the Artificial Propagation of Fish* (Burlington: Free Press Printers, 1857); G. P. Marsh, *Man and Nature* (Cambridge: Harvard University Press, 1965); P. Roppel, *Alaska's Salmon Hatcheries, 1891–1959* (Juneau: Alaska Department of Fish and Game, 1982); R. R. Stickney, *Aquaculture in the United States: A Historical Survey* (New York: John Wiley, 1996); and L. Stolte, *The Forgotten Salmon of the Merrimack* (Washington: Government Printing Office, 1981). For fish culture and management see Allard, *Spencer Fullerton Baird;* J. O. Anfinson, "Commerce and Conservation on the Upper Mississippi River," *Annals of Iowa* 52 (fall 1993): 385–417; M. Black, "Tragic Remedies: A Century of Failed Fishery Policy on California's Sacramento River," *Pacific Historical Review* 64 (spring 1995): 37–70; B. Brown, *Mountain in the Clouds: A Search for the Wild Salmon* (Seattle: University of Washington Press, 1995); Cooley, *Politics and Conservation;* D. W. Ellis et al., *Net Loss: The Salmon Netcage Industry in British Columbia* (Vancouver: Suzuki Foundation, 1996); and Smith, *Scaling Fisheries.*

The best scientific sources for fish and fish habitat are professional journals such as *North American Journal of Fisheries Management; Transactions of the American Fisheries Society;* and *Contributions to Canadian Biology* and its successor journals, *Contributions to Canadian Biology and Fisheries, Journal of the Biological Board of Canada, Journal of the Fisheries Research Board of Canada,* and *Canadian Journal of Fisheries and Aquatic Sciences.* For late-nineteenth-century ichthyological classifications see D. S. Jordan and B. W. Evermann, *American Food and Game Fisheries* (New York: Doubleday, 1902).

The best recent treatment of Pacific salmon is C. Groot and L. Margolis, eds., *Pacific Salmon Life Histories* (Vancouver: University of British Columbia Press, 1991). For syntheses of recent research on fish habitat see W. R. Meehan, ed., *Influences of Forest and Rangeland Management on Salmonid Fishes and Their Habitats*, American Fisheries Society Special Publication 19 (Bethesda: American Fisheries Society, 1991); and D. J. Stouder, P. A. Bisson, and R. J. Naiman, eds., *Pacific Salmon and Their Ecosystems: Status and Future Options* (New York: Chapman and Hall, 1997).

The problem of fluctuating fish populations has long troubled fishers, managers, and scientists. For scientific discussions about the dynamics of fish populations see M. D. Burkenroad, "Fluctuations in Abundance of Marine Animals," *Science* 103 (1946): 684–86; M. Sinclair and T. D. Iles, "Population Richness of Marine Fish Species (Temporal Variability)," *Aquatic Living Resources* 1 (1988): 71–83; M. Sinclair and P. Solemdal, "The Development of 'Population Thinking' in Fisheries Biology between 1878 and 1930," *Aquatic Living Resources* 1 (1988): 189–213; Smith, *Scaling Fisheries;* P. Solemdal, "The Three Cavaliers: A Discussion from the Golden Age of Norwegian Marine Research," in *Early Life History and Recruitment in Fish Populations,* ed. R. C. Chambers and E. A. Trippel (London: Chapman and Hall, 1997), 553–65. For case studies of these fluctuations, which often have been framed as problems of "overfishing," see M. D. Burkenroad, "Fluctuations in Abundance of Pacific Halibut," *Bulletin, Bingham Oceanographic Collection* 11 (1948): 81–129; J. Cleghorn, "On the Fluctuations in the Herring Fisheries," *Report of the British Association for the Advancement of Science* 24 (1854): 134; R. Hilborn, "Apparent Stock Recruitment Relationships in Mixed Stock Fisheries," *Canadian Journal of Fisheries and Aquatic Sciences* 42 (1985): 718–23; P. A. Larkin, "An Epitaph for the Concept of Maximum Sustained Yield," *Transactions of the American Fisheries Society* 106 (Jan. 1977): 1–11; C. G. J. Petersen, "What Is Over-fishing?" *Journal of the Marine Biological Association* 6 (1900–1903): 587–94; W. E. Ricker, "Stock and Recruitment," *Journal of the Fisheries Research Board of Canada* 11 (May 1954): 559–623; W. E. Ricker, "Maximum Sustained Yields from Fluctuating Environments," *Journal of the Fisheries Research Board of Canada* 15 (May 1958): 991–1006; E. S. Russell, *The Overfishing Problem* (Cambridge: Cambridge University Press, 1942); B. E. Skud, "Revised Estimates of Halibut Abundance and the Thompson-Burkenroad Debate," *Report of the International North Pacific Halibut Commission* 56 (1975); J. E. Taylor III, "Burning the Candle at Both Ends: Historicizing Overfishing in Oregon's Nineteenth-Century Salmon Fisheries," *Environmental History* 4 (Jan. 1999): 54–79.

Historicizing ocean and atmospheric climates is an immense challenge. Most instrument records are less than a century old and sometimes intermittent and unreliable. Moreover, most recording stations were on or near land and thus not particularly indicative of offshore conditions. Interpreting data is also hazardous because scientists are constantly revising ideas about how sea and atmosphere interact. For overviews of oceanography see M. Deacon, *Scientists at Sea, 1650–1900: Study of Marine Sciences* (New York: Academic Press, 1971); E. L. Mills, *Biological Oceanography: An Early History, 1870–1960* (Ithaca: Cornell University Press, 1989); M. Sears and D. Merriman, eds., *Oceanography: The Past* (New York: Springer-Verlag, 1980); S. Schlee, *On the Edge of an Unfamiliar World: A History of Oceanography* (New York: E. P. Dutton, 1973); H. Rozwadowski, "Fathoming the Ocean: The Discovery and Exploration of the Deep Sea" (Ph.D. diss., University of Pennsylvania, 1995); and E. Shorr, *Scripps Institution of Oceanography: Probing the Oceans, 1936 to 1976* (San Diego: University of California Press, 1978). For histories of meteorology see S. G. Brush, H. E. Landsberg, and M. Collins, *The History of Geophysics and Meteorology: An Annotated Bibliography* (New York: Garland, 1985); J. R. Fleming, *Meteorology in America, 1800–1870* (Baltimore: Johns Hopkins University Press, 1990); R. M. Friedman, *Appropriating the Weather: Vilhelm Bjerknes and the Construction of a Modern Meteorology* (Ithaca: Cornell University Press, 1989); H. H. Frisinger, *The Early History of Meteorology to 1800* (New York: Science History Publications, 1977).

For attempts to historicize the ocean see R. C. Francis, S. R. Hare, A. B. Hollowed, and W. S. Wooster, "Effects of Interdecadal Climate Variability on the Oceanic Ecosystems of the Northeast Pacific," *Fisheries Oceanography* 7 (Mar. 1998): 1–21; and R. C. Francis and S. R. Hare, "Decadal-Scale Regime Shifts in the Large Marine Ecosystems of the North-East Pacific: A Case for Historical Science," *Fisheries Oceanography* 3 (1994): 279–91. For works that integrate climate into history see R. Claiborne, *Climate, Man, and History* (New York: Norton, 1970); R. H. Grove, *Ecology, Climate and Empire: Colonialism and Global Environmental History, 1400–1940* (Cambridge: White Horse Press, 1997); H. H. Lamb, *Climate: Present, Past and Future*, 2 vols. (London: Methuen, 1972–77); H. H. Lamb, *Climate, History and the Modern World*, 2d ed. (London: Routledge, 1995); and McEvoy, *Fisherman's Problem*. For El Niño see J. M. Wallace and S. Vogel, *El Niño and Climate Prediction* (Boulder: University Corporation for Atmospheric Research, 1994); and H. F. Diaz and V. Markgraf, eds., *El Niño: Historical and Paleoclimatic Aspects of the Southern Oscillation* (New York: Cambridge University Press, 1992). For works on climate, ocean, and fish see R.

Beamish, ed., *Climate Change and Northern Fish Populations* (Ottawa: National Research Council of Canada, 1995); M. H. Glantz, ed., *Climate Variability, Climate Change, and Fisheries* (New York: Cambridge University Press, 1992); T. Laevastu, *Marine Climate, Weather, and Fisheries: The Effects of Weather and Climatic Changes on Fisheries and Ocean Resources* (New York: Halsted Press, 1993); and N. J. Mantua, S. R. Hare, Y. Zhang, J. M. Wallace, and R. C. Francis, "A Pacific Interdecadal Climate Oscillation with Impacts on Salmon Production," *Bulletin of the American Meteorological Society* 78 (June 1997): 1069–79.

Portraying Indians as dynamic figures can be as daunting a task as historicizing nature. For good discussions see T. W. Overholt, "American Indians as 'Natural Ecologists,' " *American Indian Journal* 5 (Sept. 1979): 9–16; R. White, "Native Americans and the Environment," in *Scholars and the Indian Experience,* ed. W. R. Swagerty (Bloomington: Indiana University Press, 1984), 179–204; and R. White and W. Cronon, "Ecological Change and Indian-White Relations," in *Handbook of North American Indians,* vol. 4, *History of Indian-White Relations,* ed. W. E. Washburn (Washington: Smithsonian Institution, 1988), 417–29. For methodological discussions see J. S. H. Brown, "Ethnohistorians: Strange Bedfellows, Kindred Spirits," *Ethnohistory* 38 (spring 1991): 113–23; Fixico, *Rethinking American Indian History;* C. Martin, ed., *The American Indian and the Problem of History* (New York: Oxford University Press, 1987); W. C. Sturtevant, "Anthropology, History, and Ethnohistory," *Ethnohistory* 13 (winter 1966): 1–51; and B. G. Trigger, "Ethnohistory: Problems and Prospects," *Ethnohistory* 29 (winter 1982): 1–19. The best place for researchers to begin are the essays and bibliographies of the *Handbook of North American Indians,* ed. W. C. Sturtevant, 20 vols. planned (Washington: Smithsonian Institution, 1981–). For environmental histories of Indians see W. Cronon, *Changes in the Land: Indians, Colonists, and the Ecology of New England* (New York: Hill and Wang, 1983); D. R. Lewis, *Neither Wolf nor Dog: American Indians, Environment, and Agrarian Change* (New York: Oxford University Press, 1994); R. White, *Land Use, Environment, and Social Change: The Shaping of Island County, Washington* (Seattle: University of Washington Press, 1980); and R. White, *The Roots of Dependency: Subsistence, Environment, and Social Change among the Choctaws, Pawnees, and Navajos* (Lincoln: University of Nebraska Press, 1983).

European contact wrought convulsive ecological and cultural changes for Indians. For its impact see A. W. Crosby, "Virgin Soil Epidemics as a Factor in the Aboriginal Depopulation in America," *William and Mary Quarterly* 33 (1976): 289–99; and W. R. Jacobs, "The Tip of the Iceberg:

Pre-Columbian Indian Demography and Some Implications for Revision," *William and Mary Quarterly* 31 (1974): 123–32. Drastically changing populations can make havoc for researchers. For introductions to the intellectual and political minefield of Indian demography see W. M. Denevan, ed., *The Native Population of the Americas in 1492*, 2d ed. (Madison: University of Wisconsin Press, 1992); J. W. Verano and D. H. Ubelaker, eds., *Disease and Demography in the Americas* (Washington: Smithsonian Institution Press, 1992); and D. H. Ubelaker, *Reconstruction of Demographic Profiles from Ossuary Skeletal Samples: A Case Study from the Tidewater Potomac*, Smithsonian Contributions to Anthropology 18 (Washington: Smithsonian Institution, 1974).

Numerous factors can complicate such material questions as aboriginal population or fish consumption. For an introduction to these issues see R. T. Boyd and Y. P. Hajda, "Seasonal Population Movement along the Lower Columbia River: The Social and Ecological Context," *American Ethnologist* 14 (May 1987): 309–26; D. T. Reff, *Disease, Depopulation, Culture Change in Northwest New Spain, 1518–1764* (Salt Lake City: University of Utah Press, 1991); and R. Thornton, T. Miller, and J. Warren, "American Indian Population Recovery Following Smallpox Epidemics," *American Anthropologist* 93 (1991): 28–45. For Oregon country demography see S. K. Campbell, *Post-Columbian Culture History in the Northern Columbia Plateau*, A.D. 1500–1900 (New York: Garland Publishing, 1990); and R. Boyd, *The Coming of the Spirit of Pestilence: Introduced Infectious Diseases and Population Decline among Northwest Indians, 1774–1874* (Seattle: University of Washington Press, 1999). The latter volume was in press while I was doing research, and I consulted instead Boyd's dissertation: "The Introduction of Infectious Diseases among the Indians of the Pacific Northwest, 1774–1874" (Ph.D. diss., University of Washington, 1985).

It is one thing to count bodies and fish and quite another to discern the meaning of such things. Native myths and oral histories can be rich, though problematic, sources. The two most important archival collections are at the D'Arcy McNickle Center of the Newberry Library in Chicago and at the National Anthropological Archives of the Smithsonian Institution in Washington. There are many published sources, but see especially *Smithsonian Institution Bureau of Ethnology Bulletin* (Washington: Smithsonian Institution, 1887–1971). For the limitations of these resources see M. Harkin, "History, Narrative, and Temporality: Examples from the Northwest Coast," *Ethnohistory* 35 (spring 1988): 99–130. For works on aboriginal myths and fishing see E. Gunther, "An Analysis of the First Salmon Ceremony," *American Anthropologist* 28 (Oct. 1926): 605–17; E. Gunther, "A

Further Analysis of the First Salmon Ceremony," *University of Washington Publications in Anthropology* 2 (1928): 129–73; A. Hultkrantz, "Supernatural Beings of Fish and Fishing in Aboriginal North America," in *Fishing Culture of the World,* ed. Gunda, 865–85; S. L. Swezey and R. F. Heizer, "Ritual Regulation of Anadromous Fish Resources in Native California," in *Fishing Culture of the World,* ed. Gunda, 967–89; and T. T. Waterman and A. L. Kroeber, "The Kepel Fish Dam," *University of California Publications in American Archaeology and Ethnography* 35 (1943): 49–80.

Industrial fishing was part of a tangled skein of social and cultural developments pressuring natural resources. The fates of fish and fishers were inextricably linked with political culture, technology, and science. Primary documents are critical for understanding fishers, industry, and environment. The best resources for contemporary accounts of the fisheries are the "Letters Received, 1882–1900" [120 feet] and "Press Copies of Letters Sent, 1871–1906" [696 vols., 74 feet] in the U.S. Fish and Wildlife Records, Record Group 22, National Archives, College Park, Md. Both have indexes that identify correspondents by year, name, and state. There are other files for letters to individual commissioners, and one very useful collection of letters between Spencer F. Baird and Livingston Stone. Some U.S. Fish Commission (USFC) correspondence is in the Smithsonian Institution Archives because Baird and George Brown Goode directed the USFC and the Smithsonian simultaneously during the 1870s and 1880s, and there was considerable overlap in the administration of scientific activities by the two organizations. For USFC correspondence at the Smithsonian see Record Units 26, 28–30, 33, 35–36, 38, 52–54, 201, 213, 234, 7002, 7050, 7184, and 9510.

Federal records for the twentieth century are difficult to research. In 1903, Congress transferred the Fish Commission to the Department of Commerce and Labor and changed the agency's name to the Bureau of Fisheries (and to the Fish and Wildlife Service in 1940). For histories of the USFC see Allard, *Spencer Fullerton Baird;* and T. W. Cart, "The Federal Fisheries Service, 1871–1940" (M.A. thesis, University of North Carolina, 1968). During the 1910s the USBF changed its archival policy, discontinuing the practice of depositing letters in incoming and outgoing collections in favor of topical files. The consequence for researchers is that it is much harder to track general correspondence after 1908, and while regional offices also retained copies of correspondence, their preservation policies are far from uniform. Nevertheless, visiting regional offices and research labs is strongly recommended. The Northwest Fisheries Science Center Library at the National Marine Fisheries Service in Seattle has an invaluable file of published and unpublished reports that became a crucial resource while researching this book.

But federal records can take you only so far. The *National Union Catalog of Manuscript Collections* (Washington: Library of Congress, 1959–) is useful for locating archival collections of fishing and industry records, but there is no substitute for visiting archives and scrounging around—with permission, of course. My visits to Oregon's State Archives in Salem and to Washington's State Archives in Olympia revealed remarkable, and often untapped, information on the day-to-day operations of management agencies. Local organizations are also vital sources for information. Some of the most fruitful locations include the Columbia River Maritime Museum in Astoria, Oreg.; the Fisheries Library at University of Washington, Seattle; the Fisheries Museum of the Atlantic in Lunenburg, Nova Scotia; the International Council for the Exploration of the Sea, Copenhagen, Denmark; the International Halibut Commission, University of Washington, Seattle; the International Whaling Commission archives, Cambridge, England; the Joyner Library at East Carolina University, Greenville, N.C.; the Marine Museum of the Great Lakes in Kingston, Ont.; the Mariners' Museum in Newport News, Va.; the Maritime History Archives at Memorial University of Newfoundland, St. John's; Mystic Seaport in Mystic, Conn.; the Peabody Essex Museum and Essex Maritime Museum in Salem, Mass.; the Scripps Institute for Oceanography, La Jolla, Calif.; and the Woods Hole Oceanographic Institute, Woods Hole, Mass.

Obtaining accurate fishing statistics is a huge but largely unaddressed research problem. The lying fisherman is a cultural cliché grounded in long experience, yet when it comes to documenting commercial harvests, researchers usually treat industry statistics with complete credulity. While it may be true that there is no alternative authority, researchers nevertheless need to regard with circumspection the official catch figures published by federal and state agencies. These are records of *processed* fish—not fish caught—but for centuries observers have noted the tremendous number of fish wasted between capture and can. They have also noted industry biases and problems with misreporting in different locations and seasons. For useful discussions of these problems see R. E. Mullen, *Oregon's Commercial Harvest of Coho Salmon, "Oncorhynchus kisutch" (Walbaum), 1892–1960,* Informational Report 81–3 (Corvallis: Oregon Department of Fish and Wildlife, Fish Division, 1981); and W. H. Rich, "The Present State of the Columbia River Salmon Resources," *Proceedings of the Sixth Pacific Science Congress* 3 (1939): 425–30.

Problems aside, researchers have to use some figures, and many sources are available. Sabine's *Report on the Principal Fisheries of the American Seas* and Goode's *Fisheries and Fishery Industries of the United States* are still crucial resources despite their biases. For information on fishers and capital resources see the Division of Statistics section of the annual reports by the USFC and USBF. Catch records have been kept in a haphazard fashion by the industry, state, and federal agencies. The sources cited most often include Canada, Ministry of Marine and Fisheries, *Annual Report of the Department of Marine and Fisheries, Fisheries Branch* (Ottawa: 1868–); J. N. Cobb, *The Pacific Salmon Fisheries* (Washington: Government Printing Office, 1930); G. B. Goode et al., *Materials for a History of the Mackerel Fishery* (Washington: Government Printing Office, 1883); Innis, *Cod Fisheries;* New Brunswick, Office of Lieutenant Governor, *Reports on the Sea and River Fisheries of New Brunswick*, by M. H. Perley (Fredericton: J. Simpson, 1852); Nova Scotia, Office of the Provincial Secretary, *Shore and Deep Sea Fisheries of Nova Scotia*, by T. F. Knight (Halifax: A. Grant, 1867); G. H. Procter, comp., *The Fishermen's Memorial and Record Book* (Gloucester: Procter Brothers, 1873); U.S. Congress, *American State Papers, Commerce and Navigation*, 2 vols. (Washington: Gales and Seaton, 1832–34); U.S. Department of Treasury, *Annual Report on the Foreign Commerce and Navigation of the United States* (1821–92); U.S. Department of Treasury, *Annual Report of the Commissioner of Navigation* (1893–1903); and the *Pacific Fisherman's* annual *Yearbook*.

Understanding technology is crucial for analyzing the polemic literature on declining fisheries. For fishing gear see I. J. Donaldson and F. K. Cramer, *Fishwheels of the Columbia* (Portland: Binfords and Mort, 1971); J. Garner, *How to Make Nets* (Farham: Fishing News Books Ltd., 1962); H. Krjstjonsson, ed., *Modern Fishing Gear of the World*, 3 vols. (London: Fishing News Books Ltd., 1959–71); T. G. Lytle, *Harpoons and Other Whalecraft* (New Bedford, Mass.: Old Dartmouth Historical Society, 1984); J. C. Sainsbury, *Commercial Fishing Methods: An Introduction to Vessels and Gears*, 3d ed. (Oxford: Fishing News Books, 1996); Stewart, *Indian Fishing*. For ships see H. I. Chapelle, *American Sailing Craft* (New York: Kennedy Brothers, 1936); H. I. Chapelle, *American Small Sailing Craft: Their Design, Development, and Construction* (New York: Norton, 1951); H. I. Chapelle, *The National Watercraft Collection* (Washington: Government Printing Office, 1960); H. I. Chapelle, *The American Fishing Schooners, 1825–1935* (New York: W. W. Norton, 1973); Damron, "The Emergence of Salmon Trolling on the American Northwest Coast" (Ph.D. diss., University of Oregon, 1975); and W. M. O'Leary, "The Antebellum Maine Fishing Schooner and the Factors

Influencing Its Design and Construction," *American Neptune* 44 (summer 1984): 82–95.

Rapid technological changes have had huge consequences for fish and fish environments. For food preservation see C. L. Cutting, *Fish Saving: A History of Fish Processing from Ancient to Modern Times* (London: Leonard Hill Books, 1955); P. Roppel, "The Lost Art of Mild-Curing Salmon," *Alaska Journal* 16 (1986): 230–37; and C. H. Stevenson, "The Preservation of Fishery Products for Food," *Bulletin of the United States Fish Commission* 18 (1898): 335–563. For fish processing see D. Newell, "The Rationality of Mechanization in the Pacific Salmon-Canning Industry before the Second World War," *Business History Review* 62 (winter 1988): 626–55; P. W. O'Bannon, "Technological Change in the Pacific Coast Canned Salmon Industry, 1900–1925: A Case Study," *Agricultural History* 56 (Special Issue 1982): 151–66; P. D. Schultz and F. Lortie, "Archaeological Notes on a California Chinese Shrimp Boiler," *Historical Archaeology* 19 (spring 1985): 86–95; Smith, *Salmon Fishers of the Columbia;* and T. Williams, "The Williams Lobster Factory at Neils Harbour, 1901–1935," *Nova Scotia Historical Review* 8 (spring 1988): 77–83. For transportation see F. W. Millerd, "Windjammers to Eighteen Wheelers: The Impact of Changes in Transportation Technology on the Development of British Columbia's Fishing Industry," *BC Studies* 78 (1988): 28–52. For dams see the journal *Civil Engineering* (1931–); and L. Mighetto and W. J. Ebel, *Saving the Salmon: A History of the U.S. Army Corps of Engineers' Efforts to Protect Anadromous Fish on the Columbia and Snake Rivers* (Seattle: Historical Research Associates, 1994).

Although I rejected the "tragedy of the commons" model in this study, it remains a powerful analytical tool. Anyone interested in this literature must begin with G. Hardin, "The Tragedy of the Commons," *Science* 162 (13 Dec. 1968): 1243–48. See also H. S. Gordon, "The Economic Theory of a Common-Property Resource: The Fishery," *Journal of Political Economy* 62 (1954): 124–42; G. Hardin and J. Baden, eds., *Managing the Commons* (San Francisco: W. H. Freeman, 1977); A. D. Scott, "The Fishery: The Objectives of Sole Ownership," *Journal of Political Economy* 63 (Apr. 1955): 116–24. For criticism see D. Feeny, F. Berkes, B. J. McCay, and J. M. Acheson, "The Tragedy of the Commons: Twenty Two Years Later," *Human Ecology* 18 (Mar. 1990): 1–19; D. Feeny, S. Hanna, and A. F. McEvoy, "Questioning Assumptions of the 'Tragedy of the Commons' Model of Fisheries," *Land Economics* 72 (May 1996): 187–205; M. P. Marchak, "What Happens When Common Property Becomes Uncommon?" *BC Studies* 80 (winter 1988–89): 3–23; M. P. Marchak, N. Guppy, and J. McMullan, eds., *Uncom-*

mon Property: The Fishing and Fish-Processing Industries of British Columbia (Toronto: Methuen, 1987); B. J. McCay, "The Pirates of Piscary: Ethnohistory of Illegal Fishing in New Jersey," *Ethnohistory* 31 (winter 1984): 17–37; B. J. McCay, "The Ocean Commons and Community," *Dalhousie Review* 74 (autumn 1994–95): 310–38; B. J. McCay and J. M. Acheson, eds., *The Question of the Commons: The Culture and Ecology of Communal Resources,* Arizona Studies in Human Ecology (Tucson: University of Arizona Press, 1987); A. F. McEvoy, "Toward an Interactive Theory of Nature and Culture: Ecology, Production, and Cognition in the California Fishing Industry," *Environmental Review* 11 (winter 1988): 289–305; and Warren, *Hunter's Game.* For refinements see McEvoy, *Fisherman's Problem;* D. Feeny, S. Hanna, and A. F. McEvoy, "Questioning the Assumptions of the 'Tragedy of the Commons' Model of Fisheries," *Land Economics* 72 (May 1996): 187–205; and Warren, *Hunter's Game.*

It is sometimes useful to frame regulatory issues as class conflict. For useful analyses of class and culture in American history see R. J. Oestreicher, *Solidarity and Fragmentation: Working People and Class Consciousness in Detroit, 1875–1900* (Urbana: University of Illinois Press, 1986); A. Fabian, *Card Sharps, Dream Books, and Bucket Shops: Gambling in 19th Century America* (Ithaca: Cornell University Press, 1990); L. Fink, *Workingmen's Democracy: The Knights of Labor and American Politics* (Urbana: University of Illinois Press, 1983); L. Goodwyn, *The Populist Moment: A Short History of the Agrarian Revolt in America* (New York: Oxford University Press, 1978); L. W. Levine, *Highbrow/Lowbrow: The Emergence of Cultural Hierarchy in America* (Cambridge: Harvard University Press, 1988); and S. Wilentz, *Chants Democratic: New York City and the Rise of the American Working Class, 1788–1850* (New York: Oxford University Press, 1984). For works on the roots of poaching see J. E. Archer, "Poachers Abroad," in *The Unquiet Countryside,* ed. G. E. Mingay (London: Routledge, 1989), 52–64; R. B. Manning, *Hunters and Poachers: A Social and Cultural History of Unlawful Hunting in England, 1485–1640* (Oxford: Clarendon, 1993); and R. Schulte, *Village in Court: Arson, Infanticide, and Poaching in the Court Records of Upper Bavaria, 1848–1910,* trans. B. Selman (New York: Cambridge University Press, 1994).

Index

aboriginal fishery, 6, 7, 163, 380–81; bone rights, 32–34, 36; ceremonies, 27, 32, 36, 42, 60, 64, 405–6; class, 34; commercial fishing, 135–36; Edenic fishery, 13, 22, 38, 39, 63; first-salmon ceremony, 30, 32–35, 239; food storage, 13, 15, 26–27; gender, 15, 28, 61; harvest estimates, 20–23, 63, 101, 281; history, 13; kinship, 25–26, 36–38; management, 14, 27, 31, 35–38; moderation of harvests, 36–38, 277; myths, 14, 25, 27–34, 36–38, 42, 272, 274, 405–6; pemmican, 24–25; power, 17, 25, 60; propitiation, 35; proprietary claims, 14, 26, 36–38, 63–64, 268, 278; regeneration, 30–33; respect, 30; restricted consumption, 34; rituals, 32; spatial aspects, 13, 15, 17, 23–26, 34, 60, 134–36; specialization, 14; spiritualism, 27, 28, 30, 34–35, 45, 277; subsistence, 13, 14–18, 24, 27–28, 30, 135–36, 268; taboos, 14, 28, 32–36, 64; technology, 13, 18, 38, 64; trade, 24, 25–27, 28, 40; trade after contact, 46, 60–62; treaties, 44, 134–35, 242–44, 321

Ackley, H. A., 69

African Americans, 202

Agassiz, Alexander, 86

Agassiz, Louis, 73

Alaska, 153, 155, 189, 215, 219–20, 224, 296

Albany, Oregon, 53, 174

Alsea Indians, 32, 33

Alsea River, 175, 182

American Fish Culturists Association, 75, 76, 82

American Fisheries Society, 206, 215–16

anglers, 4, 166, 178, 199, 201–2, 222, 238, 242, 253–54, 330, 340, 341, 347, 368, 395–96; class, 167–70, 193; ethics, 167–69; exotic fish, 171–74, 334; "finishing" nature, 167, 170–71, 173–74; gender, 167–68; political activities, 167, 183–99, 396; race, 169; relations to nature, 167–74, 180, 189; resistance to, 169–70, 174, 194; threats to, 168–69; urban base, 167–68, 173–74, 180, 184–85, 195–98

angling, 3, 166, 249, 395–96; growth, 180–81; spatial aspects, 167–68, 170, 181, 184–201, 330

Anthony, A. W., 53

Applegate River, 47, 50, 54

Arlington, Oregon, 191

Arrow Lakes, B.C., 233

artificial propagation. See fish culture; hatcheries

Ashland, Oreg., 198

Asians, 134, 137, 165, 169

Astoria, Oreg., 43, 59, 108, 148, 150–51, 159–62, 174, 191–92

Astorians, 46

Auburn, Oreg., 47

Babcock, John P., 210

Baird, Spencer F., 73–79, 81–83, 86–88, 95–96, 99, 104–5, 107–9, 111–12, 114–15,

Baird, Spencer F. (*cont.*)
125, 171–72, 205, 250–52; conduct of
USFC, 84, 85; endorses fish culture,
103–4; environmental analysis, 73–74,
87, 102–3; expert on fish culture, 82; re-
strictions on fishing, 74, 87, 116–18;
scientist-entrepreneur, 76, 82, 299, 302;
and scup, 73–74, 101, 171
Baker City, Oreg., 195
Baker Lake Station, 96
Bakers Bay, 144–46, 151
Bakke, Bill, 239
Bandon, Oreg., 201
Banks, Oreg., 194
barging, 4, 52, 59, 244, 246–47
Barnaby, Joseph, 230
Beals, Arthur, 191
Bean, Louis E., 126, 127–29, 213, 218
beavers, 46–47, 228–30, 364–65
Bell, Frank, 219–20
Belloni, Robert, 243
Bend, Oreg., 195
Benson, Frank, 181
Benson, Keith R., 362
Berrian, J. W., 209, 211
Big White Salmon Station, 95, 222, 228
Biological Board of Canada, 218–20, 357
Bissell, John, 92
Blackford, E. G., 86
blaming nature, 4, 213, 247
Blue Mountains, 17, 54–55, 56, 57
Blue River, 49
Boas, Franz, 28
Boise, Idaho, 51
Boise River, 49, 51, 52
Boldt, George, 243
Bonneville hatchery, 162–63, 211–13, 228
Bonneville Power Administration, 3, 226,
246
Bowers, George M., 89–94, 96, 130, 172,
174, 209–10, 214, 310, 315
Bowlby, J. Q. A., 171
Boyd, Robert, 23, 39–40, 271
Brice, John J., 89, 90–91, 92, 128, 208
British Columbia, 163, 167, 191, 210, 218,
224, 233
Brookfield, Wash., 150

Browning, D. M., 136
Bruneau River, 51, 52, 53
Bryan, E. G., 86
Bull Run River, 59, 65
Burns, Oreg., 191
Burnt River, 17, 50, 52, 175

Calapuya Creek, 49
California, 47, 49, 62, 75, 78, 84–85, 92, 104,
111, 125, 128, 130, 191, 201
Camas Valley, 17, 42
Campbell, Sarah, 40
Canada, 91, 217–20, 224, 233, 359
canneries, 137
canners, 65, 80, 107–9, 113, 116, 125, 128,
137, 147, 150–51, 164, 171, 188, 201,
209, 213, 221, 296, 297
Canyon City, 47, 49
Cascade Rapids, 17, 175
Cayuse Indians, 17, 33, 54
Celilo Falls, 17, 19, 136, 144, 148, 158
Central Station. *See* Bonneville Hatchery
Chapman, D. W., 69
Chelan County, Wash., 52
Chelan River, 49, 51
Chicago World's Fair, 86, 95
Chinese, 50
Chinook Indians, 15, 28, 43, 60
Chinook River hatchery, 127, 208
chinook salmon (*O. tshawytscha*, also called
quinnat and king salmon), 3, 6, 15, 36,
63, 64, 65, 80, 92, 108–9, 120, 184, 201,
247, 296
chum salmon (*O. keta*, also called dog sal-
mon), 6, 15, 65
Clackamas Indians, 36, 109, 134
Clackamas River, 53, 81, 108, 114, 116, 119,
121, 124, 127, 188, 222, 228
Clackamas Station, 92, 96, 118–19, 121,
124–26, 130, 209, 215–16
Clallam Indians, 41
Clanton, R. E., 189
Clark, William, 14, 24, 25, 27, 30, 34, 296
Clatsop Indians, 19, 32, 36, 46, 60
Clearwater River, 49, 175, 228, 244
Cle Elum, Wash., 49
Cleghorn, John, 66

Clemens, Wilber, 218, 220
Cleveland, Grover, 83, 86, 91
Clift, William, 75
climate: atmosphere, 65–66, 403; impact on
    history, 6; oceans, 6–7, 26, 66, 130, 403–
    4. *See also* El Niño
Clowella Indians, 134
Coast Reservation, 42, 134–36
coho salmon (*O. kisutch*, also called silver
    salmon), 6, 15, 65, 120, 184, 201, 203,
    232
Collins, Joseph W., 82–83, 85–86, 300
Columbia River, 11, 14, 15, 17, 18, 24, 40, 42,
    43, 46, 52, 55, 56, 57, 59, 62–65, 77, 80, 88,
    89, 90, 102–4, 107–8, 110, 113, 115, 119,
    124, 130, 134–35, 140, 144–48, 151, 153–
    57, 162–63, 173, 175, 182, 188–89, 199,
    204, 208–12, 215, 217, 222, 228, 230, 241,
    243–44, 246; federal jurisdiction of, 104
Columbia River Compact, 164, 329
Columbia River Fishermen's Protective
    Union, 137, 140–44, 148, 156–57
Columbia River Intertribal Fish Commis-
    sion, 244, 247
Colville Indians, 18
Comcomly, 46
Comstock, J. C., 71, 72
Conconully, Wash., 49
conservation, 79; and class, 241; history of,
    165–67; rhetoric of, 133, 146–47, 158,
    165, 167, 180, 199, 202, 239–41, 253; by
    ostracism, 137; salmon recovery, 4–5,
    241, 247, 255–57, 306
consumption, 239, 242, 254
Cook, James, 45
Coos Bay, 49, 55, 56, 155, 173, 199
Coos Bay, Oreg., 195
Coos Indians, 30–31, 33, 36, 43
Coos River, 182
Coquille Indians, 33
Coquille River, 17, 49
Corbett, Henry, 75
Corvallis, Oreg., 174
Cowlitz River, 46, 81
Craig, Joseph, 22
Cronon, William, 242
Cross, H. E., 121–25

Cultee, Charles, 28
culture, 7, 38
Cultus Lake, 218

Dalles, The, 17, 24–25, 26, 33, 34, 62, 63–64,
    65, 136, 144
Dalles, Oreg., The, 47, 192, 195, 212
Dalton, C. C., 151
dams, 4, 39, 70–71, 101, 154, 174–77, 179,
    201, 221–22, 225–35, 244–49, 254, 256;
    Bonneville Dam, 225, 228–29, 321; con-
    centrate reproduction, 175, 233; Dalles
    Dam, The, 199; Dryden Dam, 232;
    fishways, 54, 121, 175, 222, 228; flooding,
    65–66, 244, 246; Gladstone Dam, 121–
    26, 149; Grand Coulee Dam, 175, 225,
    228–29, 232–33, 248; hydroelectricity, 59,
    242, 244, 246–47; irrigation, 53; John Day
    Dam, 246; logging (splash dams), 56–57,
    228; Lower Granite Dam, 244; mills, 54,
    56; mining, 51; municipal water, 59; prob-
    lems with, 121, 225, 232, 235, 244–47;
    Rock Island Dam, 229; Savage Rapids
    Dam, 244; turbines, 229–30
Darwin, H. L., 180
Day, Thomas, 54
demography, 7, 18, 20–23, 67; epidemics,
    20–22, 40–43, 60, 61, 404–5; Euro-
    American, 43–45, 57; Indian, 39–43, 44–
    45, 405; Pacific Northwest, 45; and sal-
    mon, 18
Denny, R. B., 193
Depoe Bay, 201
Deschutes River, 51, 53, 56, 81, 116
dipnets, 7, 18, 19, 65, 199
dog salmon. *See* chum salmon
Dolph, Joseph, 116, 124
Dominis, John, 60–61
Donaldson, Lauren, 230, 235, 250
Douglas County Sportsmen Association,
    194
Downs, A. K., 182
Dupree, A. Hunter, 165

Edmunds, Ernest, 193, 195
Edmunds, George F., 73, 75
Edmunds, M. C., 75, 78–79

Egan, Tim, 247
Elkins, Stephen B., 91
El Niño, 6, 66; 1876–77, 105–7, 111–12,
114–15, 206; 1890s, 106, 115; 1925–26,
106, 189–91; 1982–83, 106, 235; 1997,
308
Elwha River, 244
Endangered Species Act, 3, 247, 254, 257
Entiat River, 49, 51, 229
environmental change, 4, 7, 45–59, 67, 68,
70–71, 83, 88–89, 104, 168, 184, 201,
203, 220–22, 229, 232, 235–36, 253–54;
and capitalism, 45, 52, 72
environmentalism, 239–42, 249
environmentalists, 4, 239–42, 244, 253, 255
epidemics. *See* demography
Eugene, Oreg., 174, 185, 191, 195
Eugene Register Guard, 198
Evermann, Barton W., 88–89, 90, 124, 214,
216–17, 220, 251

Fairchild, H. A., 150
farming, 7, 44, 45, 47, 51, 53, 55, 59, 67, 102,
171, 192, 201, 238, 242, 246, 253–54
fire, 42, 56
fish culture, 7, 68, 75, 250–53; barging salmon,
245–46; in Canada, 219, 235; capitalism,
78; concentrate reproduction, 127–30,
215, 222, 225, 228, 233; criticism, 10, 91–
92, 98, 100, 212–13, 216–19, 221, 235–36;
disease, 203, 212, 230–32, 236, 350; doubts
about, 71, 230, 235; ecological consequences, 184; egg transfers, 77, 83, 84–85,
90, 95, 97, 104, 111, 113–14, 121–25, 128,
130, 155, 162–63, 193–94, 208, 211–13,
222, 231, 232–33; endorsements, 81–83,
91–92, 94, 100–103, 107–8, 111, 114–
15, 118–19, 126, 128–31, 146, 208, 216,
222; expertise, 78–79; evolutionary
change, 203–4, 206, 225, 232–33, 236, 251;
"finishing" nature, 78–79; fiscal politics,
107, 109, 113–14, 121, 125–26, 194, 212–
13; fishery politics, 211; fish feeds, 209,
212, 230–33, 350, 366; fry vs. fingerling,
203, 205–6, 210–11, 215–16; genetics,
129, 204, 212, 232–33, 251; history, 69,
96–98, 219, 251–52; institutionalization,

10, 68, 83, 86, 92–94; panacea, 69–70, 87,
103, 104, 105, 146, 175, 222, 228, 236, 250;
political economy of, 109–11, 115–16,
125–29, 131, 214, 217, 236, 250–51, 318;
pond raising, 203–4, 205, 212, 219, 225,
230, 232–33, 236; private efforts, 72, 73,
340; problems, 10, 111, 114, 119–20,
126, 128–32, 209–10, 212–13, 217–19,
229, 232, 251; proof of efficacy, 69–70,
114–15, 119, 206–7, 212; as science, 70,
71, 79, 81, 83, 91, 104, 112, 131, 208, 211,
219, 232, 235–36; and scientific research,
89–90; spatial aspects, 109, 111, 121, 127,
131, 150–51, 154–57, 162–63, 172–74,
221–22, 314, 316, 318; techniques, 7–8;
wild fish, 204, 235
fish culturists, 4, 10, 74, 99, 133, 168, 212,
219, 225, 252; criticize scientists, 210, 215,
218, 221; practical knowledge, 203, 210,
213, 215–16; understanding of nature,
100, 204–5, 207–8, 210, 235–36. *See also*
individual names
fishery management, 13, 68, 393, 406–7; in
Alaska, 220; boundary disputes, 150–53,
156, 162, 329; in Canada, 220; class conflict, 145, 162, 166–67, 202, 253; dependence on fish culture, 87, 113, 146, 250–
52; ethnicity, 149, 253; federal jurisdiction, 156, 163–64; gear elimination, 104,
112, 144–47, 185–202, 254, 323, 342, 368;
history of, 77, 103; joint regulation of
Columbia, 101, 102, 105, 124–25, 131,
163–64, 188; political economy of, 70–
72, 74, 79, 82–83, 87, 89, 92, 96–100,
109–12, 116–18, 120, 147, 149, 179–80,
214, 219–26, 230, 236, 238–39, 245, 249–
53; politics, 156–65, 181–84, 303; race,
202, 249, 253; reliance on fish culture, 72,
74, 77, 104–5, 115, 120–21, 130–31; restriction attempts, 131; science, 400–
401; spatial aspects, 72–73, 102, 130–31,
133, 146–65, 172–74, 191–92, 201, 221,
228, 252–53, 300; Spencerian process,
133, 165, 202, 238
fishery science, 10, 46–47, 66, 80–81, 191,
211, 217–19, 221–25, 236, 399–404; in
Canada, 217–20

fishery scientists, 203, 212, 213, 215–16, 222.
   See also individual names
fish fights, 133, 165; election results, 162,
   186–88, 196–98; history of, 158
fishways. *See* dams; fish culture
fishwheel owners, 144, 147–48, 157, 159–63,
   211, 238
fishwheels, 7, 63–64, 124, 140, 144–45, 147–
   49, 156–57, 165, 199, 215
Florence, Oreg., 172
Foerster, Russell E., 218–20, 224, 230–32
Forbes, Stephen A., 81, 214–15
Fort Gaston Station, 96
Fort George, 46
Fort Vancouver, 46, 60
Foster, Fred, 230
Fraser River, 60, 137, 189, 215, 218, 241
Freeman, Miller, 163
fur trade. *See* trapping fur-bearing animals

Galice Creek, 47, 50
Garibaldi, Oreg., 195
Garlick, Theodatus, 69
Gebhard, A. E., 171
Gilbert, Charles, 88, 89, 90, 114, 137, 201
Gill, Herbert, 85
gillnets, 7, 18–19, 62, 63, 73, 134, 140, 145,
   149, 157, 199, 249, 323
gillnetters, 4, 107, 109, 113, 121, 124, 131,
   140–44, 150, 188–90, 192–93, 195, 211,
   222, 238, 254, 368; vs. fishwheel owners,
   147–48, 156–65, 185; vs. poundnet own-
   ers, 141–47
Gilman, Daniel C., 86
Goode, George B., 78–79, 83–84, 86, 118,
   137
Gorham, Charles, 88
Gorton, Slade, 243–44, 247
Grande Ronde River, 17, 51, 52, 54, 55, 56,
   57, 175
Grand Ronde Agency, 43, 134–35
Grange, 192
Grants Pass, Oreg., 174, 192, 198
Grave Creek, 50
grazing, 3, 44, 45, 52, 54–55, 102, 179, 242,
   254
Green, Seth, 69, 72, 74, 76, 168

Grey, Zane, 169–70, 198–99, 330
Grover, Lafayette, 100–101, 105
Gunther, Erna, 33–34

Hacker, Robert, 22
Hager, Albert, 204–5
Haime, Jules, 71–72, 225
Hale, W. C., 156
Hallock, Charles, 170
Halver, John, 365, 366
Hankinson, T. L., 214
Hapgood, Andrew, 62, 63
Hardy, Ron, 350
Harrison, Benjamin, 86
hatcheries, 4, 69, 83, 88, 98, 99–100, 103,
   133, 137, 140, 175, 180, 194, 228, 236,
   246, 256. *See also* fish culture; individual
   stations
Hawthorne, J. O., 156
Hays, Samuel, 165
Helix, Oreg., 191
Hermann, Binger, 149
Hewes, Gordon, 22, 271
Higgins, Elmer, 224
Hilgard, Oreg., 54
Hines, Gustavus, 43
Hispanics, 202
history, 237–38, 396–97, 399
Holmes, Harlan, 229
Hood River, 52
Hoover, Herbert, 221
Hubbard, Waldo, 111, 114, 118, 120–21,
   124–26, 314, 316
Hudson's Bay Company, 41, 43, 46–47; sal-
   mon trade, 46, 60–62
Hume, George, 62, 63
Hume, Robert D., 62, 63, 80, 153–56, 158–
   59, 163, 188, 206–11, 214, 250, 350
Hume, William, 62, 63
humpie salmon. *See* pink salmon
Hunn, Eugene, 14
Huntington, J. W. P., 135, 321
Hymes, Dell, 30

Idaho, 49, 50, 51, 80, 173, 175
Idaho City, Idaho, 51
Illinois River, 47

Independent Scientific Group, 246
Indians, 3, 4, 13, 99, 134–37, 163, 169, 180,
    183, 202, 222, 243, 252, 255, 330, 341,
    404–6; coastal groups, 15, 18, 25, 29, 37,
    135; interior valley groups, 15, 17, 41–42;
    land use, 7, 42; lower Columbia groups,
    15, 17, 18, 25, 30, 33, 41, 59, 135; Plateau
    groups, 15, 17, 25, 29, 33, 37, 41, 44, 134,
    136; settlement patterns, 14–17, 27–28.
    See also individual groups
industrial fishers, 4, 70, 80, 99, 116, 131,
    137, 164, 180, 183–84–85, 252–53, 255;
    culture, 141; ethnicity, 140–41, 165; gen-
    der, 141, 394–95; history, 141
industrial fishery, 3, 7, 13, 45, 59, 99, 102,
    185, 251, 254, 406–10; canning, 62, 64;
    capitalism, 64; class, 11, 134, 140, 144–
    45, 147–48, 157, 162, 165, 393–94, 410;
    concerns about, xvi–xvii, 100–101, 107,
    113, 116, 131, 305; decline, 65, 66, 179–
    80, 189, 212, 242, 343; ethnicity, 11, 134,
    140–41, 148–49, 165; fresh fish, 65, 201,
    343; gender, 11, 61; global trade, 62, 64;
    greed, 64, 66–67, 105, 158, 180, 193, 344;
    growth, 62–63, 65, 105, 114–15, 120,
    137–40, 144, 201; harvests, 343, 407–8;
    history, 6, 10–11, 60, 100–101, 105,
    379–80, 383–89; mild curing, 65, 201;
    overfishing, 4, 39, 65, 66–67, 83, 88, 101,
    119, 191, 308, 402; race, 11, 62, 134–37,
    165; record keeping, 65; salted salmon,
    60–62; spatial aspects, 11, 60, 62, 63,
    110, 140–41, 144, 147, 153–56, 199–
    201; violence, 141–45; waste, 64, 65
industrialization, 168, 179, 394
industry, 3, 4, 67, 246, 368
Inland Empire Waterways Association, 175,
    244
irrigation, 3, 4, 7, 52–53, 59, 67, 154, 179,
    199, 228–29, 246–48, 251–52, 254, 314
Irvine, Clare, 170, 172–73
Izaak Walton League, 177

Jacksonville, Oreg., 47
Jay, Tom, 239
Jefferson City, Oreg., 53

Jensen, Adella, 192
Jewett, Stanley, 173–74
John Day River, 17, 47, 49, 51, 52, 54, 57,
    116
Johnson, Frances, 28
Johnson, George, 144
Jones, W. A., 115, 136, 146
Jordan, David S., 80, 91, 114, 119, 137, 159,
    169, 172, 182–83, 215, 297

Kalapuya Indians, 26, 33, 36, 42
Karluk Lake, Alaska, 219
Kathlamet Indians, 31, 32, 33
Kellogg, E. C., 69, 71
Kerr, Andy, 239–41
Kershaw, T. R., 131
Kettle Falls, 18, 62
king salmon. *See* chinook salmon
Kipling, Rudyard, 169
Klamath Falls, Oreg., 174, 193
Klamath Lakes, 33
Klamath Lakes Indians, 265
Klamath River, 54, 182
Klickitat Indians, 238
Klingle, Matthew, 362
Knight, A. P., 218, 220
Krieger, Alex, 22–23

La Grande, Oreg., 51
Lampman, Ben, 171, 173–74
Langston, Nancy, 55
Larkin, Peter, 233, 252
Leavenworth hatchery, 228, 232
Lewis and Clark Centennial Exposition, 95–
    96, 173
Lewis and Clark expedition, 14, 27, 46
Lewiston, Idaho, 47, 175, 244, 246
Lincoln City, Oreg., 198
Little Spokane River, 54, 59, 88, 116
Little White Salmon River, 127
logging, 3, 7, 45, 55–57, 59, 67, 154, 170, 179,
    199, 201, 242, 249, 251–52, 254; log jams,
    56, 228; spatial aspects of, 55–56
Long, Judge, 86
Loughery, A. S., 43–44
Lyman, Theodore, 74

Malheur River, 51, 52
Marchak, Patricia, 64, 67
maritime traders, 45–46, 238
Marsh, George P., 70–72, 73, 74, 77, 83, 94,
96, 99, 102, 168, 171, 251; environmental
analysis, 70, 87
Marshfield, Oreg., 192
Mazamas, 171
McAllister, Herman C., 158, 162, 181–82,
188, 211, 215, 250
McCloud River, 79, 85, 111, 114, 208
McCloud Station, 77, 82, 84, 101, 206
McCormac, Johnston, 147
McDonald, Marshall, 3, 81, 83–91, 95, 99,
118, 120–21, 125–26, 128–29, 147–49,
172, 184; attacks on, 85–86; conduct of
USFC, 84, 89; environmental analysis,
87–88; faith in fish culture, 87; restric-
tions on fishing, 87, 124–25; on science,
88, 89–90
McEvoy, Arthur F., 6, 220
McGowan, H. S., 210–11
McGuire, Hollister D., 120–21, 124–26,
129, 149, 181, 205, 250
McKenzie River, 182, 210
McKinley, William, 90–91
McLaughlin, John T., 192
McLeod, Alexander, 26
McLoughlin, John, 41, 43, 60, 61
McMinnville, Oreg., 191, 194
McPhillips, Arthur, 191
Medford, Oreg., 155, 174, 185, 188, 242
Meek, Seth E., 90, 127–28
Megler, J. G., 150
Methow River, 49, 52, 229
Milhan, George, 57
mills, 7, 53, 99, 179; sawdust, 57
Milwaukie, Oreg., 53
Miner, Roy Waldo, 214
mining, 7, 44, 45, 47–51, 59, 67, 175–79, 238,
242, 251–52, 254; class, 50; coal, 49; cop-
per, 49; ditches, 50–52; dredge mining,
51, 175, 179; gold, 47, 49–53, 175; gravel,
175; hydraulic mining, 50–51, 53, 62;
iron, 49; placer mining, 49–50; quicksilver, 49, 175; race, 50; silver, 49

ministers, 238
Mitchell, Hugh C., 175, 222
Mitchell, John H., 104–5, 107–8, 112–13,
116
Molalla Indians, 134, 268
Molalla River, 49
Montana, 88, 247
Morning Oregonian. See Oregonian
Morris, Scott, 172
Morse, Kathy, 296
Multnomah Hunters and Anglers Club, 193
Myrtle Point, Oreg., 191

Naches River, 56
National Wild Life Federation, 177
Needham, Paul, 224, 230
Nehalem River, 182
Nestucca Indians, 25
Nestucca River, 56, 193–95, 198, 343
Nettle, Richard, 72
Nevada, 49
Newfoundland cod fisheries, 382–83, 384, 386
Nez Perce Indians, 17, 20, 31, 33, 49, 54, 244
Norblad, A. W., 192
Northern Paiute Indians, 33, 37, 238
North West Company, 46
northwesterners. *See* Pacific northwesterners
Northwest Power Planning Council, 246–47

ocean. *See* climate
Ogden, Peter Skene, 27
Okanogan River, 49, 51, 52, 54, 65, 229
Olcott, Benjamin, 182
O'Malley, Henry, 198–99, 201, 213, 215–16,
221, 250
oral traditions. *See* aboriginal fishery
Oregon, 44, 47, 49, 50, 54, 55, 57, 62, 99,
104–5, 108, 110–11, 120–21, 124, 148,
153, 172–74, 175, 180, 215, 219, 221–22,
243, 340–41, 368; fiscal politics, 99, 102,
113, 116, 118, 129, 226; governor, 100,
101; legislature, 101–2, 113, 115–16,
146–47, 153–54, 162–64, 181, 183–89,
191–92, 198–99, 206, 244; reliance on
federal subsidies, 102; Supreme Court,
113, 158, 163

Oregon and Washington Fish Propagating Company, 108–14, 116
Oregon City, Oreg., 43, 53, 131, 185, 188–89, 192
Oregon Department of Fish and Wildlife, 251
Oregon Department of Geology and Mineral Industries, 177–79; fish culture politics, 182–84
Oregon Fish and Game Association, 171
Oregon Fish and Game Commission, 181, 184, 216; egg transfers, 213
Oregon Fish Commission, 53, 113, 118, 120, 158, 210–12, 224, 228, 232–33; development of hatcheries, 129, 156, 182, 235; egg transfers, 128, 162–63, 193–94, 211; fish culture politics, 182–84, 214; politics within, 149–50; Smolt Program, 203, 225, 233–35, 251
Oregon Fish Protector, 92, 149
Oregon Game Commission, 230; development of hatcheries, 182; egg transfers, 173, 193–94
Oregonian (Portland, also *Morning Oregonian*), 3, 50, 57, 63, 100–101, 103–4, 107, 109, 111, 113–14, 118–19, 126, 130–31, 134, 158–63, 179–81, 188–89, 201, 206, 208–9, 211–12, 248, 256, 323
Oregon Journal (Portland), 193
Oregon Land Conservation and Development Commission, 241–42
Oregon Master Fish Warden, 158
Oregon Sportsmen's Club of Waterloo, 194
Oregon Sportsmen's League, 181–82
Oregon State Sportsmens Association, 195
Oregon Voter (Portland), 194–95
Oregon Water Resources Commission, 244
Orton, Molly, 28
Owyhee, 60–61
Owyhee River, 17, 51, 52

Pacific City, Oreg., 189, 191, 198, 201
Pacific Coast Hatcherymen's Association, 215–16
Pacific Fisheries Society, 216
Pacific Fisherman, 151, 163, 216

Pacific Northwest, 55, 71, 133, 166, 178, 180, 202, 211, 225, 236, 242, 247–48
Pacific northwesterners, 165, 237–38
packers. *See* canners
Page, George Shepherd, 75
Palmer, Joel, 44, 134–35
Payette River, 49
Pennoyer, Sylvester, 57, 124
Pierce, Franklin, 134
Pierce, S. P., 191
Pinchot, Gifford, 79, 166, 347
pink salmon (*O. gorbuscha,* also called humpie salmon), 5, 6, 15
Pisani, Donald, 347
Placerville, Idaho, 51
Plasec, E. K., 193, 195
poisons, 18
politicians, 249–50, 252–53
pollution, 101, 228–29, 246, 251, 254
Portland, Oreg., 43, 57–58, 108, 131, 162, 167, 171, 174, 179, 182, 185–88, 191–92, 194–95, 323
Portland Rod and Gun Club, 172
Portland Telegram, 195
Port Orford, Oreg., 201
poundnet owners, 144, 146, 148, 157, 159, 211, 238
poundnets, 7, 63, 140, 144–47, 149, 156–57, 165, 199, 215
Powder River, 47, 51, 52, 55
Pred, Allan, 11
Progressive Era, 184–85
Puget Sound, 55, 107, 150, 163, 189, 242, 296
purse seines, 189

Quinault River, 232
quinnat. *See* chinook salmon

Race, E. E., 86
railroads, 51–53, 54, 63, 64, 115–16, 155, 183, 222
Ranier, Oreg., 191
Ravenal, William de Chastignier, 90, 91, 92, 120, 128–30, 172–73, 208–9, 213, 314; institutionalization of ignorance, 86–87
red salmon. *See* sockeye salmon

Reed, F. C., 120–21, 129, 149, 169, 171, 213, 250
Reiger, John, 202
Rich, Willis P., 3, 217, 221, 224–25, 232, 245, 251
Ricker, William, 230, 359
Rickman, George, 209
Robinson, David, 195
Rockwell, Cleveland, 169
Rogue River, 17, 44, 47, 49, 50, 51, 54, 66, 80, 81, 107, 134, 153–56, 158, 168–69, 173, 175, 198–99, 206, 208–10, 214, 222, 228, 315, 318, 342
Rogue River hatcheries: Elk Creek Station, 125, 155, 213; Wedderburn hatchery, 154–55, 182, 208, 211
Roosevelt, Robert B., 74, 75, 108, 168
Roosevelt, Theodore, 163, 166, 168, 185
Rosalyn, Wash., 49
Roseburg, Oreg., 174, 185, 191, 194
Roseburg News, 181
Rosenberg, Charles, 76
Rosenberg, Ed, 157
Ross, Alexander, 25
Ruby, Wash., 49
Russell, Walter, 191
Ruth, Babe, 198
Rutter, Cloudsley, 90
Ryckman, Matt, 173

Sacramento River, 62, 80, 90, 147, 153, 155, 173, 241
Salem, Oreg., 43, 53, 58, 102, 147, 162, 171, 174, 185, 191–92, 194, 244
Salem Daily Statesman, 170, 172
salmon (Atlantic, Salmo), 5, 6, 69, 73, 76, 78, 79, 100, 183
salmon (Pacific, Oncorhynchus), 75, 76, 77, 82, 100, 170, 235–36, 246; biology, 5–6, 26, 78, 79–81, 108, 112, 204, 296, 297; classification, 182–83; crisis, 3, 4, 11–12, 202, 238, 251, 254; die after spawning, 78–81, 297; genetics, 81, 108; home stream spawning, 81; ideas about, 145–46, 323; range, 5, 14, 33, 126; rearing habitat, 47; runs, 78, 79, 81; smoltification, 5, 179,

233; spawning behavior, 6, 23, 42, 111; symbolic importance, 247–48, 371. See also individual species
Salmon Creek, Wash., 49
Salmon Falls, 17
Salmon River (coast), 134
Sanders, G. D., 192
Sand Island, 146, 151
Sandy River, 116, 124
San Francisco, Calif., 55, 155, 189
Santiam River, 49, 65, 182
Sapir, Edward, 28
Schalk, Randall, 23, 271, 281
science, 10, 68, 77, 96, 203, 216, 219–20, 225, 250–52, 398–99; ecology, 205, 214–15, 233, 236; oceanography, 235, 403. See also fishery science
Seal, William P., 86
sealing, 391–93
Seattle, Wash., 219, 242
seiners, 141, 211
seines, 7, 18–19, 20, 64, 140, 145, 147, 154, 157, 165, 199
Seufert, Francis A., 181, 212, 215
shad, 69, 73, 75, 76, 82
Shasta Indians, 29
Sherars Falls, 268
Sheridan, Oreg., 195
Shoemaker, Carl D., 181–82, 189
Shoshone Indians, 54
Siletz Bay, 29
Siletz River, 65, 135–36
Siletz Station, 125
silver salmon. See coho salmon
Similkameen River, 49
Simpson, George, 46
Siuslaw River, 56, 130
Siuslaw Station, 92, 125–29, 182
Sixes, Oreg., 191
Skowronek, Stephen, 73
Smith, Courtland L., 66–67
Smith, Hugh M., 86, 91, 221, 250
Smithsonian Institution, 73, 86
Snake River, 17, 20, 24, 46, 49, 65, 88, 92, 108, 116, 173, 175, 210, 241, 244–47
Snake River hatcheries, 125

sockeye salmon (*O. nerka,* also called red salmon), 5, 6, 15, 63, 65, 120, 212, 215, 229, 232–33, 247, 296; as kokanee, 5
Sommer, M., 194
Southmayd, H. W., 192
spatial analysis, 11–12, 397–98. *See also* tragedy of the commons
spears, 7, 18, 19, 114, 169
splash dams. *See* dams
Spokane, Wash., 54, 57–58
Spokane River, 54
sportfishers and sportfishing. *See* anglers; angling
sportsmen, 166
Stanford University, 89, 224
steelhead salmon (*O. mykiss,* also called trout), 6, 15, 65, 199, 242, 341; classification, 183–84; propagation, 184; rainbow trout, 5
Stevens, Isaac, 44, 134
Stone, Livingston, 53, 72, 76–80, 87, 91, 92, 96, 99, 101, 103–5, 107–9, 111, 115, 118, 121, 168, 204–5, 250; develops egg transportation, 77; relations with Spencer F. Baird, 77, 84; relations with Marshall McDonald, 84–85, 300
stories, 237, 253–54; complex stories, 5, 39, 253–57; effect of politics on, 238, 248–50; lapsarian narrative, 39, 238; simple stories, 4, 5, 11–12, 68, 238, 248, 253, 255–57
Swan, James, 19

Taffe, I. H., 148
Takelma Indians, 20, 28, 36
Teal, Joseph, 171
technology, 5, 68, 78, 96, 238, 251–54, 408–9
Tenino Indians, 268
Thayer, William, 113
Thompson, E. P., 173
Tillamook, Oreg., 195
Tillamook Bay, 55, 199
Tillamook Indians, 29, 30, 31, 32, 33, 238
Titcomb, W. C., 86, 95, 209
Toledo, Oreg., 191
tragedy of the commons, 10–11, 409–10
Transactions of the American Fisheries Society, 215

trap owners. *See* poundnet owners
trapping fur-bearing animals, 34, 45–47, 59, 67, 238
traps, 7, 18, 19, 63, 73, 112, 140. *See also* poundnets
Trask River, 65, 182
trollers, 4, 243, 254
trolling, 198–201
trout, 171, 184; reclassification, 183; and salmon, 5. *See also* steelhead salmon
Tumalo, Oreg., 182

Umatilla, Oreg., 47
Umatilla Indians, 107–8, 243–44
Umatilla River, 52, 53, 108, 116
Umpqua River, 49, 53, 54, 55, 66, 129, 175, 182, 198
Union Creek, 182
urbanization, 7, 57–58, 59, 67, 168, 174–75, 179, 241–42, 254
U.S. Army Corps of Engineers, 59, 144–46, 151, 226–28, 244, 246
U.S. Bureau of Fisheries, 94–96, 118, 163, 208–10, 212–16, 219–21, 224, 228–30, 318; egg transfers, 211–12, 222; species transplants, 171, 173–74
U.S. Bureau of Reclamation, 178, 226–29
U.S. Commission on Fish and Fisheries. *See* U.S. Fish Commission
U.S. Congress, 59, 68, 69, 73, 75, 89, 108, 112–13, 116, 128, 134–36, 164, 178, 222, 226, 244, 246, 249
U.S. Fish and Wildlife Service, 179, 228–30, 244; egg transfers, 232–33
U.S. Fish Commission, 53, 57, 68–69, 73, 79, 83–84, 87, 90, 92, 94–96, 99, 103, 108, 112–16, 118, 120, 124–26, 128, 144, 147–49, 155–56, 204, 206, 208–9, 213, 221, 318; aversion to restrictions, 148–49, 315; budgets, 75, 82, 89; Division of Fish Culture, 84, 86, 89, 91; Division of Fisheries, 84, 86, 91; Division of Scientific Inquiry, 84, 86, 87, 89, 91; egg transfers, 77, 83, 84–85, 90, 95–96, 111, 113–14, 121–25, 128, 130, 155, 162–63, 208; exhibitions, 94–96; expertise, 120, 129–30; fish culture, 75, 76, 81, 89, 90, 92, 98,

104; fish culture budgets, 82, 92; history, 91; politics, 73, 85, 90–91; science, 75–76, 83, 98, 129; science budgets, 82; and Smithsonian, 75; species transplants, 77, 95–96, 171–73
U.S. Reclamation Service. *See* U.S. Bureau of Reclamation
U.S. Supreme Court, 136, 151, 156, 180

Van Dusen, Hustler G., 129–31, 149–50, 156–59, 181, 210–11, 250, 252, 327
Verrill, Addison E., 74, 86
Vogt, Karl, 71, 72

Walbaum, Johann, 80
Walker, Deward E., Jr., 37
Walker, Gilbert, 191
Walla Walla, Wash., 47
Walla Walla River, 52, 116
Wallowa Lake, 65
Wallowa River, 52, 53
Wallula, Wash., 47
Walton, Izaak, 167
Wannamaker, John, 86
Ward, Henry, 51, 177–79, 198
Warm Springs Indians, 244
Warm Springs Reservation, 135–36
Warren, Frank M., 162, 171, 213
Wasco Indians, 18, 24–25
Washington, 49, 54, 56, 62, 80, 88, 102, 110, 118, 120, 124, 145, 148, 153, 162, 172–73, 180, 189, 215–16, 219, 221–22, 243–44, 368; legislature, 113, 116, 146, 150, 163–64, 183
Washington Fish Commissioner, 120, 131, 149, 208, 210
Washington Fishermen's Association, 140
Webster, Herman, 209–10

weirs, 7, 19–20, 37, 64, 112, 144
Wenatchee River, 49, 52, 229
West, Oswald, 182
West Linn, Oreg., 191
whaling, 389–91
White, Harley, 217–20
White, Richard, 294, 296
Whitelaw, Ed, 242
Wilcox, William, 91
Willamette Falls, 17, 26, 42, 59, 60, 61, 62, 134, 170, 180, 184, 188
Willamette River, 42, 43, 46, 51, 53, 54, 56, 65, 115–16, 134, 170, 172–73, 179, 181–82
Willamette Station, 95–96
Willamette Valley, 17, 26, 42, 43, 44, 46, 54, 57, 65, 134, 170, 174, 192, 196–98
Williams, Nancy, 14
Williams, Roger, 112
Wilmot, Samuel F., 69, 72, 91–92, 168, 250
Wilson, Woodrow, 185
Wilson River, 65
Winchester Bay, 201
Winslow, George, 191
Wishram Indians, 18, 24–25, 36
Withycombe, James, 181–82
Woods, Rufus, 175
Wright, C. A., 57
Wyeth, Nathaniel, 61

Yakama Indians, 136, 243–44
Yakima, Wash., 171
Yakima River, 49, 51, 52, 53, 54, 179
Yamhill River, 134
Yaquina Bay, 55, 56, 134, 199
Yaquina River, 53, 56
Yaquina Station, 125
Young, Chris, 362